Encyclopedia of the
AMERICAN
JUDICIAL
SYSTEM

Encyclopedia of the
AMERICAN JUDICIAL SYSTEM

Studies of the Principal Institutions and Processes of Law

Robert J. Janosik, *EDITOR*

Occidental College

Volume II

CHARLES SCRIBNER'S SONS · NEW YORK

Copyright © 1987 Charles Scribner's Sons

Encyclopedia of the American judicial system.

    Includes bibliographies and index.
        1. Law—United States—Dictionaries.   2. Justice,
Administration of—United States—Dictionaries.
3. United States—Constitutional law—Dictionaries.
I. Janosik, Robert J. (Robert Joseph)
KF154.E53   1987   349.73′0321   87–4742
ISBN 0–684–17807–9 Set   347.300321
ISBN 0–684–18858–9 Volume I
ISBN 0–684–18859–7 Volume II
ISBN 0–684–18860–0 Volume III

Published simultaneously in Canada
by Collier Macmillan Canada, Inc.

1 3 5 7 9 11 13 15 17 19 V/C 20 18 16 14 12 10 8 6 4 2

Printed in the United States of America.

The paper in this book meets the guidelines for permanence and
durability of the Committee on Production Guidelines for Book Longevity
of the Council on Library Resources.

CONTENTS

v

CONTENTS

CONTENTS

CONTENTS

Encyclopedia of the
AMERICAN
JUDICIAL
SYSTEM

Part III
INSTITUTIONS
AND PERSONNEL

ADMINISTRATIVE AGENCIES

Peter Woll

THE executive branch of the government comprises numerous administrative agencies, often called "the bureaucracy." Administrative agencies come in many shapes and sizes, and perform a wide array of governmental functions. The governmental departments, with secretaries of cabinet rank, are the largest and most important parts of the executive branch. In 1789 the First Congress created what was to be the core of the executive branch for a long time to come when it established the Departments of War (Army), Navy, State, and Treasury. It also created the office of attorney general as the government's counsel (the Department of Justice was not established until 1870). A general post office and a patent office completed the early executive branch, which in 1802 employed all of 132 persons, a number that increased to 318 by 1829. When Washington became the capital in 1800, there were more representatives and senators than bureaucrats. The growth of the executive branch did not begin in earnest until the twentieth century, and even then not until the New Deal of Franklin D. Roosevelt in the 1930s.

The vast governmental bureaucracy of the twentieth century bears no more resemblance to the original executive branch than the modern, congested, overbuilt city of Washington does to the deserted swamp and mosquito-infested land from which it arose. The Founding Fathers had a simple, straightforward conception of the executive branch, which was to be controlled by the president and fit nicely into the tripartite separation of powers and system of checks and balances. Unthinkable to the Founding Fathers would be today's vast array of administrative agencies that exercise both legislative and judicial functions.

THE CONSTITUTIONAL CONTEXT

Even though the Constitution does not explicitly provide for the bureaucracy, it has had a profound impact upon the structure, functions, and general place that the bureaucracy occupies in government. The administrative process was incorporated into the constitutional system under the heading of "The Executive Branch." But the concept of "administration" at the time of the adoption of the Constitution was a very simple one, involving the "mere execution" of "executive details," to use the phrases of Alexander Hamilton in the *Federalist*. The idea, at that time, was simply that the president, as chief executive, would be able to control the executive branch in carrying out the mandates of Congress. Hamilton felt that the president would be responsible for administrative action as long as he was in office. This fact later turned up in what can be called the "presidential supremacy" school of thought, which held, and still holds, that the president is constitutionally responsible for administration and that Congress should delegate to him all necessary authority for this purpose. Nevertheless, whatever the framers of the Constitution might have planned if they could have foreseen the nature of bureaucratic development, the fact is that the system they constructed in many ways supported bureaucratic organization and functions independent of the president. The role they assigned to Congress in relation to administration assured this result, as did the general position of Congress in the governmental system as a check or balance to the power of the president. Congress has a great deal of authority over the administrative process.

If the powers of Congress and the president

435

over the bureaucracy are compared, it becomes clear that they both have important constitutional responsibility. Congress retains primary control over the organization of the bureaucracy. It alone creates and destroys agencies, and determines whether they are to be located within the executive branch or outside it. This has enabled Congress to create a large number of independent agencies beyond presidential control. Congress has the authority to control appropriations and thus may exercise a great deal of power over the administrative arm, although increasingly the Office of Management and Budget, in the executive branch, has the initial, and more often than not the final, say over the budget. Congress also has the authority to define the jurisdiction of agencies. Finally, the Constitution gives to the legislature the power to interfere in presidential appointments, which must be "by and with the advice and consent of the Senate."

Congress may extend the sharing of the appointive power when it sets up new agencies. It may delegate to the president pervasive authority to control the bureaucracy. But one of the most important elements of the separation of powers is the electoral system, which gives to Congress a constituency different from, and even conflicting with, that of the president. As a result, Congress often decides to set up agencies beyond presidential purview. Only rarely will it grant the president any kind of final authority to structure the bureaucracy. During World War II, on the basis of the War Powers Act of 1941, the president had the authority to reorganize the administrative branch. Today he has the same authority, provided that Congress does not veto presidential proposals within a certain time limit. In refusing to give the president permanent reorganization authority, Congress is jealously guarding one of its important prerogatives.

Turning to the constitutional authority of the president over the bureaucracy, it is somewhat puzzling to see that it gives him a relatively small role. He appoints certain officials by and with the advice and consent of the Senate. He has directive power over agencies that are placed within his jurisdiction by Congress. His control over patronage, once so important, has diminished sharply under the merit system. The president is commander in chief of all military forces, which puts him in a controlling position over the Defense Department and agencies involved in military matters. In the area of international relations, the president is by constitutional authority the "chief diplomat," to use Clinton Rossiter's phrase. This means that he appoints ambassadors (by and with the advice and consent of the Senate), and generally directs national activities in the international arena—a crucially important executive function. Regardless of the apparent intentions of some of the framers of the Constitution as expressed by Hamilton in the *Federalist* and in spite of the predominance of the presidency in military and foreign affairs, the fact remains that we seek in vain for explicit constitutional authorization for the president to be "chief administrator."

This is not to say that the president does not have an important responsibility to act as chief of the bureaucracy but merely that there is no constitutional mandate for this. As the American system evolved, the president was given more and more responsibility until he became, in practice, chief administrator. At the same time, the constitutional system has often impeded progress in this direction. The President's Committee on Administrative Management in 1937 and the Hoover Commission in 1949 and 1955 called upon Congress to initiate a series of reforms to increase presidential authority over administration. It was felt that this was necessary to make democracy work. The president is the only official elected nationally, and if the administration is to be held democratically accountable, he alone can stand as its representative. But meaningful control from the White House requires that the president have a program that encompasses the activities of the bureaucracy. He must be informed as to what it is doing and be able to control it. He must understand the complex responsibilities of the bureaucracy. Moreover, he must be able to call on sufficient political support to balance the support that the agencies draw from private clienteles and congressional committees. This has frequently proven a difficult and often impossible task for the president. He may have the stated authority to control the bureaucracy in many areas but not enough power to act.

In addition to the problem of congressional and presidential control over the bureaucracy, there is the question of judicial review of administrative decisions. The rule of law is a central element in the Constitution. The rule of law means that decisions judicial in nature should be handled by common-law courts because of their expertise in rendering due process of law. When administrative agencies engage in adjudication, their decisions should be subject to judicial review—at least they should if one supports the idea of the supremacy of law. Judicial decisions are supposed to be rendered on an independent and impartial basis, through the use of tested procedures, to arrive at the accurate determination of the truth. Administrative adjudication should not be subject to presidential or congressional control, which would mean political determination of decisions that should be rendered in an objective manner. The idea of the rule of law, derived from the common law and adopted within the framework of the constitutional system, in theory limits legislative and executive control over the bureaucracy.

The nature of the American constitutional system poses very serious difficulties to the development of a system of administrative responsibility. The Constitution postulates that the functions of government must be separated into different branches with differing constituencies and separate authority. The idea is that the departments should hold each other in check, thereby preventing the arbitrary exercise of political power. Any combination of functions was considered to lead inevitably to arbitrary government. This is a debatable point, but the result of the Constitution is quite clear. The administrative process often combines various functions of government in the same hands. Attempts are made, of course, to separate those who exercise judicial functions from those in the prosecuting arms of the agencies. But the fact remains that there is a far greater combination of functions in the administrative process than can be accommodated by strict adherence to the Constitution.

It has often been proposed that a line of control be drawn from the original branches of government to those parts of the bureaucracy exercising similar functions, in order to alleviate what may be considered the bad effects of combined powers in administrative agencies. Congress would control the legislative activities of the agencies; the president, the executive aspects; and the courts, the judicial functions. This would maintain the symmetry of the constitutional system. But this solution is not feasible, because other parts of the Constitution, giving different

authority to these three branches, make symmetrical control of this kind almost impossible. The three branches of the government are not willing to give up whatever powers they may have over administrative agencies. For example, Congress is not willing to give the president complete control over all executive functions or to give the courts the authority to review all the decisions of the agencies. At present, judicial review takes place only if Congress authorizes it, except in those rare instances where constitutional issues are involved.

Another aspect of the problem of control is reflected in the apparent paradox that the three branches do not always use to the fullest extent their authority to regulate the bureaucracy, even though they wish to retain their power to do so. The courts, for example, have exercised considerable self-restraint in their review of administrative decisions. They are not willing to use all their power over the bureaucracy. Similarly, both Congress and the president will often limit their dealings with administrative agencies for political and practical reasons.

In the final analysis, we are left with a bureaucratic system that has been fragmented by the Constitution and in which administrative discretion is inevitable. The bureaucracy reflects the general fragmentation of the political system. It is often the battleground for the three branches of government and for outside pressure groups that seek to control it for their own purposes.

THE RISE OF THE ADMINISTRATIVE PROCESS

The rise of the bureaucracy can be explained in large part by observing how the transfer of legislative, executive, and judicial functions has derived from the primary branches of the government. Administrative agencies exercise legislative power because Congress and the president are unable and unwilling to cope with all the legislative problems of the nation. The president is chief legislator, and Congress is supposed to exercise the primary legislative function. Clearly, given the scope of modern government, it would be impossible for the president and Congress to deal on a continuous basis with the myriad legislative concerns that arise. Any president's legislative program is necessarily incomplete, because it must deal with the major problems that happen to be of interest to him and of concern to the nation at a particular time. Much of the president's program is formulated by the bureaucracy. In any event, it ultimately has to be carried out by administrative agencies, provided that Congress approves.

For the most part, Congress is concerned with formulating policy in very broad terms. It has neither the technical information nor the time to cope with the intricate phases of modern legislation. Moreover, it is often unwilling to deal with difficult political questions, for this would necessitate taking sides and alienating various segments of the public. It frequently passes on to the bureaucracy the burden of reconciling group conflict. The bureaucracy receives the unresolved disputes that come both to Congress and to the president, making it one of the most important political arms of the government. The concept of the bureaucracy as neutral is actually contrary to the facts.

Turning to the judicial arena, the development of administrative law has taken place because of the need for a more flexible mechanism for resolving cases and controversies arising under new welfare and regulatory statutes. The idea that the functions of government can be divided into legislative, executive, and judicial categories and segregated into three separate branches of the government is outdated because of the growth of a complex and interdependent economy requiring government regulation. Effective regulatory power often requires a combination of legislative and judicial functions.

ADMINISTRATIVE ADJUDICATION AND RULE MAKING

The existence of administrative agencies exercising both judicial and legislative functions has posed an almost irreconcilable dilemma to constitutional theory, jurisprudence, and judicial practice. At the outset, it should be pointed out that the kinds of judicial and legislative functions performed by administrative agencies are not exactly the same as those carried out by courts and legislatures. But they are very close.

Adjudication, in the generic sense, is a process by which individual cases and controversies are settled on the basis of an accurate determination of the facts relating to the adversary parties involved. It always involves a factual dispute, requiring a judgment to be made on the accuracy of the disputed facts. In private litigation factual disputes are between private parties. In administrative adjudication, factual disputes are between the government and private respondents or lower government entities. Usually, administrative agencies charged with the enforcement of a law bring an action against an individual party creating a case and controversy that must be resolved, first by the agency itself and, if the losing party decides to appeal, ultimately by an appellate court. The court, however, usually does not reach the substantive issues of the case but attempts to ensure that the agency has followed proper procedures required by law or, in extremely important cases involving individual liberties and rights, by constitutional due process. Adjudication by its very nature is retrospective, judging actions that have already taken place. Judgments of "adjudicative facts," or facts pertaining to the past actions of the litigants, determine the outcome.

Examples of administrative adjudication can most easily be drawn from areas of government regulation and disposition of benefits. For example, Securities and Exchange Commission or Federal Trade Commission complaints alleging violation of antitrust or securities laws involve the agencies in an adjudicative process. An agency acts as a prosecutor, bringing its case initially before an administrative law judge assigned to the agency but who, under the Administrative Procedure Act of 1946, is independent of agency sanctions and therefore theoretically capable of making an independent judgment of the facts. However, an agency may review the decision of an administrative law judge and, on the basis of its own judgment of evidence and policy views, overturn it. The regulatory realm is a major source of administrative adjudication, even though it has been reduced by deregulation in the 1970s and 1980s in such areas as airlines, railroads, trucking, and partially in banking. In other areas, government benefit determinations may also involve adjudication, as when the Social Security Administration determines whether or not an individual qualifies for disability payments and when the Veterans Administration decides whether a veteran can claim disability or other benefits.

438

The reference point in administrative adjudication is not only statutory law, which sets standards to be followed by the agencies, but also agency policy itself. Congress goes about as far as it can in establishing guidelines for the agencies, but both political considerations and the limitations of language leave a lot for the agencies themselves to decide. The securities laws, for example, forbid insiders from profiting against the "public interest." The Federal Communications Act, which regulates broadcasting, provides that licenses were to be given only to parties who acted in "the public interest, convenience, and necessity." The Food and Drug Administration law charges the agency with keeping unsafe and ineffective products off the market. But all of these statutory standards are intrinsically vague, requiring further administrative refinement to fill in the details of the legislation.

Administrative policy determinations can be made in two ways. First, they can be developed and applied on an ad hoc basis in case-by-case adjudication. For example, an agency, such as the Federal Communications Commission, may decide, without having previously announced its view in any policy statement or rule, that in the Boston metropolitan area ownership of a television station by a major newspaper violates the antitrust laws, which the agency is committed to carry out. The policy that opposes multimedia ownership, however, may pertain only to the Boston case and may not be applied in the future to similar ownership configurations in other cities. Agencies may also use another approach to policymaking, which involves them in holding rule-making proceedings in which interested parties participate and after which a rule or policy is announced that binds the agency in future cases in the same way that statutory law does.

CONTROLLING AGENCY ADJUDICATION AND RULE MAKING

That administrative adjudication and rule making should be controlled by an outside source is a premise of our constitutional system which cannot accommodate in theory an administrative branch that independently performs judicial and legislative functions. Moreover, common-law jurisprudence, which is an important underpinning of the American legal system,

strictly opposes the intrusion of the administrative state into the judicial realm. Political interests concerned with limiting administrative discretion have incorporated these ideas into an elaborate system of control by statute and judicial review.

Before the vast increase in the number of administrative agencies during the New Deal, scholars and leaders of the legal profession proposed ending administrative adjudication altogether by returning judicial functions to their proper home, the courts. Roscoe Pound, long before he became the head of the American Bar Association and later the dean of the Harvard Law School, sounded the alarm in a famous 1914 article entitled "Justice According to Law." He wrote,

> The experience of the past indicates that if we improve the output of judicial justice till the adjustment of human relations by our courts is brought into better accord with the moral sense of the public at large and is achieved without unreasonable, not to say prohibitive delay and expense, the onward march of executive justice will soon cease. But we [the legal profession] must be vigilant. Legislatures are pouring out an ever-increasing volume of laws. The old judicial machinery has been found inadequate to enforce them. They touch the most vital interests of the community, and it demands enforcement. Hence the executive is turned to. Summary administrative action becomes the fashion. An elective judiciary, sensitive to the public will, yields up its prerogatives, and the return to a government of man is achieved. . . . if we are to preserve the common-law doctrine of supremacy of law, the profession and the courts must take up vigorously and fearlessly the problem of today—how to *administer* the law to meet the demands of the world that is.

Pound did recognize that judicial inadequacy and unresponsiveness was one of the principal reasons for the rise of administrative adjudication.

The American Bar Association (ABA), realizing that President Franklin D. Roosevelt's rhetoric supporting an increase in government regulation would soon be translated into reality, in 1933 created the Special Committee on Administrative Law, charged with the task of reining in the expansion of agency adjudication. By that time, however, it was apparent even to the most conservative opponents of the New Deal and of "executive justice" that the clock could not be turned back. The original Pound solution, to transfer judicial functions back to the courts, was clearly both politically and practically unrealistic. The first report of the committee, issued in 1933, outlined a new tack:

> When . . . the administrative official exercises a quasi-judicial function, he may be expected to conform to the sort of procedure which has been found best adapted to the determination of the rights and obligations of the individual in his controversies with other individuals and with the government. Certain fundamental safeguards of notice, opportunity for hearing, and determination or review of issues of fact and of law by an independent tribunal (and eventually, on questions of law at least, by a court) are involved, and, indeed, are necessary if justice is to be done to the individual.

The imposition upon administrative agencies of procedural requirements similar to those imposed upon the courts was to be the new method of ensuring that administrative agencies, in the broadest sense, would uphold due process of law. The guardians of due process would be the courts. That would ensure upon judicial review that agencies followed the proper procedures.

THE ADMINISTRATIVE PROCEDURE ACT

The Administrative Procedure Act of 1946, combined with expanded doctrines of judicial review of administrative decision-making, put the new system of accountability into effect. Considered to be a milestone in bringing order, consistency, and responsibility to administrative adjudication, the act culminated more than a decade of political pressure from the ABA, administrative law scholars, and private interests concerned with administrative discretion in both adjudication and rule making. The law imposed a variety of procedural requirements on administrative agencies and expanded access to the scope of judicial review.

Originally, the act was designed to establish more-uniform procedures among the agencies in both rule making and adjudication. Formal administrative adjudication (where there is a statutory requirement for formal trial-type hearings before an administrative order takes effect) was required to follow procedures that were in many respects analogous to those of the regular courts. It provided for greater independence for those administrators called "hearing examiners" or "trial examiners" in 1946 but now called "administrative law judges" by an order of the Civil Service Commission in 1972. These officials conduct initial administrative proceedings in adjudication and rule making that involve formal hearings, which may be required by law or may be directed by the agency. The act required that the agencies publicize their formal rules in the *Federal Register.* The act also expanded the scope of judicial review.

Amendments to the law in 1966 and 1974, which together constitute the Freedom of Information Act, require agencies to disclose their records to "any person" making a request, subject to a variety of exemptions. For example, the Freedom of Information Act does not apply to agency records that by executive order have been designated to be kept secret in the interest of national defense or foreign policy or that are related solely to internal personnel rules and practices of the agency. Trade secrets cannot be disclosed, nor can personnel and medical files of an individual, the disclosure of which would constitute "a clearly unwarranted invasion of personal privacy." The move toward ending government secrecy was advanced with the passage of the Government-in-the-Sunshine Act in 1976. This legislation toughened the Freedom of Information Act, to make it more difficult for agencies to withhold information, and provided that the meetings of agencies headed by two or more persons appointed by the president and confirmed by the Senate would have to be open to the public, with certain stipulated exceptions.

Since the standards of the Administrative Procedure Act apply only to the formal administrative process (where formal hearings are required by law), they have limited applicability. Vast areas of administrative action are excluded from the purview of the act. A major criticism of the act is that it does not encompass informal administrative proceedings, thus making it an ineffective control over most administrative adjudication. In rule making, the act does require agencies to adhere to certain procedures even where there is no statutory requirement for hearing. Most agency rules must be published in the

Federal Register in advance of their official promulgation, and interested parties must be given an opportunity to comment and petition for a change or revocation of the rules. But these provisions governing rule making contain many exemptions, as is characteristic of other sections of the act. This means that the agencies have a great deal of discretion in deciding whether or not to adhere strictly to the guidelines set forth in the act.

There are the judicial standards that the Administrative Procedure Act makes applicable to hearings required by other statutory provisions. Generally, in the area of formal administrative proceedings, the act requires procedures analogous to the judicial or common-law process (although never as strict). Thus, notice must be given of formal administrative proceedings; a separation of prosecuting and adjudicative functions within the same agency is to be maintained; certain rules of evidence are to prevail; and a record of the proceedings is to be kept. The administrative law judge who presides at the hearing is to make the initial decision, which can be overruled by the agency on the basis of a different interpretation of policy or the introduction of new evidence; finally, appeal may, within limits, be taken to the courts.

The Administrative Procedure Act has clearly not fulfilled the expectations of its framers. To secure passage of the act in the first place, many exemptions had to be written into it in response to strong pressures from the agencies of Congress. The numerous escape clauses of the act lead to the exemption of large portions of the administrative process. The wording of the act is often ambiguous, leading to the courts' responsibility of determining its scope and impact. The act can be used either for judicial intervention in the affairs of the agencies or for judicial self-restraint. For example, although the act contains provisions expanding judicial review of agency action, it also provides that agency action that is committed to agency discretion by law is not reviewable. But it is not so simple to determine exactly which actions lie within the legal discretion of the agencies, and it is very simple for the courts to find that agency action is discretionary if they do not choose to review the decisions of the agency. The act has not been instrumental in increasing judicial control over the administrative process or in molding agency procedures in the image of the courts. The ineffectiveness of

the act illustrates the limitations statutes present as mechanisms to change decision processes that have developed out of political and practical realities.

One major accomplishment of the act that cannot be denied is the establishment, at least symbolically, of an independent class of administrative law judges. This has been done in conjunction with the separation of prosecuting and adjudicative functions within the agencies. Under the terms of the statute, administrative law judges are not subject to agency control either with respect to their job status or to their conduct in relation to the cases they initially decide. When a lawyer takes a case to an administrative law judge, he enters a decision process outside of the agency's immediate sphere of control. The role of the administrative law judge is based on the judicial model of decision-making, which requires personal (as opposed to institutional) and independent judgment in the determination of individual rights and obligations. The problem in the implementation of this model in the administrative process is that the act permits the agencies to overrule their administrative law judges whenever they are so inclined. This may seem rather strange, and the question may legitimately be asked, Why bother to give administrative judges independence under such circumstances—that is, why make their decisions only initially independent? One reason may have been the expectation that many of the decisions of administrative judges would not be appealed to, or taken by, the agencies for review. If this had become the situation, de facto power would reside with the judges. This has not, however, been the practice, and it is not uncommon for the agencies to overrule their own judges in cases involving important issues of public policy.

The very fact that administrative law judges are independent often creates conditions in which the agencies have to reverse or change their own judges' decisions. Lack of communication between the judges and the agencies and the inability of the agencies to control the actions of their judges cause the judges and the agencies to go in different directions on matters of policy.

The inherent differences between the administrative and judicial processes make it inappropriate to try to enforce a strict judicial decision-making model upon the agencies. Some of the most prominent scholars of administrative law, such as Kenneth Culp Davis and Walter Gellhorn, have long recognized that informal administrative processes may be far more appropriate to the resolution of issues involved in both rule making and adjudication than trial-type proceedings. Walter Gellhorn has stated that "some of this country's gravest administrative deficiencies stem from lawyer-induced overreliance on courtroom methods to cope with problems for which they are unsuited." Davis flatly states,

> The strongest need and the greatest promise for improving the quality of justice to individual parties in the entire legal and governmental system are in the areas where decisions necessarily depend more upon discretion than upon rules and principles and where formal hearings and judicial review are mostly irrelevant. We must try something that neither the legal philosophers down through the centuries nor our current study groups of the organized bar have tried—we must try to find ways to minimize discretionary injustice.
>
> (p. 216)

Regardless of the sound views expressed in these warnings, the ABA and, to a lesser extent, the Administrative Conference of the United States continue to recommend greater formalization of administrative procedures in both rule making and adjudication. The practicing bar continues to recommend elimination of most of the exemptions to the Administrative Procedure Act, greater judicialization of rule-making proceedings, expanded judicial review of agency actions, and a stricter separation of policymaking and adjudicative functions within the agencies. Proposals for administrative courts, which have a long history, are continually cropping up. Senator Robert A. Taft, Jr., of Ohio, for example, introduced a bill in 1975 to revive the old 1955 Hoover Commission proposals to create administrative courts.

Although proposals for greater judicialization of the administrative process are continually pouring out of various study groups associated with the bar, there has not been a single change made in the Administrative Procedure Act in this direction since it was originally passed in 1946. This reflects a general recognition of the exigencies of the administrative process in Congress as well as the power of the agencies to prevent general legislation that would further restrict their procedural flexibility. But the agencies continue to be restricted by their enabling statutes, and the tradition of requiring hearings (although not necessarily trial-type hearings) before administrative orders can be made has been continued in statutes governing more recently created agencies, such as the Department of Transportation, the Environmental Protection Agency, the Consumer Product Safety Commission, and the Nuclear Regulatory Commission. Statutory hearings need not be of the full-trial type (oral testimony with cross-examination) unless expressly required by the enabling statute, because the act, although it does impose certain judicial standards to be followed by the agencies, does not go so far as to mandate the right of cross-examination in administrative proceedings.

THE NATURE OF JUDICIAL REVIEW

Aside from attempting to mold internal administrative procedure to conform to the judicial model, the ABA, the Administrative Conference, practicing private attorneys in administrative law, and most legal scholars have supported the removal of obstacles to judicial review of administrative orders and, to a lesser extent, of administrative rules. But practical necessities dictate limited judicial review. Clearly, the courts cannot exercise broad review powers over all administrative decisions, even in the formal adjudicative realm. The courts cannot, and should not, review administrative matters that are nonjudicial in character. Parties seeking judicial review must have standing, which requires a case and controversy affecting their interests or their rights under statutory, constitutional, or common law. These requirements alone eliminate most administrative decisions from the purview of the courts. And even where the conditions of judicial review are met, the courts are reluctant, when considering a case on the merits, to delve too deeply into issues that they feel are more properly resolved by the agencies. In deference to the expertise of the agencies and their policy responsibilities, the courts have tended to limit review to legal questions concerning such matters as the scope of agency authority and whether or not proper procedures have been followed to protect the rights of private parties.

The right to judicial review of agency actions

stems from both statutory and constitutional law, although more from the former than from the latter. The statutes governing agency procedure contain provisions that explicitly grant judicial review to parties aggrieved by agency action, preclude review completely, or simply fail to mention the subject. Where explicit provisions exist for review, the courts designated by the statute must act as initial appellate bodies. Where there is preclusion of judicial review, the courts will receive a case only if they feel there is a constitutional right involved, which would be an extraordinary situation in terms of prevailing judicial practice. Where statutes say nothing about judicial review, the presumption is in favor of reviewability. This has particularly been the case since the passage of the Administrative Procedure Act in 1946, since it contains a general, although qualified, clause which states that "a person suffering legal wrong because of any agency action, or adversely affected or aggrieved by such action within the meaning of any relevant statute, shall be entitled to judicial review thereof."

Judicial review expands and contracts in an accordianlike fashion depending upon the political environment of the times, the vigor with which private interests pursue their goals, and the predisposition of the judges themselves. Before 1937, for example, a conservative New Deal Court closely scrutinized administrative action in cases on appeal from agency decisions. When Secretary of Agriculture Henry A. Wallace tried to impose rates on Kansas City stockyard brokers after extensive rule-making proceedings, the Supreme Court held that his action violated the statutory requirement for a "full hearing" because he had consulted off the record with expert members of his staff, who also had an interest in the case, before making his decision (*Morgan* v. *United States,* 1936, 1938). Chief Justice Charles Evans Hughes wrote in the second Morgan opinion, "If these multiplying agencies deemed to be necessary in our complex society are to serve the purposes for which they are created and endowed with vast powers, they must accredit themselves by acting in accordance with the cherished judicial tradition embodying the basic concepts of fair play."

The Supreme Court's conservatism and interventionist stance became muted as Roosevelt's second term was coming to an end in 1940, re-flecting both a change in Court personnel and greater sensitivity to attacks upon the judicial activism that had, in the 1930s, crippled the core of the New Deal program. The Supreme Court affirmed a position of judicial self-restraint in reviewing agency decisions that greatly expanded the latitude of administrative discretion. Above all, the courts did not interfere with the substantive decisions made by the agencies, which were more and more viewed by the increasing number of liberal justices on the Supreme Court as essential democratic instruments.

After a relatively dormant period in the struggle between the courts and the agencies, judicial interventionism returned with a vengeance in the 1960s and 1970s. Liberals joined conservatives in viewing the bureaucracy as a potentially despotic power with a tendency to override individual rights. Legal advocacy has always stressed more the importance of protecting the individual than the need to buttress government power and decision-making flexibility. Formal training in administrative law emphasizes the need to prevent government from acting arbitrarily against private interests, rather than teaching how to make government action more effective in the public interest. Even the government lawyer-advocate more often than not has his or her eye on more lucrative private practice and uses time spent working for an agency to learn how to fight it from the outside.

The resurgent judicial activism of the late 1960s in relation to administrative agencies reflected the political tenor of the times. Ralph Nader charged agencies with inefficiency, malingering, general neglect of duty, and being the captive of corporate interests. Young lawyers flocked to Nader, as they did to the civil rights and environmental movements, eager to challenge in the courts government actions they deemed to be against the public interest. Litigation became an important adjunct of political protest.

As they increasingly became the focus of political action, the courts responded with an accommodative stance. The primary reviewing bodies, the circuit courts of appeals, loosened the rules of standing to broaden the definition of aggrieved parties under the Administrative Procedure Act and the judicial-review provisions of the enabling statutes of the agencies. Even a group of George Washington University law students, under the tutelage of a dynamic professor who wanted them to learn by doing, were granted standing by the Supreme Court to challenge an Interstate Commerce Commission order that did not affect them directly as parties but only remotely as citizens (*United States* v. *Students Challenging Regulatory Agency Procedures,* 1973). Earlier the circuit courts had affirmed standing for representatives of civil rights and environmental groups to challenge agency action even though personal injury, once the touchstone of justiciability and standing, was remote and in some cases nonexistent. The Supreme Court, however, required at least a claim of personal injury to achieve standing in *Sierra Club* v. *Morton* in 1972, but the decision was not unanimous. Justice William O. Douglas, one of four dissenters in the case, cited favorably a law review article that argued even trees should have standing in environmental cases.

After expanding the standing doctrine, making the courts more accessible, some circuit judges began to impose procedural requirements on the agencies that went further in the direction of judicialization than the Administrative Procedure Act or agency statutes mandated. The Supreme Court, however, brought a halt to what it considered to be excessive intervention by the circuit courts in *Vermont Yankee Nuclear Power Corp.* v. *Natural Resources Defense Council* in 1978. Justice William H. Rehnquist's opinion for the Court emphasized judicial self-restraint, noting, "Agencies are free to grant additional residual rights in the exercise of their discretion, but reviewing courts are generally not free to impose them if the agencies have not chosen to grant them."

RESPONSIBILITY IN THE FUTURE

Because of the rule of law and the seeming pervasiveness of lawyers in a litigious society, judicial review is clearly an important channel that may be used to check administrative discretion. However, the delay and expense nearly always associated with litigation limits access to the courts. Moreover, the judicial concentration upon procedure rather than substance in reviewing agency actions means that in the end administrators usually can impose their policy

views without judicial interference. It is the president and Congress who ultimately have the responsibility for giving political direction to the bureaucracy.

The politics of the bureaucracy, however, often supports independent agency power. Always striving for political support, administrative agencies develop close ties with congressional committees that have jurisdiction over them and with special interests that they regulate or that are part of their clientele. These political "iron triangles" are often difficult to penetrate as they pursue policies that serve their interests.

The constitutional separation-of-powers system complements political pluralism to ensure a high degree of agency independence. The Constitution and the political system discourage the development of disciplined political parties capable of binding together the president and Congress. Congress itself rarely exhibits collective responsibility but, rather, relies upon its multiple and disparate committees to conduct legislative business and exercise administrative oversight. Under such circumstances administrative agencies will continue to comprise a semiautonomous fourth branch of the government, the components of which will act as entrepreneurs, seeking political support wherever it can be found, to buttress their power and expand their role in shaping government policies.

CASES

Morgan v. United States, 298 U.S. 468 (1936), 304 U.S. 1 (1938)
Sierra Club v. Morton, 405 U.S. 727 (1972)
United States v. Students Challenging Regulatory Agency Procedures, 412 U.S. 669 (1973)
Vermont Yankee Nuclear Power Corp. v. Natural Resources Defense Council, 435 U.S. 519 (1978)

BIBLIOGRAPHY

American Bar Association, "Report of the Special Committee on Administrative Law," in *American Bar Association Reports,* 58 (1933), contains early proposals for the judicialization of administrative procedures that, in modified form, eventually surfaced in the Administrative Procedure Act of 1946. Kenneth Culp Davis, *Discretionary Justice: A Preliminary Inquiry* (1969), examines the informal exercise of administrative power and ways to control it. Henry J. Friendly, *The Federal Administrative Agencies* (1962), comments on the need for administrative agencies to define more clearly their policy standards. Walter Gellhorn, "Administrative Procedure Reform: Party Perennial," in *American Bar Association Journal,* 48 (1962), evaluates proposals to reform administrative procedure. Joseph C. Goulden, *The Superlawyers* (1971), portrays Washington's top lawyers and illustrates how they deal with administrative agencies.

Ralph P. Hummel, *The Bureaucratic Experience* (1977), examines the environment and culture of bureaucracy, focusing upon the psychology of bureaucrats and how they deal with citizens. James M. Landis, *The Administrative Process* (1938), describes the characteristics of the administrative process and the reasons for the rise of administrative agencies. Eugene Lewis, *Public Entrepreneurship: Toward a Theory of Bureaucratic Political Power* (1984), examines the personal dimension of bureaucratic politics through the organizational lives of Hyman Rickover, J. Edgar Hoover, and Robert Moses. David Nachmias and David H. Rosenbloom, *Bureaucratic Government U.S.A.* (1980), analyzes not only the executive branch but also the bureaucratization of the presidency, Congress, and the judiciary, and examines bureaucratic politics in political parties and interest groups.

Roscoe Pound, "Justice According to Law," in *Columbia Law Review,* 14 (1914), is an important precursor of attacks upon bureaucratic despotism. Randall B. Ripley and Grace A. Franklin, *Congress, the Bureaucracy, and Public Policy* (1976), shows how different policy arenas affect congressional-bureaucratic relationships. Francis E. Rourke, ed., *Bureaucratic Power in National Politics* (1985), selects readings on various facets of administrative agencies, including constituencies, expertise, the struggle for power, elites, reform, and public control over bureaucratic power. Harold Seidman, *Politics, Position, and Power* (1980), examines the politics of government organization and administrative agencies. Aaron Wildavsky, *The Politics of the Budgetary Process* (1984), a political analysis of the budgetary process, covers agency strategies and congressional responses. Peter Woll, *American Bureaucracy* (1977), is an examination of the emergence of the federal bureaucracy as a major force in American government and the effect of its role on the constitutional system of checks and balances.

[*See also* ADMINISTRATIVE LAW *and* JURISDICTION.]

ALTERNATIVES TO FORMAL ADJUDICATION

Austin Sarat

In the United States during the 1980s there has been lively debate about the role of courts. Some believe that Americans have become too eager to litigate, to turn to courts for the resolution of a multitude of complicated personal and social problems, and it is felt that the courts have all too eagerly welcomed these new demands. Courts, it is said, have engineered a rights revolution and have become involved in problems that exceed their institutional capacities and overburden their limited resources. For those sympathetic to this argument, the search for, and development of, alternatives to formal adjudication is necessary to reduce the burden on courts and to provide mechanisms the institutional design of which is better suited to the provision of effective redress.

But not everyone believes in, or subscribes to, the theory of the litigation explosion and its associated crisis in the courts. Those skeptical of this view acknowledge that there has indeed been an increase in the rate at which cases are filed in courts. They argue, however, that this does not represent a change in the frequency with which grievances are brought to court but rather an increase in the rate at which grievances are experienced and acknowledged. In this view, Americans are no more litigious than they have ever been. There is simply more to litigate about. To suggest that those who litigate are acting inappropriately is, in fact, to blame the victims and to fail to come to terms with the sources and roots of their victimization.

The skeptics remind us that most disputes— that is, most potential lawsuits—never get to court, and they suggest that courts play a residual role in dispute resolution. Moreover, they argue that the filing of a lawsuit tells us very little about what courts actually do, because the vast majority of those suits will be settled without any court action at all. Formal adjudication is the tip of the iceberg, both in terms of the disputes that could be brought to court and in terms of the cases that are actually filed. Finally, the skeptics claim that the capacities of courts to resolve effectively the disputes that are formally adjudicated is underestimated by many critics of courts. Adjudication is, in this view, both useful and effective for most of the disputes that are brought to it. As a result, the skeptics question the urgency and necessity of the movement to create alternatives to formal adjudication and the need to channel disputes to such alternatives.

To consider alternatives to formal adjudication is, in the first instance, to presume a shared understanding of what adjudication is and what its attributes are. This essay will first examine several ideas about the nature of formal adjudication. In each of those ideas there is an implicit —or, occasionally, explicit—argument about the capacity of, and limitations on, formal adjudication, about what it is good for and what lies beyond its proper reach. Arguments about the capacities of formal adjudication provide an introduction to the world of alternatives and to the wide variety of techniques and methods through which disputes are processed without resort to adjudication. This essay considers various ways of describing and classifying those techniques and methods. It concludes by speculating about the future development of alternative methods of handling disputes and about the implication of that development for formal adjudication.

ALTERNATIVES TO FORMAL ADJUDICATION

THE ADJUDICATIVE IDEAL AND THE LIMITS OF ADJUDICATION

The term *adjudication* refers to a complex cluster of activities through which courts authoritatively decide cases and controversies and thus attempt to finally resolve them. It is one type of procedure through which disputes are submitted to a third party, in this instance a judge. As Martin Shapiro reminds us, "wherever two persons come into a conflict that they cannot themselves solve, one solution appealing to common sense is to call upon a third for assistance in achieving a resolution" (p.1). A triad—two disputants and an intermediary—provides the skeletal framework for adjudication. But not every instance of triadic conflict resolution qualifies as adjudication. Considerable scholarly energy has been devoted to the effort to specify those attributes or characteristics of triadic conflict resolution that constitute adjudication.

There are two different approaches to this problem of specification. The first looks for the essential and enduring core attributes of adjudication, attributes that must be present in order for a dispute-processing technique to be labeled adjudication. These attributes are presumed to be given and fixed. The definitional strategy employed by this first, "essentialist" approach is abstract and deductive. It seeks to isolate the central features and characteristics of adjudication without reference to any single set of practices associated with courts in any particular society or at any particular time. Essentialist definitions take the form of normative constructs or descriptive ideals that can be used to evaluate the extent to which any dispute-processing mechanism or technique approximates the adjudicative ideal.

Adjudication is seen as having rather strictly limited capabilities. Some believe that essentialist definitions of adjudication serve only to provide the basis for an argument that what courts do should be rather tightly restricted. If the attributes of adjudication are, in fact, given, then the range of things that can be appropriately asked of an adjudicative process is similarly a given. For essentialists, the functions of adjudication must be adapted to its form. Finally, essentialists typically provide long lists of the attributes of adjudication and link each of these

attributes to a specific limit on its capacity to resolve effectively some class or type of dispute.

The second approach to the definition of adjudication begins by trying to identify its essential or desired functions. It assumes that adjudication is an adaptive social process the characteristics of which may vary considerably with different times, places, and circumstances. For these "adaptationists," form follows function. Adjudication has no a priori character. Courts or courtlike processes are constructs designed by humans to serve certain purposes and are alterable as those purposes are altered.

Adaptationists look to the history of particular institutions and are less interested in establishing and protecting purity of form than in identifying the way in which those institutions develop and evolve. As a result, they are less eager than the essentialists to restrict the kinds of disputes that are, or can be, brought to adjudicative institutions. Whereas essentialists seek to find the perfect fit between the attributes of adjudication and particular disputes, adaptationists see these attributes as changing when demands on courts change.

Perhaps the most famous of the essentialist approaches to adjudication is found in the work of a former Harvard Law School professor, Lon Fuller. Fuller says that it is possible to think about adjudication "as a means of settling disputes or controversies" but that such a definition does not differentiate the process of adjudication from other means of processing disputes. Its distinguishing feature, according to Fuller, is the way adjudication allows for, and structures, the participation of persons concerned with, and affected by, its decisions.

The participation that is allowed emphasizes the presentation of proofs and reasoned arguments. This contrasts with other methods of dealing with conflict that allow affected parties to participate by voting or engaging in bargaining or negotiation. Voting allows for the play of preference unaccompanied by the need for reasons and justification; negotiation involves strategy, bluff, move, and countermove as much as, or more than, an effort at rational persuasion. It follows, Fuller argues, that "whatever heightens the significance of . . . [reasoned] participation lifts adjudication toward its optimum expression." Adjudication is, at its core, a way of making decisions that gives institutional expression to the importance of reason in human affairs. It embodies the belief that humans are rational beings, capable of exploring and justifying their actions in a reasoned fashion and of being persuaded by logical argument. Litigants seeking favorable judgments refrain from making threats or deals and, instead, present some set of principles against which their claims may be evaluated. Adjudication thus encourages normative argument and distributes entitlements in accordance with those arguments.

Fuller's is an inverted view of adjudication, a view in which the structure of formal adjudication is fixed in terms of its relationship to some a priori moral goal. His view is highly individualistic; that is, he imagines that social life proceeds through, and can be understood solely in terms of, the actions of individuals. To him, adjudication is one important method through which individuals, acting as individuals rather than as members or agents of organizations or aggregates, work to produce and maintain social order. As Owen Fiss suggests, Fuller's view of adjudication is "rooted in a horizontal world in which people relate to one another on individual terms and on terms of approximate equality." This argument reminds us that each definition of adjudication is at base deeply political in the sense that it is connected with, and serves to advance, some particular vision of the good life.

From this central emphasis on reasoned participation, Fuller and other essentialists deduce other attributes of adjudication. The first of these is impartiality. A biased judge, or one whose mind is made up before evidence is presented, makes reasoned argument an empty and meaningless effort. The adjudicator must not be an ally, tacitly or overtly, of either party. He must be persuadable and deliberative. An impartial adjudicator, in addition, must base his decision on the proofs and arguments presented by the parties.

Others, in addition to Fuller, have tried to define the essential or core attributes of adjudication by going beyond reasoned participation. Adjudication, according to law professor Marc Galanter, is "a kind of third-party processing of disputes in which disputants or their representatives present proofs and arguments to an impartial authoritative decision-maker who gives a binding decision, conferring a remedy or award

on the basis of a preexisting general rule" (1986, 9). Galanter's definition strongly resembles Fuller's except that whereas Fuller assigns priority to one element—party participation—as the defining core of adjudication, Galanter does not argue for the priority of any one element. Galanter suggests that adjudication should be examined and understood in terms of six general features—namely, how it acquires cases, how it processes these cases, the nature of its decisions, the bases of its decisions, the extent to which it is differentiated from other social processes, and the nature and extent of its connection to state power.

The first major dimension of adjudication is the manner in which it acquires its cases. Adjudication, Galanter tells us, deals with discrete cases and controversies between identifiable parties. It does not deal with general situations or issues. Adjudication is, in this sense, a process of giving particular answers to particular questions rather than a way of setting or establishing general policies. Cases are dealt with on an individual basis, each dispute being resolved on its own merits. The typical adjudicated case involves two parties, one with a claim or complaint, the other with a defense or an excuse.

Adjudication is a decisional process initiated by the action of the complaining party. It is, in this sense, reactive. Cases are brought to it. Adjudicative procedures are not self-starting. Judges do not set out or plan their own agendas. Unlike legislative bodies, in which individual legislators decide what ideas will be proposed and what issues will be discussed, judges must sit back and wait for disputes to be brought to them. This is not to say that they will hear every or any case brought forward. Judges have evolved various standards (such as standing and mootness) that allow them to decide whether a case is ripe or eligible for adjudication and to screen out or refuse to hear those that are not. Some appellate courts, such as the Supreme Court, have extensive discretionary jurisdiction, which allows them to pick and choose from among cases that are technically eligible those cases that are most important and consequential.

The second major dimension of adjudication is the way in which cases eligible for adjudication are processed. Galanter, like Fuller, emphasizes the importance of participation by affected parties and of the presentation of reasoned argument. The nature of the reasons and arguments that will be considered relevant are specified by the court. The rules of relevance that typically govern the adjudication process have the effect of narrowing the range of issues and questions that the parties themselves might wish to discuss or present to the court. As Galanter puts it, in adjudication "the case is defined by claims that specific events, transactions or relations should be measured by application of some delimited conceptual categories. The forum will only hear matters that are relevant to application of those categories" (1986, 15). Rarely do these categories require inquiry into the full range of circumstances out of which the case at hand arises. Most of the life history of the dispute and the disputants is left aside.

The third and fourth of Galanter's dimensions of adjudication are the nature and bases of decisions produced by and through adjudication. In the adjudicative process, judges are required to make a decision once a case has been properly presented. They cannot refuse to act or decide. Moreover, the decisions must be made on the basis of the reasons and the arguments presented by the parties. The judge is not free to import considerations of facts or norms that have not been presented. Decisions are made by fitting the facts of the case to a set of general norms (laws) articulated in advance and binding on the court or the judge. Judges are supposed to apply the law to the facts and, in theory, are not to consider the consequences or wisdom of the general norm being applied.

In this formal sense, adjudication is a process through which the law is applied rather than made. This is, in practice, a distinction without meaning, because the process of applying norms inevitably adds new meanings to those norms and, in so doing, changes and transforms them. In addition, since it is virtually impossible to write laws with such precise detail or comprehensiveness as to answer with clarity and exactness every question that may arise under them, judges will always have available to them a wide range of plausible readings or interpretations of applicable norms.

Moreover, the language of the applicable norm is often quite general or vague. Consider, for example, the Fourteenth Amendment's requirement that no state "shall . . . deprive any person of life, liberty, or property, without due

process of law." Nowhere in the amendment—or indeed in the Constitution—is there a definition of liberty or property. Thus, even the most cautious judge will have to reach beyond the letter of the law when asked to decide whether, for example, a state may remove welfare payments without following due process. And, as difficult as it may be to resolve the question of whether property includes welfare payments, the conscientious judge will still have to face the problem of defining what process is "due." Thus, to suggest, as both Fuller and Galanter do, that adjudicative decision-making involves the application of preexisting normative standards is not to resolve the question of how such standards will, in any case, be interpreted, understood, and applied.

The adjudicative process ends with an award or judgment for one or the other of the parties. The award or judgment embodies an all-or-nothing dimension. One party wins, the other loses; one party is branded as culpable, negligent, or at fault, and the other is portrayed as the innocent victim. Adjudicators make no effort to reconcile the parties or to arrange a resolution that will satisfy both. Decisions made through the adjudicative process are binding and final. Usually, once a decision has been made and a judgment entered, the court's involvement with the dispute and the disputants comes to an end.

Galanter's fifth dimension of adjudication is the extent to which adjudication as a process is embedded in, or separate from, other social processes. As Galanter sees it, adjudication is highly differentiated. Considerable effort is made to insure that it is separate and distinct and is readily perceived to be both. "Typically," Galanter argues, "adjudication involves special locations, persons, roles, language, postures, costumes and furniture. . . . Adjudication is . . . [in addition] conducted by professional specialists who have recourse to special forms of knowledge, discontinuous with everyday understandings not expressed in everyday language" (1986, 18). The highly differentiated quality of adjudication, with its arcane language, has the effect of making the process of adjudication seem mysterious and rather special to the outsider. The differentiation and professionalization of adjudication may, as a result, contribute to its legitimacy in the eyes of the public.

The final dimension of adjudication is its relationship to state power. Courts are typically agencies of the state, exercising public power, applying norms developed through the governmental process and ultimately dependent on the coercive force of the state to secure and ensure compliance with their decisions. Yet, while courts are part of the governmental apparatus of any society, they are not, at least in a democratic society, instruments of state policy. In order to be legitimate and to satisfy the requisites of meaningful party participation, courts must be at least partially independent. Although they are a part of the government, courts must not follow its directions. Special efforts must be made to establish judicial independence, one example being the guarantee of life tenure for judges in federal courts, a guarantee intended to protect judges from attempts at outside direction or threats of reprisal for unpopular decisions. The independence of the adjudicating body is, in turn, seen as a necessary guarantee of its impartiality. Balancing the need for independence and impartiality with the reality of its connection to the state places great stress on the process of adjudication and makes that process inherently unstable.

Those who define adjudication in terms of a list of its essential attributes regard adjudication as a moral ideal rather hard to attain. Adjudication, because its attributes are given or fixed, is considered rather strictly limited in its capabilities. For the essentialist, it is important to assess the fit between the attributes of adjudication and the needs or demands of particular types of disputes. Much of the energy devoted to encouraging the development of alternatives to formal adjudication comes from essentialists seeking to preserve courts for those disputes that are best suited to their rather limited institutional capacity.

Essentialists imagine that the typical lawsuit presents itself as a bipolar contest between two mutually opposed interests or parties each of which seeks a zero-sum, all-or-nothing resolution. The lawsuit focuses on a completed set of past events—who did what to whom, and who was responsible—and seeks a remedy commensurate with the right violated. In this view the lawsuit is what Abram Chayes calls a "self-contained episode," one with its primary impact being confined to the parties involved in it, each of whom takes responsibility for organizing and presenting what they consider the relevant facts. This kind of litigation does not, according to the essentialists, strain the capacity of formal adjudication. But change any aspect, and problems arise.

With this image in mind, essentialists often argue that the courts should avoid involvement in so-called social policy disputes, such as that about school desegregation—disputes in which there are more than two parties involved, in which the focus of the dispute is a present and ongoing condition rather than a past event, and in which there is a demand for judicial supervision and control during an extended remedial period. Such cases threaten the integrity of adjudication and strain its rather limited institutional capacity (Horowitz).

Adaptationists, in contrast, begin with the social function of formal adjudication rather than with its structural attributes. Owen Fiss puts forward perhaps the clearest statement of the adaptationists' definition of adjudication. For Fiss, "adjudication is the social process by which judges give meaning to our public values." Fiss suggests that the task of adjudication is to provide an opportunity for the clarification and application of values such as due process, freedom of speech, and personal autonomy. These values, stated in the Constitution, are not self-defining or self-enforcing. The essence of adjudication is found in moments when judges give those values specific meaning and operational content and, where there is a conflict of values, act to establish some, albeit tentative, priorities.

Adaptationists believe that while this process of finding meaning is constant, the social context out of which arise questions about the meaning of public values is not. As the context changes—for example, as society becomes much more technologically sophisticated and bureaucratically complicated—the form in which questions of public values will arise cannot be expected always to approximate the traditional image of the bipolar lawsuit. In such conditions, litigation often focuses not on a particular event but on a social condition that appears to threaten an important public value, such as the relationship between schools and patterns of residential racial segregation. The alleged victim will often be a group rather than an individual, and the remedy sought may involve a continuing effort to disentangle the strands of complicated social pattern.

ALTERNATIVES TO FORMAL ADJUDICATION

While the essentialist would worry about the fit between these attributes of a lawsuit and the essential characteristics of adjudication, the adaptationist would point to historical examples in which the courts have adapted their structure to accommodate new demands—they do so to question the argument that courts have not and cannot deal with such lawsuits successfully, and to suggest that alternatives to formal adjudication have been no more successful than the courts in dealing with such problems.

Adaptationists criticize the essentialist definition of adjudication for its arbitrary quality (Cavanagh and Sarat). That definition is, in the adaptationist view, wedded to a conception of courts that is abstract and static. Courts, so the argument goes, can take any form or adapt any procedures as long as they do not violate the relatively flexible parameters of due process of law. The structure and procedures of courts have in fact frequently changed to accommodate new types of cases. For the adaptationist, "judicial effectiveness depends on pragmatic experimentation, not on a theoretical analysis of the essential characteristics of courts. . . . By this view, what courts should do is a question distinct from what courts can do most effectively" (Council on the Role of Courts, 85). For the adaptationist, there can and should be no fixed definitions of adjudication and no attempt to arrive deductively at judgments as to what disputes do or do not belong in court.

IDENTIFYING THE ROLE OF ADJUDICATION

Essentialist and adaptationist views of adjudication share or seem to encourage two misperceptions about the role of formal adjudication. The first of these misperceptions is that courts play a major, direct role in processing society's dispute-resolution business. The second is that most of the disputes litigated are dealt with through formal adjudication.

Talk about the litigation explosion, the growth of an adversary society, or the dangers of legal pollution encourages the view that courts play a major role in processing disputes (Lieberman). There is, of course, no precise way to measure how large a role they do play. The range of disputes that come to courts is quite broad, and the sources of litigation are quite diverse. While we know that more than 100 million cases (many of which are routine) are filed in court every year, we have no comparable idea of the number of potential legal disputes that occur in a similar time period.

There has, in fact, been only one comprehensive, empirical effort to examine the extent of the involvement of courts in dealing with disputes and problems, the study by Richard Miller and Austin Sarat. It focuses on middle-range civil legal disputes, admittedly a small subset of the business of the courts. It identifies as a baseline the number of households out of a sample of 5,000 that had experienced a grievance that might give rise to a civil suit. Using that baseline it reports that approximately 45 percent of grievances lead to disputes over who did what to whom or over the appropriate remedy for an acknowledged wrong. Of those disputes, approximately 10 percent (5 percent of the original grievances) lead to litigation.

While this study is by no means exhaustive or even fully representative of the kinds of disputes that end up in court, its findings are suggestive. Courts, it appears, play a rather limited direct role in dealing with disputes, most of which are resolved without litigation through a range of techniques from "lumping it" (see below) to bilateral negotiations.

It would be neither fair nor accurate to suggest that the importance of formal adjudication is limited to its direct involvement in dispute processing. Adjudication casts a shadow within which many of the disputes that never make it to court are worked out (Mnookin and Kornhauser). It stands as a procedure of last resort, an authoritative and binding mechanism the decisions of which are beyond the immediate control of the parties. The anticipated results of adjudication must be taken into account if adjudication is to be avoided. Those results provide a set of normative expectations that structure bargaining and negotiation. The ways in which formal adjudication has in the past dealt with similar disputes establishes a framework within which current disputes can be managed. The question of what a judge or jury would do is very much in play in any dispute. Past results and decisions help establish the value of present claims and establish a baseline against which offers and demands can be judged.

ALTERNATIVES TO FORMAL ADJUDICATION

The metaphor of a shadow is apt in suggesting that formal adjudication cannot direct appropriate resolutions. Because no two cases are exactly alike, there is always room for doubt about what a court would do. Because the case is made as much as found, disputants attempt to manipulate perceptions and manufacture facts to suggest that court treatment is likely to follow one or another pattern. Nevertheless, anticipation of that treatment can be said to establish "bargaining endowments," chips that each party can play to its advantage. In divorce cases, for example, the "rules governing alimony, child support, marital property and custody give each parent certain claims based on what each would get if the case went to trial. In other words, the outcome that the law would impose if no agreement is reached gives each parent certain bargaining chips—an endowment of sorts" (Mnookin and Kornhauser, 968). What is true in divorce is also true in other areas of the law. In criminal cases, for instance, the sentencing dispositions of judges help to establish the "going rate," against which plea bargains can be worked out.

The shadow of the law reaches to questions of facts and procedures and to substantive outcomes. The rules of relevance that courts employ may provide an incentive for the transformation of disputes, for recasting them in terms that would receive favorable treatment in court. Formal adjudication provides a modal definition for all potential legal disputes, a definition to which parties can refer as they try to construct and reconstruct their disputes and as they present their case to the other side. Rules of relevance may also serve to enable disputants to defend themselves or to ward off claims. Claims unlikely to receive favorable treatment in court have a much reduced "street value."

Finally, the shadow of adjudication includes the procedures through which disputes are treated. The procedures of formal adjudication provide a model for dispute resolution generally. Rules of evidence used in courts may communicate to disputants the expectation that particular kinds of evidence or testimony do not count. Rules of procedure may suggest ways in which disputants must proceed if their claim is to be taken seriously or to be regarded as legitimate. Moreover, informal procedural barriers, such as delay and cost, work to confer bargaining advantages or disadvantages on disputants.

The shadow of adjudication does not fall into a social vacuum (Galanter, 1986, 128). First, the skills and resources of the disputants are critical in determining the worth of the endowments created by substantive, factual, and procedural shadows. Some disputants are able to take advantage of these endowments; others are not. In addition, the shadow of formal adjudication falls into a complex and dense pattern of informal norms and customs that also work to shape disputant behavior. The impact of the shadow of adjudication is as highly varied as it is difficult to track in practice.

If one false perception of formal adjudication concerns the extent of its direct involvement in dispute processing, a second and equally pervasive misperception involves the role of formal adjudication within the judicial process. Formal adjudication is by far the most remote and least frequently invoked aspect of the judicial process. In both criminal and civil courts, approximately 10 percent of cases filed end up in a formal trial. Most are settled with very little, if any, intervention by the court. Of those that are settled, as many are simply abandoned or withdrawn as are pursued to formal adjudication. "The master pattern of American disputing is," according to Marc Galanter, "one in which there is an invocation . . . of an authoritative decision maker, countered by a threat of protracted or hard fought resistance, leading to a negotiated . . . settlement in the anteroom of the adjudicative institution" (1986, 100). In the usual case, litigation does not mark the end of efforts to reach an agreement. It often is simply a stage along the way, a stage that focuses attention, indicates a higher level of seriousness, and helps to reinvigorate faltering efforts. Thus, adjudication is to the judicial process as the judicial process is to the structure of dispute processing, in that it is a rather remote but highly influential arena.

Just as we recognized the influence of the norms, rules of relevance, and procedures of formal adjudication on dispute processing outside of courts, we must acknowledge its comparable significance in the much smaller universe of litigated cases. The power of formal adjudication as example, prediction of outcome, or threat is intensified as cases get closer to it. The decision to file a lawsuit is, in a sense, a decision to bring one's dispute more directly under the umbrella of the law, to invoke the norms and practices of a particular court and its local legal culture. The effect of filing a lawsuit may be to transform the culture of argument: it decisively puts at the center of attention the question of how this case would be dealt with through formal adjudication.

Yet, filing a lawsuit as a tactic to promote settlement—thereby moving more fully into the shadow of adjudication—is not without its risks. The most important of these risks is an escalation of the hostility that accompanies litigation. Because litigation is threatening, it may, if only for a brief period, harden positions and increase defensiveness and suspicion. In most cases, adjudication is avoided, and agreement is reached or resignation prevails.

ALTERNATIVES TO FORMAL ADJUDICATION: TECHNIQUES AND PROCESSES

Alternatives to formal adjudication can be approached in several ways. One way highlights the distinction between those alternatives involving third-party intervention as against bilateral dispute processing, in which the parties manage their own conflict. Another distinguishes between those that are in some way connected to state power and those that are not. Yet another emphasizes the formality or informality of the procedures that are utilized. Still others emphasize the political dimensions of dispute processing, contrasting alternatives, on the one hand, that, like adjudication itself, employ a specialized discourse and a relatively closed, private setting and thus allow third parties to define the operational content of the dispute, with, on the other hand, those employing more generalized discourse in an open setting to allow the parties themselves, and their allies and supporters, to retain control of their dispute and its definition. There is, of course, no right way to divide up and speak about the world of alternatives to formal adjudication. Each of these approaches has its advantages; each emphasizes a somewhat different aspect of the alternatives that are surveyed.

Perhaps the most common alternative to formal adjudication is in many ways the least recognized and least recognizable. This alternative involves unilateral action on the part of a potential disputant to avoid voicing a grievance or complaint or to avoid making a claim. This alterna-

tive, variously called lumping it, endurance, avoidance, and denial, stops the disputing process before it begins. It occurs when people self-consciously refuse to define some event or transaction in their lives as troubled or problematic. This occurs at the stage of problem recognition and is, in many ways, the predominant or modal response to potential disputes. Social life is, for the most part, inert. The world as it is, fraught with problems and difficulties, is perceived to be the world as it has to be. People invest substantial energy in resisting attempts to define events within life as either injurious or blameworthy. It is almost always easier to endure the familiar than to seek redress or compensation (Felstiner, Abel, and Sarat).

Moreover, there are formidable social and cultural barriers to the voicing of a claim. First, it is all too infrequently acknowledged that disputing, no matter what its outcome, may create greater problems for the parties involved than suffering in silence. To enter a claim for redress involves a social declaration of trouble, a declaration that may lead to considerable social disruption and disorientation. We need only consider the situation of the employee who begins to perceive herself as a victim of employment discrimination. In such a situation, the declaration of trouble is really just the beginning of trouble.

Even in less complex situations, blaming and claiming entail numerous risks, risks that arise in breaching public presumptions of order and in indicating and acknowledging in a public way that one's life is troubled. These risks deter potential claimants. Notions of civility encourage people to ignore trouble and, in so doing, to display tact. Given these notions, alleging trouble almost always brings some trouble on the self, making it uncomfortable, dirty work to be avoided. Those who seize on any normative ambiguity in interaction as an opportunity to register dissatisfaction develop reputations such as obnoxious or neurotic. Thus, risks of loss of face, reputation, or status commonly accompany social declarations of trouble.

In addition, those who allege that another has caused trouble may confront problems stemming from the admission of their personal involvement in social messes. Clearly, this has been an acute problem in rape cases. While severe penalties reflect society's supposed moral horror of the crime, the social stigma of acknowledging such a violation, as well as the law's insensitivity to the victim, frequently results in a refusal to report or to prosecute such crimes. To acknowledge publicly that there is trouble in one's life is to run the risk of being stigmatized, gossiped about, or ostracized, because claimants may be held causally or morally responsible for not doing something to prevent or avoid the trouble in the first place. Blaming the victim is, indeed, a common cultural preoccupation. When, for example, parents label children as disturbed and bring them in for treatment, psychiatrists may agree with them but suspect that the parents are themselves to blame. Those who acknowledge trouble seem somehow to be troubled themselves.

Claimants pay a high price for disturbing the peace and for not being able or willing to "take it." As a result, social life often proceeds with one or both parties of an interaction believing that something is wrong in their relationship, without ever communicating this feeling to the other person. To do so would be to risk engendering hostility in the other party and in others who learn of the accusation or the claim. Thus, private endurance has its attractions. When endurance becomes unbearable, however, catharsis may help. People cope with trouble by collusively discussing it with associates, a kind of displacement. At mealtime debriefings, workers may use the family as a forum to voice suppressed criticism of fellow workers, business associates, or others in the workplace. Returning to work, however, they may complain about their insensitive spouses to the very co-workers who were the object of the earlier criticism. In these ways, public allegiance to definitions of civility and order are maintained and trouble is avoided, evaded, or rendered manageable.

It is important not to underestimate the social pressure to repress grievances or claims. A repressed trouble may be less troubling than what results when it is made public. The revelation of grievances or of long suffering that may come to light in the wake of socially acknowledged trouble gives but one indication of the value of the effort to endure without complaint. While the social declaration of trouble always has the potential to restore order and harmony, such declarations almost inevitably open the floodgates of recrimination and retribution. Society is, in truth, held together by the implicit promise not to tell "the whole truth and nothing but the truth" about our grievances, anger, or offense. Imagine the horror that would result if everyone were, in psychological terms, to become congruent and to fully express their grievances. Such a society would lead any sane person to the brink. The burden of raising a claim is the fear of opening a Pandora's box of retribution. As anyone who has ever had a marital quarrel knows, often the simple suggestion that you pick up your underwear leads to the recitation of a surprisingly long list of comparable grievances given by the alleged offender. As a result, claiming is often accompanied by a sense of foreboding about what the alleged wrongdoer may himself allege or do in return.

If these barriers are overcome and a claim is made, a second alternative to formal adjudication—bilateral bargaining and negotiation—may be employed. Bilateral negotiation can be implicit and indirect, or it may be relatively formal and direct. It occurs within a framework of norms and expectations about how reasonable people ought to behave, how responsibility ought to be assessed, and what constitutes fair and equitable compensation for wrongs and injuries. These expectations both shape and reflect legal norms and the patterns of formal adjudication. They are, at the same time, autonomous from, and often resistant to, those norms and patterns. Bilateral dispute processing may be more or less embedded in a common folk culture, which exerts as much or more influence than the legal culture.

Bilateral dispute processing is likely to continue throughout the course of a dispute. Invocation or intervention of third parties seldom ends, although it significantly alters, the negotiation phase. We must recognize the overlapping quality of alternatives to formal adjudication and the way in which the various mechanisms of, and strategies for, processing disputes interpenetrate. It would be inaccurate to assume that there are rigid boundaries between dispute-processing techniques, that when one is invoked others are abandoned. There is no neat pattern in the way dispute processing occurs. Choices are tentative and revocable. What happens in the process of negotiation structures the way in which triadic processes are employed, just as the expectation or threat of resort to those processes influences the negotiation process itself.

ALTERNATIVES TO FORMAL ADJUDICATION

The content and form of bilateral negotiation is, of course, highly varied. It is difficult for an outsider to know the extent to which disputants bargain over norms and facts, whether negotiation is highly ritualized or ad hoc, and whether the negotiation process is oriented toward compromise or toward establishing the conditions under which one or another of the parties will feel comfortable and secure enough to concede or surrender. Indeed, even what is most central to the process of bilateral negotiation—namely, the fact that the parties themselves retain control over the final outcome—may be blurred through the intervention of allies and supporters and the use of intermediaries, such as lawyers. Bilateral dispute processing is, then, in many ways the most idiosyncratic and difficult to understand of the various alternatives to adjudication.

Perhaps the most prominent type of bilateral dispute processing is plea bargaining in criminal courts. Plea bargaining is, of course, one example of the overlap and interpenetration of dispute-processing mechanisms, since it generally occurs only after a criminal case has been formally initiated. Like other types of bilateral negotiation, plea bargaining is highly varied in its application. It can focus on an exchange of a plea of guilty for a reduction in the number and seriousness of criminal charges or for an agreed-upon and more lenient sentence recommendation. Judges may be more or less actively involved in trying to facilitate agreement. Moreover, because local norms and conventions often dictate the range of appropriate punishments for different offenses, bargaining may focus on the question of what was done rather than on what should be done about it. Thus, when fixing the type of offense requires rather precise knowledge of the circumstances and conditions surrounding a crime, what is most at issue is what type of offense was committed. Bargaining may take the form of an exchange of information rather than a succession of offers and demands, an exchange designed to produce an agreed-upon definition of the offense so that a rather standardized response can be applied. Thus, as Malcolm Feeley notes,

discussion of plea bargaining often conjures up images of a Middle Eastern bazaar, in which each transaction appears as a new distinct encounter, unencumbered by precedent or past association. Every interchange involves higgling and haggling anew in an effort to obtain the best possible deal. The reality . . . is different. [It is] more akin to modern supermarkets, in which prices for various commodities have been clearly established and labelled in advance. To the extent that there is any negotiation at all, it usually focuses on the nature of the case and the establishment of relevant "facts."

(p. 462)

Third-party, or triadic, alternatives to formal adjudication are both less common and easier to understand than either the unilateral or bilateral type (Sarat and Grossman). Each triadic dispute-processing institution has its own special set of participants, perhaps a different set of rules, and a distinctive style. Each alternative provides its own kind of "justice"; some proceed without reference to general rules known and articulated in advance; others operate according to such rules. Some provide a process of judgment in which it is the status of the parties in dispute or the preferences of the third party that determine the outcome; others require impartiality. Courts, for example, generally emphasize greater procedural regularity than do other dispute-processing institutions. Furthermore, while adjudicative decision-making is, as we have seen, supposed to encompass the marshaling of reasons and justifications by an impartial arbiter, triadic processes do not always produce reasoned decisions and equitable results.

The structure of a third-party dispute-processing institution has an important influence on the way the dispute is presented; indeed, it may alter the basic nature of the dispute itself. This is as true in moving from informal to more formal means of conflict resolution as it is in moving from trial to appellate courts. Finally, any particular institution has inherent some limitations on the available remedies and thus indirectly on the nature of the settlement that is possible. Participants have to agree to play by the rules of the institution; often this requires that they redefine their interests, goals, and strategies.

The third-party technique that displays the greatest family resemblance to adjudication is arbitration. Like adjudication, arbitration seems to produce a result on the basis of some principle; unlike adjudication, it need not establish that principle in advance. Arbitration is, in general, although it need not be, entered into voluntarily. Often arbitration provisions are written into contracts as a way of avoiding the need to resort to formal adjudication, should disagreements arise.

The arbitration process is similar to adjudication in that each party has the opportunity to present its "case" to the arbiter, who is most often a subject-matter specialist rather than a generalist trained in law. Some believe that the tailor-made expertise of the arbiter gives arbitration a major advantage over adjudication in technically complex disputes. Arbitration procedures are supposed to be less formal and more flexible than those used in formal adjudication, and it is argued that as a result, arbitration is speedier and simpler. At least in theory, arbitration places considerably less emphasis on adversariness and on the establishment of guilt or responsibility. As in adjudication, the arbiter is assumed to be neutral and impartial. Nevertheless, the arbiter may, with agreement of the parties, undertake some independent fact-finding and, in such instances, render decisions on grounds that go beyond those that are established or presented by the parties themselves.

Another type of triadic dispute processing that is much less like adjudication is mediation. Mediation differs from both adjudication and arbitration in that the third party is not empowered to enter a binding decision. Instead, the mediator attempts to bring about an agreement between the parties by listening to each side, trying to identify areas of common concern, and building on those areas by proposing solutions in areas of disagreement (Eckhoff). In mediation the disputants thus have control over the process and the results. A successful mediation is one in which the parties are enabled to reach an agreement that they were, or would have been, unable to reach bilaterally and that is truly satisfactory to both parties, so that they will be willing to comply with it even in the absence of coercion or threat. While the third party in mediation is supposed to be neutral and unbiased, mediators are encouraged to actively shape proposals and develop conditions out of which an agreement might arise. Finally, mediation is ad hoc in the sense that the mediator is bound by neither abstractly stated and codified normative principles nor by previously mediated agreements.

There is an important danger to any discourse about alternatives to formal adjudication that proceeds as this one has. This danger, roughly equivalent to the danger of essentialist definitions of adjudication, is the danger of the ideal type, the danger of relying on abstract, ahistorical descriptions of complex social processes. With respect to both arbitration (Kritzer and Anderson) and mediation (Merry), there is some suggestion that many of their advertised differences from formal adjudication are not realized in practice. Arbitration, especially in commercial disputes, has become increasingly formal and rule-bound, increasingly lawlike in its procedures. This again demonstrates the power of adjudication as a model for dispute processing. Mediation, on the other hand, despite its advertised emphasis on voluntariness and on the retention of its control by the disputants, has been found to be highly coercive and often unfair or inequitable in the results it produces, especially in situations in which there are significant power differentials between the parties or in which it is used as an adjunct to more formal processes.

We have to this point talked about alternatives to adjudication in terms of the number of parties most directly involved as participants, but there are, as suggested above, several other ways in which we can talk about them. One approach emphasizes both the level of formality of adjudication and its alternatives (that is, the presence or absence of a specialized third-party role, specialized rules of evidence and procedure, written records, and established channels of appeal) and their connection to the established governmental apparatus (that is, whether the coercive power of the state can be used to enforce their decisions).

In this view, exemplified by Sarat and Grossman, the first type of third-party dispute-processing alternative to adjudication is informal and private. The adjusters of disputes in a private, informal setting do not have any formal connection with the state, although in some cases they may have to be licensed by the state or by a quasi-public organization of professionals that exercises a delegated licensing function. The third party may be chosen because he has status, position, respect, power, or money. Or he may simply be the designated agent of an organization set up to handle specific disputes. The technique of bringing disputes to a private, informal third party may be the choice of both disputants or of one but not the other party to a conflict. Or it may be the result of private norms or expectations of a subcultural group which "require" that disputes be settled, as much as possible, within the group.

Private, informal dispute resolution is found in the United States in religious and ethnic communities, in the work of trained professionals such as marriage counselors, in various commercial relationships, and even in large shopping malls. In all of these settings private, informal dispute processing is based on the assumption that the parties to a dispute will agree about what matters are in dispute and will trust the person called upon to act as a judge.

Societies differ in the extent to which private, informal modes of dispute settlement predominate and in the extent to which the norms of private settlement affect the operations of more public and more formal institutions. Japan, for instance, seems marked by the ubiquity of such private, informal conflict-resolving devices. Private, informal dispute settlement has also been found to be relatively more extensive in underdeveloped societies. In such societies, dispute settlement most often occurs within primary groups or within a village setting. A respected elder intervenes and, after listening to the disputants, makes a decision. His decision will be accepted by the disputants because of their respect for his position or their allegiance to a closely knit social community.

In both underdeveloped and developed societies, private, informal processes may be favored over litigation because of their "proximity" to the disputants. This proximity facilitates dispute settlement by allowing people to work out their problems without clearly having to acknowledge that their relationship is "in trouble." Members of distinct subcultural groups may feel more comfortable being judged by "their own kind" or at least by someone perceived as similar in lifestyle and values. They may be reluctant to participate in formal processes of adjudication because they lack faith in the fairness and justice of results that might be obtained from these processes. This lack of faith is accentuated where public dispute settlers (including lawyers) are predominantly of a different race, religion, ethnic group, or social status from that of the disputants.

Third-party processing of disputes also pro-

ceeds through public, informal methods. These methods involve the informal intervention by agents of the state to solve disputes. Such dispute processing is utilized to complement the needs of public, formal institutions by reducing their operating burdens through the delegation of discretion to actors whose behavior in working out disputes is less often guided by standardized norms or procedures than by role-relevant routines. Dispute treatment in this context reflects not only official norms of substance and procedure but also, within broad limits, the organizational commitments of the public agents involved.

Avoidance of procedural regularity in the pursuit of more immediate and more efficient conflict resolution is also characteristic of plea bargaining, the practices in the early juvenile courts, and the pretrial conference, which has come to play an increasing role in facilitating the settlement of civil suits in the United States. In the case of plea bargaining the defendant is induced to settle his "conflict with the law" through an informal, bargaining process. Thus, plea bargaining may be less like other third-party mechanisms in which the roles of judge and adversary are clearly separated than the kind of dyadic negotiation that generally begins before resort to adjudication. The public prosecutor becomes the "dispute settler" and has virtually complete discretion as to whether to prosecute or on what charge. He has available both the coercive power of the state (in the form of a probable guilty verdict if the case goes to trial) and the discretion to work out an acceptable compromise.

Mediating toward a compromise is also in the prosecutor's interest. It reduces the risk of (too many) acquittals, and it gives him better control of the outcome. His role becomes managerial and bureaucratized in place of the formality of court adjudication of guilt or innocence. The prosecutor becomes the manager of a ritualized conflict-resolution ceremony. While in some ways his handling of guilty pleas resembles the resolution of private, informal disputes, it is much less open-ended. The prosecutor is a public official designated to resolve such conflicts, and the defendant cannot simply drop out of the relationship.

The thread connecting all public, informal methods of dispute resolution is their proximity to the formal arena of the courts and to third-party adjudication by a judge, and their reliance on private bargaining within this context. There are no formal rules, but a set of norms and mutual expectations gives these processes some structure. Indeed, in some cases, the process by which informal settlements are reached (plea bargaining is the best example) has become bureaucratized. A relatively small group of actors is involved in any one jurisdiction, regularized relationships and mutual dependencies develop, and the needs of the bureaucracy for compromise and accommodation frequently predominate.

Unlike private, informal alternatives, which act to deflect disputes from formal processes before they are carried into litigation, these examples, although not all, of public, informal processes act to deflect disputes from formal processes only after the process of litigation has been initiated. In a sense, these devices do not act as alternatives to such formal adjudication; they function instead to reduce it from a highly conflictual process to one in which all that is sought is certification of an informally agreed-upon solution.

A third category—private, formal alternatives —involves dispute settlers who remain private actors but carry out their functions in accord with certain agreed-upon and standardized procedures. They are more likely to act as judges than mediators, although role definitions may be fluid. Such formal but private tribunals are found within the confines of organizations or associations, professional groups, and within certain subcultural groups. These tribunals exist to settle conflicts between group members, conflicts that cannot be settled informally but that, for some reason, the parties are reluctant to move into the public arena. Where group membership is conditioned by a voluntary or imposed acceptance of certain norms or a code of conduct, the enforcement of such norms will typically be handled at several levels within the group. Those breaches that cannot be settled or sanctioned informally will usually have to be settled by more formal means. Although the rules and procedures followed by such tribunals may bear some resemblance to those of the courts, those rules and procedures remain private and often diverge substantially from those employed in the public sector.

Many trade associations have established their own formal arbitration machinery for the settlement of disputes between members. Similarly, labor-management disputes are often brought before arbiters, designated in advance, whose decisions are binding by mutual consent of the disputants and ultimately enforceable by private sanctions and by the courts. Agreement to submit disputes to private but formal arbitration is characteristic of parties whose relationship involves long-term performance or other aspects of permanence.

Private, formal dispute-processing devices employ courtlike procedures for settling disputes between group members. Decision-makers are not agents of the state but may be regarded by group members as possessing some sort of jural authority based on the stipulation of a prior contract or on delegated state authority. Compliance may be purely voluntary, as in the case of a religious court, or induced by potential sanctions (loss of license, loss of hospital privileges for a doctor, and the like) or the ultimate threat of a spillover into the public courts, with greater potential consequences.

The final type of dispute-processing mechanism includes adjudication in courts. This type is both public and formal. The rules that govern access and establish the procedural framework of these bodies are variables of critical importance. What kinds of disputes are to be decided, who can bring these disputes, and what kinds of solutions are possible are among the most important determinants of the involvement of public, formal mechanisms in defining, managing, and interpreting conflict. In contrast to private, informal mechanisms, the "rules" for decision in courts do not come from the parties themselves. Their sources are many—statutes, prior decisions governed by the rule of predecent, and evolving policy considerations responsive to current demands.

Unlike other dispute-processing institutions, those that are both public and formal generally require, either explicitly or implicitly, that parties in dispute be represented by legal specialists, people who claim unique knowledge of the procedural and substantive rules governing access to, and the operation of, public, formal institutions. These specialists act on behalf of the parties to shape and structure the issues presented to these institutions and the way in which the issues are perceived and handled by them.

ALTERNATIVES TO FORMAL ADJUDICATION

Legal specialists play a critical role in influencing and determining the conditions under which courts and similar types of adjudicative institutions become involved in conflict management and in defining the goals and objectives of litigation.

Public, formal dispute mechanisms are usually more oriented toward zero-sum decisions than are the less formal mechanisms noted above. Additionally, they generally require disputants to narrow their definitions of issues in such a way as to identify unambiguously, if sometimes artificially, the nature of their problems. In spite of the zero-sum nature and formality of many of their procedures, public, formal institutions occasionally do seek compromise and flexibility. Since they are substantively more concerned with right or wrong and with enforcing general norms than with the resumption of normal relations between the parties, the processes through which this flexibility is introduced may be quite unique.

A number of means have been devised for reconciling new experiences and expectations with past values while preserving at least the illusion that the law is consistent over time. The development of equity has provided one well-known technique of providing justice to the parties where a strict application of the law would be unjust. Furthermore, the formal adjudication of disputes is, at least in some countries, an essential, if somewhat awkward, means of reinforcing or changing public policy. This is bound to have an important effect on the way in which essentially private or localized disputes are settled. For those who seek to bring public norms to bear in essentially private disputes and thus broaden the range of perspectives relevant to their problem, litigation is an attractive mode of participation. For them the "public regardingness" attached to all disputes brought to the courts is an advantage that outweighs group ties or cultural norms designed to discourage this form of political participation.

This way of talking about alternatives to formal adjudication has recently been criticized for overemphasizing the discontinuity of dispute-processing institutions, for artificially separating those institutions from their social context, and for not being useful in helping to explain differences in outcomes typically associated with different types and styles of dispute processing (Yngvesson and Mather). Critics suggest that attention be given to the social accessibility of such institutions and the nature of the language and procedures that they employ. In this view, the significant differences between the various dispute-processing institutions are the extent to which they are open and accessible or closed and inaccessible to informal audiences and participants and the extent to which they rely on specialized language and procedures. Institutions that are closed and inaccessible and those that rely on specialized language and procedures concentrate and centralize power and stratify the disputing process much more than those that are open and rely on generalized discourse.

The value of this way of thinking is that it alerts us to the power and control dimensions of dispute processing—that is, to the extent to which particular techniques and approaches confer control over the dispute on specialists or officials or allow continuing control on the part of disputants. In this view, formal adjudication, because of its relative inaccessibility and its specialized language and procedure, would be seen as a disempowering way for individuals to deal with disputes, while mediation would be seen as keeping power in the hands of the disputants.

THE FUTURE OF ADJUDICATION AND ITS ALTERNATIVES

However one chooses to describe and discuss formal adjudication and its alternatives, it is clear that during the 1980s in the United States, there is considerable dissatisfaction with the former and considerable energy being devoted to the development and encouragement of the latter. Whether because of doubts about the competence and effectiveness of courts in resolving the kind of complex social policy disputes that now seem so much a part of the American judicial process, or out of a sense that courts are all too often violating and ignoring the essential attributes of adjudication, many observers now seem to feel that there is a serious crisis in the courts. For them the preferred solution is often to encourage the development of or greater reliance on alternatives to adjudication, and to divert particularly troublesome cases from formal adjudication to one or another of those alternatives.

The years 1970–1985 produced an explosion

ALTERNATIVES TO FORMAL ADJUDICATION

of activity in support of alternative dispute resolution. Yet the sources and consequences of this development are little understood. Some critics, such as Laura Nader, have taken the alternatives movement to task for uncritically assuming that procedures appropriate in one social context can be readily transplanted to another, for neglecting the task of strengthening legal institutions upon whose power the efficacy of all alternatives ultimately depend, and for failing to devise better ways to prevent injuries and social troubles. Others, like Jerold Auerbach, worry that alternatives to formal adjudication provide a kind of second-class justice that will be increasingly meted out to the poor and disadvantaged while the first-class justice provided by formal adjudication is reserved for the social and political elite. Sarat and others fear that the interest in developing alternatives has yet to take account of the social and cultural difficulties that repress and discourage people from voicing complaints or making claims. Still others, such as Richard Abel, see formal adjudication as providing an effective arena in which to struggle for significant social change, and they worry that the energy behind the push for alternatives is rooted in a desire to expand and strengthen society's mechanisms for control and regulation.

Those who support the further development and encouragement of alternative dispute resolution believe that it will not only alleviate the problems of courts but also that it will make justice more accessible, efficient, and effective (Council on the Role of Courts). For them, formal adjudication should be even more of a last resort than it has been in the past; for them, public policy ought to be devoted to the efficient allocation of disputes among various dispute-processing techniques with an eye to insuring the best fit between the demands of different kinds of cases and the resources and capacities of those techniques. The crisis of the courts provides, in this view, an opportunity to assess the proper role of courts and of adjudication and to take steps to bring both back within the bounds of that role.

In the final analysis, it seems unlikely that the nature and role of formal adjudication will soon undergo significant alteration. In this sense, the adaptationists, who see in the history of adjudication a history of incremental change, seem correct. Formal adjudication plays and will continue

to play a secondary, but major, part in the dispute-processing apparatus of American society. The primary, if not the most significant, part will continue to be played by the least visible and least manipulable processes of unilateral and bilateral adjustment. The energy devoted to the proliferation of nonadjudicative third-party mechanisms will not, it seems, much alter this basic pattern of disputing and dispute processing.

BIBLIOGRAPHY

Richard Abel, "The Contradictions of Informal Justice" in Abel, ed., *The Politics of Informal Justice* (1982), presents a radical critique of informal alternatives to courts with special emphasis paid to their function in extending the sphere of state-sponsored social control. Jerold Auerbach, *Justice Without Law?* (1984), reviews the history of alternatives in the United States and emphasizes their relationship to the value of community.

Ralph Cavanagh and Austin Sarat, "Thinking About Courts . . ." in *Law and Society Review,* 14 (1980), is one of the few scholarly pieces to take issue with the alleged crisis of judicial capacity. Abram Chayes, "The Role of the Judge in Public Law Litigation," in *Harvard Law Review,* 89 (1976), is a classic discussion of recent changes in the nature of adjudication. Chayes shows how courts adapt to changing demands.

Council on the Role of Courts, *The Role of Courts in American Society* (1984), is a "blue-ribbon panel" report on the differences between essentialist and adaptationist views of courts.Torstein Eckhoff, "The Mediator and the Judge," in Vilhelm Aubert, ed., *Sociology of Law* (1969), reviews in a formalistic fashion the differences among various modes for handling conflict. Malcolm Feeley, *The Process Is the Punishment* (1979), describes the informal processing of cases within a criminal court.

William Felstiner, Richard Abel, and Austin Sarat, "The Emergence and Transformation of Disputes," in *Law and Society Review,* 15 (1980–1981), describes the emergence of disputes and the way different types of dispute processing alter and transform those disputes. Owen Fiss, "The Forms of Justice," in *Harvard Law Review,* 93 (1979), is the clearest and most important statement of an adaptationist perspective. Lon Fuller, "The Forms and Limits of Adjudication," in *Harvard Law Review,* 92 (1978), is the authoritative statement of essentialism by its leading proponent.

Marc Galanter, "Reading the Landscape of Disputes," in *UCLA Law Review,* 31 (1983), and "Adjudication, Litigation and Related Phenomena," in Leon Lipson and Stan Wheeler, eds., *Law and the Social Sciences* (1986), review the evidence concerning the alleged litigation explosion and finds it inadequate to sustain the allegations. The author also discusses the attributes of adjudication and changes in the functions of courts. Nathan Glazer, "Toward An Imperial Judiciary," in *The Public Interest,* 41 (1975), is a broad and general indictment of the courts impinging on the functions of other branches of government.

Donald Horowitz, *The Courts and Social Policy* (1977), provides the best book-length treatment of the problem of judicial capacity. Herbert Kritzer and Jill Anderson, "The Arbitration Alternative," in *Justice System Journal,* 8 (1983), provides a short, careful, empirical examination of arbitration as an alternative to courts. Jethro Lieberman, *The Litigious Society* (1981). Sally Merry, "The Social Organization of Mediation in Nonindustrial Societies," in Richard Abel, ed., *The Politics of Informal Justice* (1982), expresses skepticism about the ability to transplant mediation models from preindustrial to industrial societies.

Richard Miller and Austin Sarat, "Grievances, Claims and Disputes" in *Law and Society Review,* 15 (1980–1981), reports on an empirical study of the incidence of disputes and litigation and suggests that measured against the potential civil lawsuits, the actual incidence is quite small. Robert Mnookin and Lewis Kornhauser, "Bargaining in the Shadow of the Law," in *Yale Law Journal,* 88 (1979), demonstrates that the power and the influence of adjudication is seen most clearly in terms of its impact on informal, bilateral bargaining.

Laura Nader, "Dispute Resolution—Law as Marginal or Central," in *A Study of Barriers to the Use of Alternative Methods of Dispute Resolution* (1984), expresses concern that the movement for alternative dispute resolution will be both culturally insensitive and part of a more general movement to provide second-class justice for the poor. Austin Sarat, "The Emergence of Disputes," in *A Study of Barriers to the Use of Alternative Methods of Dispute Resolution* (1984), describes a variety of barriers which inhibit the emergence of disputes and argues that alternatives to formal adjudication should work to facilitate the emergence of conflict.

Austin Sarat and Joel Grossman, "Courts and Conflict Resolution," in *American Political Science Review,* 69 (1975), offers a typology for comparing alternative forms of dispute resolution and an analysis of factors associated with the decision to use those alternatives. Martin Shapiro, *Courts* (1981), is a comparative study of the form and function of courts in different societies. Barbara Yngvesson and Lynn Mather, "Courts, Moots and the Disputing Process" in Keith Boyum and Lynn Mather, eds., *Empirical Theories About Courts* (1983), draws on anthropological research and carefully critiques the way social scientists have written about alternatives to formal adjudication.

[*See also* EQUITY AND EQUITABLE REMEDIES.]

APPEALS AND APPELLATE PRACTICE

Robert J. Martineau

O NE of the few aspects of the American judicial process about which there is a consensus is that every loser in a trial court should have a right to appeal to a higher court. This principle is best expressed by the statement, often made by real-life litigants as well as fictional ones, "I'm going to take this all the way to the Supreme Court"—a statement indicating that the matter is of such importance that the person will not rest until all efforts to obtain justice have been exhausted. Notwithstanding the unanimous agreement on the importance of the right to appeal, the Supreme Court of the United States has held that the right to appeal is not mandated by due process. There are in fact two states, Virginia and West Virginia, in which there is no right to appeal; appellate review is at the discretion of the appellate court. The right to seek appellate review is thus dependent solely upon statute. If a legislature decided to abolish either the right to appeal or even the right to seek discretionary review in an appellate court, it could do so without violating the requirements of due process. In spite of this anomaly of constitutional principle, the fact remains that there is, in the federal system and in every state, a process by which an action of a trial court is reviewable in an appellate court. It is the purpose of this article to explain how this process developed and how it works.

DEVELOPMENT OF CONCEPT OF APPELLATE REVIEW

In examining the history of the development of appellate review, it is important to understand that appellate review as it now exists in the United States reflects to a substantial degree the structure of government, which divides governmental power into the legislative, executive, and judicial branches, each having a particular role. The separation of powers as a basic element of governmental structure dates back only to the eighteenth century, but the concept of a judicial process and appellate review goes back much further. Appellate review originated in the civilizations that developed around the Mediterranean Sea. During the Middle Ages in Europe the development of a structured legal system with an appeal process depended upon the existence of a central governmental structure. As power became centralized in an individual sovereign, procedures developed whereby a person dissatisfied with the decision of a judicial official could have the decision reviewed by one or more higher judicial officers. The sovereign, as the repository of all governmental authority, was the final judicial authority.

In England, as in the continental countries, an increase in royal power resulted in the development of a national legal system. In the thirteenth and fourteenth centuries, appellate review was initiated by the filing of a new lawsuit in the reviewing court by the losing party against the judge whose decision was contested. By the time of Edward I, however, the prevailing party rather than the judge was required to defend the judgment of the trial court. During this same period the formal record in the lower court became established, as did the jury as the finder of fact and the distinction between finding of facts and discovering and applying legal principles to those facts.

At the beginning of the eighteenth century there were two principal procedures for appellate review in the English legal system, writ of error and appeal. The writ of error was a common-law writ that grew out of the earlier procedures under which the losing party filed suit against the judge who rendered the original decision. The writ of error initiated a new lawsuit with the parties, known as the plaintiff in error (the losing party in the lower court) and the defendant in error (the winning party in the lower court). The writ of error could be obtained as a matter of right. When it was obtained, it automatically stayed the enforcement of the judgment of the lower court if a bond was posted to secure the amount of the judgment and any costs or damages that would be caused by delaying enforcement of the judgment. The plaintiff in error arranged for a copy of the record in the lower court to be sent to the reviewing court. The record consisted of the writ of error, the pleadings, the judge's notes of the trial, the verdict, the proceedings after the verdict, and the judgment.

To raise any matter in the appellate court not included in the original record, the plaintiff in error had to prepare a bill of exceptions recording alleged errors of law made at the trial but not shown on the record. A record had to be made of each exception in writing at the time that the adverse ruling was made. At the end of the trial all the exceptions were put together to constitute the bill of exceptions. This bill, once approved by the trial judge, was then appended to the record.

After the record and bill of exceptions were transmitted to the appellate court, the plaintiff in error prepared an assignment of the errors, which in the appellate court served the same function as a complaint in the trial court. The defendant in error then filed a plea in response to the assignment of errors. Review was limited to errors of law made by the judge. Any factual errors made by the jury could not be reviewed. Oral argument was heard at the request of either side, and a copy of the record was given to each judge.

There also existed in England during this time another legal system called equity. Proceedings in this system were held in the Court of Chancery. The decisions of the Court of Chancery were subject to review in the House of Lords. An unsuccessful litigant in the Court of Chancery desiring to challenge the decision filed a petition and appeal with the House of Lords. That document recited the proceedings in the lower court and presented the grounds for appeal. The successful party in the Court of Chancery then filed an answer. The papers were printed, and oral argument was held in the House. The House could review any matter in the case, whether or not it was in the record and whether it was a factual or legal issue, and could render any judgment it thought appropriate. After 1873 the House of Lords could even accept new evidence.

In the American colonies, appellate review was virtually nonexistent until the eighteenth century because there were no well-developed legal systems. Usually the colonial legislature or the governor and his council were the highest court of review except for the privy council in England. The review was similar to that in the House of Lords in an equity matter; the legislature or the governor and his council had the power to render any judgment thought appropriate. During the eighteenth century the colonies began to develop legal systems with an appellate review procedure that increasingly resembled the English writ of error rather than the equity appeal. This change developed in large part because larger numbers of colonial lawyers obtained their legal training in England. They brought back with them the common-law concept of appellate review as reflected in the writ of error rather than the equity appeal. Although there was continuing conflict between the two approaches to appellate review, the writ of error system clearly prevailed. This continued to be true in the states after the Revolution began in 1776 and in the federal system after the Constitution became effective in 1789.

Because the technical writ-of-error procedure became generally applicable rather than the more flexible equity appeal procedure, the appellate process as it developed in both the federal and state systems became overridden with procedural technicalities. As a result, at least six separate steps were required before an appellate court would review an issue on the merits: (1) making a timely objection; (2) taking an exception; (3) preserving the objection, the ruling on the objection, and the exception to the exception in the bill of exceptions; (4) moving for a new trial; (5) specifying the overruling of the objection in the assignment of errors; and (6) specifying the issue in a "brief." The same insistence on procedural technicalities affected every step in the appellate process.

Even though the procedural requirements of the writ of error became applicable to the equity appeal, the appeal in equity was nonetheless preserved. The major difference between it and the writ of error was in the scope of review. Following the English practice, under the writ of error only errors of law could be reviewed. In an equity appeal, however, both questions of law and questions of fact could be reviewed, and the appellate court had full authority to render any judgment it thought justice required. The appeal in equity was thus considered a trial de novo rather than a review of the lower court judgment, even though no new evidence was admissible in the appellate court. Even in equity appeals during the nineteenth century, however, appellate courts began to give such deference to the factual findings of the judge that the scope of review in the equity appeal became very similar to that of the writ-of-error review.

The result at the end of the nineteenth century was a very formalistic procedure. Appellate review was to be denied if any of the technical procedural requirements had not been complied with completely. To the extent that there was appellate review, it was of a very limited nature. Since early in the twentieth century, there has been a continuing effort to reform the appellate process. The objective has been to make the procedure for appeals more simple, to make sure that appellate courts review cases on the merits, and to expand the scope of review from the narrow review of errors of law as shown by the record to include a broader review of both questions of law and questions of fact.

NATURE OF THE APPELLATE PROCESS

Beginning in the 1960s, the increase in the number of cases being brought to the trial courts and the simplification of the appellate process have created what has been termed a "crisis of volume" for appellate courts. The increased burden on appellate courts has prompted a wide range of responses. In most jurisdictions the initial steps were to add additional judges to existing courts and to create new appellate courts. These remedies, however, were not long-range solutions. Furthermore, the creation of intermediate appellate courts made it easier for persons to appeal, thereby increasing the appellate court

case load. The most dramatic fact of the appellate process in the federal courts of appeals has been the growth in the number of appeals from decisions of the federal court. The number of appeals increased from 4,204 in 1961 to 29,630 in 1983, an increase of 705 percent. During the same period, the number of circuit judges increased by only 100 percent. The growth in appeals at the state level has been almost as dramatic as at the federal level. Although statistics for the same period are not available, between 1972 and 1983 the number of appeals filed in the state appellate courts grew by 151 percent, whereas the number of judges increased by only 33 percent.

A whole range of techniques designed to reduce a court's backlog and to reduce the time for a case to move from judgment in the trial court to judgment in the appellate court were also implemented. It was recognized that if courts continued to do business as usual, appellate review would become an empty remedy because the delay in obtaining it would make review ineffectual in many, if not most, cases. There was also recognition, however, that speed and efficiency were not ends in themselves and that an undue emphasis on them could deny litigants the thoughtful review traditionally characteristic of the appellate process. For these reasons the appellate process since the 1960s has been in an evolutionary state. On the one hand, there have been efforts to preserve the essential features of appellate review, while on the other hand, the process has been adjusted to accommodate the demands of an ever-expanding case load. The consensus on the essentials to be preserved include prompt review, by a group of judges, of the merits of a final judgment of the trial court; a statement of reasons by the appellate court; and, after the parties have submitted their views on the issues, consideration by the judges as dictated by the complexity of the appeal.

STRUCTURE OF FEDERAL APPELLATE SYSTEMS

In Article III of the United States Constitution, only the Supreme Court of the United States is specifically mentioned. All other federal courts, trial and appellate, are created by act of Congress pursuant to a grant of power under Article III. The basic court of original jurisdiction in the federal system is the United States district court. In almost all cases, appeals from the district court are taken to one of the United States courts of appeals and thereafter, by appeal or petition for certiorari, to the United States Supreme Court. There is a right to appeal every final judgment to a court of appeals. To obtain further review in the Supreme Court requires a vote of at least four justices of the Supreme Court. As a practical matter, the Supreme Court is not required to review any decision of a court of appeals; thus, in all but a relatively small percentage of cases, the decision of the court of appeals is final.

The United States is divided into twelve geographic circuits, eleven comprising various states and one for the District of Columbia. There is a United States court of appeals in each circuit and another in the District of Columbia. There is also the United States Court of Appeals for the Federal Circuit, which sits in Washington, D.C. An appeal is taken from a district court to the court of appeals for the circuit in which the district is located, except for certain types of cases such as patent, trademark, and copyright cases, which go to the Court of Appeals for the Federal Circuit. Each court of appeals has a number of judges specified by statute, based upon the size of the circuit and its case load. In 1985 there were 168 circuit judges, assigned on the basis of the case load of the circuit and historical circumstance, as follows: First, 6; Second, 13; Third, 12; Fourth, 11; Fifth, 16; Sixth, 15; Seventh, 11; Eighth, 10; Ninth, 28; Tenth, 10; Eleventh, 12; District of Columbia, 12; and Federal, 12.

The court of appeals' decisions are usually made by three-judge panels. If a majority of the active judges so vote, however, the court of appeals may hear a case either initially or on rehearing while sitting en banc—that is, with all the active judges of the circuit plus any senior judge who participated in the original decision. The chief judge of each court of appeals is the judge senior in commission under seventy years of age.

STRUCTURE OF STATE APPELLATE SYSTEMS

The appellate systems of the states differ greatly in their structure and organization. As of 1985, fifteen states did not have intermediate appellate courts between their trial courts and supreme courts. In these states the highest courts generally have little discretionary jurisdiction, with the losing party having the right to appeal from most final judgments. In the remaining states, intermediate appellate courts have been established between the trial courts and supreme courts. These intermediate courts differ greatly in subject-matter jurisdiction, which can fall within two extremes. At one end is Wisconsin, which gives its court of appeals jurisdiction over all appeals from the trial courts. At the other end are Idaho and Iowa, which limit the jurisdiction of their intermediate appellate courts to cases assigned to them by the supreme court. Five states have created two intermediate appellate courts with jurisdiction divided between criminal and civil matters. Texas and Oklahoma have in effect two supreme courts, one for civil cases and the other for criminal cases.

The majority of the states with intermediate appellate courts allow no appeals of right to the highest court. States allowing an appeal of right limit it to specific classes of cases. All states with intermediate appellate courts provide for appeal from those courts to the highest court of the state, usually in the discretion of the supreme court. Most states with intermediate appellate courts have also enacted statutes that permit direct appeal from the trial court to the highest court in certain classes of cases.

The organization and internal structure of state intermediate appellate courts also vary greatly. The two main structures are a single court with statewide jurisdiction, and several courts each with distinct territorial jurisdiction. Under both types the court may sit in panels or en banc. Intermediate appellate courts in states with distinct territorial jurisdiction usually sit only in those districts.

JUSTIFICATION FOR APPELLATE REVIEW

The most basic justification for appellate review is stated in terms of the desire for uniformity of decisions among the trial courts. Chief Judge John J. Parker expressed this position in the following terms:

> The judicial function in its essence is the application of the rules and standards of organized

society to the settlement of controversies, and for there to be any proper administration of justice these rules and standards must be applied, not only impartially, but also objectively and uniformly through the territory of the state. This requires that decisions of trial courts be subjected to review by a panel of judges who are removed from the heat engendered by the trial and are consequently in a position to take a more objective view of the questions there raised to maintain uniformity of decisions throughout the territory.

There are additional justifications for appellate review. Appellate review aids in creating the appearance of providing justice—often just as important as actually providing justice. It protects against outside interference because it permits the judicial system both to correct itself and to develop as society changes. It offers psychological relief by providing the aggrieved party with a way to save face, at least temporarily, by taking additional steps to assert the justice of his or her cause.

FUNCTIONS OF APPELLATE COURTS

Although there is general agreement as to the necessity for appellate review, there is less agreement as to an accurate description of the functions of appellate courts. Error correction and law development are the two functions most often set forth. Some authorities also include "doing justice" as one of the functions of appellate courts.

The most obvious function of appellate review is to correct errors made by the trial court. It is inevitable that mistakes will be made in any process that depends upon humans to ascertain facts and law and to apply one to the other in thousands of cases involving adverse parties. The potential for error is high, and it is perhaps remarkable that the system produces as few appeals as it does. Error correction is concerned primarily with the effect of the judicial process in the trial court upon the individual litigants; it is intended to protect those persons from arbitrariness in the administration of justice. In most cases the error-correction function will be exercised only when the law is clear and the action of the trial court is inconsistent with the demands of the law. The issues often involve a ruling on

a matter of procedure or evidence, the application of the wrong legal principle, or the misapplication of the correct legal principle. In any case, the function will be exercised only if the error is not harmless; that is, the impact of the error upon the losing party must be such as to deny something to which the party is clearly entitled.

As noted, error correction is concerned with the impact of the lower court's decision on the parties in the case. An equally important concern of appellate review is the impact of the lower court's decision upon the law and the legal process. Review so concerned has been termed "institutional review." Its purpose is to provide an opportunity for the common law to develop, thereby permitting it to reflect the demands of the individuals and institutions the law serves, as well as to accommodate factual situations substantially different from those in prior cases. The development function is crucial in a common-law jurisdiction, which has a body of judge-made law as well as law declared by a legislative body or in a constitution.

The functions of error correction and law development have uniformity as their ultimate objective. Yet appellate judges neither can nor should forget that their decisions are not rendered on abstract legal questions but have a direct and immediate effect upon the parties before them. They also cannot forget that their decisions should not be good only for one case and irrelevant to all other cases. Precedent and stare decisis are essential features of a common-law legal system, and appellate courts, like trial courts, cannot ignore the requirements of the law in deciding individual cases. Judge Albert Tate, Jr., of the United States Court of Appeals for the Fifth Circuit expressed the principle in the following terms: "The result that seems 'just' for the present case must be a principled one that will afford just results in similar conflicts of interest. The judge has an initial human concern that the litigants receive common sense justice, but he also realizes that the discipline of legal doctrine governs his determination of the cause."

Doing justice, if it means having the most deserving party prevail, cannot be divorced from doing justice in the context of the entire legal system. Obviously the legal system does not exist for the purpose of doing injustice. But justice is not done by ignoring the applicable substantive and procedural law to achieve a particular result in an individual case. In every case, consequently, the judge's function can be summarized as doing justice in accordance with the law. This means that the judge should try to treat the parties fairly, in accordance with the equities reflected by the facts of the case, and not simply to apply the law mechanically, without regard to the effect upon the persons before the court. At the same time, the judge is not free to disregard the law simply to do what he or she thinks is right as between the parties. There is a tension involved in virtually every case between these two interests, and the judge must try to balance them. When the judge goes too far in the interest of justice and bends the law to accommodate the individual case, he or she gives rise to the type of result that is characterized by the maxim "Hard cases make bad law."

PRESERVING ISSUES FOR APPEAL

One of the basic features of the appellate process is that it begins not when the notice of appeal is filed but at the very start of the litigation process when consideration is first given to filing suit. The principal reason for this is one of the basic rules of appellate procedure: only those issues raised in the trial court can be raised on appeal.

The origin of the requirement that issues be raised first in the trial court goes back to the development of the writ of error in England and its subsequent influence on appellate procedure in the United States. If the appeal is looked at from the perspective of the original form of the writ of error—that is, as a new lawsuit filed by the losing party in the trial court against the trial judge and attacking the errors made by him—then the necessity for having the issues presented to the trial judge is obvious. The trial judge cannot be charged with making a wrong decision on an issue if it was never presented to him.

Even though the appeal is no longer considered a separate suit against the trial judge, the requirement that issues be presented at the trial level has been retained primarily because the rule has several important justifications beyond the merely historical. If the function of the appellate court is considered to be error correction,

error can be committed only on an issue raised in the trial court. If the losing party can raise a matter on appeal for the first time, he may be able to build in an error to ensure a successful appeal by failing to make a timely objection; that is, had the objection been presented in the trial court, it is possible that no error would ever have been committed. Allowing new issues on appeal also may diminish the need to be fully prepared for the trial itself, a result contrary to the current concern over the competency of trial attorneys. Finally, the requirement also promotes efficient judicial administration because it results in fewer new trials or remands for further proceedings.

Even though the rule requiring issues to be raised first in the trial court is applied by almost every appellate court, there are many refinements or exceptions to the rule. These include fundamental or plain error, particularly if it involves constitutional questions; questions that first arise after the judgment appealed from was entered; jurisdiction of the trial court over the subject matter; failure to plead a claim upon which relief can be granted; and new arguments or theories to support the position of a party originally presented to the trial court.

These exceptions or refinements are usually discussed in terms of issues that a party can raise in the appellate court even though they were not presented to the trial court. It is also generally accepted that an appellate court can and will on occasion consider certain types of issues on its own motion even though they were not raised by either party in the trial court or the appellate court. The subject-matter jurisdiction of the trial or appellate court is always open to question by the appellate court. In addition, two other issues are considered under this principle: the appellate court may wish to review an error committed by the trial court that is not recognized by the appellant, or the appellate court may decide to consider a change in the controlling legal rule that had been accepted by the parties and the trial court.

In addition to the rule that an issue first be presented to the trial court, there are a number of other requirements for preserving an issue for appeal. Some jurisdictions require that an issue, even if originally presented at the trial, must also be presented to the trial court in a posttrial motion to give the judge an opportunity to correct his or her own error. Although this was once the general rule, very few jurisdictions continue this requirement, because posttrial motions usually build in additional delay and are seldom granted. Another important requirement is that the alleged error be reflected in the record on appeal. There is also a requirement that the issue be raised and discussed in the brief.

In summary, the basic requirements for appellate review are that issues initially be presented to the trial court, that this fact be reflected in the record, and that the issue be submitted to the appellate court in the brief filed in that court. These requirements will be enforced, absent one or more of the circumstances set forth above.

APPEALABILITY

Probably the best-known rule of appellate procedure is that a judgment must be final before it can be appealed. A final judgment is defined as one that determines all the issues as to all parties in a case, leaving only execution of the judgment to be completed. Although most jurisdictions have adopted the final-judgment rule, the application of the rule is a source of great difficulty for both federal and state appellate courts. The final-judgment rule has several goals. A single appeal that consolidates all issues is economic in that it prevents "piecemeal adjudication" of intermediate orders. It prevents potential harassment of opponents, reduces the cost to the parties and the courts, prevents delay in the trial court, and reduces congestion in appellate courts. The ultimate goal is efficient judicial administration.

Unfortunately, the application of the final-judgment rule has not been as simple as the statement of the rule may imply. Competing with the goals of the rule is the litigants' need for effective review of intermediate rulings that may irreparably harm them, such as revealing information claimed to be confidential or defending a case in a foreign jurisdiction. To avoid arbitrary harshness in particular cases or classes of cases, the finality requirement has been refined or exceptions created by either legislative or judicial action. Each refinement or exception has reduced the effectiveness of the final-judgment rule, with the result that it is often unclear when the rule will be enforced or ignored.

The final-judgment rule as it is applied in the federal judicial system is representative. The rule is embodied in section 1291 of Title 28 of the United States Code, which provides that "the courts of appeals shall have jurisdiction of appeals from all final decisions of the district courts." The Supreme Court has interpreted the statute to mean that a decision is final if it "ends the litigation on the merits and leaves nothing for the court to do but execute the judgment" (*Catlin* v. *United States,* 1945).

A judgment must meet two provisions of the Federal Rules of Civil Procedure before it will be declared "final": it must be set forth separately (Rule 58), and it must be entered by the clerk of the district court in the civil docket (Rule 79[a]). Even after a final judgment has been properly entered, the time limitation on appealing it may be tolled by the timely filing of postjudgment motions such as a motion for judgment notwithstanding the verdict, a motion to amend or make additional findings of fact, a motion for a new trial, or a motion to alter or amend the judgment. A judgment's appealability is restored only when such a motion is denied.

The Supreme Court has said that the finality requirement of section 1291 should be construed in a pragmatic rather than a technical sense (*Cohen* v. *Beneficial Industrial Loan Corp.,* 1949). The pragmatic approach has resulted in three major refinements or exceptions to the final judgment rule. One is in a statute, one in a court rule, and one in judicial decision. Under section 1292 of Title 28 of the United States Code, Congress has provided for the appeal of certain types of interlocutory orders. These include orders concerning injunctions and orders that present "controlling questions of law" about which there is a "substantial ground for difference of opinion" and whose immediate review will "materially advance the ultimate termination of the litigation." (An example would be the applicability of a statute to the facts of a case.) For the latter the trial judge must certify that the requirements of the section are met, and the appellate court must agree. Both courts have wide discretion in making these determinations.

Another exception to the final-judgment rule is Federal Rule of Civil Procedure 54(b). This rule applies only when a case involves multiple claims or multiple parties. The rule permits the trial court to direct entry of a final judgment "as to one or more but fewer than all of the claims or parties only upon an express determination that there is no just reason for delay" in entering judgment. The principal difficulty in applying this rule is determining when a claim is separate. Under the most common approach, a claim is considered separate when it arises from a legal theory different from that under which the other claims arose.

The most significant judicially created exception to the final-judgment rule is the collateral-order rule. This rule makes final, for purposes of section 1291, certain orders that do not finally determine the entire controversy between the parties. Under the rule the order must conclusively determine the issue and not be subject to revision; resolve an important issue completely separate from the merits of the action; and be effectively unreviewable upon appeal of the final judgment. An example would be whether the defendant is immune from suit under the facts alleged by the plaintiff. Some courts of appeals have tended to use the collateral-order rule as a basis on which to review any order they have deemed important to review immediately rather than waiting for the final judgment, even though the order did not technically fit any of the other exceptions to the final-judgment rule. The Supreme Court in recent years, however, has rendered several decisions that reject these efforts, beginning with *Coopers and Lybrand* v. *Livesay* (1978).

Although most states, in theory at least, follow the final-judgment rule, there are, as in the federal system, many exceptions to its universal application created by statutes, rules, and judges. In addition, some states either enforce the final-judgment rule strictly or ignore it almost completely. An example of the first is Wisconsin, where an appeal of right can be taken only from a true final judgment. Wisconsin does provide, however, that an appellate court has discretion to review almost any order made by a trial court. New York, in contrast, allows an appeal of right from virtually every kind of intermediate order.

The Wisconsin approach is based upon the Standards of Judicial Administration of the American Bar Association, which recognize the significant distinction between an appeal of right and an appeal within the discretion of the appellate court. Given the tendency of both legislatures and courts to create exceptions to the final-judgment rule to avoid hardship in individual cases or to treat special-classes cases differently, the standards reflect the position that it is better to give the appellate court discretion to review any order when it thinks it appropriate. This restricts the final-judgment rule to appeals of right but allows discretionary review for all other orders.

PARTIES

Almost as important as determining what can be appealed is the question of who can appeal, who defends the judgment rendered by the trial court, and what special problems are created when there are multiple parties and multiple claims on each side of the case in the trial court. These issues suggest that the status of parties in the appellate courts is extremely complicated. An analysis must be made to determine the status of persons affected by the judgment of the trial court and their rights and duties in the appellate court.

The first and most basic question is who can appeal. The general rule is that only a person who is aggrieved by a judgment can take an appeal from it. The rule is often contained in the statute that provides for the right to appeal, but even without a statutory provision the courts apply the rule. Essentially the rule is one of standing. To bring a lawsuit, a person must have a legally recognized interest that is claimed to be harmed by the defendant. So, too, must a person have an interest adversely affected by the judgment to be able to take an appeal from the judgment.

The person who files the initial appeal is designated as the appellant. If other persons with the same interest as the first appellant also appeal, they are designated as coappellants. Those persons who are not designated as appellants become appellees. Usually their role is to defend the judgment rendered by the trial court. On some occasions the appellee will also seek to challenge some order or ruling of the trial court. In such a case the appellee files a cross-appeal and becomes both an appellee and a cross-appellant; the appellant acquires the additional status of cross-appellee.

As with almost every other rule in appellate practice, the rule that permits only an aggrieved party to appeal has some exceptions. One is on the question of subject-matter jurisdiction. The winning party in the trial court can always appeal to attack the jurisdiction of the trial court over the subject matter of the case. The winning party can also appeal if the party has not recovered all that it sought as relief in the trial court. A party receiving less than the full amount requested is technically aggrieved by the judgment and thus can appeal. A successful party accepting the benefits of the judgment, even though less than requested, cannot appeal. The court treats the person who accepts the benefit of a judgment as though he or she consented to the judgment and thus is prevented from challenging it. For the same reason, the unsuccessful party who voluntarily pays the judgment cannot appeal from it.

There often are persons who are not formal parties in the trial but who may be adversely affected by the judgment. These persons can appeal the judgment if they petition the trial court to intervene in the case for the purpose of taking the appeal. A trustee or other fiduciary who is a formal party in the proceeding can appeal to protect the interest of the estate but not the interests of individual beneficiaries. An attorney does not have a right to appeal in his own name a judgment adverse to his client, even if the fee of the attorney is dependent upon recovery by the client or even when the attorney's fee is an item of recovery and includable in the judgment. This rule does not apply, however, in those cases in which the attorney files a fee petition in his own name. In those situations the attorney can appeal an adverse decision on the fee petition.

INITIATING AND PERFECTING THE APPEAL

The single most important procedural step in the appellate process is the filing of the notice of appeal. Most appellate courts treat timely filing as mandatory and jurisdictional. The failure to file a timely and proper notice of appeal results in dismissal of the appeal.

Most jurisdictions have placed minimal formal requirements upon the filing of the notice of appeal. Usually the notice of appeal is filed with the clerk of the court from which the appeal is taken, although in some jurisdictions it is filed with the court to which the appeal is taken. The content of the notice of appeal usually requires only the name of the party taking the appeal, the judg-ment or order from which the appeal is taken, and the name of the court to which the appeal is taken. Most courts are very liberal in construing a notice of appeal. The absence of some of the required information is not fatal so long as the opposing party has a reasonable notice of the intent of the appellant to appeal.

Every jurisdiction has established a time limit within which the notice of appeal must be filed. Sometimes the time limit will vary with the nature of the case or the type of party involved. Time limits are strictly enforced because they are treated as though they are statutes of limitations. A typical rule provision is that an appellate court can waive any failure to comply with the appellate rules except the timely filing of the notice of appeal. Trial courts are often given limited authority to extend the time in which to file the notice of appeal. In addition, the filing of certain types of postjudgment motions, such as a motion for a new trial, delay the time for filing the notice of appeal until the motion is acted upon by the trial court.

In addition to the filing of the notice of appeal, there are several other requirements for perfecting the appeal. These include the payment of the required filing fee, the docketing of the appeal in the appellate court, the filing of a bond to guarantee payment of court costs if required, and the filing of the appeal record in the appellate court.

CROSS-APPEAL

If an appellee desires only to support the judgment entered by the trial court, the appellee may make any argument in support of the judgment, even that the trial court was correct in entering the judgment but for the wrong reason. The appellee must file a cross-appeal, however, if the appellee seeks to change the judgment of a lower court.

The notice of cross-appeal must follow the same form as the notice of appeal. The cross-appeal must be filed within a limited period specified in the appellate rules.

RELIEF PENDING APPEAL

When an appeal is taken, it is not automatic that the enforcement of the judgment appealed from is stayed—that is, unenforced temporarily —while the appeal is pending. Most jurisdictions provide that a money judgment is stayed if a bond is filed, the amount of bond being either specified by statute or rule or as established by the trial court. In all other cases a stay is granted only if the trial court so directs and only under the terms and conditions specified by the trial court. In many situations a stay is absolutely necessary to preserve the status quo while the appeal is pending. Otherwise, the matter may become moot before the appeal is decided. This can occur whenever the lawsuit involves the doing or the not doing of an act, such as the demolition of a building.

In considering whether to grant a request for relief pending appeal, the trial court normally considers four factors: the likelihood that the appellant will prevail upon appeal; the probability that the appellant will suffer irreparable harm in the absence of relief; the harm that the appellee may suffer if relief is granted; and the public interest. The trial court must balance all four of these factors, no one of which is controlling. The action of the trial court in granting or denying the relief requested can be challenged in the appellate court by either party.

RECORD ON APPEAL

The general rule is that a reversible error must appear in the record on appeal and that, for the purposes of the appeal, if it is not in the record, it did not happen. The record on appeal can consist either of all the papers and exhibits filed in the trial court plus the transcript of testimony or of only those items in the trial court record designated as the appeal record by the parties. In either case, the record on appeal is crucial to the appellate process because it is the only means by which the appellate court may ascertain what happened in the trial court. Appellate rules generally provide that within a specified period of time, usually thirty days after notice of appeal is filed, the clerk of the trial court or the appellant must have the record on appeal transmitted to the appellate court. Appellate rules also provide for an agreed-upon statement of facts as a substitute for the record on appeal, but this procedure is not often followed.

An important part of the record in most cases is the transcript of testimony at the trial. A major cause of delay in the appellate process traditionally has been the preparation of the transcript of testimony. This transcript is prepared by the court reporter who was present in the courtroom during the trial and recorded the testimony by stenographic, mechanical, or electronic means. The court reporter often has difficulty finding time to transcribe the notes into a typewritten record because when one case is finished, the reporter usually must begin working immediately on the next case. Preparation of the transcript has been one of the major focuses of efforts to expedite the appellate process. Probably the most significant step has been for the appellate court to supervise the preparation of the transcript and to ensure that it is filed within the time period allowed by the rules. Disputes over the content of the record on appeal or the accuracy of the transcript of testimony are decided by the trial court, which retains jurisdiction for this purpose. Only in rare circumstances will this matter reach the appellate court.

THE BRIEF AND APPENDED MATERIALS

The brief is the principal written communication from each party submitting the factual and legal basis on which the appellate court should decide in the party's favor. The relative importance of the brief and the oral argument in the appellate process has been changing slowly over the past two centuries and has changed dramatically since the mid-1960s. In late eighteenth-century England and the United States, communication from the attorneys for the parties to the court was almost exclusively oral. Arguments often lasted several days. Briefs, to the extent that there were any, were merely summaries or outlines of the oral argument and were not of major consequence. In the middle of the nineteenth century, courts became busier, and so they began to impose limitations on the length of the oral argument. At first each side was allowed several hours, then one hour, and then thirty minutes; arguments of fifteen or twenty minutes per side are now common. Written briefs became the substitute for lengthy oral argument. The shortened oral argument became primarily an opportunity for lawyers to emphasize principal points made in their briefs. Since the mid-1960s it has become the opportunity for judges to ask attorneys questions about issues raised in the briefs. In most busy appellate courts, oral argument is heard only in a portion of the cases —sometimes in even less than 50 percent of all appeals. In these courts the brief affords the primary, and perhaps the only, opportunity for the attorney to present arguments on behalf of the client to the appellate court.

The brief is a formal document usually limited in length and following a format specified by the appellate rules. Most jurisdictions allow only three types of briefs as a matter of right: an appellant's brief, an appellee's brief, and an appellant's reply brief. Other briefs may be filed only with the consent of all the parties or by leave of court.

A brief usually includes a table of contents and authorities; a statement of the issues; a statement of the case; a statement of facts; an argument; and a conclusion. Each part of the brief plays a particular role. The table of contents is simply a listing of each of the sections of the brief and the page on which it is found. The table of authorities is an alphabetical listing of all the cases, statutes, and other authorities cited in the brief. This is followed by a statement of the issues or questions presented. These are the issues that in the opinion of the party will determine the outcome of the case. Usually only the two or three most important issues are presented, and they are framed in such a way as to incorporate the essential factual and legal elements in the case. The statement of each issue is usually only one sentence long.

The next section, the statement of the case, gives in one or two paragraphs the procedural history of the case, including the status of the parties in the trial court, the relief sought, and how the matter was resolved by the trial court. Essential dates of the most significant procedural events are also given.

After the statement of the case comes the statement of facts. This is supposed to be a neutral statement written in narrative form and giving the essential facts of the dispute between the parties as revealed by the record. Each statement of fact must be supported by a reference to the place in the appendix or the record that supports it. Facts are presented in chronological order rather than in the order presented at the trial. Facts that are in dispute should also be noted.

Next follows the argument, which has as many sections as there are issues presented, with one section of the argument addressed to each issue presented. It is here that the attorney must relate the relevant law to the facts as set forth in the statement of facts and show why both the facts and the law compel a decision in favor of the attorney's client. This is usually the longest section of the brief and the one in which the art of persuasion comes to the fore. The final section of the brief is a conclusion, which is nothing more than a short paragraph stating the precise relief sought. (The appellee's brief follows the same format except that the statement of the case, the statement of facts, or the statement of issues can be omitted when the appellee agrees with the appellant's statement.)

The brief must be prepared in accordance with the appellate rules, which specify the size of paper, whether it is to be printed or typewritten, and, most important, the maximum length. Each brief must be filed within a specified time. For the appellant this is usually thirty days after the appeal record is filed, and for the appellee it is usually thirty days after the appellant's brief is filed.

An appendix is filed at the same time as the appellant's brief. This is a document prepared in the same manner as a brief. It includes the items in the record that both parties think are essential to a decision in the case. Because of the expense of preparing the appendix, some courts have dispensed with it and require only photocopies of portions of the record.

ORAL ARGUMENT

After the briefs are filed, the case is then scheduled for oral argument or, if oral argument is not heard in every case, a decision is made as to whether oral argument is necessary. Cases are usually scheduled either in the order in which the record is filed or in the order in which the last brief is filed.

As noted above, the relative importance of the brief and the oral argument has changed dramatically since the 1960s. Oral argument in most cases now plays a subsidiary role to the brief, and its primary function is to allow the judges to ask questions about the case that have occurred to them in reading the briefs. Judges prepare for oral argument not only by a careful reading of the briefs but also by having a memorandum prepared by a law clerk or staff attorney and, in some courts, by discussing the case with the other judges on the panel.

Oral argument in an appellant court has a very stylized protocol. The court sits on a raised bench facing the attorneys; the chief or presiding judge sits in the middle, and the other members of the panel alternate to the right and the left of the presiding judge in the order of their seniority. The attorneys sit at a table or tables facing the court with a lectern in the middle. Thirty minutes per side is usually the maximum, but in many courts only fifteen or twenty minutes per side is allowed. The appellant always speaks first and usually will save a few minutes of the allotted time for rebuttal. Each attorney starts off with the statement "May it please the court" and then identifies himself or herself and the client. At one time it was traditional for the appellant to give a shortened version of the statement of the case and the statement of the facts, but because of the advance preparation for oral argument undertaken by most judges, this is no longer necessary. The attorney begins to address the most significant issues in the case but often spends most of the time responding to questions from the bench. By their questions the judges make known to the attorneys the issues that they think are the most important.

The appellee's argument follows the same format except that the appellee has no opportunity for rebuttal. When the appellee is finished, the appellant uses whatever time was reserved to respond to points made by the appellee or simply emphasizes one or two points made in the main argument. At the conclusion of the argument, the presiding judge thanks the attorneys and advises them that the court takes the case under advisement.

THE DECISIONAL PROCESS

Following oral argument or, if there is no oral argument, when the court begins to consider the case on its merits, the decisional process of the court starts. The first step is a conference of the members of the panel, usually held immediately following the last oral argument of the day. A tentative decision is reached, and the case is as-

signed to a member of the panel to write the opinion.

The judge to whom the case is assigned then proceeds to prepare a draft opinion, assisted by the judge's law clerks. After a draft opinion has been prepared, it is circulated to the other members of the panel for their comments. Draft opinions are subject to substantial or little criticism, depending upon their acceptability to the other judges. When the opinion is finally approved by the entire panel, it is filed with the clerk of the court, who sends copies to the parties. A second conference may be held in some courts for final approval of the opinion. The number of conferences may depend upon whether the judges have their offices in the same building. If the court decides that the case is not significant enough to warrant the writing of an opinion, it may simply enter an order disposing of the case.

The decision of the court is not implemented immediately when the opinion and judgment are filed. The parties usually have a certain period, ordinarily fourteen days, in which to petition the court for a rehearing or reconsideration. If the panel that heard the court is less than the full court, the party may also request that the matter be reheard by the entire court rather than just the panel. It is rare for either type of rehearing to be granted, but if one is, supplemental briefs may be called for and the case may be argued again.

SEEKING REVIEW IN HIGHER COURTS

If the first appellate court that decided the case was an intermediate rather than a supreme court, it is also possible to seek review in the higher court. There is usually a limited time in which to seek review. The normal procedure is to file a petition with the supreme court along with a copy of the opinion of the intermediate court. There are three common grounds for seeking review in the supreme court. First, the decision of the intermediate appellate court may be in conflict with prior decisions of the supreme court or with decisions of other panels of the intermediate appellate court. Second, if the decision is consistent with prior decisions, the supreme court should consider changing the law. Third, if there are no prior decisions on the issue, the supreme court should give an authoritative decision. If the supreme court accepts the case, oral argument is almost always heard.

JUDGMENT AND MANDATE

After all appellate proceedings have been completed, whether after rehearing or after the matter has been taken to a higher court, the final appellate court issues its judgment. It will either affirm or reverse the trial court's judgment or vacate it. The case is then returned to the lower court for execution of the original judgment, entry of another judgment as directed by the appellate court, or any other action ordered by the appellate court, such as conducting a new trial. The formal communication from the appellate court is called the mandate, which notifies the trial court of the judgment of the appellate court and returns the record in the case.

Upon receipt of the mandate, the trial court must then take action as directed by the appellate court. If further proceedings are required, they must be consistent with the appellate court's decision. There are, however, certain circumstances under which the trial court can reconsider a matter decided by the appellate court. This can occur when a new trial establishes facts different from those found at the first trial or when the statutory or case law is changed retroactively before the trial court acts in accordance with the mandate.

CASES

Catlin v. United States, 324 U.S. 229 (1945)
Cohen v. Beneficial Industrial Loan Corp., 337 U.S. 541 (1949)
Coopers and Lybrand v. Livesay, 437 U.S. 463 (1978)

BIBLIOGRAPHY

American Bar Association Commission on Standards of Judicial Administration, *Standards Relating to Appellate Courts* (1976), is a report with standards and commentary on most aspects of the appellate process from functions of appellate courts to internal operating procedures. American Bar Association Task Force on Appellate Procedure, *Efficiency and Justice in Appeals: Methods and Selected Materials* (1977), is an anthology of pieces on various aspects of the appellate process. Paul D. Carrington, Daniel J. Meador, and Maurice Rosenberg, *Justice on Appeal* (1976), is a general overview of the appellate justice systems, with special emphasis on problems created by the crisis of volume in appellate courts. Frank M. Coffin, *The Ways of a Judge: Reflections from the Federal Appellate Bench* (1980), is a highly introspective analysis of the work of an appellate judge written by a federal court of appeals judge. Commission on Revision of the Federal Court Appellate System, *Structure and Internal Procedures: Recommendations for Change* (1975), is a study of the problems of the federal courts of appeals in coping with an ever-increasing case load with some recommendations.

J. Woodford Howard, Jr., *Courts of Appeals in the Federal Judicial System* (1981), is a study of the federal courts of appeals written from a political science perspective, with concentration on three circuits. Robert A. Leflar, *Appellate Judicial Opinions* (1974), is a collection of excerpts from articles and books on the role of the opinions of appellate courts and how they are crafted; and *Internal Operating Procedures of Appellate Courts* (1980), describes how appellate courts function internally and provides a broader review of the appellate justice system. Robert J. Martineau, *Modern Appellate Practice: Federal and State Civil Appeals* (1983), a text for practicing attorneys covering all aspects of the appellate practice, is a general treatise on the appellate process; and *Fundamentals of Modern Appellate Advocacy* (1985), a text written for use by law students in courses on brief writing and oral argument, gives additional material on the appellate process. Thomas B. Marvell et al., *State Appellate Caseload Growth: Documentary Appendix* (1983), a documentary summary of appellate court statistics for thirty-eight states from 1970, includes filings, reversal rate, time to decision in intermediate court, pending and disposed cases, and trial-court case loads. Marlin O. Osthus and Mayo H. Stigler, *State Intermediate Appellate Courts* (1980), surveys varieties in jurisdiction and structure of state intermediate appellate courts, with compilations of arguments for and against their creation.

John J. Parker, "Improving Appellate Methods," in *New York University Law Review*, 25 (1950), describes prevailing procedures in appellate courts in the 1940s and efforts to improve them. Roscoe Pound, *Appellate Procedure in Civil Cases* (1941), is an historical examination of the appellate process from earliest times, with concentration on development of the English and American appellate systems through the 1930s. Albert Tate, Jr., "The Art of Brief Writing: What a Judge Wants to Read," in *Litigation*, 4 (1978), is an article on the changes in brief-writing technique caused by the greatly increased case load of appellate courts, written by a federal appellate judge. Stephen L. Wasby, Thomas B. Marvell, and Alexander B. Aikman, *Volume and Delay in State Appellate Courts: Problems and Responses* (1979), is a report on statistical data on appellate court delay and the responses to delay, including adding of new resources and more efficient use of existing resources.

[*See also* CERTIORARI; EQUITY AND EQUITABLE REMEDIES; FEDERAL COURT SYSTEM; *and* SUPREME COURT OF THE UNITED STATES.]

BAR ASSOCIATIONS

Albert P. Melone

B AR associations are societies of lawyers formed to advance the legal profession. Most express an interest in elevating standards of integrity and education and in promoting legal reform. As with all associations, bar associations profess a public service mission.

Bestowing high honors upon select attorneys, bar associations in America were in the beginning largely exclusive clubs requiring the consent of the membership for admission. This elitist conception has been supplanted by a broader view that holds that bar associations should be open to all attorneys within a given jurisdiction for the purpose of benefiting both the bar and the public by unifying the bar and exposing its members to its professional norms. Although important, professional norm articulation, promulgation, and enforcement are not the only functions to be performed. Some bar associations are actively involved in public policy choices that touch upon not only professional concerns but also matters that affect society more broadly. This article will focus primarily upon the political activities of two bar groups that are very different in terms of size, ideology, and political style. The American Bar Association (ABA) and the National Lawyers Guild (NLG) present an interesting contrast, one that serves to paint lawyers as central figures on the American political canvas.

BAR DEVELOPMENT

The growth of the legal profession in the American colonies was very slow, and for the period from the Revolution through the last third of the nineteenth century, bar associations were, with few exceptions, little more than social clubs. The circuit riding days of the American frontier provided a shared experience among the itinerant bench and bar that translated into personal camaraderie and a degree of professional cohesion. However, this quintessential rural experience did not provide a tradition for a stay-at-home bar, which was to develop by the 1870s.

The development of the modern bar association is closely associated with urbanization and the dominance of big cities by political machines, which were opposed by the leading lawyers of the day. Well-established attorneys in New York City formed in 1870 what is today the nation's most prestigious city bar association—the Association of the Bar of the City of New York. Attempting to free the bench from what was felt to be undue political control and corruption, the formative years of the association were spent in bitter conflict with the political machine of Boss Tweed. The Chicago Bar Association was formed a few years later, and it, too, was interested in municipal reform. Ostensibly interested in bar admission standards and professional discipline, bar-association founders of the day were also concerned with the increased competition at the bar, primarily from persons without white, Anglo-Saxon, Protestant, and Ivy League backgrounds. In short, political reform, professional standards, competition, and stratification served as prime motives for genuine bar-association development after 1870; in twelve states, eight city and eight state bar associations were founded in eight years. The ABA was founded in 1878.

Bar leaders understood that group development, maintenance, and survival depended upon more than shared interests. Indeed, by the 1920s, only about a quarter of all lawyers belonged to local bar associations, and even fewer to the ABA. If bar associations were to exert control over the profession and to influence political decisions important to bar leaders, then reliance upon the spirit of professionalism and voluntarism would not suffice. Compulsory bar-association membership became an obvious solution. Following the Canadian model, North Dakota in 1921 became the first state to pass a statute requiring all persons wishing to practice law in that jurisdiction to belong to the state bar association and to pay its dues and to live by its rules of professional conduct. Today, either by statute or by state supreme court ruling, thirty-three states have this closed-shop arrangement, which is euphemistically termed either an integrated or a united bar.

Every state now has a bar association, whether integrated or not. There are also voluntary city and county bar associations and functional or special-interest associations, such as the Federal Bar Association, the Association of Trial Lawyers of America, the National Association of Women Lawyers, and the Decalogue Society of Lawyers, a Chicago organization of Jewish lawyers. There are nationwide, broadly function-oriented bar associations. The ABA and the NLG are both voluntary. However, they differ significantly in terms of organization, membership, political access, and policy preferences.

AMERICAN BAR ASSOCIATION

From 1878, when the ABA was founded, until 1889, Saratoga Springs, New York, was the scene of the organization's annual meetings. The resort spa was a favorite summer retreat for the social elite of the day. The location seems appropriate because in its early years the ABA was a selective and highly personalized organization. It closely resembled an exclusive social club to which members were elected, and no serious attempt was made to open the organization to lawyers generally. Although the organization had a strong social component, the ABA was led by men with strong wills and sharply defined ideological proclivities. They worked hard at improving legal education, spearheaded early efforts at creating uniform state laws; proposed amendments to the nation's patent and bankruptcy laws, which were enacted later by Congress; advocated uniform federal rules of procedure, which many years later were promulgated into law as the Federal Rules of Civil Procedure; and

agitated for a code of professional ethics. These same ABA leaders were clearly identified as conservative ideologues. They launched a program against the Progressive movement's demand for the recall of judges and of judicial opinions. Under the banner of property rights, ABA leaders were at the forefront of the constitutional attack upon economic legislation designed to end what was viewed by the progressives of the period as the worst abuses of monopoly capitalism.

Although the ABA enjoyed successes in its formative years, agitation grew within the organization for a new internal structure that would render it more representative of the profession and more efficient and effective. Adopted in 1936, the new constitution provided for a federal structure, which with minor modifications has endured. Before 1936 the governing body consisted of the entire membership, operating through a quorum of the members present at any annual meeting. A thirteen-member executive committee exercised plenary authority between annual membership meetings. The new federal system permits greater oligarchical control and, theoretically, greater effectiveness by lodging authority in a body known as the House of Delegates. Ostensibly, membership within the House of Delegates was designed to afford the ABA a broad base of lawyer representation. A weakness of the pre-1936 constitution was that policy was made by an executive committee responsible to the 2,000–3,000 lawyers attending the organization's annual conventions. The 1936 federal constitution afforded representation immediately to 78,000 state bar members, whether they paid ABA dues or not.

Originally, the 1936 constitution provided for fifteen categories of delegates, and in 1940 and 1942 two additional membership designations were added. In 1986 the House of Delegates was composed of thirteen broadly designated membership categories. Delegates from state and local bar associations, representatives from a wide variety of special interest sections within the ABA, judicial administrators, the attorney general of the United States, and delegates from affiliated organizations, including the American Judicature Society, the American Law Institute, and the Association of American Law Schools, are given representation in the House of Delegates. This wide representation of various bar elements in the House of Delegates is the basis

476

for the ABA's claim that it is the representative of the legal profession in America.

The creation of a federal structure did not change the ABA's basic conservative policy bent. From the early days of the administration of Franklin D. Roosevelt to the present era, the ABA has been regarded as an opponent of the policy orientation of the New Deal. It strenuously opposed Roosevelt's Court-packing plan, a variety of health insurance bills, and labor and welfare legislation. In the 1940s and 1950s the ABA supported such probusiness legislation as the tidelands oil bill and such conservative internal-security legislation as the Mundt-Nixon bill, going so far as to commend the House Un-American Activities Committee and the Senate Internal Security Subcommittee for their conduct. The Genocide Convention was opposed for many years, but it is now supported by the association.

Between 1953 and 1968 the association sanctioned about 124 official appearances by its representatives before congressional committees. Analysis of these appearances indicates that the ABA displayed a high rate of agreement with big business enterprises, and business interest groups, including the United States Chamber of Commerce and the National Association of Manufacturers. At the same time, the ABA stood in opposition to the policy preferences expressed by organized labor and consumer groups; for example, the ABA has consistently opposed changes in the strengthening of the antitrust laws and opposed tax-reform packages offered during the Kennedy administration. During the same period, the association continued to oppose what later became Medicare legislation. Studies indicate that in the 1970s the ABA continued to concern itself with policy matters that could adversely affect the interests of big business. In brief, throughout its history, the ABA has a consistent record of support for big business interests and opposition to labor and consumer demands.

It should not be concluded that the ABA is only interested in serving vested business interests. Sometimes it pursues just about everyone's version of the public good. Two examples from the mid-1960s are striking. The first is the proposal and successful adoption of the Twenty-fifth Amendment (the presidential-disability amendment), and the second is the attempt to reform the electoral college system.

A special ABA commission working closely with the chairman of the Senate Subcommittee on Constitutional Amendments recommended the chief guidelines for the Twenty-fifth Amendment. The association opened its Washington office as a central clearinghouse for information and promotion of the effort. The goodwill earned from this project was exclaimed by its chief ABA operative, Herbert Brownell. The former United States attorney general and chairman of the ABA's Special Committee on Presidential Inability reported to the House of Delegates at the association's 1965 annual meeting that he did not believe

> there has been an instance in the long and honorable history of the American Bar Association when our Association has obtained more favorable mention and more credit with the Congress of the United States than it has in the instance of this Constitutional amendment. There is not an iota of partisanship involved in that amendment. There is not an iota of personal advancement of anyone in the legal profession involved. It is purely a public service.

Another special ABA commission recommended a drastic change in the presidential election process: that the president and vice-president be elected as a team by popular vote of the people and that the electoral college be completely eliminated. The commission further suggested that the winning candidates must receive a minimum of 40 percent of the vote to be elected and that if no candidate received this limited vote percentage, a national runoff election be held. This particular ABA proposal failed but demonstrates once again the association's concern for the public interest.

A noteworthy feature of its congressional behavior has been the ABA's support for the United States Supreme Court. Its leadership believes that as the ostensible representative of the legal profession the ABA has a duty to support the legal system generally and the Supreme Court in particular. But this task has been complicated by the fact that many ABA leaders have opposed a host of Supreme Court decisions, particularly those handed down during the tenure of Chief Justice Earl Warren.

A high point in ABA-Court relations was the 1954 drafting of a proposed constitutional amendment that would have frozen at nine the number of Supreme Court justices, relinquished congressional control over the Court's appellate jurisdiction, and provided for a mandatory retirement age of seventy-five. The Senate approved the proposal, but it eventually died in the House of Representatives.

Segregationists and many ultra-security-conscious members of Congress were deeply disturbed by the school desegregation case, *Brown* v. *Board of Education of Topeka* (1954), and the federal preemptive case, *Pennsylvania* v. *Nelson* (1956). The *Brown* decision ended de jure segregation in public education. The *Nelson* decision struck down state antisedition acts, which the Court held were "preempted" by federal sedition legislation. Southern segregationists and northern congressmen concerned with internal security found a way to vent their Court-induced anger with the introduction in 1955 of a bill declaring that Congress had not intended to preempt the sedition field but instead favored concurrent federal-state jurisdiction. The ABA supported passage of the bill, though its argument was not limited to the field of state sedition laws. The ABA Standing Committee on Jurisprudence and Law Reform reasoned that concurrent state laws in the fields of banking, commerce, communication, and labor were subject to federal preemption under the rule in *Nelson*. This perception was shared by business organizations, which offered testimony on behalf of the bill, and labor unions, which appeared to testify in opposition to passage.

The introduction of the Jenner bill in 1957 was the strongest attack on the Court in the postwar era. This bill would have removed appellate jurisdiction from the Supreme Court in five classes of cases including contempt of Congress, federal loyalty-security programs, state antisubversive statutes, regulation of employment and subversive activities in schools, and admission to the practice of law in any state. Each of these provisions was included as a response to various Supreme Court decisions.

The ABA's testimony on the Jenner bill reveals its general strategy on Court-related matters. It reserved the right to disagree with any Supreme Court decision. However, ABA representatives argued that the Jenner bill contradicted the balance-of-powers principle established in the Constitution by weakening the authority of the judiciary. It therefore eschews

direct attacks upon the Court as an institution; yet the ABA is willing to recommend ways to overturn decisions deemed undesirable by the device of specific legislation, namely statutory reversal, as it did when it endorsed the 1955 bill. At the same time, the legitimacy of the constitutional amendment as a Court-curbing device has been recommended by the association. But constitutional amendments may be used only as a remedial measure, not in diminution of the Court's constitutional authority.

During the 1970s and early 1980s the Supreme Court once again became an object of conservative attack. However, the ABA has continued to abide by its general support for the Court as an institution. This time the issues were the social ones of abortion, busing, and school prayer, but the principled stance of the association remains firm.

Another more positive way in which judicial decisions may be affected is through the selection of those to serve on the bench as judges. Many organized bar groups, including especially the ABA, have sought to convince decision-makers and the public alike of the advisability of instituting nonpartisan and merit-based plans of judicial selection. As early as 1936 the ABA endorsed a plan to eliminate the direct election of judges or the direct appointment of judges by political party organizations and governors. Instead, the plan—alternatively called the Missouri plan, the merit plan, or the commission plan—has a commission composed of bar representatives, the state judiciary, and laypersons appointed by the governor, to select a specified limited number of nominees for the governor's approval. The selected nominee serves for a specified time period, after which his or her name is put before the electorate for approval on a nonpartisan, noncompetitive retention ballot.

The ABA has been especially active in the selection process of judges for the federal judiciary. The ABA Committee on the Federal Judiciary was created in 1946; in 1947 the committee was empowered to promote the nomination and confirmation of competent persons to the federal judiciary. Since the days of the Eisenhower Administration, the attorney general has sought the advice of the ABA committee before a candidate for a federal judicial post is proposed to the Senate. Moreover, the ABA is often called upon to make its recommendations known on nom-

BAR ASSOCIATIONS

inees during formal sessions of the Senate Judiciary Committee. Although its recommendations on particular candidates have not always been followed, the ABA's success rate is high, and it is regarded as a most influential actor in the selection process.

The ABA Federal Judiciary Committee has been charged with allowing conservative political ideology to dictate judgments about nominees' temperaments. Evidence is available to support both sides of this question. What is agreed upon is that the role of the ABA committee is now accepted by both Democrats and Republicans. The institutionalization of ABA influence in the judicial selection process is a fact of political life.

The fact is that the ABA possesses all the necessary ingredients for the exercise of political influence within the political system. These desirable attributes include high status, effective organization, and skilled leadership. Its high status stems from the number of lawyers it represents and the sociology of its leadership. Although less than 50 percent of all lawyers are ABA members (approximately 300,500 members in 1984), no other bar organization can claim to represent as many United States lawyers. As previously noted, the association's constitution provides for wide bar representation. Nonetheless, it is also true that with respect to a variety of professional characteristics, the leadership is unlike the rank-and-file lawyers of the country. For example, about 50 percent of all United States lawyers are individual practitioners, having small businesses and private parties for clients. Their practices involve such matters as personal injury, divorce, criminal, and other assorted low-status endeavors. Figures for the 1960s and 1970s establish that less than 10 percent of ABA leaders were solo practitioners. Rather, three-quarters were associated in partnerships specializing in such high-status practices as corporation, antitrust, estate, and appellate work. They have for clients some of the wealthiest business enterprises in America. However, the unrepresentative character of ABA leadership may add to its status.

First, a large number of public figures, including somewhere between 50 percent and 60 percent of members of Congress, are lawyers. By the criteria of professional success, most ABA officials offering congressional testimony and lobbying government in general are at the zenith of the profession. Thus, lawyer-congressmen may be flattered when ABA officials ask their indulgence and treat them with great respect. Second, the high status enjoyed by the ABA may be due in part to the clients of ABA leaders; in other words, the association enjoys high status because its leaders are counsel for big corporations, successful individuals, and trade and business associations.

The ABA as an organization is known to have participated in national interest-group alliances, predominantly big-business-oriented and dominated. Two such alliances, almost completely unknown to the media and public, are the Conference of National Organizations and the Greenbrier Conference. The membership of these alliances includes such notables as the American Bankers Association, the American Farm Bureau Federation, the American Medical Association, the Association of American Railroads, the Association of Stock Exchange Firms, the Chamber of Commerce of the United States, and the National Association of Manufacturers. The Conference of National Organizations was founded in 1944 when sixteen national associations met for two days of roundtable sessions on national topics. The Greenbrier Conference got under way in 1951 when Farm Bureau leaders were introduced to a vice-president in charge of interassociational relations for the National Association of Manufacturers. Both organizations discuss national policy issues and suggest legislative strategy; member groups then lobby before congressional committees. ABA participation in these alliances has afforded the association a communication network linking it with other influential groups sharing similar ideological perspectives.

Beyond involvement in formal alliances, ABA leaders are well known in their communities and to power brokers of all kinds, including elected officials. They often know personally members of the Congress. They are active for their alma maters. And, again, many of the major American corporations have for general counsel persons who have, at one time or another, occupied positions of leadership within the ABA.

The high status enjoyed by the ABA is to some extent attributable to its effective organization. Because its many sections are subject-matter-oriented, outstanding expertise can be brought to bear on virtually any problem with legal content. For example, during the 1970s subject specialists in antitrust, taxation, corporation, business, banking, international law, and criminal law studied and made carefully worded recommendations to the Senate Judiciary Committee on proposed bills to rewrite the massive federal criminal code. There is considerable evidence that this expertise had a significant impact on the debate over the proposed code revision. Further, ABA presidents are empowered to appoint ad hoc committees to study specific problems outside the competence of particular association sections or divisions.

The House of Delegates, the central structure within the organization, passes upon resolutions containing public-policy recommendations. Usually, resolutions coming from subject sections receive the association's official imprimatur. Sometimes, however, serious debate ensues, as in 1963 when the influential Council of State Governments proposed a constitutional amendment to remove appellate jurisdiction from the Supreme Court in the matter of legislative apportionment—this a response to the Court's 1962 decision in *Baker* v. *Carr*. The ABA Standing Committee on Jurisprudence and Law Reform endorsed the council's proposal and asked the association's House of Delegates at its 1963 annual meeting to approve the recommendation. The house not only failed to accept the committee's recommendation, but it voted to disapprove and oppose the Council of State Governments' proposal. Two years later, however, the House of Delegates voted to support a less drastic attack upon the Court but one nonetheless that would amend the Constitution to effectively overturn the decision in *Baker*.

Between meetings of the House of Delegates, the Board of Governors is empowered to perform any act, including the authorization of official ABA lobbying, not inconsistent with any action taken by the House itself. The organization possesses additional flexibility. Section leaders and other interested ABA members may testify before congressional committees even without specific House or Board authorization so long as they make mention of their lack of authorization. In fact, the rule is that whenever the House of Delegates or the Board of Governors has not authorized official ABA testimony, mention of this fact must be made. However, once having made the obligatory disclaimer, ABA representatives are free to lobby Congress and mention the results of ABA studies or even section or council recommendations concerning particular legislative proposals.

In recent years the association has maintained the Governmental Relations Office in Washington, D.C., to monitor and coordinate ABA political activities. Because of a perception of diversity and complexity of views within the ABA there was a felt need to isolate major issue concerns for the attention of the leadership. So, for example, in 1980 this office aided in the development of a "presidential legislation priorities list," which included fifteen items. Though this operation has not been studied carefully enough to draw firm conclusions, future researchers should pay it special attention. It has potential for contributing to the ABA's already considerable organizational prowess.

The political skills possessed by ABA leaders are likewise impressive. Chief among these skills is the ability to present the association as a group of impartial experts aiding policymakers to serve the public interest. This may seem extraordinary, given the history of ABA policy stands. Nonetheless, in view of the cultural responsiveness to legal symbols, it is possible. In his 1969 report on the state of the ABA, President William T. Gossett put the matter rather well. He said in part:

> We should remind ourselves from time to time . . . that the Association as an adviser of government has uncommon attributes, not only with respect to investigative and analytical competence, but in terms of basic motivation; that is, a capacity to act and speak with detachment and independence regarding the issues involved. And its views generally have been accepted as nonpolitical and impartial. The recently appointed commission to study the Federal Trade Commission, at the request of President Nixon, has an opportunity to add luster and credibility to the Association's *aurora popularis* as a dispassionate investigator and advocate of the public interest.

ABA recommendations are often treated by the mass media as dispassionate judgments of objective experts. Indeed, ABA representatives often present themselves as impartial experts, not as hired guns for special interests.

As adept as ABA leaders are at argumentation, other political skills abound as well. The ABA publishes a number of journals, including the *American Bar Association Journal.* Other periodicals are published as a service to specialist audiences. These media are used to communicate with attentive publics within the association. Interested persons may then communicate policy recommendations to government officials and other elites either by writing letters or speaking with political figures directly.

Consider the tactics employed by Charles S. Maddock, a representative of the ABA Section on Corporation, Banking, and Business Law. After testifying in 1971 and 1973 before a Senate subcommittee against certain proposed provisions on the revision of the United States criminal code, Maddock wrote an article entitled "The Proposed Criminal Code: Business Lawyer Beware" in his section's official organ, *The Business Lawyer.* The article outlined the section's objections to certain proposed criminal code provisions and admonished business attorneys to become familiar with its terms and to inform public officials of their objections. A reprint was submitted to, and made part of, the record of the Senate Subcommittee on Criminal Laws and Procedures. In this way the valuable political information was communicated to Senate members that business lawyers and executives were apprised of the stakes at issue. In brief, Maddock presented the party line to the membership. In turn, members were asked to join with the leadership in pressuring Congress to make changes in the proposed code consistent with its recommendations. The relevant policymakers, in this case members of the Senate committee with jurisdiction over code reform, were provided with important political intelligence to consider in their own deliberations. Tactics such as these are well known. The fact that the ABA leadership employs such maneuvers underscores its sophisticated understanding of the workings of the political process.

An interesting exercise of political skill entails the regular interaction with government officials and staff personnel to both educate and persuade those in a structural position to affect policy outcomes. It is known that some ABA sections—those concerned with taxation, corporations and banking, and antitrust matters—have permanent, floating meetings with public officials. Ostensibly, these meetings take place so as to provide government with technical advice. The regular interaction between the ABA's antitrust section and Justice Department personnel is particularly instructive.

Past, present, and potential Justice Department personnel are included as ABA antitrust section officers and council members. Between 1968 and 1980 more than 24 percent of the antitrust section leaders were at one time or another associated with the Justice Department's antitrust division. Moreover, since 1970 the antitrust section has formally included on its governing council Justice Department and Federal Trade Commission (FTC) representation. Communication is further enhanced by the inclusion at section meetings of antitrust and FTC officials in a variety of participatory roles, including making introductory comments and speeches and acting as panel moderators or discussants.

In summary, the ABA enjoys high status, effective organization, and abundant political skills—all the necessary conditions for sustained political influence. Nevertheless, it is not always successful. But no interest group always wins. What is important to note is that by all accounts the ABA is the most powerful of lawyer groups on the national scene.

NATIONAL LAWYERS GUILD

The NLG provides a stark contrast to the American Bar Association. The ABA is clearly an accepted establishment institution; the NLG is not.

The election of Franklin Roosevelt in 1932, the establishment of organized labor as a permanent group in American life, and the use of the federal bureaucracy ostensibly to aid the needy set the scene for the founding of the NLG in 1937. Lawyers aligned ideologically and in their work with these political developments felt a need to organize. The bar in general and the ABA in particular were viewed by NLG lawyers as representative of society's reactionary elements. The ABA, which then excluded black lawyers from membership, was viewed as part of a conservative alliance that included such notables as the National Association of Manufacturers and the Liberty League.

In 1933, Maurice Sugar, a Detroit attorney,

circulated a letter suggesting a new association of progressive lawyers to alleviate "their suffering [of] virtual ostracism because of their defense of those who otherwise would have been defenseless." Several New York City attorneys took up Sugar's challenge and the guild's founding national convention took place on 21 and 22 February 1937 at a Washington, D.C., hotel. New Yorker Frank P. Walsh presided as temporary chairman of the estimated 425–600 attending lawyers. Included at the founding were two federal judges, justices of two state supreme courts, two members of Congress, two state governors, and five law professors. An experienced group of individuals was elected as the first national executive committee. Members included Sugar, the counsel for the American Civil Liberties Union, a justice of the Domestic Relations Court of New York, a federal district court judge, and the general counsel for the American Federation of Labor. Chief Justice John P. Devaney of the Minnesota Supreme Court was elected as the first NLG president.

Reflecting a commitment to human rights over property rights, the founders included in the preamble to the NLG constitution the following:

> The National Lawyers Guild aims to unite lawyers of America in a professional organization which shall serve as an effective force in the service of the people, to the end that human rights shall be regarded as more sacred than property rights. The organization aims to bring together all lawyers who regard adjustments to new conditions as more important than the veneration of precedent, who recognize the importance of safeguarding and extending the rights of workers and farmers upon whom the welfare of the entire nation depends, of maintaining our civil rights and liberties and our democratic institutions, and who look upon the law as a living and flexible instrument which must be adapted to the needs of the people.

In keeping with these sentiments and establishing the ideological path the guild would follow throughout its history, the first national convention debated, and went on record concerning, important controversial issues. It supported President Roosevelt's Court-packing plan, which was vigorously opposed by the ABA. It passed a resolution calling for the removal of all restrictions on suffrage and removing restrictions on minority parties, including poll taxes and all-white primaries. It responded to the decisions in the infamous Scottsboro cases by calling for more public defenders to replace the prevailing practice of bench-assigned counsel. It formally committed itself to the formation of legal aid clinics aimed at making legal services available to the poor. In fact, a pilot program was instituted the next year in Philadelphia involving the establishment of four neighborhood offices, which, by 1942, had grown to ten.

The guild also considered a constitutional amendment designed to restrict the power of the federal courts, so as to ensure congressional authority to legislate with respect to labor relations, child labor, social security, and the ownership and operation of transportation, natural resources, utilities, and banks. The assembled lawyers also considered but rejected a resolution endorsing the sit-down strike as a legitimate tool of labor against business. Finally, at this first national convention the guild's commitment to worker rights was affirmed with resolutions providing for the right of labor to organize fully; labor should be permitted all necessary weapons, including the right to strike, picket, and boycott. It also called for legislation that would outlaw company unions, the private employment and compensation of law enforcement officers by companies, and the imposition of restrictions on the use of antilabor court injunctions.

By the end of its first year, 1937–1938, NLG nationwide membership had grown to more than 3,300 attorneys. The membership included notable legal figures, such as University of Chicago law professors Edward H. Levi and Malcolm Sharp and future Supreme Court justices Robert H. Jackson, then solicitor general, and Arthur J. Goldberg, a Chicago-based labor lawyer. Prominent women members included Pearl M. Hart and Ruth Weyand of Chicago and Carol King of New York.

The first issue of the *National Lawyers Guild Quarterly* appeared in November 1937. That issue, totaling five thousand copies, sold out within two months of its release. Contributing authors included Senator Robert La Follette; the historian and political scientist Charles Beard; and chairman of the Securities and Exchange Commission (later Supreme Court justice) William O. Douglas. Thus, regular communication with guild members and other lawyers got an auspicious start.

For the brief period between its founding and the outbreak of World War II the guild busied itself with a variety of projects. The neighbor-hood-office project for low-income citizens pros-pered. In the face of ABA opposition, the guild promoted social security protection for self-employed attorneys. It filed amicus curiae briefs involving labor, civil rights, and other constitu-tional issues. It urged a policy of asylum for polit-ical refugees fleeing fascism. It also sought jury trials for immigrants facing deportation. The guild's International Law Committee prepared a brief that argued that it was legal under the 1935 Neutrality Act to provide United States military assistance to Republican Spanish forces to be used against the fascists under Generalissimo Franco. Involvement in foreign affairs created serious debate within the newborn lawyer orga-nization about its goals and purposes. Some guild members argued that the organization should focus its attention strictly upon legal mat-ters, but others carried the day with the argu-ment that law and politics are inseparable. Guild interest and involvement in foreign affairs con-tinues to this day.

While the country was fighting World War II, guild members publicly advocated tax reform and rent control through their association with the War Labor Board and the Office of Price Administration. Members also urged the Na-tional Labor Relations Board to deny exclusive bargaining rights to unions practicing Jim Crow segregation in the organization of locals. At war's end, the guild provided consultants to the San Francisco founding of the United Nations, and it helped to establish the International Asso-ciation of Democratic Lawyers.

It was just before and during World War II that the guild's left-of-center sentiments and ac-tions attracted patriotic suspicions. The guild opposed the antialien Voorhis Registration Act, the antisubversion Smith Act (used for the first time during the war against the Socialist Workers party), and it denounced FBI tactics employed against Harry Bridges in an effort to deport the left-leaning labor leader. In the case of Judith Coplon, a Justice Department employee con-victed of illegal copying of documents relating to internal security, the guild reported numerous instances of FBI misconduct, including illegal

entry, use of unlawful wiretaps, and the use of unreliable informants. Internal disunity was most evident on the Communism issue. At one point, prominent guild members, including Abe Fortas, Morris Ernst, Robert Jackson, Jerome Frank, and Arthur Goldberg, left the organiza-tion because members refused to adopt a resolu-tion repudiating Communism. The guild was not the only left-of-center group experiencing the ill effects of anti-Communist sentiments awash in the nation. In fact, the most civil-libertarian of voluntary organizations, the American Civil Lib-erties Union, in 1940 expelled Elizabeth Gurley Flynn because of her Communist party member-ship, an action it repudiated thirty-six years later.

Guild problems multiplied in the 1950s when the country entered the period commonly re-ferred to as the McCarthy era. In 1950 the House Un-American Activities Committee (HUAC) charged the NLG as being "the foremost legal bulwark of the Communist Party, its front orga-nizations, and controlled unions." Guild leaders attempted to respond but their efforts had little impact. At the ABA's annual meeting in August 1953, Attorney General Herbert Brownell an-nounced his intention to list the guild as a "sub-versive" organization. The guild made unsuc-cessful attempts to block the blacklisting in the courts. These efforts were followed by adminis-trative proceedings within the Justice Depart-ment. The battle against blacklisting lasted four and one-half years, ending finally in April 1958 when Attorney General William Rogers dropped the entire proceeding against the guild. The NLG was but one of many groups and individu-als that was made to suffer during this period. Nevertheless, the epithet was damning and the effects were real.

Membership had dwindled from about 4,000 at the beginning of World War II to about 560 by the late 1950s. The guild was unable to solicit the growing law student population because of fears that guild membership might provide com-mittees passing on fitness of character a cause to deny licensure to young lawyers. But the 1960s visited new problems upon the country. The mood of the country had changed, and the guild found itself back in business. The guild was espe-cially active in the civil rights struggle and the anti–Vietnam War movement of that dramatic and eventful decade.

It established in early 1962 the Committee to

Aid Southern Lawyers, to assist blacks in achieving racial equality. The guild openly criticized the southern bar for what it termed a "refusal" to provide effective legal representation for black Americans and their white supporters. This committee, working with other civil rights groups, prepared briefs and pleadings, conducted interracial conferences in southern cities, and made northern lawyers available to try cases and to conduct appeals. The guild also published a practical manual for civil rights lawyers and activists, the *Civil Rights and Liberties Handbook.* During the summers of 1962 and 1963, law students from northern schools were sent south to clerk in the offices of civil rights lawyers. The guild organized in 1964 and 1965 the migration of more than one hundred northern attorneys who devoted a week or more of their time in the state of Mississippi on behalf of the civil rights movement.

As was often the case in the 1960s, those who actively supported the civil rights movement also found it necessary to oppose United States involvement in Vietnam, and that included the guild. Guild chapters represented clients who resisted the military draft and those military personnel seeking discharge after induction. The guild, as it did for the civil rights movement, published a practical manual, one concerning draft law. It also operated a great number of draft counseling centers and antiwar coffeehouses where military personnel opposed to the Vietnam War could gather. The guild went as far as Asia itself, where in 1971 it established law offices near military bases in the Philippines, Japan, and Okinawa.

The decade of the 1970s was a period when the guild expanded its interests. Members became active in issues surrounding prisoner rights, gay liberation, sexism, abortion, native Americans, Palestinian rights and the recognition of the Palestinian Liberation Organization, and farm worker unionization. It also expanded contacts with other groups, such as the National Conference of Black Lawyers and the organization of Hispanic lawyers, the La Raza Legal Alliance. In cooperation with these minority-centered groups the guild devoted manpower to affirmative action and related matters. The 1970s were also a time in which the guild reaffirmed its historic interest in worker rights. It counseled a group of dissident Teamsters Union members called Teamsters for a Democractic Union. To provide resources to labor lawyers and union organizers from around the country, the NLG established during the fall of 1979 the Washington-based National Labor Center. The center specialized in the particular problems of occupational health and safety, union democracy, and organizing workers. This project survived for about four years; the center had to close its doors in March 1983 because of a lack of funds.

A review of guild programs and activities for the early part of the decade of the 1980s provides the opportunity to describe how it goes about attempting to influence events. Although each mode of political involvement may be illustrated for previous decades, five prominent activities were employed in the 1980s to challenge the economic policies of the Reagan administration, racism, sexism, civil liberties violations, and United States foreign policy. These include initiating and supporting litigation; legislative lobbying; involvement in electoral politics; grassroots organizing and education; and publication.

Litigation may be viewed as a practical and pragmatic skill employed by uniquely well qualified professionals. Many guild lawyers no doubt share a common faith with other lawyers, including leaders of the ABA and many members of the public, that through litigation justice may be realized. Indeed, many view the courts as the means by which preexisting rights are protected and legitimate social change consistent with justice may be achieved. It is little wonder, then, that guild efforts have often focused on the courthouse—this despite expressions by the guild that the law is an instrument of a dominant ruling elite.

In the 1980s, guild attorneys coordinated the defense team that represented native Americans prosecuted for violating federal and state fishing laws on what the defendants argue are Indian lands rightly belonging to them under treaties entered into with the United States government. The Buffalo, New York, guild chapter won a suit in a United States district court that challenged that city's denial of advertising space on city buses to a proabortion group. Police brutality cases in Georgia, Louisiana, and Connecticut have been handled by guild attorneys. They have, in cooperation with others, mounted legal challenges through case filings involving Reagan administration policies in Grenada, El Salvador, Guatemala, Nicaragua, and Cuba. The NLG also participated as amicus curiae in numerous United States Supreme Court cases.

Perhaps the most dramatic litigation involving the guild is its own suit filed in 1977 against the FBI, CIA, and other government intelligence agencies. The guild alleged in *National Lawyers Guild* v. *Attorney General* that the government had engaged in a campaign of surveillance and harassment against the guild since its 1937 founding. The suit sought a declaratory judgment that the alleged government spying and disruptive activities were and are illegal, an injunction against the government ordering it to refrain from such activities, and monetary damages.

As already noted, it was in its formative years that the guild expended some energy on legislative lobbying. But this was before it became tainted by charges of subversion. It made nine known appearances before congressional committees during the period 1970–1981. The ABA, on the other hand, during this same decade made 285 hearing appearances. Note that the ABA possesses great prestige, respectability, and therefore, access and probable influence. The guild, except in a very small congressional circle, lacks the prerequisites for influence and therefore a sustained legislative lobbying effort. Devoting energy to political areas in which it might enjoy greater success is a reasonable guild strategy. The National Immigration Project of the guild lobbied Congress to defeat the controversial Simpson-Mazzoli immigration bill, the same bill debated in Congress and condemned on the floor of the Democratic National Convention at San Francisco in July 1984. At the local level, guild members in Massachusetts played a role in convincing the state legislature to hold hearings on the impact on residents of that state of United States intervention in Central America. By and large, however, traditional forms of legislative lobbying at the state and local levels of government are not, as is also the case at the national level, a tool prominently employed by the guild.

Guild members in recent years have become involved in municipal campaigns. During the 1982 mayoral race in Chicago, the local guild organized a five-hundred-member lawyer's committee for successful black candidate Harold Washington. It raised money and performed many of the functions associated with winning local elections. A similar effort on behalf of an unsuccessful mayoral candidate in Boston was mounted by guild members. The National Executive Committee of the guild involved the organization in the 1984 presidential campaign by putting together a voter registration program urging members to get involved in the campaign to build a multiracial coalition.

As the guild was particularly active in the civil rights and antiwar movements in the 1960s and 1970s, it has also been active in grass-roots and other front-line educational efforts during the 1980s. For example, it has participated in training programs to deal with problems associated with economic recession. In Milwaukee it participated in a university program on unemployment benefits. In San Francisco and Los Angeles it held classes on plant closings. In Ohio and Illinois it addressed public budget cuts. And in Gary, Indiana, it held forth on home mortgage foreclosures. These more recent education activities are consistent with the civil rights and anti–Vietnam War activities of the 1960s and 1970s and with the legal-aid clinics for the poor and union organizing of an earlier era. They are an explicit recognition that legal rights are not automatically enforced and are predicated on the belief that affected persons must know their rights and the political options open to them.

Publication is the last of the five political tools at the guild's disposal. Publication activities range from a quarterly dealing with a variety of legal issues to how-to manuals and polemical materials designed to persuade others of the guild's viewpoint. The NLG publishes practical litigation manuals on police misconduct, draft and military matters, gay rights, grand juries, immigration, labor, native Americans, and prisoners. Examples of the guild's more polemical tracts are *The Illegality of U.S. Intervention: Central America and Caribbean Litigation* and *Don't Let the Draft Blow You Away*.

The NLG is no longer exclusively an organization of lawyers. For this reason, one might question whether the NLG should properly be regarded as a bar association. Broadening membership criteria began with the July 1968 convention in Santa Monica, California. Law students played an active and forceful role at that time in staffing various guild projects and in participating on each convention committee. Some members, including Doris Walker, the Guild's first woman president (1970), had serious reservations about admitting law students as regular members. It was felt that the expanded membership to nonlawyers would change the character of the guild. Nonetheless, the guild at its 1970 meeting voted to admit law students.

A year later the most radical departure from the traditional bar-association format took place. At its 1971 national convention in Boulder, Colorado, the NLG voted to include legal secretaries, paralegals, legal assistants, legal administrators, investigators, jury workers, and law clerks. Perhaps reflecting the guild's historic labor orientation, this group was given the generic label *law workers.* Prison inmates who study law independently to prepare defenses for their own legal problems, the so-called jailhouse lawyers, were also included. Prior to 1971, legal workers labored on many NLG projects but were unable to vote in the guild. The victory for legal workers reflected a conviction, based upon experience, that law workers can contribute to the development of legal strategies; lawyers, it was argued, do not possess a monopoly on such talent.

The inclusion of jailhouse lawyers reflected the development of the guild's prison activity in several regions of the country. Members came to respect the success of self-trained legal experts. Again, as occurred with the law-student admission question, some guild members objected to the organization's metamorphosis; but, a motion for the inclusion of the legal workers and jailhouse lawyers carried the day.

Despite the opening of the organization to nonlawyers, attorneys still hold numerical dominance in the guild. For the year 1983, 55 percent of the 7,300 NLG members were lawyers, 34 percent were law students, and 11 percent were legal workers and jailhouse lawyers.

In terms of organizational structure, the guild is composed of a national executive committee, eight regional bodies, and more than one hundred local chapters. A president, two executive vice-presidents, and a treasurer are elected at the guild's national meetings and are members of the National Executive Committee. They play prominent roles in the operation of the guild, including those of the national office, located in New York City, which is the administrative and communications heart of the organization. It collects the dues and processes hundreds of requests each month for information, legal assistance, and a host of other functions, such as coordinating speaking tours and fund-raising projects. The national office also communicates with the membership through the bimonthly *Guild Notes,* a newspaper produced by a staff editor and backstopped by an editorial board based in New York City.

Depending upon current NLG priorities, subject-matter interest groups within the organization are represented on the National Executive Committee. During the 1983–1984 period, that representation took the form of five designated vice-presidents, for antiracism and affirmative action, antisexism, economic rights, law-student organizing, and Third World caucus organizing. Reflecting the obvious importance of funding the guild, the National Finance Committee is also represented on the National Executive Committee.

At its 1973 convention, the guild officially recognized regionalism. The guild is organized around eight geographic areas, with each region represented on the National Executive Committee by a regional vice-president. Each region is composed of a number of local chapters that include city, geographic designations, and law schools. As members of the National Executive Committee, the regional vice-presidents communicate regularly and directly with the national organization through quarterly meetings. Thus, regional perspectives are brought to the attention of the national officers and presumably have an impact on the guild's national programs.

Each region communicates with its chapters and memberships directly through personal contacts and through the publication of regional newsletters. Some regions maintain regional organizers responsible for promoting the development of new chapters and strengthening existing chapters and programs. Each region has its own conference, usually held on an annual basis. Previous conference themes have focused on poverty, social services, and United States intervention in Central America.

Presently, there are more than one hundred guild chapters, ranging from small groups of less than twenty-five in southern Illinois to large groups in such places as San Francisco and New

York with membership in the one thousand range. Much of the guild's activity takes place within the local chapters, which are actively involved in local political and legal projects. Many national committees are administered within local chapters. The Boston chapter, for example, houses the National Immigration Project and the National Committee to Combat Women's Oppression. The San Francisco chapter was the guild's original home for its Central American projects. Litigation on behalf of the national organization is also often handled by local chapters.

Local chapters sponsor seminars designed to equip members and others to meet the ideological objectives of the guild. Topics such as suing the government, legal rights of activists, and police misconduct are standard fare for chapter legal education programs. Thus, city chapters, in cooperation with law school chapters, provide a continuing legal education component to guild activities with trial skill workshops for lawyer activists.

Local activities that directly benefit local attorneys are likely to be very important for the future of the guild. Although idealism must play a central role in motivating persons to join the guild, ideology alone is not sufficient to maintain an organization. When organizations can provide members with divisible material benefits, the likelihood of group survival and prosperity is enhanced. Indeed, the Massachusetts chapter has gone so far as to institute a program of group purchasing of law office supplies and services. Also, most guild chapters provide an informal attorney referral service, and some chapters publish referral directories.

What unites guild members is the view that the legal system is a tool of a corporate elite. The law is often referred to in guild publications as an instrument of class, sexual, and social oppression rather than as an agent of some mystical concept called justice. The guild presents a striking contrast to the ABA.

FREEDOM AND THE BAR

Both the ABA and the NLG are voluntary associations. If a member does not concur in the views expressed by the group then the available options are to stand mute, to attempt to change undesirable policy positions, or to leave the organization. That members may vote with their feet and take their financial support elsewhere is among the more serious threats to organizational viability. However, this option may not be open to attorneys in the thirty-three states that compel lawyers to be members of the state bar association.

State bar groups have used dues to pay for a host of lobbying activities associated with the regulation of the practice of law, disciplinary matters, continuing legal education, public education, and improvement of the administration of justice. Beyond these commonly accepted activities, many state bar associations have lobbied state and national legislatures on matters that do not directly affect lawyers in the conduct of their profession. Taking public stands and attempting to influence legislatures on nuclear power, minority-college funding, the right to life, and other matters of popular concern are a few of many such examples. Beyond legislative lobbying, state bars are known to have influenced public policy through amicus curiae briefs, participating in judicial and administrative rule-making proceedings, conducting and publicizing the results of bar polls in which candidates for judicial elective office are evaluated, and offering technical advice on legislative drafting. It is these attempts to influence public policy that have induced disaffected members of integrated bars to raise serious constitutional objections.

In the Supreme Court case of *Lathrop* v. *Donohue* (1961), a Wisconsin lawyer argued that his First Amendment rights of speech and association were violated because he was forced to belong to, and pay dues to, the state bar association, which in turn used some of the compulsory dues to take positions on public policy matters with which he disagreed. The Court rejected the lawyer's claim, and integrated bars continued to engage in legislative activities, with very few concessions made to dissidents. However, in *Arrow* v. *Dow* (1982) bar members won a similar suit, and in so doing placed in question the political activities of the thirty-three unified bars. This federal district court case held that the use of compulsory state-bar dues for legislative lobbying violated the plaintiff's rights because such activities did not in this case serve an important state interest that would justify the infringement of the First Amendment.

Some bar leaders have begun to wonder publicly whether political activity is worth the organizational difficulties such activity creates. Less reclusive steps than giving up political activity are open to the bar. First, a checkoff system by which members could request and obtain a refund on that portion of dues otherwise devoted to support lobbying could be instituted. Second, a voluntary fund could be established; members might contribute financial support to special lobbying funds that are expressly and separately administered from other bar activities. As some state bars have already done, political action committees may be established to support candidates for political office. A final option championed by opponents of the integrated bar is the logical step of the abolition of the compulsory bar association in favor of the voluntary bar association model currently found in nineteen jurisdictions. There, it is argued, the regulatory functions of the bar are effectively managed while legislative lobbying programs are maintained.

Whatever the course of future bar activities might be it is certain that lawyer influence in this political culture will live on. That keenly perceptive foreign observer of nineteenth-century America, Alexis de Tocqueville, put it best when he wrote in *Democracy in America*,

> The lawyers of the United States form a party which is but little feared and scarcely perceived, which has no badge peculiar to itself, which adapts itself with great flexibility to the exigencies of the time and accommodates itself without resistance to all the movements of the social body. But this party extends over the whole community and penetrates into all the classes which compose it; it acts upon the country imperceptibly, but finally fashions it to suit its own purposes.

CASES

Arrow v. Dow, 544 F. Supp. 458 (1982)
Baker v. Carr, 369 U.S. 186 (1962)
Brown v. Board of Education of Topeka, 347 U.S. 483 (1954)
Lathrop v. Donohue, 367 U.S. 820 (1961)
National Lawyers Guild v. Attorney General, pending
    Pennsylvania v. Nelson, 350 U.S. 497 (1956)

BIBLIOGRAPHY

Jerold S. Auerbach, *Unequal Justice: Lawyers and Social Change in Modern America* (1976), critically analyzes the modern history of the legal profession and contains references to a variety of bar associations. Charles L. Cappell and Terence C. Halliday, "Professional Projects of Elite Chicago Lawyers, 1950–1974," in *American Bar Foundation Research Journal* (1983), reports on the composition and politics of the leaders of the Chicago Bar Association. Joel B. Grossman, *Lawyers and Judges: The ABA and the Politics of Judicial Selection* (1965), studies the efforts of the ABA to influence judicial selection. James Willard Hurst, *The Growth of American Law: The Law Makers* (1950), contains much information on the history of the bar and its associations. Herbert Jacob, *Justice in America: Courts, Lawyers, and the Judicial Process*, 4th ed. (1984), discusses bar associations and their political involvement. Richard Katz, ed., *The National Lawyers Guild: An Inventory of Records, 1936–1976; An Index to Periodicals, 1937–1979* (1980), is the first stop for researchers investigating the guild.

Dayton David McKean, *The Integrated Bar* (1963), discusses the history of the integrated bar and the political involvement of the profession in politics. Charles S. Maddock, "The Proposed Criminal Code: Business Lawyer Beware," in *The Business Lawyer*, 29 (1974), exemplifies internal group lobbying, rallying ABA lawyers to lobby Congress for reforms in the criminal code that will not adversely impact business interests. George W. Martin, *Causes and Conflicts: The Centennial History of the Association of the Bar of the City of New York, 1870–1970* (1970), details the history of this very important bar association. Albert P. Melone, *Lawyers, Public Policy and Interest Group Politics* (1979), analyzes the ABA's policy positions and interest-group alliances during the period 1953–1968; "The American Bar Association, Antitrust Legislation and Interest Group Coalitions," in *Policy Studies Journal*, 11 (1983), studies the ABA's policy toward antitrust legislation and the pattern of agreement with other interest groups at the national level; and "The Interest Group Politics of the American Bar Association and the Reform of the United States Criminal Code," in Erika S. Fairchild and Vincent J. Webb, eds., *The Politics of Crime and Criminal Justice* (1985), examines the ABA's position and politics on criminal code reform.

National Lawyers Guild, *The Challenge of the Eighties: National Lawyers Guild 1983 Organizational Report* (1983), reports information about the guild. John R. Schmidhauser, *Judges and Justices: The Federal Appellate Judiciary* (1979), discusses in chapter 6 the ABA's influence on state and federal courts. John R. Schmidhauser and Larry L. Berg, *The Supreme Court and Congress: Conflict and Interaction, 1945–1968* (1972), contains, in chapter 5, a discussion of ABA political involvement in court-related conflicts. Theodore A. Schneyer, "The Unified Bar: A Historical Perspective," in *Bar Leader*, 8 (1982), discusses the case law and implications of court decisions on the First Amendment and the integrated bar.

Edson R. Sunderland, *History of the American Bar Association and Its Work* (1953), describes the history of the ABA, especially the association's early years. United States Congress, Senate Committee on the Judiciary, *Hearings Before the Subcommittee on Representation of Citizen Interests, The Organized Bar: Self-Serving or Serving the Public?* 93rd Cong., 2nd sess. (1974), reports the testimony of bar leaders who answer charges that the organized bar is self-serving. Doran Weinberg and Marty Fassler, "A Historical Sketch of the National Lawyers Guild in American Politics, 1936–1968," in United States Congress, House Committee on the Judiciary, *Hearings on Nomination of Nelson A. Rockefeller to be Vice President of the United States,* 93rd Cong., 2nd sess. (1974), is a warm interpretative history of the guild. Mary H. Zimmerman, ed., *Seventy-five-Year History of National Association of Women Lawyers: 1899–1974* (1975), gives the history of this women's group, with references to the personalities of the officers and directors.

[*See also* JUDICIAL SELECTION.]

CIVIL LAW SYSTEMS

Henry W. Ehrmann

SINCE colonial times the legal system of the United States has followed the common-law tradition imported from England. It is true that some regions have a legacy of non-English law derived from earlier settlers and conquerors. As one would expect, Spanish and French influences were strong and survived for some time in such states as Florida, Texas, New Mexico, Arizona, and California.

The question as to whether and to what extent law of French, Spanish, or Mexican origin was still operative in these territories after annexation by the Union is quite controversial. The foremost French scholar of comparative law (David, 339) states that while these territories "might in theory have been subject to French, Spanish or Mexican law as well, such laws were really unknown for all practical purposes." Other historians have described the "legal chaos" that prevailed for a number of years during which neither legal practitioners nor judges were certain which traditions and rules to follow: those of the civil or the common law. But before long, and often before these territories achieved statehood, previously existing laws were revoked and replaced by explicit adherence to the common law. In some of these states certain features of the old law have not completely disappeared. This is particularly true in such fields as land titles, mining law, riparian and water rights, matrimonial property, and in regard to some aspects of procedure, such as forms of pleading. But these "remnants" are often "hidden under a thick layer of common law" (Schlesinger).

Only Louisiana and the Commonwealth of Puerto Rico have preserved a legal culture different from that prevalent in the rest of the nation. For historical reasons, distinctive features of their legal systems belong to the civil-law, rather than to the common-law, tradition.

In countries adhering to the civil law tradition, law and legal science have developed on the basis of Roman law as it is known by the extensive compilations which were produced in the sixth century upon the orders of Emperor Justinianus. Not the judges, as in countries of the common-law tradition, but legal scholars developed the concepts and what was called the "doctrine" of the civil law. On the basis of these concepts legislators and administrators fashioned, and frequently modified, the actual legal rules in accordance with the assumed needs of the society or, more often, of the ruling elites. Of late differences between these two "families" of law, those of the common- and the civil-law, have diminished; yet they have by no means disappeared altogether. The conditions under which part of the civil-law traditions have survived in Louisiana and Puerto Rico illustrate both the narrowing of the differences and their continuing salience.

Louisiana was first settled by France under a private charter granted by Louis XIV in 1712. That charter provided that a body of French customary law, the *Coutume de Paris* ("Custom of Paris"), and royal ordinances were to be observed as laws and customs in Louisiana. Since the Custom of Paris harbors not only Roman but also rather strong Germanic traits, both French and Teutonic customary law entered the region. France ceded Louisiana to Spain in 1762. Overcoming opposition from the French-speaking population and the indigenous jurists, the Spanish governor, Alexander O'Reilly, abolished all French law (except for the *Code Noir*, or "Black Code," dealing with slaves) and replaced it with Spanish law. But at this time Spanish law was incorporated into a multiplicity of legal institutions dating from different periods. A digest of Spanish laws was published in French to familiarize Louisianians with the complicated legal system under which they were living.

In 1803 France regained control of Louisiana. But after a mere twenty days the territory was purchased by the United States. During his brief tenure the French prefect abolished all Spanish courts but had no time to reintroduce French law. Hence, the American governor, William Claiborne, transferred to New Orleans from a similar post in Mississippi, found an all but complete juridical vacuum, which he hoped to fill by the common law. The resistance he met proved that in spite of political vicissitudes, the mixture of French and Spanish laws and customs under which the population had lived for at least a century had endowed the region with a solid legal culture. The influx of citizens from the United States that followed the Louisiana Purchase was not strong enough to overcome these traditions, supported by the fact that for a time French remained the predominant language.

The attractiveness of staying within the older traditions was enhanced by legal developments in Napoleonic France that gave an example of stability and convenience. By enacting the comprehensive French Civil Code of 1804, or Code Napoléon (to be followed by some supplementary codes), the French had put an end to the legal disorders that the declining ancien régime and the French Revolution had engendered. The new code incorporated existing law, both customary and statutory, which it reorganized, clarified, and elaborated with the help of the extensive legal learning in which French jurists excelled.

The three major sections of the code deal with "persons," with "property," and with "modes of acquiring property rights." Under these general headings a great variety of matters are treated: the rights and the civil status of individuals; family relations, including divorce and adoption; the various forms of ownership and of servitudes; torts; contracts of all kinds; sales; loans; partnership agreements; liens; mortgages; and successions. The code treated these in straightforward language, eliminating the technicalities of the feudal terms that abound in prerevolutionary French law as well as in the common law. It addressed all citizens without distinction of class or caste. Napoleon had boasted that even the poorest peasant would find in the code a description of his rights and of his duties.

But what the code also did was to invite imita-

tion. A compact code is more easily exported than either customary law or a long line of judicial precedents, both, by their very nature, closely tied to the culture in which they have developed. In fact, the Code Napoléon served as a model in countries on all continents. After two centuries its influence is not yet spent. In the country of its origin, it has survived political revolutions and drastic economic changes with very few of its articles altered. All attempts at a thorough overhaul of the code have been abandoned.

Louisiana's was the first (in 1808) legal system to draw its inspiration from the Code Napoléon. Having been frustrated in his effort to make the common law prevail, Governor Claiborne directed the Louisiana legislature to draft a civil code out of the existing law. The code, enacted in 1808 and written in French, was presented as a digest to guide the judges in their decision-making. When this method proved insufficient, the code was replaced in 1825 by a more detailed code covering the same subject matters as the French code.

Careful research has shown that a great majority of the articles of the earliest Louisiana code reproduced literally, or almost so, corresponding articles of the Code Napoléon. The later, more comprehensive version of 1825 incorporated supplementary materials from older Spanish and even Roman sources; when interpreting the code, some judges felt free to use Spanish precedents with which they were familiar. In addition, a very few provisions were lifted from Blackstone's *Commentaries.* If this made the legal heritage of Louisiana somewhat intricate, the revised Civil Code of 1870, still in force today, clarified and simplified the law. But no important changes were made. At least half, and the most important, of the older rules patterned after the Code Napoléon survived in the modern code. But unlike its predecessors, the 1870 code was written in English. The change of language had a considerable impact on further developments of Louisiana law.

Federal law became applicable to Louisiana with the incorporation of the territory into the United States, and Louisiana state law did not long resist an early and progressive "Americanization." Whatever touched on the various aspects of public order—the frequently amended or altered state constitution, administrative and criminal law, both civil and criminal procedure (including the rules of evidence)—followed almost exclusively common-law traditions. To have chosen another way would not only have been impractical but would also have created uncertainties detrimental to the rule of law. It is therefore not correct to describe Louisiana's legal system as one of civil law. It is rather to be regarded as a mixed jurisdiction, accommodating both civil and common law and thereby two of the world's foremost legal traditions and cultures. The significance of the coexistence of a comprehensive code regulating the legal relations of Louisiana citizens in ways derived largely from continental law and a court and administrative system firmly embedded in the American common-law tradition remains a fascinating subject for scholars. It also appears frequently as a bewildering reality to Louisiana's jurists and citizens.

SOURCES OF LAW

Following its French model, and in similar terms, the Louisiana code sets out to advise the judges about the sources of law on which they should draw when called upon to settle legal disputes. Its first article proclaims a principle and establishes a priority: "Law is a solemn expression of legislative will." (*Law* in this context means legislation enacted by the legislature.) A subsequent provision admonishes the judge to construe all legislation as literally—and, by implication, as narrowly—as he can: "When a law is clear and free from all ambiguity, the letter of it is not to be disregarded, under the pretext of pursuing its spirit" (Article XIII). There are subsidiary sources to help judges in their task: "Customs result from a long series of actions constantly repeated, which have by such repetition, and by uninterrupted acquiescence, acquired the force of a tacit and common consent" (Article III). If the tests that custom must meet in order to be recognized as a source of law are quite strict, the code also acknowledges that customs meeting these tests might clarify legislative intent.

Another code article envisions situations in which there exists in the eyes of jurists raised in the civil-law tradition a gap in the law: "In all civil matters, where there is no express law, the judge is bound to proceed and decide according to

equity. To decide equitably, an appeal is to be made to natural law and reason, or received usages, where positive law is silent" (Article XXI). It is often remarked that, at least in their explicitness, these later articles of the Louisiana Code have no counterparts in the Code Napoléon. It might therefore be assumed that by their very explicitness the drafters of the code wanted to give particular weight to these guidelines.

Even such apparently detailed guidelines do not settle the question of the relative weight and the appropriate interpretation to be given the code and other statutory provisions. Since the Louisiana code insists on the overriding importance of legislation, an examination of enacted texts and the code itself will be the judges' first concern.

What might be called the classical view of an older generation of Louisiana jurists has been laid down in an often-quoted text, stating that:

> When conflicts occur and litigation becomes necessary, the first question is whether the problem is controlled by one or more Code articles. In the great majority of cases this will be so, and an elaborate apparatus of interpretation will be called into play. Regard will be had to the language of the text and the sense it conveys, the influence of other articles, considerations of the textual arrangement of the Code as a unit, historical factors, the clarifying effect of the *motifs* on obscure passages, and the allowable areas within which the legislator has indicated that judicial discretion may be used in taking account of special factors. The whole import of the process is the ascertainment of the genuine significance of the Code text.
>
> (Morrow, 549)

If such an analysis appears, at least on the surface, to provide a contrast to the methods of the ordinary common-law judge, a younger generation of Louisiana judges insists less on differences than on similarities of judicial reasoning. They think that there has been in the past a tendency to overemphasize distinctions that do not amount to real differences.

One associate justice of the Louisiana Supreme Court, Albert Tate, Jr., has suggested that a Louisiana judge applies to the civil code and other legislation the type of reasoning which a common-law judge applies to a constitutional provision and that "he may thus disregard interpretations of past generations in order to apply the principles underlying legislation to the resolution of contemporary problems" (Dainow). As is well known from American constitutional law, the discovery of the "underlying principles" cannot be free from more or less subjective evaluation of what Oliver Wendell Holmes called the "felt necessities of time." At common law, as in civil law, this leads to the exercise of rather broad discretion when judges evaluate what Tate called the "interpretations of past generations." As the same justice has stated, "The Louisiana judge, like his common-law brother, is a law-announcer as well as a case-decider" (Dainow). This disposes of the folklore according to which the role of the judiciary in a civil-law jurisdiction is merely mechanical, a description that amounts to a fiction masking the actual role played by civil-law judges not only in Louisiana but also in most civil-law countries.

It remains true that to the common-law jurist the code's enumeration of the sources of applicable law leaves a gap of its own: Judicial precedents are not mentioned. Can they not be relied upon as positive law? Do they have, especially when they originate in a higher court of the state, binding force for subsequent decisions turning on similar questions of law? Is a particular interpretation that a higher court has given to the text of the code or of other statutes to be considered as authoritative?

An eminent Montreal jurist, Jean-Louis Baudouin, has stated in a study of the impact of the common law on the civil-law systems of Louisiana and Quebec, "Perhaps the most significant and critical point of disagreement between common- and civil-law lawyers concerns the role and impact of 'jurisprudence' or judicial decisions upon the legal system as a whole" (Dainow). (In civil-law countries *jurisprudence* means case law rather than legal philosophy, as it does in Anglo-American writings.)

THE FORCE OF PRECEDENTS

According to transmitted theory and announced principle, the common-law doctrine of stare decisis, the binding force of precedent, is not recognized by Louisiana courts. Civil-law judges, it is sometimes said—and not in Louisiana alone—will never let today become either the slave of yesterday or the tyrant of tomorrow. When the attitude of Louisiana judges toward precedents is described as less reverent than that of judges in common-law courts, one tends to minimize the ease with which an American judge can overrule a precedent by "distinguishing" the case before him from previous ones. Yet the freedom with which, especially in the recent past, the Louisiana Supreme Court has overruled prior decisions is not equaled in common-law countries. Cases are quoted in which lower courts have refused to follow state supreme court decisions. The court of appeal has sometimes won out, when it declared erroneous a supreme court decision, and has been upheld by a subsequent supreme court decision acknowledging its previous error.

Nonetheless, it would be wrong to assume that, because they are not formally binding, precedents do not carry weight in Louisiana courts. They are, or at least have become, a persuasive force in judicial decision-making. What remains are differences of degree. Louisiana follows the civil-law practice of heeding what has long been called in France the doctrine of *jurisprudence constante,* according to which a single decision might not be sufficient to establish a precedent, but a series of adjudicated cases, all agreeing on a point of law, especially on the interpretation of a legislative text, will sooner or later be considered as binding. Courts might still shy away from openly acknowledging that in these cases judge-made law has become a binding rule. They prefer to regard a more or less long line of concordant precedents as establishing rules of customary law. And customs have been described by the Louisiana code as one of the legitimate sources from which the courts may draw their conclusions and rulings. A. N. Yiannopoulos states, "Theoretical differences notwithstanding, the use of precedents in practice is often similar in civil-law and in common-law jurisdictions. The essential difference may merely relate to the degree of sanctity with which precedents are regarded" (Dainow).

What this means for the "practice" of the courts and for the style of the attorneys appearing before them has been described by another associate justice of the Louisiana Supreme Court, Mack E. Barham, seeking to sort facts from long-accepted fiction:

Under our code and through the historical civilian tradition, jurisprudence is not a major source of law, yet it has been and remains such in reality. . . . Though we may really believe that legislation is the primary source of law, we practice under the principle that jurisprudence is a major source of law. Lawyers may only perfunctorily examine legislative expression before they turn for final authority to the jurisprudence to resolve the legal question posed by their clients' cases. Often when the court asks the lawyer in argument to give the authority for a point which he advocates, the court expects a case citation even where there is positive codal or statutory authority. As a result of the pressure under which we perform our various roles in our legal system, there has been a tendency to stray from strict civilian methods and concepts.

(Dainow, 39–40)

In the civil-law systems of Europe and Latin America, another source of law, the *doctrine,* has long been considered an important element of judicial decision-making, often attracting more attention than judicial precedent. *Doctrine* stands for the body of opinions on legal matters expressed in books and articles, including often elaborate and learned commentary on decided cases. The prestige of such writings has no counterpart in common-law jurisdictions. It derived from the role that the legal faculties of medieval universities had played in the growth of the law at a time when there existed no sovereign states to develop a legal system (such as the English throne).

In France and to an only slightly lesser extent in Spain, legal treatises, many dating from the sixteenth and seventeenth centuries, enjoyed great authority. Napoleon may have hoped that his codification would put an end to such scholarly influence, but French courts continued to rely on the writings of law professors. The professors considered their contribution to the exegesis of codes and statutes at least equal to that of judges, and their role in legislative reform was in fact considerable.

In Louisiana, *doctrine* never acquired the status it did in other civil-law systems. The drafters of the two earlier versions of the code had been familiar with, and had used some of, the works of French and Spanish legal scholars. But when, after the American Civil War, English became the dominant language in Louisiana, the judges were no longer able to follow the doctrinal development that continued apace in France. Although some outstanding scholars teaching at Louisiana law schools were well versed in the civil law, the practical needs of their students moved them to give their greatest attention to common-law thinking and techniques.

SUBSTANTIVE LAW

The Louisiana civil codes have now been in operation for almost the same span of time as the Code Napoléon in France. In both France and Louisiana, the codes have been admired and indeed "deified," ensuring the survival of these bodies of law. In order to make an antiquated code's provisions workable under totally changed economic and social conditions, the Louisiana courts have had to develop new concepts and, frequently, new institutions. While in some fields new legislation has been forthcoming, in many others the judges were called upon to fill old forms with new substance. As in common-law systems, there have been landmark decisions that settled newly arising problems in line with the urgent needs of society and the prevalent sense of justice. The Louisiana judges take pride in referring to the often-quoted admonition of a German scholar of world renown, Rudolf von Jhering, writing in the civil-law tradition, "Through the Code but beyond it!" Here a few examples of such development must suffice.

Like the French code, Louisiana's recognized liability for damages only in cases where the defendant had been at fault. But by reworking principles, the courts have established strict liability for damage from hazardous or inherently dangerous activities. The vicarious responsibility of the master for his servants' delicts committed in pursuit of the master's economic interest was established by extending the liabilities foreseen by the code. Product liability of the seller was awarded in similar fashion, protecting not only the buyer but also third persons.

To evaluate the validity of contracts and the extent of contractual obligations, the courts have resorted to the concept of public policy, developed principally in English law. But the concept is quite congenial to civil-law judges in Louisiana (and elsewhere) because the French *ordre public* fulfills a similar function as a standard by which acts or agreements that offend the public order or good morals may be set aside (Friedmann).

Changes in property law have been substantial. When Louisiana became one of the largest producers of oil and gas in the United States, new legal problems arose. Without waiting for the somewhat hesitant enactment of special legislation, the courts fashioned on a case-by-case basis a new mineral law, for which there were, of course, no provisions in the code. Taking the property concepts of the code as a point of departure, the courts used analogies, the "doctrine" developed in learned treatises and other methods of civil-law methodology but also economic data and statistics to arrive at results that strive to combine the defense of business interests with community concerns for reasonable conservation and environmental protection.

When faced with these and similar tasks, Louisiana judges claim that the mixed jurisdiction under which they operate offers them certain advantages over their common-law colleagues and, by implication, over European civil-law judges, to whom common-law traditions are altogether alien. In the words of Tate,

> As with the common-law judge, he [the Louisiana judge] views himself not merely as a technician but also as a scholar and law-maker and exponent of doctrine. However, as with a modern-day civilian judge, he is essentially more free than his common-law counterpart from the mechanical effects of "binding" precedent; more free to return, independent of intervening judicial precedents, to the initial legislative concepts and to use creative analogies and constructs based upon them; or, in the absence of legislation expressly intended to apply, more free to devise socially just and sound rules to regulate the unprovided-for case.
>
> (Dainow, 36)

The frank eclecticism praised and practiced by Louisiana judges results in a judicial output hardly different from that of common-law courts. In Louisiana, as everywhere, it is the output of the system that interest the citizens who appeal to the law for settlement of conflicts. This is true of all of the major fields to which the civil code applies: individual rights and family relations, succession among the living and after death, conditions making a contract valid or null, liability, and property rights. Existing differences are hardly greater than those between American states sharing common-law traditions and can therefore not result from differences in the legal culture of common-law and civil-law systems. On the other hand, such a convergence is not peculiar to Louisiana and therefore cannot be interpreted as the overwhelming of Louisiana law by the common law prevalent elsewhere in the United States.

The gap between common-law and civil-law systems has been narrowed, and in certain fields closed, the world over and especially in advanced industrial societies. Similar problems and ever-new needs pressing for recognition have put similar demands on the legislative and judicial processes of many countries. Progressive assimilation was unavoidable and has in general not been resisted. To arrive at solutions deemed adequate and equitable, both systems had to free themselves from the shackles of obsolete traditions.

Authors who have convincingly argued that the difference between common-law and civil-law cultures is vanishing in countries of similar socioeconomic structure have nonetheless concluded that in regard to procedure and the rules of evidence, the differences between Anglo-American and civil-law principles remain "important, and in some respects, spectacular" (Friedmann). But, as we have seen earlier, in procedural matters Louisiana law has long since followed common-law patterns. This further eliminates differences between the practice of Louisiana and other state courts.

By adhering to the so-called adversary system of the common law, trials in Louisiana courts follow a scenario different from that enacted in the courts of other civil-law systems. European judges do not fit into the role of an umpire between contending parties, a role the common-law judge strives to fill. European judges are expected to be far more active in elucidating the facts underlying the conflicts they are called upon to settle. There also is a traditional lack of orality in the civil law, whereas in common-law proceedings most arguments will be stated explicitly in the courtroom. This, by itself, shapes not only form but also the content of admissible evidence. In all these matters the Louisiana courts consistently follow common-law, rather than civil-law, practices.

495

In one rather important instance, Louisiana law follows civil-law procedure. The state constitution has preserved the civil-law rule under which intermediate appellate courts may review not only the law but also the facts of the case under scrutiny. Since Louisiana admits jury trials in civil cases (they are unknown in continental Europe), Louisiana appellate courts have used their power to review the facts of a case to overturn jury verdicts in tort claims, by declaring that the findings of the jury were "manifestly erroneous." In this way the Louisiana appellate courts are able to do what other American appellate courts are generally prevented from doing—namely, to reduce excessive damage awards, which the jurors may have granted out of sympathy with an injured plaintiff. But in more recent times, civil jury trials have become a rarity in Louisiana (Schlesinger).

AMERICAN JUDGES IN A CIVIL-LAW SYSTEM

It is not the operation of the courts but the careers and personalities of their operators that continue to provide the clearest and often very important contrast between civil-law and common-law cultures. Practically all judges in Western Europe and Latin America are career bureaucrats; their status is little, if at all, different from that of other civil servants. They enter the judicial career immediately after academic preparation, followed perhaps by a period of in-service training. They are chosen and promoted to the higher judicial posts of a tightly organized hierarchy according to their skills as evaluated by their superiors. They are expected, and prefer, to remain anonymous. If they sit on collegial courts, their views are absorbed in the majority decision, reached behind closed doors. If there are dissenting opinions, they remain unreported.

The experienced practitioner who assumes judicial office in a common-law country, either by election or by nomination, but always by the political process, neither thinks of himself as a bureaucrat nor is regarded as such. The psychological differences between him and the bureaucrat are great, and their consequences are significant. Common-law judges are known, respected, and criticized for their opinions. Their prestige in society is in general immensely higher than that of the "faceless bureaucrats." Their independence might be impinged upon by politics, but since they seldom seek promotion, they have no reason to be subservient to a judicial hierarchy.

The career, the professional position, and the mentality of the Louisiana judge, even though he applies civil law, are those of his common-law brethren. The bureaucratic model of the civil-law judiciary developed in Europe over many centuries has never taken root in Louisiana. This could hardly be otherwise "in a 'new' country, devoid of ancient traditions and settled on the frontier of the civilized world in comparatively recent times," as Tate says (Dainow). The style of Louisiana court decisions is the one customary in English and other American courts: lengthy elaborations of opinions that mirror frequently, and sometimes without restraint, the judges' values, instead of the summary, often curt statements of facts and applicable rules characteristic of continental jurisprudence. Elaborate dissents are characteristic of Louisiana reports. After judgment day, judges do not hesitate to explain their views in legal journals. Louisiana judges have thereby joined the honored tradition of legal pluralism. Sometimes minority decisions of the Louisiana Supreme Court have become important for the progressive development of the law, like those of the United States Supreme Court.

THE RENAISSANCE OF CIVIL LAW IN LOUISIANA

During the 1930s the practice of the civil law in Louisiana had reached a low ebb. An article appearing in 1937 in the law review of Tulane University stated bluntly, "Louisiana is today a common-law State." One might say that in fact its civil-law system was undergoing a crisis of identity. Many of the developments described here contributed to the widely shared view that civil law in Louisiana had become nothing more than an empty shell. The interpretation given to the code, the weight attached to precedents, the convergence of substantive rules of law, and the role of the lawyer in Louisiana society seemed to indicate that an insular legal culture was losing out to the one dominant in the nation.

A comparison with Quebec, that other civil-law system in North America, illustrates the special difficulties encountered in Louisiana. In Quebec, certain concepts of the common law had also penetrated theory and practice. But the use of French by the bench and bar, and by most of the parties appearing before the courts, kept civil-law traditions strong. For this very reason, Quebec was not isolated from sources that are of such great importance in the civil law: French legal doctrine and the evolving jurisprudence of the French courts were well-known and quoted by the Quebec practitioners. Not so in Louisiana. Over the course of a century, the use of French had become restricted to a few not highly developed regions of the state. Because of the language barrier, Louisiana jurists were, at least up to the period here evoked, almost completely cut off from other civil-law jurisdictions. Common-law sources, including textbooks and casebooks, were more readily available and therefore more attractive for judges and attorneys pressed for time. The training in civil-law methods by the universities came to be thought inadequate.

Especially since the end of World War II, this trend toward an extinction of the civil-law tradition has been reversed. Those who speak about a renaissance of Louisiana civil law seem to be justified. A number of factors are responsible for this reversal. The war and its aftermath have evoked throughout the Western world a renewed interest in comparative law: the interdependence of nations has intensified the need for familiarity with foreign legal systems; the legal elites of different nations are intermingling as never before. For those who wish to understand and compare not only the legal rules of other nations but also their legal cultures, a mixed jurisdiction such as that of Louisiana (or Quebec, Puerto Rico, and the Philippines) offers great opportunities for informed observation. Indeed, Louisiana could become an almost ideal laboratory for the sociologically interested comparatist.

The law schools were the first to take up the challenge of bringing lawyers, legislators, judges, and professors themselves back to the civilian tradition. The increasing postwar enrollment at law schools permitted the enlargement of faculties, with preference given to teachers with a broad comparative and civil-law background. This in turn led to the extension of libraries and to an expansion and revitalization of

the law reviews. Two institutions, the Louisiana State Law Institute, created by legislative act in 1938, and the Institute of Civil Law Studies, founded in 1967 by Louisiana State University, give evidence of, and support for, the reawakened interest. Under a broadly conceived mission, the former envisions a reform of the civil code; to prepare for it, extensive doctrinal studies have been undertaken. A complete overhaul will take time, but single articles of the code that have proven inadequate are being revised. Those who prepare the drafts submitted to, and voted on, by the legislature are fully familiar with the latest developments of French law.

An extensive publication program was launched. It includes comprehensive treatises and commentaries on the Louisiana Civil Code and English translations of some of the best-known multivolume French textbooks, which are being quoted with increasing frequency in briefs and decisions. Comparative studies, encompassing not only the French but also the codes of West Germany and other civil-law countries, supplement the program.

The impact of these efforts on the outlook and practice of Louisiana judges and attorneys has been noted. Like other civil-law jurists, Louisiana's are readily inclined to turn for help with interpretation to doctrinal sources, but they have heretofore suffered from a dearth of appropriate materials. Annual seminars, attended at first by appellate judges and devoted to discussions about the role of judges in a civil-law jurisdiction, have been enlarged to address the entire judiciary. Other meetings are organized by the Civil Law Section of the Louisiana State Law Institute to benefit attorneys as well. It is hoped and expected that once the lawyers have become more familiar with the revived civil-law tradition, they will abandon their earlier inclination to turn for problem solving to more easily accessible common-law sources. "To fully accomplish a rebirth of the civil-law tradition," Barham has written, "and to assure its survival in Louisiana in a mixed jurisdiction require a reeducation of some of the practitioners and a program of continuing legal education for all practitioners" (Dainow).

It is taken as an index of the resurgence of the civil-law tradition that during the 1970s the number of cases in which courts overruled previous decisions, either expressly or implicitly, increased sharply. As mentioned earlier, the Louisiana courts had come to treat precedents with a respect that amounted almost to the common-law practice of stare decisis. If the adherence to precedents has been replaced or at least modified by reasoning along the lines of a doctrinal development of code provisions, this may be taken, probably correctly, as a sign of a return to judicial methods more congenial to a dynamic civil law.

THE COMMONWEALTH OF PUERTO RICO

When the Treaty of Paris established United States sovereignty over Puerto Rico in 1899, the island had lived for centuries under a system of Spanish law. Hence, the hold of a unified civil-law tradition was stronger than in Louisiana, where French and Spanish law had competed and where incorporation into the United States had taken place ninety years earlier. Initial suggestions by military and civilian governors for a wholesale "Americanization" of the Puerto Rican legal system were discarded. But as in Louisiana, only the established civil and commercial codes were left intact. Other laws in force were rescinded, if frequently under protest. The wholesale introduction, in 1902, of a new penal code, the California code of 1873, was resented as being too abrupt and unnecessary; it was finally revised by the Puerto Rican legislature in 1974.

Spanish civil law had been codified in the 1880s and extended to Puerto Rico shortly thereafter. The modern codes show clearly the influence of the widely admired *Siete Partidas* ("seven parts"), the code promulgated by the Castilian King Alfonso X ("el Sabio") in the thirteenth century; the *partidas* incorporated much of Roman and canon-law rules and principles and went into effect in 1348. But the modern Spanish civil code was also heavily influenced by the Code Napoléon. The fields covered by them and the organization of the Spanish and French codes are almost identical. The versions of the civil code enacted in 1930 by the Puerto Rican authorities left the Spanish model largely unchanged, except for the rectification of a few errors and for some clarification of obscure clauses. However, the Puerto Rican code was given a form designed, as was officially stated, to facilitate future additions that might be found appropriate to "regulate the relationships of man's private life in its three principal phases: family, property, contracting."

Unlike the Louisiana code, the Puerto Rican law does not specifically enumerate the sources of law, but the introductory provisions place the code squarely in the civil-law tradition. The interesting Section 7 (in language differing from a corresponding provision in the Spanish code) admonishes the judge to apply, in cases not covered by a statute, either equity, "which means . . . natural justice, as embodied in the general principles of jurisprudence," or "established usages and customs." Section 19 of the code gives the judge guidelines for "discovering the true meaning" of "a law" (and that includes the code itself) "when its expressions are dubious." What the article prescribes amounts again to long-established civil-law practice. But it also differs little from the famous rules in the English *Heydon's Case* (1584), still the basis for statutory interpretation in common-law courts.

Puerto Rico shares with Louisiana the problems of a mixed jurisdiction; the richness derived from the coexistence of different legal cultures has to be paid for by the uncertainties about which techniques of judicial decision-making will predominate. There are reasons to presume that the Puerto Rican system would be more impervious to the penetration of common law. As in Quebec, most of the legal business is conducted in the original language of the civil code. Unlike Louisiana, Puerto Rico has a strong cultural identity.

However, in important respects the legal culture of the island has been affected even more by the common-law culture than has that of Louisiana. This is best illustrated by the treatment of judicial precedents by Puerto Rican courts. In line with the civil-law tradition, the code does not mention judicial precedents as a source of law. Spanish courts have never recognized the principle of stare decisis, but not long after Puerto Rico became part of the United States, the Puerto Rican Supreme Court ruled that, for provisions derived from the Spanish Civil Code or from the Louisiana Civil Code, Puerto Rican courts should follow the "construction given to said provisions by the magistrates of the respective countries" *Olivieri* v. *Biaggi* (1911). This grants Spanish precedents more binding force than they ever could claim in Spain (Schlesinger).

Even more generous was a 1962 decision stating that it has always been the tendency of the island's supreme court to give, through its interpretation of the law to the citizens, "the full benefit of the two juridical systems prevailing in Puerto Rico until one is created which embodies the most just of both" *Infante* v. *Leith* (1962).

A study exploring the Puerto Rican practice of attributing binding force to appropriate precedents concluded that stare decisis was essentially nothing more than an expression of that Anglo-Saxon empiricism, which has "exercised so profound an influence on Puerto Rican jurists" (Mouchet and Sussini). Helen Silving, a prominent professor of the University of Puerto Rico, argued in similar terms before the Legislative Legal Reform Committee that the spirit and the methodology of common law form an "integral part of the inarticulate philosophy of law reflected in each and every decision of our supreme court."

This should not be understood to mean that Puerto Rican courts are relinquishing their autonomy. Because of the constitutional position of the island, autonomy is a concept of great importance to it. Quite significantly, a United States congressional enactment ruled in 1961 that it is no longer possible to appeal to any federal court against interpretations of the civil code or of other local laws given by the Supreme Court of Puerto Rico (Schlesinger). In spite of the strong influence that the common law has exercised on the decisions of judges and the practice of attorneys, Puerto Ricans wish to determine by and for themselves the scope and the survival of their own and other legal traditions.

CASES

Infante v. Leith, 85 P.R.R. 24 (1962)
Olivieri v. Biaggi, 17 P.R.R. 676 (1911)

BIBLIOGRAPHY

Joseph Dainow, ed., *The Role of Judicial Decisions and Doctrine in Civil Law and in Mixed Jurisdictions* (1974), contains excellent up-to-date articles authored by Louisiana Supreme Court justices and eminent law professors. René David and John E.C. Brierley, *Major Legal Systems in the World Today,* 2nd ed. (1978), is a broad, nontechnical survey with major emphasis on civil- and common-law systems, with extensive bibliographical information. Henry W. Ehrmann, *Comparative Legal Cultures* (1976), presents a global view, historically and sociologically oriented, and is addressed mainly to the American college student.

Wolfgang Friedmann, *Legal Theory,* 5th ed. (1967), a leading treatise, gives an enlightening discussion of the background and development of civil-law and common-law cultures. Frederick H. Lawson, *A Common Lawyer Looks at the Civil Law* (1955), is a vivid account, treating both practical and more fundamental aspects. John Henry Merryman, *The Civil Law Tradition* (1969), is the best short introduction to the field, discussing the legal systems of Europe and Latin America but not treating the civil-law systems of North America. John Henry Merryman and David S. Clark, *Western European and Latin American Legal Systems* (1978), is a comprehensive collection of cases and materials, with an interesting comparative discussion of the Louisiana and French codes.

Clarence Morrow, "Louisiana Blueprint: Civilian Codification and Legal Method for State and Nation," in *Tulane Law Review,* 17 (1943), presents a classical view, still respected but not always honored in practice. Carlos Mouchet and Miguel Sussini, *Derecho hispanico y "common law" en Puerto Rico* (1953), is a realistic look at the common-law inroads on Puerto Rican legal practice. Marcel Planiol and Georges Ripert, *Treatise on the Civil Law,* 12th ed. (1956), is an eminent French textbook frequently quoted in Louisiana civil proceedings. Rudolf B. Schlesinger, *Comparative Law: Cases, Text, Materials,* 4th ed. (1980), a lively discussion and collection of pertinent materials, contains valuable references to Louisiana and Puerto Rican law.

Bernard Schwartz, *The Code Napoléon and the Common-Law World* (1956), of great general interest for an understanding of the civil-law tradition, contains an article on Louisiana practice. Arthur Taylor Von Mehren and James Russell Gordley, *The Civil Law System,* 2nd ed. (1977), a very comprehensive introduction to comparative law, provides lengthy excerpts in English from the French code. Kate Wallach, *Research in Louisiana Law* (1958), is a concise bibliographical guide; and Wallach et al., "Bicentennial Survey of Civil Law Influences on American Legal Development," in *Law Library Journal,* 69 (1976), is a valuable symposium, including Puerto Rico, as well as Louisiana and a number of other states.

[*See also* ADVERSARY SYSTEM.]

COMMON LAW AND
COMMON-LAW LEGAL SYSTEMS

Calvin Woodard

C OMMON law is a term central not only to Anglo-American law but also to some of the
most treasured institutions and values in modern
society. Accordingly, in this article the subject
will be treated from a general point of view.

DEFINITIONS OF COMMON LAW

Common law is a term with several different
meanings, depending upon the context and the
level of generality in which it is used. In its least
familiar, yet perhaps oldest, form, it refers to that
law which is of general, as contrasted to limited
or restricted, applicability. Thus, local laws (peculiar to particular geographical areas), special
laws (limited in scope to specific categories of
persons, such as coal miners, veterans, or aliens),
and private laws (enacted on behalf of certain
named individuals) are, though law, not common
law, which applies to all subjects throughout a
nation, state, or jurisdiction.

In this usage of the term, the Roman law or
one of its derivatives was, and still is, the common law in many European states. It is of general
applicability, and it was in many instances "received," usually by royal fiat during the Middle
Ages, for the specific purpose of supplanting the
particularism inherent in local, customary law. F.
W. Maitland suggested that the origin of the
phrase may have been the jus commune of canon
law, which denoted the general laws of the
church universal.

The more familiar use of the term, however,
is in the context of English and American law.
Even in this more limited context, the phrase
may have two widely differing meanings, depending again on the level of generality on which
it is used. It may refer either to an entire legal
system or to a particular form of law within that

system. When used to connote an entire legal
system, it refers to that of England and, still more
generally, to that shared by Britain, the United
States, and many other nations—including Canada, Australia, and India—most of which are former members of the British Empire and some of
which are still members of the Commonwealth.
Together, they make up a community of nations
bound together by a distinctive common-law
legal system and tradition. It was this most general usage of the term—within, that is, the limited context of English law and legal history—
that Sir Frederick Pollock had in mind when he
called the common law the "fountainhead of Anglo-American jurisprudence."

So defined, of course, the common law includes, in addition to the various common-law
principles applicable to specific areas of law,
such as contracts and torts, the complex array of
legal institutions, procedures, practices, and
jurisprudential values that collectively make up
what R. Meredith Jackson called the "machinery
of Justice" in England and that gives the common law its own unique character. As such, it is
comparable to, and to be distinguished from, the
other great legal systems of the world, such as
those of civil-law countries, mostly in Europe
and Latin America (based on some code derived
from Roman law), Islamic law (based on the
Koran), and Soviet law (based on philosophical
and jurisprudential teachings of the Communist
party of the Soviet Union). In the United States
the term *common law* is probably most often used
to refer loosely to a legal tradition stemming
from England and translated to the United
States, where it, in combination with the federal
Constitution, has become the foundation of
the nation's law and its increasingly distinctive
legal system.

Still within the limited context of the Anglo-

500

COMMON LAW AND COMMON-LAW LEGAL SYSTEMS

American legal system, the term *common law* may, and among practicing lawyers usually does, have a rather specific meaning: it refers to that body of law stemming from a specific source, custom, and embodied in the reported decisions of common-law courts since the Middle Ages. As Chancellor Kent long ago observed, "It includes those principles, usages and rules of action . . . which do not rest for their authority upon any express and positive declaration of the will of the legislature." In this context the common law is a form of unwritten law, and it is to be distinguished from all forms of (written) law—such as codes, statutes, and administrative regulations—that derive their authority from some determinate enacting body, whether it be Parliament, Congress, or any other legislative office or agency.

The common law, so defined, is also to be contrasted to equity, a technical (as well as jurisprudential) term in Anglo-American law. Historically, equity stems not from custom but from the king, as the "Fountain of Justice," and consists of maxims, principles, rules, and remedies created (not "discovered") by chancellors, acting on behalf of the crown (as the keepers of the king's conscience) for the purpose of ameliorating the harshness of, or rectifying injustices caused in specific instances by, the common law. Although law (that is, the common law) and equity have long been merged in most Anglo-American jurisdictions, the distinction is still recognized in common legal usage.

ORIGIN AND DEVELOPMENT OF THE COMMON LAW IN ENGLAND

The common law, as a basis of a legal system, has long been something of a mystery to those not trained in the Anglo-American legal tradition. Its mystical character is derived in part from its inscrutable nature, as viewed by outsiders, and in part from guild barriers (including a measure of consciously perpetuated ritualism) grown up around a profession long possessed of quasi-monopolistic control over its own affairs, including criteria for admission to its ranks, methods of education and training, and standards of professional conduct.

What invariably puzzles laymen most about the common law is, however, a matter of form. How, laymen always want to know, can a legal system be based on unwritten law? If law is un-

written, how can anyone—whether lawyer, judge, client, or the public—know what it is? Would not each of us be free to assert that the unwritten law is what we believe, or want, it to be? And who is to say that my (or your) version of the unwritten law is less valid than theirs? And if I (or you) can say what the law is, do we have law or anarchy? Such is the major confusion most laymen, and no doubt many lawyers trained in non-common-law traditions, experience when first acquainted with the unwritten character of the common law. And the cause of the bewilderment hinges upon that most tiresome of questions, What is law?

Virtually everyone, except common-law lawyers, assumes law to be a body of concrete rules expressed in statutory or constitutional form, prescribing a permissible or prohibited course of action. The Code of Hammurabi, the Code of the Manu, the Ten Commandments, the Twelve Tables, and the Code of Justinian of Roman law come to mind; and in the United States, the federal and state constitutions are regarded as definitive statements of the most fundamental law. All of these are law—real law—and they are written.

We are thus inclined to think of law in terms of more or less crisp commands expressed in bold, black letters, and accordingly, laymen readily assume that learning law, like learning multiplication tables, must mean learning the various concrete rules that make up the law. Hence, the very idea of law not being written—somewhere, anyway—is perplexing to the layman. Yet the unwritten common law has for centuries served as the basis of a legal system. How can that be?

Any discussion of the common-law system must therefore seek to explain how such a system could have come into being in the first place and how it has survived and flourished for so long. The answer to the question has two aspects, one historical and the other jurisprudential: the former explains how the common-law system came into being, and the latter deals with how lawyers, committed to it, justify its existence.

With respect to the jurisprudential aspect, it is worth noting at the outset that common-law lawyers have traditionally not regarded the popular notion that law is a body of concrete rules to be so much wrong as insufficient—insufficient because it artificially constricts the meaning of law to static declamatory commands, carved or carvable in stone. Common-law lawyers think of law as including the totality of activities and procedures by which actual disputes are resolved in courts. Accordingly, they are likely to think of law not so much as a body of previously promulgated (and hence static) commands but as a dynamic process by which the correct rule or principle of law is discovered and applied to specific human problems when framed in legal terms, rigorously examined in accordance with established legal procedures, and resolved in terms of legal practice and precedent. Thus, to them, the existence or lack of existence of black-letter rules is not crucial. What is of capital importance is the court system and how it functions. Hence, Justice Oliver Wendell Holmes's famous definition of law as prophecies of what courts will do. Hence, also, Anglo-American legal education has long stressed not the memorization of hornbook rules but the cultivation of those forensic skills and that peculiar kind of reasoning essential for students to participate effectively in a creative and dynamic process of finding, making, and applying law. Understanding the common law and the common-law legal system means in large part understanding why it was, and how it came about, that common-law lawyers associate law with a dynamic process rather than with a body of static rules.

The explanation can only be found in the historical circumstances that gave rise to the common-law tradition in England. The common-law legal system developed gradually over long spans of time in response to a series of some quite unrelated historical circumstances; and it is that history, not legal theory, that explains how and why it developed as it did in England and only in England.

The history of the common-law system involved much more than the growth of legal doctrine or even a body of judicial precedent. Specifically, it was a response to a series of power struggles and political crises plaguing an island kingdom in the throes of a traumatic transformation into a modern state, for law—the very idea of law—carries with it the authority to exercise a particular kind of coercive power, and who has the right to wield that power, in the name of what authority, and for what purposes are always more than mere legal questions. In fact, the major social institutions of English society—the crown, the church, the family (especially the great landed families, first as feudal barons and later as gentry), Parliament, and even the guild of lawyers—all claimed, at one time or another, the authority to wield the power of law; but it was not until the eighteenth century that the authority to wield the legal sanction in England seemed to be finally vested in the common-law judges, subject only to the largely quiescent legislative powers of Parliament. And so it was until the emergence of the welfare state in the twentieth century.

In the evolution of the common-law system, the influence of such struggles for control over law is vividly evident. Specifically, each of the major attributes of the English legal system, which came to make up the common-law tradition, and which subsequently spread throughout the English-speaking world, bore the marks of at least four different struggles for the right to wield the force of law with some claim to legitimacy. Those struggles were between the Norman kings (or conquerors) and their vanquished subjects (Anglo-Saxons, Danes, and Englanders generally); the crown and the feudal barons; the crown and the Roman Catholic church; and the crown and the landed gentry (including the legal profession) in Parliament. The nature of these struggles and their impact on the development of the common law will be summarized.

The Norman Kings. The most distinctive—and to non-common-law lawyers and laymen, the most puzzling—attribute of the common law is its very lack of definitive form. To many, perhaps most, laymen the idea of law connotes an authoritative word, and law without such a word is, if not a contradiction, virtually incomprehensible. Yet, the English common law not only did not begin with such a word but has for some eight hundred years largely defied codification. In fact, the legal system associated with the common law started with a writ, or a form of action, which raised technical questions of procedure, or what is sometimes called adjective law; and it was not until late in its history, well into the eighteenth century, that the substantive-law rules became sufficiently developed for the first great common-law commentator, Sir William Blackstone, to extricate them from procedure and to present them as such.

How, then, can a legal system come into being, thrive and spread throughout the world without the word? The answer, or the beginning of the answer, is found in the Norman Conquest. William, duke of Normandy, found it politically expedient to claim the English crown not as a conqueror, which he surely was, but as the legal heir to his English uncle, the late King Edward the Confessor. He thus took the throne subject to the Anglo-Saxon law existing during his uncle's reign, prior to his military conquest; and the nature of that preconquest law—or laws—would be for centuries a burning political and legal question. Some protagonists found it politic to construe narrowly the ancient law, limiting it to various indigenous codes, such as those of Alfred and Canute; and others referred more generally and more vaguely to ancient customs that had long prevailed. (The "time immemorial" of ancient custom eventually came to be defined to mean anything before the coronation of Richard I in 1189.) Later, others spoke of "fundamental law," with Parliament as its guardian; and in the stormy seventeenth century, especially in the era of James I and Charles I, Lord Coke and his parliamentary allies conjured up, and vehemently held the king to, what they called the "Ancient Constitution," a venerable medley that included the Magna Charta and various other ancient statutes and ordinances as well as custom. Whatever the designation, however— and "the common law" is but one, albeit an ancient and persistent one—the unwritten law of ancient origin and hallowed authority acknowledged by William the Conqueror and construed and reconstrued by others became (to paraphase Jeremy Bentham in another context) "a formidable nonentity" guiding and censoring the behavior not only of Englishmen but also of the English crown. It is the ancient common law— not the natural law of Thomas Aquinas—that Henry de Bracton had in mind when he said the king was *sub deo et sub legis* ("under God and under law"). And it is the fact that English kings came to be regarded as under some law greater than that of their own making that left an indelible mark on English legal and constitutional history and, at bottom, distinguished the English from the various continental legal systems. In the context of English history, that unwritten ancient custom, which in time took the name of *common law,* would not only serve to curb royal power; it would lead ultimately to the famous doctrine of parliamentary sovereignty. It would also be the legal basis for what Blackstone called "the Rights of Englishmen" (most of which were written into the Bill of Rights of the United States Constitution) and A. V. Dicey called the "Rule of Law."

The Crown and the Feudal Barons. The general and widespread commitment to a form of ancient customary law obviously provided the theoretical foundation for a legal system based on unwritten law. But the common-law system did not develop in England simply because some form of customary law prevailed. After all, virtually every nation-state has, at one time or another, been largely governed by customary law and, in Western Europe, never more so than in that period during which the common-law system began to take its unique form and character in England. Indeed, the chaotic particularism created by, or attendant to, customary law accounts in large part for the widespread reception of Roman law in the fourteenth and fifteenth centuries on the Continent. Hence, once again, the question, Why did the deference to, and glorification of, ancient customary law in England lead to the development of a sophisticated and complex legal system while on the Continent it spawned and perpetuated a debilitating kind of balkanization? And why did the English kings not follow the pattern of so many other continental rulers during those tumultuous times and adopt the Roman law?

The answer to these questions is to be found in the policies adopted and pursued by early English kings, most notably Henry II (reigned 1154–1189) and Edward I (reigned 1272–1307), in struggling to establish and maintain a stable political order in the face of strong divisive forces that threatened to undermine the power of the crown itself. The early English kings struggled endlessly against the grim possibility of anarchy. The threat stemmed from two seemingly contradictory circumstances: too much law and not enough law. The threat of anarchy stemming from not enough law—or, which was the same thing, not enough power to enforce the king's law—came from the landed barons, who claimed the right (backed up, as King Stephen learned, by might) to exercise suzerainty over their fiefdoms. Being Normans, many of whom claimed their lands and titles from William the Conqueror, the barons had brought with them ideas of feudalism (whether theretofore unknown to England remains an open question) that were certainly inimical to the interest of the crown and its desires to unify the nation under law. Thus, the early English, especially Norman, kings had a very rational reason for acknowledging their allegiance to the ancient custom of the Anglo-Saxons: it gave them a claim to legitimacy that not only commanded the respect of their less than enthusiastic Anglo-Saxon subjects; it was also an additional club to use against the vulgar demands of powerful barons and their alien brand of feudalism. But much more was needed to tame the barons and to neutralize the anarchistic tendencies of their rule if royal justice were to prevail. The first problem was how to deal with the proud barons in a way that would enhance the king's authority without exciting more anarchistic misrule.

Even as the early kings faced treasonable anarchy from feudal barons whose power often appeared to be greater than the crown's law, they also struggled with yet another form of anarchy: a nation rendered virtually ungovernable because of too many legal systems and forms of law. Consider the various other courts existing in medieval England. Beside the feudal (manorial and honorial) courts, there were local (hundred, wapentak, and borough) courts; a whole phalanx of ecclesiastical courts; mercantile (fair, staple, and pie-powder) courts; and, in virtually every harbor town, admiralty courts. Each of these courts, and others, administered a kind of law more or less peculiar to itself. Thus, the local courts relied chiefly upon customary law, much of which was applicable only to specific geographical areas, and a medley of Anglo-Saxon, Celtic, Danish, and even a bit of Roman law (lingering from Hadrian's day). The feudal courts imposed some form of Norman or French law. The ecclesiastical courts, which made up a sophisticated legal system with a network of courts ranging from parishes to archbishoprics, relied upon the canon law and Roman law, with which the former had become inextricably bound in its scholastic form. The mercantile and admiralty courts were largely governed by special custom and, more generally, by the law merchant, the law of the sea, and the nascent forms of international law.

Faced with such a panoply of law and competing legal systems, the crown clearly had a major problem in establishing the superiority and ultimate authority of its own law. It was Henry II who, in combating the two forms of anarchy, set English law on its own course, culminating in what we now know as the common-law legal system. He sensed that the key to the success of any legal system lies not so much in the law that reposes in the statute books as in the practical means by which law, however defined, is administered. Thus, rather than focus his energy and resources on promulgating yet another authoritative text to compete with the sundry other forms of law then extant, he threw the full weight of his authority, power, and influence behind his nascent court system, taking pains to make it the source of the fairest, cheapest, and most effective remedies to legal problems. By so doing, he lured private suitors of all kinds and all persuasions away from the various rival courts into his own; and in time those courts became so popular that the law administered in them became that law common to all quarters of the realm. By the end of the fourteenth century the three royal courts—Common Pleas, King's Bench, and Exchequer—could be said to be common-law courts. But it was a commonality based more on nationwide jurisdiction than it was on a common text, for it was precisely in those courts that the unwritten law prevailed. And the fact that private parties seeking legal redress repaired to such courts of their own free will gave them an added aura of legitimacy, as well as popular support, conspicuously lacking where law, especially an alien code, was imperiously imposed upon the people by royal command.

Thus was laid the foundation for a legal system based on courts, not a code; and the venerable idea that the process by which the legal sanction is administered is far more important than the form of the law itself would persist. Consequently, the common-law courts were given a centrality of importance and made the focus of a degree of scrutiny and attention largely lacking in other legal systems. The courts became not only the forum in which the common law is administered but also the sole place in which the amorphous unwritten law could be authoritatively declared and applied; they also became the birthplace of those judicial decisions which, as precedent, become the best evidence of the unwritten law, adding to the common law new life and dimensions.

The Crown and the Church. At the time the common-law legal system was taking its form and shape, the controversy between the crown and the Roman Catholic church was also reaching fever pitch in England. That conflict—which would not be resolved definitively until the Reformation and the troubles of Henry VIII—had important implications for the development of English law. At stake was more than the question of religion and the souls of men; there was a very practical, and intrinsically secular question of who governed—or, more prosaically, whose law was supreme, that of the pope or that of the king.

That conflict was exacerbated by yet another historical circumstance of great, albeit indirect, import in the development of the common law: the revival of Roman law in Italy in the eleventh and twelfth centuries. The rediscovery and systematic study of the long-lost Code of Justinian at Pavia and Bologna gave rise to more than a new field of academic research; it led to the subsequent spread of Roman law throughout Europe. No less important, it precipitated the rise of a wholly new Western institution of enormous influence, the university.

Closely identified with the church, the new universities quickly became centers of higher learning. Among the chief subjects studied were canon law and Roman law, the latter very often being treated by laymen and clergy alike as a semischolastic subject. Certainly the modes of interpretation adopted by, and the exegetical methods of, the commentators were sufficiently similar to those of biblical scholars to warrant the double conclusion that as university-studied law was semitheological, so university-studied theology was quasi-legal in character. Thus, the European legal mind developed, from its very inception, a scholastic and abstract quality of thought that is still reflected in modern civil law and that has perhaps always been closer to medieval Scholasticism than it has been to its Anglo-American counterparts. But early English law, and especially the common law, escaped the theological and academic influences that played such an important part in forming the European legal tradition.

During the period that the first European universities were coming into being, Oxford and Cambridge became centers of learning in England, and like most of the others, they, too, were essentially ecclesiastical institutions in which the influence of Rome and the pope was both patent and palpable. As law was one of the major subjects taught in the new universities, it would have been natural for English lawyers, like continental lawyers, to be trained at Oxford and Cambridge by those immersed in Roman and canon law; and it would also have seemed natural for them, as practicing lawyers, to regard and to pursue Roman and canon law as the supreme law of the land. This no doubt they did. Or tried to do.

But they failed. They failed largely because of, again, historical circumstances. At the time the universities were becoming eminent centers of higher learning, the royal courts, which were increasingly the object of the English crown's full support and concern, were located chiefly in London; and the power of the crown and the taste for practical affairs lured many ambitious young men there, away from the quasi-monastic universities. There a different legal tradition developed: law students learned to speak the language of the court, French, not that of the church and the universities, Latin; they learned skills needed to deal with practical legal problems— the intellectually barren but legally essential procedural technicalities required to obtain a writ and to establish a cause of action, not the mastery of the Pandects (the sixth-century Roman civil-law digest) or the Decretum of Gratian (1140), the authoritative texts of Roman and canon law. They learned, in short, to practice common law.

Thus, a cadre of professional lawyers developed in England outside the emerging scholastic tradition of European universities. Looking to the crown and not to the pope for authority, to Westminster and not to Rome for preference, those Englishmen who were collectively most responsible for implementing the royal court system (and who thereby gave life, tone, and tenor to the unwritten common law) were trained for their task in an intellectual tradition that is peculiar to themselves and unknown to the Continent. The key institutions in the development of that tradition and, hence, that legal system were not Oxford and Cambridge but the Inns of Court, which by the fifteenth century Sir John Fortescue called England's "third university."

By developing their own court system (based on the unwritten common law) administered by a bench and bar trained in its own unique manner, the English kings staved off the pope's

COMMON LAW AND COMMON-LAW LEGAL SYSTEMS

efforts to make the canon law, as administered by the courts Christian, the law of England. Thus, though the political struggle between the crown and the church would continue down to the Reformation, the tone and character of the common law was, by the fifteenth century, firmly established. It would not be taught in the English universities until the mid–eighteenth century, and as late as 1901, Maitland could give a lecture at Cambridge entitled "Is There a Place for Law in a University?" He answered the question with ambivalence—and to this day wherever the common-law tradition is strong, it must still be answered with doubt.

The Crown and the Landed Gentry. The lawyers and judges who inherited the task of translating the unwritten law into a court-based legal system shared a unique form of intellectual discipline, and they provided the common law with that which customary law always lacks: a systematic and disciplined methodology for determining the indeterminate and a rational means for accommodating legal change. The central institution providing those essential elements to the royal court system were the Inns of Court.

The origin of the Inns of Court is shrouded in mystery. Probably they started as hostels located close to the king and his court where courtiers, including aspiring lawyers, took lodging. In time, however, they became more: they became guild halls for a closely knit medieval mystery, or guild, which came to hold the exclusive right to practice before the three royal courts. By the fourteenth century, no one could be "called" to the bar (entitling one to appear in the courts) who was not a member of one of the four major Inns. (Attorneys, solicitors, proctors in admiralty, civilians—all legal practioners—were not members of the Inns and, hence, were excluded from the common-law courts.) Later, through custom and practice, the Inns would also gain power, albeit indirectly, over the judiciary, for no one would be elevated to the bench who had not been previously called to the bar and risen to the rank of serjeant, the highest rank in the guild of barristers.

Thus, the common law—that law practiced in the royal courts—came to be intimately linked, by the bond between bench and bar, to the Inns of Court. All cases in the common-law courts were argued exclusively by barristers, who were still members of the Inns of Court, and decided by judges, who were themselves trained therein. And it was through their labors in the common-law courts that the unwritten law was rendered into a coherent legal system: professional craftsmen whose perception of their function and duty had been shaped almost exclusively by serving long apprenticeships in a close-knit guild, absorbing its conventions and traditions while mastering the technicalities of pleading and practice. Consequently, the common-law legal system they created took on the tone and quality of those practices adhered to in the Inns of Court.

The major convention of the Inns of Court that came to be a distinctive attribute of the common law was the doctrine of precedent. As in any guild or rigid hierarchical association, the behavior of the seniors sets the tone of the group, and the lead of the most respected and influential members is followed scrupulously by ambitious juniors. And so it was in the Inns of Court. The decisions of the more esteemed serjeants-made-judges, duly noted, repeated and scrutinized, became precedents for others to follow; and it was the disciplined adherence to those precedents, together with other established practices in a guild governed largely by an oral tradition, that gave the legal system based on unwritten law a semblance of stability and its own distinctive form of reasoning.

With the rise of the printing press, the Inns of Court monopoly over the law was weakened, for the most authentic evidences of the mysterious unwritten law, notably the cryptic and often erratically reported judicial opinions, became more readily available to a wider reading public. Also, a number of general treatises appeared shedding unwonted light on the arcane subject.

But by then the principle had become firmly established: the only authoritative statements of the unwritten law are to be found in the decisions of the common-law courts, and the barristers and judges honor the guild custom of following the lead of their seniors, superiors, and predecessors. Important cases on important issues become, in short, precedent to be acknowledged and, where appropriate, followed.

As a result of this convention, the unwritten common law began to take form piecemeal as judges followed or distinguished earlier decisions. In time the precedential value of certain cases involving recurring issues became so compelling that the questions with which they dealt

506

would appear to be settled. Also, in time, legal thinkers—judges and scholars—ventured to ferret out of the mass of decisions those kernels of viable principles in order to restate them free of procedural complications. When they succeeded, the common-law legal system generated a body of substantive law rules, also known as common law, which certainly had not existed when the court system had come into being. Hence, many commentators have noted that such common-law rules grow out of cases actually litigated in court and hence can only be developed by judges through time. Thus, they are knowable only relatively late in the historical development of a legal system. In this respect, the common-law system differs dramatically from those legal systems based on codes, for it generates (rather than begins with) rules of law.

As the common-law legal system came to be so closely associated with the Inns of Court and the conventions and rituals of their members, so the members naturally developed a proprietary attitude toward the common law and the common-law court system. So much so that, in time, the members of the Inns would dare to challenge the power of the king—in the persons of James I and Charles I—to tamper with, or alter, that law over which they had peculiar custodial dominion. When that happened, but only then, the modern doctrine of judicial independence, one scarcely known on the Continent to this day, became a distinct, albeit inchoate, feature of the English legal system. But it would take revolutionary radicals, Englishmen overseas in America, to work out the ramifications of a legal system in which the judiciary alone has the power to determine that law which binds even the king. (Though some of the Founding Fathers would attribute the United States' constitutional doctrine of separation of powers, with its independent judiciary, to Montesquieu, he admitted deriving the idea from his study of English legal institutions.)

The forces at work in England tending toward an independent judiciary did not lead (as they later did in the United States) to judicial supremacy. Rather, they culminated, in the late seventeenth and early eighteenth centuries, in the doctrine of parliamentary sovereignty. The English bar joined the landed gentry in the House of Commons in resisting the crown's efforts to assert, through the royal prerogative, its powers over English law, common law and statutory law alike; but it took a bloody civil war and a beheaded king (Charles I), followed by another absconding king (James II), to reestablish law and order. It was done finally, in 1688, when William and Mary were offered the throne on conditions laid down by Parliament. From that time onward, there has been no question but that Parliament—or technically the "King in Parliament"—is sovereign: it alone has the power to make and to unmake law, and its laws are presumably as binding upon the common-law courts as they are upon ordinary citizens.

But within the courts, the common-law principles still prevail, and it has always been a nice question as to what extent, in modern Britain, Parliament is, like the medieval kings, under God and under the (common) law—and, if so, who (if not the judges) would have the power to hold Parliament to the law. Notwithstanding a few anomalous cases, English courts have steadfastly refused to strike down parliamentary enactments as unconstitutional. In sum, perhaps no single development more sharply delineates the difference between the English and American common-law traditions than the articulation of the doctrine of judicial review in the United States.

DISTINCTIVE ATTRIBUTES OF THE COMMON-LAW TRADITION

By 1800, when the legal system in the still new country of the United States was coming into being and taking its form and shape, the English common law, as a legal system, had attained its distinctive characteristics, five of which deserve note. First, the common law consists of a body of unwritten principles and practices that did not derive their authority from any single or positive declaration of will by any explicit legislative or executive source. The common law was an unshakable legacy from a remote past; but vague and amorphous though it was, it was nevertheless widely believed to be supreme to, and binding upon, all Englishmen, the mightiest and lowest, public officials and private citizens, lawmakers and subjects.

Second, the distinction, well-known in the United States, between constitutional law and private (common) law was scarcely recognized in England. As the English Constitution remains to this day unwritten, it is obviously part of that *lex non scripta* applicable to private citizens in their private affairs. For example, the difference, analytically, between the common law of contract and the constitutional right to contract is not so sharply drawn there as it is under the written constitutions of the United States and of the several states.

Third, except for criminal law (itself a problem), the distinction between private and public law was scarcely known. Thus, English public officials have long been held personally accountable at common law for their misdeeds in office; and a notion so familiar on the Continent—that a separate body of law should apply to the government, its activities, and all civil servants—was peculiarly obnoxious to the common law. The result was a long tradition hostile to the development of what we now call administrative law.

Fourth, the principles of the semimystical common law, though stemming from ancient custom, can only be authoritatively known (or "discovered") and applied ("declared") in the strictly controlled context of court proceedings. Hence, the authoritative source of the unwritten law was the decisions of the royal (or common-law) courts, King's Bench, the Court of Common Pleas, and the Court of the Exchequer. The power to give finite meaning to the unwritten common law was vested exclusively in a single body of less than fifteen men: the judges of the three common-law courts, who were selected exclusively from members of the Inns of Court who had been called to the bar. The circumstances and conditions under which these "oracles of the law" (as Blackstone called them) could declare the common laws were, however, limited: they could do so only in actual (not hypothetical) cases, or causes of action, properly brought before the court and tried in accordance with established procedural and evidentiary rules.

In dealing with the cases coming before them, the common-law judges (in contrast to their continental counterparts) in effect delegated part of the task to others. By so doing, they were able to keep their numbers small (thereby increasing their chances of consistency) and also share their awful responsibility. Specifically, they relied upon ad hoc panels of laymen (the jury) to determine the relevant facts in each specific case and barristers—members of the Inns of Court trained in the same legal tradition as the judges

—who represented private parties in cases coming before the court. As counsel, it was the responsibility of barristers to frame the issues in legal terms; to uncover, assemble, or present the relevant facts; to identify the legal questions; and to assist the judges (through their arguments on behalf of their clients) in discovering, among the welter of legal precedents, the appropriate common-law principle and authority. In addition, appeal was permitted but limited to questions of law, giving other judges (and barristers) the opportunities to review and, after further reflection, to overturn or approve the first ruling.

Thus, the amorphous common law came to be authoritatively discovered, declared, and applied piecemeal in specific cases by means of a collective enterprise involving lay and professional, as well as judicial, participation. Moreover, it was carried out altogether in a forum that, by the eighteenth century, had become relatively immune to blatant extralegal or political interferences. The autonomy of the courts—and hence the integrity of the judicial process—was thus generally assumed to be an essential aspect of the common-law system.

The judges, in declaring the common-law principles applicable to specific cases, were obliged to honor a doctrine of precedent—that is, to acknowledge earlier holdings in similar cases and either to distinguish the case at bar from such earlier holdings or to follow them in reaching their own decisions. Furthermore, they were obliged not only to make a decision but to explain it, stating individually from the bench their own reasons for deciding as they did.

Each holding by a common-law court was thus based in earlier decisions even as it became in turn a precedent binding on other judges in deciding future cases involving the same or similar legal questions. As each case represented a fresh application of ancient principles to a current (and therefore different) set of facts, the immutable principles were constantly being restated and refined, taking on new dimensions. Thus, the common-law principles, though ancient in origin, were always exhibited in modern form.

Finally, the common-law system was overwhelmingly practical, not theoretical, in character. At its center lay the adversary proceeding within the courtroom—a confrontation between two contending parties, each making (through their lawyers) different allegations and claims in the specific context of an actual controversy. Accordingly, common-law lawyers spent their time and energy in mastering the skills, forensic or otherwise, needed to engage in such proceedings effectively and successfully. Hence, also, they tended to eschew speculation about the nature of law in general and to make little effort to extricate—for analytical purposes—legal rules (that is, substantive law) from the procedural context in which they were embedded. Among common-law practioners, such intellectual activities came to be openly derided as useless and idle speculation. Thus, members of the bar and the public came to associate the common law rather pridefully with a wholly practical legal system and a pragmatic calling, as distinguished from a theoretical or philosophical subject; and as befitted the common law's early development outside the universities, it long remained the least scholarly of the learned subjects. Peculiarly the province of severely client-oriented practitioners preoccupied above all with proceedings in court, the common law came to be traditionally identified more with procedural technicalities than with substantive issues and essentially as a subject that could only be learned (like the skills of any craft guild) by observing and emulating practioners at work and not by teaching it as a scholarly or philosophical subject (as on the Continent) in academic classrooms. Thus, a strong anti-intellectual bias for centuries alienated the common law from the seats of higher learning. Only in the twentieth century has this bias been materially challenged, thereby dramatically changing the character of the modern common law, especially in the United States, as discussed below.

THE COMMON-LAW TRADITION IN MODERN BRITAIN

Taken together, the foregoing attributes describe the nature of the English legal system during what is sometimes called the golden age of the common law. Certainly as of about 1800, its distinctive institutions, procedures, and practices had crystallized into a coherent jurisprudential system, and most of the famous leading common-law cases—those by such luminaries as Sir Edward Coke, Sir Matthew Hale, Sir John Holt, Lord Mansfield, and Lord Ellenborough—

had by then been decided. Thus, at that time, the English legal system could be, and was, clearly differentiated from those on the Continent. Furthermore, as Britain's colonial and imperial star was then in the ascent, so was the prestige and reputation of the common law, for the English legal system, as it then existed, became the model—occasionally, it is true, for contemptuous rejection but far more often for sincere imitation—in the various colonies and dependencies where new legal systems were being established as parts of a rapidly expanding empire. Thus, the history of the common law since that golden age has been largely one of exportation (or, depending upon the point of view, reception) and reform.

In England, reform of the common law was the keyword throughout the nineteenth century, as a most significant and radical retreat from the common law was during much of the twentieth century. The age of common-law reform included simplification of the technical rules of procedure; the merger of law and equity; countless efforts to codify the appallingly complex common-law rules in particular fields of law, most notably real property and, later, aspects of commercial law (such as sales, bills of lading, and negotiable instruments); a complete reorganization of the court system; and a systematization of the publication of law reports under the direction of an official editor.

The unmistakable trend toward codification during that heady period of reform was set by Jeremy Bentham and his followers in Parliament, the so-called philosophical radicals. Outraged by the idea of law being hidden in the mysteries of a legal process known only to barristers and controlled by an uncontrollable "Judge and Company"—and hence knowable to the lay public only after the court has discovered and applied it to hapless parties—they called for the total abolition of the common-law system. They demanded, in its place, a code based on utilitarian principles, which were as controversial as the common law.

Though they failed, they nonetheless directed the major energies of Victorian law reformers toward making the unwritten law clearer and more rational by reducing the various common-law principles to some positive form, if not a code.

The most serious attack on the common-law

system in England did not come until the twentieth century. The movement for a welfare state, which started with the Minority Report of the Royal Commission on the Poor Laws in 1909 and came to fruition with the White Paper of 1944, was really a renewal, or continuation, of the ancient struggle for control over the legal sanction. Traditionalists, including most of the bar, insisted that the common law—the law discovered and applied by the judges—should continue to govern economic and social relationships in the modern industrial state. The radicals (especially Fabian socialists and trade-union leaders) insisted that the law should be vested in the hands of local government and administrative agencies that were responsible to the public for carrying out socially determined policies and achieving socially defined goals. In their view, the judges, coming from a privileged social class and trained in a narrow legalistic tradition, wielded the arbitrary power of the common law to ignore or evade pressing "social issues" and preserve and perpetuate an unjust social hierarchy. Hence, another classic struggle over the right to define the law and to determine the ends to which it was put.

Down through the middle half of the twentieth century the status of the common law and the legal profession in England fell precipitously as the welfare state, with its own agencies, rules, and regulations became an ever more compelling reality. Judges, unable to declare statutes unconstitutional, became more like civil-law judges, interpreters, and construers of written texts, implementing policies established by Parliament or those agencies to which it delegated power; judges, sensitive to the various charges of arbitrariness and class bias, retreated behind an ironclad rule of stare decisis, regarding themselves bound absolutely to defer to earlier decisions. The image of the common-law judges as robust, creative, and fearless champions of the law to be respected as well as feared faded as they became, in the eyes of many, faceless civil servants. Only a few, most notably Lord Denning, kept alive the golden-age tradition of the heroic (or demonic) common-law judge.

Since about 1970, the common law and the bench have taken on new life in England. The various attacks on the welfare state have included serious charges that the rights of individuals have been abused by the administrative process. And as traditionalists have come back in power, the judges have begun to assert themselves more robustly and more conspicuously. Some observers have recently asserted that the future may well see a renaissance of the common-law tradition—a period during which new Mansfields and Hales will write a rich new chapter in the history of the common law in England.

THE COMMON LAW IN THE UNITED STATES

The history of the common law in the United States is marked by ambivalences inherent in the American Revolution, which was waged not only against England but against everything English, including English law. The ambivalences are complex. The major grievance of the colonists against the mother country was that the British government had violated the ancient, unwritten English law in trampling upon their (common-law) rights. Thus, the famous English constitutional principle "No taxation without representation" became one of the rallying cries of the Revolution; and the First Amendment to the United States Constitution, ratified shortly after independence, is but a skillfully drafted itemization of what Blackstone called "the rights of Englishmen"—rights anchored deep in English legal history, not (like the abstract ones claimed in the Declaration of Independence) an expression of natural law or natural rights.

In fact, the American legal system reflects, to this day, the same deep ambivalences. Thus, Americans proudly acknowledge that theirs is a common-law country, though they have either rejected or severely modified the most distinctive characteristics, such as the jury trial in civil cases, of the classical common-law legal system. Even so, it is probably accurate to say that they have retained, and still cling fiercely to, the values of the common law. Or, they still have what some have called a common-law frame of mind, which gives tone and character to a legal system that has become increasingly different in form from both the classical common-law model and that of modern Britain.

The nature and extent of the common-law influence in the United States today is best indicated by comparing its modern legal system with the classical common-law model referred to above specifically with respect to the source and form of American law; the importance of the court system; the role of the guild of lawyers in the governance of the legal system; and the intellectual character of American law.

Source and Form of American Law. The basic premise of the common-law legal system—that the highest law was based on the unwritten authority of ancient custom—was emphatically rejected by the Founding Fathers. They insisted on a Constitution that would be the highest and most fundamental source of American law; and that Constitution (unlike the English Constitution) was reduced to clear writing—a legal document—the authority of which derived not from ancient custom but from its ratification and acceptance by the people of the several states.

Therefore, United States law, certainly that of the federal government, has always been, both in theory and form, at odds with the common-law model. But the United States Constitution was really a blueprint for a novel form of government. Primarily concerned with the structure of the federal government and its relationship with the several states, it said almost nothing about the law governing the relationships between private individuals. Other than creating a United States Supreme Court with jurisdiction over cases "in law and equity" and a few specified circumstances, it left open the question of the nature of the law that is to be administered by the federal courts in such cases. It also delegated to the several states the freedom and the responsibility of creating their own legal systems and administering their own (local) state law. Accordingly, many states incorporated by statute the English common law into their own law; and notwithstanding the federal and state constitutions, the unwritten common law of England became the basis of the private law in all the states except Louisiana. Criminal law, a form of public law left to the states, was, however, quickly codified or put into statutory form: the very idea of common-law crime was obnoxious to Americans.

One major common-law controversy that plagued the law in the United States for more than a century grew out of the unique form of federalism in which two court systems, state and federal, exist side by side. The question was whether there was such a thing as federal common law—that is, a body of unenacted law enforceable by the federal courts in the absence of specific congressional legislation. In 1842, Justice Joseph Story of the United States Supreme Court struck down a New York statute that defined the terms of negotiability of commercial paper in ways that deviated sharply from the (unwritten) law merchant, which, he said, was binding upon all civilized commercial nations and states. As such, he concluded that it was a part of the law, albeit unwritten, that federal courts were obliged to recognize, uphold, and implement. This decision led to a prolonged legal debate over the nature of the law applicable by federal courts in private lawsuits in the absence of specific congressional legislation. The issue was not conclusively resolved until 1938 in the celebrated case of *Erie Railroad* v. *Tompkins.* At that time, the Supreme Court declared, once and for all, that in the absence of explicit constitutional or federal legislative authority, federal courts were bound to follow applicable state law. Thus ended the specter of a kind of federal common law hovering alongside the Constitution over the states and enforceable by federal courts.

Perhaps the greatest jurisprudential change and controversy in American legal theory since the Civil War centered on the orthodox or classical common-law premise that its ultimate authority lies in ancient custom. The various codes, statutes, uniform state laws, and administrative regulations that have been enacted in the twentieth century make up a huge corpus of law totally different in character from the classical common law, in that it stems from some determinate body—Congress, legislatures, governmental agencies, and the like. It takes a positive form, and its authority stems from, and is found in, sources other than the judicial opinions of common-law courts.

If the essence of the common-law system is that law stems from ancient custom and is only discoverable by judges sitting in actual cases and consulting earlier law reports, it, too, has been firmly rejected. The overwhelming consensus of American legal thought, especially since about 1900, is that even in the most traditional common-law areas (torts and contracts, for example) judges do much more than discover the law.

Thus, the heresy of heresies—that judges make law, at least to some extent (to use Cardozo's word) "interstitially"—is now an accepted fact, almost indeed a dogma of American jurisprudence. If this be so, modern American judges are, whatever else they may be, different from the classical common-law model.

Again, the premise that the common law consists of principles embedded in "ancient custom" has undergone even more devastating criticism during the same period. Of course, in the United States the question of whose "custom" was inevitable from the outset; and whether it was that of pre-Norman England or that of the New World was largely settled pragmatically by the colonies long before the Revolution. By 1789, when the Constitution was ratified, each of the original states already had a legal system based, at least in part, on its own experience as a colony, giving rise to its own local custom (which often included its own version of ancient English custom); and in the nineteenth century, as the number of indigenous law reports expanded astronomically, American courts relied on, and cited ever more frequently, other American cases in their searches for the unwritten common law. By so doing, of course, the courts increasingly discovered principles based on American, not English, custom.

Paradoxically, that development, which led to a body of case law different in many respects from that of England, was more in keeping with, than a rejection of, the common-law tradition. After all, Blackstone defined the common law to be the "general custom" of the realm; and insofar as American decisions reflected evidence of the general custom of the United States, they represented the growth of an American common law. Americans were, in short, emulating the English common-law legal system even as they rejected English law.

But a different and more serious conceptual challenge to the common-law theory came toward the end of the nineteenth century. Many influential legal reformers lamented the fact that some of the most controversial and explosive social issues of the day were being decided by judges who, in keeping with their common-law training, felt constrained to base their decisions exclusively on case law, thereby shutting out all other legal and extralegal considerations, however pertinent, and felt bound absolutely by the

doctrine of stare decisis to follow, as closely as possible, earlier decisions wherever they might lead and whatever the social consequences of their holdings might be. The reformers, or many of them, thus urged a totally new and conceptually alien approach to law: they urged judges to give more attention to the "real" (not merely the "legal") interests at stake in such controversies and to weigh the social consequences of their decisions rather than mechanically following earlier cases. Thus, the famous calls for a "sociological jurisprudence" and later for "legal realism."

In time, these movements accomplished a veritable revolution in the theory of American law by shifting the emphasis of legal thought from the traditional common-law preoccupation with what H. L. A. Hart called the "pedigree of rules" to ever more sophisticated tests for identifying and balancing the interests at stake in lawsuits. Regarding all law, including judicial decisions, to be expressions of social policy, they believed judges should strive to reach decisions that would best further the goals of a free, democratic society. This overt shift in emphasis marked a de facto rejection of the classical common-law model. The law, ceasing to be the reflection of ancient custom, became a tool useful for building a better future. The difference between judges dispassionately declaring what law had always been and judges affirmatively seeking results that would have desirable future effects was a difference of more than mere words: it implied a novel legal system with attributes strikingly different from those of the common-law model.

The new approach to law went even further: it made significant breaks from conventional law practice as defined through the centuries by a monopolistic guild of lawyers. The search for the real interests at stake in litigation and for ways to predict the most desirable consequences of various alternative solutions to legal problems obviously extended the parameters of lawsuits to include a whole host of extralegal considerations far beyond the ken of traditional legal skills and concerns. Increasingly in the twentieth century, sociology, economics, psychology, anthropology, and other scientific and social scientific disciplines have become credible sources of knowledge concerning various aspects of human behavior simply unknown to earlier generations, and much of that knowledge had obvious bearing on the issues in law cases, at least when framed in terms of sociological jurisprudence and legal realism.

Accordingly, the leaders of those movements, most of whom were law professors, urged that legal education should be broadened to include the interaction of law with these other fields of knowledge and further insisted that court pleadings and briefs should not be limited to citing strings of cases but should make reference to, and incorporate, such extralegal data, where relevant, so that judges might consider them in making their decisions. In short, they believed judicial decisions should be based not only on custom and not only on unwritten principles buried in earlier cases but also on all relevant knowledge produced by the researches of scientists and social scientists unconnected in any direct way with the legal profession. Of course, no approach to law could more seriously undermine the rationale of a legal system based solely upon judicial precedent, and no innovation could, conceptually anyway, do more to crack the legal profession's guildlike monopoly of the law. Thus, these developments marked yet further deviation from the classical model of the common law.

The Court in Modern Society. The revolution in American law, radical as it was, effected in another way a significant rejuvenation of the common-law system. However heretical it may have seemed to the traditional common-law lawyers, the movement served to make the American judiciary more responsive to practical needs and (in an age of information) more susceptible to new forms of knowledge. It thereby strengthened the utility, credibility, and influence of the central institution of the common-law system by making courts less dependent upon a single semimystical form of authority; and by potentially widening the base for its involvement in areas outside the purview of law, at least as defined by legal tradition, it came to constitute a kind of declaration of independence from the narrow limits of law as defined by English lawyers. Since about 1940, American and English law and legal education have drifted conceptually further apart.

But this development has also led to a paradoxical result: as the classical model of the common law has become less and less realistic, the common-law tradition of a jurisprudence based

on the common-law court has taken on new life. Today it flourishes in areas scarcely dreamed of in England—so much so that many observers lament that America has become a litigious society, one in which going to court has become a way of life. Whatever else the "litigation explosion" may mean, however, it certainly demonstrates that the public has confidence in the courts and the court system as a forum for both protest and conflict resolution. In this sense, it is an affirmation of the ancient common-law tradition—begun by Henry II—that the nation would be unified by a responsive court system, not by a draconian black letter imposed from above.

The Modern Bar and Law School. Perhaps the most important institution in bringing about these revolutionary changes in American law has been the law school, which has developed in its modern form since about 1870. For its first hundred or so years, America struggled, like England, with the inherent problems of a legal system based on unwritten law; but unlike England, it did so without the Inns of Court, a powerful guild, capable of training and restraining lawyers in a responsible legal tradition. The United States thus had the worst of both worlds: the uncertainty of law that a code could have provided and an undisciplined, self-serving, often corrupt cadre of poorly trained judges and lawyers responsible for administering a systemless system. As a result, the legal system often appeared to be capricious and arbitrary.

It was not until after the Civil War—when the legitimacy of American law, as well as the Union itself, had been called into doubt—that the nation seriously faced the problem of training a responsible legal profession capable of engendering faith in the United States legal system. The task fell to the law schools, which came into existence with spectacular success and in extraordinary numbers toward the end of the nineteenth century. They not only undertook to train a responsible bench and bar but also undertook a searching criticism of American law and legal institutions generally. American law has not been the same since.

Unlike the Inns of Court, the American law school is almost invariably a part of a university, and accordingly, the major movements in American jurisprudence—be it the scientific study of cases, sociological jurisprudence, legal realism, legal process, law and economics, critical legal studies, or what not—have all evolved in academic centers, inspired on the whole by legal scholars, and not by practitioners. And here, too, the change from the classical common-law model is striking. Law is now studied, taught, and researched by a genre of lawyers—a professoriat, many of whose members have never practiced. They have, through their critical researches, publications, and teachings significantly imported non-common-law theories into American common-law legal institutions.

Moreover, it is no longer quite fair to say that the anti-intellectual tradition of the English common law, being born and growing up outside the walls of universities in medieval England, still dominates the legal profession in the United States. Blackstone, insisting that the "sciences are sociable," first took the mysterious common law to Oxford in the mid–eighteenth century to make it more accessible to laymen; and the Americans followed his lead, far more so than his countrymen, in making law a university subject. The result is a form of law that has become richly influenced by, and conversant with, both nonlegal forms of learning and scholarship in non-common-law legal theory.

The Common-Law Frame of Mind. When we compare the modern United States legal system with the classical common-law model, the conclusion seems inescapable that Americans have so thoroughly rejected, so totally ignored, or so drastically modified the basic common-law tenets that their legal system cannot truthfully be described as a common-law one. If, therefore, the essence of a common-law system is that the great bulk of its law must be unwritten in form, the evidence of which can be found only in the decisions of common-law courts, the United States has surely long since ceased being a common-law jurisdiction. Even most of American case law today involves statutes or regulations rather than unwritten common-law principles. In fact, the greater portion of American law today is, in form, far more similar to that of the civil-law countries of Europe than it is to that of England during the golden age of the judge-made common law, and increasingly, American judges, like their European counterparts, are engaged in the task of interpreting legislation and implementing legislative policy.

If, however, the essence of the common-law system is not so much a matter of form and

source of the law but of more general attitudes toward law, then the common-law tradition surely still prevails and sets the tone of American law, for Americans still hold their highest leaders to be under law, even though it be a written Constitution, and in keeping with the common-law tradition, they still expect and demand that law apply equally to all. The notion that law applies equally to all, irrespective of rank and status, has in recent years been extended to race and sex, as it was earlier to religions and social classes, through the constitutional guarantee of "equal protection of the laws." This societywide egalitarian movement, though constitutional in form, is firmly based on a venerable common-law ideal, which, while never attained, has never ceased to inspire and to give direction to legal change in Anglo-American law. As such, it represents the continuation, rather than rejection, of a traditional common-law pursuit.

Another fundamental attribute of the common-law tradition that still flourishes in the United States is a distinctive attitude toward authority. Based on a form of law that for generations took no definite, determinate form, the common law engendered a state of mind that both deferred to the idea of higher authority in principle and was skeptical of all manifestations of it in fact. Thus, common-law courts became not so much agencies for applying the law as public places in which the appropriate form of legal authority was sought in a common-law way; the judges were not so much human repositories of law as they were exacting critics of that search for law, who had to be persuaded, by counsel and by the evidence, that the correct rule of law had in fact been found.

This searching attitude toward law engendered a judiciary open to voices and influences other than that of some omniscient lawgiver, and in time, it gave rise to a tradition of extraordinary judicial autonomy, if not judicial independence in the larger, political sense. Judges, called upon to state publicly their findings and to justify their conclusions and having the power to dissent from their brethren, were readily identified with their own holdings. Thus, the common-law judiciary became something more than, and certainly different from, a typical nameless bureaucracy mechanically implementing state policy. In fact, individual judges became so well known that a unique personality cult developed,

COMMON LAW AND COMMON-LAW LEGAL SYSTEMS

making many of them—such as Marshall and Holmes—genuine folk heroes, a status virtually unknown in non-common-law legal systems. And to this day, American judges—the last generalists in a world of specialists, technicians, and experts—make up a group of unique public officials in whom are vested the most awesome and delicate powers, upon whom falls responsibility for making some of the gravest moral decisions, and to whom is permitted the greatest autonomy. They are the living legacy of the common-law tradition.

Another, perhaps even more important, consequence of the traditional common-law attitude toward authority, including its robust skepticism of all assertions claiming to be authoritative, is a marked lack of that institutional dogmatism, or certitude, that laymen and others are likely to associate with the law. The indeterminate essence of the common-law renders it inherently inconclusive in form, and it is only by what modern philosophers call "argumentative techniques," or a kind of open dialogue between disputants—what common-law lawyers call a trial, in which the parties, the jury, witnesses, the bar, and the bench are all volatile participants— that legal decisions are rendered. Decisions reached under such circumstances tend to take the form of findings rather than bald proclamations and tend to be grounded in reason rather than based on dogma. As such, they encourage, rather than discourage, credulity and moderation and the great social virtue of tolerance.

Thus, the common-law process is both skeptical and creative. Each case involves a new search for the law, and that attitude continues to prevail today, though the form of American law has become ever more determinate. In American courts even the clearest statutes, codes, and regulations are treated with studied irreverence, and like unwritten common-law principles, their authority must be clearly established in each case before they are acknowledged to be the law. So the common-law legal tradition survives and flourishes even in America's increasingly non-common-law legal system, which has retained the flexibility, relative lack of dogmatism, and responsiveness to changing social conditions that characterize the common law at its zenith, largely because of the attitudes toward law and authority that evolved from the common-law tradition.

CASE

Erie Railroad v. Tompkins, 304 U.S. 64 (1938)

BIBLIOGRAPHY

The history of the English common law has long been associated with the legendary names of Frederick Pollock and Frederick W. Maitland, the authors of *The History of English Law Before the Reign of Edward I,* 2 vols. (1899; 2nd ed., 1968), and William Holdsworth, the indefatigable author of *A History of English Law,* 16 vols. (1901–1965). T. F. T. Plucknett, *A Concise History of the Common Law* (1929), served as the staple introduction for more than one generation of law students in both Britain and the United States, as it went through five editions.

When modern scholarship began to reveal fallibilities in the earlier established authorities, two major revisionist histories appeared. The first was S. F. C. Milsom, *Historical Foundations of the Common Law* (1969; 2nd ed., 1981); it was Milsom who in 1968 edited (with a most perceptive introduction) the 2nd ed. of Pollock and Maitland. The second was J. H. Baker, *An Introduction to English Legal History* (1971; 2nd ed., 1979), which is certainly the most reliable introductory survey now available. R. O'Sullivan, *The Inheritance of the Common Law* (1950), is also helpful.

Two brief, but valuable, studies are John P. Dawson, *The Oracles of the Law* (1968), part I of which deals with the rise of the English judiciary, and R. C. Van Caenegem, *The Birth of the English Common Law* (1973). Both of these studies have the additional virtue of putting the history of the English legal system in the wider context of continental legal developments. For that purpose and in the still wider context of ancient Roman law, see also P. Stein, *Legal Institutions: The Development of Dispute Settlement* (1984), and for a comparison of modern European and common-law legal systems, see F. L. Lawson, *A Common Lawyer Looks at the Civil Law* (1953).

For a jurisprudential introduction to some of the most fundamental institutions of the common-law legal system— specifically, custom, precedent, equity, and legislation—see C. K. Allen, *Law in the Making* (1927; 6th ed., 1958), and A. W. B. Simpson, "The Common Law and Legal Theory," in Simpson, ed., *Oxford Essays in Jurisprudence,* 2nd ser. (1973). For the role of the jury, see Patrick Devlin, *Trial by Jury* (1956). For an exhaustive discussion of the procedural aspects of the common-law legal system, see Robert W. Millar, *Civil Procedure of the Trial Court in Historical Perspective* (1952). For a contemporary overview and comment on the virtues of the adversary system generally, see S. A. Saltzburg, "Lawyers, Clients, and the Adversary System," in *Mercer Law Review,* 37 (1986). See also Karl N. Llewellyn, *The Common Law Tradition: Deciding Appeals* (1960), a late production of an American iconoclast who spent much of his scholarly career attacking some of the most cherished legal conventions associated with the common law but who ended up a champion of what he called the "Grand Style" of the common-law tradition.

For the fate and changing shape of the common law in the United States, see Roscoe Pound, *The Spirit of the Common Law*

515

(1921) and *The Formative Era of American Law* (1938). M. Radin, *Handbook of Anglo-American Legal History* (1936), is a sophisticated melding of New World developments with the Old World tradition. Other useful accounts are found in M. Horwitz, *The Transformation of American Law* (1977); William E. Nelson, *The Americanization of the Common Law: The Impact of Legal Change on Massachusetts Society, 1700–1830* (1975); and, more generally, Lawrence M. Friedman, *A History of American Law* (1973; 2nd ed., 1986).

[*See also* AMERICAN JURISPRUDENCE; AMERICAN LEGAL CULTURE; CIVIL LAW SYSTEMS; COMMERCIAL LAW; CONTRACTS; EQUITY AND EQUITABLE REMEDIES; FRAMING THE CONSTITUTION; LEGAL EDUCATION; LEGAL PROFESSION AND LEGAL ETHICS; LEGAL REASONING; PROPERTY LAW; *and* TORTS.]

COURTS OF LIMITED AND SPECIALIZED JURISDICTION

Russell R. Wheeler

Courts of limited and specialized jurisdiction constitute the bulk of America's judiciary. They include the municipal courts, police courts, justice-of-the-peace courts, small-claims courts, traffic courts, probate courts, juvenile, family, and domestic-relations courts, landlord-tenant courts, and other trial courts distinguished by the fact that they have been established to try only a particular kind of legal dispute.

These courts occupy a peculiar place within the American citizen's frame of reference about the legal system. In one sense, people generally know less about courts of limited and specialized jurisdiction than they do about the general-jurisdiction trial courts and the appellate courts. It is the work of these latter tribunals that gets reported in the popular press and depicted in dramatizations. Public interest is sparked by appellate rulings that announce new rules of public policy. Moreover, people want to know about trials involving major public figures or issues, trials of notorious crimes, or unusual civil suits. That popular desire is whetted perhaps by the related folklore of the trial as a crucible of eternal verities. Asked to describe a court of law, most people would refer to a dignified chamber in which a judge presides over the lawyers' examination of witnesses before a jury while the parties sit to the side, occasionally conferring with counsel. Those who know courts professionally know that this picture reflects little of what transpires in most courts, given the high proportion of dispositions occurring before trial procedures.

What typically happens in the limited- and special-jurisdiction courts, workhorses of the American judicial system, has little to do with the layperson's notions of what happens in court. In these courts, as in other courts, many of the cases are disposed of without trial. They differ from general-jurisdiction trial courts in that in them even cases that get a hearing are heard rapidly, frequently absent procedural details, and often without the benefit (and costs) of counsel, or even law-trained judges.

The great majority of criminal offenses that get judicial attention get it only in the limited- and specialized-jurisdiction courts, which hear primarily misdemeanors rather than felonies. They also hear many civil cases, disputes about broken contracts, broken marriages, and broken homes. Thus, to the degree that people know courts from actual experience, it is the limited- and specialized-jurisdiction courts that most people know best, because they are the courts with which most people are likely to have contact.

Limited- and specialized-jurisdiction courts reveal the tension between two fundamental but largely conflicting goals of American judicial procedure: strict, formal adherence to the letter of the law, on the one hand, and concessions to principles of equity and demands of expediency, on the other hand. Limited- and special-jurisdiction courts have long been bemoaned as dangerous to the unified and effective administration of justice. Their judges are said to be poorly trained and their procedures haphazard; neither their judges nor their procedures, critics charge, can give litigants justice according to accepted standards of due process. Plaintiffs and prosecutors are overwhelmingly victorious. The need to process large masses of cases helps explain why they substitute a rough approximation of judicial justice for the ideal. There is little debate that the assembly-line nature of many limited- and special-jurisdiction courts is undesirable, but little is done to change it.

Limited- and special-jurisdiction courts vary

COURTS OF LIMITED AND SPECIALIZED JURISDICTION

from strict adherence to legal standards in another way that is not so universally deplored. At the same time that they are damned for the laxness of their procedure and the unprofessionalism of their judges, others praise these same aspects and refer approvingly to "people's courts." Many defend them as providing justice closer to the people, often without the reliance on procedural rules and the trappings of formality that more accurately characterize the general-jurisdiction courts and that some say interfere with doing substantive justice. Limited- and special-jurisdiction courts provide a "day in court," an opportunity to present one's story to an impartial arbiter, who may fashion a solution to a problem that reflects common sense rather than the dictates of legal precedent. They are thus a paradox. Depending on the court and the viewer's perspective, they present the best and worst of American courts.

DEFINITIONS AND OBSERVATIONS

Courts of limited and specialized jurisdiction is not a formal or official label. Rather, it reflects a long-standing and commonly observed way of categorizing certain trial courts. In one sense, all courts are courts of limited and special jurisdiction, which is simply the converse of the obvious proposition that no court has unlimited jurisdiction. The United States Supreme Court, which has more authority than any other court in the United States, may only accept jurisdiction over a limited range of cases, most of which have been tried in another court. In at least two states, Oklahoma and Texas, separate courts exercise final appellate jurisdiction in civil and criminal cases, respectively. Federal district courts have obvious legal limits on their jurisdiction.

The label is not used to capture these pervasive jurisdictional limitations, which characterize all courts in one way or another, but rather to distinguish the two basic kinds of state and local trial courts. One kind consists of those state trial courts with jurisdiction to hear all varieties of civil and criminal cases without limits as to the penalties that can be imposed or the damages that can be awarded. They are typically referred to as the general-jurisdiction trial courts, and have various official names, such as *circuit courts* and *district courts,* depending on the particular state.

Limited- and special-jurisdiction courts alludes to the other kind of state trial courts or, more typically, local trial courts, a larger group of courts that are distinguished by the quantitative and/or qualitative limits on the types of cases they may try. These quantitative limits are the maximum dollar amounts in controversy that can be litigated (for example, no civil claim more than $1,000) or the maximum punishment that the court may impose (for example, no more than a six-month incarceration or a $500 fine). Qualitative limits are those that restrict the courts to hearing only certain kinds of cases—criminal, probate, juvenile—from among those lawsuits over which courts in the particular state or locality have jurisdiction to find facts and apply the law to the facts so found.

Two special final definitional points should be mentioned. First, in defining limited- and special-jurisdiction courts, it is important to realize that the rubric does not embrace any tribunal other than the well-recognized general-jurisdiction trial and appellate courts. Most specifically, specialized courts are not generally thought of as including the many administrative law courts that are creatures of both the state and federal governments but are in fact executive branch agencies, rather than judicial bodies, and are expected to find facts and apply the law to those facts, subject only to review by appropriate appellate procedure. Second, the rubric is sometimes used to include particular units of general-jurisdiction courts that are established to hear particular kinds of cases—such as a landlord and tenant branch of a general-jurisdiction trial court. The concept of special units of general-jurisdiction courts reflects the current conventional wisdom of court organization; and thus, save for small-claims courts, these special units, or parts, are generally not considered to be specialized trial courts.

Some generalities about special courts override the great variety of their shapes and sizes. First, specialized courts exist both for civil and criminal disputes. Probate and small-claims courts are examples of specialized civil courts. Traffic courts and misdemeanor, or municipal, courts are examples of specialized criminal courts.

Second, cases tried in the limited-jurisdiction courts, especially criminal cases, are frequently reheard in general-jurisdiction trial courts. They do not hear appeals from these courts, in the sense of reviewing whether the law was properly applied. Rather, they give the dispute another full-blown trial, a *trial de novo,* when litigants request it and according to procedures that vary from state to state.

Third, the role limited- and special-jurisdiction courts play in the administration of justice is determined not by the notoriety of the cases they decide but by the quantity of cases brought to them. Most handle only civil cases involving comparatively small amounts of money or other damages, or only less serious criminal offenses. But they handle such a great proportion of all cases that the cumulative impact of their actions is very large. As Table 1 indicates, their proportion of the total case load is typically about 90 percent in any particular state jurisdiction. It also bears mention that not all limited- and specialized-jurisdiction courts are involved only in petty squabbles. The dollar amount in controversy in some courts with specialized jurisdiction can be very high; state probate judges, for example, may handle multimillion dollar estates.

Fourth, specialized courts in the United States are created by local government and, to a lesser degree, state government; relatively few of them are federal courts. This is inevitably true simply because the federal judiciary is tiny in comparison with the state court systems. In the federal judicial system, unlike the state systems, the district courts, which are the general-jurisdiction trial courts, are the predominant trial courts. The limited and specialized federal judiciary comprises mostly two specialized units of the district courts. One is the United States magistrates, who try misdemeanors, conduct various preliminary proceedings in civil and criminal cases, and can enter final judgments in certain civil cases with the consent of the parties. The other is bankruptcy courts, adjuncts of the district courts, which hear claims arising under the federal bankruptcy laws. Although the number of matters filed with magistrates and bankruptcy judges exceeds the civil and criminal filings in the district courts, many of those matters are relatively simple to handle.

There are several other specialized federal courts. They deal with such matters as the appointment of special prosecutors to investigate allegations of official misconduct, the authorization of eavesdropping in national security cases, the arrangement for the consolidation of complex civil actions that produce filings in more

than one federal judicial district, and the hearing of appeals involving wage and price guidelines. Judges of these latter courts serve in addition to their duties on the regular federal trial or appellate courts.

General statements about special courts are very risky once one goes below a high level of generality. Beyond some pervasive organizational and behavioral characteristics, it is difficult to develop common descriptive denominators for them or to ascribe measures of performance that are universal. Special courts, like all courts, exist in widely varying legal-political cultures and thus will vary widely. A few generalizations are safe. It is clear, for example, that defendants rarely win in special courts; in fact, the abbreviation *J.P.* for "justice of the peace" is often said to stand more accurately for "judgment for the plaintiff" or "judgment for the police." But there can be significant variation in the specific levels at which plaintiffs prevail in different courts, just as there will be variations in the percentage of defendants sentenced to incarceration or fines, the use of juries, and the quality of the judges. Thus, even when patterns of behavior are fairly pervasive from court to court, it is important to be alert for exceptions. More important, though, beyond the basic and pervasive pattern, are countless individual differences.

EVOLUTION OF SPECIAL COURTS

Courts of limited and specialized jurisdiction are in a constant state of evolution. Changes in them over the years mirror changes in society and the judiciary's link to those changes. Roscoe Pound's succinct description of the foreign antecedents to the American judiciary is worth quoting:

> Multiplying of tribunals is a characteristic of the beginnings of judicial organization. When some new type of controversy or new kind of situation arises and presses for treatment, a new tribunal is set up to deal with it. So it was at Rome. So it was in England from the twelfth century to the sixteenth, and indeed, on the whole, down to the nineteenth century. In the same way we in the United States have set up administrative tribunals in the present century with no system, with no uniform provisions for or practice as to review, and not infrequently with no clear definition of jurisdiction as between one and an-

other. The reason in each case is the same. Every new condition is met at first by a special act, and so for every new problem there is likely to be a new court.

(1940, 5)

In England, there were numerous different courts handling different kinds of cases. In the American colonies and then in the American states, the same phenomenon occurred. Various legislative acts established, for example, justice-of-the-peace courts, orphans courts, or admiralty courts. New York established the Court of the Mayor, Recorder, and Aldermen for municipal disputes. Virginia established "Hustings courts" for commercial disputes, and South Carolina established the Court of Pleas, Assize, and Jail Delivery for civil and criminal cases. Many of the courts established in colonial times and shortly after the Constitution have long since been abolished. Today's justice-of-the-peace courts are the primary legacies of those earlier tribunals.

The special courts that populate the judicial landscape near the end of the twentieth century are largely the products of the era of industrialization and urbanization that began toward the end of the nineteenth century. Again, court organization mirrored the conditions that were created by social and technological change or that were illuminated by an increased sense of social responsibility. Newfound problems led to the creation of new courts to resolve those problems when they took shape in legal form. Municipal courts were established around the turn of the century, as in Chicago in 1906 and Cleveland in 1912, to replace justice-of-the-peace courts in those urban areas. Small-claims (or "small-cause") courts, or branches, were frequently established within those new courts. At about the same time, reflecting the Progressive Era's craving for agencies of social improvement and order, cities created juvenile courts, family courts, and domestic-relations courts, to join various misdemeanor and other limited-jurisdiction criminal courts.

Court reorganization has been a staple reform effort of the twentieth century, and a major element of that effort has been to abolish a state or city's many special courts serving many different purposes in favor of a single trial court of general jurisdiction, perhaps with special branches. It is almost obligatory, in this context, to quote from Pound's famous address on the causes of popular dissatisfaction with the administration of justice. "Our system of courts," Pound told the American Bar Association in 1906, "is archaic in three respects: (1) In its multiplicity of courts, (2) in preserving concurrent jurisdictions, (3) in the waste of judicial power which it involves. . . . Multiplicity of courts is characteristic of archaic law."

Court reformers are wont to quote this passage in the course of bemoaning how unenlightened legislatures must be not to have understood Pound's indictment. Those reformers apparently fail to wonder whether the proliferation of courts is not an organic condition of dispute-resolving organizations. Even where court reorganization efforts have succeeded in eliminating many special courts, the legislature proceeds to create new tribunals with specialized or limited foci, such as courts to handle environmental disputes. In the 1970s and 1980s, many cities created various mechanisms of alternative dispute resolution. Mediation and arbitration forums were created for disputes that established courts could not handle well or would not handle at all, given the small amounts of money in controversy or the reluctance of the disputants to bring them to courts.

COURTS AND CASE LOADS

Courts and Financial Support. Although each state differs in the precise configuration of its judicial structure, there is a typical, three-tiered, organizational pattern: limited- and specialized-jurisdiction trial courts; general-jurisdiction trial courts; and appellate courts. Typically, the general-jurisdiction trial and appellate courts are agencies of the state government, while the special courts are agencies of cities and counties. Thus, special courts within the same state vary by name and function from locality to locality. They certainly vary from state to state.

In almost all states, financial support for the general-jurisdiction trial courts is a mixture of state and local funds, with the state providing the basic salary funds for the judges. By contrast, special courts receive their operating funds from local rather than from state treasuries. In some situations, the fines and fees they bring in are a source of considerable revenue for courts themselves or their parent governments or both. For example, Texas municipal courts collected five times as much revenue as their actual operating expenses in the mid-1970s. However, that the courts are money producers does not necessarily mean that they enjoy the benefits of that production. As regards Texas municipal courts, for example, the same 1977 American Judicature Society survey that identified their revenue potential also found that they lacked adequate courtrooms, office space, and supplies. The same pattern was identified in Louisiana, where, for example, a small rural court in the early 1970s budgeted $10,200 but generated $15,277 in revenue, and an urban court budgeted $206,500 while generating $233,000.

Supporting courts with the revenue they produce may pose a danger to due process if the financing scheme biases the judge to favor dispositions that promise the greater financial return to the court. In *Tumey* v. *Ohio* (1927), the Supreme Court was asked to review a local ordinance because it provided that the town mayor, who was authorized by state statute to try state liquor-prohibition offenses, would receive his costs from each convicted defendant's fine (part of which also went to the municipal treasury). The Court held the ordinance to be unconstitutional as a violation of due process because it provided the mayor "a direct, personal, pecuniary interest in convicting the defendant who comes before him for trial, in the twelve dollars of costs imposed in his behalf, which he would

not have received if the defendant had been acquitted."

In a minority of the states there is a statewide, state-funded limited-jurisdiction court; both Alaska and Maryland, for example, maintain a statewide district court, with limited criminal and civil jurisdiction and with general right of appeal to the state superior and circuit courts. This pattern increased in the 1970s as various states (Maryland, for example) revised their judicial systems, abolishing a patchwork of limited-jurisdiction courts that varied from city to city and county to county. In most states, however, local governments continue to support a variety of courts for probate, family, juvenile, and other matters.

Case Loads. It is by now well recognized that variations in jurisdiction, in methods of categorizing cases, and in counting and reporting them make it very difficult to generalize about the business of state courts. For example, including or excluding traffic cases or, more obviously, parking violations in the court's total case load will have a major effect on any effort to quantify the business that courts handle and the proportion of such business in any state handled by general-jurisdiction (as opposed to special-jurisdiction) trial courts.

Some patterns do emerge, however. Perhaps most important is that any state's special courts receive about 90 percent of the total filings in all of the state's trial courts. Table 1 bears this out. It shows the percentage of filings by case cate-

TABLE 1

Filings in Limited-Jurisdiction Courts by Case Category as a Percentage of Total Cases Filed in General- and Limited-Jurisdiction Courts, 1978[1]

State	Percent of total case load	Proportion by case category			
		Civil	Criminal	Traffic	Juvenile
Hawaii	88.2[2]	32.5	94.8	99.9	0.0
Alaska	89.5	52.4	94.1	100.0	0.0
California	90.6[2]	60.0	92.7	100.0	0.0
Washington	91.8	41.1	89.7	100.0	0.0
North Carolina	92.2	78.8	87.1	100.0	100.0
Virginia	93.4	86.4	84.3	100.0	100.0
Vermont	93.9	69.2	99.6	100.0	100.0
Connecticut	95.0	86.5	95.8	100.0	100.0
New Jersey	95.2[2]	84.0	92.8	100.0	100.0

[1]Adapted from National Center for State Courts, *The Business of State Trial Courts* (1983), p. 19.
[2]Proportions exclude parking violations.

gory in limited-jurisdiction courts of nine states as a total of filings in both general- and special-jurisdiction trial courts for 1978.

Thus, for example, in Hawaii, limited-jurisdiction courts received more than 88 percent of all the cases filed in that state's general- and limited-jurisdiction courts. The limited-jurisdiction courts received almost one-third of the civil matters filed in both types of courts but almost 95 percent of the criminal matters, including virtually all traffic filings.

SELECTION OF JUDGES

The judges who serve in specialized courts are almost as varied as the types of courts themselves. Data given for each state in a National Center for State Courts study (1981, 14–18) indicates that in 1980 there were almost 19,000 authorized limited- and specialized-jurisdiction court judgeships, full- and part-time. Most of these positions, moreover, are filled by election rather than by "merit selection" systems, which have come increasingly to control access to the general-jurisdiction trial courts and appellate benches.

The most striking characteristic of the limited- and specialized-jurisdiction judgeships is the large proportion filled by nonlawyers. A 1979 study published by the Institute of Judicial Administration estimated a total of 20,280 limited- and special-jurisdiction judges serving nationwide (part-time and full-time), of which probably as many as 14,000 were nonlawyers. The discrepancy between this figure and the total judgeship figure reported by the National Center for State Courts reflects not a decline in actual numbers of judges but different methods of ferreting out and categorizing judges and courts on the local level. For these purposes, systematic statewide data are unavailable.

Some states, concerned about the quality of justice that nonlawyer specialized court judges are likely to render, have insisted that they complete minimum in-service continuing-education programs. In Texas, for example, at the last survey in 1975, only 55 of the 934 justices of the peace and 220 of the more than 1,000 municipal-court judges were lawyers. However, at that time, more than two-thirds of the justices of the peace had completed a forty-hour training

course. About half the states mandate continuing-education programs for judges, and these mandates are enforced most rigorously for the limited- and specialized-jurisdiction courts, where virtually all the nonlawyer judges serve.

In *North* v. *Russell* (1976), the Supreme Court gave constitutional sanction to nonlawyer judges when it held that Kentucky did not deny due process to a drunk-driving defendant who was convicted before, and sentenced by, a nonlawyer judge. Due process was protected, the Court held, because trial de novo was available to the defendant in the lawyer-judge circuit court. The Court also approved, in the face of equal-protection claims, Kentucky's scheme of requiring that police-court judges in more populated areas be lawyers but allowing nonlawyer judges to serve in those courts in less-populated areas.

PROCEDURE IN SPECIALIZED COURTS

It may be helpful to take a closer look at two of the best-known types of specialized courts, the criminal-jurisdiction misdemeanor courts, and the civil jurisdiction small-claims courts.

Misdemeanor Courts. Misdemeanors, generally those criminal offenses with sentences of incarceration for less than a year and fines below a specified, relatively modest amount, constitute the vast majority of criminal offenses that move through the courts. They are heard by the limited-jurisdiction criminal courts, typically called misdemeanor courts, or municipal courts, in the urban areas. (Justice-of-the-peace courts hear misdemeanor violations in some rural areas.) Misdemeanor courts have long been singled out for their inadequate facilities and procedures. The *Task Force Report: The Courts* of the 1967 President's Commission on Law Enforcement and Administration of Justice stated that "no findings of this Commission are more disquieting than those relating to the conditions of the lower criminal courts" (p. 29).

There is ample, albeit impressionistic, documentation of the current problems of these courts. That documentation echoes complaints that extend well back to the nineteenth century. The more recent studies have not upset the basic picture painted by scholars of an earlier generation, such as Felix Frankfurter and Roscoe

Pound, who wrote about Cleveland's criminal courts in 1922. What more recent research has done is to illuminate the variations in conditions between misdemeanor courts—between urban and rural, for example, or between municipal courts in different cities.

The most common complaint about limited-jurisdiction criminal courts, especially municipal courts, is that they move defendants from filing to disposition in the fashion of an assembly line. Misdemeanor courts handle the great number of defendants brought before them by a batch-processing system that tracks the various stages in the criminal process. Defendants are rarely arraigned individually; rather, the judge makes a speech to all defendants brought into court for the day. Impediments to speedy disposition, even if they compromise the defendant's constitutionally protected rights are often ignored in the interest of quick disposition. The result, a study in one court found, is that the judge did not inform one-fourth of all defendants of their rights. As Neubauer puts it, "appraisal of rights is treated by the court as a clerical device to be dispensed with before the taking of guilty pleas can begin" (p. 367). On average, most defendants are before the judge for about one minute.

In *Argersinger* v. *Hamlin* (1972), the Supreme Court held that the constitutional right to be represented by a lawyer cannot be denied any defendant, even those accused of only petty offenses or misdemeanors. The Court's decision, however, was evidently a change more in the form of the law than in what actually happens: the right to counsel remains an empty right for most defendants in limited-jurisdiction criminal courts. Indeed, in these courts, most defendants' initial appearance is their only appearance. About 90 percent plead guilty; thus, trials are exceptional events.

The factorylike way in which defendants are quickly brought into court and just as quickly sent out, usually with a short jail sentence or a fine, is of a piece with the physical appearance of most municipal courts—dirty, drab, often as much beyond repair as the defendants who shuffle through them. Behind this picture, however, is a subtle but pervasive reality: the conditions in most municipal courts are a function of the value society has collectively ascribed to the work it assigns to them. One can infer an unarticulated, generally even unrealized, collective judgment that public drunks, disorderly persons, and minor offenders are due a limited dose of punitive attention and that the misdemeanor courts are there to administer it. In most cases, there are few valid legal defenses to the charges brought against the defendants. In fact, political scientist Malcolm Feeley has argued that the process by which these persons are taken from the street to jail and a brief court appearance is as much a part of the punishment they receive as the typically brief imprisonment or mild fine imposed on them. Misdemeanor courts, in other words, may not provide a sentence carefully calibrated to the offense in question, but they do provide a punishment of sorts simply by the process through which defendants are herded.

The underlying social purpose served by criminal processing in municipal courts calls into question one of the least-questioned explanations for the courts' behavior: that the pressure of heavy case loads leads them to procedural shortcuts and heavy reliance on guilty pleas rather than to full-blown criminal trials to dispose of cases. Put another way, even without the pressure of heavy case loads, most cases in misdemeanor courts would probably be disposed of by guilty pleas. In a paper presented to the American Political Science Association in 1975 Feeley observed, based on a study of lower criminal courts in Connecticut, that

> regardless of caseload, there will always be *too many cases* for many of the participants in the system since most of them have a strong interest in being some place other than in court. . . . They are presented with a predetermined total daily workload, everyday, and when this task is completed, many of them can leave. . . . In each instance, the faster the work is done, the sooner court can be adjourned and many people can go home or back to their offices.
> (quoted in Wheeler and Whitcomb, 36–37)

Small-Claims Courts. One civil justice counterpart to the municipal court is the small-claims court, created in the early part of the twentieth century to provide access to justice for citizens aggrieved by injustices that are small in comparison to other civil wrongs but significant to the aggrieved citizen. Small-claims courts were established to allow wage earners, small businessmen, tradespeople, and consumers to seek redress of grievances without having to negotiate the regular courts' maze of procedural rules, which were in fact much more formal and much more unforgiving of their violation than are today's procedural rules.

In 1978, small-claims courts were found in all but eight states. Small claims include efforts to gain redress for faulty service, such as a garment being ruined by a dry cleaner; to force individuals to pay debts, such as installment payments on an appliance; or to force dealers to repair or replace faulty goods. The maximum claim that most small-claims courts can hear is about $1,000, and typically the remedies they can order do not extend to equitable relief, such as injunctions. The formal standard of proof in small-claims proceedings is the same as in a plenary civil trial—proof by a preponderance of the evidence. Most judges in small-claims proceedings adhere as best they can to that standard. There are no juries; the judge applies the law and finds the facts.

The organization of the small-claims courts provides another illustration of the great diversity of the special courts, because in fact the label *small-claims court* does not refer to an autonomous court but rather to a special procedure carried out in a special part or division of an existing limited- or general-jurisdiction trial court. Judges of the parent court rotate in and out of small-claims assignments, typically for a week's term.

As in misdemeanor courts, summary procedures characterize small-claims courts. Most small-claims hearings last fifteen to thirty minutes, but into that period is crammed everything from gaining initial familiarity with the case to the judicial order that, in most cases, directs the defendant to compensate the plaintiff and thus terminate the proceeding. Judges are beset by the pressure of volume and may terminate the hearings themselves when they believe they have heard enough to satisfy themselves as to the proper disposition. The logic of simplified small-claims procedures does not allow for pretrial conferences or discovery, but even if it did, the reality would probably resemble misdemeanor court proceedings: such steps would typically fall by the wayside.

The most reliable generalization about all special-jurisdiction courts—that plaintiffs overwhelmingly prevail—is not jeopardized by an examination of small-claims outcomes. In a recent survey of fifteen small-claims courts the plaintiffs won—generally in the 80 percent to 90 percent range—regardless of education, income, or race. Furthermore, the impact of attorney services (not all small-claims courts allow attorneys) appears to be minimal on determining who wins.

The same phenomenon that explains the high conviction rates in misdemeanor courts explains the high plaintiff success ratios in small-claims courts: defendants are rarely able to present a valid legal response to the charges brought against them. When small-claims plaintiffs lose, it is typically not because they lack sufficient evidence to support a claim but because they state a claim that does not come within the jurisdiction of the small-claims court.

Finally, just as the "process is the punishment" in misdemeanor courts, the small-claims procedures may serve a social purpose apart from providing litigants a specific monetary gain or loss as the result of a judicial order disposing of the claim. Specifically, small-claims courts probably work a therapeutic effect, at least when black-robed judges take the time to listen to plaintiffs and defendants explain their sides of a dispute. As Ruhnka and Weller reported in 1979, all the judges they interviewed in a fifteen-court survey, regardless of whether they were active or passive as judges, "recognized a therapeutic function in small-claims trials and said they often let litigants explain their sides of the story long past the point where the judge had enough facts to decide the case, although they viewed fifteen or twenty minutes as an average time they had to keep in mind in hearing a case" (p. 21).

CONTROVERSY OVER SPECIALIZED COURTS

A former state court administrator once quipped that if limited- and specialized-jurisdiction courts did not exist, court reformers would have to invent them. They have indeed provided a stable target for standard court-reform groups and are a staple of their complaints. The controversies about special-jurisdiction courts can be grouped into three main categories. There are controversies over whether such courts should be merged into a single, unified state court system; whether the procedures in specialized courts are adequate to assure the proper administration of justice; and whether the judges in such courts are minimally competent. Usually, these issues emerge together, as when court reformers claim that establishing one class of trial courts with specialized units will result in more efficient administration and proceedings of greater dignity and justice, and lump this recommendation with a parallel recommendation for restricting the trial bench to lawyer judges selected by a nominating commission that will allegedly assure the selection of meritorious judges.

Ridding the nation of specialized- and limited-jurisdiction courts has been a major objective of conventional court reform organizations and "good-government" organizations. Reorganizing the court system was only one element of the Progressive Era's effort to make government more orderly, efficient, and, in the reformers' wistful phrase, less political. The American Judicature Society, established in 1914 to promote the efficient administration of justice, developed a model judicial article in 1920 for the National Municipal League to propose to state legislatures. The model article proposed a unified statewide court structure. It would consist of a single appellate court (supreme court), a single trial court for trials of all kinds (district court), and a county court for the special convenience of each separate county.

There have been variations on this basic idea through the years. Some models, for example, would have the states adopt constitutions creating a single court of justice for the entire state, leaving it to the legislature to specify court levels. When the National Municipal League proposed such a scheme in 1942, however, the American Judicature Society roundly condemned it, fearing, not without reason, that legislatures would be unlikely to create a streamlined judicial structure. More recent conventional wisdom is seen in the 1973 *Report* of the Courts Task Force of the National Advisory Commission on Criminal Justice Standards and Goals and the American Bar Association's 1974 *Standards Relating to Court Organization*. Both of these documents embrace the notion of a single trial court, with more specialized divisions as necessary to accommodate more specialized and limited civil and criminal case needs. This approach comported with Pound's basic assumption that specialized courts were to be avoided in favor of specialized judges.

CONCLUSION

The pervasive efforts of various court reform groups to eliminate limited- and special-jurisdiction courts will never succeed. Changing social conditions inevitably prompt the creation of new forums to deal with the disputes among persons and organizations that those changes inevitably create. Limited- and specialized-jurisdiction courts, moreover, serve a valuable political function, meting out dispositions that impose a rough justice on a great many lawbreakers, civil and criminal. That they serve a valuable social function, however, does not mean that their procedures, or their personnel, are not in need of considerable refinement in many ways.

The best approach is to regard these courts as neither a necessary evil nor a positive good, but rather as a permanent, if fluctuating, feature of the American judicial landscape. As such, they should provide the basic procedural rights that are the due of every person who seeks, or is subject to, judicial review. At the same time, however, it is important to bear in mind that they serve one of their most important functions precisely when they broker the law's demands with the dictates of common sense and community values.

CASES

Argersinger v. Hamlin, 407 U.S. 25 (1972)
North v. Russell, 427 U.S. 328 (1976)
Tumey v. Ohio, 273 U.S. 510 (1927)

BIBLIOGRAPHY

American Bar Association, *The Improvement of the Administration of Justice*, 5th ed. (1981), provides some good examples of the court reform perspective on limited-jurisdiction courts, including family and traffic courts. Allan Ashman and James J. Alfini, *Courts of Limited Jurisdiction: A National Survey* (1975), analyzes the structure and operation of limited- and specialized-jurisdiction courts in six states and includes helpful information and references to the history of efforts to reform these courts. Malcolm M. Feeley, *The Process Is the Punishment* (1979), analyzes lower criminal court operations and dynamics, based on the author's study of lower criminal courts in Connecticut. Milton Heumann, "A Note on Plea Bargaining," in *Law and Society Review,* 9 (1975), uses Connecticut criminal courts for illustrations of the underlying behavioral motivations in criminal courts. Herbert Jacob, *Debtors in Court: The Consumption of Government Services* (1969), analyzes the operation of a civil limited-jurisdiction court.

Karen M. Knab, ed., *Courts of Limited Jurisdiction: A National Survey* (1977), is a state-by-state review of limited-jurisdiction courts' organization and structure. "Misdemeanor Courts," in *The Justice System Journal,* 6 (1981), is a special issue on misdemeanor courts, with special attention to their cultural and management characteristics. National Advisory Commission on Criminal Justice Standards and Goals, *Report on Courts* (1973), reports on the criminal justice system. National Center for State Courts, *State Court Organization: 1980* (1981), presents state-by-state data on numbers of courts, judges, and characteristics; and *The Business of State Trial Courts* (1983), presents information on the comparative case loads of limited- and general-jurisdiction trial courts and of appellate courts. David W. Neubauer, *America's Courts and the Criminal Justice System* (1983), is an excellent introductory analysis of the lower criminal courts, with extensive bibliographic references to social science literature.

Roscoe Pound, *Organization of Courts* (1940), provides im-

portant historical details on the evolution of limited-jurisdiction courts; and "Causes of Popular Dissatisfaction with the Administration of Justice," in Leo A. Levin and Russell R. Wheeler, eds., *The Pound Conference: Perspectives on Justice in the Future* (1980), is his 1906 ABA speech. Roscoe Pound and Felix Frankfurter, *Criminal Justice in Cleveland* (1922), is a good example of the early, Progressive Era studies of the administration of limited-jurisdiction criminal courts. President's Commission on Law Enforcement and Administration of Justice, *The Challenge of Crime in a Free Society* (1967), the report of President Johnson's so-called crime commission, redirected attention toward conditions in misdemeanor and municipal courts; and *Task Force Report: The Courts* (1967).

John Robertson, ed., *Rough Justice: Perspectives on the Lower Criminal Courts* (1974), is an anthology of writings on lower criminal courts. John C. Ruhnka and Steven Weller, *Small-Claims Courts: A National Examination* (1979), surveys small-claims courts. Linda Silberman, *Non-Attorney Justice in the United States: An Empirical Study* (1979), gives the results of an Institute of Judicial Administration study of nonlawyer judges. Jerome Skolnick, *Justice Without Trial* (1966), analyzes the informal dynamics of criminal case processing. Russell Wheeler and Howard Whitcomb, *Judicial Administration: Text and Readings* (1977), treats the history of the court reform movement and contains a relatively complete bibliography of items on limited-jurisdiction courts.

[*See also* STATE COURT SYSTEMS.]

THE CRIMINAL JUSTICE SYSTEM

Herbert Jacob

THE criminal justice process is marked by five characteristics. First, it consists of many closely interconnected segments and may be thought of as a system in which one part affects every other. These segments also enjoy a high degree of autonomy; thus, the second characteristic is fragmentation. Third, all major participants in the process enjoy a high degree of discretion in making their decisions. That discretion is in every case limited by the fourth characteristic, an intricate set of legal rules. Fifth, the process is marked by intense conflict between two sets of competing values. On the one hand, a lively distrust of governmental authority pervades the process and displays itself in elaborate rights for those accused of crime; on the other hand, criminal justice officials feel a strong commitment toward promoting public safety by dealing swiftly and, if necessary, harshly with those who have committed crimes. These five characteristics are evident in every phase of the criminal justice process. Before exploring the separate elements of the process, we shall briefly discuss each of these fundamental characteristics.

First, the criminal justice process consists of many segments that are connected to each other in intricate ways. The police, prosecutors, defense counsel, courts, judges, and prisons each respond to actions one of the others undertakes; their actions affect, and are affected by, every other element of the criminal justice process. For instance, although the police are responsible for making arrests, they sometimes modify their actions to accommodate pressure from prosecutors and judges who want them to direct their energies toward different types of crimes or to observe legal technicalities more carefully. These modifications may entail, for example, a shift in police attentions from prostitution to illegal gambling, or the exercise of greater diligence in obtaining search warrants. And although prisons are filled through court convictions, judges ration prison sentences when penitentiary facilities become overcrowded. The systems metaphor has become the conventional way to conceptualize the criminal justice process since the President's Commission on Law Enforcement and Administration of Justice adopted it in its report in 1967. Yet it remains mostly a metaphor. Scholars rarely succeed in examining the entire set of interrelationships. Most research on the criminal justice process focuses on single segments, with some attention being paid to their links to other elements of the system.

Second, the system paradigm is difficult to execute, because the criminal justice process is in reality only a loosely coupled system of many autonomous fragments. Most criminal justice agencies operate with independent grants of authority based on a statute or constitutional provision. For instance, elected mayors usually control the police, but they have little influence and no control over prosecutors, judges, and prisons. Similarly, judges only control their own bailiwick, the courtroom, but they have no control over police, prosecutors, or prisons. The same is true of prosecutors and prison administrators. There is no true hierarchy among criminal justice agencies; one is not the superior of others, but all are more or less coequal. Moreover, every institution exists in triplicate—at the local, state, and national levels. No other large nation has such a decentralized, fragmented criminal justice system as the United States. Nevertheless, these agencies constitute a loosely coupled system because they remain interdependent.

527

Third, decisions to invoke the law must fit an enormous array of situations. For instance, while the police have rules governing the firing of handguns, every officer must make a split-second judgment when confronted with a dangerous situation on the street about whether the rule governs. Such judgmental decisions permeate the criminal justice process. Officials constantly must use their judgment to determine whether to invoke a rule or to choose among alternative rules. Many such discretionary decisions are barely visible to outside observers and often are scarcely checked by higher authorities. Thus, the process entails a high degree of discretion.

Fourth, law dominates the criminal justice process in the United States. It limits allowable discretion, and sometimes it may override discretionary decisions. The rule of law in criminal proceedings is reinforced in the United States by the deep commitment to it by the principal decision-makers in the process, all of whom are lawyers: prosecuting and defense attorneys, judges, and the legal counselors of the police and prisons. These officials do not view the law as a mere technicality that hinders appropriate action. Rather, they are usually imbued with the lawyer's view that constitutional rights establish overriding obligations.

Finally, a constant tension between individual rights and community protection marks the criminal justice process. On the one hand, an elaborate set of procedures has been designed to protect the rights of persons accused of crimes. Those procedures seek to protect persons against self-incrimination and unfair police practices and require that the accused be allowed to face their accusers at trial. These and other safeguards are usually encompassed in the term *due process of law*. On the other hand, every important criminal justice official feels the heat of public opinion and the public's fear of crime. Public opinion polls often reveal a desire for safer streets and better protection of private property. Officials fear being accused of coddling criminals. Consequently, the criminal justice process is constantly engaged in seeking to balance two conflicting values: maintaining defendant's rights and promoting public safety.

These five characteristics will be evident in our discussion of the separate elements of the criminal justice process. The process itself consists of six parts. First, laws must be passed that define which acts are to be considered criminal.

Second, someone must commit such an act. Third, the police must intervene and label the act as illegal and press charges against the perpetrator. Fourth, a prosecutor must decide to take these charges to a court for adjudication. Fifth, the court must decide on the innocence or guilt of the alleged offender. Sixth, if the court convicts, the offender is punished, often with some form of incarceration in a jail or prison. The remainder of this article will examine each of these segments and show how the overriding characteristics pervade each of them.

THE ADOPTION OF CRIMINAL LAWS

Congress may pass criminal laws effective for the entire nation, but most criminal laws in the United States are the product of the legislatures of the fifty states and are valid only within each state's borders. In addition, local legislative bodies, such as city councils and county boards, enact ordinances defining minor offenses for their jurisdictions. No empirical study has encompassed all three of these levels of lawmaking.

Criminal laws are complex, providing many opportunities for legislative tinkering as well as for fundamental policy shifts. Criminal codes in the first instance define activities that are considered illegal. That, however, is not enough. They may also need to define the persons who are prohibited from engaging in the activities, the occasions on which activity is prohibited, and the circumstances in which it is outlawed. Finally, the penalty must be specified. Consider, for instance, killing. All killing is not criminal. A soldier may kill at the front line; mentally ill persons may not be convicted of killing if their lawyers can prove that they did not know what they were doing. Penalties may vary with the particular mix of characteristics that happen to exist. The penalty is greater for intentional killing than for accidental deaths. It may be different for killings committed by adults and those committed by youths. It may be different if committed with a weapon than with a car.

Another example is the crime of carrying a concealed weapon. The law must first define which weapons are to be included (rifles as well as handguns; pocket knives as well as daggers). It must distinguish between persons who carry weapons as part of their trade, such as policemen and bank guards, and those for whom carrying concealed weapons is illegal. It must distinguish places where weapons are carried, differentiating between hunters in the field and criminals in urban alleyways. It may distinguish between minors and adults. Once more, a whole range of penalties may be provided in order to accommodate varying circumstances.

Since World War II, state legislators have adopted many minor and major changes in their state's criminal codes. One major change has been legislative attention to "the drug problem," which has been exhibited in many ways. Laws have been revised to include entirely new narcotic substances. In many states, legislatures have mandated harsh sentences for narcotics suppliers and sometimes for users. On the other hand, possession of small quantities of marijuana has been decriminalized by some state legislatures. Legislatures have not treated all narcotic substances in identical ways. They have paid no attention to caffeine or nicotine abuse. Alcohol abuse in the form of public drunkenness has been decriminalized in most states, although drunk driving has attracted increasingly severe penalties.

Another area of major legislative action has involved the adoption of laws that constrain the discretion of judges when they hand out sentences to persons convicted of crimes. The range of prison time that can be given has been severely limited in many states, with some adopting "flat," or determinate, sentences and other states adopting legislatively mandated sentencing guidelines that specify not only the range of discretion but also the factors that may be considered in exercising that discretion. Those actions reflected a loss of confidence in the possibility of rehabilitating offenders. Prison increasingly became considered an instrument of punishment rather than an opportunity to rehabilitate. Consequently, legislatures have deprived both judges and parole officials of much of their discretion to alter sentences on the basis of prisoner behavior.

These and other changes in criminal law were the product of the intricate play of political forces. An important factor in determining the content of legislation and the time of its adoption was the interplay of interest groups in state legislatures. Law enforcement agencies and their officials often played a prominent role in lobbying for changes in criminal codes. Arrayed against them were groups representing defense attorneys and civil liberties groups, such as the American Civil Liberties Union (ACLU). Occasionally, a dominating personality such as Harry J. Anslinger, a long-term commissioner of the Federal Bureau of Narcotics, seemed to have a substantial impact on the development of the law. Political parties had notably little interest in such legislation, with the legislative coalition in favor of or opposed to particular changes usually crossing party lines. However, during the 1960s and 1970s, Republicans on the national level were widely perceived to be more concerned about "law and order" than their Democratic rivals and Republican administrations generally provided more national funds for law enforcement activities than their Democratic counterparts.

Legislative changes in state criminal codes appeared to reflect general unease in the American population about the rise in official crime rates that characterized most of the period between the end of World War II and the late 1970s. However, no direct relationship existed between changes in the official crime rate and the adoption of changes in the criminal code. The existence of model laws and exemplars appears to have been important in the legislative process. For instance, the prominent abandonment of indeterminate sentences by California in 1976 played a large role in convincing other state legislatures to reconsider their own state's commitment to such practices. The Uniform Controlled Substances Act, as proposed by the National Conference of Commissioners on Uniform State Laws, also was influential in the adoption of revised narcotics laws by the states in the 1970s.

A major result of legislative revision of state codes and of city-council actions regarding ordinances was to reduce the variability of criminal law in the United States. Provisions of the criminal code still vary considerably from place to place, but the differences were narrowed during the thirty years before 1978. Their administration, however, continued to show great diversity from place to place.

CRIMINAL BEHAVIOR

The effect of criminal law depends in the first instance upon the behavior of violators. While it is true that without criminal acts, there is no crime, the relation between law and criminal behavior is at best a subtle one.

Crime and *criminals* are generic terms, for they include a wide variety of phenomena. In a technical sense, a crime is any act that violates a law that provides for criminal sanctions such as a fine or imprisonment. It not only includes common offenses such as murder, assault, and theft but also the sale and use of some narcotics (but not all), "unnatural" sex acts, gambling in certain circumstances, and the pollution of air and water. Scholars commonly distinguish between three categories of crimes: those involving violence and principally directed against persons; those principally aimed at property; and so-called victimless crimes, in which the "victim" (for instance, the buyer in a drug transaction) is a willing participant. According to the 1984 Uniform Crime Reports, property crimes known to the police are more common than violent crimes, by a ratio of approximately 8 to 1. However, violent crimes are generally more feared and considered more serious by the general public than are property or victimless crimes.

Another important distinction separates crimes committed calculatingly and those committed as the result of uncontrolled passion. Calculating crimes are often considered to be instrumental in the sense that they are planned and the result of a calculation that the gain is likely to outweigh the cost. Many crimes against property fall into this category; they are committed in order to enrich the offender. In contrast, other crimes occur on the spur of the moment as the result of anger or unexpected opportunity. They are often committed while under the influence of alcohol. Many violent crimes fall into this category.

The law is likely to have a greater direct deterrent effect on instrumental crimes. When legislatures impose severe penalties on some actions, they may deter calculating offenders because the possible costs have been raised far beyond the expected benefit. However, most of those who commit crimes unthinkingly will not be deterred. Nevertheless, laws may create a deterrent climate indirectly by stigmatizing certain actions and mobilizing social pressures to prevent illegal actions.

Deterrence is also considered to be the result of the probability of swift enforcement. Criminals in the United States face a low likelihood of arrest and imprisonment and can often count on long delays between arrest (when it comes) and punishment (if it comes).

Much controversy exists over the real deterrent potential of law. Most of the research has centered on the deterrent effect of the death penalty on homicides. Some researchers, most notably Ehrlich, believe that they have detected a substantial deterrent effect; many others doubt it (Blumstein, Cohen, and Nagel). In any case, one would expect less deterrent effect for homicides, which are mostly committed in the heat of passion, than for burglary and theft, which are often planned. However, even property crimes are not prevented by extraordinary safeguards and harsh laws, as can be inferred from the regular occurrence of bank robberies, a serious federal offense that usually leads to arrest, conviction, and imprisonment.

Persons committing crimes represent a broad spectrum of the American population. Most are men, although the participation of women in crime has increased since World War II. Most are youthful; involvement in crime drops markedly when people get beyond their mid-thirties. Many are minorities; the proportion of known offenders who are black is much larger than their share of the general population. Most, but not all, identified offenders have low incomes and poor educations. Some are career criminals in the sense that they do little else for a living. However, a substantial number of offenders are moonlighters; they hold full-time jobs in the legitimate world, but when they need additional cash or when an unusual opportunity beckons, they rob or burglarize. We possess little reliable information about these patterns of behavior because our knowledge rests entirely on research about criminals who have been caught and are studied in prison. More successful criminals may possess quite different characteristics.

For most of the period following World War II, official crime rates rose sharply in the United States, despite harsher criminal laws. In the late 1970s, official crime rates began to drop. According to many criminologists, this drop in the official crime rates may be the result of a decline in the number of youths in the American population. However, it is very difficult to draw any firm conclusions about the rise and fall of official crime rates, because they are calculated on unreliable data.

Two sources exist in the United States for counting crime. The most widely used is the count of offenses known to the police made by the Federal Bureau of Investigation (FBI) and published annually under the title *Uniform Crime Reports*. Although the FBI and other agencies have vigorously sought to standardize these counts, they remain dependent on factors that are beyond their control. These factors are of two kinds. The first are the habits of citizens in calling the police when something that might be a crime has occurred. Citizens call the police only in the minority of such occurrences, although the proportion varies by kind of offense, apparently being higher in violent crimes than in property crimes. People have a variety of reasons for not calling the police. Some do not trust the police; many believe that no benefit will come from reporting an offense. There is reason to believe that the number of people reporting crimes may have risen during the period that official crime rates rose, because new telecommunications technologies (such as the simple 911 telephone number to reach the police) came into widespread use and dramatically increased the calls for service received by the police.

The second factor affecting the reliability of official crime rates is the manner in which police record offenses. Some cities have been known to be much more lax than others, with the result that changes in recording practices have periodically produced substantial jumps in city crime rates. For instance, in Chicago a television station discovered that the police were "unfounding" about one-third of all crimes originally recorded by patrol officers, thereby artificially reducing the city's crime rate. That practice was halted in 1983, but for that year Chicago was excluded from the FBI's crime statistics. Consequently, an unknown but substantial error exists in official crime rates. Small differences between cities or from one year to the next are as likely to be the result of changes in counting practices as they are to reflect changes in criminal behavior.

The second source for crime statistics in the United States is the annual victimization survey conducted by the Census Bureau and known as the National Crime Survey. The survey identifies victimizations by asking a random sample of residents in the United States whether anything that might be considered a crime happened to them during the previous six months. It also suffers from problems. It does not cover such crimes as homicide, where the victim obviously cannot be interviewed, or victimless crimes, where the ostensible victim will not report his own behavior. It is likely to be unreliable for offenses where the assailant is a relative or friend, as in the case of child or spouse abuse. The most serious shortcoming of the National Crime Survey, however, is that it provides information only about the nation as a whole and not for individual cities, where most law enforcement activities occur and are controlled.

Because crime statistics are inherently unreliable, it is very difficult to discern whether harsher laws or more vigorous law enforcement makes a difference. It appears that many policymakers disregard the unreliability of the statistics. When crime rates rise, they point with alarm to that statistic; when rates fall, they point with pride to their past efforts to pass harsher laws or to provide more funds for law enforcement activities.

THE POLICE

The application of criminal laws depends almost entirely on local police in the United States. Police activity responds to many factors within the criminal justice process and outside it.

Discretion is the key characteristic of police actions. The police are in fact first-instance judges of the citizen actions they encounter. If a police officer thinks citizen behavior warrants an arrest, he sets in motion the criminal justice process, from which the alleged offender cannot escape without considerable trouble and cost. If a police officer decides to ignore the behavior or deal with it by some action short of an arrest or summons, no one is likely to second-guess that decision, and the citizen will escape all the consequences of being accused of a crime.

These discretionary powers are routinely exercised by officers with little legal training and no immediate supervision. Unlike judges, police officers are not graduates of law school; many are only high school graduates. Their police academy training covers only the rudiments of criminal law. They work out of sight of their immediate supervisors. When they encounter a situation on their beat, they must immediately make decisions on which their lives and the lives of bystanders sometimes hinge. Consequently, although patrol officers are the foot soldiers of the police, they work with considerable autonomy and make many discretionary decisions.

The police officer's discretion is affected by many elements of his or her environment. Some of those elements expand or support police discretion; many of them constrain it. The most important of them include the degree of citizen involvement, the requirements imposed by courts, the political environment, the available technology, and the degree of professionalization.

In some situations the police are fully in charge, while in others they depend on citizen initiative to involve them. The difference is one between "proactive" and "reactive" police patrolling. When the police engage in proactive patrol, they search for violations and themselves initiate any action. Typical proactive activities involve "sting" operations, such as when the police open a fencing operation to trap burglars into selling their stolen goods before hidden cameras, which will lead to their later arrest. Many narcotics investigations depend on proactive undercover operations in which police officers act the role of drug dealers in order to obtain evidence against real narcotics traffickers. Proactive policing is particularly important for combating victimless crimes because such offenses usually occur with the compliance of those who are victimized. Few outside constraints govern proactive patrolling. The police determine their target and the means for snaring their prey. Only after an arrest has been made do external constraints begin to impose themselves on the results of proactive patrolling.

Reactive patrolling, by contrast, depends on the cooperation of ordinary citizens. It is triggered by a call from either the victim or a bystander. Police have little choice about responding to such calls, because they risk severe public criticism if they ignore a call that turns out to have involved a serious crime. When the police respond, they encounter citizens, who must be accommodated. Although the police retain discretion founded on their authority and expertise, they must also often justify its use to those who called them to the situation. Consequently, they may make an arrest when confronted with disorder, to mollify neighbors, even though they might prefer to handle the situation through a

warning. However, in many instances, they cannot make an arrest, for the simple reason that the offender has already escaped because the victim delayed in calling the police. For instance, a householder who finds his house burglarized often conducts a search of the premises himself and then confers with neighbors before calling the police. Such a delay, even when it takes only half an hour, usually makes it impossible for the police to find the burglar. In reactive policing, the police are also constrained by social relationships in the situation. Being themselves mostly of working-class or lower-middle-class origins, they tend to treat the poor with brusque authority and the rich with inordinate respect. Finally, they cannot ignore the interpretation that citizens have imprinted on the situation to which they are called. If the caller considers the matter a very serious one, police have difficulty in downgrading it. Thus, reactive patrolling places many more constraints on the use of police discretion than does proactive patrolling.

The choice between proactive and reactive patrolling is to a large degree dictated by the resources of a police department and its technology. Since the mid-1960s, most large police departments have installed communications systems that permit citizens to call the police quickly and easily through the installation of the 911 telephone number. That has greatly increased the number of calls for service. Most departments have not obtained commensurate increases in resources, so that patrol time that might once have been devoted to proactive patrol now must be committed to reacting to calls for service.

Police behavior is also subject to constraints of the law as interpreted by the courts. During the 1960s the United States Supreme Court issued a series of decisions intended to control abuse of police discretion. One set of decisions was based on the Fourth Amendment's prohibition of illegal searches and seizures. In *Mapp* v. *Ohio* (1961), the Court extended the exclusionary rule, which had already applied to federal courts, to state courts. That rule required the exclusion of evidence in criminal trials if it was illegally seized. In practice, the exclusionary rule required a police officer to obtain a search warrant from a judge before searching for evidence or seizing it. To obtain a search warrant, police officers had to show reliable evidence of a probable crime, thus sharing discretion with judges. The number of situations covered by *Mapp* and subsequent rulings of the Supreme Court has been the subject of continuing controversy. The fact that searches and seizures are the object of continuing litigation indicates that police compliance with these rulings has been far from complete. Searches and seizures, however, do not apply equally to all crimes. They are most important in narcotics and weapons offenses; they are rarely invoked in crimes of violence or ordinary property crimes. Thomas Davies suggests that the bulk of empirical evidence collected seems to indicate that compliance with the exclusionary rule has not substantially reduced the number of persons convicted of crime.

A second set of court rules involves the interpretation of the Fifth Amendment's prohibition against involuntary self-incrimination. The police may not force a person to testify against himself. The Supreme Court in *Miranda* v. *Arizona* (1966) extended this rule by requiring that police warn persons whom they arrest that anything they say may be held against them and by forbidding police interrogation until the detained person has been informed of his right to obtain a lawyer and, if he or she wants an attorney, until the lawyer has arrived and is present during the questioning. This has led to the formulation of the "*Miranda* warning," which almost all police officers now read to persons whom they arrest. As with the exclusionary rule, the *Miranda* warning has constrained police discretion by forcing the police to share the questioning of suspects with defense attorneys. The warning has reduced the number of spontaneous, "voluntary" confessions, but because few convictions depend entirely on confessions, it, like the exclusionary rule, has not substantially reduced the number of convictions obtained after an arrest.

The exclusionary rule and the *Miranda* warning are only two examples of the ways in which the criminal law attempts to control police discretion. They operate only to control abuse of the arresting power of the police. If the police abuse their discretion by not intervening in some situations, the courts rarely intervene.

The political environment might be thought to constitute the most appropriate constraint on inactivity by the police, as well as affording additional constraints on the active abuse of police powers. In fact, it does not consistently do so.

One reason is that the police are not centrally controlled. Control over the police in the United States is scattered among thousands of municipalities, counties, states, and federal agencies. In most metropolitan areas, dozens of police agencies vie with each other. It is not easy for the public to identify the official they should hold responsible for police actions; public officials often cannot control police who violate priorities and standards.

In addition, city politics are themselves too diffuse to render effective control over the police in many cities. Although the police chief is often a key mayoral appointee, in many cities a city manager appoints the chief. Control over the police budget is shared with the city council. However, the principal obstacle to effective political control over police activities is the obscurity of most police operations. Knowledge of police operations comes mostly from the police department itself.

Police departments cannot be readily penetrated. They are often more autonomous than other city agencies because the police are a socially isolated group operating under a quasi-military discipline. Police harbor an intense distrust of "civilians." Consequently, they have worked hard and successfully in avoiding the establishment of civilian review boards that might investigate and punish instances of police abuses. In addition, supervisory personnel are almost entirely recruited from the department itself or from similar departments in other cities.

Therefore, although a mayor or city-manager appointee, the chief is usually the only political appointee in the department and is still more representative of the department than of the political leadership of the city. Police departments that avoid major scandals usually evade political supervision.

Still another factor affecting the exercise of police discretion is the technology employed by the police. Two characteristics of American police forces have particularly strong effects on the use of patrol discretion. The first is the deployment of most patrol officers in motor vehicles. Few patrol on foot. Their use of cars insulates patrol officers from citizens. It would also insulate them from supervisors, were it not for another technology—sophisticated radio communications systems. Radio systems permit supervisors to contact patrol officers in their cars

THE CRIMINAL JUSTICE SYSTEM

and direct them to locations where they are needed. The radio may even allow headquarters to keep silent track of the location of police cruisers. Consequently, the command echelon of the police can direct the deployment of their officers, but that fact does not yet permit control over officers' actions when they have stepped out of their cars.

Finally, increasing professionalization of the police has both increased their autonomy and subjected them to a new set of external standards. The more the police manage to convey an impression of possessing arcane skills and professional ethics, the more they can resist control by civilians and politicians. On the other hand, professional ethics themselves may constrain use of police discretion. Thus far, few instances of internal professional control exist among American police forces. Professionalization has usually meant resistance to political control by increasing the civil service protection available to police officers and opposition to the creation of civilian review boards.

CRIMINAL COURTS

After the police have made an arrest, the case moves to the courts. However, police share control over access to the courts with prosecutors. Together the police and prosecutors may be considered the gatekeepers of the criminal courts.

Except for minor offenses (such as traffic violations), where the police act in the prosecutorial role, police charges must be brought into the courts by prosecutors. Once prosecutors have decided to accept some version of the police charges, the criminal prosecution process begins. Prosecutors play a major role in the process, but it is not dominated by any single participant. At various decision points, defense counsel, defendants, judges, and jurors exercise considerable influence over the proceedings. Rarely can a single participant ramrod a verdict through the criminal courts; rather, verdicts of innocence or guilt are the product of intricate interactions between these participants.

To clarify the criminal justice process, we will examine each participant separately. However, their close dependence upon each other needs to be kept in mind.

Prosecutors. Every criminal courtroom in the United States except those handling the most minor matters has a prosecutor assigned to it. These prosecutors, however, are not part of a single hierarchy. They work for different superiors with different policies and priorities.

When a federal police agency, such as the FBI, charges someone with violating a federal criminal statute, the offender is brought to a federal magistrate and prosecution is brought by a federal prosecutor, the United States attorney, before the federal district court. United States attorneys are presidential political appointees who must be confirmed by the United States Senate, just as federal judges must be. They serve for a term of four years and generally resign when a new president takes office. Consequently, federal prosecutors are usually aligned with the party controlling the White House. The office is a patronage appointment. However, United States attorneys operate under the bureaucratic control of the Department of Justice, which controls their budgets and guides their actions. These prosecutors generally handle routine violations of federal laws, such as narcotics probes; prosecution of labor-law violations; interstate crime, such as racketeering and kidnappings; and tax fraud. Unusually important or sensitive prosecutions, such as those involving prominent officials or crimes affecting national security, may not be initiated without approval from Washington.

Because the office of United States attorney is under presidential patronage and has the potential for focusing public attention on official corruption as well as on routine crimes, it possesses considerable visibility and prestige. Appointees usually have close political connections with congressional as well as executive party leaders. They often later seek high elective office themselves. Because of the high prestige of the office, United States attorneys also frequently succeed in recruiting extremely able young attorneys as their assistants. In many places, the office has a very large staff of attorneys, many of whom serve for only a few years before moving on to private-sector legal positions.

When local police bring charges against someone for violating state or local criminal statutes, they do not take those charges to the federal court or to the United States attorney. Rather, they go to local criminal courts and local

THE CRIMINAL JUSTICE SYSTEM

prosecutors, who operate independently of the United States attorneys. In most areas prosecutors are county officials elected on a partisan ballot for a term of four years. In only a few states do they serve larger areas than counties or are chosen by some method other than election. Such county prosecutors—usually holding the title of state's attorney or district attorney—handle the bulk of police arrests. There are many more state's attorneys offices than United States attorneys. Many operate in rural areas with part-time personnel. In metropolitan areas, however, the local prosecutor's offices are large, full-time, professional establishments. In many cities, they rival in size the largest private law firms and the United States attorney's office. Most of the staff consists of assistant prosecutors who are appointed in most jurisdictions through a civil service examination system.

While the elected prosecutor in a large office is almost always an important political figure in his locale, assistants are usually anonymous civil servants or beginning lawyers. Young attorneys seek appointment to the local prosecutor's office because it provides good trial experience and a way to begin a legal career if the lawyer has not succeeded in obtaining a position in a private law firm. For many assistants the prosecutor's office is only the first step of their legal career. They remain in the office just long enough to obtain a better position. Consequently, assistant prosecutors often work hard to build good reputations among local lawyers, with an eye toward getting an offer to join a local firm. Such rewards are as significant for young assistants as those offered through internal promotions in the prosecutor's office.

The local prosecutor's office is not part of a larger bureaucratic hierarchy, as is the United States attorney's office. Each state's attorney is accountable only to the electorate. No superior office formulates policy or priorities for an entire state, and important cases are not referred to some superior officer. In terms of formal authority, the local prosecutor is an independent official who does not need to coordinate actions with local police, local judges, or the United States attorney.

Nevertheless, many informal forces lead to considerable collaboration between prosecutors and the police. They have a common interest in controlling crime. The police depend upon prosecutors to convict those whom they arrest, and prosecutors rely on the police to collect evidence that they need for successful prosecutions.

Circumstances constantly force police and prosecutors to respond to each other. The largest police department in a jurisdiction generally controls the prosecutor's work load. That means that it not only sets the number of cases that prosecutors process, but it also determines the kinds of cases that prosecutors must handle. The most serious charges simply arise because the crimes have been committed. But even with such serious charges as murder, police and prosecutors have discretion to charge intentional homicide or accidental manslaughter. In most cases, charges can be upgraded or downgraded by the police. When the police regard them as serious incidents, they place a greater burden on the prosecutor. When they treat incidents as minor crimes, the prosecutor's office can handle them with less effort.

The police also control the quality of the evidence with which prosecutors must work. Most evidence is collected at the crime scene by the responding officers. They take down the names of eyewitnesses and gather physical evidence, such as shell casings, guns, narcotics substances, or stolen goods. When the prosecutor receives these bits of evidence a few days or weeks later, it is usually impossible to supplement them. Much of the prosecutor's success depends on the quality of initial police work. When police are thorough and careful, the task of the prosecutor is eased. However, if the police miss significant pieces of evidence, make mistakes in recording the names and addresses of witnesses, or are careless in handling the evidence, so that it cannot be clearly linked with the offender, the prosecutor may be unable to obtain a conviction. This organizational interdependence sometimes leads to conflict as when the police and prosecutor exchange charges of incompetence. On the one hand, the police often do not appreciate the need for attention to the details of evidence collection; they generally dislike the paperwork required. It is often more important to them to control offenders or victims at the scene of the crime. On the other hand, prosecutors have little sense of the situation on the street but must face the threat of a courtroom challenge to the evidence they must present to a judge. Consequently, although the police and prosecutor normally work together, they often do so with considerable tension.

Constituency differences between the two agencies add to those tensions. One significant difference in constituency is geographical. Police serve municipalities that usually are much smaller than the county. Prosecutors work with police from cities and towns with varying degrees of commitment toward combating the kinds of crime that the prosecutor's office is presently targeting. Neither a mayor (or the police chief) nor the prosecutor can set law enforcement priorities for the entire community. The mayor may be most concerned about vice, while the prosecutor may see child abuse as the number-one priority. In such an instance, the police may find that the vice arrests they make get dismissed by the prosecutor's office but the prosecutor tries to obtain indictments about child abuse through office-based investigations. Another source of conflict lies in the different electoral base of mayors (who control the police) and prosecutors. It is not unusual for the mayor of a large city to be the political rival of the prosecutor serving the same area. They occasionally try to embarrass each other with charges of inefficiency or corruption.

Another potent source of conflict between police and prosecutors lies in their social and intellectual roots. Police generally come from working-class and lower-middle-class backgrounds and possess at most a college education. Most prosecutors come from middle- or upper-middle-class backgrounds and have a law school education in addition to their college degrees. Prosecutors are always lawyers and have the lawyer's respect for judicial procedures and legal technicalities, matters that simply seem irksome to many police officers. Moreover, while police officers must deal with the reality of life on the street, prosecutors must deal with the reality of life in the courtroom. Thus, they begin with different perceptions of what is proper and necessary and respond to different imperatives.

The first task facing the prosecutor is to determine whether to accept the charges brought by the police. The prosecutor's mandate in the United States is to see that justice is done. That means that prosecutors must dismiss charges if evidence is insufficient. Alternatively, prosecutors may alter the charges originally brought by the police so that they accord more closely to the situation as reflected by police reports and the evidence forwarded to the prosecutor. Consequently, prosecutors enjoy enormous discretion. That discretion is exercised by decisions to change charges and to drop charges as well as to control the speed with which charges are processed.

If a prosecutor decides to proceed, formal charges are drawn up. The defendant is then notified of the charges before a judge. That hearing, called an arraignment, must generally take place within twenty-four hours after the defendant's arrest. At arraignment, the defendant is notified of the formal charges and is given an opportunity to obtain legal counsel and to post bail. Both are crucial to the later outcome of the case. As we shall see below, defendants may have several choices about which defense attorneys will represent them. The bail decision determines whether a defendant awaits the outcome of the case in jail or at home.

Prosecutors play a major role in the bail decision. The level of bail ordinarily is closely related to the seriousness of the charge facing a defendant. Consequently, when prosecutors decide on a charge, they also influence the range of bail that might be set. In addition, prosecutors normally make specific recommendations about bail, which in many instances influence the presiding judicial officer. Bail is usually an amount of money that the defendant must post (or get someone else like a bail bondsman to post) before he or she may be released from jail. However, in some instances, defendants are released on their own recognizance (known as an ROR release) on the basis of their roots in the community. Usually, ROR defendants have lived a long time at their current address, are married, have a job, and do not possess long arrest records. While the prosecutor's recommendations about bail do not always prevail, they usually receive serious consideration. Thus, the prosecutor has considerable influence over whether defendants are free or sit in jail while awaiting their trial. Defendants who await disposition of their case in jail are in fact punished before trial and are seriously disadvantaged in their attempts to defend themselves.

When the charges are minor (usually called misdemeanors), trials occur almost immediately after arraignment and usually end with guilty pleas. Elaborate plea bargaining rarely occurs in such matters. Sentence is pronounced by the presiding judge—but once again, the prosecutor plays an important role in recommending a sentence. In these cases, as Feeley has shown for New Haven, Connecticut, the prosecutor and police possess inordinate influence because their joint decision about the charge against a defendant usually determines the punishment. Relatively few defendants contest minor charges; an overwhelming proportion result in a conviction resulting from the defendant's guilty plea.

Prosecutors exercise less influence when serious charges are involved, because the procedure is more elaborate and involves other participants more actively. In serious cases (called felonies), prosecutors must generally first demonstrate that probable cause exists to believe that a crime has been committed and that the defendant committed it. Probable cause is a lighter burden of proof than the standard of "beyond a reasonable doubt," which is ultimately required for conviction. However, prosecutors must present sufficient evidence to a judge in a preliminary hearing or to a grand jury to meet the standard of probable cause. Failure to do so means that the charge will be dismissed. Such dismissals are a common outcome for criminal charges because prosecutors find that they lack sufficient proof to proceed further. That occurs when an eyewitness fails to identify the defendant in the courtroom, when a complaining witness decides not to testify, or when the powder the police seized on the assumption that it was heroin turns out to be sugar. The preliminary hearing requires prosecutors to share decision-making with police, witnesses, defense counsel, and judge. Unless the coordinated effort of all of these leads to a ruling of probable cause, the charges are dismissed.

Dismissal of charges does not mean that the person involved escapes without punishment. The arrest, the loss of time, the expense of defense (even at this stage), and the embarrassment of being involved in a criminal proceeding may be a substantial price for whatever behavior led the police to make the initial arrest. In all but extreme cases of police harassment, persons whose charges are dismissed have no possibility of recovering damages or costs incurred.

When prosecutors have obtained a ruling that probable cause exists, the case proceeds to a trial. However, few cases actually get to trial.

Most are plea-bargained. In exchange for a guilty plea by the defendant, prosecutors may promise to dismiss some charges (when multiple charges face the defendant), reduce the charge upon which the guilty plea is made, or make a recommendation for a sentence that might be more lenient than that which might be given after a trial. As Eisenstein and Jacob have shown, negotiations leading to guilty pleas take place in a variety of conditions. In some jurisdictions, all such negotiations are centralized in a single bureau of the prosecutor's office. Cases routinely flow through that bureau. The attorneys who work there do nothing but negotiate plea bargains with defense counsel. In other jurisdictions, bargains are struck in the courtroom, in adjoining hallways, or in the judge's chambers. A much larger portion of the prosecutor's office is involved when the negotiations are decentralized. Even judges may be explicitly drawn into the negotiations.

In all plea negotiations prosecutors hold the controlling cards. They do so because they possess more information about the offense than anyone else in the negotiations. Prosecutors possess the police report and have information about the prior record of the defendant. They also have the results of any interrogations conducted by the police or prosecutor. Defense counsel may obtain similar information, but in ordinary cases they do not have sufficient funds to finance independent investigations. Moreover, the prosecutor's information has the authority and imprimatur of the police, while the defense counsel's information usually consists of undocumented assertions by defendants and their friends or relatives, assertions that can easily be depicted as being self-serving.

Plea negotiations usually proceed informally. No one testifies under oath; no one is cross-examined. Rather, prosecutors typically present a narrative description of the incident and give their characterization of the defendant. Defense counsel then attempt to counter some or all of the assertions made by the prosecutor. When judges participate, they may hasten agreement by suggesting particular sentence or charge reduction, an arrangement that carries the weight of prior approval by the judge. Even with judicial participation, however, prosecutors retain their dominant position in plea negotiations. Defendants rarely join these negotiations. Only after an agreement is struck must the defense counsel present it to the defendant for his or her approval.

If a bargain is struck and the defendant agrees to it, the accused pleads guilty and is sentenced accordingly. If no bargain is reached, a trial must be held. At trial the dominant position of the prosecutor is diminished by the larger role that defense counsel, witnesses, and judges play.

Defense Counsel. The conventional view of the criminal justice process puts defense counsel on an equal plane with prosecutors. Defense attorneys are, in that view, simply the defense counterparts of the prosecuting team. In reality, however, substantial differences exist between the resources and roles of defense lawyers and prosecuting attorneys.

Whereas all prosecutors are members of a government office, only some defense attorneys are. Defendants in the United States may be represented by attorneys from various sources. If defendants can afford to pay legal fees, they must hire their own private lawyer. In practice, the means test imposed is whether the defendant can afford to make bail. Many courts require that defendants who can afford to buy their pretrial liberty by making bail must also pay for their own attorney. In some jurisdictions, that arrangement is promoted by directing the bail refund (when the case is finished) directly to the attorney rather than to the defendant. Attorneys hired by defendants vary considerably in their characteristics. Most come from small partnerships or individual practices rather than from large law firms. Many are attorneys who hang out around criminal courts to seek clients from among those just arraigned. Such defense attorneys are particularly expert in the folkways of the courthouse, even though they may not be highly sophisticated in legal doctrine. Since they normally defend routine accusations of common crimes, their organizational expertise is often quite appropriate to the task. They ordinarily take cases for set fees (called retainers), which they often require in advance. Such payment up front is important to these lawyers because clients who are convicted and sent to prison (and most are) usually cannot and will not pay their fee.

Many defendants cannot afford a private attorney. If they win pretrial release, they do so on personal recognizance rather than on a mone-

tary bail payment. Under Supreme Court decisions dating from *Gideon* v. *Wainwright* in 1963, almost all defendants must be offered an attorney if they cannot afford to retain one themselves. Most use their opportunity. Such lawyers come from two sources. In some jurisdictions, the trial court assigns private attorneys to defend the accused with the county or state paying their fee. Those fees are generally less than the going rate charged by private attorneys. In some places, every attorney must take such cases when his or her turn comes up. In most places, however, attorneys volunteer to accept these cases. Some of these attorneys are young lawyers just beginning their practice and eager for some paying cases and experience; others are courthouse regulars who also take many paying clients.

Defense attorneys may also be provided by the public defender's office. Public defenders are government employees funded from local taxes and supervised by the court or by the county board. In most cases, the chief public defender is appointed, as are the other members of the office. Only in a few jurisdictions does the public defender run for election like the prosecuting attorney. The public defender's office rarely offers the political advantages of the prosecutor's office. Defense of accused criminals is often an unpopular task; a successful office boasting a high acquittal rate is unlikely to obtain favorable public notice. Consequently, the office attracts fewer politically ambitious lawyers. In many places, it is an alternative to the prosecutor's office for young lawyers who want a steady income and an opportunity to develop the skills and contacts needed to develop a private trial practice. Assistants in the public defender's office, like those in the prosecutor's, are mostly civil service appointees who serve for three to five years before moving on to a private legal career.

Defense attorneys work with far more meager resources than the prosecutor's office. Whereas the police serve as a rich source of information for prosecutors, defense counsel have no counterpart. In most routine cases they conduct no independent investigation of the incident that led to the arrest of their client. Rather, defense attorneys generally rely on the same police reports that the prosecutor holds. They obtain those reports from the prosecutor rather than directly from the police. Often they only gain access to the reports just before trial, and thus, there is insufficient time to resolve any contradictions between their client's story and the police report through additional investigation. Consequently, the plea-bargaining session or trial ordinarily becomes a credibility contest between police officers and defendants, with the police usually winning because they come with better reputations. Unusual cases are handled differently. When the defendant is well-off, he or she can finance independent investigations. Moreover, in the most notorious cases, such as those involving mass murderers, defense counsel are given more resources to conduct a more vigorous defense, lest the accused be released upon appeal because the trial was judged to have been unfair. The public knows much more about such cases because they receive far more publicity than routine ones, where defense counsel operate under severe resource constraints.

Defense attorneys exercise less discretion in the criminal justice process than do prosecutors. Prosecutors are in the driver's seat and control the pace of the proceedings; defense attorneys usually respond only to prosecutorial initiatives. However, in a few instances, the rules of the courtroom give defense lawyers considerable influence. In the many jurisdictions where a time limit is set for conducting a prosecution, defense attorneys gain bargaining power as the time limit approaches. When a prosecutor is on the verge of losing a case simply because it was not processed according to schedule, a more lenient bargain may be reached. Defense counsel can also delay cases by asking for continuances on the ground that they are not yet prepared, that they have to try another case in a different courtroom, or because "Mr. Green" is not in the courtroom. Mr. Green is not a witness but a reference to the fact that the attorney has not yet been paid by his client. Such continuances are not always granted, and when they are, they do not count against the prosecutor's deadline for finishing the case. Delay creates problems for prosecutors because it provides a way through which defense attorneys can prolong a case until witnesses become forgetful or unwilling to appear in court. Nevertheless, the defense lawyer's ability to delay is a meager weapon compared to all of the information at the disposal of prosecutors.

A final difference between prosecutors and defense counsel is that defense lawyers must defer to their clients' preferences. Those wishes are often less predictable than the policy directives that prosecutors must obey. When a prosecutor and defense attorney have agreed upon a plea bargain, it must be accepted by the defendant before becoming binding. He or she may refuse. Refusals are not common, because defense attorneys can exert considerable psychological pressure upon clients. Clients often possess only a fragmentary knowledge of the alternatives available to them. They may be frightened by the prospect of a trial and by the uncertainties of the sentence that may await them upon conviction at trial. Clients may not fully understand that they are in charge. Yet despite such considerations, some clients give considerable trouble to defense lawyers.

The defense counsel's role is not entirely unique; defense attorneys share some important characteristics with prosecutors. When defense lawyers work for the public defender's office or when they are criminal law specialists, they face much the same work-load strain as do prosecutors. Ordinarily defense attorneys have too many cases to give each of them individual attention. Public defenders cannot afford to try every case before a jury or judge because that would take too much time. Private attorneys also cannot afford trials in every instance, because the fees that they have collected are insufficient. Private attorneys who have collected only $1,000 will then be reluctant to devote more than $1,000 worth of their time to the case. If they commit more time, they are unlikely to be reimbursed. The constraints that lead defense attorneys to prefer plea bargains are quite similar to those we described for prosecutors. Neither attorney has enough time or money to go to a full-fledged trial in every case.

Moreover, like the prosecutor, defense counsel in most jurisdictions are courthouse regulars. That means that they intermittently confront the same prosecutors over a long period of time. Prosecutors and defense counsel become associates in the same task—disposing of cases. Although defense lawyers have a fundamental commitment to their clients, they also share with prosecutors a commitment to keep the process viable. They cannot treat each case in total isolation from the flow of cases they handle. Today's negotiations with a prosecutor are likely to reflect the relationship established in previous negotiations and must be conducted with an eye on future interactions with a prosecutor. Similar constraints impinge on prosecutors. Consequently, the actions of defense attorneys cannot be understood solely from the perspective of their obligation to their clients. While that responsibility is primary, the secondary obligations incurred through their contacts with prosecutors and other persons working in the courthouse exert some influence on their decisions.

Thus, courtroom encounters are not simply contests between two equal contenders, the prosecution and defense. The prosecution enjoys a considerable advantage, and in many instances the process is not a contest at all but rather a joint venture in which both prosecutor and defense counsel seek to dispose of pending cases expeditiously. But they are not the only participants in the process. They must share that concern and their power with judges.

Judges. Judges are conventionally thought to control the criminal justice process. It is true that they preside over trials, but as we have already seen, judges are only one of several officials with considerable influence on the outcome of criminal prosecutions. In a few instances judges are truly in charge; in many they must take into account what other officials want done.

The power of judges is greatest in formal proceedings; it is least when discretion is exercised before a trial is scheduled. Thus, although the Supreme Court has fashioned many decisions to constrain abuse of police discretion, the effectiveness of those decisions is questionable. Judges never see the potential defendants whom the police fail to arrest. Likewise, judges rarely can intervene if prosecutors decide not to press charges, and they do not have much influence on the nature of the charges that prosecutors choose when they proceed against a defendant. When plea bargaining centers on dismissal of concurrent charges rather than on the promise of a specific sentence, judges usually remain powerless to intervene. Only when a defendant stands before the judge at trial or for sentencing do judges assume the power that the public associates with their title.

Nevertheless, it would be inaccurate to portray judges as powerless in the preliminary stages of the criminal justice process. Their in-

fluence is indirect rather than direct; it is exerted in subtle ways. Judges are part of the same courtroom work group as prosecutors and defense attorneys. Through many informal contacts, they convey their preferences without seeming to command compliance. Judges obtain compliance in part out of respect for their superior position. But they also possess powers to enforce compliance. Judges possess the formal power (which they rarely invoke) to speed up or slow down proceedings. They can insist that a case begin or continue at a time that is very inconvenient to the others. Judges can compel attention to the minutiae of court proceedings or wink at minor lapses. Judges not only control appointments of defense attorneys in some cases but also may publicly praise or chide an attorney before a full courtroom. All of these powers make prosecutors and defense attorneys attentive to the judges' preferences. In the normal course of courtroom proceedings, judges do not intervene in matters that they cannot directly control; rather, they rely on the informal deference that is paid them, to maintain their influence.

During formal proceedings the judge appears to be clearly in charge. The judge makes all important decisions as to the admissibility of evidence, the length of a sentence, and the guilt or innocence of the defendant in juryless trials. However, even at formal proceedings, the other participants have considerable influence. While judges make the formal decisions, the information on which those decisions are based usually comes from prosecutors, defense counsel, or other participants. A judge's sentence, for instance, is normally heavily influenced by the prosecutor's recommendation (itself often the result of a plea bargain) and information about the defendant supplied by the prosecutor, defense counsel, and probation officer. Decisions on the admissibility of the evidence depends on testimony submitted to the judge and on legal briefs on which trial judges heavily rely. Even instructions to a jury are the result of negotiations in the judge's chambers at which prosecuting and defense lawyers present alternative versions of disputed instructions. Judges normally choose one or the other rather than drafting their own.

Moreover, judges also respond to pressures from their hierarchical superiors—the appellate bench. While most judicial decisions are not appealed, appeals occur much more frequently in criminal matters than in civil cases. Judges are sensitive to being overruled by appellate courts, especially because it occurs infrequently. However, appellate courts do not usually directly supervise the actions of trial judges in their jurisdiction. Trial judges do not wait to have their decisions overturned. Rather, they pay attention to the drift of appellate decisions and respond to legal arguments citing those decisions.

On the other hand, judges are much less responsive to local political pressures than are elected prosecutors or police departments under the control of mayors. In many jurisdictions, judges win office by a gubernatorial appointment process called merit selection, in which the bar association has more influence than local politicos. Under this plan, candidates for judgeships must win endorsement from a selection panel composed of lawyers and judges rather than from local government officials. Judges so appointed usually face retention elections in which they run only against their record rather than against an opponent. Where such merit-selection schemes are not used, trial judges are elected either on a party ballot (as congressmen are) or on a nonpartisan ballot. In both cases their campaigns attract little attention from the electorate, and few judges lose office because of decisions they have made. Moreover, judicial ethics and the culture surrounding the judicial office stigmatize judicial behavior that responds to public opinion. Instead, judges are supposed to be above partisan politics. Consequently, judges are much more insulated from day-to-day fluctuations in public opinion. Because they typically have deep roots in their communities and many social ties to them, they are not entirely isolated from community pressures, but political responsiveness is not their strong suit.

Other Participants. Private citizens play an important part in many criminal court proceedings. They may serve as witnesses or as jurors. Both are important roles, because they significantly break into the professional monopoly held by prosecutors, defense attorneys, and judges. They also contribute a large degree of uncertainty in the proceedings in which they take part.

As witnesses, private citizens provide testimony either for the prosecution or defense about charges facing a defendant. During a trial their task is to respond to questions that attorneys put to them. First, they testify in direct examination by the prosecutor (or defense attorney, if a defense witness) and then under cross-examination by the other attorney. Judges occasionally intercede in the questioning and make their own queries. The experience can be an intimidating and frightening one for witnesses. In some cases, it can be degrading, as when a rape victim is asked to testify about her own virtue as well as about the assault that occurred. Witnesses introduce a considerable degree of uncertainty into trials because their performance can vary greatly. In many routine criminal trials, attorneys spend little time preparing them and may be surprised by the answers they give. Sometimes witnesses become confused under the pressure of testifying in court; often they are not very articulate.

Jurors participate in fewer cases than witnesses. Only a tiny proportion of all cases are decided by juries in the United States; the remainder are tried by judges alone or result in guilty pleas. If a defendant wants a jury trial, he or she can obtain it, but most attorneys will advise against it. Jury trials tend to occur in cases where there is considerable doubt about guilt; in very serious cases, where the defendant has nothing to lose; and in cases involving very prominent defendants.

Juries listen passively to the presentation of evidence and to the summations presented by defense and prosecuting attorneys. They are then instructed by the presiding judge about the applicable law on such matters as how to weigh the evidence, what outcomes they may choose, and what vote is required for a decision. When all these proceedings have been completed, the jury withdraws to its room to deliberate. Jury deliberations are entirely private; no outsider is permitted to observe them. Sometimes, a jury reaches its decision almost immediately; on more rare occasions, a jury may deliberate for days. When its decision is reached, the jury reports to the judge and announces its decision in open court.

Juries are notoriously unpredictable. Each jury is different. None belong to the web of relationships that composes the courtroom work group. Few courtroom professionals feel confident that they can accurately guess the outcome of jury trials, because it is difficult to gauge the impression testimony made on jurors or the dynamics of jury decision-making.

CONVICTION AND PRISON

The final institutional actors in the criminal justice process are those involved in punishing the guilty. Prisons and other correctional agencies resemble the police more than courts in many respects. They are organizationally independent of courts in most instances. Their staffs do not share the legal training common to key court personnel. They respond to different imperatives than do courts.

Two entirely different kinds of agencies handle persons who are convicted of a crime. First are parole and probation agencies, which supervise persons who are convicted but not incarcerated. Second are jails and prisons, which house those who are. Both are as fragmented as all the other agencies of the criminal justice system.

Probation and parole agencies exist at the local, state, and national levels. At each level, agencies are often autonomous from those at higher levels. The local agencies generally work under the supervision of local courts, although their staffs generally consist of persons with backgrounds in law enforcement or social work rather than in law. State-and national-level agencies usually are part of the prison system rather than of the courts. Their autonomy makes coordinated policy as unlikely in the field of probation and parole as in other segments of the criminal justice system.

The work of probation and parole agencies share many similarities, although they intervene at different stages of the process. Probation is generally an alternative to prison or jail. Parole occurs after part of a prison or jail sentence has been served. In both cases, convicted persons must subject themselves to supervision of their daily activities. They must periodically report to their parole (or probation) officer. That report may be no more than a phone call indicating that they still live at the same address. It may, however, involve a detailed probing into their lives, with orders to avoid certain friendships of which the officer disapproves, to maintain a job, or to

reside in a particular section of the city. Serious violations of parole or probation—generally involving an arrest for a new offense—may result in revocation proceedings and in the subsequent jailing of the probationer or parolee.

Intrusive as parole or probation may be, incarceration is far more severe. It involves the total control of prisoners from the moment they enter the institution until they leave it. Violations of institutional regulations may result in severe punishment such as solitary confinement, in which all social contact with other prisoners becomes impossible.

Prisons are expensive, highly labor-intensive institutions. It costs as much or more to incarcerate someone in the United States for a year as to send a college student to a private university; in 1979, prison costs averaged $9487 per prisoner. Most of the prison staff are relatively unskilled persons serving as guards. They work under close supervision by the prison warden. While regulations vary considerably from one institution to another, the warden ordinarily provides detailed guidance for guards and inmates. But like others in the criminal justice process, prison officials exercise considerable discretion over inmates because much of their work is out of sight of supervisors and out of the limelight of public attention.

Prisons are not simply the passive recipients of court decisions. All prisoners come to them because of court decisions. But while one set of courts may be increasing the number of prisoners, another set may be setting limits on the numbers prisons may hold. That was particularly true during the 1970s and early 1980s when prison populations increased dramatically in the United States. Between 1974 and 1983 the number of inmates in state and federal prisons rose from 229,721 to 438,830, but the size and number of the facilities hardly changed. Consequently, in response to prisoner complaints that the increasingly crowded conditions violated the Constitution's ban on "cruel and unusual punishments," courts imposed limits on the number of inmates that could be housed in existing facilities. Such court decisions typically also established minimal food and health conditions that state and local authorities had to establish and maintain. Therefore, in many places, trial-court decisions to impose a prison sentence on those convicted could be accommodated only by a parallel decision by prison authorities to release some other person. Often such releases come many months or years before the expiration of inmates' formal sentences. As long as most sentences were of indeterminate length, prison authorities or parole boards enjoyed considerable discretion about the actual length of sentences to be served. Whereas a robber might be sentenced with considerable fanfare to a ten- to thirty-year prison term in court, the actual sentence served was often as little as four years. With the passage of determinate sentence laws by many states in the 1970s, much of this discretion disappeared. Yet, even in states with determinate sentences, early-release programs existed in order to make room for new prisoners. Alternatively, new prisoners were kept in local jails until there was room in the state penitentiary or until the local jail also became overcrowded.

It is at this final stage of the criminal justice system that its lack of coordination becomes most evident. Both police and courts make decisions with little regard for the ability of prisons to accommodate the persons sent there. Often indeed, police and courts lack information about the level of available prison capacity. Decisions to build more prisons or to staff them differently are made at the state level by gubernatorial appointees and by state legislatures. Proposals to expand prisons must compete for funds with highways, schools, mental health, and all other programs, many of which have much more powerful political support than do prisons. At the national level, prisons are administered by the United States Department of Justice; they usually receive little attention amidst the many programs and agencies that the federal government administers.

Prisons incur much of the wrath of the public about the apparent ineffectiveness of the criminal justice system. The police often point to persons whom they have arrested and whom the courts have convicted but who reappear in the community in a few months to commit new crimes. Prosecutors often recommend long sentences, and judges impose them only to find the prisoner on the street a little while later in order to make room for new inmates. Indeed, as stated by Martinson, studies of the rehabilitative function of prisons indicate that they more often fail than succeed. At most, prisons appear to be warehouses for those adjudged guilty. In some instances they teach crime; in a few cases they provide an occasion for reform. In most, the persons leaving are no better than when they entered. Uniformly they are worse off because of employment difficulties they normally encounter, because of their difficulty in readjusting from the regimented life of prison to the free life outside its walls, and because of the fractured families to which they return.

CONCLUSION

The principal characteristics of the criminal justice process should now be apparent. The process is a system—albeit a loosely coupled one—because each of the many agencies involved in criminal justice affect the others. It is also one marked by a high degree of fragmentation and decentralization. Each of the major participants enjoys a high degree of discretion in making decisions, but that discretion is contained by intricate legal rules. Finally, each portion of the criminal justice process is marked by the tension between a desire to control crime and a distrust for excessive governmental authority. These characteristics make criminal justice in the United States unique and difficult to reform.

CASES

Gideon v. Wainwright, 372 U.S. 335 (1963)
Mapp v. Ohio, 367 U.S. 643 (1961)
Miranda v. Arizona, 384 U.S. 436 (1966)

BIBLIOGRAPHY

Richard A. Berk, Harold Brackman, and Selma Lesser, *A Measure of Justice: An Empirical Study of Changes in the California Penal Code, 1955–1971* (1977), is the most comprehensive existing study of the political activity leading to change in parts of the criminal law; however, it deals only with the situation in California. Donald Black, *The Manners and Customs of the Police* (1980), a collection of articles about policing, is by one of the leading sociological scholars of the police in the United States. Alfred Blumstein, Jacqueline Cohen, and Daniel Nagin, eds., *Deterrence and Incapacitation: Estimating the Effects of Criminal Sanctions on Crime Rates* (1978), addresses the deterrence question in this collection of papers by eminent criminologists and statisticians that was commissioned by the National Academy of Sciences. Greg A. Caldeira and Andrew T. Cowart, "Budgets, Institutions, and Change: Criminal Justice Policy in America," in *American Journal of Political Science*, 24 (1980), examines the politics of budgeting for criminal justice activities in the United States. William J. Chambliss, ed., *Crime and the Legal Process* (1968), is standard but critical criminology text. Thomas Y. Davies, "A Hard Look at What We Know (and Still Need to Learn) about the 'Costs' of the Exclusionary Rule," in *American Bar Foundation Research Journal* (1983), analyzes the effects of the exclusionary rule.

Isaac Ehrlich, "Participation in Illegitimate Activities: An Economic Analysis," in G. S. Becker and W. M. Landes, eds., *Essays in the Economics of Crime and Punishment* (1977), is regarded as the opening salvo in the dispute between conventional criminologists and economists about the efficacy of the death penalty and is considered a classic by some and a seriously faulted piece of research by others. James Eisenstein and Herbert Jacob, *Felony Justice: An Organizational Analysis of Criminal Courts* (1977), describes and analyzes felony case processing in Baltimore, Chicago, and Detroit in the early 1970s; particularly noted for its application of organizational analysis to criminal court processes. Malcolm M. Feeley, *The Process Is the Punishment: Handling Cases in a Lower Criminal Court* (1979), is an account of misdemeanor processing in New Haven, Connecticut. David F. Greenberg, ed., *Corrections and Punishment* (1977), is an excellent collection of articles on various elements of the work of correctional agencies. Anne M. Heinz, *Legislative Responses to Crime: The Changing Content of Criminal Law* (1982), analyzes the politics of criminal legislation at the state and local level in the United States. Anne M. Heinz, Herbert Jacob, and Robert L. Lineberry, *Crime in City Politics* (1983), analyzes the politics of crime control between 1948 and 1978 in ten large American cities.

Alfred R. Lindesmith, *The Addict and the Law* (1965), studies the interaction of drug addiction and legal prohibitions. William F. McDonald, ed., *The Defense Counsel* (1983), is a useful and up-to-date collection of articles on various modes of providing counsel for criminal defendants. Robert Martinson, "What Works? Questions and Answers about Prison Reform," in *Public Interest* 35 (1974), is a scathing critique of the rehabilitative potential of prisons. Jonathan Rubenstein, *City Police* (1973), offers a study of the police in Philadelphia by a participant-observer. Jerome H. Skolnick, *Justice Without Trial* (1966), gives sociological study of the use of discretion by the police and is considered by many to be a classic.

United States Department of Justice, Bureau of Justice Statistics, *Career Patterns in Crime* (1983), one of a series of reports by the bureau, summarizes current research on participation in criminal activities by various elements of the American population; "Prisoners in 1983," *Bulletin*, April 1984, is a statistical summary of distribution of prisoners within American prisons, published annually; and *Criminal Victimizations in the United States*, published annually, reports a sample survey estimating the number of criminal victimizations in the United States. United States Department of Justice, Federal Bureau of Investigation, *Uniform Crime Reports*, published annually, is the most frequently cited count of crime in the United States. Franklin E. Zimring and Gordon J. Hawkins, *Deterrence* (1973), examines empirical evidence on the deterrent effect of criminal laws and analyzes the potential for empirical research on this effect.

[*See also* JUDICIAL SELECTION; PLEA BARGAINING; PROSECUTORS; SENTENCING ALTERNATIVES; *and* TRIAL JURIES AND GRAND JURIES.]

EQUITY AND EQUITABLE REMEDIES

W. Hamilton Bryson

EQUITY is the system of justice that arose in the court of the lord chancellor of England in the late fourteenth or early fifteenth century. (In order to avoid confusion, this essay will not use the word *equity* to refer to the nontechnical concepts of fairness and justice.) Equitable remedies are those remedies granted by courts of equity as opposed to legal remedies, which are granted by courts of common law. The system of remedies we call equity arose to supplement and to complement, but not to supplant, the common law of England.

ENGLISH ANTECEDENTS TO MODERN EQUITY PRACTICE

The common law of England in the Middle Ages, whether administered in the royal courts or the county courts, was an unwritten system of law that was thought to be totally comprehensive; it governed all situations, and it was the duty of the courts to "discover" the law and to apply it to each particular case. In the thirteenth and fourteenth centuries, common-law remedies grew to combat all types of injuries; in some cases the royal courts were granting remedies to deal with problems formerly handled only in the county courts and, in other cases, to deal with newly invented injuries. This was a period of luxuriant growth for the English common law. However, the fourteenth century saw the rise of Parliament as a legislative body and, by midcentury, the development of a substantial body of judicial precedent stating the common law. The result was that common-law judges were becoming trapped by their own precedents and in time became unable to change the law without trespassing upon the legislative prerogative of Par-

liament. Judicial restraint is a good thing, but it can be carried too far, for there is no such thing as a general rule (or a statute) that cannot be avoided or perverted by persons of bad intentions. Furthermore, the medieval Parliament was not a very efficient legislature by modern standards; for one thing it met only irregularly, usually being called when the king needed more money.

As the common-law courts became unable to grant new types of remedies to deal with new types of problems, litigants turned to the king, and the king sent them to the lord chancellor, the head of the royal secretariat, for special aid. As these special petitions were regularly accepted and decided, the chancery developed into a law court, and the system of justice administered there became known as equity. Equity thus arose several centuries later than the common law and was that much more modern in terms of procedure and substantive law. It is to be remembered that chancery is a court that applies the system of law called equity. A chancellor is an official who is the keeper of someone's seal; the lord chancellor of Great Britain is only incidentally a judge. Thus, an equity judge is not usually a chancellor, though in the United States the term *chancellor* is sometimes used to refer to an equity judge and the term *chancery* is used loosely to refer to an equity court and equity jurisdiction. This article will use the word *chancery* to refer only to the court of the lord chancellor and not to any other court of equity.

Equity arose in the court of chancery in order to provide remedies when the common law proved inadequate to do justice in a particular case. (From the middle of the sixteenth century onward, the court of exchequer also granted equitable remedies.) Some of the substantive improvements of equity were the enforcement of trusts and the use of various defenses to contracts. A trust, or a use, was a type of contract, usually in reference to land, which was invented after the common-law writs (which controlled the jurisdiction and procedures of the common-law courts) had become fixed and unchangeable. A trust is the situation in which the common-law ownership of property is given to a person (the trustee) to hold and manage for the benefit of another person (the beneficiary of the trust). Since there was no common-law writ available to enforce a trust and since the chancery clerks and the common-law judges could not change the law by inventing a new one without unconstitutionally usurping the legislative power of Parliament, the chancellor enforced them. It was clear to the entire legal profession that justice required the enforcement of trusts and uses. Since the common-law courts could (or would) not, everyone agreed that equity should. Thus, the beneficiary of the trust is said to be the equitable owner of the property in question. The trust, which is completely unknown in European law, is a magnificent device for managing property or companies in both personal and commercial settings. This device has been steadily refined over the centuries to serve more and more needs of society.

In the area of contracts, justice required that each party receive "consideration"—that is, something of value for the performance of his part of the agreement. The common-law courts required proof of consideration "flowing" from the plaintiff to the defendant (the obligor) before a plaintiff (the obligee) could recover on an oral contract. However, if the contract was in writing and under the defendant's seal, the written and sealed instrument was sufficient proof for a common-law recovery, even though there was no consideration. A sharp dealer would be able to take advantage of others by always having such an unfair bargain reduced to writing with an eye to future litigation, relying on well-established common-law precedent. The common-law courts could not change their law, but the court of equity came to require the unconscionable obligee to forgo his unfair gain. The courts of equity required that all contracts be supported by consideration on both sides.

The mortgage is a common-law conveyance of land to secure a loan; the mortgage contract is written so that if the loan is repaid, the debtor gets his land back; if it is not repaid in full, the creditor keeps the land, even if only one payment is not made or if payment is made only one day late. In many cases a debtor may be in technical default only, but the common-law courts must enforce the contract that was freely entered into by the debtor. To prevent such harsh results, penalties, and forfeitures, the courts of equity allow the debtor to redeem his land by making the payments late (with appropriate additional interest); thus, the equity courts have created what is called an equity of redemption. (To protect fair-minded creditors, the courts of equity allow a creditor to come into the equity court and prove the hopeless insolvency of his debtor, and the equity judge will foreclose the debtor's equity of redemption; this will give the creditor clear title to the land being held as security so that he can sell it and recoup the amount of the defaulted loan.) Although the general common-law rule that contracts should be kept is well respected by society, everyone's sense of justice will acknowledge that the equity of redemption is a fine tuning by the courts of equity that results in substantial justice in the individual case where the debtor is acting in good faith but has had a bit of bad luck.

In more recent times the courts of equity have evolved a law of fiduciary responsibility, which did not exist in medieval England. Thus, administrators of estates, guardians of mental incompetents, and trustees are held to higher standards of loyalty than are ordinary businessmen.

The equity jurisdiction of the chancellor's court grew in the fifteenth century also to cure problems in the administration of justice caused by various defects in the procedures of the old common-law courts. One common-law rule of evidence was that a party could not testify in court as a witness. Much has been written about the aspect of this rule that a person cannot testify against himself, but we will consider here that a person also could not testify for himself. Thus, where the only witnesses to a transaction or occurrence were the parties thereto, the person injured could not prove his case in a court of common law, because there was no admissible evidence; and since the plaintiff always has the burden of persuasion, the defendant would win by default. Thus, if one were assaulted in a dark alley, one had no practical remedy at common law. To aid the injured party, the courts of equity, where the defendant was required to plead under oath, would allow a person with a common-law grievance to sue in equity in order to force the defendant to respond under oath and "discover" (make known) the truth, and then this sworn statement would constitute a binding admission for use in the common-law court. In time, the courts of equity, where discovery was needed, began to retain the case and to decide the common-law dispute in order to avoid the multiplicity of litigation that would have been, involved by sending the plaintiff back to the court of law. This was the origin of the bill of discovery.

One of the most glaring archaic features of the medieval common law was trial by jury. Although the criminal jury was usually up to its task, life was too complicated for the civil jury; civil juries were seldom sufficiently educated or experienced to understand complex issues of financial importance. But regardless of how good the jurors might have been, the jury system required a single verdict of liability or not and, if so, what damages. Thus, where there were multiple plaintiffs or defendants, the common-law jury was inadequate to sort out issues of, for example, which of the defendants might be liable for what proportion of the damages. In the courts of equity, which arose long after the common-law courts had settled upon the use of the jury as the trier of the facts of the case, the judge heard all of the issues of the case and, being an educated and highly competent person, was able to determine complicated issues.

Another jury-related problem was the common-law action of account. When the parties presented an accounting dispute to the court, the jury was required to render a separate verdict on each line in the account; this clumsy procedure was beyond the abilities of a jury of ploughmen, and the courts of equity took over accounting litigation to remedy this deficiency in the common law.

If two different persons claimed an object or a fund in the hands of a third party, problems could arise in the common-law courts. For example, if an expensive diamond necklace had been given to a jeweler to be repaired, the owner had died, and the jeweler had then been sued at common law for the necklace by both the heir and the widow, there would have been a very real danger that the different juries in the two common-law cases would both find against the jeweler. To prevent the likelihood of inconsistent jury verdicts and double liability, the courts of equity would allow the defendant jeweler to come into equity and to bring both common-law plaintiffs into the case, thus forcing them to litigate in equity their competing common-law claims.

A more serious defect of the common-law procedure was that when any party died, the lawsuit died, and the plaintiff had to restart his suit from scratch. Where there were many parties, it was frequently the case, particularly where a whole family was involved, as in litigation over a family inheritance, that parties would die and new parties be born, so that the case could never be brought to a conclusion. This problem was remedied by the courts of equity, because there a case could be easily revived when there was a change in parties and the litigation would not be frustrated by such accidents.

The fifteenth century in England was a period of political weakness as a result of the drawn-out Wars of the Roses; even during periods of peace, the authority of the crown was weak. England was at the mercy of private armies; the county administrators, the sheriffs, were usually either powerless or beyond the control of the courts. It was a period during which the rich and the powerful of the county could manipulate or intimidate juries and thus pervert the course of justice. Frequently weak and poor litigants had to resort to the court of the lord chancellor, the most powerful political figure in the country, to obtain justice against their strong neighbors. The chancellor was the king's prime minister in fact, though not in name, and he could do justice and enforce his orders without fear or favor. Many common-law disputes were therefore heard in the court of chancery in the fifteenth century.

Thus did equity come into existence to supplement and complement the common law. Equity does not compete with the common law but tunes it more finely. The common law is, in theory, a complete system; equity is not a system within itself but rather relates to the common law and aids the common law. Justice came to consist of both common law and equity; English justice would be defective without both. This was recognized as early as the fifteenth century, and so lawyers and judges had to work out in the pleading stage of the litigation whether justice in a particular case was to be served in a court of common law or a court of equity.

Equity does not deny the validity of the common law but rather recognizes it and fulfills it. Equity does not change the common law, but where a person is using the common law to an unjust purpose, the equity judge will order that person not to sue in the common-law court or not to enforce a common-law judgment. The court of equity does not change the common law or reverse, overrule, or annul any common-law judgment, for to do so would be an unconstitutional usurpation of legislative power and an illegal appellate power over the common-law courts. But all disinterested persons would agree that the common-law courts should not be used in an unjust manner, and thus, the equity court orders that person not to do it. It is against good conscience to do injustice. Equity courts simply force defendants to act according to conscience; consequently, they have frequently been called courts of conscience.

St. German was the first scholar to attempt to explain the activities and jurisdiction of the chancellor's court. He spoke in terms of *epikeia* and conscience. The former concept is that, although all law must be framed in general terms, it should be applied to individual cases with flexibility and mitigation. The concept of conscience is the same today as it was in the sixteenth century, a sense of absolute right versus wrong. A party should not be allowed to use the common law to perpetrate a wrong. For example, if a person made a written contract under seal, an agreement to pay money for an assignment of contract rights, and then it turned out that the assignment was invalid and worthless, the general common-law rules allowed the enforcement of the written contract. However, the injustice of enforcing this contract was obvious, because while contracts should be kept as a general rule, where one party did not get what he thought he was getting, he should not have to give up what he promised to pay. The remedy for the mistaken person is to sue in equity for an order to the other party not to sue on the contract and to return the written agreement to him or, if he had already been sued, not to ask the sheriff to execute the com-

mon-law judgment. Thus, the contract and the common-law judgment remain in force, but if they are taken advantage of, the obligee will be put in prison for contempt of the equity court's order.

Since the courts of equity grant remedies only when the ordinary common-law remedies are inadequate, the jurisdiction of the equity courts is said to be extraordinary. The term *extraordinary* is used here in the sense of going beyond the basic rather than in the sense of unusual; equity is both extraordinary and quite usual and frequent.

One aspect of extraordinary equity powers involves the personal order. A personal order does not change the law or the parties' strict common-law rights and is enforced by the court's holding the defendant in contempt and keeping him in prison until he obeys. Thus, equity is said to act in personam. A common-law court acts in rem (that is, on the property of the defendant), declaring the money or land in dispute to belong to the successful plaintiff. The common-law court thus changes ownership and orders the sheriff to take the money or land from the defendant and to give it to the plaintiff. It should be noted, however, that in modern practice, statutes have given the courts of equity power to act in rem so that, for example, a sheriff can execute an equity order or a commissioner can be appointed to make a common-law conveyance or release in the defendant's name.

The procedure of the equity courts, sometimes referred to as English bill procedure, which was developed in the fifteenth-century chancery, was clearly more modern and much more efficient than the common-law procedure, with its forms of action and trial by jury. Every court that was set up by act of Parliament or evolved on its own in England from the fifteenth century onward used this English bill procedure rather than the procedure of the common-law courts.

It has been argued that the origin of equity procedure and substantive law is to be found in the procedure of the canon-law courts. Most of the medieval English chancellors were bishops in whose courts the canon law was used. It is my opinion that equity was an evolution native to England and that the bill grew out of an ordinary petition or request, that depositions grew out of administrative inquisitions, and so on. The fact that the chancellors were bishops does not mean that they could not keep their courts entirely separate. Indeed, many common-law judges were bishops. Furthermore, many leading medieval politicians were given bishoprics so that the king could have administrators without having to pay them salaries; the bishops could do the king's work in person and their ecclesiastical work by deputy. Most ecclesiastical courts were presided over by the bishop's official or deputy anyway. There are similarities and dissimilarities between the canon law and equity.

The peaceful coexistence of law and equity continued until the chancellorship of Cardinal Wolsey during the early reign of Henry VIII. Thomas Wolsey, a person of modest social background, came to the notice of Henry VIII, who recognized in him a competent administrator and so put him into the highest seats of power in the kingdom, civic and ecclesiastical. As lord chancellor, archbishop of York, cardinal, and papal legate, he was exalted over all men in England except only the king himself and the pope. The power went to Wolsey's head, and he alienated people. The odium that became attached to Wolsey personally spilled over onto his court of chancery and from there to the rules of equity that were administered in chancery courts.

In 1529, Cardinal Wolsey, having failed to get Henry VIII's divorce from Queen Catherine, was stripped of all his offices and wealth. He died shortly thereafter of a broken heart, having lost his power, his only love. He was succeeded in the office of lord chancellor by the common lawyer Sir Thomas More. This was an interesting succession in that More was the first layman to be appointed chancellor since 1454; he had not been, and was not to become, the king's prime political adviser; and he was a well-known practicing lawyer. It was believed that he would restore the proper relationship between common law and equity. Soon after his appointment, he called the judges together to settle this relationship. He proposed not to enjoin common-law litigation if the judges would reform the common law, but the judges said that they did not have the power to change the law, and this forced More to continue to grant injunctions, in personam orders, as Wolsey and all earlier chancellors had done. Thus, More's appointment did not change or restore anything; but because he was a courteous man, the antagonisms between common law and equity were quickly forgotten, and equanimity prevailed until the reign of James I.

In the first decade of the seventeenth century, two very ambitious and aggressive men began to compete over personal dominance of the English legal system. The two were Thomas Egerton, Lord Ellesmere, who became lord chancellor, and Sir Edward Coke (pronounced "Cook"), a common-law judge who became lord chief justice of England. The chancellor has always been the administrative head on the English judiciary, but tradition was for Coke a servant, not a master. When Coke became lord chief justice of England, he began a systematic attack on every court and legal system but his own.

In the early seventeenth century, the concept of res judicata—the doctrine that once a court has decided a matter, it cannot be litigated again—had not been worked out between the courts of law and courts of equity. Therefore, if a person was sued at common law on a contract to which he had a defense in equity, he could sue in equity at once to stop the plaintiff (the obligee) from suing at common law, or he could wait and, if the common-law result was against him, sue to prevent the enforcement of the judgment. Thus, the defendant (the obligor) had two chances of success. Today, the defendant at common law must resort to equity at once or lose his equitable defense.

This situation was galling to Coke because the equity order, the injunction, appeared to be an appeal to his rival, the lord chancellor. Coke therefore let it be known that he was prepared to stop this practice. Soon a most unworthy plaintiff, Richard Glanvill, appeared in Coke's court to sue on a contract that was the result of his gross fraud and deceit. (He had sold a topaz, representing it to be a diamond.) He got judgment; the court of chancery issued an injunction to stop enforcement of the common-law judgement; the injunction was disobeyed; Egerton put Glanvill in prison for contempt of court; and Coke ordered him released on a writ of habeas corpus. This matter ended inconclusively, but this case and several others made a public issue of this problem of the practice of law and the administration of justice. The whole matter of the boundaries between common law and equity were then referred to the king's counsel for full debate and resolution. The result was in favor of the courts of equity, as should have been expected. Even though equity practice was not perfect, it was more modern and more flexible than the common law. The old rule was thus reestablished in 1616 without any further serious dispute. Simply stated, the rule was that where the results of an equity order and a common-law order were in disagreement, the equity rule and decree would prevail. Otherwise, equity would have been unable to perform its function of seeing justice done in the individual case. Shortly thereafter, Coke was removed from his judgeship and Egerton died, and things returned to normal in the English courts. A generation later, personalities and politics, rather than jurisprudence, again impinged on the relationship between common law and equity. Soon after his accession to the throne in 1625, Charles I decided to follow the French theories and methods of government and to rule England without the interference of Parliament. When Parliament was removed as a political forum, the opponents of the king's policies took their fights to the area of the law courts. Lord Coventry, the lord chancellor, was identified with the king and his policies. And again the dislike of the chancellor resulted in dislike of his court and of its jurisprudence.

It was during this period that John Selden, the famous legal scholar and antiroyalist, published his famous jibe at equity: "Equity is a roguish thing; for [in] law we have a measure [we can] know what to trust to. Equity is according to the conscience of him that is chancellor, and as that is larger or narrower, so is equity. 'Tis all one as if they should make the standard for the measure we call a foot to be the chancellor's foot; what an uncertain measure this would be."

The political, military, and personal defeats of Charles I are well known. As the king, the bishops, and the aristocracy were one by one removed from power, the radicals turned against Oliver Cromwell and the moderate Puritans, and in their zeal and ignorance they attacked the law itself. One of their proposals was to abolish the court of chancery. This attack was the low point of equity. This ill-conceived move was referred to a commission set up under Sir Matthew Hale to study the issue of law reform in general, and nothing more was heard of the taking-away of the chancery. During the interregnum, the court of chancery was presided over by a committee of three commissioners, and this assured that it

would have no political power. The normal course of equity jurisprudence in the courts of chancery and exchequer continued unabated during the time of Cromwell.

After the Restoration, the commercial empire of England began to grow by leaps and bounds. As English wealth became more and more based on commerce, the patronage of the lord treasurer became greater than that of the lord chancellor, and so the politician closest to the king sought to be appointed the former rather than the latter. The result was that the chancellor became less important politically than he had been in the past and thus had more time for the performance of his judicial duties. Furthermore, the legal ability of the candidate for the position of lord chancellor became more important than his political connections. Thus, the period extending from the Restoration into the middle of the nineteenth century produced a series of scholarly and legally adept chancellors whose opinions were systematically reported.

First and foremost was Heneage Finch, earl of Nottingham, a lawyer and a judge without equal. Since the Middle Ages, the court of chancery had been loosely called a court of conscience. Lord Nottingham put the theory of conscience into its proper perspective when, in *Cook* v. *Fountain* (1676), he stated that he was not ruling according to the personal conscience of any particular party litigant, himself, or the king but according to the civic conscience of the English legal system. The concept of conscience as administered in the courts of equity is general and institutional; it is to be found in the established practices and precedents of the courts of equity; it applies equally to all persons. Since Nottingham expounded equity doctrine in lucid and rational opinions based on precedent and since his opinions were the first to be systematically published, he has been called "the father of equity."

Equity jurisprudence was developed throughout the eighteenth century by a series of most excellent jurists: Charles Talbot, Lord Talbot; Philip Yorke, Lord Hardwicke; Charles Pratt, Lord Camden; and Edward Thurlow, Lord Thurlow, among others. The lord chancellor during the long and difficult later years of George III was John Scott, earl of Eldon. We must pause to consider Lord Eldon as lord chancellor.

Lord Eldon, who was as politically and personally traditional as the king, was a brilliant equity judge, but there were problems. Eldon was pilloried by the novelist Charles Dickens in *Bleak House* as being the perpetrator of endless judicial delay, and the bar agreed with Dickens; Eldon blamed the truly excessive delays in his court on the bar and on the litigants themselves. (The true villain in *Bleak House* was a testator who made a series of wills without destroying the earlier ones.) However, frequently Eldon would hear the evidence in a case, take it under advisement, and then two years later, when he was ready to render an opinion, have to have the case reargued. (If these delays were really so irksome to the legal profession, they could have divided their equity practice between the chancery and the exchequer, but they for some reason preferred the delays of the chancery to quick results in the exchequer.)

Lord Eldon's opinions were carefully reasoned and drafted; many are still cited today. Eldon was judicially conservative, and he felt bound to follow the traditional practices and the established law. Thus, when justice required him to grant a mandatory injunction in the case of *Lane* v. *Newdigate* (1804), even though no such order had ever been granted before, he felt obliged to disguise it as a prohibitory injunction by phrasing the order as a double negative. Perhaps Eldon's judicial philosophy was caused by Selden's jibe of 150 years before. In *Gee* v. *Pritchard* (1818), Eldon said, "Nothing would inflict on me greater pain . . . than the recollection that I had done anything to justify the reproach that the equity of this court varies like the Chancellor's foot." And thus, by the conclusion of Eldon's influential chancellorship, equity had become as rigidly bound by precedent as was the common law. And indeed ever since, equitable remedies have been dispensed with the same understanding of precedent and stare decisis as have common-law remedies. This will vary according to the judicial philosophy of a particular judge or generation of judges; history shows that the pendulum is always in motion.

EQUITY IN THE UNITED STATES

By the time of the first English settlements in America, equity was an integral part of English law. The "Articles, Instructions and Orders" dated 20 November 1606 for the government of Virginia required that litigation be determined "as near to the common laws of England and the equity thereof as may be." Once the Virginia courts and an educated legal community was established, which happened sometime before the mid-1640s, equitable remedies were fully available. In Virginia, equity was administered by the same courts that heard the common-law cases. In some of the New England colonies, equity was resisted. The probable reason for this was the identification of equity and arbitrary royal power in the minds of nonlawyers. In eighteenth-century New York, an attempt was made to set up a court of chancery to administer equity; this was strenuously opposed because the governor was to be the sole chancellor and this was not politically desirable.

The substantive doctrines of equity can be administered in separate courts, as in England the court of chancery had only equity jurisdiction whereas the court of common pleas and the court of king's bench had only common-law jurisdiction. In 1826 there were separate courts for law and equity in Delaware, New Jersey, South Carolina, and Mississippi. Today there are separate courts in Arkansas, Delaware, Mississippi, and Tennessee.

An alternative is the system of fused courts, in which common-law and equity cases are administered by the same court but common-law cases are tried by common-law procedures and equity cases by equity procedure. Here the courts are said to have a common-law side and an equity side. Although the same judge hears both types of cases, a case must be brought as either one or the other; the court sitting as a common-law court cannot grant an equitable remedy, but if the case is transferred to the court's equity side, it can. The courts of Virginia from 1607 to the present, except for the period 1776–1831, have been thus fused. In 1826 the lower courts of New York, Maryland, Virginia, Missouri, North Carolina, and Kentucky were examples of this type of judicial organization, as were the federal courts before 1938. Today this system of justice exists in Iowa, Maryland, New Jersey, Pennsylvania, and Virginia.

In the 1820s many equitable doctrines were being administered in the common-law courts of Pennsylvania, and a limited amount of equity had slipped into the common-law practice in New

England. It was against this background that Joseph Story of Massachusetts published his encyclopedic treatises on equity practice and equity jurisprudence. In the southern states, equity was freely available. (It is to be recalled that the first reports published in Virginia were a selection of equity opinions of George Wythe, which were collected for publication in 1795, and the second volume of Conway Robinson's *The Practice in the Courts of Law and Equity in Virginia* was published in 1835.) On the other hand, in the northern states, a general undercurrent of skepticism of equity remained.

In the 1840s a movement for law reform through codification was initiated in New York by David Dudley Field. His most notable achievement involved civil procedure, including the abolition of the common-law forms of action and the merger of the procedures of common law and equity. The most remarkable aspect of the New York "Field Code" of 1848 was that the substantive doctrines and remedies of common law and equity could be freely combined in the same lawsuit; this was the first procedural system in Anglo-American jurisprudence to provide a merged system of law and equity. The substantive rules were not altered, but the old procedures of judicial administration were merged into one. It is to be noted that Field's new statutory procedure was a modernized and streamlined one based on equity procedure; the common-law procedures, with the exception of trial by jury, were discarded. The success of the merger of law and equity procedure in New York was followed by its successful adoption in most states, in England (in 1873), and in federal practice (in 1938).

Equity procedures and practices, then, have come to dominate American civil procedure through the influence of Field. In particular, masters and receivers and the equity devices of pleading by petition and answer, discovery, interpleader, class actions, third-party practice, injunctions, and contempt-of-court proceedings have all taken their place in all courts in the United States.

Masters (also known as commissioners) in chancery are officers of the court appointed on an ad hoc basis to aid the equity judge in performing some routine but time-consuming task. The most frequent use of masters is to take complicated accountings and to conduct judicial sales of property. But a master can also be appointed to hear evidence on some part of the case or to draft and execute a conveyance or other document.

Receivers are officers of the court who are appointed to take possession of property that is the subject of litigation. Such a seizure of property may be necessary to prevent its being hidden, destroyed, or lost during the course of the judicial proceedings. The receiver, at the direction of the judge, takes possession of the property and holds it safely until further order of the court. A receiver may be appointed simply to hold an object or a fund, or he may even run a corporation to preserve it as a going concern, pending its sale or reorganization. Receivers are appointed to sell off the assets of a bankrupt business.

Equity has also had a deep and lasting impact on the content of American law, as well as on its procedure. In the area of contracts law, the equitable remedy of specific performance is vital. In some cases the ancient common-law remedy of money damages as compensation for the wrongful breach of a contract is not adequate to satisfy a person; where it is not, a court will exercise its equity powers and force the defaulting party to do what he contracted to do. Thus, where there is a contract to sell a unique object, the seller will not be allowed to back out and pay damages for his breach, but he will be compelled specifically to deliver the item sold. Note that the equitable remedy is granted only where the common-law remedy will not do complete justice; the ancient relationships survive in a merged system of administration.

Contracts for the sale of agricultural land will be thus "specifically enforced," as the expression goes. No farm is like any other one, and thus, the disappointed buyer cannot go and buy another farm to replace his lost bargain, as can the purchaser of a ton of gravel. In agricultural England, the specific enforcement of land sales contracts became so much the normal remedy that all land is now considered unique as a matter of law and the remedy of specific performance is always available, no matter how indistinguishable one unit of a condominium may be from another.

As to suits to enforce contracts, there are many defenses that are of equitable origin, such as dishonest conduct that does not involve a direct lie or dilatory conduct that harms another. An unforeseeable accident or a catastrophe of nature may relieve a person from a contractual obligation. A grossly unfair and harsh bargain that "shocks the conscience" will be set aside by principles of equity, even though the common-law rules of making the contract were followed.

Equity has also created a means for assuring the adequate supervision of the actions of fiduciaries. Thus, the executor of a will may ask an equity judge to interpret the will, and the administrator of a dead person's estate may ask him for advice and guidance as to the accounting for, and distribution of, the assets. Directors and officers of corporations have fiduciary duties to their corporations, and therefore, most of the problems of corporations and corporation law are solved by equitable principles. Trustees and guardians are also fiduciaries and are supervised by the equity courts.

The courts of equity also have the power to issue orders to forbid the commission of future torts where the threatened wrongful act is likely to occur in the near future and common-law damages will not afford adequate compensation. This is known as the court's *quia timet* jurisdiction; the suit is brought by a person "because he fears" that a tort will be committed against him. For example, if your next door neighbor threatens to cut down an ornamental tree that is on your land or to throw poisoned meat onto your land so that your dog will eat it, you can get an injunction to forbid such acts. Usually the likelihood of imprisonment for contempt of the injunction is a sufficient deterrent to the threatened tort.

Thus, equity has become an integral part of American law. The major misconception about equity—that it is administered at the whim or caprice of the judge—is not, and never has been, true. The "discretion" exercised by the equity judge is a sound judicial discretion regulated by the established principles of equity that have, over time, come to play an invaluable role in American legal practice.

CASES

Cook v. Fountain, 3 Swanston 585 at 600, 36 Eng. Rep. 984 at 990 (Ch. 1676)

Gee v. Pritchard, 2 Swanston 402 at 414, 36 Eng. Rep. 670 at 674 (Ch. 1818)

Lane v. Newdigate, 10 Vesey 192, 32 Eng. Rep. 818 (Ch. 1804)

BIBLIOGRAPHY

J. H. Baker, "The Common Lawyers and the Chancery: 1616," in *Irish Jurist*, 4 (1969), discusses the disputes between the courts at the time of Coke and Ellesmere. W. H. Bryson, *The Equity Side of the Exchequer* (1975), describes the equity courts and procedures in sixteenth- and seventeenth-century England. E. R. Daniell, *A Treatise on the Practice of the High Court of Chancery*, 3 vols. (1837–1845), is the best English encyclopedic work on equity. J. A. Guy, *The Public Career of Sir Thomas More* (1980), discusses the court of chancery at the time of Wolsey and More. W. J. Jones, *The Elizabethan Court of Chancery* (1967), describes the court of chancery and its procedures. F. W. Maitland, *Equity: A Course of Lectures*, 2nd ed., edited by J. Brunyate (1936), gives the historical background of equity.

J. N. Pomeroy, *A Treatise on Equity Jurisprudence*, 5 vols. (1941), is a basic American encyclopedia on equity. E. D. Re, ed., *Selected Essays on Equity* (1955), concerns itself primarily with equity in America. Baron Redesdale (J. F. Mitford), *A Treatise on the Pleadings in Suits in the Court of Chancery* (1784), influenced equity practice in England and America. C. St. German, *Doctor and Student*, edited by T. F. T. Plucknett and J. L. Barton, Selden Society, vol. 91 (1974), a sixteenth-century explanation of equity jurisprudence, was very influential. E. H. T. Snell, *Principles of Equity*, 28th ed., edited by P. V. Baker and P. St. J. Langan (1932), is the basic English treatise on equity. Joseph Story, *Commentaries on Equity Jurisprudence, as Administered in England and America*, 2 vols. (1836), influenced the doctrines of equity; and *Commentaries on Equity Pleadings* (1838) was a widely used work on equity procedure. [*See also* DISCOVERY.]

THE FEDERAL COURT SYSTEM

Howard Ball

THIS essay will examine the growth of the federal judicial system, in particular, the United States district courts, the courts of appeals and the United States Supreme Court, from the Constitutional Convention and the First Congress (1789) to the activities of the Reagan administration and the Ninety-eighth Congress. An examination of the development of the federal judicial system is an examination of controversial political issues pitting federalism and states' rights against each other. From the beginning of the Republic, the issue has been whether there was a justification for the federal judicial system, given the existence of an energetic state court system with a fairly well developed common law in each state. Through political compromise, the federal judiciary was created in 1787 and 1789. After the Civil War and again after the Great Depression there were dramatic expansions of federal judicial power and authority. The essay describes these various periods of growth and stability in the federal judicial system.

HISTORICAL EVOLUTION

The evolution of the federal court system to its present jurisdictional and organizational shape and authority is a reflection of the general growth of central powers in a federal system. In the beginning of the Republic, there was dramatic mistrust of the federal judicial system, and from 1789 to 1875, the lower federal courts did not have very much authority. However, after the Civil War, with its clear resolution of the question of an organic versus a compact form of government, the growth of the federal judiciary, like the growth of the federal system generally, was inexorable.

Constitutional Convention of 1787. Throughout the period of the Articles of Confederation, an active state judiciary and viable state judicial systems provided adjudicative relief for persons with conflicts in need of resolution. Article III of the Constitution of 1787 created a second federal judicial system: "The judicial power of the United States shall be vested in one supreme Court and in such inferior courts as the Congress may from time to time ordain and establish." The creation of this separate federal court system inspired a great deal of contemporary controversy. During the Constitutional Convention in Philadelphia in the summer of 1787, heated debate took place over the necessity for a national court system. According to the noted constitutional historian Charles Warren, Article III was the subject "of more severe criticism and greater apprehension than any other portion of the Constitution."

There were serious concerns, especially among the Antifederalists (later called Jeffersonians) at the Constitutional Convention, that such a federal court system, with its obvious commitment to adjudication as the basic form of conflict resolution in the new social and political system, would dampen efforts that were under way in the states to develop nonlegalistic approaches to conflict resolution. Among Antifederalists, the legal profession was not the most popular vocation and the lawyer was not seen as the best or only person to act energetically to resolve conflicts in the community. Furthermore, as states'-rights advocates, they favored decentralized government, shorter tenure for judges, and an easier removal process and so were extremely concerned about the "monstrous appearance" of a new system of federal courts. Such a federal court system, even though its exact parameters were not worked out in 1787, was a manifest threat to those at the Constitutional Convention who believed in the dominance of state power in the new system of government. The Antifederalists felt that the state courts could continue the business of dispensing justice under the watchful eyes of the local populations. Luther Martin, one of the delegates opposed to the creation of the federal court system, said that the creation of these federal courts "would create jealousies and oppositions in the state tribunals with the jurisdiction of which they will interfere."

At the Constitutional Convention, the Antifederalists were opposed by the Federalists, or Hamiltonians, who believed that a strong, central government and a national commercial economy—with a strong federal judicial system to enforce the national government's rulings—were important for the continued viability of the new nation. The nationalists argued that the success of the new political system, federalism, "depended on the existence of a supreme national tribunal, free from local bias or prejudice, vested with power to give an interpretation to Federal laws and treaties which should be uniform throughout the land . . . and to control State aggression on the Federal domain" (Warren, vol. 1, 9). The Federalists did not trust the state courts to act objectively regarding property issues that would come into the court involving citizens of the local community. Said Warren, "The Courts of the states cannot be trusted with the administration of the national laws. The objects of jurisdiction are such as will often place the general and local policy at variance."

The 1787 Constitution finally incorporated two articles that attempted to satisfy both Federalists and Antifederalists: Article III vests "the judicial power . . . in one supreme Court, and in such inferior courts as the Congress may from time to time ordain and establish," and Article VI contains the supremacy clause, which states that the Constitution and the federal laws and treaties are the "supreme Law of the Land" and that "the judges in every state shall be bound thereby, any thing in the Constitution or laws of any state to the contrary notwithstanding." In

the end the general concept of a federal, or national, court system was accepted in 1787–1788; it would be for the new national legislature to develop the specifics of the new court system.

Judiciary Act of 1789. To the First Congress, meeting in 1789, was given the delicate task of determining the composition of the Supreme Court, erecting those inferior federal courts referred to in Article III, and establishing the jurisdiction of the Supreme Court and the inferior federal courts because, as a check on federal judicial power, Article III gave the Congress the power to limit the appellate jurisdiction of these federal courts. The fundamental differences of opinion between the Antifederalists and the Federalists that had existed in 1787 came out sharply during the debates from April to September 1789. Out of this intensely partisan discussion emerged the Judiciary Act of 1789.

For the Antifederalist legislator of 1789, such as James Jackson of Georgia, the creation of a federal court system "swallows up every shadow of a state judiciary." But, for the Federalist, such as Roger Sherman of Connecticut, "it is necessary that the National tribunal possess the power of protecting those [federally developed] rights from such [state court] invasion." Two basic questions were addressed by the national legislators in the First Congress: Should inferior federal courts be created at all? If so, should there be narrow jurisdictional limits so that federal courts will not "swallow up" the state court systems?

Two politically astute legislators, Oliver Ellsworth of Connecticut and William Patterson of New Jersey, led the fight in the First Congress for the creation of a federal court system. Political compromise ensued in the Congress, and the result was a federal court system that was structurally acceptable to the Federalists and functionally tolerable to the Antifederalists. Section 34 of the 1789 Judiciary Act was a basic restriction on the new federal courts' jurisdiction. It stated that the laws of the states "shall be regarded as rules of decision in trials at common law in the courts of the United States in cases where they apply." In effect, this meant that the state common law controlled the decisions of the federal courts in all cases except those involving "federal questions." State law controlled the actions of federal judges in cases heard in federal district courts, primarily diversity and maritime litigation. Furthermore, "federal question" jurisdiction—that is, the judicial power to hear cases involving clashes between a federal statute and a state law—was left with state courts in the first instance. While the Supreme Court could review these state actions, as is evident from Section 25 of the 1789 Judiciary Act and *Cohens* v. *Virginia* (1821), lower federal courts did not have jurisdiction to hear these types of cases until 1875. And, in 1793, Congress passed legislation that barred the new federal courts from enjoining proceedings in the state courts. This was a major bar to federal judicial power until the post–Civil War congressional statutes gave power to the three-judge federal district courts to remove certain civil rights cases from state courts.

The system of inferior federal trial courts established at that time placed severe restrictions on the jurisdiction of those courts. Although the federal trial courts, called United States district courts, were created to hear cases and controversies, the federal judges had to apply state law, the boundaries of the district courts followed state lines, the federal district court judges were given very limited jurisdiction by the First Congress, and the federal judges who would sit on these trial benches would be nominated by the president but the chief executive's selections would have to receive the advice and consent of the United States Senate.

As passed by the Congress, the Judiciary Act of 1789 established the structure of the federal court system that still exists today. There were thirteen federal district courts created by Congress in the 1789 legislation, with a federal district court judge assigned to each district. There was one federal district court in each of the eleven states in the federal Union at that time. Two other district courts were placed in Maine, then a part of Massachusetts, and in Kentucky, then still part of Virginia. (North Carolina and Rhode Island, after they ratified the Constitution, each received a federal district court and judge.)

Additionally, the Congress created three federal circuit courts—the southern, middle, and the eastern circuits. There were, however, no permanent circuit court federal judges. Instead, two justices of the United States Supreme Court and one judge from a federal district court would ride circuit to hear appeals from the district courts. The Congress also determined that the Supreme Court, the only federal court specifically mentioned in the Constitution, would have one chief justice of the United States and five associate justices.

Finally, much of the Judiciary Act's language focused on congressional development of the appellate power of the federal courts. For example, Section 25 of the 1789 act gave the United States Supreme Court the jurisdiction to review, on writ of error, certain actions of the state supreme courts that involved federal questions. This section was very controversial and led to a number of interesting Supreme Court opinions, notably *Martin* v. *Hunter's Lessee* (1816) and *Cohens* v. *Virginia* (1821). Section 13 of the 1789 statute led to the famous case of *Marbury* v. *Madison* (1803).

Organizational Development, 1789–1891. By 1791, Federalists in Congress had begun attempts to expand the organization and the power of the federal court system. In 1799 the Federalists introduced legislation, passed and signed into law by Federalist President John Adams in February 1801. In addition to expanding the jurisdiction of the federal courts, the Judiciary Act of 1801 eliminated the burdensome circuit-riding responsibilities of the Supreme Court justices, created six circuit courts of appeals, and created sixteen federal circuit court judges to sit permanently on these newly created circuit courts.

However, as soon as the new Antifederalist President Thomas Jefferson took office in 1801, along with a Jeffersonian-Republican Congress, that body passed the Circuit Court Act of 1802, which effectively repealed the 1801 Federalist legislation. Jefferson's repeal argument was simple and political: "The Federalists have retired into the Judiciary as a stronghold . . . and from that battery all the works of republicanism are to be beaten down and erased." In 1803 the solidly Federalist Supreme Court, with Chief Justice John Marshall writing the opinion in *Stuart* v. *Laird,* validated the 1802 repeal statute. Charles Warren commented of this opinion that "no more striking example of the nonpartisanship of the American Judiciary can be found than this decision by a Court composed wholly of Federalists, upholding, contrary to its personal and political views, a detested Republican measure." It was also, however, the better part of wisdom for the outgunned Federalist judges to withdraw from this battle; the Republicans were on the ascendancy politically and it would have been political suicide for the Federalist judges to have fought the Republicans on that issue.

With the validation of the 1802 repeal act, no further change in the structure of the federal court system occurred until 1891. Periodically, bills were introduced in Congress to change the organization of the federal court system. Essentially, these changes revolved around concepts of a viable intermediate federal court of appeals with permanent sitting federal judges given substantive jurisdiction to hear cases and controversies and thereby reduce the reviewing burden of the Supreme Court. Friedman notes, "In Congress, a strong states-rights bloc was hostile to the federal courts. . . . Again and again, reform proposals became entangled in sectional battles or battles between Congress and the President, and went down to defeat" (p. 126).

The Removal Act of 3 March 1875 was the first major breakthrough in the nationalists' efforts to give more power and responsibility to the federal court system. A removal act enables defendants in state courts to request a removal of their conflict from the state court into the local federal district court. Earlier removal act legislation had, in Warren's words, been introduced "out of a fear of prejudice in state courts against the national government." The successful 1875 Removal Act accomplished the following: Any action asserting a federal right could begin in a federal district court or, if begun in a state court, could be removed through a writ of habeas corpus to the federal courts. Functionally, after 1875, the federal courts took on a new, vastly important role in the federal system. Organizationally, however, it was not until 1891 that legislation was passed creating the new intermediate appellate courts with permanent sitting federal judges presiding over the appeals process.

Friedman has stated that the creation of the federal court of appeals was the outcome of "one of the most enduring political struggles in American political history." By 1890 the Supreme Court had a docket of over eighteen hundred cases. (By contrast, the Supreme Court's case load in 1950 was less than fifteen hundred cases.) The Court's case load was high because in the absence of an intermediate federal appel-

late court system, it had to hear all appeals from the district courts. As a result of this case-load problem, the nationalists prevailed in Congress and legislation was passed creating nine new intermediary federal circuit courts of appeals. Each of these new courts would have three federal judges sitting permanently on these appeal courts. Under the legislation passed in 1891, most appeals from the federal trial courts (the district courts) would end in these courts, subject to discretionary review by the Supreme Court.

Organizational Development, 1891–1937. In 1903 the three-judge United States district court was created by Congress to hear the Interstate Commerce Commission or Sherman Antitrust Act cases on appeal. All cases involving violations of this substantive legislation were to be heard by the special district court—made up of two court of appeals judges and one judge from the district court in that area—with appeals as of right directly to the Supreme Court. In 1910 the Mann-Elkins Act empowered these courts to hear cases brought by private individuals involving the constitutionality of state or federal statutes and to issue injunctions to prevent enforcement of these challenged statutes. In the 1960s these three-judge courts would play an important role in the resolution of civil rights clashes in the South.

Prior to 1960 these three-judge district court hearings were a rarity. However, civil rights litigation groups such as the National Association for the Advancement of Colored People (NAACP) began using these courts to remove hard cases from state courts. In 1956 there were 50 three-judge district court hearings; in 1976, there were 208 cases heard in these courts, including 161 civil rights cases. Given criticism of the use of these courts, Congress, in 1976, passed legislation that greatly restricted the use of these three-judge district courts, to lighten the burden of the federal judges. Additionally, during the early years of the Burger Court, the Supreme Court justices themselves took action to limit the activities of the three-judge district court, as in *Younger* v. *Harris* (1971). By 1983 the number of three-judge district court cases had dropped to a low of 27 cases.

By 1911, with passage by Congress of the Judicial Code, the basic contours of the federal system were established. There were the federal trial courts (the district courts), the intermediate-level appellate courts (the courts of appeals), and the Supreme Court. In 1925, Congress passed the Judge's Act. Prodded by the national organized bar and Chief Justice William Howard Taft, the national legislature, in a purely Hamiltonian move, expanded the jurisdiction of the federal courts, especially the Supreme Court, and dramatically improved the administration of a very decentralized federal court system. Congress accomplished this by authorizing the Supreme Court to have total control of its appellate docket by allowing the Court to use its certiorari power in a purely discretionary manner. With this very important change, the Court has had broad discretion to decide which cases it will resolve on the merits. In addition, the chief justice was allowed to assign federal judges to temporary duty anywhere in the federal court system, and he could create the Conference of Senior Circuit Judges (later called the Judicial Conference), which would meet annually in Washington, D.C., to discuss common federal court problems.

Roosevelt's Court-Packing Plan. When Franklin D. Roosevelt became president in 1933, he confronted a Supreme Court of nine elderly justices. Characteristically conservative (Chief Justice Taft had derisively referred to President Herbert Hoover as a "bolsheviki"), the federal justices on the High Bench did not like Roosevelt's energetic brand of governing. This was especially true of a handful of the justices known as the "Four Horsemen"—Justices Willis Van Devanter, James C. McReynolds, George Sutherland, and Pierce Butler. These "direct descendents of Darwin and Spencer," according to Henry Abraham, "were totally antagonistic to the New Deal, and they could usually count on support in their antagonism from Justice [Owen] Roberts and Chief Justice [Charles E.] Hughes."

By 1937 the Supreme Court, led by the Four Horsemen, had struck down over a dozen major pieces of New Deal legislation. Roosevelt was extremely frustrated because of these judicial actions and because he had not yet had a single occasion to select his first justice to sit on the Court. Consequently, on 5 February 1937, President Roosevelt sent to Capitol Hill his plan to enlarge the Supreme Court. His plan was simple: for every justice over seventy years of age who had served ten years on the federal bench and who had failed to retire within six months after

reaching his seventieth birthday, the president would be allowed to appoint a new federal judge, up to a maximum of fifty such appointments in the entire federal court system and fifteen on the Supreme Court.

The public justification for the plan was that the elderly men on the High Court needed the assistance of younger jurists to reduce the burdens on these federal courts. If successful, the Roosevelt plan would have given the president six new Supreme Court seats to fill. It would have given the country a new Court, a Court that would not invalidate New Deal legislation. Indignant letters from Chief Justice Charles Evans Hughes and Justice Louis D. Brandeis to influential senators helped kill the legislation in the Senate.

However, two critical events made such a draconian change of the federal court system unnecessary. First, two of the justices who had voted with the Four Horsemen, Hughes and Owen J. Roberts, switched their votes in key New Deal cases, thereby validating these controversial measures, notably in *West Coast Hotel* v. *Parrish* (1937) and *National Labor Relations Board* v. *Jones & Loughlin Steel Corp.* (1937). Second, in May 1937, the oldest of the Four Horsemen, Justice Van Devanter, announced his retirement effective 1 June 1937. Roosevelt's first appointee was a loyal New Deal legislator, Senator Hugo L. Black, a Democrat from Alabama. Roosevelt would ultimately appoint a total of nine men to the Supreme Court. As a consequence of vote switches, retirements, and death, Roosevelt did not have to push through his "organizational" reform of the federal system.

Growth of the System After 1939. The case load of the federal court system has increased dramatically in the years since the New Deal. Another section will examine the reasons for the growth of this case load; for now, it is enough to note its existence and to examine the response by Congress to these new developments. Ideally, in an adjudicative conflict resolution environment, "a litigant should have his case heard and decided within a reasonable time by an unhurried, highly qualified judicial officer" (Comment).

The reality of the federal court system is that since the Roosevelt administration, it has moved away from a purely deliberative, and toward a bureaucratic, response to increased litigation pleadings. As a recent United States Department of Justice Commission on the Revision of the Federal Judicial System report entitled *Needs of the Federal Courts* (1977) indicated, "We are creating a workload that is even now changing the nature of Courts, threatening to convert them from deliberative institutions to processing institutions, from a judiciary to a bureaucracy."

Administrative Office of the United States Courts. In 1939, at the behest of the Judicial Conference, the Administrative Office of the United States Courts was created by the Congress. The basic function of the office, reflecting this growing federal court system tendency toward "bureaucratization," was to collect statistics on the case load and related judicial activities of the federal courts. Its director was charged with the responsibility for issuing *Management Statistics for United States Courts for the Chief Justice of the United States.* This annual report provides the federal judges and the federal judicial administrators with extremely useful data to be used to deal with problems associated with the rise of the case load.

Office of United States Magistrates. In 1961 the case load for the district court judges across America totaled 98,000 criminal and civil filings. By 1976 the total number of filings was almost double the 1961 figure: 171,000 filings. One congressional response to this dilemma, which forced courts to choose between careful and efficient justice, was to free up the federal district court judge by providing relief in the form of better use of the United States magistrate.

In 1968, Congress passed the Federal Magistrate Act, which formally established the office of United States magistrate. According to Steven Puro, the office was created to "provide a first new echelon of judicial officers in the federal judicial system and to alleviate the increased work load of U.S. District Courts." Magistrates, appointed and supervised by the federal district court judges, relieve the federal judges of certain routine duties. Consequently, the federal judges are free to hear and monitor the cases that go to trial, while magistrates handle the various pretrial activities in both civil and criminal filings. Rather than enlarging the federal court system with another layer of federal courts, the 1968 legislation attempted to ease the work-load problem by enabling federal judges to get away from performance of purely administrative functions.

In 1985 over 500 full- and part-time magistrates served in the federal court system. The magistrate performs certain pretrial and post-trial functions in civil and criminal cases. These duties are ministerial (taking depositions, administering oaths), advisory, adjudicative, and quasi-judicial (hearing petty offenses cases, issuing search warrants, receiving prisoner petitions, disposing of motions, conducting postindictment arraignments). Magistrates must be members of the state bar; they are appointed by the federal judges in the United States district court for an eight-year term during which they can only be removed for "good cause."

A National Court of Appeals. As the case load handled by the judges in the federal court system increased in the middle decades of the twentieth century, there were increased demands by federal judges and others for organizational changes and substantive modifications in federal appellate court jurisdiction to parallel the kind of assistance the trial court judges of the federal court system received with the creation of the office of United States magistrate. In the 1960s and 1970s, renewed concern over the increased work load of the appellate federal judges, especially the United States Supreme Court justices, led to a debate over the creation of another federal court that would be situated, organizationally, between the federal courts of appeals and the Supreme Court.

In December 1972 a seven-person panel appointed by Chief Justice Warren Burger, an advocate of some kind of plan to relieve the justices of the work-load dilemma, presented its findings. In arguments reminiscent of the nineteenth-century arguments for a federal court of appeals, the *Federal Judicial Center Report of the Study Group on the Case Load of the Supreme Court,* chaired by Professor Paul A. Freund (the report is commonly referred to as the *Freund Report*), said that "relief is imperative" and called for the creation of a new tribunal, a national court of appeals, to ease the work load of the Supreme Court. The *Freund Report* envisioned a special appellate court, composed of seven United States court of appeals judges sitting in Washington, D.C., for (staggered) three-year terms, that would receive all cases (except original jurisdiction pleadings) presently petitioned to the United States Supreme Court. It recommended that this seven-judge appellate court "screen all petitions . . .

and hear and decide on the merits of many cases of conflicts between circuits. . . . The great majority . . . would be finally decided by that court. Several hundred would be certified annually to the Supreme Court for further screening and choice of cases to be heard and adjudicated there."

Once certified to the Supreme Court, the justices would use their discretionary powers to grant, to dismiss, or to deny. In addition, the report recommended that the Supreme Court be given the power to "make rules governing the practice in the National Court of Appeals." By mid-1975, five of the nine Supreme Court justices had indicated their support for the Freund plan—the four Nixon appointees (Chief Justice Burger, Justices Harry A. Blackmun, Lewis F. Powell, and William H. Rehnquist) and Justice White.

In 1975 a report was published by the Commission on Revision of Federal Court Appellate System, chaired by United States Senator Roman Hruska. It, too, recommended that a national court of appeals be created, but its vision of the relationship between the Supreme Court and the national court of appeals differed radically from the Freund committee's vision. The Hruska Commission urged that the new court "furnish additional authoritative decisions on issues of national law through the adjudication of cases referred to it by the Supreme Court."

Neither report was enthusiastically received. Supreme Court justices such as William O. Douglas, Potter Stewart, and William J. Brennan were highly critical. Douglas' response to these proposals: "It's about a four-day-a-week job." Stewart's comment was that "the very heavy caseload is neither intolerable nor impossible to handle." Other constitutional scholars pointed out that the concept of a national court of appeals, if implemented, would take away the Supreme Court's critically important power to review, to select the cases it wished to hear, and to decide them definitively as the final court of the federal system.

As a consequence of these criticisms, those who have been calling for an easing of the work load of the appellate courts, especially the Supreme Court's work load, including Justices White, Stevens, and Blackmun, have refocused their lobbying efforts in two directions. First is remedial legislation that would, in Chief Justice

Burger's language, "reduce the load on nine mortal justices," including Burger's recommendation that the three-judge federal district courts be eliminated entirely by Congress. Second is a narrowing of the jurisdictional doors of the appellate process to litigants, which, according to Burger, could be done by eliminating the abolition of the federal courts' diversity of citizenship jurisdiction.

In December 1978, in an opinion attached to a Supreme Court denial of certiorari, in the case of *Brown Transport* v. *Atcom* (1978), Chief Justice Burger pointed out that the Court was "accepting more cases for plenary review than [we] can cope with in the manner they deserve." Burger, in his opinion, called for a national reexamination of the Freund Committee recommendations. Referring to the fact that there were additional judgeships created recently, Burger concluded by stating that they "may solve short-term problems, but the long-term problems of the Supreme Court analyzed by the Freund committee . . . remain as they were a decade ago." In his *Brown* dissent, Justice White noted ominously "There is grave doubt that the appellate system has the capacity to function in the manner contemplated by the Constitution." Justice Brennan, however, in that same case, indicated that he was "completely unpersuaded . . . that there is any need for a new National Court."

In 1983 and again in 1985, Chief Justice Burger called for the creation of a temporary five-year experimental intermediate federal appeals court staffed by court of appeals judges. This court's prime task would be to resolve inter-circuit conflicts, which account for about fifty cases on the Supreme Court's docket. Nothing has happened in Congress to lead to the creation of this novel federal judicial experiment.

Recent Changes. In 1978, Congress passed the Omnibus Judgeship Act, which created 152 new federal judgeships at the district court and court of appeals levels. With this legislation, an effort by Congress to deal with the increased work load at the federal trial-court level, the federal judgeships were increased by one-third. (In 1985 there were 513 federal district court judges and 168 court of appeals judges.) President Jimmy Carter used the opportunity to appoint a large number of minority, female, and partisan Democratic jurists to the federal bench across America.

In 1980, the United States Court of Appeals

for the Fifth Circuit, the largest in terms of work load and number of judges, was divided into the reduced Fifth Circuit and the new Eleventh Circuit. The new Fifth Circuit, with its fourteen judges, covers the appeals from federal trial courts in Texas, Louisiana, and Mississippi. The new Eleventh Circuit, with its twelve federal appellate judges, receives appeals from trials conducted in the federal district courts in the states of Alabama, Florida, and Georgia.

In 1982, Congress passed the Federal Courts Improvement Act, which led to the creation of the United States Court of Appeals, Federal Circuit. In early 1986 the Reagan administration revealed plans to ask for the creation of a new federal court called the Social Security Court. This new entity would, if created by the Congress, hear the more than fifty thousand social security cases that are presently heard in the federal district courts.

Organizational changes in the federal court system will continue to take place. The debate does not have the same sharpness of focus that the Jeffersonians and Hamiltonians brought to the Congress about the role and function of the federal judiciary. There is an acceptance of the important role of the federal court system in the larger society. The discussion surrounding the creation of a national court of appeals centers around the need for such a body and the effect it might have in eroding the discretionary power of the Court.

CONTEMPORARY FEDERAL COURT SYSTEM

Since the Roosevelt New Deal, we live in the age of the Leviathan. Consequently, the federal courts have expanded to deal with the litigation that has developed as a consequence of new responsibilities that the central government has taken since 1933. More than 300,000 cases are heard annually in the federal judicial system, involving constitutional issues as well as commercial ones. The case load per judge in the federal district court has increased to over 508 per judge in the 94 district courts and the Supreme Court receives over 5,000 petitions annually. There is clearly a dramatic growth in the federal judicial case load. However, to place matters in perspective, there are over 26 million cases that are initi-

ated annually in the fifty state court systems. Thus, while the federal judicial personnel are struggling to deal with the increased case load, the state judicial personnel are still, much as in 1789, handling the bulk of the litigation in the federal system.

The federal court system in the 1980s (Fig. 1) is essentially the same one envisioned by the Federalists in 1787. There are the trial courts, an intermediate layer of appellate courts, and the Supreme Court. In addition, over the past century a small number of specialized, Article I federal courts, such as the Tax Court, the Court of Military Appeals, the Court of Claims, and the Court of Customs and Patent Appeals, have been created by Congress to handle special kinds of controversies that arise in America.

Process in the Federal Courts. An overview of the legal process in the federal court system (Fig. 2) emphasizes the point that adjudication in the system is essentially a time-consuming, procedural flow from trial court to appeal court. Most civil and criminal cases are settled prior to the formal trial, but most of the remaining transactions end at the trial level. The remaining sections will focus on the process in each of the three Article III courts in the federal court system: the district courts, the courts of appeal, and the Supreme Court.

The Federal District Court as an Organization. Federal district courts have become organizations that administer justice in a bureaucratic manner. This change from pure adjudication to "jurocracy" has led many people to review the process in an effort to return to the judicial process. The difficulty lies with the case load that the federal district courts have had to shoulder since the end of World War II. Jack Weinstein, a federal district court judge, summarized the development of the problem: "As the law has become more compassionate and the guarantees of equality and due process have begun to be realized, the quantitative problems of the courts have increased. The increased load on the courts because of the fact that we are doing more than merely paying lip service to the Constitution and our democratic ideals is great" (p. 145).

Because of the renewed legal emphasis by the Warren Court on "fundamental fairness" and on "equal protection of the laws" and because of the character of federal legislation that has created the additional load (that is, statutes

THE FEDERAL COURT SYSTEM

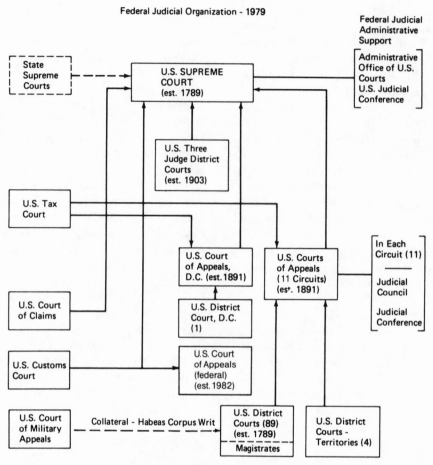

Federal Judicial Organization - 1979

FIGURE 1
Federal Court System in the 1980s

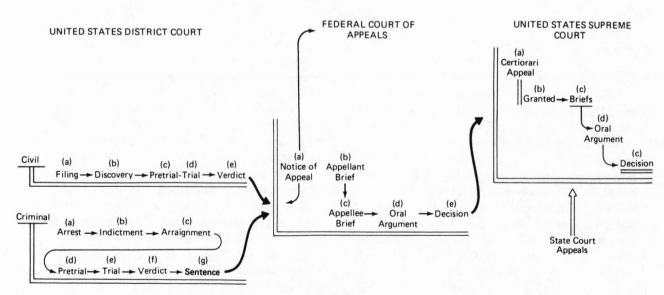

FIGURE 2
Federal Judicial Process from Trial to Final Appellate Review

creating civil rights and legislation providing more social and remedial-type legislation, with judicial review sections built into these statutes), the federal judge has become, in effect, a managing partner in a small law firm. On average, filings for district court judges were 77 in 1964 but almost 200 in 1980. In 1958, the staff–judge ratio in federal district courts was 11–1; by 1982, it had risen to 17–1.

In the federal district court, there exists an organized network of relationships centering about the federal judge. The judge has, minimally, two secretaries, two law clerks, a docket clerk, a court reporter, and several United States magistrates and probation officers as intimate support mechanisms in the effort to administer justice. In addition, in each district court system there is the office of the United States attorney, a chief clerk, private counsel (officers of the court), bailiffs, United States marshalls, and others.

The District Court Judge. The federal district court judge is the trial judge in the federal court system. The judge is also responsible for making that small federal court system function effectively. As Flanders and Sager put it, "the responsibility of the judge is to be superintendent of the production of justice" in the courtroom environment. Judicial bureaucratization occurs because the federal district court judge has begun to perform a great many administrative functions in addition to the judicial function.

As trial judge, the district court judge occasionally has to judge in an emotionally charged trial atmosphere. In sharp contrast to the serenity of the federal appellate courts, the federal trial judge must make instantaneous decisions on points of law during the trial itself. Most of the district court judge's judicial career is spent enforcing technical, procedural, and legal rules about which there is little disagreement. Even a policy-oriented district court judge spends a great deal of time issuing rulings on motions brought to him by attorneys involved in the litigation.

The trial judge must know the rules of federal civil and criminal procedure, as interpreted by the court of appeals and by the Supreme Court, and must also control the trial-court flow and personnel so that things get done in the organization. In this regard, the trial judge is assisted by major sets of subordinates: personal law clerks, court clerk, United States magistrate, United States attorneys, and private counsel.

At least two law clerks work for each federal district court judge. These young men and women assist the federal judge by working with the judge on legal briefs and requests for motions. The court clerk, appointed by the federal judge, is responsible for case management in the courtroom. The clerk maintains the judge's calendar and handles scheduling communications with the attorneys. In sum, the clerk is responsible for making sure that the basic court operations run smoothly and that things happen in the trial court when they are supposed to happen. The magistrates relieve the judge of administrative chores such as dealing with pretrial motions and prisoner petitions and trying minor cases. The United States attorney is responsible for prosecuting defendants in these district court trial proceedings, while the defense attorneys provide the legal counsel for those charged with violation of federal civil or criminal statutes.

Case Flow in the District Courts. Over 298,000 cases are filed annually in the federal district courts; these filings have increased by as much as 10 percent annually in recent years. There are essentially two broad types of cases that make up the work docket of the federal trial judges: private cases involving tort liability suits and diversity of citizenship; and public cases in which the United States attorney initiates criminal actions against individuals or in which the federal government is a defendant in a civil proceeding.

Civil Case Flow. As noted in Figure 3, the civil process begins in federal trial court with a plaintiff filing a complaint against the defendant. In 1938 the Federal Rules of Civil Procedure were developed by Congress to assist the parties in a civil suit in federal court. Two very important elements in this process are discovery and the pretrial conference. The former practice, carried on extensively under the guidance of the United States magistrate, allows both parties to a dispute to engage in a thorough review of the facts and an examination of the witnesses in order to find out the dimensions of the controversy. The pretrial conference between the judge (or the magistrate in many cases) and both parties to the dispute is carried on with the hope that out-of-court settlement will result. Most civil suits (90 percent nationally) are settled without going to trial.

THE FEDERAL COURT SYSTEM

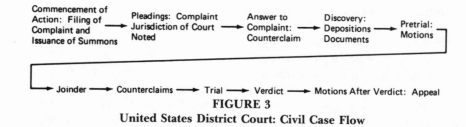

FIGURE 3
United States District Court: Civil Case Flow

Criminal Case Flow. The criminal-suit case flow was streamlined by virtue of congressional passage of the Speedy Trial Act of 1973. Criminal cases seldom reach the trial stage; generally, there is either dismissal of charges or a guilty plea through the mechanism of plea bargaining. Fewer than 10 percent of the criminal prosecutions initiated in the federal trial courts ever get to the trial stage. Figure 4 highlights the process since the passage of the 1973 legislation.

The 1973 federal law calls for the commencement of trial in criminal proceedings no more than one hundred days after the arrest. Between arrest and trial, there is the indictment phase, wherein the grand jury finds probable cause that a defendant has committed the act. This is followed by the arraignment phase, wherein the defendant formally responds, in the federal court, to the charges against the person. Within ten days there is a pretrial hearing, where the lawyers review the charges and evidence and attempt to settle the case prior to formal trial. If the charges have not been dismissed and if there has not been a successful plea bargaining, then the criminal case goes to trial before the federal district court judge.

Appeals of District Court Judgments. Federal law provides persons with the opportunity to appeal final decisions of the federal district courts to the United States courts of appeals. In addition, the federal courts of appeals hear appeals from federal administrative-agency or commission judgments. These intermediate appellate courts are required to hear all appeals brought to them from the federal trial courts, although the judges do not devote equal time to all cases. Every case that comes into the court of appeals from the trial courts or from the federal agencies is an attempt to, in the words of Richardson and Vines, "undo a previous judicial or administrative determination" (p. 115). Generally, less than 4 percent of the federal trial court judgments are appealed to the federal courts of appeals; most of the courts of appeals judgments end at that level.

The Court of Appeals as an Organization. Each of the courts of appeals, covering the entire federal system, including those lands that are the nation's territorial responsibility, consists of a number of judges who do most of their work in panels of three judges randomly selected by the chief judge of the circuit. The First Circuit has

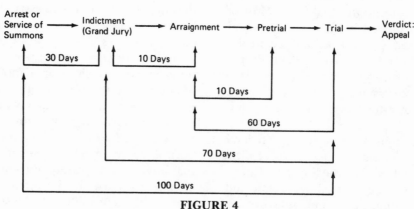

FIGURE 4
United States District Court: Criminal Case Flow

four judges and meets in Boston. The Second has eleven jurists and meets in New York. The Third has ten and meets in Philadelphia. The Fourth has ten and meets in Richmond, Virginia, and Asheville, North Carolina. The redrawn Fifth has fourteen and meets in New Orleans; Fort Worth, Texas; and Jackson, Mississippi. The Sixth has eleven judges and meets in Cincinnati, Ohio. The Seventh has nine judges and meets in Chicago. The Eighth has nine judges and convenes in Saint Louis, Missouri; Kansas City, Missouri; Omaha, Nebraska; and Saint Paul, Minnesota. The Ninth Circuit has twenty-three judges and meets in San Francisco and Los Angeles; Portland, Oregon; and Seattle, Washington. The Tenth has eight judges and convenes sessions in Denver; Wichita, Kansas; and Oklahoma City, Oklahoma. The new Eleventh Circuit has twelve jurists and meets in Atlanta; Jacksonville, Florida; and Montgomery, Alabama. In addition, there is the District of Columbia Circuit, with eleven judges, which meets in Washington, D.C., and the new Federal Circuit, with twelve judges, which meets in the District of Columbia and "in any other place listed above as the court by rule directs."

Each court of appeals, as a small organization, has its support staff to assist these judicial panels. Included in the support picture are the court clerk and the clerk's staff assistants, the law clerks that each federal appeals judge brings into the judge's chambers to assist the judge with case preparation (at least two for each federal judge and three for the chief judge of a circuit), librarians, bailiffs, messengers, criers, marshalls, United States attorneys, and the private counsel, considered officers of the court. A recent personnel addition to the federal courts of appeal support staff reflects the growing "bureaucratization" of the federal courts: each chief judge of a circuit court of appeals may appoint a senior staff attorney as well as a senior technical assistant to further assist the court in the management of the case flow in the federal courts of appeals.

The chief judge of each circuit is a senior judge, which means a judge who is at least sixty-four years of age, has served at least one year in a circuit court role, and has not previously been a chief judge. He presides at en banc sessions of the circuit court and is responsible for the administration of the circuit's legal responsibilities.

In addition, he plays a major role in the assignment of the other federal judges in the circuit to the three-judge panels, which hear the vast majority of appeals. The court, through the judgment of the chief judge, authorizes "the hearing and determination of cases and controversies by separate panels, each consisting of three judges."

Case Flow in Courts of Appeals. In 1940 the courts of appeals received 3,446 filings; in 1964 the filings rose to 6,000; in 1984 there were 28,000 appeals taken to the courts of appeals. In addition to the quantitative increase that has confronted federal court of appeals judges, there are the qualitative differences. Many of these appeals to the federal appellate court are highly complex cases that, unlike the one- or two-issue appeals of the 1940s, involve dozens of legal issues.

While judges have been added to the courts of appeals and the size and number of courts have increased to deal with the increased case flow into the federal courts of appeals, these changes have not kept pace with the case-load increase. Much like the explosion of the case load at the district court level, the explosion at the court of appeals level has had a qualitative impact on the amount of time a federal judicial panel can give to the multi-issue case before that small group.

The new Federal Circuit Court of Appeals, with its large contingent of federal judges, is available for relocation to the most crowded and burdened of the other circuits. Consequently, the process provides for short-circuiting of the full appellate review process. Figure 5 suggests that all appeals have oral arguments scheduled before the court's decision is announced. However, due to the case-load crunch, one-third to one-half of these appeals are not argued orally before the court of appeals.

En Banc Proceedings in Courts of Appeals. When, in the estimation of the chief judge, a case raises major policy issues, the chief judge will convene an en banc panel of that circuit. The en banc panel consists of all the judges sitting on that circuit. A classic example of a chief judge convening the court en banc was the 1973 litigation involving then-President Richard M. Nixon and the Watergate tapes. Judge John Sirica's decision in the district court was appealed by both the president's attorneys and the special prosecutor

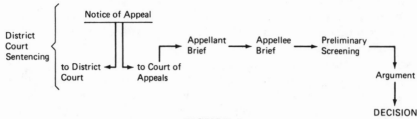

FIGURE 5
Case Flow: United States Courts of Appeals

in the Court of Appeals for the District of Columbia. Because of the historic nature of the constitutional and political and policy issues, the chief judge convened that court of appeals en banc.

Filing the Briefs in the Court of Appeals. After an adverse judgment in a federal trial court or a federal administrative agency, a person must file papers in both the trial court and in the court of appeals informing the courts of the intent to appeal. The appeal brief (stating the reason for the appeal and suggesting certain remedies that the court of appeals may apply to the case) must be filed in the court of appeals. The appeal brief must be accompanied by a transcript of the trial proceedings so that the court of appeals panel of judges will know with certainty what took place at the trial and will have the record to pore over as they and their clerks examine the legal points raised by counsel.

Informal discussions are then conducted between counsel for both parties to the dispute and officers of the court of appeals, including the staff attorney or an assistant staff attorney. The presubmission screening in a federal court of appeals, done by the court staff, sets aside those appeals called consensual—that is, those where there is general agreement on how the case ought to be disposed of by the court of appeals. These cases are disposed of summarily by the court of appeals without oral argument. Many cases, between a third and one-half of the total that begin this process, are screened out of the appellate process at this stage. Wheeler and Whitcomb note that "attorneys may 'settle' the case before court consideration, or they may withdraw the appeal, or the court may dismiss it on one party's motion that the court does not have jurisdiction."

Oral Arguments. Appellate oral argument is older than the written brief. It assists the federal appellate judge in a number of ways; the human connection between the bench and the bar is one important function of the oral argument. (Cases not settled or summarily decided are then scheduled for oral argument before a three-judge panel.)

During oral argument, counsel for both parties to the dispute elaborate upon points developed earlier in their written briefs and respond to questions by the sitting judges. These cases are the most difficult ones to be heard by the federal court and the resolution of these conflicts occasionally leads to intracourt conflict. (Statistically, J. W. Howard's study of three courts of appeals found that these middle-level appellate courts upheld the lower federal trial court judgment about 67 percent of the time.)

Appellate Decisions. On many occasions, a court of appeals panel will render its judgment immediately after oral argument has ended, without meeting in conference session to vote and to assign someone to write the opinion. There is also the per curiam opinion, a short written opinion that announces the judgment without an elaborate judicial justification for the decision. The balance of the cases are discussed in conference session after oral argument, a formal vote is taken, and then the opinions are written, based on the law of the circuit and the precedents of the Supreme Court. After the opinion has been written, printed, and approved by the panel, it is announced by the court of appeals.

Courts of Appeals as Final Reviewers. Congress' purpose in creating the courts of appeals in 1891 was to alleviate some of the federal appellate burden that rested solely with the Supreme Court justices. The courts of appeals have

THE FEDERAL COURT SYSTEM

fulfilled that purpose. They have relieved the Supreme Court of that burden. The federal courts of appeals, to the extent that very few appeals go from them to the Supreme Court, have functionally become the "court of last resort" for many claimants. What justice a person receives when appealing an adverse district court or administrative-agency ruling will be found generally in the federal court of appeals in that person's geographical area.

Appeals to the Supreme Court. Appeals to the Supreme Court come from federal courts of appeals, three-judge district courts, and state supreme courts. To be considered by the Supreme Court, these appeals must fall into the Court's constitutionally and statutorily defined jurisdiction and the case must be seen by the justices as justiciable.

By the mid-1980s the Supreme Court was receiving around 5,000 petitions yearly from these various sources. Annually, the justices of the Supreme Court decide between 130 and 150 cases. The rest, almost 95 percent of the number, are either denied the writ of certiorari or their appeals are dismissed for want of a substantial federal question.

The important point here is that the Supreme Court virtually controls its docket, for it hears only those petitions it wants to hear. The Supreme Court is not an appellate court in the traditional sense. The fact that the Court has decided to grant certiorari in a particular case means that the federal justices have decided to use that particular litigation as a vehicle for making known their policy preferences on one of the issues raised in the litigation and in the briefs.

SUMMARY

The development of the federal court system over two centuries of American history mirrors the tensions and dynamics of the growth of American society. The early years of the Republic were stressful ones; even after the Civil War, federal-state conflicts inhibited the full development of a functioning national judiciary. Not until 1891, with the creation of a fully functioning court of appeals network, did the federal court system begin to realize its potential—perceived a century earlier by the Federalists.

The development of the federal court system since 1891 has come full circle. In 1973, Chief Judge Irving H. Kaufman, of the United States Court of Appeals for the Second Circuit, sardonically said, "I submit that we [federal judges] are being smothered with confidence." By that decade, the federal court system was in the process of turning into a jurocracy—that is, a judicial bureaucracy. Because of the activism of the Warren Court and several Congresses, the jurisdiction of the federal courts has grown geometrically. The federal courts were being "smothered," but it was the paperwork—the thousands and thousands of pages of complex filings, the jurisdictional briefs, the briefs on the merits, the amicus curiae briefs—that was choking the federal jurists.

It is a great paradox that the system finds itself trying to build more federal courthouses and hire more federal judges—trial and appellate—and continuing to increase the jurisdiction of these federal courts. What was labeled a "monstrous appearance" in 1787, the federal courts, has become the very basic foundation of America's functioning republican system of self-government. Hamiltonianism has finally triumphed: there is a strong, independent, somewhat overworked federal judicial system in place, providing the citizens of a great nation with the opportunity to resolve conflicts in the context of a national court system.

CASES

Brown Transport v. Atcom, 439 U.S. 1014 (1978)
Cohens v. Virginia, 19 U.S. 264 (1821)
Marbury v. Madison, 1 Cranch 137 (1803)
Martin v. Hunter's Lessee, 14 U.S. 304 (1816)
National Labor Relations Board v. Jones & Loughlin Steel
    Corp., 301 U.S. 1 (1937)
Stuart v. Laird, 1 Cranch 299 (1803)
West Coast Hotel v. Parrish, 300 U.S. 379 (1937)
Younger v. Harris, 401 U.S. 37 (1971)

BIBLIOGRAPHY

Henry J. Abraham, *The Supreme Court in the Governmental Process* (1975), provides the reader with a good view of the

THE FEDERAL COURT SYSTEM

functions of the Supreme Court and its interactions with other political agencies in Washington, D.C.; and *Justices and Presidents* (1985), is a chronological political study of all presidential appointments to the Supreme Court from Washington to Reagan. Howard Ball, *Courts and Politics* (1980), examines roles, functions, and organization of the federal court system as well as the processes of decision-making in each of the three major federal constitutional courts. Warren Burger, "Annual Report on the State of the Judiciary," in 96 *U.S. Reports*, no. 9 (1 March 1976), focuses on the problems facing the federal judiciary and suggests organizational and management improvements. Comment, "An Expanding Civil Role for U.S. Magistrates," in *American University Law Review*, 26 (1975), describes the rapid growth of the responsibilities of United States magistrates in the district courts. James Eisenstein and Herbert Jacob, *Felony Justice* (1977), explores the organizational and policy relationships between the federal judge and his or her staff.

Steven Flanders and Alan Sager, "Case Management Methods and Delay in Federal District Courts," in Russell Wheeler and Howard Whitcomb, eds., *Judicial Administration* (1977), carefully examines and explains the rapid growth of the case load problem in the federal courts. Lawrence M. Friedman, *A History of American Law* (1973), is a well-written history of the development of the American legal profession. Sheldon Goldman and Thomas Jahnige, *The Federal Courts as a Political System* (1971), is a very good collection of essays focusing on the Supreme Court's judicial behavior as a part of the larger political process. J. Woodford Howard, "Role Perceptions and Behaviors in Three U.S. Courts of Appeals," in *Journal of Politics*, 39, no. 4 (1977), is a perceptive essay that analyzes judicial self-perceptions relative to the role and function of a federal judge. Roman Hruska, *Commission on Revision of Federal Court Appellate System* (1975), is the report that recommended the creation of a national court of appeals and was one of a number of proposals developed in the mid- and late 1970s that called for organizational modifications of the federal judicial system in order to deal with the increasing case load. Steven Puro, "U.S. Magistrates: A New Federal Judicial Officer," in *Justice System Journal*, 2 (1976), is a fine essay that examines the growth of the powers and responsibilities of magistrates.

Richard J. Richardson and Kenneth N. Vines, *The Politics of Federal Courts* (1970), is an early, yet still valuable, examination of the nature of federal judicial decision-making processes. United States Department of Justice, *Needs of the Federal Courts* (1977), is a government report that reflects on the growing case load dilemma of the federal courts. Charles Warren, *The Supreme Court in United States History*, 3 vols. (1922), is the classic recording of the history of the United States Supreme Court up to the early 1920s. Jack Weinstein, "The Role of the Chief Judge in a Modern System of Justice," in Russell Wheeler and Howard Whitcomb, eds. *Judicial Administration* (1977), written by a federal judge, clearly illuminates the role and functions of the federal judge who handles the administrative chores for his or her federal district court. Charles Wright, *Federal Courts* (1972), is an excellent examination of the federal court system from a legal perspective.

[*See also* CERTIORARI; DISCOVERY; JUDICIAL ADMINISTRATION; JURISDICTION; PLEA BARGAINING; *and* SUPREME COURT OF THE UNITED STATES.]

JUDICIAL ADMINISTRATION

Peter G. Fish

THE distinctive function of the judiciary is the adjudication of cases, and the immediate context of that function is judicial administration. Russell R. Wheeler and Howard R. Whitcomb define that context as including "*all* the directions and influences . . . that affect the behavior of a certain set of people . . . who are expected to contribute to just and efficient case processing." This broad definition necessarily nets a wide variety of elements internal to the judicial system: judges, clerks, court administrators, jurors, lawyers, and institutional structures relating to judicial selection and removal, court organization, jurisdiction, procedures, and management. It also encompasses immediate external elements—preeminently legislators and members of the executive branch, whose activities, or lack thereof, determine the personnel and institutional resources available for judicial administration. More remote external elements are manifested in societal changes to which the judicial function reacts or which it may even stimulate. These remote directions and influences affect court administration but lie largely beyond its control. Nevertheless, their impact, whether quantitative or qualitative, may prove so dramatic as to transform the contours of judicial administration.

In accord with the separation-of-powers doctrine, Article III of the Constitution vests "the judicial power of the United States" in the third branch of government. But except for the constitutionally established Supreme Court and its original jurisdiction, the system of "checks and balances" functions to render the judiciary a resource-dependent branch of government. Creation by Congress of tribunals inferior to the Supreme Court is specifically authorized by both Article I, Section 8, and Article III, Section 1;

Article III, Section 2 endows Congress with power to regulate appellate jurisdiction. Administrative elements of the judiciary likewise lie within the realm of congressional genesis and oversight. Article I, Section 8, grants to Congress power not only to effectuate powers delegated to it but also those vested in other branches. Thus, Congress enjoys sweeping authority to regulate courts and judges so long as its purposes and means are consistent with the letter and spirit of the Constitution. Legislative power may not encroach upon the judicial function because, as the Supreme Court stated in *United States* v. *Will* (1980), "a Judiciary free from control by the Executive and the Legislature is essential if there is a right to have claims decided by judges who are free from potential domination by other branches of government." But except for abolition of the Supreme Court and of its original jurisdiction, diminution of judicial salaries, and removal from office inconsistent with the "good behavior" standard, Congress, subject to judicial review, is broadly empowered to delegate its authority by establishing, maintaining, and overseeing institutions and programs of federal judicial administration.

As a result, the "mixed constitution" bequeathed by the eighteenth century and the intrinsic nature of judicial administration render virtually impossible effective separation of that subject from politics and the law. That which is pronounced judicial administration may in fact be public policy merely garbed in the shrouds of administration. President Franklin D. Roosevelt's famous 1937 court-packing proposal illustrates the inextricable links that exist between putative administrative reform, politics, and the law as developed through exercise of the judicial function.

JUDICIAL ADMINISTRATION

ADMINISTRATIVE HERITAGE

As mandated by the Constitution and congressional statute at the nation's inception, the federal judiciary manifested characteristics of a hierarchy of courts, not of judges. Independence, decentralization, and individualism stood as the system's hallmarks into the twentieth century. These features received recognition and reinforcement in the Judiciary Act of 1789. That formative measure created district courts, manned by solo judges, the boundaries of which were coterminous with those of the several states. It also combined into three circuits the eleven states along the eastern seaboard that had ratified the Constitution by the time the act became law. The circuit boundaries were drawn according to divisions used for military administration in the first year of the American Revolution. Thus began a venerable tradition of circuit lines bearing a dubious relationship to court conditions but a close one to state and regional political and legal cultures.

The foremost theme of national judicial administration during the federal judiciary's first century was creation of additional judgeships, courts, places of courts, and circuits intended to bring justice to an ever-growing but widely dispersed people. Within "watertight" geographical compartments created by the Judiciary Act of 1789, performance of the judicial function dominated courthouse activities. Managerial imperatives did not receive much attention. For instance, the 1789 act authorized adjournment of district court sessions when the judge found himself unable to attend or when a trial bench became vacant. The statute merely directed that all pending judicial business be continued "as of course until the first regular term after the filling of the vacancy." This casual management approach accorded with other elements of the federal judiciary's administrative context.

Judicial selection, patronage appointment by judges of subordinate court officers, fee-based financial autonomy, dominance of local law and procedure, and sheer geographic isolation marked a judicial system emphasizing localism over nationalism and administrative decentralization over centralization. Under such conditions federal judges enjoyed virtual autonomy. In administering their courts, they were independent of Congress, the president, and even

each other. Although Supreme Court justices had responsibilities in their assigned circuits, they exerted only sporadic influence on administration.

On a much reduced scale after 1866 and until the Court of Appeals Act of 1891, the circuit justices sat with district judges to constitute the old circuit courts finally abolished in 1911. But they sat primarily to perform the judicial function. Infrequently they played a role in judicial administration, as Chief Justice Salmon P. Chase did. He advised district judges and court officers in his Fourth Circuit on convening of the circuit court, settling jurisdictional conflicts with military courts in the postbellum occupied South, avoiding race discrimination in jury selection, and promptly deciding long-delayed cases.

Statutory acknowledgment of national judicial administration imperatives existed only in rudimentary form. Beginning in 1850, Congress authorized the chief justice of the United States to meet district court congestion by intercircuit transfer of judges, but only when the need arose from physical disability of the resident judge and could be satisfied by intercircuit transfer of a judge from a contiguous circuit. Two years later the act was amended to permit such transfers if warranted by exigencies caused by "the accumulation or urgency of judicial business in any district." Not until 1907 were all geographical restrictions on intercircuit assignments lifted when related to judicial disability. Six years later, Congress empowered the chief justice to assign a consenting judge from any one of the then existing nine circuits to the Second Circuit when the senior circuit judge in New York certified the existence of a case overload, whether or not caused by disability. All other circuits were made eligible recipients of such intercircuit transfers in 1922.

JUDICIAL REFORM

The incremental development of judicial transfers indicates the emergence of systemwide administration as a twentieth-century phenomenon. Reflective of political and jurisprudential developments in American society, the modern form of judicial administration was shaped by turn-of-the-century judicial reformers, who were participants in the broad-flowing Progressive movement. From their evaluation of the judiciary's condition in an industrializing and urbanizing nation, they concluded, as did William Howard Taft, that there existed nothing warranting criticism "in the decisions of the courts, or the character of the judges, or the result of litigation" (quoted in Fish, 1975, 129). Rather, the reformer's diagnosis revealed a preeminently administrative problem. Roscoe Pound had sketched in 1906 the specific steps demanded by the condition of the third branch. In his famed address "Causes of Popular Dissatisfaction with the Administration of Justice," presented at an American Bar Association (ABA) meeting, he called for centralizing changes in court procedures, flexible assignments of personnel, and chief-justice-based managerial systems using modern business methods.

Challenging this judicial-reform orthodoxy was the social progressivism associated with the urban liberalism advanced by Robert F. Wagner of New York, the Progressive party of Theodore Roosevelt, and the midwestern populism articulated by George W. Norris and Robert La Follette. These reformers emphasized government as the most efficacious means of ameliorating defects in the fabric of society, the foremost of which was the perceived maldistribution of political power and economic wealth. Achievement of popular democracy would pave the way for a more fundamental reallocation of national resources. Consequently, they attacked assessments of the judiciary's status that were concerned only with that branch's administrative shortcomings. The problems with courts, as these critics saw it, lay not in the dilatory nature of the judicial process but in the erroneous essence of its decisions. La Follette Progressives thus took direct aim at judicial decisions that were highly protective of private property rights.

Judicial reformers in the Taft tradition promoted reforms in judicial administration. They called for institutional autonomy from political influences and judge control of the courtroom, to be facilitated by the unification, simplification, and centralization of court systems. Chief Justice Taft advanced a three-pronged plan of reform. The first aimed at nationalizing procedural rules used in federal courts; it bore fruit in 1938 with the promulgation of civil procedure rules and in 1946 with the publication of criminal rules. Another resulted in the 1925 "Judge's Bill." A third prong fostered centralization of federal judicial management and spawned in 1922 the Conference of Senior Circuit Judges (later known as the Judicial Conference of the United States).

Nationalization of federal procedure under Supreme Court control was seen by proponents as a means of unshackling federal courts from legislatively drafted state rules reflecting interests of local plaintiff-lawyers and from subordination of judges to the will of contending lawyers in the courtroom. Simple and uniform judge-drafted procedures would elevate judges from mere umpires to actual controllers of litigation in their courtrooms.

The Judge's Bill was intended to enhance case-flow management in the Supreme Court by screening out unimportant cases and thereby rendering final the decisions of federal courts of appeals. In addition to augmenting the status and power enjoyed by these appellate courts, the measure spoke directly to jurisprudential issues by the confidence it manifested in the exercise of the judicial function by judges of the several federal courts of appeals. Review of their handiwork by the Supreme Court was discretionary. But dramatically different treatment was accorded judicial products emanating from state courts of last resort. Afflicted with an infusion of popular democracy, including elected judges and recall, state decisions were seen to embody a potential threat to the development of harmonious national law and consequently required mandatory review by the Supreme Court.

Development of a national administrative system looked to rendering federal judges accountable in some degree for their nondecisional acts. The Judicial Conference of the United States, chaired by the head of the judicial department, would become a catalyst to promote speedy, economical, honest, and efficient justice. That institution would thereby safeguard the core judicial function by deflecting public criticism of, and political attacks on, the end products of that function—legal decisions.

For Taft's successor, Charles Evans Hughes, threats to the judicial function emanated not from tides of popular democracy engulfing individual states but from the rise of executive-centered national governments at home and abroad. He therefore promoted major institutional changes that became embodied in the 1939 Administrative Office Act. The act established the

Administrative Office of the United States Courts. Its creation separated the judiciary's business and budgetary operations from the Department of Justice, thereby enhancing symbolically and realistically the third branch's independence from the executive in a wide range of nonadjudicatory matters. The new bureaucratic institution did not constitute an autonomous center of power within the branch, although neither the chief justice nor the Supreme Court sought control over its operation.

Not enamored of Taft's enthusiasm for a judge-centered hierarchical administrative system and with the court-packing bill fresh in his mind, Hughes successfully diverted supervisory power over the office from the chief justice to the Judicial Conference and shifted responsibility for hands-on administration in the several circuits from himself and his Court to circuit-based judicial councils. This decentralized system accorded with his jurisprudential belief in "dual federalism" and evidenced his deep-seated fear that scandals or maladministration in remote federal courts might reflect badly on, and induce political attacks against, the chief justice "as the responsible officer who apparently had been neglectful in a matter which did not seem important perhaps at the time, but later developed importance" (quoted in Fish, 1973, 137). Also authorized by the 1939 act were circuit judicial conferences patterned on those held annually in the Fourth Circuit since 1931. Attendees at these judge-controlled forums include members of federal and state benches, the bar, and law schools. The broad purposes served by the conferences are socialization of federal judges in national judicial norms, public relations and education, and mobilization of regional political support for the federal judiciary's administrative programs.

No further institutions of federal judicial administration emerged until 1967. In that year Congress established the Federal Judicial Center, intended to support the third branch's extensive administrative bureaucracy, then beginning to confront a case-load crisis of impressive proportions. It was designed to meet the challenge of "congestion and delay, untrained supporting personnel, inadequate facilities, uneven distribution of case loads, and the general absence of administrative expertise" (quoted in Fish, 1973, 370). Congress charged it with (1)

coordination and conduct of "research and study of the operation of the courts of the United States"; (2) developing and conducting "programs of continuing education and training for personnel in the judicial branch of Government, including, but not limited to, judges, [bankruptcy] referees, clerks of court, probation officers, and United States [magistrates]"; and (3) providing "staff, research, and planning assistance to the Judicial Conference of the United States and its committees."

STATE TRENDS

Changes in federal judicial administration in the 1930s were accompanied by stirrings at the state level. In 1938 the ABA endorsed standards advanced by two key actors in the struggle leading to the Administrative Office Act of 1939: Chief Judge John J. Parker of the Fourth Circuit and Arthur T. Vanderbilt, president of the ABA. The latter expounded on the virtues of these standards in *The Challenge of Law Reform,* in which he urged the consolidation of fragmented court systems into unified systems that featured a simplified plan of organization and distinct centralizing elements. In this manner states might achieve judge-centered administration of justice free of legislative control over procedures and free of executive-branch dominance of budgets and purely administrative functions. A "scientific" policy planning component was embodied in judicial councils to be established by the states.

The Parker-Vanderbilt "Minimum Standards of Judicial Administration" advanced in 1938 and amplified in 1949 sought to render the doctrine of separated powers a reality by enhancing third-branch autonomy. The specific elements of the reform platform found their way into the 1947 New Jersey Constitution. As explained by "midwife" Vanderbilt, that document vested in the state's supreme court

exclusive power not only to make rules of practice and procedure but also rules of administration for all of the courts in the States. In matters of administration the Supreme Court therefore acts as the policy-making body for the judicial system, occupying a position in the administration of the courts comparable to that of the board of directors of a business corporation. The Constitution also provides that the Chief Justice of the Supreme Court shall be administrative head of all the courts and grants him broad powers with respect to the assignment of judges. His position therefore, is comparable to that of chairman of the board and president of a business concern. He is concerned both with the establishment of policies and with their execution. For the Supreme Court and the Chief Justice to exercise intelligently their policy-making powers and to enable the Chief Justice to carry adapted policies into effect, they must have an organization. This is primarily afforded by an Administrative Office of the Courts headed by a director who is appointed and serves at the pleasure of the Chief Justice.

The Parker-Vanderbilt executive model of judicial administration received approval from the ABA and the National Municipal League and became the bellwether of judicial reform during subsequent decades.

In the decades after 1938, states implemented to varying degrees the model system of judicial administration advocated by reformers. A comprehensive survey, *State Court Organization 1980* executed by the National Center for State Courts, reported on fifty-five court organizations and found management centralization much in evidence. The chief justice or presiding judge of the court of last resort served as the administrative head of all courts in thirty-one jurisdictions. In another eighteen the Supreme Court held responsibility for general administration of the full court system but usually acted through the chief justice. Court budgeting and funding constituted paramount and continuing issues of judicial administration. Funding of many state court systems is derived from different sources, including the state and local governments as well as fines and fees imposed on litigant-users. Overcoming decentralization and localistic influences promoted by such fragmented funding sources is sought by full state financing of the courts. This step toward centralization has usually been accompanied by centralized or unitary judicial budgeting. Transfer to the courts of their budgets embedded in executive budgets subject to gubernatorial veto is discerned as enhancing third-branch power while reducing local court autonomy. These factors tend to spur resistance to transfer of budgeting from local and political

entities, as Carl Baar has observed. Nevertheless, the survey reported that in thirty-four of the fifty-five jurisdictions examined, judicial budgets could be classified as separate from, and coequal with, those of the executive branch. In twenty-six systems, the courts' budgets were free of executive-branch authorization for transfers across budget categories.

Although each of the fifty states possesses its own system of judicial administration, since 1978 the National Center for State Courts in Williamsburg, Virginia, has provided "a focal point for state judicial reform, . . . a catalyst for setting and implementing standards of fair and expeditious judicial administration, . . . and . . . answers to the problems of state judicial systems" (Fetter, iii). The institution thus bears a similarity to the Federal Judicial Center. It operates a communications network to publicize innovations, undertakes training programs, and sponsors studies on state court organizations, jurisdictions, managements, technologies, and procedures. Its program has been complemented by the National Judicial College at Reno, Nevada, which since 1964 has offered educational opportunities to state judges. By the 1980s both these nonprofit institutions found themselves in difficult financial straits. To aid them as well as state courts whose judicial function had been impacted by federal legislation and United States Supreme Court decisions, Congress considered establishment of an independent federally chartered and funded state justice institute. This corporation would disburse funds directly to state and local courts as well as to such intermediaries as the National Center for State Courts.

THE JUDICIAL CONFERENCE

Institutions of federal judicial administration serve a twofold purpose. First, they develop, promote, and implement integrative policies affecting administration. Second, because the courts are dependent on coordinate political branches for resources, their administrative institutions engage in legislative clearance activities, including lobbying.

The intrabranch administrative function is challenged by a historic sense of autonomy and professionalism felt by individual lifetime judges. Judges prize independence as a bulwark of their essential judicial function, but Chief Justice Warren E. Burger's administrative assistant, Mark Cannon, once noted, "Without a similarly compelling societal need . . . judges have long extended this traditional independence to the administration of their own courts, valuing independence from both the other branches of government and other courts and institutions within the judiciary." This tendency is exacerbated by the geographical organization of the courts, a selection process based on that organization, which produces locally oriented judges; by the decentralized administrative system written into law in 1939; and by what Cannon termed a "tradition of civility and camaraderie associated with their profession." The presence of these elements has meant that "hierarchical chains of command, formal rules of interaction among judges, and impersonality are the exception" (p. 37). These aspects have encouraged judicial autonomy and rendered difficult the development of accountability in the realm of judicial administration.

The Constitution, with its separated powers and built-in checks and balances, likewise poses dilemmas for the modern judiciary. From 1922 to 1939 the creation of largely self-contained and autonomous administrative institutions had the paradoxical result of facilitating "clearance," presentation, and enactment of the judiciary's legislative programs. Simultaneously, it largely eliminated links with the politically powerful executive branch and enhanced the import of governmental fragmentation for judicial administration. Predictably, congressional attention to court-related programs has been episodic. Political inertia is surmounted only by the development of a real or perceived crisis in federal judicial administration—usually related to a case-load inundation exceeding the judiciary's capacity to process it. Such propitious conditions for change are dimly perceived by the general public unaffected by delayed justice. Consequently, as Chief Justice Burger observed, the judiciary's needs for resources "reach the attention of the other branches and the public only if they are pressed forward by someone—and often not even then" (quoted in Cannon and Cikins).

The Judicial Conference of the United States is the linchpin of national judicial administration. This supreme oracle of policies affecting administration of the federal courts began as an annual gathering of presiding judges of the then existing nine courts of appeals, Chief Justice Taft, and President Warren G. Harding's attorney general. Since 1949 the conference has met in Washington at least twice each year and sometimes more frequently. Participants include not only the chief justice and the chief judges of each of the eleven numbered circuits and of the District of Columbia and federal circuits but also, since 1957, a district judge representative from each circuit with the exception of the federal circuit, which lacks a trial-court tier. These twenty-six conference members are joined by nonmember invitees drawn from the judiciary and its administrative offices, from Congress, and from the Department of Justice. Although not a court and not specifically performing a judicial function, conference sessions are held in secret. A cryptic summary of its proceedings is published with the annual report of the director of the Administrative Office of the United States Courts.

The Chief Justice. Chairmanship of the Judicial Conference has, in some degree, transformed every chief justice beginning with William Howard Taft into the "third-branch chieftain." Only first among nine equals on the Supreme Court over which he presides, the chief is first among judges and others clothed with distinctly inferior formal status. Even under relatively weak leaders, the conference has served as a vehicle for advancing administrative policies favored by him. The chief justice, as third-branch chieftain, is essentially the glue holding together a diverse and fragmented administrative system. In his hands are the levers of power, such as they are, vital to the operation of that system. He is statutorily required to preside at sessions of the Judicial Conference. But every chief since Taft has done more than merely preside.

The chief justice controls the agenda, and he votes. More important, he determines the composition of more than a dozen standing and special conference committees, appointment to which confers enhanced status on otherwise undifferentiated legal professionals. The Administrative Office acts under "the supervision and direction" of the Judicial Conference, and its director and deputy director are appointed by the Supreme Court. But in practice the High Court justices defer to the chief's preferences, on grounds that he chairs the conference, to which the administrative officers are responsible. The chief justice also influences the agenda of the Federal Judicial Center. As chairman of its governing board, he is in a position to promote his candidate for director of the Center and to shape the agency's research programs and its training programs for court personnel. Chief Justice Burger proved decisive in establishment of the Study Group on the Case Load of the Supreme Court, the controversial report of which urged creation of a national court of appeals as an adjunct to the Supreme Court.

Judicial Conference Committees. The work of the Judicial Conference, with its numerically large membership and relatively brief sessions, is performed in committees. Their subject matter indicates the range of the agency's interests. In addition to an executive committee, there are committees classified as either "general" or "special." In the former category is that on court administration, with subcommittees on such matters as federal jurisdiction, judicial improvements, judicial statistics, supporting personnel, and intercircuit assignments. Special committees include those to implement the Criminal Justice Act, judicial ethics, admission of attorneys to federal practice, codes of conduct, and judicial branch. The standing Committee on the Rules of Practice and Procedure replaced in 1958 both the Supreme Court Advisory Committee on the Rules of Civil Procedure and Practice and the Committee on the Rules of Criminal Procedure. The work of the rules committee is facilitated by separate advisory committees on criminal, civil, appellate, and bankruptcy rules. Recommendations of this committee approved by the conference are subject to Supreme Court adoption, modification, or rejection in order "to promote simplicity in procedure, fairness in administration, the just determination of litigation, and the elimination of unjustifiable expense and delay."

INTRABRANCH ADMINISTRATION

From its inception in 1922, the Judicial Conference has worked to promote third-branch administrative centralization and uniformity to ends identical with those statutorily articulated for procedural rules. The act of that year, incorporated in Title 28 of the United States Code, charges it with duties to "make a comprehensive survey of the condition of business in the courts"; to "prepare plans for assignment of judges to or from circuits or districts where necessary"; and to "submit suggestions and recommendations to the various courts to promote uniformity of management procedures and the expeditious conduct of court business." The first duty imposed stimulated development of judicial statistics, which eventually involved the Administrative Office, a parallel Judicial Conference committee, and the Federal Judicial Center. Intercircuit assignment of judges, which Taft regarded as an administrative panacea for congested court dockets, has always produced both costs and benefits for the judicial system. A variety of transfer motives exist, one of which looks to influencing the doctrinal results shaped by transient judges' exercises of the judicial function.

Just as administration and law are sometimes inseparable in the realm of intercircuit assignments, so administration may closely relate to politics. Congressional denunciation of the organization in 1959 and use of judicial manpower followed an earlier Judicial Conference "cover-up" of an incipient scandal involving questionable maintenance expenses charged by judges on assignment to "foreign" courts. Legislative agitation produced the Committee on Intercircuit Assignments. Intended to foster rational nationwide deployment of federal judges, it also serves to insulate the chief justice against unwise assignments, possibly subjecting him to criticism and the federal judiciary to political attacks.

The power of the conference to make "suggestions and recommendations" to judges on management of their courts promoted an important and enduring theme of judicial administration. The conference has attempted to shift control of local judicial administration from the adversaries to the judges before whom they contended. It worked to convert judges from umpires to potent administrators of a system that increasingly manifested attributes of the continental inquisitorial model.

Pretrial practices authorized by the Federal Rules of Civil Procedure and promoted by the Judicial Conference Committee on Pretrial Procedures in the 1940s and 1950s eroded lawyer control of the litigation process. Kenneth M. Holland has noted that "the rules authorize judges to manage the discovery phase of litigation and to sanction dilatory attorneys; judges may broaden the scope of litigation by forming all litigable issues between the parties; and because the [Federal Rules of Civil Procedure] abolished the distinctions between law and equity, judges may deny the right to trial by jury where it existed before." Pursuit of a judge-controlled court system has continued into the 1980s. In accord with Chief Justice Burger's long-held view on the dismal quality of advocacy, the Judicial Conference, through one of its committees, considered plans for imposing special admission requirements on attorneys seeking to practice before federal courts. Perceived implications of the proposal for lawyers from racial minorities and for legal education gave proponents pause.

Much of the conference's business relating to administration in lower courts is of a housekeeping variety. Yet the stake for individual courts can be high indeed and the accompanying intrabranch politics intense. Committees on the budget; on administration of the federal magistrates system, the bankruptcy system, and the probation system; on implementation of the Criminal Justice Act; as well as the subcommittee on supporting personnel of the Committee on Court Administration, all determine who gets "what, when, where, and how" within the limitations imposed by the congressionally authorized judicial budget. Related intrabranch distributive politics involves individual trial and appellate judges, chief judges, circuit judicial councils, and national organizations of court officials, such as the National Council of United States Magistrates. A decisive actor in the allocation of judicial resources is the Administrative Office, the judiciary's central bureaucracy. Its interest lies in maintenance of fairness, equality, and uniformity in management of the personnel systems prevailing among classes of court employees. These widely dispersed individuals range from secretaries to probation officers, to court reporters.

CIRCUIT JUDICIAL COUNCILS

Judicial councils in the federal circuits provide the court system with an areal administrative organization. For more than four decades following establishment of the councils, authorized by the act of 1939, council membership consisted of all judges sitting on the court of appeals in each circuit. Effective 1 October 1981, the Judicial Councils Reform and Judicial Conduct Act of 1980 mandated district judge representation, a tacit acknowledgment of the consensual basis of authority among legal professionals in the federal judiciary. The value of representativeness was augmented by that of expertise when a professional administrator was provided each circuit court of appeals by the Circuit Court Executive Act of 1981. Charged with performing specific supporting services for the councils, circuit executives are certified by a special board whose five members are named by three different judicial institutions, each of which is headed or dominated by the chief justice of the United States.

Like the Judicial Conference, the councils utilize committee systems and operate in secret. But unlike the national agency, these regional institutions issue no public reports on their proceedings. However, minutes of a council meeting may be distributed to all federal trial and appellate judges within the circuit, and a brief digest of council work may be included in a circuit executive's published annual report. Partial justification for such secrecy is that the business transacted relates to largely mundane administrative matters.

Councils actually perform a variety of duties consistent with the statutory charge to ensure "the effective and expeditious administration of the business of the courts within its circuits," a charge broadly construed to reach the appellate court as well as the more numerous trial benches. Purely housekeeping matters, sometimes confined to management of the court of appeals, have included plans for public presentation of a retired circuit judge's portrait and authorization of sets of circuit court briefs and opinions in unbound form. Similar matters have related to the circuit as a whole, such as laying plans for its social event of the year, the circuit judicial conference.

Notwithstanding attention devoted to administrative trivia, the councils were conceived as key units of federal judicial administration. Language carried in the act of 1939, as revised in 1948 and incorporated in Section 332(d) of Title 28 of the United States Code, states that "each judicial council shall make all necessary orders for the effective and expeditious administration of the business of the courts within its circuit. The district judges shall promptly carry into effect all orders of the judicial council." The "orders" contemplated reflected the councils' sweeping mandate. As affirmed by Congress in 1961 and reaffirmed by the 1974 Judicial Conference, that mandate embraced "not merely . . . the business of the courts in its technical sense (judicial administration) such as the handling and dispatching of cases, but also to the business of the judiciary in its institutional sense (administration of justice), such as the avoiding of . . . loss of public esteem and confidence in respect to the court system, from the actions of a judge or other person attached to the courts" (Flanders and McDermott, 83). To this end, councils have exercised docket supervision; review and clearance of administrative acts of trial courts; and review of allegations of misconduct on the part of court personnel, officers, and judges.

As the more inclusive entity in federal judicial administration, councils were charged by the 1974 Judicial Conference with an affirmative responsibility to review district court administrative issues, such as case flow, number of prisoners awaiting trial, assignment of counsel for indigent defendants, and jury selection. "Where it appears that the court of appeals or any district court in the circuit has a large backlog of cases," the conference demanded that "the circuit council should take such steps as may be necessary to relieve the situation" (Flanders and McDermott, 84). Notwithstanding the responsibilities imposed, a thorough 1978 Federal Judicial Center study determined that council performance of its docket supervision function fell short of expectations.

Congress has continuously augmented council responsibilities with specific review or clearance functions. Some of these are shared with, and typically devolve upon, the chief judge of the circuit. Thus, councils must review and approve district court plans for random jury selection, appointment of counsel under the Criminal Justice Act of 1964, requests for court quarters and accommodations, and pretermission of district court sessions; and prior to subsequent review by the Administrative Office and the Judicial Conference, they approve and transmit recommendations for additional and continuing court personnel, ranging from secretaries to new judgeships.

Variations on the review-and-clearance function enhance the councils' role and, to some degree, obscure the distinction between administrative and judicial functions. The councils appoint, on recommendation of relevant district courts, federal public defenders and are empowered by the Bankruptcy Amendments and Federal Judgeship Act of 1984 to establish courts. A consenting district court majority may authorize referral of appeals from a bankruptcy judge to a council-established "bankruptcy appellate panel, comprised of bankruptcy judges from districts within the circuit." While these "executive" acts are unlikely to impinge on the judicial function, other duties may have that effect or permit the council to do in its administrative capacity what the court of appeals might do, should the relevant issue be raised in a live "case and controversy." The Jury Selection and Service Act of 1968 requires that councils receive the names of all persons excluded from jury service, "together with detailed explanations for the exclusions." In the absence of any case and controversy, these administrative agencies are empowered "to make any appropriate order . . . to redress any misapplication" of a statutorily prescribed bar to jury service.

JUDICIAL DISCIPLINE

The framers of the Administrative Office Act of 1939 clearly intended for councils to act as the system's troubleshooters. Each was to "make all necessary orders" to remove obstacles to "effective and expeditious" judicial administration. Hard tests confront a council when the obstacles are posed by court personnel and especially by judges. Councils may or may not grapple with the hard tests; they may defer to the chief judge of the circuit to resolve the problem in an informal diplomatic style, or they may seek to remove the problem to, or invoke the authority of, the more inclusive element of judicial administration—the Judicial Conference.

Disciplinary measures to remove from office subordinate supporting personnel and non–Article III court officers, such as magistrates and bankruptcy judges, test the will, but not the power, of councils. Judges appointed to hold office during "good Behaviour" (Article III, Section 1) present a more perplexing problem.

It is a dilemma not faced to the same degree in the several states where judges, however selected, hold their offices for terms of years. All fifty states have central institutions for disciplining their judges. In each, a variously constituted commission is organized in either a single tier or many tiers, depending on the perceived desirability of separating fact-finding from judgment-recommendation tasks. Commission recommendations are transmitted to the state supreme court for its authoritative imprimatur, except in a handful of states where they are received by legislatures that retain judicial removal power.

Disciplinary power, such as it is, remains largely decentralized in the federal system. When a circuit council has to cope with a wayward judge, it is confronted by a dilemma. On the one hand, its duty is to promote efficient judicial administration; on the other, the 1974 Judicial Conference warned that in making "all necessary orders" to achieve that end, councils must be aware "that the independence of individual members of the judiciary to decide cases before them and to articulate their views freely be not infringed by action of a judicial council." In the exercise of powers related to docket supervision, councils have issued to judges rare formal orders freezing, reducing, or removing case assignments. Among them was the Tenth Circuit Council, the action of which received Supreme Court consideration in *Chandler* v. *Judicial Council of the Tenth Circuit* (1970).

Ongoing debate inside and outside of Congress over removal of federal judges by means other than impeachment and a vast increase in the number of Article III judges during the Carter presidency led Congress to enact the Judicial Councils Reform and Judicial Conduct and Disability Act of 1980. The act explicitly empowered the councils to receive complaints about judicial conduct opaquely described as "prejudicial to the effective and expeditious administration of the business of the courts, or alleging that such a judge or magistrate is unable to discharge all the duties of office by reason of mental or physical disability." An elaborate judicialized procedure for processing such complaints within the administrative system of the councils and the Judicial Conference was prescribed. Armed with power to subpoena witnesses, primarily attorneys reluctant to testify against judges before whom they practice, council proceedings bore "inquisitorial" characteristics.

Available sanctions are largely those which preexisted the act: (1) public or private censure or reprimand; (2) request for voluntary retirement; (3) certification of disability with reduction of the subject judge's status to that of most junior in commission, his judgeship to terminate upon death or retirement, together with creation of an additional permanent judgeship; (4) freeze "on a temporary basis for a time certain" case assignments; and (5) "such other action as it considers appropriate under the circumstances." What these actions might include is unexplained. Conceivably, councils could impose monetary fines on Article III judges. Noncompliance could be referred by councils to the Judicial Conference for issuance of an order to the director of the Administrative Office of the United States Courts to deduct the fine from the errant judge's salary. Whatever actions a council may take, it is explicitly barred from removing a judge from office. Should a council determine that the conduct constitutes grounds for impeachment or, as in past instances, decide that the conduct "is not amenable to resolution" by council, the case may be certified to the Judicial Conference of the United States, which may take "appropriate action." If impeachment is deemed warranted, the conference is empowered to transmit the record and its determinations to the House of Representatives.

In the fiscal year ending 30 June 1983, the Judicial Conference reported that 148 complaints had been filed under the act. Most were directed at the conduct of district judges, and nearly half related not to administrative shortcomings but to allegedly defective exercises of the judicial function. As mandated by the statutes, such complaints were dismissed, usually by the chief judge of the circuit acting as a screening agent rather than by the full council. Of the 148 filings, only 5 reached the Judicial Conference Committee to Review Circuit Council Conduct and Disability Orders.

THE JUDGES' LOBBY

Separation of powers prescribes third-branch dependency on the legislature for needed resources. The federal courts in particular have traditionally looked to Congress for their financial and other resources, including changes in court organization, jurisdiction, and procedures.

Chief Justice Taft early perceived the Judicial Conference as an apt vehicle for enabling "the judiciary to express itself in respect of certain subjects in such a way as to be helpful to Congress." Objections from one conference participant to this function, on the grounds that it contravened the separation-of-powers doctrine, were squelched by word from the chief that "Congress was waiting upon the Conference for such recommendations" (quoted in Fish, 1973, 61–62). Appropriations and creation of additional judgeships comprised the earliest legislative proposals and were soon augmented by those for changes in institutional structures and procedures. The establishment of the Administrative Office, accompanied by the transfer to it of subject matter previously within the purview of the Justice Department and by the related development of the Judicial Conference committee system, brought more and different legislative recommendations to Congress. Reflecting this enhanced liaison orientation, Congress embodied in statute what had been actual practice since 1922: the Judiciary Act of 1948 required that the chief justice submit to Congress recommendations for legislation adopted by the conference.

Legislative liaison as an integral part of judicial administration unavoidably draws judges into the political process, thereby introducing a chronic tension. Should or should not members of the third branch adhere to a self-effacing policy of "judicial lockjaw" rooted in the separation of powers? Chief Justice Burger admitted the existence of "a long tradition of isolation of judges from day-to-day controversy. That tradition means not only that judges do not take part in political affairs or other public controversies but also that it is inappropriate for them to be involved with matters not relating to the administration of justice." But in practice, he and other judges have found it difficult to remain distant from "public controversies," even (perhaps especially) in advancing matters relating to the administration of justice.

The involvement of judges in legislative politics reflects the dependency of the judicial branch on Congress and the nature of the legislative process. Consequently, Judicial Conference committee chairmen spend many hours lobbying on Capitol Hill for enactment of the third branch's program. Especially involved are the chairman of the Court Administration Committee and representatives from the Administrative Office, who appear regularly on behalf of conference programs before subcommittees of the congressional judiciary committees. Traditionally, mobilization of public support for low-visibility court programs is difficult. Chief justices, in their capacity as third-branch chieftains, use media-saturated forums provided by meetings of the ABA and the American Law Institute to broadcast the judiciary's resource needs. But long-pursued efforts have failed to result in congressional authorization of an annual "state of the judiciary" address to be made by the chief justice to a joint session of Congress, comparable to the president's State of the Union message.

The conference's legislative program includes additional judgeships, a highly volatile political issue in that success brings creation of valuable patronage positions to be filled by the president with the consent of the Senate. Proposed jurisdictional changes may alter relationships between federal and state court systems, as manifested by endemic proposals to eliminate federal diversity jurisdiction and to alter habeas corpus procedures. Proposed changes in court organization may likewise take on a political hue by virtue of their projected impact on both litigants' access to justice and the status of judges on benches of existing tiers of courts.

The distinction between promoting legislation on "the administration of justice" and that of a more general public-policy nature is sometimes a fine one. In fact, judges may find it advantageous to rephrase as a judicial-administration issue a question with far-reaching substantive public-policy implications. Thus, as Carl Baar has stressed, their preferences on such substantive policy issues may be enacted into law as conference-endorsed proposals for revision in procedural rules or for improved administration of United States courts; many such proposals have the potential for embroiling the judiciary in visible and controversial legislative politics. The administrative system thus affords the federal judiciary a vehicle for supporting or sapping substantive law as laid down by the Supreme Court. In the 1960s the conference came to the Court's defense of its pre-*Miranda* "Mallory rule," which excluded all evidence obtained from defendants who, after arrest, had not been brought before a magistrate without unnecessary delay. In 1963 it condemned pending legislation aimed at abrogating the rule. On the other hand, the September 1967 Judicial Conference threw its support behind one of six pending "crime control" bills, one that would have permitted court-supervised electronic surveillance. It endorsed a bill that, in the words of the *Washington Post* reporter John P. MacKenzie, "was clearly unconstitutional under existing Supreme Court precedents." Taking cognizance of the public uproar ignited by the bill, the 1968 Judicial Conference added the caveat that any wiretap legislation must meet applicable constitutional standards.

The federal judiciary's administrative system was established in part to deflect encroachment of democracy on the judicial function. Development of that system has enhanced the political autonomy enjoyed by the judiciary, an autonomy so marked that the federal courts, in exercising their judicial function, have been viewed as neither predictable nor controllable. Attempts to exert popular control evoke mobilization of the judiciary's major institutionalized self-defense force—the Judicial Conference and its committees.

COURT, CRISES, AND RESPONSES

Notwithstanding reliance on the administrative system to buffer the judicial function from democratic impulses, the foremost issue for state and federal courts since the 1960s has been the tendency toward subordination of the judicial function to the administrative function. The increase in litigation volume and the changing nature of the traditional judicial function whereby the two-party adversary model has been eclipsed by a model characterized by multiple parties and complex legal issues requiring courts to engage in more than dispute resolution have led to pressure for ever-greater administration. Policymaking, ongoing administrative oversight, and social change have all become attributes of the judicial function. As J. Woodford Howard, Jr., has put it,

> Whatever the causes, the effects are plain. Both in volume of litigation and in tasks undertaken there have been quantum leaps of judicial power

and corresponding risks. Courts have become surrogate lawmakers in vacuums of public choice. Courts have become administrators of great enterprises, including schools, prisons, mental institutions, and personnel systems. Courts have become ombudsmen of bureaucratic mistakes. All this happened without pruning customary business. The combined results are sea changes in what courts do and how judges work.

And, he asks whether under such circumstances, judges can "provide services, formerly reserved to elites, *en masse* without cheapening the product?" The question becomes salient in light of the responses made to the perceived judicial crisis. They have followed two paths: expansion of the capacity of the court system to accommodate the incoming case-flow tide and reduction of that incoming tide.

Adding more judges has traditionally expanded judicial capacity to meet problems of increased case loads. But this administrative "quick fix" in turn creates administrative problems associated with cost, space, and management of the new judges. At the appellate level, such horizontal expansion creates problems of vertical control. The difficult question of how to preserve intracircuit decisional uniformity in the presence of more appellate judges and more rotating three-judge panels may induce consideration of so dramatic a remedy as circuit splitting. Geographical realignment of circuits and of districts is almost always a political issue, as is attested by the twenty-year-long struggle for division of the sprawling and congested Fifth Circuit. Such division and realignment strategies effectively expand administrative oversight exercised by the more inclusive entity—the circuit councils in cases of district splitting and the Judicial Conference in cases of circuit divisions.

A new profession has emerged to meet court crises. Professional court administrators, specialists in management techniques, have their own training program. Established in 1970 and sponsored by Chief Justice Burger, the Institute for Court Management in Denver is supported by the ABA, the American Judicature Society, the Institute of Judicial Administration, and the American Academy of Public Administration. Its graduates become court managers responsible to the chief judge of a court or to the whole bench. Such administrators essentially relieve the chief judge and the court clerk of supervisory and managerial duties concerning personnel, public information, jury and witness services, calendaring, finance, space and equipment, data processing, systems analysis, and assorted liaison functions. Execution of these duties poses inherent friction-inducing consequences for displaced court clerks as well as for judges. Whether the administrator stands "on top or on tap" has been a perennial concern, leading James A. Gazell to suggest that "because court administrators are experts, they may be gaining de facto control of state judicial bureaucracies just as the technostructures dominate other organizations." If so, he warned, these professional managers "may be acquiring more line functions, may be reversing the downward flow of authority, may be providing judicial leadership themselves instead of merely facilitating it for their titular superiors" (p. 47). Others, like David J. Saari, take a more sanguine view of the growing court-level administrative component. Administration and adjudication are separable in his view; judges may perform both, but clerks, administrators, and others perform only managerial functions without which the judicial function faces sure evisceration.

The presence of a professional administrator, court executive, administrative assistant, or even a corps of such management experts may not afford the chief judge relief from managerial duties sufficient to permit performance of the judicial function comparable to that of peers. Legislatures tend to load administrative duties on the office of chief judge, at least in part because that officer alone has the power, responsibility, and position to handle problems. Such transformation of presiding judges from "jurists" to "administrators" prevails in both state and federal systems.

The trade-off between the judicial and administrative function may be unavoidable, but the chief circuit judges themselves often resist any reduction in their court case loads. Furthermore, such trade-offs tend to inject friction into collegial relationships between chief justices and associate justices, who resist an independent executive.

The conferral of often statutorily imposed administrative duties on chief judges became a congressional issue in the 1980s. Attention focused on the chief-justiceship of the United States, then held by Warren E. Burger, who, having served in that office for more than fifteen years, had reached his late seventies. He occupied an office that had become the locus of a vast number of legislatively mandated duties that served to make the incumbent, with or without his consent, the third-branch chieftain. One proposed remedy has looked to the creation of an administrative judge of the United States courts. Accorded the title chancellor of the United States, this Article III judge-administrator would assume the chief justice's nonjudicial managerial duties for all federal courts except those which relate to the Supreme Court. Unresolved were the qualifications for chancellorship candidates, the locus of the appointing authority, the specific scope of administrative duties within that officer's purview, and the extent of any judicial functions performed by the judiciary's chief executive officer.

Speed-up strategies for case-load problems are also legion. Elimination of appellate briefs, curtailment of oral arguments, decisions based on counsel's written submissions, nonpublication of opinions (oral decisions), and bench memoranda prepared by law clerks or central staff attorneys constitute some of the strategies developed for streamlining adjudication. Some of these shortcuts clearly strike at the heart of the judicial function, at its reliance on written and reasoned elaboration of the law. They suggest the bureaucratization of that function.

Separating the wheat from the chaff, the meritorious from the less meritorious or frivolous cases, determines whether litigants receive retail or wholesale exposure to the judicial function. Courts have developed screening systems in order to route cases. Such systems may be operated by judges. But the screening task may well be delegated to law clerks, central staff attorneys, or other paralegals. Symptomatic of creeping bureaucratization in federal courts is the rising proportion of the judiciary's budget devoted to expenditures for nonjudge resources. The Administrative Office director reported in fiscal year 1941 that nearly one-third of the court system's budget went into judicial salaries. But by fiscal year 1960 that proportion had fallen to 19 percent and to 18 percent a decade later. In 1983, judicial salaries constituted a minuscule 9 percent of the budget. Meanwhile, total judicial branch employees increased slowly in the three decades following establishment of the Judicial Conference. From 1922 to 1953, their numbers only doubled from 1,880 to 3,954. And, during Chief Justice Earl Warren's tenure, they grew from 4,045 to 6,561. But a decade after Chief Justice Burger's confirmation in 1969, the judicial branch employed 13,493 persons, a number that continued to rise to 15,992 in 1982.

A variant of the gatekeeping and shortcut strategies involves diversion of specific classes of cases from courts to different forums. As with the operation of screening mechanisms, tasks once part of the judicial function may be delegated to others. Mediators, arbitrators, and neighborhood dispute-resolution centers constitute available channels for diversion of case flows.

In the federal system the use of this strategy has assumed several forms. The first is the United States magistrates model. By legislation the jurisdiction of this officer appointed by Article III district judges has been expanded from minor and chiefly criminal justice matters to include trying, with consent of the parties, of civil cases and entering of final judgments. District judge appointment and case references and withdrawals by the Article III judge to and from the magistrate led the Court of Appeals for the Second Circuit in *Collins* v. *Foreman* (1984) to validate such vesting of Article III judicial power in a non–Article III officer.

Second is the bankruptcy-judge model, which clearly indicates the constitutional pitfalls that envelop case-diversion strategies. A congressional attempt to vest extended federal bankruptcy jurisdiction in non–Article III judges not subject to district judge supervision and control analogous to that exercised over magistrates led the Supreme Court to exercise its power of judicial review in declaring unconstitutional the Bankruptcy Reform Act of 1978. In *Northern Pipeline Construction Co.* v. *Marathon Pipeline Co.* (1982), the Court ruled that the broad grant of jurisdiction accorded the bankruptcy courts was unconstitutional. It reasoned that in clothing the judges of those courts with power over such significant ancillary elements as contract and tort claims against bankrupt estates, the act had "impermissibly removed most, if not all, of 'the essential attributes of the judicial power' from the Art. III district court, and has vested those attributes in a non–Art. III adjunct." The Bankruptcy

Amendments Acts of 1984 resolved the long-festering issue by resort to the magistrates model. Bankruptcy judges appointed by courts of appeals as judicial officers of district courts were empowered to hear "noncore" bankruptcy matters in which either final orders of judgments were entered by district judges or parties had consented to finality of the bankruptcy judge's conclusions.

The third, the "national court of appeals" model, is characteristic of alterations in court organization and allied jurisdiction proposed to meet problems of judicial administration, in this instance the alleged overload on the Supreme Court's appellate capacity. Proposed as a fourth tier in the federal judicial system standing between the several courts of appeals and the Supreme Court, the national court of appeals would screen cases on appeal to the High Court, a gatekeeping task immediately perceived by critics as fraught with far-reaching implications for judicial policymaking. Opposition thus ignited transformed the nature of the perceived problem from one of Supreme Court undercapacity to one of intercircuit conflicts of law. To remedy what proponents contended was rampant development of a disharmonious national law, the contemplated operation of the new court was revised to permit case transfers to it from courts of appeals and voluntary case references to it from the Supreme Court.

Congress eventually created the Court of Appeals for the Federal Circuit with highly specialized jurisdiction. And, in the mid-1980s, discussion centered on establishment of an intercircuit tribunal to resolve intercircuit conflicts of laws, thereby relieving the Supreme Court of at least a portion of its historic task of developing a uniform national law. In the wings lurked a number of proposed specialized courts, establishment of which would ostensibly facilitate efficient judicial administration: a science court, an environmental court, an administrative appeals court, and social security and welfare claims courts. The fragmentation of both administration and the judicial function was posed by the court-proliferation model. Lying in the misty past and largely forgotten was the political demise that befell another specialized tribunal—the Commerce Court in 1913.

Finally, the increased capacity of courts is predicted as springing from another variant of the diversion strategy. This remedy promotes revision and reallocation of jurisdiction to reduce sharply the classes of cases flowing into particular courts. Judge Henry J. Friendly of the Court of Appeals for the Second Circuit is a leading exponent for the shedding of federal jurisdiction in case categories wherein the federal interest is slight or unimportant. Ranking high on his reallocation list is the federal power to adjudicate state questions in cases involving parties who are citizens of different states. Eliminating the residue of obligatory or mandatory appellate jurisdiction of the Supreme Court left by the act of 1925 has also been promoted as a means of affording the Supreme Court greater gatekeeping discretion and thus providing administrative relief—at the expense of civil rights groups who would lose guaranteed access to the High Court and to the benefit of intermediate appellate tribunals that would gain status by virtue of the increased finality of their judgments.

The inevitable joinder of judicial administration with politics and law raises the fundamental question of how to maintain the integrity of the judicial function. Answers come hard when the threat emanates not from the political branches but from within the third branch itself. Beguiling panaceas ostensibly divorcing administration from law and politics may well be capable of eroding the very purpose for which courts exist. Most beguiling of all is bureaucratization, if for no other reason than because of the minimal political and financial resources required for its implementation as compared to those needed for structural and jurisdictional changes. But for the judiciary especially, costs incurred by bureaucratization may be high. As long ago as 1925, Justice Louis D. Brandeis noted such costs in commenting on the relationship between the Supreme Court's legitimacy as an institution of government and the manner in which its members performed the judicial function. The High Court was "venerated throughout the land," he told then Harvard law professor Felix Frankfurter, because "the duties of the Court have . . . been kept within such narrow limits that the nine men, each with one helper, can do the work as well as can be done by men of their calibre, i.e. the official coat has been cut according to human cloth." Not so in other departments where, he lamented, "increasing work has been piled upon them . . . [and] the high incumbents, in many cases, perform in name only. They are administrators, without time to know what they are doing or to think how to do it. They are human machines" (p. 160).

CASES

Chandler v. Judicial Council of the Tenth Circuit, 398 U.S. 74 (1970)
Collins v. Foreman, 729 F.2d 108 (2nd Cir. 1984); cert. denied, 105 S. Ct. 218 (1984)
Northern Pipeline Construction Co. v. Marathon Pipeline Co., 458 U.S. 50 (1982)
United States v. Motlow, 10 F.2d 657 (7th Cir., 1926)
United States v. Will, 449 U.S. 200 (1980)

BIBLIOGRAPHY

American Bar Association, *Standards Relating to Court Organization* (1974), sets out the received wisdom on court organization, an enduring legacy of the era of Pound, Taft, Parker, and Vanderbilt. Carl Baar, *Separate But Subservient: Court Budgeting in the American States* (1975), considers questions of court budget power from a political perspective. Larry C. Berkson and Susan J. Carbon, *Court Unification: History, Politics, and Implementation* (1978), is a Department of Justice study of the history of court unification in the states and of such related issues as court management, centralized intrajudiciary rule making, budgeting, and state funding. Larry C. Berkson, Steven W. Hayes, and Susan J. Carbon, *Managing the State Courts* (1977), provides wide coverage within the context of state courts. Louis D. Brandeis, *Letters of Louis D. Brandeis*, vol. 5, *1921–1941: Elder Statesman* (1978), edited by Melvin I. Urofsky and David W. Levy, is a rich source of material on the distinguished associate justice.

Mark Cannon, "Innovation in the Administration of Justice, 1969–1981: An Overview," in Dubois, *Politics*, is a noteworthy essay by the administrative assistant to Chief Justice Warren E. Burger. Mark Cannon and W. I. Cikins, "Interbranch Cooperation in Improving the Administration of Justice: A Major Innovation," in *Washington and Lee Law Review*, 38 (1981), addresses problems in judicial-legislative relations and strategies for ameliorating them. Philip L. Dubois, *The Politics of Judicial Reform* (1982) and *The Analysis of Judicial Reform* (1982), comprise essays that explicitly seek to link judicial administration with politics and law.

Theodore J. Fetter, ed., *State Courts: A Blueprint for the Future* (1978), contains the Proceedings of the Second National Conference on the Judiciary. Peter G. Fish, *The Politics of Federal Judicial Administration* (1973), analyzes the development of national institutions from the nineteenth century up to the end of Warren's chief-justiceship in 1969 and includes an extensive bibliography; "William Howard Taft and Charles Evans Hughes: Conservative Politicians as Chief Judicial Reformers," in *Supreme Court Review* (1975), delineates the nexus of law, politics, and administration; and *The Office of Chief Justice of the United States: Into the Federal Judiciary's Bicentennial Decade* (1984), considers the multiple functions performed by the chief justice and proposals for their reduction. Steven Flanders and John T. McDermott, *Operation of the Federal Judicial Councils* (1978), is one of several studies on various aspects of federal judicial administration issued by the Federal Judicial Center.

James A. Gazell, *State Trial Courts as Bureaucracies* (1975), provides a wide-ranging, if abbreviated, survey of administrative problems in the lower tiers of state judiciaries. Henry R. Glick, "The Politics of State Court Reform," in Dubois, *Politics,* is noteworthy. Kenneth M. Holland, "The Twilight of Adversariness: Trends in Civil Justice," in Dubois, *Analysis,* is a perceptive essay. J. Woodford Howard, Jr., *Courts of Appeals in the Federal Judicial System: A Study of the Second, Fifth, and District of Columbia Circuits* (1981), based on extensive empirical data for the period 1965–1970, is a definitive work on judicial administration and decision-making in three federal courts of appeals.

National Center for State Courts, *State Court Organization 1980* (1982), is a comprehensive survey that provides voluminous data on court personnel, organization, jurisdiction, and administrative systems. Richard A. Posner, *The Federal Courts: Crisis and Reform* (1985), links judicial administration to proposed changes in substantive law and provides valuable statistical data. Roscoe Pound, "The Causes of Popular Dissatisfaction with the Administration of Justice," in *American Bar Association Reports,* 29 (1906), his historic ABA address, has become a reference point for modern reformers. David J. Saari, *American Court Management: Theories and Practices* (1982), with a six-page bibliography, regards court management as an all-purpose prerequisite for performance of the judicial function.

Irene A. Tesitor, *Judicial Conduct Organization* (1978), comprehensively surveys judicial disciplinary commissions and procedures in the states, and is supplemented by Kathleen Sampson and Joseph B. Cahill, eds., *1984 Update,* 2 vols. (1984). Arthur T. Vanderbilt, *The Challenge of Law Reform* (1955), describes this leading reformer's program and its implementation during the late 1940s, especially in his native state, New Jersey. Russell R. Wheeler and Charles W. Nihan, *Administering the Federal Judicial Circuits* (1982), is another study issued by the Federal Judicial Center. Russell R. Wheeler and Howard R. Whitcomb, *Judicial Administration* (1977), surveys both state and federal systems and includes an excellent twenty-two-page annotated bibliography.

[*See also* DISCOVERY; FEDERAL COURT SYSTEM; JUDICIAL SELECTION; *and* STATE COURT SYSTEMS.]

JUDICIAL SELECTION

Sheldon Goldman

THE question of how American judges are selected might be thought a relatively simple one to answer, but this is decidedly not so. At the surface level there are five principal methods of judicial selection, or recruitment, as it is sometimes called. Yet, for most intents and purposes the formal process does not reflect behavioral and political realities or their transactional complexities. Let us first examine the formalities of the selection methods in use in the 1980s before considering their empirical dimensions. We will subsequently turn to a consideration of a variety of issues that surround judicial selection and finally focus our attention on the subject of judicial tenure and the disciplining of judges, including removal from office.

FIVE SELECTION METHODS

There are five methods for selecting judges in use in the United States. They are legislative election; executive (gubernatorial or presidential) appointment with the approval of another body; partisan election; nonpartisan election; and merit selection. Of the five appointment methods, the oldest are legislative election and executive appointment with the advice and consent of another body.

Legislative election, still in use in Rhode Island (for state supreme court judges only), South Carolina (for most judges), and Virginia, was the method adopted by a majority (seven) of the states after the former colonies won their independence from Great Britain. Under this method both houses of the legislature must vote to elect judges to judicial office. The governor has no constitutionally mandated role in the process. This selection method was a reaction to one of

the grievances held by the colonists, that the King of England unilaterally appointed and removed colonial judges. Indeed, among the list of "repeated injuries and usurpations" found in the Declaration of Independence is the charge that the king "has made judges dependent on his will alone, for the tenure of their offices, and the amount and payment of their salaries." Election by legislators as representatives of the people was considered to be a major step toward democratizing the selection of judges.

Gubernatorial appointment with the approval of another body, typically the executive council or the state senate, is the method used in eight states (nine, if Rhode Island, which appoints most lower court judges this way, is included). This method dates back to the years following the Revolution, when five of the thirteen states chose this scheme and one, Connecticut, adopted a variation, still used, whereby the governor nominates and the legislature (both houses) appoints. The federal Constitution also provides for the President to appoint federal judges with the approval ("advice and consent") of the Senate. Delaware, Maine, Maryland, New Jersey, and Rhode Island have their governors appoint some or all judges with the consent of the state senate. In Massachusetts and New Hampshire the executive (or governor's) council is the body that is authorized to approve judicial appointees, while in California the Commission on Judicial Appointments must give its approval.

The age of Jacksonian democracy, with its democratic and egalitarian impulses, gave rise to some dissatisfaction concerning the ways judges were chosen. The judiciary was seen as being drawn from too narrow an economic and political base and too far removed from democratic accountability. Although "reform" was gradual, by the mid-nineteenth century the move to have the voters directly elect judges in normal partisan elections was well under way. The partisan election method has voters elect judges who run for office under a party label that has been designated by the party primary or convention. There are generally no special restrictions on the conduct of judicial campaigns, which means that they are conducted in as partisan a manner as campaigns for other public offices. Partisan election at one time was used by a majority of states. Today twelve states (thirteen if New York, which chooses most lower court judges this way, is included) use partisan elections to select most or all of their judges.

The move to elect judges on a nonpartisan ballot—that is, without any party designation—dates back to the progressive era at the beginning of the twentieth century. Progressives saw urban political machines dominate the electoral process, and they were determined to end what they saw as an insidious pattern of corruption reaching from city hall to the local courthouses. One way to achieve this objective was to alter the election law so that political parties would no longer be designated on the local election ballot. The assumption was that candidates for local office would no longer need the political machine to be elected to office and therefore would not be beholden to the party bosses. As for judicial elections, progressives argued that there was no valid reason to elect judges on a partisan ballot and no justification for judicial candidates to conduct a partisan campaign. The result of this movement, primarily in the Midwest and West, was the adoption of the nonpartisan election method to select judges. Today ten states use nonpartisan ballots to elect most or all of their judges.

The newest of the selection methods is the merit plan, which is sometimes called the Missouri plan because it was first established there, in 1940. Merit selection is the method favored by the organized bar and, since the early 1960s, has been the subject of extensive campaigns for its adoption. The merit scheme is simply that a nominating commission submits to the governor a list of names to fill a particular judicial post. The governor is legally required to make the appointment from that list. The heart of this method is the selection by the nominating commission of those who are presumably best qualified, chosen on their professional merits. Under the original nominating commission concept of the Missouri plan, the commission consists of lawyers selected by the bar (elected or appointed), gubernatorial appointees who are not lawyers, and one or more members of the judiciary. Today seventeen states have established by constitutional or statutory law some form of the merit plan for selecting their highest judicial officials. Most of these states select their lower-level judges in a similar way.

The names and composition of merit-selection nominating commissions vary; for example, Alaska and Idaho call it the Judicial Council, Arizona calls it the Commission on Appellate Court Appointments, and Vermont's is the Judicial Nominating Board. Some statutes specify that the nominating commission must be bipartisan or nonpartisan. In three states (New York, Utah, and Vermont) the state senate must still approve the governor's selection from the list provided by the commission.

Merit plans were adopted by three states during the years 1940–1961. Eight states adopted it during the 1962–1971 period, and six states from 1972 through 1983. In some states (notably Delaware, Maryland, and Massachusetts) and localities, governors and mayors have, by executive order, established nominating commissions similar to the merit plan, but they do not have the force of constitutional or statutory law; that is, the commissions are not binding on the executives' successors in office and even the originators can return the list of names and ask for others if the original list is unsatisfactory. Further, the nominating commission can be dissolved at any time by the public official who created it. In contrast, where merit selection has been established in the state constitution or by statute, the governor can neither unilaterally dissolve the commission nor reject its nominees.

Complicating the picture of judicial selection is the fact that only twelve states initially select all their judges by one method. In a large majority of states there are different selection methods for different court levels. For example, in New York the highest state court's membership is selected by a variation of the merit plan: the bipartisan Judicial Nominating Commission is required to present the governor with from three to five names for associate judge and seven for chief judge, and the governor must select from the list of names provided by the commission. The state senate must then approve the choice. Selection of other New York judges utilizes the partisan election method. However, the gubernatorial appointment method is used for the selection of judges of courts of claims and the appellate division of the state trial court. The mayor of New York City appoints judges of the city criminal and family courts but has voluntarily used a merit process.

Another complicating factor is that the formal selection methods discussed here are for initial selection. In the forty-seven states in which judgeship tenure is for a fixed term of office, there is the possibility of an interim appointment when a judge dies or resigns. However, only twelve states use the same method to fill interim vacancies as they do the initial selection. Proponents of the merit plan have achieved some success in persuading states that initially select judges by other methods to use the merit plan to fill interim appointments. Kentucky, Montana, Nevada, and North Dakota have formally adopted the merit plan for the filling of interim appointments. In five other states governors have issued executive orders to establish a merit plan by which to make interim appointments.

THE POLITICS OF SELECTION

To understand why one particular individual received an appointment and not another, similarly qualified person, it is necessary to be privy to the series of backstage transactions that propelled the appointee to the judgeship. To understand how a specific judicial recruitment method works in practice, it is necessary to study the actual process as it has concerned numerous appointments. Fortunately, the subject of judicial recruitment has received so much scholarly attention that we are in a position to make reasonably accurate generalizations about how the process works. It should be understood that generalizations apply in most but not necessarily all instances and that there are occasional exceptions to the rule. We will examine first the political reality of judicial selection in the states and then federal judicial selection.

State Judicial Selection. Common to all selection methods regardless of the intent of their proponents is that judicial selection is a political pro-

cess. This is not to say that all methods have the same form of politics or necessarily the same extent or mix of the various forms of politics. There is the most obvious form of party organizational politics, and at the local level it is most felt with the electoral methods for selecting judges. This is obviously true for party-label ballots where the party designation has been obtained during the party primary or convention. In some states and localities where the nonpartisan ballot is used, local party leaders even endorse a candidate and otherwise make it known that a person running for judicial office has party backing. At the state level, party organizational politics have a hand in both the legislative and gubernatorial selection methods. Judicial appointments can be viewed then as rewarding the faithful who have been active in behalf of the party. Also, appointments can be seen as "rewarding" certain party constituency groups, such as ethnic minorities.

Akin to party organizational politics is the politics of personal patronage, best manifested in those methods involving the governor. Governors at times seek to appoint close associates and supporters (presumably otherwise qualified) to the state bench. Obviously, the gubernatorial appointment method is the most straightforward way for a governor to secure a judgeship, but even with merit selection the governor's friends and appointees on the nominating commission can influence the selection of the names to be presented to the governor.

One can also consider the politics of policy—that is, judicial appointments being made because of the policy views or orientation of the appointees. Interest groups have been known to be concerned about appointments to the bench, particularly at the highest court levels. Civil rights and civil liberties groups are sensitive to the views of potential appointees and can be counted on to actively oppose the appointment of one with a poor record on those issues. Conservative or right-wing groups are alert to the policy or ideological perspective of appointees. This concern of interest groups exists under all five methods but potentially can be most effective with electoral selection methods. Methods involving the governor also may involve the politics of policy, with the governor taking the initiative or responding to group pressures.

Still another form of politics is bar association

politics, and while the involvement of the organized bar cuts across all selection methods (for example, the bar may rate or even endorse candidates for judgeships), it is clearly most involved with merit selection. The judicial nominating commissions under the Missouri plan include members of the bar elected by the bar associations. A study of such elections in Missouri found that a quasi-party system emerged with contested elections between distinctly different groupings of lawyers with different interests and outlooks. Some merit plans leave the means of selection of the bar representatives on the commissions up to the bar groups themselves, but there is a political type process at work there, too.

All selection methods involve negotiation. With electoral methods much of the activity is concerned with obtaining backing for the placement of the name on the ballot and achieving electoral support. For the merit plan the negotiation occurs in the legal community and concerns pressures, however subtle, that are brought to bear on the nominating commissions. This may include not only personal contact with commission members but also the mobilization of bar groups and individual lawyers and judges who send to the commission letters of support in behalf of candidates. For gubernatorially involved methods, negotiations may include state legislators, party leaders, interest-group representatives, bar association leaders, and judges—all of whom may also be involved in one form or another with the other selection methods. It is also of interest to observe that for the most part those who want to become judges have to wage a campaign. This is obviously true for the electoral methods but also for the other methods. Aspiring judges need to mobilize bar support as well as political support and other forms of public backing, such as newspapers and civic organizations.

A variety of considerations have been seen as playing a part in judicial selection, regardless of formal method. First, particularly for the highest state court bench, the legal credentials of potential judges come into play. Governors do not relish being attacked in the newspapers or by bar associations for nominating clearly unqualified persons. Similarly, bar associations will be highly sensitive to the professional qualifications of potential or actual judicial nominees and will wage campaigns against the clearly incompetent.

Second, partisan considerations are present with every selection method—not only with electoral, gubernatorial, and legislative selection but also with merit selection. Under the merit scheme the governor appoints most or all members of the commission, which assures at the very least that commission members will be minimally sensitive to his or her political needs (for example, the need to make some or most appointments to members of the governor's party). Under merit selection the governor selects from the names presented by the commission, and unless the commission deliberately stacks the panel with people not belonging to the governor's party (which has been known to happen), the governor is free to select along partisan lines. As to political considerations, those selection methods in which the governor has a role may have the governor making selection decisions on the basis of what may best enhance reelection or even what may best enhance passage of legislation favored by the governor (for example, selection of a close associate of a key state legislator whose legislative support is needed).

Finally, policy considerations can be seen as playing a part in all selection methods. The policy orientation of a candidate for a judgeship may surface during an electoral campaign as well as at different points with the other selection methods. The governor may consider the policy outlook of judicial candidates, particularly when constituent groups from within the governor's party take a lively interest in policy views. For example, a conservative Republican governor in a conservative state will generally not appoint a liberal reformer to the highest state bench.

Electoral methods of judicial selection have received some scholarly attention, and it has been found that in practice judicial elections tend to be largely ignored by the electorate, with low voter interest and turnout at the polls. Another significant aspect of the electoral method of judicial selection is that research findings reveal that the majority of judges are initially selected by the governor to fill vacancies that occur between elections. When judges resign, retire, or die in states whose formal method of judicial selection is by the partisan or nonpartisan ballot, the governor is authorized to make interim appointments. This means that at the next election such judges are able to run as incumbents with all the advantages of that position, such as name recognition and whatever mystique surrounds the occupants of judicial office. It has also been found that with partisan elections, the party label is the most significant factor in the voter's choice. Normally, judicial elections are uncontested; but on relatively few occasions there are contested elections, particularly for the highest state court positions, and invariably the organized bar strenuously objects to the conduct of such campaigns. In New York State, after several contested high-court elections, the state switched to a merit plan. Similarly, the Missouri plan was adopted in Missouri after several acrimonious contested elections to the state supreme court.

Merit selection plans have been examined by scholars. It has been found that gubernatorial politics is inherent in the merit selection method because of the provision for the governor to select some or even all (depending on the state plan) of the membership of the judicial selection commission and to make the final selection from the names submitted by the commission. Bar association politics is also institutionalized by merit plans that provide for bar association selection of bar representatives for service on the commissions. In the major study of how the merit plan has worked in Missouri, it was found that rival bar associations with contrasting socioeconomic interests contested the elections for the slots on the nominating commissions. The commissions were also found to be characterized by intense negotiation and internal politicking, and in some instances the commissions sought to dictate the selection outcome by stacking the list of names so that the commission favorite would be the likely person to be picked by the governor. In other cases, the governor quietly let be known a preference for certain individuals being included on the lists. It has also been found that the partisan makeup of the commissions has at times resulted in partisan considerations being taken into account in preparing the lists.

Federal Judicial Selection. There are a number of similarities between state and federal judicial selection. Federal judicial selection involves a negotiation process in which the varying types of politics discussed earlier can be seen at work. Party-organizational politics, the politics of personal patronage, the politics of policy, and bar association politics all come into play, as do the considerations examined previously.

Federal judges are nominated by the president after a recommendation from the attorney general. This has meant that the center of selection activity lies in the Justice Department and in practice today is located in the Office of Legal Policy. Participants in the negotiations, particularly for lower-court judgeships include not only Justice Department officials but also United States Senators and other major leaders of the president's party from the state in which there is a federal judgeship or the state that is "entitled" (that is, as a matter of expectation but not as a legal requirement) to be represented on a federal court of appeals. In addition, since 1953 the American Bar Association (ABA) Standing Committee on Federal Judiciary has investigated and rated leading candidates for judgeships as part of its informal working relationship with Justice officials during the prenomination stage. The Justice Department officials request a preliminary or tentative report, and the ABA committee if given more than one name can potentially influence the selection process by a finding of "not qualified" for one candidate as opposed to an "exceptionally well-qualified" rating for another. (The other ratings used by the ABA committee are "qualified" and "well-qualified.")

A senator of the president's party expects to be able to influence heavily the selection of a federal district judgeship in the senator's state; indeed, most such senators insist on being able to pick these judges, and they expect judgeships on the federal courts of appeals going to persons from their states to be "cleared" by them—that is, to meet with their approval. Judgeships in the federal territories, including the District of Columbia, on specialized courts, and especially on the United States Supreme Court are considered more within the prerogative of the president, and free from such senatorial pressures. When a senator from the president's party promotes a candidate not acceptable to the Justice Department, when a state has two senators of the president's party and they are in disagreement over the filling of a judgeship, or when senators and state party leaders are at odds, extensive negotiations may result. The senators are of such importance in the prenomination stage because the president's nomination must be sent to the Senate to be voted on and approved (confirmed) by a majority of those voting. Once a nominee has been confirmed, the president makes the formal appointment.

There are at least four major categories of considerations that tend to be of great relevance in the selection of federal judges. First are the professional qualifications of the candidates. This is so not only because of the active participation of the ABA and intense interest on the part of other bar groups but also because senators and presidents can be damaged politically if they are seen as promoting or choosing clearly unqualified persons for federal judgeships. Justice Department officials, furthermore, normally take pride when the administration is able to select people with outstanding legal records.

Second are partisan considerations. The political reality of federal judicial selection is that from the administration of George Washington to the present, the large majority of judicial appointments has gone to members of the president's party. Typically, the proportion has been more than 90 percent.

A third consideration from the standpoint of the administration is approval of the senator or senators of the president's party from the state of the prospective nominee. No administration deliberately seeks to alienate senators of their own party or to run the risk of a senator's sabotaging a nomination once it has been sent to the Senate. Although rarely invoked, a senator can claim senatorial courtesy, which would mean that the senator's colleagues would refuse to confirm.

A fourth principal consideration is the policy or even ideological outlook of judicial candidates. The Republican Reagan Administration, for example, shied away from political liberals or those who were publicly identified as supporters of a woman's right to choose abortion. The Democratic Carter Administration placed a considerable number of political liberals on the bench and few political conservatives. In assessing the relative importance of these four considerations, one can say that in general, political considerations have taken priority over the ideological or policy views of the candidates, which in turn have tended to be more important than the recruitment of the best legal talent available.

During the Carter Administration there was an attempt to bolster the relative importance of legal qualifications by the introduction of presidentially appointed merit selection commissions to recommend to the president the best available candidates for judgeships on the federal courts of appeals. By executive order President Carter established the Judicial Selection Commission. When a vacancy on an appeals court occurred, the eleven-member selection panel for that circuit was given sixty days in which to choose five persons qualified to fill the position. The selection panel was authorized to advertise for applicants, and the only way to be considered for the judgeship was for the aspiring judge to file an application and be investigated and interviewed by the panel. President Carter was pledged to select the nominee from the list of five names submitted by the selection panel.

In practice, the commission panels, whose membership was chosen by the White House, consisted of primarily Democrats, a large chunk of them active Carter supporters prior to his winning the Democratic party presidential nomination in 1976. Studies of the panels found that a majority of the panelists were political liberals and that approximately 40 percent were women and approximately 30 percent were black. It was also found that the selection panels were not only concerned with the professional qualifications of prospective nominees but also their policy outlook.

The creation of these selection panels resulted in a unique opening up of the recruitment process to women and minorities in terms of being able to choose potential nominees and being chosen as nominees. Of the fifty-six courts-of-appeals appointments by the Carter Administration, an unprecedented eleven appointments went to women, nine to blacks, two to Hispanics, and one to an Asian-American. They were also primarily Democrats. The selection panels used by the Carter Administration established merit selection of Democrats regardless of sex or race.

The Carter Administration also encouraged senators to establish similar selection commissions for federal district judgeships, and in a majority of states, such commissions were created. However, when Ronald Reagan became president, he eliminated use of the selection commission and reverted to the traditional negotiation process centered in the Justice Department. Nevertheless, some Republican senators have still retained their versions of selection commissions, although the result has typically been the merit selection of Republicans.

A change in the federal judicial selection process that carried through the Reagan years is the change in procedures within the Senate Judiciary Committee. Since 1979 the committee has utilized its own investigatory apparatus to help it independently determine whether the nominees are qualified for office. Each judicial nominee is required to complete an extensive questionnaire on his or her personal, professional, and financial background. There is also a section on the nominee's views on the proper scope of the exercise of judicial power. The questionnaire is the starting point for the committee's investigation. A further change since 1979 is that the chairman of the Senate Judiciary Committee no longer automatically buries the nomination of someone opposed by the senator from the nominee's state. Under the changed procedures the nomination is discussed by the full committee, with the possibility that the nomination will be reported out of committee to the full Senate.

Any consideration of federal judicial selection should devote special attention to appointments to the Supreme Court. These appointments generally hold the greatest interest for the general public. The Supreme Court is widely acknowledged to be the leading judicial policymaker for the nation; thus, appointments to the Court are the subject of keen concern and occasional controversy. Since the 1960s, a frequent presidential campaign issue has been what sorts of people will be named by the person elected president.

Supreme Court nominations, it should be clear, are in a class by themselves and are considered to be the personal choice of the president. Presidents have made their selections on the basis of a variety of considerations, including the personal, the political (such as party affiliation and effect on constituent groups in the president's coalition), and the ideological. Sometimes these considerations coalesce and reinforce each other. This was true, for example, with President John F. Kennedy's appointments of Byron White and Arthur Goldberg and with President Lyndon B. Johnson's appointment of Abe Fortas. Political considerations, as well as ideological or policy orientation, governed President Johnson's selection of Thurgood Marshall, the first black American to serve on the Court and President Reagan's appointment of Sandra Day O'Connor, the first female Supreme Court Justice and Antonin Scalia, the first Italian-American. It should also be mentioned that the Senate does not necessarily rubber-stamp presidential nominations. During the nineteenth century close to one out of three nominations were not confirmed by the Senate. In the twentieth century there have been four occasions when nominations died in the Senate (three of the four in the 1968–1970 period). Thus, appointments to the Supreme Court must be handled with some care by the White House and with a sensitivity to the concerns of senators.

ISSUES IN JUDICIAL SELECTION

The subject of judicial selection has been a source of continuing controversy. Some of the issues have been of long standing; others, such as affirmative action for the judiciary, are of more recent vintage. Without attempting to be exhaustive, several issues and questions surrounding judicial selection will be briefly discussed.

Partisanship. The organized bar and the American Judicature Society have long decried the partisan aspects of judicial selection. Party affiliation has no place, they have argued, in the selection of judges and is, or should be, irrelevant to the administration of justice. It is demeaning for those with judicial ambitions to have to court party bosses or otherwise play the political game. The best selection process, they insist, is one in which party affiliation and party connections are minimized, if not eliminated altogether, and professional qualifications are maximized, so that they become the decisive factors.

Those on the other side of the issue have argued that for every judicial vacancy there are many individuals who have similar legal credentials and are qualified to serve. Party affiliation and partisan activity are legitimate concerns on the part of those who select judges and ought to play a role in the method of selection. They argue further that the party system is crucial to American democracy and that service on behalf of the party and its candidates for public office helps to maintain the system. If political parties are to remain viable institutions, it is important that men and women of talent, skill, and commitment be active in politics. A selection method that rewards an individual on the basis of party activism, if not party affiliation, over a similarly qualified individual without such political credentials is a method that provides incentives necessary for viable political parties. Moreover, by choosing partisans, the party makes it reasonable for voters to hold the party responsible for the judges' performance in office. Political considerations of this sort, it is argued, thus foster a responsible party model of American politics and should be encouraged, rather than discouraged, by anyone concerned with the health of American democracy.

Personal Patronage. Similar to the debate over partisan considerations is that over the use by governors and presidents of their selection powers to advance their friends and associates. Again, legal reformers argue that personal patronage as a selection variable demeans the bench and, at least initially, stigmatizes those chosen. The determinants should be not "who you know" but "what you know" about law and the administration of justice and whether you possess the professional skills necessary to be a successful judge. Courts should not be the repository of cronyism; while some close personal associates of governors, senators, and presidents have distinguished themselves, others have been pedestrian, or worse, on the bench.

The counterargument is that a personal association or relationship with a key participant in the selection process should not disqualify an otherwise qualified person from judicial office. To do so would penalize individuals who already may have made personal sacrifices to serve in public office, and that would not only be unfair but also cause dysfunction in the workings of government. When a governor, senator, or president turns to a close associate, that should be taken as a sign of confidence in the caliber of the individual. It should be recognized that the judicial performance of an individual so chosen will reflect more on the politician responsible for the appointment than if there were no prior personal relationship. Substituting a Missouri plan will not eliminate personal variables. Rather, it has been argued, these considerations are shifted to a different sphere, the bar association. Instead of party politics, there is bar association politics. Instead of politicians' associates having the inside track, bar leaders' associates are in that enviable position.

Policy, or Ideological, Screening. When the Republican platform of 1980 contained a provision that pledged a future Republican administration not to appoint to the federal bench anyone who favored the right to have an abortion, opponents of the plank offered several criticisms. First, they argued that it is not right to have an ideological or policy litmus test for prospective judges. A judge is called on to handle a wide variety of matters and to single out only one of a multitude of legal issues before the federal courts for ideological screening distorts the nature of the judicial process and is unfair.

Second, they argued that an individual's personal views on a controversial question of public policy should play no part in the decisions that an individual will make as a judge. As such, one's private views are irrelevant to judicial decision-making, and to suggest otherwise is to undermine the professional integrity of the judiciary.

Third, it was argued that to specify a preferred policy position on a controversial issue and to seek out individuals sympathetic to that position means that the courts are being stacked with biased persons. Even if these individuals conduct themselves in a thoroughly professional manner and decide on the basis of law and not their personal predilections, they will have come to the bench with an image of being biased and already committed on the particular issue. Each judicial action will then be suspect and placed in the most damaging light, and the confidence of the public will be undermined.

And finally, on the specific issue of a woman's right to choose abortion of a nonviable fetus rather than childbirth, the Supreme Court has already spoken and has established that right as a constitutional one and the law of the land. To search for active opponents of that right and the Supreme Court's constitutional determination in that sphere is to search for potential saboteurs of the very court that in theory heads the judicial system. This cannot be good for the workings of the system nor for the public image of the courts.

The counterargument is that courts, particularly at the higher levels but also at the trial level, cannot help but make policy by their interpretations of precedents, statutes, and the Constitution. Where there is room for judicial discretion, a judge's personal values and judicial philosophy come into play. A concern with a judge's policy or ideological orientation is then a concern with how the judge will use the very discretion that is inevitable and is inherent in the judicial function. What is wrong, these rebutters ask, with a political administration or body that is responsible for choosing judges being concerned with how prospective judges will behave when faced with alternative, if not conflicting, solutions to the judicial questions before them? Should a political official ignore the overwhelming evidence that from among viable alternatives, judges choose those consistent with their judicial philosophies and ideological or policy outlook? Should a political official appoint judges who stand for that which the official is publicly committed to oppose?

This issue is a particularly sensitive one with regard to appointments to the Supreme Court. President Eisenhower apparently regretted that he had not been concerned with the policy outlook of Earl Warren when Eisenhower named him to the chief-justiceship of the Supreme Court. Presidents Nixon and Reagan, on the other hand, were quite pleased with their appointees because they had been ideologically screened before being named. Senators, however, may be uneasy about Supreme Court nominations of those whose views are diametrically opposed to theirs. But senators usually recognize that more than ideological opposition is needed to oppose successfully a Supreme Court nomination. The debate over whether judicial selection should permit the ideological stacking of a court is bound to continue, particularly concerning the Supreme Court.

Affirmative Action for the Judiciary. The Carter Administration introduced the concept of affirmative action for the judiciary, a determined effort (in the words of the executive order establishing the circuit judge nominating commission) "to seek out and identify well-qualified women and members of minority groups as potential nominees." Carter's selection commission panels, particularly with their women and minority membership, were thought to constitute a useful means for accomplishing this goal. However, the application of affirmative action to the judiciary was met with severe criticism that included the arguments also applicable to efforts at the state level.

First, it has been argued, affirmative action in practice means the imposition of quotas to achieve a sexual and racial balance on the bench and that use of quotas is incompatible with merit selection and can result in the appointment of marginally qualified or unqualified persons.

Second, affirmative action promotes reverse discrimination in that persons of the "wrong" sex or race are not seriously considered and are thereby discriminated against because of their sex or race.

Third, by ignoring individual merit and focusing on group affiliation in the initial screening for a judicial position, affirmative action places the government in the position not of being neutral but of playing favorites. Rather than simply ending racial and sexual discrimination, the government perpetuates a new form of sexual and racial favoritism.

Fourth, by engaging in affirmative action, the government—meaning government bureaucrats—must classify people by their race, which in turn requires clumsy and arbitrary definitional standards such as how many black parents or grandparents are necessary in order to classify a person as black.

Finally, it has been posited that affirmative action is inappropriate for the judiciary because the need for highly skilled legal practitioners requires that the best people be selected and so a person's race, sex, or national origin is totally irrelevant to job performance as a judge.

Answers have been offered to these objections. First, the supporters of the Carter Administration's affirmative-action efforts and similar programs elsewhere emphasize that they never intended to implement rigid quotas but rather wished to widen the recruitment net and actively seek out qualified women and minorities. Rather than being incompatible with merit selection, affirmative action assures that all potential candidates will be considered on their individual merits. There is no evidence at all that affirmative action applied to judicial selection has resulted in marginally qualified or unqualified appointments. To the contrary, at least for the appointments of women, blacks, and Hispanics by the Carter Administration, the evidence suggests that these nontraditional appointees were as qualified, if not more so, as traditional, white male appointees.

Second, proponents of affirmative action stress that white males have not been discriminated against and in fact still constitute the large majority of appointments. During the Carter Administration there was no reverse discrimination, but instead, all other things being roughly equal, preference was given to the person belonging to the group that was victimized by past discrimination.

Third, affirmative-action supporters argue that individual merit is still the most important consideration and that government's role in ending racial and sexual discrimination and becoming truly neutral is enhanced by its active recruitment of women and minorities. Neutrality is not the same as indifference, and a meaningful end to past practices of discrimination must be heralded by vigorous and conspicuous attempts to open up the judicial recruitment process.

Fourth, while supporters of affirmative action are generally not enthusiastic about bureaucratic procedures to classify people as to their race and ethnicity, the fact that this is being done with benign, positive, antiracist motives and for antidiscriminatory purposes justifies this excursion into racial classification.

Last, defenders of affirmative action vigorously deny that sex or race are irrelevant to the judicial process. Issues of sexual and racial discrimination have come before the courts in relatively large numbers since the early 1960s. Women and minorities personally familiar with discrimination bring to the bench life experiences and sensitivities that the typical white male does not. There are certain qualities of the heart and mind that, when brought to bear on issues of discrimination, may well add a new dimension of justice to the courts. The visibility of women and minority judges on the bench may inspire confidence in the courts within those groups in the population. And on the bench these judges cannot help but educate and sensitize their colleagues. Indeed, given the wide range of variables and personal attributes associated with judicial selection, the deliberate recruitment of qualified women and minorities may indeed result in the "best" people to fill certain judgeships.

Defining and Finding Good Judges. A perennial issue surrounding judicial selection is how to define and then find "good" judges. There are certain traits associated with being a good judge that most observers seem to agree on, although they might describe them somewhat differently. They include neutrality toward the parties in litigation; fair-mindedness in the conduct of a trial, with special emphasis on a scrupulous concern for procedural due process; knowledge of, and experience in, the law; an ability to think and write clearly and logically; great personal integrity; good physical and mental health; a judicial temperament (being even-tempered, courteous, cooperative, patient); and the capacity to handle judicial power sensibly. This last characteristic is

the most controversial as it is open to more widely differing interpretations than the others. Some believe that a good judge will defend and promote human rights and personal freedom and be particularly sensitive to the plight of the racially, sexually, and economically oppressed. Others believe that a good judge will recognize the place of the judiciary in a democratic society and not arrogate power and behave imperiously (as a philosopher-king).

How to find good people for the judiciary, assuming that the qualities of a good judge have been adequately defined, is an exceedingly difficult task for at least two reasons. First, it is hard to establish an objective indicator for each quality, with a precise measurement rather than a subjective evaluation. Second, the selection methods in practice are concerned with factors other than those that define a good judge; thus, considerations of what makes a good judge are rarely given close attention.

Nevertheless, it is essential to make every attempt to be thorough in assessing these qualities and to use such methods as surveys of the bar, former clients, and sitting judges, along with close analysis of briefs written by the candidate. If the candidate is already a lower-court judge or has had previous judicial experience, a qualitative and quantitative assessment of the candidate's judicial record may be in order. For federal judgeships, the Federal Bureau of Investigation (FBI) conducts extensive background investigations as does the staff of the Senate Judiciary Committee. There is considerably less extensive investigation for most state judgeships. Despite the likelihood of some errors of evaluation, a systematic evaluation of the qualities previously mentioned can identify those who are clearly suitable for judicial office, as opposed to those clearly unsuited. Undoubtedly, the success of judicial selection depends upon the intelligence, perceptiveness, skill, and sensitivity of those involved in the choosing and the wisdom of their subjective evaluations.

Evaluation of Selection Methods. To evaluate the five principal selection methods, it is first necessary to establish the criteria according to which the selection methods are to be assessed. There are a variety of standards that bar groups offer, such as the desirability that the selection method results in the "best" available people being chosen and minimizes "politics" as a factor in selec-

594

tion. Four basic principles are useful in efforts to maximize the likelihood of selecting good judges.

First, the selection process should be an open one in at least two ways: compilation of information about all possible candidacies and provision for expansion of the recruitment net to include all those who wish to be considered.

Second, the selection process should provide for the active recruitment of women, blacks, and other ethnic groups that have been the victims of discrimination. By actively seeking out those who may have been shut out of the system, it is likely that there will be an increase in the numbers of well-qualified people from which to choose. Furthermore, a sincere effort to recruit more women and minorities can reassure certain segments of the population of the neutrality and fairness of the judicial process. The presence and interaction of women and minorities on the bench can enhance other judges' sensitivity to issues of race and sex discrimination thereby enhancing further the judiciary's qualities of neutrality and fair-mindedness.

Third, a thorough investigatory apparatus of the leading candidates is necessary to ensure that all relevant facets of these individuals are consistent with the qualities that constitute a good judge. The investigators should do more than compile allegations: They should follow through and evaluate the information collected.

Fourth, some form of political accountability may be useful in the quest to maximize the possibility of selecting good judges. It is taken for granted that judges exercise discretion and by so doing can act as policymakers. The challenge is to place the judiciary within a democratic framework of accountability so that judges' choices of policy and other aspects of their performance in office will be subject to review either directly at the polls or indirectly (that is, holding those who selected them responsible), while at the same time not compromising their independence while they sit.

Taking these four selection principles as the basis for evaluation, we can suggest that on the surface the electoral methods seem to provide for the most open selection process in that anyone can choose to run for judicial office. Those running for office are subject to the scrutiny of bar groups, the media, and citizens' organizations, so that theoretically a great deal of investigation of the candidates occurs. Direct election of judges would appear to be the highest embodiment of the democratic process and to provide for the greatest accountability when limited terms of office require judges to run for reelection. Of the four principles of selection, only that of affirmative action appears inadequately addressed. In reality, electoral methods fall far short of the idealized portrait, although partisan elections do ensure a rough sort of political accountability.

The legislative and gubernatorial appointment methods hold legislators and particularly governors accountable. In the case of gubernatorial appointment, governors have the opportunity to appoint those in tune with their own overarching values, if not more specific policy perspectives. Accordingly, gubernatorial appointment can produce a "responsible party model," whereby policy coordination among the branches of government occurs and the party takes the credit or the blame at the next election. Gubernatorial appointment is also a selection method potentially flexible enough to employ the openness principle and the use of affirmative action. Whether or not there is openness and affirmative action depends on the particular individuals in office and the political pressures they face. The executive appointment method appears to allow the complete investigatory resources of the state to be made available for investigating judicial candidates, and this may be more systematic and reliable for the gathering of information about candidates than reliance on bar groups and the print and broadcast media (as is the case with electoral selection methods). In practice, however, there is a heavy reliance on political processes that do not place much of an emphasis on the qualities that make for a good judge.

Merit selection in theory would seem to embody all four of the principles suggested earlier and to result in good judges being chosen. The selection commission is supposed to be concerned with precisely the sorts of considerations suggested earlier as being the indispensable qualities of the good judge. The process is thought to be an open one, whereby any interested individual can apply. The commission can also try to interest people in applying and herein lies the potential for affirmative action. It could also be argued that emphasis on merit and searching for the best available candidates should overcome the racial and sexual biases of the past and bring well-qualified women and minorities before the commissions. Both the merit commission and the governor who must make the formal appointment will have had the opportunity to investigate the backgrounds of the candidates. And last, the merit tenure concept, whereby the judge periodically goes before the electorate in what is essentially a plebiscite, is consistent with the principle of accountability.

In practice, as seen earlier, merit selection fails to live up to the goals of its founders in that political considerations and bar association politics can be seen at work. It has not automatically guaranteed affirmative action absent a vigorous commitment on the part of the governor. The selection commission, consisting largely or entirely of gubernatorial appointees, can be shaped so that certain outcomes are more likely than others. Yet, in the public's eye the governor is not held politically accountable because the process was ostensibly based on merit.

Federal judicial selection, like gubernatorial appointment, has the virtues of political accountability and the potential for openness, affirmative action, and thorough investigation. Under President Carter the Judicial Service Commission had a mandate to open up the process and to vigorously proceed with affirmative action. The Senate's more independent investigatory role also enhanced the fact-finding aspects of the process. It can be argued that judicial selection during the Carter administration came closer to satisfying the four selection principles than any other method. In that respect the Reagan administration's abandonment of the Judicial Selection Commission, its explicit rejection of affirmative action, and its reversion to the more closed selection process of the past can be seen as a move away from the principles suggested earlier.

Nonetheless, there is no evidence that any one selection method produces more good judges than any other method. In terms of state judicial selection, while the merit concept has become increasingly favored, there has yet to be any definitive evidence that any one method produces superior judges or judges with vastly different backgrounds or qualifications. Given the available evidence, no one selection method can be said to be a superior method for the appointment of judges with the qualities that make for good judges or judges whose on-the-bench performance is adjudged to be of the highest caliber. There is no hard evidence linking the method of judicial selection with judicial decision-making trends.

One final point to keep in mind is that the methods currently in use are not the only possible methods of judicial selection. For example, the Constitution suggests in Article II that Congress could authorize the Supreme Court or the attorney general to appoint lower-court judges. Similarly, state supreme courts or attorneys general could be given the responsibility for state judicial selection. Article II also indicates that lower-court judges could be appointed by the president alone if Congress so provided. Still another method of judicial selection could be modeled after the process used in Europe, which essentially considers the judiciary a specialized type of civil service. Would-be judges complete a special course of study, take special examinations, and work their way up the judicial hierarchy—all outside the political appointment process. It is not appropriate here to evaluate these alternative methods, but it is relevant to observe that there is no movement in the United States to adopt any of these alternative judicial selection methods.

JUDICIAL TENURE AND JUDICIAL DISCIPLINE

The mirror image of judicial selection is judicial tenure, with the subsidiary issue of judicial discipline. Once a judge comes on the bench, how does he or she retain office and what means are there for disciplining gross misconduct?

There are six principal provisions for tenure in current use. First, three states and the federal government appoint most or all their judges for life tenure or its close approximation, tenure to age seventy. Second, in six states tenure for most or all judges depends upon reappointment by the governor with the consent of the state senate. In Connecticut, the governor nominates and the full legislature elects. The terms of office vary from six to fourteen years. Periodic partisan or nonpartisan elections are the third and fourth methods of tenure with terms of office ranging from four to ten years. (Appellate court judgeships tend to have the longest tenure, with terms of office at least six years.) Ten states, eight of them southern, use partisan elections to determine tenure in judicial office. Twelve states, eleven of them midwestern or western, use non-partisan elections for establishing tenure. Two states, South Carolina and Virginia, use legislative reappointment, the fifth tenure method. Sixth, in seventeen states the tenure provisions of the merit plan or a close facsimile are in effect. Terms of office vary, but the ranges are similar to those in states with other than life tenure.

Under merit tenure, judges run unopposed "on their records" in nonpartisan retention elections. Typically the question on the ballot is "Shall Judge X be retained in office" and the electorate votes yes or no. Of the seventeen states that use merit selection, thirteen use merit tenure. (In Hawaii, the Judicial Selection Commission, not the electorate, makes the retention decision.) Of the other four states that use merit tenure, Illinois and Pennsylvania use partisan elections for selection while California and Maryland use gubernatorial appointment with the advice and consent of the Commission on Judicial Appointments and of the state senate, respectively.

In practice, most judges serve for as long as they wish or until a mandatory retirement age, usually seventy, is reached, regardless of the formal method for tenure. Most judicial incumbents running for reelection run without opposition. Those who do run against opposition are seldom defeated, although on rare occasions an upset has been known to occur. In states that use the merit plan's provisions for tenure, it is almost a certainty that judges win retention. In Missouri, for example, in the two decades or so following the adoption of merit selection and tenure, only one judge failed to win the retention election. Even where there is a concerted effort to oust a judge by voting no at the retention election, as has happened on several occasions with the justices of the California Supreme Court, it has been difficult (but not impossible as the 1986 elections showed) to defeat an incumbent judge. The fact remains that a judge who does not conspicuously court notoriety will be reappointed, reelected, or retained in office. This has meant that it has been extraordinarily difficult to discipline, if not remove, judges who are unwilling or unable to perform their duties satisfactorily. Until the 1960s the difficult process of impeach-

ment and conviction begun during the term of office (rather than other efforts at reelection or reappointment time) was the only potential means of disciplining the judiciary. Only the most serious and public offenses triggered such extreme action, and as a consequence, such removal machinery has been infrequently employed.

The problem of the lack of judicial disciplinary institutions began to be faced in the early 1960s, and within two decades all states had established or strengthened judicial qualifications commissions or otherwise named investigatory and disciplinary boards. At the federal level Congress enacted the Judicial Councils Reform and Judicial Conduct and Disability Act of 1980, which authorizes each of the circuit judicial councils to exercise disciplinary authority, short of removal from office, over federal judges within their respective circuits.

That disciplinary machinery now exists does not mean that all methods are equally effective or that the machinery will necessarily be used. A few states seem to have made little better than token gestures in this regard. For example, in 1977 the state of Arkansas enacted legislation establishing a judicial ethics committee with the authority to investigate allegations of judicial misconduct and to report its recommendation to the state legislature. However, the removal from office of the major state judicial officials, including judges of trial courts with general jurisdiction, must be done through the traditional process of impeachment or by the governor upon the joint address (vote) of two-thirds of each house of the legislature.

A somewhat stronger method exists in Massachusetts, where the Commission on Judicial Conduct was established by state statute in 1978 and given authority to investigate allegations of misconduct. However, it can only recommend disciplinary action to the Supreme Judicial Court, which in turn can discipline, short of removal from office. Removal from office must be accomplished either through impeachment (only six states do not make this provision) or upon the address of both houses of the legislature to the governor (seventeen states have such provisions), with the governor needing the consent of the executive council. Another method used in several other states is the recall election, whereby a retention election is held upon the signing of a petition by a certain number or percentage of registered voters. These are cumbersome methods.

By contrast, in Michigan the Judicial Tenure Commission was established by an amendment to the state constitution in 1968. Under its provisions the Michigan Supreme Court, upon recommendation of the commission, may censure, suspend with or without salary, retire, or remove from office a judge convicted of a felony, found to have a physical or mental disability, found to have persistently failed to perform duties or to have engaged in other misconduct in office, or found to have engaged in conduct clearly prejudicial to the administration of justice. In fact, thirty-nine states have similar strong disciplinary mechanisms that permit removal from office by a commission or the highest state court. In the District of Columbia the local judges (with a fixed term of office) may be removed from office by the Commission on Judicial Disabilities and Tenure. However, federal judges appointed for life under the authority of Article III of the Constitution may only, according to the Constitution, be removed by impeachment in the House of Representatives and conviction after trial in the Senate, a rarely used method (although used successfully in 1986 to remove convicted felon Harry Clairborne from the federal district bench).

The qualifications commissions vary in membership, but they generally consist of judges, lawyers, and lay persons. How they operate in practice and how effective they have been are questions that must await systematic empirical investigation, although the anecdotal evidence suggests that in some states, such as New York, they have had some impact.

CONCLUSION

The problems posed by judicial selection, tenure, and discipline are not easy to resolve for several reasons. First, there are fifty different state governments and the federal government, each with its own laws and unique combination of methods and machinery. Second, the formal methods do not necessarily suggest what happens in practice. Finally, there are numerous issues of some degree of complexity that surround judicial selection. What might superficially seem

to be a process that ought to be straightforward is not in reality and for good reason. The people who are selected to serve on the American bench determine the course of the administration of justice. Particularly at the higher levels of the judiciary but even at the trial level, these judges, in their rulings, formulate public policy that may affect the lives and fortunes of many people. That is why there has been, and will continue to be, a lively interest in the processes of judicial selection and in the people selected. That is also why there will continue to be controversy.

BIBLIOGRAPHY

Henry J. Abraham, *Justices and Presidents* (2nd ed., 1985), provides a comprehensive descriptive account of appointments to the Supreme Court from Washington to Reagan. Burton Atkins and Henry Glick, "Formal Judicial Recruitment and State Supreme Court Decisions," in *American Politics Quarterly,* 2 (1974), puts the relationship between formal judicial recruitment and judicial decisions to an important test. Griffin Bell et al., *Whom Do Judges Represent?* (1981), offers differing views on the issues surrounding judicial selection in this edited transcript of a television panel discussion.

Larry C. Berkson and Susan B. Carbon, *The United States Circuit Judge Nominating Commission: Its Members, Procedures, and Candidates* (1980), extensively examines the nominating commission created by President Carter. Harold W. Chase, *Federal Judges: The Appointing Process* (1972), analyzes and discusses in rich detail federal judicial selection from Eisenhower to Johnson. Nancy Chinn and Larry Berkson, *Literature on Judicial Selection* (1980), is a valuable annotated bibliography of the judicial selection literature.

John H. Culver, "Politics and the California Plan for Choosing Appellate Judges," in *Judicature,* 66 (1982), analyzes California's method of judicial selection and examines alternative methods in use in the states. David J. Danelski, *A Supreme Court Justice Is Appointed* (1964), analyzes the events leading to the appointment of Pierce Butler to the Supreme Court and is still the best theoretical work on the transactional nature of selection. Phillip L. Dubois, *From Ballot to Bench: Judicial Elections and the Quest for Accountability* (1980), provides a systematic analysis of judicial election and related data and draws many important insights and conclusions.

W. Gary Fowler, "Judicial Selection Under Reagan and Carter," in *Judicature,* 67 (1984), systematically analyzes comparisons between the two administrations, including the use of selection commissions. Sheldon Goldman, "Judicial Selection and the Qualities That Make a 'Good' Judge," in *Annals of the American Academy of Political and Social Science,* 462 (1982), considers various aspects of the linkage between judicial selection methods and the recruitment of "good" judges and considers the challenge of determining and applying objective criteria to particular individuals; and "Reaganizing the Judiciary," in *Judicature,* 68 (1985), offers an analysis of the selection process of lower federal court judges during President Reagan's first term. Sheldon Goldman and Thomas P. Jahnige, *The Federal Courts as a Political System* (1985), examines federal judicial selection and places it within the context of the workings of the federal judicial system.

Kenyon N. Griffin and Michael J. Horan, "Patterns of Voting Behavior in Judicial Retention Elections for Supreme Court Justices in Wyoming," in *Judicature,* 67 (1983), provides a valuable analysis of the problems associated with merit tenure. Joel B. Grossman, *Lawyers and Judges* (1965), although dated, is the most thorough book-length account available of the workings of the ABA Standing Committee on Federal Judiciary. Kermit L. Hall, *The Politics of Justice: Lower Federal Judicial Selection and the Second Party System, 1829–61* (1979), offers a valuable, methodologically sophisticated, historical perspective on federal judicial selection from the Jacksonian period to the outbreak of the Civil War.

Alan Neff, *The United States District Judge Nominating Commissions: Their Members, Procedures and Candidates* (1981), has written a comprehensive account of selection commissions used by senators during the Carter Administration. Charles Sheldon, "Influencing the Selection of Judges: The Variety and Effectiveness of State Bar Activities," in *Western Political Quarterly,* 30 (1977), scrutinizes the role of state bar associations in judicial selection. Elliot E. Slotnick, "Judicial Selection: Lowering the Bench or Raising it Higher?: Affirmative Action and Judicial Selection During the Carter Administration," in *Yale Law and Policy Review,* 1 (1983), provides a systematic and insightful empirical analysis of the backgrounds and professional qualifications of the affirmative-action appointees of the Carter Administration; and "The ABA Standing Committee on Federal Judiciary: A Contemporary Assessment," in *Judicature,* 66 (1983), gives an up-to-date, extensive, and excellent survey of the workings of the ABA committee.

Mary L. Volcansek, "Money or Name? A Sectional Analysis of Judicial Elections," in *The Justice System Journal,* 8 (1983), is an analysis of certain variables and their effect on the outcomes of judicial elections. Richard A. Watson and Rondal G. Downing, *The Politics of the Bench and the Bar* (1969), is the classic study of the Missouri plan.

[*See also* FEDERAL COURT SYSTEM; JUDICIARY; JUDICIAL ADMINISTRATION; JUDICIAL REVIEW; *and* STATE COURT SYSTEMS.]

THE JUDICIARY

John R. Schmidhauser

THE judiciary, as it evolved in the Western legal tradition, is often described as an institution that resolves conflicts on the basis of fair, predictable, and objective principles and procedures. It achieves its purposes by developing and maintaining its independence from external institutional influences, such as governmental leaders and bureaucracies, political parties, and religious leaders and organizations. Its judges and supporting legal personnel are trained and socialized to develop and apply doctrines and procedures that are rational and predictable. Such legal officials are selected on the basis of merit, professional training, and experience. Ascriptive criteria, such as race, caste, tribe, socioeconomic status, or gender, are rejected.

The judiciary serves as a neutral arbiter of relations between equals before the law. It assumes the responsibility for safeguarding economic rights, such as contract or property, and protecting noneconomic rights and liberties, such as freedom of speech and religion. Its decision-making procedures and customs are characteristically objective and nonpartisan with respect to individuals, groups, political parties, and ideologies. These attributes contain fundamental components of the ideal conception of a judiciary. Most elements of this ideal conception are embodied in the analyses of a number of perceptive scholars of the Western legal tradition, such as Max Weber and Harold J. Berman.

These characteristics of a model or ideal judicial system may not, of course, be fully attained in the actual judicial and legal systems of nations under most circumstances. For example, it is generally recognized that a judicial system is not likely to maintain its independence and objectivity in periods of dangerous political unrest. Neither can such a judicial system maintain fair standards and render objective doctrines in a nation driven by bribery, nepotism, and conflicts of interest. Nor can a judicial system function fairly in a nation that abides bitterly divisive class or caste societal distinctions. Thus, it is not surprising that in a revolution, a national judicial system and its judicial and legal elite may be considered significant contributors to the oppressions and grievances which led to the revolt. This is, in part, what occurred in the 1776 revolution of colonists in the portions of British North America that became the original thirteen American states.

ORIGINS OF THE AMERICAN JUDICIARY

Convinced that their rights and privileges as Englishmen had been tyrannically denied them, many Americans fought for independence from Great Britain. While broad issues such as taxation without representation were salient, other conflicts involving the legal and judicial system controlled by Great Britain were very important. Chief among the latter were issues involving corrupt use of the legal system and the arrogant manner in which the British chose unqualified individuals for judicial posts sought by able Americans. For example, John Jay, destined to become the first Chief Justice of the United States, was outraged by British selections of "needy ignorant dependents [of] great men . . . to the seats of justice, and other places of trust and importance" (Wood, 78). Another colonial was less restrained. He resented the advancement "to the most eminent stations men without education and of dissolute manners . . . sporting with our persons and estates, by filling the highest seats of justice with bankrupts, bullies, and blockheads" (Wood, 145). Their ex-

600

periences and disillusionment with British corruption and legal imperialism during the events that led to the American Revolution sharpened their ideas about judicial organization and the need for judicial independence.

When the former colonials succeeded in winning their national independence, they were confronted by a dilemma. Their entire legal culture was based upon the English common law. When the founders of the new American constitutional system met to create a stable foundation for their federal governmental system, would they totally reject the fundamentals of the British legal system under which they had been nurtured as British colonials and denied equality and fair play as transatlantic subjects? What emerged after the momentous sessions of the Philadelphia Convention of 1787 was not only a Constitution that delineated the powers of the new federal government but also specified limitations on those powers as well. A new judicial system was developed to fulfill a central role in defining those powers and enforcing limitations. The entire American legal cultural foundation remained fundamentally within the framework of the English common law tradition, but the organization and structure of the new federal judicial system represented a departure from the eighteenth-century British model. The key elements of the new system were significantly influenced by the prevailing notion of the separation of powers and checks and balances as safeguards of the independence of the three branches of the national government and by the notion of federalism as a determinant of the relationship of the national government to the governments of the states. The new judiciary was also the product of political compromise in the protracted meetings of the Philadelphia Convention of 1787.

Because the members of the convention vividly remembered the undue influence of the crown, safeguards against excessive executive authority were provided. The president nominated justices of the new Supreme Court and the judges of such inferior federal courts as the Congress chose to create. But presidential nominations and appointments were subject to the advice and consent of the Senate. Justices of the Supreme Court and judges of the regular federal judiciary were provided two very important protections for judicial independence—life tenure on good behavior and a prohibition of the reduction of their salaries.

The powers of the federal judiciary, spelled out specifically in Article III, Section 2 of the Constitution as jurisdictional authority, ensured that the new system would play a determinative role as interpreter of the safeguards of the separation of powers and as final arbiter in conflicts between the states and the national government. The founders of the American constitutional system were keenly aware of the intimate relationship between a sound and independent judiciary, political and economic stability, and individual freedom.

The first decade of the new national American judicial system was very significant for the future development and expansion of judicial powers. The First Congress passed the seminal Judiciary Act of 1789, in which the appellate jurisdiction of the new Supreme Court was given statutory substance. Significantly, there was enacted the framework of a complete organization for an inferior federal judiciary consisting of courts of first instance, denominated district courts, and three initial intermediate appellate courts, the federal circuit courts for the three major regions of the new nation, New England, the Middle Atlantic states, and the South. Provision was made for regular federal district judges, but not for separate judges for the circuit courts, which were manned during congressionally designated periods each year by federal district judges serving as circuit judges and by members of the United States Supreme Court serving as chief judges or members of the circuit to which they were assigned. The Supreme Court members and district judges chosen by the first president, George Washington, were all Federalists, thus establishing partisan selection as the general appointing policy of subsequent presidents. The justices of the 1790s did not receive the recognition accorded to Chief Justice John Marshall, but they did contribute in a number of significant ways to judicial supremacy and the sanctity of contracts —two principles central to Federalist and neo-Federalist doctrinal judicial influences.

JUDICIAL INDEPENDENCE AND POLITICAL PRESSURE

When John Marshall was appointed chief justice of the United States by President John Adams, the Supreme Court was destined to face major tests of the independence and stability of the judicial system. The Jeffersonian Republicans, enraged by Adam's selection of many Federalists for new circuit judgeships created by the Judiciary Act of 1801 (a product of the lame-duck Federalist Congress), promptly repealed the act in 1802. Since the Federalist circuit judges were protected by the constitutional provisions providing life tenure on good behavior, the question arose whether Congress could constitutionally remove regular federal judges by the exercise of its power "to ordain and establish" or disestablish "inferior courts." When the repealing act came before the Supreme Court in *Stuart* v. *Laird* (1803), the Federalist justices (Marshall abstaining) provided a cryptic yes to the question. The major companion decision, *Marbury* v. *Madison* (1803), by contrast, contained Marshall's articulation of the power of judicial review, establishing the principle in American constitutional law that the Supreme Court possessed the authority to determine the constitutionality of congressional enactments and executive decisions.

The intense partisanship of some of the early Federalist judges and justices and the lame-duck partisanship of the first Adams administration stimulated strong Jeffersonian Republican reactions. The conflicts involving the judiciary in the Jacksonian era were occasionally intense but did not result in institutional setbacks as direct and severe as in both the era of Jefferson and the era of President Abraham Lincoln. Several clear patterns of political-judicial conflict and interaction emerged by the end of the nineteenth century. Particularly after the great, albeit contemporaneously controversial, era of Chief Justice John Marshall, the Court's institutional independence emerged in fact as well as in constitutional clause. But such institutional independence was subject to at least two practical political limitations and had been threatened by others. In rare instances, a politically controversial Supreme Court decision could be overturned by the complex but occasionally politically responsive amending process. Significant amending-process reversals of Supreme Court decisions followed *Chisholm* v. *Georgia* (1793); *Dred Scott* v. *Sandford* (1857), and *Pollock* v. *Farmers' Loan and Trust Company* (1895).

The first decision had held, contrary to Philadelphia Convention understandings, that a state could be sued by a citizen of another state. The decision aroused strong Antifederalist reactions.

The initial call for a constitutional amendment to overturn the *Chisholm* decision came in 1795, two years after the Court had acted. On 8 January 1798, after the requisite three-fourths of the states had ratified the amendment, President Adams formally announced that the Eleventh Amendment was part of the Constitution.

The reaction to the *Dred Scott* decision of 1857 was perhaps the most intense adverse response, because of the intimate relationship of the case to the bitter decisions that ultimately led to the Civil War. The Thirteenth Amendment, ratified in 1865, makes major portions of the *Dred Scott* decision irrelevant because the amendment's prohibition of slavery and involuntary servitude repudiates the portions of the decision that upheld the concept of slaves as property and the doctrine that slavery could not be territorially limited in the United States. The Fourteenth Amendment, adopted in 1868, similarly repudiates the *Dred Scott* decision's doctrine that national citizenship is contingent upon state citizenship. Section 1 holds that "all persons born or naturalized in the United States and subject to the jurisdiction thereof, are citizens of the United States and of the States wherein they reside." The Pollock decision struck down a congressionally passed federal income tax statute on the ground that it was a direct tax requiring apportionment among the states in accordance with state population distributions determined by the decennial census. In 1913, with the impetus of Progressive legislators, the Sixteenth Amendment was ratified, eighteen years after the Pollock decision was handed down. Repudiation of Supreme Court decisions by constitutional amendment obviously does not occur frequently and is often a slow and politically complex procedure. But it is important to note that the amending process has been invoked successfully in periods of great political tension and thus represents a constitutionally valid source of restraint on the judiciary.

The most direct political weapons available to antagonistic Congresses or presidents are the impeachment process, the removal of judges of inferior federal courts by abolishing their courts, and the occasional, politically motivated withdrawal of appellate jurisdiction. After the bitter conflicts of the Federalists and Jeffersonian Republicans that resulted in the removal of Federalist District Judge John Pickering in 1804, and the near impeachment of Justice Samuel Chase, impeachment has not been successfully invoked as a method of political removal of judges or justices, although the threat of the impeachment process has stimulated judicial resignations, such as those of Circuit Judge Martin Manton and Associate Justice Abe Fortas. The abolition of courts with the resultant removal of their judges could not constitutionally be applied to the Supreme Court of the United States but has been utilized on two separate occasions in the nineteenth century—first, to abolish the Federalist-created circuit court system of 1801 and, second, during the Civil War, to abolish the circuit court for the District of Columbia. The latter was replaced immediately by President Lincoln and the Republican Congress with a new court with virtually the same jurisdiction called the Supreme Court for the District of Columbia.

Adjustments of the appellate jurisdiction of the Supreme Court of the United States have been generally made for straightforward legal purposes unrelated to conflicts between the branches of the national government. But the precedent created by the Radical Republican Congress in the hasty repeal of a provision of the statute of 1867 affirming the appellate jurisdiction of the Supreme Court in cases involving habeas corpus, the writ providing that a person held in custody be brought before the court to establish whether he or she is being detained lawfully, is instructive. In acknowledging the power of Congress to repeal portions of its appellate jurisdiction in *Ex parte McCardle* (1869), Chief Justice Salmon P. Chase summed up the effect of such denial of jurisdiction: "Without jurisdiction the court cannot proceed at all in any cause. Jurisdiction is power to declare the law, and when it ceases to exist, the only function remaining to the court is that of announcing the fact and dismissing the cause."

After the unpopularity of President Franklin D. Roosevelt's Court-packing plan of the 1930s, it was commonly assumed that the Court enjoyed an attitude of reverence in Congress and support among the public. But the main portion of the congressional opposition to Roosevelt's plan consisted of a conservative coalition composed of conservative southern Democrats and northern Republicans. When the balance of Supreme Court appointments shifted to the New Deal and its successor, Harry Truman's Fair Deal, the conservative coalition became the political center of anti–Supreme Court political activity. By the 1980s, many elements of an anti-Court conservative coalition had shifted further to the right, augmented by younger conservatives elected to the House of Representatives and the Senate with the support of the Moral Majority and its political-action committee, which was controlled by Senator Jesse Helms of North Carolina. The "social agenda" goals of the new right included repudiation of a number of Supreme Court decisions, such as the key abortion ruling in *Roe* v. *Wade* (1973). Senator Helms, with the support of President Ronald Reagan, recommended selective statutory curtailment of the appellate jurisdiction of the Supreme Court to accomplish Moral Majority legislative goals. One such Helms bill was only narrowly defeated in the Senate in 1982. In short, direct political action against the Supreme Court is not merely a nineteenth-century phenomenon.

In sum, the independence of the Supreme Court and regular federal judiciary against direct political attacks by Congress or the president has generally been maintained. But while twentieth-century Supreme Court crises have been fewer and less intense, the institutional weapons to mount such attacks, from the cumbersome amending process to statutory manipulation of the appellate jurisdiction of the Supreme Court, are still intact and have tempted some contemporary critics of the doctrines and personnel of the Supreme Court.

THE RELATIONSHIP OF THE FEDERAL AND STATE COURTS

One of the most interesting and initially unpredictable aspects of the adoption of the Constitution of 1787 was the creation of an entirely new court system that operated as the judicial arm of the new nation upon individuals who were used to utilizing the court systems of their respective states. The initial conflict between the two systems occurred even before the national court system was created. There was little disagreement over the establishment of a Supreme Court of the United States with jurisdiction sufficiently broad to encompass cases and controversies that involved the scope of national authority or the violation by states of claimed federal rights. The Philadelphia Convention of 1787 left to the Congress the question of whether a system of inferior federal courts would be created or not. The First Congress was controlled by Federalists, who wanted to create a complete federal court system. They succeeded in passing a comprehensive framework, but as the comments above about the first circuit court system indicate, no separate federal circuit judges were included. In Section 25 of the Judiciary Act of 1789, Congress provided for a means by which any state court challenge to federal powers or rights could be finally decided by the Supreme Court of the United States. The section stated that final judgment in any suit in the highest court of law or equity of a state,

> where is drawn in question the validity of a treaty or statute of, or an authority exercised under the United States, and the decision is against their validity; or where is drawn in question the validity of a statute of, or an authority exercised under any State, on the ground of their being repugnant to the Constitution, treaties or laws of the United States, and the decision is in favour of their validity, or where is drawn in question the construction of any clause of the Constitution, or of a treaty, or statute of, or commission held under the United States, and the decision is against the title, right, privilege or exemption specially set up or claimed by either party, under such clause of the said constitution, treaty, statute, or commission, may be re-examined and reversed or affirmed in the Supreme Court of the United States [upon writ of error].

The Antifederalists argued that Supreme Court oversight was enough and also argued on states' rights and economic grounds that inferior federal courts were not needed. The Federalists prevailed, and the two judicial systems were paired in every state.

The most dramatic confrontations between the two systems occurred in situations in which the highest court of a state directly challenged the authority of the Supreme Court of the United States. Chief Justice Marshall firmly rejected such assertions of state judicial authority in *Cohens* v. *Virginia* (1821), as did Justice Joseph Story in *Martin* v. *Hunter's Lessee* (1816). Both invoked the supremacy clause as the ultimate source of federal judicial authority. But it should be noted

that the relationship and relative positions of the federal and state courts were not determined by dramatic constitutional confrontations alone, although such conflicts ultimately established the subordinate positions of the state courts when valid federal judicial authority was at stake. As the relative positions of the federal and state judicial systems changed over the nineteenth and early twentieth centuries, other factors, such as the prestige and relative independence of the two sets of courts, were important. For example, a notable and very conservative New York state jurist, James Kent, concerned about the successes of the Jacksonians in gaining state approval of public election of judges, suggested that

> the judiciary of the United States has an advantage over many of the state courts, in the tenure of the office of the judges, and the liberal and stable provision for their support. The United States are, by these means, fairly entitled to command better talents, and to look to more firmness of purpose, greater independence of action, and brighter displays of learning. The federal administration of justice has a manifest superiority over that of the individual states, in consequence of the uniformity of its decisions, and the universality of their application. Every state court will naturally be disposed to borrow light and aid from the national courts, rather than from the courts of other individual states, which will probably never be so generally respected and understood.

Perhaps more important, the Supreme Court of the United States and the inferior federal courts became, especially during and after the era of John Marshall, rather clearly identified as the legal tribunals that reliably sustained property rights via the contract clause. Commercial and banking interests increasingly avoided state courts in favor of federal courts where the jurisdictional requirements could be met. Chief Justice William Howard Taft candidly and accurately summed up some of the reasons for such forum preference. Addressing the American Bar Association, Taft stated that

> litigants from the eastern part of the country who are expected to invest their capital in the West or South, will hardly concede the proposition that their interests as creditors will be as

sure of impartial consideration in a western or southern state court as in a federal court. . . . No single element in our governmental system has done so much to secure capital for the legitimate development of enterprises throughout the West and South as the existence of federal courts there, with a jurisdiction to hear diverse citizenship cases.

(Parker)

It should be noted that jurists of several of the highest appellate courts of the states have, over the nearly two centuries of dual court systems, achieved notable reputations. These include Chief Justice Lemuel Shaw and Chief Justice Oliver Wendell Holmes of the Supreme Judicial Court of Massachusetts, Chief Justice Benjamin N. Cardozo of the Court of Appeals of New York, Chief Justice Roger Traynor of the Supreme Court of California, and Chief Justice Arthur Vanderbilt of New Jersey. The prestige and doctrinal influence of some of the highest state courts have been rather substantial and contribute a degree of diversity and intellectual stimulation that would be lacking in a single judicial system. Just as several conservatively oriented Midwestern state supreme courts doggedly opposed New Deal Supreme Court doctrine when the jurisdictional properties permitted, so did contemporary liberally oriented state supreme courts, such as California's, provide doctrinal counterpoint to the Burger Court's narrowing of the rights of criminal defendants.

THE SOCIOPOLITICAL CHARACTERISTICS OF FEDERAL APPELLATE JURISTS

Federal appellate judicial selection has, since 1789, involved characteristics that in a number of important respects have contributed both to the strength and stability of the American national judiciary and, on occasion, to the political controversies that have engulfed the system. In sociopolitical terms, such selection has not generally been very responsive to the democratization of American politics and society, which purportedly has progressed since the era of government by gentry class of the late eighteenth and early nineteenth centuries. Particularly, by the twentieth century, ethnic and religious groups in the United States began to indicate greater interest in a concept of judicial representation. This concept resembles the suggestion of Walter F. Murphy and Joseph Tanenhaus that many "national constitutional courts typically display a large element of representation" because the political authorities making judicial selections may "consciously try to staff constitutional courts with personnel of diverse background characteristics that are more or less shared by the various politically relevant groupings within the polity." Another characteristic of the American selection process that has occasionally contributed to political conflict is the age of appointees and the possibility that justices or judges chosen in an earlier political generation may, under the system of life tenure on good behavior, be doctrinally at odds with legislative and executive leaders of a totally different political generation.

An ideal model of a judicial recruitment system would presumably be based upon attributes such as professional training, educational proficiency, and, as in the continental European system from which it was derived, judicial training and experience. The American system of national judges and justices (and the systems of the numerically increasing states, for that matter) did not evolve in accordance with the continental European model. The selection of federal appellate judges and justices has usually combined partisanship with an interesting composite of judicial skill and practical experience. The importance of background and careerist attributes has changed in certain respects with political eras, but in certain matters they have remained remarkably consistent. One key indication of social status, parental occupation, is a good example. Approximately 90 percent of the members of the Supreme Court have been products of economically comfortable families, largely the prestigious and politically powerful gentry class in the late eighteenth and early nineteenth centuries and the professionalized upper middle class thereafter. The circuit court judges come from the same sorts of families.

A special type of occupational heredity includes the transmission of a family tradition of political participation, which generally entails the prestige of a political name, and a family apprenticeship in political education. Two-thirds of all the justices have come from such a background, but after the Civil War few of the circuit court judges came from such families. One-third of the justices came from an even more unusual type family, those with a tradition of judicial service, a relationship generally not present for circuit court judges.

Ethnicity and sex have become factors of increasing importance in the politics of judicial selection in the twentieth century. For more than the first hundred years of the Supreme Court, it was a complete monopoly of white men and a virtual monopoly of white men of western European background. Indeed, throughout the entire history of the Court, approximately 85 percent of the appointees have been of English, Welsh, Scotch, or Irish heritage. It was not until the 1960s that a black, Justice Thurgood Marshall, was nominated and appointed. The first woman chosen, Justice Sandra Day O'Connor, was selected in the 1980s. The federal circuit courts were ethnically diversified earlier than the Supreme Court, with President Truman selecting the first black circuit judge, William H. Hastie, in 1949; President Richard M. Nixon chose the first circuit judge of Asian extraction, Herbert Y. C. Choy, in the early 1970s. President Franklin D. Roosevelt chose the first female circuit judge considerably earlier, nominating and appointing Ohio Supreme Court Justice Florence E. Allen in 1934.

Religion has often proved a complex issue for presidents because religious issues and attitudes occasionally stimulate serious political conflict. Historically, Roman Catholics and Jews have been subjected to nativist and religious criticism, and as a result, few of either denomination have been chosen, with most selected in the twentieth century. The overwhelming number of nominations made were of Protestants, with high-status denominations such as Episcopalian, Presbyterian, and Congregationalist constituting most of the selections. The nineteenth-century nominations of Roman Catholics and Jews did not involve the beginning of a tradition of such denominational choices but were made for contemporary political reasons largely unrelated to religion. President Andrew Jackson's choice of Chief Justice Roger B. Taney had little to do with Taney's Roman Catholicism, but Taney was the very first of his denomination on the Court. President Millard Fillmore's offer to nominate Louisiana senator-elect Judah P. Benjamin also was

primarily political and had little to do with Benjamin's Jewish faith. Like the choice of Taney, this was the first such denominational choice. Benjamin preferred to keep his newly won Senate seat. Thus more than six decades lapsed before President Woodrow Wilson nominated and, after a bitter Senate fight, appointed Louis D. Brandeis as associate justice, an appointment accepted by Brandeis.

It was not until the twentieth century that political controversy arose over the concept of a Catholic seat or a Jewish seat on the Court. For example, President Truman was asked after the death of Justice Frank Murphy whether the Court "should have at least one representative of each major minority religious community?" Truman replied that he did "not believe that religions had anything to do with the Supreme Bench." This certainly appeared to be the case when Republican President Herbert Hoover selected New York Court of Appeals Justice Benjamin N. Cardozo as associate justice despite the fact that he would be the second member of the Jewish faith currently on the Court (Brandeis was still serving), the second New Yorker, and a moderately liberal Democrat as well. However, the political controversies over alleged failures to fulfill a custom of maintaining a Roman Catholic and Jewish seat on the Court are likely to intensify as group consciousness increases in American society. In fact, a considerable number of smaller and more unusual religious groups in the United States have never been represented on the Court. Of the members of major religions that have on occasion experienced discrimination, only three have been represented—Catholics, Jews, and Quakers—and throughout the entire history of the Court they have collectively constituted only 16 percent of all appointments. The proportion for circuit judges has been similar.

Because geographic representation has often been an important political consideration for presidents making judicial nominations, states having greater electoral-college significance have had more selections and those states entering the Union most recently have generally produced fewer justices and judges. A small number of foreign-born jurists have been chosen, the greatest number having been selected in the early decades of the Republic.

The framers of the Constitution did not specify that members of the federal appellate judiciary be lawyers. In practice, all the justices and circuit judges have been lawyers, although a number of the selectees in the earliest periods were primarily politicians and a few in the New Deal era were drawn from the ranks of law professors, notably Felix Frankfurter, William O. Douglas, and Wiley Rutledge. But most nominees to the Supreme Court after the 1870s have been former corporate lawyers. The New Deal interrupted the trend, but it was reinstated at the levels of the Supreme Court and the circuit courts after Truman's presidency and was particularly important under the presidencies of Eisenhower, Nixon, Ford, and Reagan.

Education, both undergraduate and professional, has been one of the most important background variables in the American judicial selection process. While the educational backgrounds of justices and circuit judges of the late eighteenth century and early nineteenth century were frequently superior to those of most contemporary lawyers, this dimension of the qualitative relationship of the public and private sectors of America's legal culture has changed. Perhaps the most significant changes took place after a frequently close relationship evolved between the emergent corporate law firms and the law schools that largely supplanted other modes of legal education by the late nineteenth century. An analysis of legal-educational background of the young associates hired by two large prototype law firms, the Cravath firm of New York City and O'Melveny and Myers of Los Angeles, indicates that in comparison to the Supreme Court justices and circuit judges who attended law schools, a far higher proportion of associates graduated from highly ranked law schools located in states that were highly industrialized, commercially active, and culturally influential. Such schools and regions do not, of course, have a monopoly on legal talent, as Thurman Arnold indicated in his witty and perceptive autobiographical chapter entitled "Law and Politics in Wyoming and Why I Left." Differences in salaries had been a source of dispute over the relative positions of state and federal courts in the nineteenth century. For example, a federal judicial salary increase proposed in 1838 was defeated on the ground that higher salaries would lure many state judges to the federal judiciary. But the most significant salary differential in the late twentieth century was between the public and private sectors. Judge Henry J. Friendly of the U.S. Court of Appeals for the Second Circuit provided an unusually candid commentary on the problem while arguing against substantial increases in the number of federal judges. He pointed out that

> prestige is a very important factor in attracting highly qualified men to the federal bench from much more lucrative pursuits. Yet the largest district courts will be in the very metropolitan areas where the discrepancy between uniform federal salaries and the financial rewards of private practice is the greatest, and the difficulty of maintaining an accustomed standard of living on the federal salary the most acute. There is real danger that in such areas, once the prestige factor was removed, lawyers with successful practices, particularly young men, would not be willing to make the sacrifice.

The trends in private-sector and public-sector legal and judicial salaries, especially when the incomes of corporate law firm partners are measured against those of federal judges and justices, have steadily enhanced the position of the private sector with consequences for the federal appellate judicial system still largely unexplored.

Of all the background and career factors that may influence the federal appellate judiciary, chronological age appears at first glance to be the simplest and least important. But when age is assessed in relation to stage of career at judicial selection and at termination of service, it assumes considerable importance because of the constitutional provision for life tenure on good behavior. This complex of age and constitutional factors practically ensures periodic policy conflict and doctrinal dissonance in the American political system. In elementary terms, the House of Representatives is totally renewed every two years, although in modern times renewal has often been a matter of course for congressmen who combine a strong instinct for survival and a "safe" one-party district. The Senate, similarly, is renewed regularly with one-third of the members up for election for a six-year term every two years. The most important potential generator of fundamental political change is the election for renewal of the presidency every four years. Unlike the House and Senate, where politically entrenched members may seek reelection as often as their health or constituents permit, the presidency was subjected to a two-term limitation in 1951 by the Twenty-second Amendment, in reaction to the four-term Roosevelt administration. The prospect of a conflict between political generations is considerably diminished in periods of political stability and concomitant legislative seniority but is especially likely in the aftermath of critical elections in which a long-controlling political party loses the White House, the House, and the Senate, and a new or rejuvenated party takes electoral control of those three institutions for a long period of time.

Major conflicts involving the federal appellate judiciary have occurred in connection with four of the five critical elections. In the first such election, that of 1800, the Federalist-controlled federal courts were the only remaining party positions after the victory of the Jeffersonian Republicans. Despite the effective elimination of the "midnight" circuit judges created by the lame-duck Federalist Congress, Federalists controlled the Supreme Court and the single remaining circuit court, that for the District of Columbia. The persistence of Federalist doctrinal influence is dramatically underscored by John Marshall's thirty-five years as Chief Justice and by Federalist William Cranch's astonishing fifty-five years of service as a member of the Circuit Court for the District of Columbia. The Federalist party never captured the White House, the House, or the Senate after 1800, but the Federalists' conservative judicial principles were perpetuated in the federal appellate judiciary in doctrines such as judicial review, broad constructionist interpretations of the commerce clause, the implied-powers clause, and the contract clause. The Federalist justices had a numerical majority for twelve years after Jefferson's first presidential election and maintained effective doctrinal influence well into the Jacksonian era because of the ideological defection of Joseph Story and the neo-Federalism of Thomas Todd and Robert Trimble.

The critical election of 1828 did not directly involve the federal appellate judiciary, but the incoming president, Andrew Jackson, soon found himself in disagreement with Chief Justice Marshall and with his congressional opponents, the political successors to the Federalists, the Whigs. Their leaders, Henry Clay and Daniel Webster, frequently invoked Federalist judicial arguments in defense of the Bank of the United States. The bitter congressional battles over the Bank and the senatorial confirmation fights over Jackson's nominations of Roger B. Taney and other Jacksonian judicial nominees made clear the importance attached to control of the Supreme Court by both parties in the 1830s, 1840s, and 1850s. During the latter two decades especially, Court-related controversies shifted more and more away from the economically oriented battles that began to dominate political controversy. By the late 1850s Jacksonian justices and judges controlled the federal appellate judiciary. On a number of slavery-related issues, they became identified, generally correctly, as proslavery jurists. The *Dred Scott* decision catapulted the Supreme Court fully into the mounting slavery controversy. Chief Justice Taney's references to blacks as individuals who "had for more than a century before been regarded as beings of an inferior order . . . [having] no rights which the white man is bound to respect" inflamed abolitionists. His decision to declare unconstitutional the Missouri Compromise on the ground that Congress could not constitutionally exclude slaveholders and their property in slaves from any territory of the United States aroused wide opposition. Indeed, Taney asserted that the "only power conferred [upon Congress] is the power coupled with the duty of guarding and protecting the [slave] owner in his rights." This portion of the decision eliminated the major plank of the new Republican party—free soil. As a result, the Jacksonian Court majority found itself pitted against not only the abolitionists but also the Republican party, which achieved victory under the leadership of its presidential standard-bearer, Abraham Lincoln.

The critical election of 1860 not only included the Court-president confrontation but was soon followed by a bitter, divisive, and violent revolution by the secessionist Southern states. The Jacksonian Democratic majority, which held all but one of the nine seats of the Court on the eve of the election, lost control of the Court in an astonishingly short period. Unlike the Federalists of 1800, the Jacksonians did not extend their influence beyond the era of Jacksonian electoral ascendancy. Justice Peter V. Daniel died in 1860, Justice John A. Campbell resigned to join the Confederacy in 1861, the Republicans increased the size of the Court to ten members in 1863,

THE JUDICIARY

Chief Justice Taney died in 1864, and Justice John Catron died in 1865. President James Buchanan's only appointee, Justice Nathan Clifford, died in 1881 after vainly hanging on to his seat awaiting election of a Democratic president. Had the full Jacksonian Democratic judicial majority of 1859 remained on the Court throughout the Civil War years, a very serious confrontation with the new Republican president and Congress would have been highly likely. Most of the Jacksonians had been proslavery in doctrinal orientations and the non-Southerners on the bench had been accurately identified as "Northern men with Southern principles."

When President Lincoln was confronted with the prospect that the three proslavery judges for the circuit court for the District of Columbia were likely to apply Chief Justice Roger B. Taney's *Merryman* doctrine of habeas corpus, Lincoln ordered the judges placed under house arrest. In order to maintain the military authority he deemed vital to the defense of the capital city, he then successfully asked Congress to abolish the circuit court, thus eliminating the judges. His Congress soon replaced the circuit court with a larger judiciary, denominated the Supreme Court for the District of Columbia, and granted similar judicial authority over the District of Columbia.

As in 1860, the critical election of 1896 was in part fought over issues related to the Supreme Court. This time the controversies related to the conservative doctrinal tendencies limiting the capacity of Congress to curb monopolies in restraint of trade and to the power of state legislatures and state regulatory agencies to regulate the rates of grain elevators and railroads. The Court also managed to limit congressional regulatory power over railroads, too. It struck down the income tax and upheld racial segregation in public transportation, adopting the separate-but-equal doctrine, which was destined to dominate public education for decades. Overall, the Court substantially broadened constitutional protections for corporations and minimized protections for individuals' noneconomic rights and liberties under the equal protection and due process clauses of the Fourteenth Amendment. At the Democratic convention of 1896, the nominee, William Jennings Bryan, adopted the strong anti–Supreme Court plank of the Populist party as a Democratic party plank, thus making the

Court a major issue in the presidential campaign. Bryan's Republican opponent, William McKinley, won, and the Court's conservatism seemed electorally vindicated.

However, within a few years, progressive Republican Theodore Roosevelt and progressive Democrat Woodrow Wilson were both critical of the Court's conservatism and sought by appointments and public exhortation to change the Court's doctrinal direction, efforts that only achieved limited successes. These progressive efforts at liberalizing the Court failed in part because both Roosevelt and Wilson each made one serious error in selection—Day, by the former, and McReynolds, by the latter. And, more important, both progressive presidents were totally overshadowed by the conservative appointment opportunities available to Presidents William Howard Taft, Warren G. Harding, and Calvin Coolidge.

A dramatic change occurred after the last critical election, in 1932. Although little serious discussion of a possible confrontation took place before the election, the presence of a majority of conservative justices who had been chosen largely during more than a decade of solid Republican presidential and congressional control provided the foundation for the major constitutional crisis of the mid-1930s. The conservative majority struck down a number of key New Deal economic recovery statutes. By the end of President Franklin D. Roosevelt's first term, not a single justice had left the Court. Although conservative justices had served for decades, McReynolds since 1914, and Sutherland since 1922, there was no indication of a possible resignation or retirement. Roosevelt was confronted by a situation similar to that which apparently prompted Thomas Jefferson to state resignedly that "judges never die, and seldom resign." After the beginning of his second term, Roosevelt urged passage of the most direct legislative effort at neutralizing a Court majority short of impeachment based on political orientation. The statute, generally referred to as the Court-packing plan, would have enlarged the Court to as many as fifteen members by in effect matching new members with sitting members of the Court who were more than seventy years of age and had served ten years. The plan was not successful in Congress, but by 1937 the two most flexible of the conservatives had changed their posi-

609

tions abruptly, thereafter generally supporting the very forms of New Deal legislation that they had earlier deemed unconstitutional. The year 1937 also proved to be the one in which President Roosevelt, for the first time in his long tenure, could fill a vacancy on the Supreme Court. Thereafter, the transformation was rapid. After the appointment of Hugo Lafayette Black in 1937 came those of Stanley Reed in 1938; William O. Douglas and Felix Frankfurter in 1939; Frank Murphy in 1940; James Byrnes, Robert H. Jackson, and the promotion of Harlan Fiske Stone to chief justice in 1941; and Wiley Rutledge in 1943.

The high tide of positive judicial policy-making by the Supreme Court came with the unique combination of Eisenhower nominees for chief justice and associate justice plus enough New Deal Democrats to fashion a working liberal majority. Chief Justice Earl Warren, chosen in 1953, and Associate Justice William Brennan, selected in 1956, were the two important additions in this development. The defeat of President Lyndon Johnson's effort to name Associate Justice Abe Fortas as Chief Justice Warren's successor set the stage for resurgent conservatism on the Court. On the eve of the 1984 presidential election, only a few members of the old liberal coalition remained on the Court, all elderly, several in reported poor health. Associate Justice William Brennan, a nominal Democrat, who was chosen after a distinguished career on the Supreme Court of New Jersey, was the last Eisenhower appointee remaining on the Court. Moderate Associate Justice Byron White, chosen from a western corporate law firm in 1962, is the last of only two Kennedy selectees. Former civil rights attorney and NAACP legal strategist Thurgood Marshall is similarly the last of only two Johnson appointees. Marshall has served since 1967.

To Johnson's successor, President Richard M. Nixon, fell the most significant prize, the chief justiceship, and with the resignation of Associate Justice Abe Fortas in May 1969, a second vacancy. Nixon chose a sitting court of appeals judge, chosen for the District of Columbia circuit by President Eisenhower. The new chief justice, Warren E. Burger, had a visible track record as a strong 'law and order' judge on the circuit court, thus fitting Nixon's criteria established in the 1968 campaign. After the defeats of his nominees Haynsworth and Carswell, President Nixon chose another circuit judge and friend of Burger, Harry A. Blackmun. In 1971, President Nixon chose two corporate lawyers to replace Justices Black and Harlan. Former American Bar Association President and Richmond, Virginia, firm member Lewis F. Powell, and former corporate law firm member and Assistant Attorney General William H. Rehnquist were often described as advocates of judicial restraint but were in the forefront with Chief Justice Burger as conservative judicial activists. After Nixon's resignation and presidential pardon, President Gerald R. Ford chose moderate circuit judge John Paul Stevens in 1975. Stevens became a severe critic of the conservative judicial activism of some of his colleagues in August 1984. President Jimmy Carter did not have a vacancy on the Court to fill. In 1981, when Associate Justice Potter Stewart resigned, President Ronald W. Reagan chose a former corporate law firm member serving on an Arizona appellate court, Sandra Day O'Connor. She was the first woman chosen for the Supreme Court.

An overview of the significance of the background and career factors in the selection of members of the Supreme Court suggests that the highest appellate court of the United States embodies a relatively unique institution. The Court does not completely conform to the ideal model often associated with the contributions of the sociologist Max Weber. Its members in modern times have conformed to the main attributes of American social stratification, with upper-middle-class professional family backgrounds predominating. Education in general and legal training in particular have generally screened out most lower socioeconomic class potential candidates, yet the quality of education has not matched that of corporate law firm members nor has the salary and life-style. The selection process makes it highly likely that most justices are political activists of some sort. This factor, in combination with jurisdictional grants of judicial authority in subject-matter areas of great political sensitivity, such as federalism, virtually ensures that the Supreme Court normally renders constitutional decisions of major political importance. This political emphasis is generally enlarged in those periods of fundamental political change when an entrenched Court majority, safeguarded by life tenure on good behavior, thwarts judicially the executive and legislative purposes of a different political generation.

THE INTERNAL PROCEDURES AND CUSTOMS OF THE SUPREME COURT

A countervailing institutional factor is summed up in Justice Felix Frankfurter's argument that the role changes the man. The extent to which such an institutional tradition has influenced Supreme Court or circuit court voting behavior varies by individual. There is no question that the procedures and customs of such higher appellate courts are related to the internal performance of an appellate court as a collegial body, while the broader political policy issues are external in certain respects. The line between external political purposes and internal institutional goals is, of course, not very precise. Chief Justice John Marshall's major change in the mode of rendering Supreme Court decisions is a good example. For the first decade of the Supreme Court, under the chief-justiceships of John Jay and Oliver Ellsworth, the justices followed the practice of writing separate opinions, technically referred to as seriatim opinions. Marshall was chosen as chief justice of the United States after the defeat of the Federalists in 1800. As a matter of fact, Marshall continued to fulfill his duties as Secretary of State after he assumed the chief justiceship, an example of dual office-holding that would not be permitted under modern standards. Soon after becoming chief justice, Marshall persuaded his fellow Federalists to adopt modes of procedure that would enable the Court to present a unified front. The practice of writing seriatim opinions was completely abandoned, dissent was discouraged, and the writing of concurring opinions was virtually eliminated. During the first four years of Marshall's leadership, Marshall himself wrote every majority opinion except two coming from his own circuit court.

President Jefferson's first appointee, William Johnson, eventually succeeded in getting a compromise procedural arrangement. A return to seriatim opinions was not accepted, but a compromise procedure, majority opinion-writing, with the concept of dissents and concurring opinions, was established. In the initial years of Marshall's chief-justiceship, Court unity was es-

sentially Federalist unity. After the compromise procedure was adopted, the greatest internal pressure was still against dissents and concurrences. But in eras of great national political divisions, individual justices tended to assert their independence by accentuating their differences. The crises of slavery and states' rights in the decades immediately preceding the Civil War; the late nineteenth-century and early twentieth-century public and judicial disputes over the power of corporations and the scope of state and federal regulatory authority; and the contemporary societal and judicial dissonances regarding such matters as police behavior related to criminal defendants, pornography, racial desegregation, and abortion provide the best examples of divided decisions.

Throughout much of the history of the Supreme Court, the mainstream of American legal culture held a rather conservative opinion on the matter of a divided Court. Through much of the most bitter post–Civil War judicial eras, very strong conservative professional opinions on the question were stated by a number of judges and by leaders of the American Bar Association. The association itself adopted Canon 19 of the Canons of Judicial Ethics, which provides that

it is of high importance that judges constituting a court of last resort should use effort and self-restraint to promote solidarity of conclusion and the consequent influence of judicial decision. A judge should not yield to pride of opinion or value more highly his individual reputation than that of the court to which he should be loyal. Except in case of conscientious difference of opinion on fundamental principle, dissenting opinions should be discouraged in courts of last resort.

It was not until the flowering of dissent and concurring opinions of the 1940s, 1950s, and 1960s that a clearly stated countervailing body of liberal legal opinion began to emerge. One of the most direct of the advocates of separate opinion-writing was Justice William O. Douglas. Douglas not only wrote rationales for dissents in some of his own dissenting opinions (as did several of his colleagues) but he also contributed to the debate in journals. For example, in response to a veritable flood of critical articles about an allegedly divided Court, Douglas not only argued that justices were often divided because they were dealing with issues over which society was divided but he also equated dissent with the Jeffersonian conception of the role of judges in a democracy. It may be noted that although the practice of writing separate opinions was attacked as a procedural shortcoming of liberal justices in the 1940s and 1950s, members of the conservative majority headed by Chief Justice Warren E. Burger continued the practice with undiminished intensity.

The disagreements among the justices are usually muted by the use of language that tempers the degree of dissonance. On the rare occasions when sharp disagreement becomes public, such as in the aftermath of the *Dred Scott* decision or the period of deep divisions between New Deal chief justices, considerable public and professional interest is aroused. But there are other institutional practices, many developed under the chief justiceship of John Marshall, that militate against frequent public disagreement. The chief justice presides at the conferences in which individual cases are discussed. When, after each justice has freely discussed the issues, a vote on the outcome of the case is called for, each justice responds in reverse order of seniority. If the chief justice is with the Court's majority, he designates the associate justice (or himself) who will write the majority opinion. If not, the senior justice with the majority makes the assignment.

These procedural matters and the incidence of dissents and concurring opinions have created far fewer problems than those associated with the burgeoning case load of the Supreme Court and the federal circuit courts of appeal. Since the Court has not appreciably increased since 1925 the number of cases that are actually decided annually, the case load pressures are serious for the institution and for the individual justices themselves. Justice Harry Blackmun's moving commentary about the effects of the huge case load ably sums up the problem for the justices as individuals. He pointed out that

> the question is how long we can continue so to function and to do our work adequately. The heavier the burden, the less the possibility of adequate performance and the greater is the probability of less-than-well considered adjudication. Personally, I have never worked harder and more concentratedly than since I came to

Washington just five years ago. I thought I had labored to the limits of my ability in private practice, in my work for a decade as a member of the Section of Administration of the Mayo organizations, and as a judge of the Court of Appeals. Here, however, the pressure is greater and more constant, and it relents little even during the summer months. One, therefore, to a larger degree, relies on experience and an innate and hopefully already developed proper judicial reaction. One had better be right! Good health is an absolute requisite. The normal extracurricular enjoyments of life become secondary, if it can be said that they exist at all. What I am saying, I suppose, is that there is a breaking point somewhere at which one's capacity will be exceeded or at which one's work becomes second-rate. The nation, in my opinion, deserves better than this.

Considerable attention has been given in Congress, the legal profession, and the federal judiciary to a variety of suggested solutions. The recommendations have ranged from adding more inferior federal judges to the creation of yet another appellate court with authority greater than the courts of appeals of the circuits but less than that of the Supreme Court. A commonly accepted solution has not been found.

CONCLUSION

The Supreme Court of the United States is unique in the manner in which it often exercises policy-making authority, which on occasion thwarts the purposes of the politically elective branches of the national government. To be sure, the Court has on occasion suffered serious setbacks in its policy-making endeavors.

In the context of an ideal Weberian conception of a judiciary based upon nonpartisan professionalism, the highest appellate judiciary of the United States does not totally fulfill the criteria, nor do any other judiciaries throughout the world. The Founding Fathers quite consciously anticipated a political role for the Court, especially as final arbiter of federalism. They could not have fully anticipated its generally consistent commitment to corporate power. Perhaps the greatest test to be anticipated by the American appellate judiciary is that of reconciling such corporate preference with the more objective requirements of equal justice.

THE JUDICIARY

CASES

Chisholm v. Georgia, 2 Dallas 419 (1793)
Cohens v. Virginia, 6 Wheaton 264 (1821)
Dred Scott v. Sandford, 19 Howard 393 (1857)
Ex parte McCardle, 7 Wallace 506 (1869)
Marbury v. Madison, 1 Cranch 137 (1803)
Martin v. Hunter's Lessee, 1 Wheaton 304 (1816)
Pollock v. Farmers' Loan and Trust Company, 157 U.S. 429;
    158 U.S. 601 (1895)
Roe v. Wade, 410 U.S. 113 (1973)
Stuart v. Laird, 1 Cranch 299 (1803)

BIBLIOGRAPHY

Thurman Wesley Arnold, *Fair Fights and Foul: A Dissenting Lawyer's Life* (1965). Harold J. Berman, *Law and Revolution: The Formation of the Western Legal Tradition* (1983). Testimony of Associate Justice Harry Blackmun, Report of the Commission on the Revision of the Federal Court Appellate System, U.S. Government Printing Office (1973). William O. Douglas, "The Dissent: A Safeguard of Democracy," in *Journal of the American Judicature Society,* 32 (1948) and "Stare Decisis," in *Columbia Law Review,* 49 (1949). Henry J. Friendly, *Federal Jurisdiction: A General View* (1973).

James Kent, *Commentaries on American Law,* 1 (1844). Walter F. Murphy and Joseph Tanenhaus, "Constitutional Courts and Political Representation" in Michael N. Danielson and Walter F. Murphy, eds., *Modern Democracy* (1969). John J. Parker, "The Federal Judiciary," in *American Bar Association Journal,* 24 (1938). C. Herman Pritchett, *The American Constitution* (1977). Guenther Roth and Claus Wittich, eds., *Max Weber: Economy and Society: An Outline of Interpretive Sociology* (1968). Gordon Wood, *The Creation of the American Republic, 1776–1787* (1969).

[*See also* FEDERAL COURT SYSTEM; JUDICIAL ADMINISTRATION; JUDICIAL REVIEW; JUDICIAL SELECTION; LEGAL EDUCATION; LEGAL PROFESSION AND LEGAL ETHICS; MARSHALL COURT AND ERA; *and* STATE COURT SYSTEMS.]

LEGAL EDUCATION

Jay M. Feinman

From the early eighteenth century through the early twentieth century, apprenticeship was the principal device for the study of law. A young man (women were not considered to be fit candidates for legal practice until about 1870) who wished to learn the law would pay an established practicing lawyer a fee to take him into his office. There the extent and quality of the apprentice's legal education would depend on the nature of his master's practice and on his master's ability and willingness to teach. Many apprentices complained that they were no more than clerks, engaged in office drudgery such as copying documents, and receiving no instruction beyond occasional glances at the lawyer's books. Others enjoyed a better experience, being directed in extensive programs of reading in law, economics, history, and philosophy, and receiving systematic lectures and less formal instruction in legal doctrine and legal practice.

Some practitioners became well known for the high quality of the education they provided their apprentices, and the demand for instruction by these practitioners outgrew their ability to provide it in an office setting. To meet the demand, some of these attorneys established formal programs of instruction, creating the first law schools. The most famous of these schools was the Litchfield Law School in Connecticut, founded in 1784 as an outgrowth of the office instruction of Tapping Reeve. During its forty-nine-year existence Litchfield attracted students from all over the country and numbered among its graduates three justices of the Supreme Court and two vice-presidents.

Some of these private law schools attempted to teach law in a comprehensive, scholarly manner. The Litchfield program encompassed more than a year of daily lectures based on Sir William Blackstone's *Commentaries on the Laws of England* and on American precedents. Students were examined regularly on the material covered in the lectures and in assigned collateral readings. Other law schools, however, provided little more than dry lectures on local doctrine and practice.

During the same period, legal education became available in several colleges. At the College of William and Mary in Williamsburg, Virginia, the first American law professorship was established, held by George Wythe, the former teacher of Thomas Jefferson. The Universities of Maryland and Pennsylvania, and Yale, Columbia, and Harvard Colleges also established early chairs in law.

Like the private schools, the college professorships varied greatly in quality. Some of the early professors were appointed for political or personal reasons and provided little enlightenment to students. Other professors, however, delivered scholarly lectures and produced learned treatises that became the basic literature of the law in the early Republic. In several colleges, law was taught as one of the liberal arts and was thought to be important training for citizenship in the new nation.

NINETEENTH-CENTURY LEGAL EDUCATION

In the early 1820s the two forms of legal schooling began to find a common ground as a few private schools were absorbed by colleges. These mergers provided the private schools with added prestige and with the ability to grant academic degrees, a power given by state law to chartered colleges. It also served the colleges by associating them with a powerful interest group

614

—the lawyers—and by increasing their student bodies. The mergers did not always breed strength, though. College-affiliated law schools, like private schools, came and went as economic and political pressures and intellectual and professional interests changed.

Through the middle of the nineteenth century, then, varied forms of legal education were available. College-affiliated law schools became more popular, but apprenticeship and practice-oriented schooling still had their adherents. Because the standards for admission to legal practice were generally low, no single form of educational preparation was necessary. That began to change about 1870, when the format for the modern law school was set at the Harvard Law School.

The changes initiated at Harvard were part of a broad movement toward institutionalization and professionalization in the second half of the nineteenth century. During that period, major private universities and land-grant institutions were organized for the first time in the form with which we are now familiar. Academic disciplines such as history, sociology, and political science were conceptualized and formalized. The modern professions, including law, medicine, and engineering, were elevated and made more restrictive.

The principal architects of the changes at Harvard were university president Charles W. Eliot and law dean Christopher Columbus Langdell. Eliot, formerly a chemistry professor at the Massachusetts Institute of Technology, introduced the spirit of experimental science and evolutionary theory in rigorous programs throughout the university. Langdell held similar views about law as science and attempted to carry out his and Eliot's program in the law school. In a famous statement Langdell expressed the core of his educational philosophy: "First, that law is a science; secondly, that all the available materials of that science are contained in printed books."

Eliot and Langdell implemented this philosophy at the law school in a dramatic fashion. The scientific approach led Langdell to formulate the case method of law study. Instead of reading expository texts and listening to lectures, students read and discussed sequences of English and American judicial opinions. The cases in these sequences were carefully edited by the teacher to illustrate the historical development of fundamental legal principles. In class the teacher would direct the discussion by asking questions about the cases and posing hypothetical situations to be resolved using the cases that had been read as precedents.

The experience required of a teacher in a case-method classroom was the ability to analyze the cases in this way, and not the experience of long years of practice. Accordingly, in a departure from tradition Langdell hired as professors young graduates of the law school, rather than experienced practitioners. James Barr Ames, the first of these professional law teachers, would later become Langdell's successor as dean of the law school.

Eliot, Langdell, and later Ames also attempted to elevate the prestige of the law school by introducing structural reforms. The goal, which was met only in the twentieth century, was a professionally oriented postgraduate institution. Only students with a college degree would be admitted, and three years of study in the law school would be required. The law school curriculum would be sequential, with students required to take a series of courses in a certain order. Only "pure law"—common-law doctrine—would be taught; international law, legal philosophy, and legal history would be eschewed in favor of professionally oriented courses.

The Harvard reforms had considerable impact but were controversial. They were attractive to some legal educators because they raised the power and prestige of the law school within the university and within the legal profession. The new law school became a device for raising the status of the legal profession generally and for restricting entry into the profession. However, many lawyers and law schools resisted the Harvard innovations on intellectual and political grounds.

The limits of the case method and the doctrine-based, professional curriculum (both still important aspects of legal education) are discussed more fully below. The early criticism may be summed up in the remark that law school sharpens a student's mind by narrowing it. The case method was designed to develop particular analytic skills and to convey particular kinds of knowledge. In doing so, critics charged, it ignored important aspects of a lawyer's education. The Harvard law student learned only one of the many skills a lawyer would need in practice. The professional curriculum also ignored issues of the history, social context, and morality of the legal system, which many thought necessary for the development of a well-rounded lawyer. The case method was criticized as an ineffective teaching method for many students and an inefficient method when used exclusively.

Critics also attacked the exclusivity inherent in the new type of law school. Requiring both undergraduate education and a full-time commitment for three years limited the ability of many students of lesser means to attend law schools. The next logical step, requiring attendance at law school for admission to practice or making attendance at a prestigious law school an informal condition of employment for the most advantageous legal positions affected social and economic groups in different ways. Law had always been a public-regarding profession, and an important tenet of the democratic ideology of the profession, access to the bar, was being eroded.

These criticisms engendered resistance to the spread of the Harvard structure and style. At some law schools—Columbia was a notable example—the struggle over the introduction of Harvard methods caused faculty splits, with some members resigning in protest. Many law schools continued to employ text and lecture methods. A few experimented with training students in clinical programs in which they performed or simulated a range of lawyer functions. Others attempted to integrate the study of jurisprudence, international law, or the social sciences into the professional curriculum.

A different trend in legal education was a response to the elitism of the Harvard method. This was the spread of proprietary (privately owned) and part-time law schools. Located in many of the large cities, these schools primarily served the expanding urban population, especially immigrant groups. The proprietary schools increased the places available in law school. For immigrant and other students who did not have college preparation or who could not afford full-time schooling, the part-time schools offered the only means of access to a legal career. Proponents of these schools hailed them as the heirs of the tradition represented by Abraham Lincoln, the self-made man and self-educated lawyer. The education they provided, unlike that in the elite law schools, was more

likely to address the everyday concerns of the practicing lawyer. Lectures on local law and instruction in the preparation of pleadings and documents replaced discussion of general principles of law and case-method teaching.

Despite resistance, the Harvard innovations spread and provided a new model for law schools. One important factor in this success was economics. A law school curriculum made up of courses concerned with legal doctrine and taught by the case method permitted very high student-faculty ratios. At Langdell's Harvard, for example, there was one faculty member for every seventy-five students. Further, the professional curriculum required only minimal resources, such as a small law library. This model was more attractive financially to a university than a program requiring expensive tutorial instruction or supervision of student law practice.

Although the Harvard method came to predominate, over time its inadequacies became apparent. At many schools modifications of one sort or another were introduced. The increasing importance of the federal government and of administrative agencies, especially during the New Deal era, caused the introduction of public law topics into the curriculum. Seminars in advanced topics were offered for upper-level students. During the 1960s clinical training programs and lawyering courses became more widespread. All of these changes, though, were viewed as minor modifications to the basically sound structure of the modern law school, which is now in essential part more than one hundred years old.

LEGAL EDUCATION TODAY

From its beginnings in the Litchfield Law School, law school education has grown enormously. In 1985 there were about 240 law schools in America, most of them affiliated with universities. Together they enroll about 130,000 students, a remarkable number considering that there were about 570,000 lawyers in the nation in 1985. Much of the growth has been recent; during the decade of the 1970s, for example, the number of lawyers in America increased as much as it had in the previous hundred years.

Law schools are of two types: accredited and unaccredited. Most states require graduation from an accredited law school for admission to law practice. (Four states still permit admission to practice after a period of study not in a law school, a modern version of apprenticeship. Three other states require one or two years' attendance at a law school but do not require graduation.) Most states have delegated the accreditation function to the American Bar Association, a lawyers' professional organization. Of the 240 law schools, 174 are approved by the ABA. California is an important exception to this system; in California, law schools are separately accredited by the California bar examiners. Graduates of these law schools are eligible for admission to the California bar, but not usually to the bar of other states. Because of this special situation, most of the law schools unaccredited by the ABA are in California.

In addition to the formal system of accreditation, there are important but less formal hierarchies among law schools. One distinction is membership in the Association of American Law Schools, an organization with no official functions but with considerable unofficial influence; about 150 law schools are members of the Association. Schools are admitted to the Association if they adhere to standards higher than those required for ABA accreditation.

Another distinction relates to the prestige and reputation of the law school and its affiliated university. Reputation is not necessarily a measure of the quality of the education or of the richness of the experience that a school provides for its students, but it can be a significant factor in the recruitment of faculty and in the future employment of students.

Legal education is both a complex system and an individual experience. The remainder of this article describes both the system and the experience. The system may be thought of as composed of institutions, law schools, and organizations, but the experience is that of people, students, and teachers: how they come to be in law schools and what they learn and teach there.

LAW STUDENTS

Students come to attend law school through a filtering process. Despite the relatively large number of law schools, not everyone who wishes to attend can find a place in law school. Students

compete for admission to law schools, especially for admission to the most prestigious schools, and law schools compete for the students believed to be the most desirable. Student motivation, academic preparation, and a variety of other characteristics all figure into the determination of who attends which law school.

Most law schools require completion of a bachelor's degree before a student may enroll. No particular undergraduate major or prelaw course of study is necessary. Law schools frequently suggest the desirability of courses in any field that develops analytic skills and writing ability. Although students come to law school with diverse educational backgrounds, many students will have taken courses relevant to the study of the legal process, such as economics, history, political science, and philosophy. In recent years, an increasing number of students pursue graduate study in other fields prior to attending law school. Many others do not attend law school immediately after college, preferring to work first.

The quality of the student's performance in college is as important to law school admission as the content of the undergraduate education. Because law school admission is competitive, the grades a student received in college, the rigor of his or her program, class rank, and the quality of the undergraduate institution are considered in assessing the likelihood of success in law school.

In addition to the undergraduate record, the second important factor that law schools use to measure the quality of applicants is the score on the Law School Admission Test, or LSAT. The LSAT is a national standardized examination designed to test reasoning ability, language skills, and other abilities necessary to pursue a legal education. When the LSAT was originally devised in the late 1940s at the urging of a number of law schools, its purpose was to screen out those students highly likely to fail in law school. As admissions became more competitive, the test became a measure of the relative likelihood of individual success. The LSAT is the only means that law schools have to rate all applicants by the same measure, so it is used extensively in the admissions process.

Heavy reliance in law school admission on undergraduate records and LSAT scores influences the composition of law school student bodies. Students who have done well at better-known colleges, and students who have the educational background that enables them to excel on the LSAT, on the average represent a narrow segment of the general population. Children of families with high incomes and children of parents in white-collar or professional jobs are disproportionately represented in the law student population. These are the students who are most likely to have received the type of educational opportunities that prepare them for success in college, on standardized tests such as the LSAT, and therefore in the law school admissions process.

They are also the students best able to afford the high costs of college and law school. At many private colleges and law schools, tuition alone costs more than $10,000 per year. Added to the tuition cost is the cost of living expenses, books, and the income foregone by not being able to work fulltime. Despite extensive financial aid programs, money is an important direct filter in the law school admission process and serves as an indirect filter through its relationship to prior education.

These filters and others have produced a law school student body that is not representative of the country as a whole. For a long time, the great majority of law students were white, male, and upper class; at the most prestigious law schools, these tendencies were even more exaggerated. This unequal representation was seen to be a problem because of the view of the importance of access to the law. Access to the law often depends on the availability of an attorney. If certain social groups are systematically underrepresented in the legal profession, it is harder for them to avail themselves of our system of justice because of the limited availability of attorneys who are sympathetic to their situation or with whom they identify.

Law schools, under pressure from the civil rights and feminist movements of the 1960s and 1970s, initiated efforts to correct these inequalities. In the admissions process, schools began seeking diversity in the student body by considering factors other than undergraduate record and LSAT score. Membership in traditionally underrepresented groups, such as minority groups, and volunteer or work experience, for example, were considered to be relevant criteria. These efforts have had their effect; in 1985 about 10 percent of law students were minorities and

40 percent women. In terms of social background and experience, too, many law schools now have more diverse student bodies. However, to a great extent the inequalities inherent in a system that relies so much on prior academic work still remain.

Attempts have been made to describe the characteristics of law students beyond demographic features. There is a tradition of anecdotal accounts of law school life that describe the personalities of law students, and recently this literature has been supplemented by more scientific surveys. These accounts suggest that many law students embody the character traits usually associated in the public mind with lawyers. Law students are generally "tough-minded." With developed analytic skills, they tend to enjoy conceptualizing and solving problems. That finding is consistent with the emphasis on analytic skills in the law school admissions process. In law school, this trait is reinforced and produces an intellectually competitive atmosphere in which the manipulation of ideas is more important than the consideration of feelings. In legal practice, the same trait produces a particular kind of relationship with clients. In the lawyer-client situation, the lawyer usually focuses on the client's legal problem, rather than on the client's emotional situation or the complex circumstances that led up to the legal problem. These generalizations overstate the case and do not apply to all students of law, yet they represent a recurrent theme.

LAW FACULTY

Depending on the size of the institution and its finances, a law school may have a faculty of as few as ten or more than seventy full-time members. The full-time faculty bears the principal responsibility for the teaching and governance of the law school. Accordingly, the character of the faculty is crucial in shaping the character of the law school.

Like law students, law teachers are the product of a filtering process. Many law professors have followed what has been a traditional (but by no means exclusive) path to appointment to a law faculty position. The traditional path includes high grades and service on the editorial board of the law review while in law school and, following graduation, a clerkship with a judge and a few years' practice experience, often in government or with a large law firm.

The theory underlying this traditional career path proceeds directly from the faculty appointment of James Barr Ames at Harvard in 1873. In this view, the law teacher's work focuses on the particular kind of case and statute analysis taught in a case-method classroom, not on the broad range of knowledge and skills required for actual law practice nor on the social context of law. The appropriate credentials for teaching law are demonstrated excellence in academic work and some experience in settings that do not depart greatly from the academic approach, such as a judge's chambers.

As with the selection of law students, this narrow approach to the selection of law teachers has produced a bias in the interests, orientations, and abilities of faculty members. Faculties have tended to reproduce themselves, hiring as new teachers those who best emulate the old. Persons who had extensive experience or interest in the nonacademic side of law practice, especially public interest or other less elite forms of practice, and persons whose perspective was less focused on pure law and more on historical or social context have been less likely to be hired.

To be sure, there were exceptions; the University of Chicago Law School, for example, has had a strong tradition of including among its faculty economists, social scientists, and others with varying perspectives. As with law students, to some extent this problem has been recognized and attempts have been made to correct it. Some law schools have begun to look beyond the traditional criteria in appointing faculty. The result has been a limited but perceptible change in the composition of these faculties.

Once appointed to a law school faculty, a professor's responsibilities include teaching and scholarly publication. Typically a professor develops a specialty in one or two areas of the law, and both teaching and writing are concentrated in those areas.

On the average, a professor teaches about four courses or seminars in an academic year. In addition, he or she supervises student research, counsels students on academic and nonacademic matters, and participates in the administration of the law school.

Like other university professors, law professors engage in scholarly research and writing. Scholarship usually takes the form of articles published in student-edited law reviews (described below) but may also include books and other works. For most law professors, scholarship consists of the analysis of recent developments in their areas of interest: organizing confusing areas of doctrine, criticizing recent court decisions, proposing modifications in the law. Others engage in historical research or bring to bear on legal issues the insights of other disciplines—philosophy or economics, for example. Many professors edit casebooks, the collections of judicial opinions and other materials used as the primary teaching resource. Few professors devote their scholarship to practice-oriented issues other than the development of doctrine, or to the process of legal education itself.

Some law teachers engage in law practice in addition to their teaching and research. They may consult with law firms or for government agencies in their areas of expertise or take individual clients. There is some feeling that limited amounts of practice aid a professor in keeping in touch with legal developments. However, by rule and custom (which are not always observed), excessive involvement in a practice is frowned on at most law schools as distracting professors from their primary obligations.

At many law schools the full-time faculty is supplemented by part-time or adjunct professors. Most often these are practicing lawyers who teach one or two courses a year. Often these courses are advanced offerings best taught by a sophisticated practitioner, or practice-oriented courses such as trial advocacy. Law schools may also have professors from other disciplines teach subjects such as legal history or legal accounting. By regulation of the accrediting agencies, the adjunct faculty must be used only to supplement the offerings of the full-time faculty. Usually, their sole function is teaching, and they do not otherwise participate in law school administration or do much scholarly publishing.

Finally, law schools that sponsor their own clinical programs may have faculty members to staff the programs. These programs for giving students education and experience in practice settings require teachers with qualifications and teaching abilities different from those of the traditional professor. Lawyers with more practice experience or those who are sensitive to the issues arising in client contact and in practice may teach in these clinics. At some schools these teachers are regular members of the faculty with the possibility of life tenure. At others they may be hired for a term of years. Recently, in recognition of the importance of this type of teaching, efforts have been made by the accrediting agencies to require the integration of the clinical faculty with the regular faculty by mandating that they be given a status substantially equivalent to that of regular full-time faculty members.

In a sense, the role of the law professor is ambiguous. The law professor straddles two worlds, the academic life of the university and the professional life of the lawyer. The professor teaches, but teaches more with the goal of preparing students for legal practice than of generally imparting knowledge and enlightenment, as is often perceived to be the task of professors in other disciplines. The professor writes scholarly works, but the writing most often has a relatively narrow professional focus. Thus the law professor does not fit comfortably in the university and at the same time has an uneasy relation to practicing lawyers. Much of what the professor does in the classroom and in scholarship has little immediate relevance to law practice.

This personal dilemma is mirrored in the creation of the institutional identity of the law school. Defining the law school's relation to both the university community and the professional community is at the heart of many of the debates about what law schools should teach and how they should teach it: debates about curriculum.

LAW SCHOOL CURRICULUM

The law school curriculum has two aspects. One is the formal course of study: the courses taught and the stated objectives of the courses in terms of the knowledge conveyed and the skills developed. The other aspect is the implicit curriculum: the attitudes, values, approaches, and feelings that the law school process frequently inculcates in students. The first is the easier to identify and thus is the more often described, but both aspects are important elements of the process by which students learn to become lawyers.

The full-time law school curriculum encompasses three academic years, in each of which a student normally is in class about twelve to fifteen hours per week for thirty weeks. In a part-time program a student takes eight to ten hours of classes per week for four academic years. In addition to time in class, many more hours are spent reading and studying.

Typically, the first-year program consists of required courses, while most or all of the second-year and third-year courses are elective. The core first-year subjects at most law schools include contracts, torts, property, civil procedure, and criminal law. Other courses sometimes taught in the first year include constitutional law and criminal procedure. Some law schools have attempted to compensate for the heavy common-law orientation in the first year by including a course in which statutory law predominates, such as administrative law, labor law, or federal income taxation. Other schools seek to provide their students with a broad perspective on the law by offering a first-year course in legal history, jurisprudence, or law and social science.

In addition to these substantive courses, the first-year curriculum often contains one or two courses that seek to develop basic lawyer skills. A legal methods or legal process course concentrates on introducing students to the legal system and teaching the skills of case analysis and statutory interpretation, without concern for conveying particular information. A legal research and writing course introduces students to the tools of legal research available in the law library and to the unique forms of expression used by lawyers. In conjunction with the legal research and writing program, students often participate in moot court, in which they write briefs and make oral arguments in a simulated appellate court setting.

In the upper level, law schools offer a variety of courses. All law schools teach the subjects regarded as generally useful for preparation for law practice: courses in the judicial process, such as advanced constitutional law and procedure courses; courses in business and commercial law, such as corporations, sales, and bankruptcy; courses in economic regulation and public law, such as labor law, environmental law, and antitrust; and courses concerning domestic relations, such as family law and estate planning.

Beyond these basic subjects a school may offer advanced courses in the same areas. In the property area, for example, advanced courses include landlord and tenant law, real estate development, and urban planning. Many schools have courses that provide perspectives on the law and the legal process, such as legal history, jurisprudence (legal philosophy), and law and literature. Others have offerings in international law and courses comparing the law of foreign countries with American law. The choice among these offerings depends on the traditions of the school and the availability of faculty members to teach in the areas. It also depends on changes in the law. As new fields of law develop, law schools introduce corresponding courses. For instance, courses in environmental law became widespread following the surge of environmental activism and the environmental legislation of the 1960s and 1970s.

Students usually are free to select from among these courses. Nearly all students take a foundation of basic courses: evidence, corporations, taxation, and so forth. After that, course selection depends on the extent to which a student is inclined toward practice in a particular legal area, or on whether he or she seeks a broader approach while in law school. For example a student interested in a career in business law will take several courses in commercial law, taxation, and corporate law. Students who have not yet defined their career choices may try out a number of areas. Some will pursue their intellectual interests even if the courses selected do not appear immediately relevant to their careers, taking a variety of perspective courses. A few law schools offer formal concentration programs in specialized areas, but no major course of study is required in law school, as it is in college. In fact many students select their courses on the basis of their assessment of the quality of the teacher or their affinity for his or her approach, rather than on the specific subject matter.

A distinctive feature of the law school curriculum is the attempt to integrate skills training with the imparting of broad knowledge. In the traditional view every course is a skills course, because in every course an important objective is the development of the particular analytical techniques used by lawyers. This pervasive approach to skills training so dominates thinking about legal education that in most law schools no specific skills courses are required beyond the basic legal research and writing course.

This integration of method and substance is most pronounced in the first year, when the pre-dominant method of instruction is the case method. In its extreme form, embedded in the popular mind by Professor Kingsfield's classroom in *The Paper Chase*, the case method presents students with a sequence of judicial opinions or "cases" to be read, dissected, and discussed as the sole body of material for a course. In preparation for class a student reads the opinion and then prepares a case "brief." The brief contains in outline form the student's analysis of the case: the nature of the lawsuit, the parties involved, the legal issues presented, and the court's resolution of the issues. In class a student is called on to present his or her brief. The instructor asks questions that are designed to expose errors and ambiguities in the brief and in the reasoning of the opinion itself. The instructor also poses hypothetical variations on the facts of the case that test the soundness of the principles extracted and suggest how the case and its rationale might be used in deciding future cases.

In most courses the student's grade is determined by a single examination given at the end of the course. Final examinations usually are constructed to parallel the kind of process engaged in during class sessions. Seldom are students asked to simply state a legal rule. Typically the student will be presented with a complex fact situation to analyze. The analysis requires both knowledge of relevant legal principles and the ability to apply the principles to a new situation. Successful performance on the examination will depend as much on the demonstrated ability to do legal analysis as on reaching a particular answer to the problem.

The theory of the case method is that it requires the student to learn by doing, to acquire lawyerly skills by engaging in the same process lawyers do, under the direction of an experienced guide. The student learns to analyze facts for their legal significance, generalize from cases, abstract rules and principles of law from particular opinions, and make the kinds of arguments that courts find persuasive. The student's grappling with cases alone before the class and the discussion in class led by the experienced professor provide both an illustration of and experience in lawyer's work. In the classroom, it is thought, all students participate in this process, vocally or silently.

A frequent criticism of the case method is that

it can easily be abused to become an instrument of oppression rather than learning in the classroom. The lore of legal education is replete with tales of brutal professors who terrorized their students in case teaching. The nature of the method is that it requires every student to be well prepared. But no matter how well prepared a student is, the professor can ask penetrating questions and produce hypotheticals to demonstrate that the student's analysis is incomplete or inadequate. At its best this process teaches students the uncertainty and flexibility of legal principles. At its worst this approach causes students to be afraid to participate for fear of humiliating consequences. Fortunately the current approach to case teaching in most schools is one of rigor, not terror.

In the case method may be seen all of the strengths and weaknesses of the integration of method and substance in law teaching. Its greatest strength is that it engages students in the process of lawmaking and law-applying in a way that traditional lectures or readings cannot. Many students come to law school with the belief that the study of law is the study of a body of knowledge; terms, rules, and answers to problems all are in a set of mysterious books, and law school is designed to show the students how to use those books. But law study like law practice is more appropriately characterized as an activity or a process. As such, it can be learned only by participation and practice rather than by reading and observation. Learning law is like learning a sport. Reading books about playing baseball is no substitute for getting out on the field and trying to hit a ball. This is just what happens in a case-method classroom: the student tries out the activity of using legal principles and precedents under the direction of a "coach," the professor.

But the case method has its weaknesses. One is that it commonly attempts to teach skills without ever giving students an explicit and comprehensive statement of the nature and content of the skills. The usual assertion is that the case method teaches students to "think like a lawyer," but students are never told exactly what thinking like a lawyer means and how it is different from the way nonlawyers think. In this way the case method assumes almost mystical proportions; at the end of some period of time during which they have practiced by imitating the professor, stu-

dents are presumed to have acquired this mysterious skill without ever being sure how or why.

"Thinking like a lawyer" constitutes a core of distinctively legal skills. It is not that lawyers engage in different analytical processes than lay people or other professionals. Instead, lawyers operate in unique contexts with unique materials. Teaching students to think like a lawyer simply means grounding them in those contexts and those materials. This involves acquiring a legal vocabulary (understanding the special meaning lawyers give to common words and the meaning of words used only by lawyers), understanding how legal rule systems are constructed and how they may be manipulated, being able to use judicial opinions as precedents, and understanding the systematic nature of legal argument and the kinds of arguments lawyers and judges use repeatedly.

Few law students could give as explicit an account as this of the goals of the case method. Perhaps the goals are seldom articulated because they reveal the serious limits of the case method as a lawyer training device. Case teaching can be effective analytical training, but it is inefficient for the conveyance of information. To compensate, most law teachers supplement the case method in their courses with lectures, supplementary reading, and discussion classes.

A more important limitation is that the case method, even with modifications, focuses on a limited range of the skills students need to become capable novice lawyers. Lawyers confront complex and disorganized sets of facts presented to them by clients, but a judicial opinion in a student casebook presents a refined set of facts neatly arrayed. Lawyers deal with flesh-and-blood human beings, with all their emotions and difficulties, but the people described in cases are as two-dimensional as the printed page on which they appear. Lawyers plan transactions, invoke legal procedures, and evaluate strategic courses of action, but case analysis encourages only retrospective discussion of principles and rules. Case-centered legal education is equivalent to permitting medical students to complete their education having seen pictures of the body but without having examined live patients.

Fortunately no law school curriculum is composed entirely of case teaching. Efforts to compensate for the limits of case teaching and purely doctrinal courses take a variety of forms: skills courses, integration courses, clinical experience, and extracurricular activities.

Most law schools offer a variety of courses designed to teach students particular lawyering skills and to simulate in the classroom the settings in which lawyers do their work. The most common examples are moot court and trial practice experiences. These courses place students in the lawyer's advocacy role in simulated appellate- and trial-level courts, respectively. In moot court students are presented with the kind of written record that would be before an appellate court. Taking the position of one party or the other, they research the legal issues, write an advocacy document known as a "brief" on behalf of their position (not to be confused with the case brief), and then present oral arguments to a court composed of actual judges, professors, practitioners, or upper-level students. In most schools a first-year experience in moot court is required. Participation in advanced programs in the second and third years is voluntary, with intraschool competitions leading up to various national moot court competitions.

Trial practice courses are similar except that they are focused on trial advocacy, not appellate advocacy. In these courses, often taught by adjunct professors who are experienced litigators, students learn to present evidence, examine witnesses, make motions to the court, and argue to a jury. This type of course usually culminates in the students acting as counsel in a complete simulated trial before a real judge.

Other skills courses follow the same pattern of providing instruction in lawyer skills and then placing the student in a role to practice the skills under supervision and with expert criticism. In addition to the advocacy courses, these skills courses include efforts to develop the skills of interviewing and counseling clients, negotiating with other parties, and drafting legal documents such as contracts.

Integration courses attempt to merge doctrinal learning with strategic thinking and practice skills. In these courses students may discuss complex legal problems in a classroom setting and also perform a role. Often integration courses cross doctrinal boundaries. Examples include courses in business planning, which involve corporate law, tax, and antitrust aspects, and constitutional litigation courses, which develop sophisticated understanding of constitu-

tional law doctrine, procedural issues, and litigation strategy. In a business planning course a student might be given a set of facts concerning a complex corporate transaction and then be asked to advise the parties as to an appropriate course of action and to prepare the legal documents necessary to implement the advice.

The integration courses suggest that the distinction between learning substantive law and learning lawyer skills is illusory. The functions of the lawyer cannot be neatly divided into acquiring substantive knowledge and the techniques of applying that knowledge. Theory and practice, substance and process, knowledge and technique all merge in the lawyer's work. The principal attempt to expose students to this unity in law school is through clinical legal education. The antecedents of clinical legal education include the earliest forms of office apprenticeship and the efforts at clinical teaching in a few law schools in the early part of this century. However, only in the past twenty years has clinical education acquired a highly sophisticated theory and methodology that has spread to many law schools.

Two kinds of clinical programs are common. In one kind, upper-level students are placed with agencies such as public defender offices and legal services programs, where they work under the supervision of the agency staff. A different form of clinical legal education is the operation of a law office by the law school. Usually this office provides legal services for low-income people, often in association with a local legal services program or a public defender office. The attorneys in the clinic are regular or specially appointed members of the law faculty.

The final supplement to the traditional curriculum includes a variety of extracurricular activities. The most common of these is the law review or law journal, a student-edited scholarly publication. The law review is supported and published by the law school but administered and edited by second- and third-year students. Usually students are selected to work on the law review because of their academic performance or proficiency in legal writing. The student members of the law reviews write notes and comments on recent developments in the law and edit articles submitted to the review by professors or practitioners. This produces an unusual situation: the basic source of legal scholarship is largely in the hands of novices at the trade. Nevertheless, participation on the law review is often regarded as good training in legal writing and the more academic forms of legal analysis.

Other extracurricular activities allow students to be involved in areas of individual interest. In most schools the moot court programs are run largely by students. Also popular are organizations that provide forums for activities in particular areas of the law or for students with particular interests. Examples are an international law or environmental law society for students who wish to be involved in those areas, and the National Lawyers Guild for politically progressive law students. Finally, schools usually also have a student bar association, which organizes social activities and other programs.

All of the activities of the law school, curricular and extracurricular, are designed to teach students about the law and about being a lawyer. Some of the lessons to be learned are explicit and obvious: the body of legal rules, the organization of courts, the forms of legal procedure, and lawyer skills such as legal research and appellate advocacy. The law school experience also teaches less obvious lessons. These lessons concern the nature of legal theory and legal reasoning, the professional role of the lawyer, and the structure of the legal system. Although they are seldom included in the formal statement of the law school program, they are an important aspect of legal education.

The first element of the implicit curriculum involves a theory of legal reasoning. In case-method classes students learn that there is a special kind of reasoning known as legal reasoning. Legal reasoning is both a mode of discourse, a way of talking and arguing about problems, and a method for deciding the correct results in individual cases. Legal reasoning is distinct from ordinary methods of analysis and argument about values, fairness, and the like. In law school these ordinary methods are lumped together as involving "policy," not "law." Courts and lawyers employ legal reasoning to formulate doctrines and decide cases, and that process is completely unlike the political process engaged in by a legislature in enacting a statute.

This theory of legal reasoning has consequences for the students' view of the legal process and of the body of substantive law. The special form of legal reasoning may be used to justify the special position of courts and lawyers. Their expertise in reasoning, it is argued, makes it appropriate that they should have a lawmaking function in society and a significant position in the social hierarchy. Further, in general lawyers using their special position have served society well. The uniqueness of the process of legal reasoning means that in large part the law formulated by the courts is sound. Legal reasoning permits courts to fashion legal rules and principles that are just and responsive to the current needs of society.

At the same time that the law school conveys this satisfying message of certainty, it also teaches about uncertainty. In case-method classes students learn about the open-ended character of legal discourse. The discussion of a particular case often does not converge on a single correct result but opens up to indicate the wide range of reasonable arguments that can be made as to how the case should be decided. Students learn how it is possible for a lawyer to argue either side of a case, depending on who is his or her client. This message contradicts the idea of certainty. The contradiction is resolved by distinguishing core issues of doctrine, which have been resolved through the objective process of legal reasoning, from issues at the periphery of doctrine, often involving new fact situations, about which there can be argument and controversy without subverting basic principles.

The second element of the implicit curriculum is a set of ideas about the lawyer as professional. Students learn what it is like to be a lawyer and what attitudes lawyers should have. Although the law school classroom may be far removed from the realities of the lawyer's office, the classroom is the students' initial intensive exposure to the culture of the profession.

Important messages about professionalism are communicated in the style of classroom discussion. In discussing cases and doctrines, professors emphasize the importance of narrowing the issue. When students raise issues of fairness, the professor often either rejects the relevance of the issue of fairness as involving nonlegal considerations or recasts the student comment into a narrower, legal conception of fairness. Similarly when students express their intuitive feelings about doctrines or decisions, the comments are often dismissed as insignificant unless they can be reconceptualized in legally cognizable terms.

This narrowing of the realm of relevant discussion teaches students that legal issues are separate from moral issues. As lawyers the students can divorce their actions from their personal ethics. They can detach themselves from their work and from the consequences of their actions. The irrelevance of feelings also permits them to detach themselves from personal involvement with their clients. The lawyer's role is not that of counselor, helper, and friend, but of a technician who translates the client's problem into legal terms and then applies technical expertise to the legal resolution of the translated problem. Because the issue has been recast in legal terms, the relationship between client and lawyer is always one in which the lawyer, as the expert, is in control.

Finally, students acquire messages in law school about the structure of the legal system and the organization of law practice. In a variety of formal and informal ways, professors communicate their views about the quality and importance of different parts of the system of government and of different kinds of law practices. Legislatures are often denigrated as messy or corrupt political bodies. Courts are arrayed in a hierarchy that depends on the extent to which they emulate the law school classroom. Appellate courts are more highly valued than trial courts because they engage more often in the forms of abstract legal reasoning that professors do. Federal courts are preferred over state courts because they are believed to deal with more complex and interesting legal issues. Corporate law practice also is viewed as more significant than small general practice. In fact practice settings are evaluated as desirable and important in inverse relation to the extent to which the lawyer in them has contact with everyday life situations. Criminal and divorce law, for example, are downgraded because they require dealing with ordinary people in emotionally charged situations.

These implicit messages about law and lawyering obviously are not often proclaimed explicitly. Nor are the messages the same from school to school or from professor to professor. Schools have different orientations in this respect, and students even in the same school will acquire different attitudes on these issues. But the implicit curriculum described here is an important element of the current system of legal education.

EDUCATION AFTER LAW SCHOOL

Since the rise to dominance of the modern law school, any account of legal education centers on the law school experience. The education of lawyers, however, does not cease upon graduation. The true professional keeps abreast of changes in the law and grows and develops his or her own knowledge and skills throughout a career. Ideally, the law school graduate is sensitive to the need for further learning and possesses the tools to continue to learn.

Probably the most important means of continued learning is the learning a lawyer does on his or her own in practice. When faced with new situations—an everyday occurrence in most practice settings—the lawyer goes to the law books in an attempt to find background, new approaches, and relevant materials. In addition the lawyer is likely to consult with other lawyers on many matters. For new lawyers this collaboration is an important form of legal education and an important element of professional acculturation. Much of the lore and custom of legal practice is not written down in books but resides in the oral tradition of members of the local bar. Important aspects of local procedure, customary practice, attitudes, and values must be acquired through consultation with others and through trial and error.

Some employment settings try to formalize this informal process. Large law firms and large public agencies may provide training programs for new lawyers and more experienced practitioners. Also, bar associations and other organizations organize programs, known as continuing legal education programs, in which experts in particular fields present lectures and discussions concerning current legal topics. Even the most experienced lawyers are likely to attend such programs, for they understand that no single lawyer can keep up on all relevant legal developments alone, and that every lawyer can benefit from the experiences of others.

LEGAL EDUCATION

BIBLIOGRAPHY

Jerold S. Auerbach, *Unequal Justice: Lawyers and Social Change in Modern America* (1976), critically accounts the changes in legal education and the legal profession in the twentieth century. Dusan J. Djonovich, *Legal Education, A Selective Bibliography* (1970), is a comprehensive bibliography of publications on legal education, although now somewhat dated. Stephen Gillers, ed., *Looking at Law School* (1977), introduces law study and law school, including basic subjects, teaching methods, and current issues. Duncan Kennedy, "Legal Education as Training for Hierarchy," in David Kairys, ed., *The Politics of Law* (1982), critiques the political and ideological content of the law school process.

Karl Llewellyn, *The Bramble Bush* (1950), is a series of introductory lectures first given at the Columbia University Law School in 1920 by this leading legal thinker. He discusses legal education, legal reasoning, the case method, and other topics. Herbert L. Packer and Thomas Ehrlich, *New Directions in Legal Education* (1972), surveys contemporary issues in legal education. Alfred Z. Reed, *Training for the Public Profession of the Law* (1921), is a major, controversial study of legal education and its relation to the structure of the legal profession. Joel Seligman, *The High Citadel* (1978), gives a history and analysis of the Harvard Law School and its influence on legal education, including discussion of admissions, curriculum, and faculty.

Robert Stevens, *Law School: Legal Education in America from the 1850s to the 1980s* (1983), has written the leading history of American legal education, with comprehensive notes and bibliography. Scott Turow, *One L* (1977), offers a journalistic description of a student's first year of law school.
[*See also* FULLER COURT AND ERA; JUDICIARY; LEGAL PROFESSION AND LEGAL ETHICS; *and* LEGAL REASONING.]

THE LEGAL PROFESSION
AND LEGAL ETHICS

Frances Kahn Zemans

THE very term *profession* implies a high level of social prestige, to which many occupational groups aspire and which lawyers clearly enjoy in American society. Such high social status emerges in part out of the special skills and knowledge that are allegedly peculiar to a profession. Affirmation of these special competencies is found in licensing requirements and laws that grant the designated group an exclusive right to perform certain tasks. In the case of the legal profession, licensing in almost every state requires graduation from a law school accredited by the American Bar Association (ABA), successful completion of a state bar examination, and approval by a character and fitness committee. In an increasing number of states, membership in the state bar association is also required. A monopoly is granted to the legal profession for a wide range of services, from such clearly defined ones as representing a client in court to those ambiguously labeled the practice of law. Bar associations, particularly at the state level, work actively to protect the monopoly granted by the state. In a majority of states, membership is a mandatory condition of practice.

Another aspect of professionalism to which many groups aspire is self-regulation. Given that only members of the profession have the special skills and knowledge that are the core of their work, it follows that only other lawyers are in a position to evaluate and regulate lawyers' conduct. Such independence is also presumed by the profession to be necessary if it is to operate autonomously so as to perform its social role. In the case of the legal profession, this entails two sometimes conflicting roles: the representation of client interests and the representation of the legal system as officers of the court. The latter implies some professional responsibility to serve the society at large. In recent years questions have been raised about the professionalism of lawyers. Has the profit motive overtaken the commitment to service? Does working as a so-called hired gun representing any and every point of view conflict with the obligation to act as an officer of the court committed to improving the system of justice?

The privileged status of lawyers implies a uniformity within the profession that is difficult to substantiate. Not only is the legal profession very heterogeneous, but there are direct conflicts of interest between different segments of the bar. For example, trial lawyers who generally represent plaintiffs in personal injury cases may have a view of what would qualify as an improvement in the judicial system very different from that of lawyers who represent insurance companies. The former argue that justice would be best served by creating rules that would make it easier for plaintiffs to succeed in their claims; the latter argue just the opposite.

LAWYERS IN SOCIETY

Beyond the status enjoyed by professions generally, the legal profession derives great power from its control over the law that is central to the American political and social system. The tendency for basic social issues to become questions of law in the United States implies an obvious role for lawyers in the determination of public policy. This was recognized early in the twentieth century in a study of legal education in which the practice of law was distinguished as "a public function, in a sense that the practice of other professions, such as medicine, is not. Practicing lawyers do not merely render to the community a social service. . . . They are part of the governing mechanism of the state. Their functions are in a broad sense political" (Reed, 3).

Lawyers are the primary gatekeepers to the administration of justice. This means that to get a case before the courts, it is generally necessary to have a lawyer present it. Although lawyers are available for a fee to take a case to court, there are a number of reasons they might decline to do so. Examples include the lack of valid legal claims, the settlement of the case more expeditiously without going to court, and a claim insufficient to justify the costs of litigation. Without a lawyer's agreement to take a case to court, there will be no public decision in the case. By screening cases, lawyers thus influence which laws will be enforced and which will be challenged. The highly structured educational and licensing requirements of the bar give lawyers control of what enters the courts and what is therefore subject to judicial decision.

Lawyers' advice also determines how economic exchanges are arranged and whether legal rights are pursued. A national survey found that in addition to the extensive use of lawyers by businesses, nearly two-thirds of the adult population had consulted a lawyer at least once about a personal nonbusiness legal problem (Curran, 1977, 186). Indeed, lawyers appear to be ubiquitous in American society.

The United States has long had more lawyers per capita than any other nation. In the decades since 1950, the number of lawyers both absolutely and in relation to the population as a whole has increased dramatically. At the beginning of the 1950s, there were more than 220,000 lawyers. By 1980, there were more than 540,000 lawyers. The estimated figure for 1984 is almost 650,000 lawyers, or 1 for every 364 people (Curran, 1985, 2). The most dramatic growth occurred in the 1970s as more students sought admission to law schools, which in turn grew to accommodate the increased demand.

Growth of the profession has been greeted with a mixed response. Some believe that the more lawyers there are, the more they will be available to do the less remunerative work of the middle- and lower-income populations. This will, it is argued, increase the access to justice that is required in a democratic society. Others argue that the increase of lawyers only means more litigation, which will further clog the

courts. These two arguments are of course not unrelated. Almost by definition, the more access there is, the more litigation there will be. Whether this is good or bad depends on one's views as to the cases that should be heard by the courts.

THE WORK OF LAWYERS

The public's image of the lawyer at work is the courtroom advocate arguing a client's case before a jury. While courtroom advocacy is lawyer's work, it constitutes but a small part of what lawyers do. The legal profession is in fact quite heterogeneous. Lawyers differ in workplace and specialty; they also differ in how they spend their time and in the skills needed to do their jobs. With the focus of legal education almost exclusively on legal rules, there has been continuing concern over how, when, and where lawyers learn to do their work. A prominent law professor wrote,

> Meantime, what pictures should we of today be making about the actual workings of "the" heterogeneous Bar? *Not rules, but doing, is what we seek to train men for.* Rules our men need. Rules do in part control or shape, do in still greater part set limits to, their doing. But the thing remains the doing. What *is* this doing of lawyers? Whither we are to head our students? We do not know.
>
> (Llewellyn, 1935, 654)

Practicing lawyers, whether in the office or the courtroom, are in the business of representing the legal status of others. Although law schools concentrate on the analysis of rules, practicing lawyers consider facts the more important in their work. For most situations the rules are a given; what is important to preparing the individual case or document is the facts of a situation. Lawyers who practice different specialties, however, also tend to use different skills. Thus, selection of a specialty is critical to determining the actual tasks in which a lawyer will be engaged. In the larger law firms, one's status within the firm may also determine the nature of one's work, with younger associates doing the research and more-senior members dealing more directly with clients.

THE LEGAL PROFESSION AND LEGAL ETHICS

Although analytic skills are most characteristic of the practice of law, more-generalizable skills like fact-gathering, effective oral expression, and interviewing are at the core of much of the practice of law. Many of these competencies are, of course, equally important to other occupations and may be learned in a variety of contexts. In the practice of law these skills are used to write contracts that will be enforceable in court, to help collect debts, to give tax advice, to write wills, to arrange a real estate transaction, or to reach a divorce settlement. The same skills and many of the same tasks apply to the lawyer's special preserve: the representation of clients before courts and other government agencies.

With the exception of prosecutors, public defenders, and attorneys working for organizations who are specifically seeking judicial rulings, only a very small percentage of lawyers ever argue a case in a courtroom. A somewhat larger proportion file cases in court but settle most of them outside of court. In fact, the filing of a case in court is often a strategic move to encourage an opponent to settle a case. Even the categories of cases that require a judicial decision, such as divorce and probate, only rarely are actually litigated; in most cases the judge merely affirms arrangements entered into by the affected parties. Lawyers employed or retained on an ongoing basis are more likely to be engaged in anticipating and avoiding legal problems in such activities as negotiating contracts or writing wills. If problems do develop, it becomes their job to reach the best possible result within the confines of the law and legal process. The work of lawyers who largely serve individuals on a case-by-case basis is not very different except that since they are not engaged until a client perceives a need for legal assistance, they are usually not in a position to anticipate and therefore assist the client in avoiding legal trouble.

There are, of course, many lawyers admitted to practice in one or more states who do not practice law. Some enter completely different, nonlegal careers. Others, though not practitioners, pursue alternative legal careers in academia, on the bench, or in judicial administration. Still others serve as legislative staff, government examiners, trust officers of banks, lobbyists, and policymakers and executives at all levels of government. These last two positions, while often filled by lawyers, do not require legal training

and background, and there is some debate as to whether the lawyer credential should in fact be an advantage, as it clearly now is, to obtaining such a position. Many lawyers, of course, have chosen to enter politics. Indeed, young people attracted to politics often enter law school as a step toward building a political career. While few offices require candidates to be lawyers (district attorneys and attorneys general who are legal counsel to governmental entities are obvious exceptions), the representation of lawyers in political office is out of proportion to their numbers in the society at large.

The dominance of lawyers as public office holders and advisers is well documented by Peter Irons, among others. They are prominent in both elective and appointive office. Most United States presidents and vice-presidents have been lawyers, and the majority of United States senators are lawyers, as they have been since the 1940s. The United States House of Representatives has also been historically dominated by lawyers, although not to the same extent as the Senate. Lawyers are not nearly so prominent in state governments. At the end of the 1970s, in only one state legislature was the proportion of members who were lawyers as much as 40 percent; most states had substantially fewer. It can be said that lawyers are prominent in politics but do not predominate. Although many lawyers enter local politics to develop a reputation and clientele and to secure business relationships, most lawyers in political office have made a career out of politics. Except for their ability to begin political careers as state or federal prosecutors, lawyer-politicians are in most ways quite similar to those who are nonlawyers.

Aside from the power that accrues to roles with obvious political influence, the public power of the legal profession stems largely from the part lawyers play in applying and interpreting the law, in advising private clients in the settlement of legal matters, and thereby in the shaping of the law in action. Lawyers effectively transform real-life events into a legal formulation. Issues are narrowed to fit into legal categories and to meet required standards of evidence. The legal profession sets the policy agenda of the third branch of government by filing cases in court and influences judicial decisions and the development of the law by formulating (framing) the issues in legal arguments. It influences which laws will be enforced by virtue of advising clients to seek the benefits of their legal rights. Lawyers decide which cases to pursue as a means of changing the laws. Thus, it is in allegedly private capacities that the greatest public power of the legal profession is exercised.

STRUCTURE AND ORGANIZATION

The traditional image of the lawyer has been that of the solo practitioner who represents individual clients on a case-by-case basis. It implied a knowledgeable client who could recognize a legal problem and seek the services of a lawyer, who could then provide independent professional advice in the client's best interests. Even though most of the adult population have sought a lawyer's services, businesses rather than individuals are the major consumers of legal services.

Individuals generally use lawyers intermittently. Writing a will, buying or selling a house, and suing one who has caused an injury (as in an automobile accident) are discrete events not often repeated in the average individual's life. Businesses, by contrast, seek legal assistance on a more continuous basis, often to prevent legal problems from developing. The relationship between the lawyer and the individual client more closely approximates the traditional lawyer-client relationship, in which professional services were sought in connection with a particular event or difficulty. The relationship between the lawyer and the business client is much more likely to be ongoing; many lawyers are kept on retainer for general legal counsel, with additional work billed on an hourly fee basis. That relationship makes the lawyer more knowledgeable of the client's affairs and better able to provide legal advice, absent a discrete legal event. Such relationships raise questions as to how independent the lawyer's advice is, particularly if the client accounts for a substantial proportion of the lawyer's income. This problem is further exacerbated in those situations in which lawyers and clients become business partners or the lawyer sits on the client's board of directors.

Questions have been raised as to the degree of independence that counsel can exercise under such circumstances. On the other hand, there has been criticism of the legal profession for ex- erting too much control in the lawyer-client relationship where the client is an individual and the relationship is on a one-time-only basis (Rosenthal). Of particular concern has been the degree of control exercised by the lawyer over the client's affairs and whether the interests of the client rather than the lawyer remain paramount.

Even if it is agreed that the lawyer owes loyalty to the client and must represent the client's interests, in contemporary America it is sometimes difficult to determine exactly who is the client. Identification of the client is complicated by work settings that include lawyers working for other lawyers, for legal-services organizations, for interest groups, and for business corporations whose management and stockholders may be in conflict.

Still, most lawyers (68 percent) are in private practice (that is, not employees of government, industry, or other organizations), and about two-thirds of those still practice alone or in association with one or two other lawyers (Curran, 1985, 8). There has, however, been a growth in both the number and size of large law firms, particularly in large cities. This trend has developed during a period when the legal profession as a whole has become increasingly urban both as a reflection of population trends and as a response to the concentration of economic activity in urban areas. At the same time, solo practice has been on the decline.

While most lawyers are still private practitioners, law firms have many associates (the larger the firm, the greater the proportion of associates) who are employees, not partners. Partnership is typically granted after five to eight years of associate status. Promotion to partnership was once nearly automatic, but it has become more competitive, with disassociation from the firm usually the only alternative to partnership. (A new job category, the permanent associate, has so far been limited to a small number of the largest law firms.) Traditionally, once a lawyer was elevated to partnership, particularly in large firms, it meant that an entire career would be spent in that firm. This is less true today, with more movement between firms by individuals and groups of attorneys. Movement by a group sometimes results in the spin-off and creation of a new firm. At the same time, large firms are getting larger, not only by hiring new lawyers but also by merging with other firms. In addition, since the mid-1970s the multioffice law firm has become more common. Firms are increasingly opening branch offices in major cities around the United States, enabling them to serve the national legal needs of their clientele. This trend, while much examined in the legal media, is confined to large law firms located in major metropolitan areas.

Since 1960, the proportion of the bar in private practice has been on the decline, in large measure because of the increase in the number of lawyers working for government or private industry (Curran, 1985, 7). Among government lawyers, the greatest number work for the federal government, most for the Department of Justice; at the state and local levels, the largest number work as prosecutors. Most industry lawyers work for very large corporations, which are increasingly conscious of the cost-savings of employing in-house counsel and which have become more selective about the aspects of their legal work that they refer to private attorneys. This trend has been in response to the recognition by corporations that their outside legal fees were growing at a faster rate than their profits and that lawyers, by virtue of their orientation to asserting rights, are often counterproductive to the furtherance of business relationships and interests. An executive with a major corporation put it this way:

> I think lawyers too often assume a combative posture best likened to gladiators in an arena, a fight to the death . . . victory at all costs. The client's interests may be ignored consciously or unconsciously as the highs and lows of battle ensue.
> I think that the combative nature of some lawyers converts important litigation into personal episodes for counsel, which tends to cloud opportunities for amicable disposition. I think this tends to extend the litigation and certainly increases the cost of litigation.
> ("A Businessman's View of Lawyers," 834)

In addition to employment arrangements, lawyers are also often characterized by the specialty or area of the law in which they practice. Corporate law, family law, tax law, and criminal law are among the areas identified as legal specialties. Greater specialization has occurred in virtually all facets of American society, but despite similar trends, the legal profession is not nearly as specialized as other occupational groups, particularly the medical profession. Even those lawyers who consider themselves specialists only rarely practice exclusively in one area of law. With the exception of prosecutors and public defenders who practice only criminal law, specialization among lawyers typically means that a large share or most of one's time, not the whole of it, is devoted to a particular area of the law.

In private practice, specialization varies with both the context of practice and the nature of the clientele, which are interrelated. Although specialization is often identified as characteristic of lawyers in firms, rather than of solo attorneys, the difference is really between lawyers in large firms, who tend to be highly specialized, and lawyers who practice in other settings.

The larger the law firm, the greater the degree of specialization in the individual lawyer's work. With members of large law firms specializing in different areas of the law, the firms can provide for all the legal needs of their business clientele. These include corporate law, securities, antitrust, and tax. In some areas, such as antitrust, the bar is further divided, with some lawyers specializing in plaintiff work (that is, representing those bringing suit) and others specializing in defending the corporations being challenged. It has in fact been argued that the emergence and rise of large law firms was a result of the development of large corporations that demand specialized legal services (Ladinsky). As such, the trend toward specialization was noted at least as early as the 1930s in a commentary on the modern metropolitan bar: "Most of its best brains, most of its inevitable leaders, have moved masswise out of court work, out of a general practice akin to that of the family doctor, into highly paid specialization in the service of large corporations" (Llewellyn, 1933).

Individuals' legal needs are serviced by quite a distinct segment of the bar, one that tends to be less specialized. To the extent that lawyers who handle legal work for individuals do specialize, it is a function of their clientele; specialties include family law, real estate, wills and estates, criminal law, and personal-injury work. These are the areas in which individuals are most likely to seek legal services, and so they are often practiced together.

Among lawyers who do legal work mostly for

businesses, a single attorney may do corporate, tax, and securities work. Some specialties, such as tax and real estate, are practiced by all segments of the bar, but while the large firm is engaged in corporate tax work and real estate development, the solo attorney is more likely to be involved in individual estate and tax planning and the sale of individual homes. These distinctions, however, are most likely to occur in large cities; in small towns, lawyers are more likely to do many varieties of legal work.

Although the substantive specialty that a lawyer practices may determine the skills used in practice (Zemans and Rosenblum), the clientele served, and the lawyer's status within the bar (Heinz and Laumann), very little is known about the factors that influence who will practice which specialty. With the exception of engineering graduates entering patent law and of accounting and business students practicing tax law, there is little predictability as to who will specialize in what legal areas. Law students do not major in a particular area of the law; in fact, law schools pride themselves on training generalists. Determination of specialization generally occurs after the lawyer enters the practice of law. This is particularly curious because of the importance of specialty in defining the actual nature of one's practice.

In most cases the context within which one practices appears to be the most important determinant of both the degree of specialization and the areas of specialization. The precise area in which a lawyer practices is largely the result of the expertise needed by the firm early in one's career. There may be a general need in the tax area, or the firm may require work on a particular case. A firm that is handling a very large case is likely to assign to it many junior members of the firm. In the course of that case, some of the lawyers will become the firm experts in that area of the law. This applies particularly to younger lawyers not only because they have not yet developed an area of expertise but also because firms are structured to assign them as the need arises. In private practice, expertise and therefore specialization is developed in response to client demand. In contrast to the medical profession, which requires substantial formal training in a self-selected specialty, lawyers almost universally develop their specialty on the job in the course of representing clients. Thus, the determination

of the tasks in which a lawyer is engaged are to a substantial degree determined by others. To the extent that the specialty practiced determines one's prestige within the bar, the same can be said of a lawyer's professional status.

PRESTIGE WITHIN THE PROFESSION

Although the bar as a whole enjoys a high level of prestige within American society, there is a hierarchy of prestige within the profession. Since formal requirements for entry to the profession are nearly universal (graduation from an ABA-accredited law school and passage of a state bar examination), more subtle distinctions are made. At the point of hiring, the law school attended and class standing in law school are the most important criteria. Those who obtain judicial clerkships upon graduation from law school have an additional credential. This is particularly important for those seeking a teaching position in a law school.

The difference in the jobs obtained and specialties practiced by graduates of different law schools has been recognized at least since the publication of Reed's 1921 study of legal education. The more prestigious the law school attended and the higher one's class standing, the more likely a law graduate is to join a larger, more prestigious firm and to do law work for high-status clients. Clients with higher social status tend to use lawyers in selected specialties. It has been argued that lawyers who mainly practice in areas of the law such as securities and antitrust are accorded high status within the bar by virtue of the nature of their clientele (Heinz and Laumann). The lower end of the bar's status hierarchy is occupied by criminal lawyers, whose clients are almost all of lower social status.

Appropriate social, religious, and ethnic credentials have also played an important role in the distribution of lawyers within the bar (Auerbach). Many of the most prestigious firms were for many years the bastions of white, Anglo-Saxon, Protestant males. Catholics, Jews, those of southern and eastern European ancestry, and, more recently, blacks and women have entered the most prestigious and powerful big-city law firms, although in most cases they remain decided minorities. To some extent, exclusions in the early days could be based simply on the allegedly objective criterion of law school attended. In practice, immigrants, the children of immigrants, women, and minorities had only limited access to the very law schools whose attendance was a prerequisite for consideration for hiring.

It should be made clear, however, that access to the profession has been quite open to those seeking upward mobility. This was reflected in the conscious decision in the early part of the century to maintain part-time night law schools, thereby maintaining variations in legal educational opportunities. This contrasts with the policies adopted by the medical profession. Still, those coming from low-status backgrounds often attend law school at night because they cannot afford to be full-time students.

In the distribution of law school graduates, it is the largest law firms (more than fifty lawyers) that are most likely to recruit graduates from the more prestigious law schools. Although class standing plays a significant role, in the metropolitan bar the law school attended is the best single predictor of both the size of the firm in which one practices and the prestige of the specialty practiced. Despite the importance of law school attended to legal career, it must be noted that lawyer markets are relatively localized; with a half dozen exceptions, so are the reputations of law schools. That is to say that even law schools unknown outside of their own locale get their graduates hired by the most prestigious firms within their own geographic area. Most lawyers attended law school in the same general locale in which they practice.

PREPARATION FOR THE PRACTICE OF LAW

In the colonial era, one aspiring to a legal career sought an apprenticeship with a practicing lawyer. The nineteenth-century emergence of university-based study of the law did not supplant the need for an apprenticeship if one was to practice law. Such university-based instruction was tied to philosophy, political economy, and ethics and linked law with the broader social order; it prepared men for prominent positions of leadership. Concurrently, the practicing bar began to establish its own schools to train future lawyers. These trends merged as law schools

were established within universities. Still, apprenticeship was the major route to the profession and remained so well into the twentieth century.

The most radical change in the preparation of lawyers was instituted in 1870 at Harvard Law School by the new dean Christopher Columbus Langdell. For him the study of law was a science whose tools were housed in the library. The case method, as it came to be called, based instruction exclusively on the examination of appellate court opinions and was aimed at developing analytic skills. This mode of instruction was distinct from both the philosophical approach and the apprenticeship model; it was to become the basic model of instruction in law schools nationwide. This uniformity became particularly important as the organized bar successfully encouraged states to require law school attendance as a prerequisite for admission to the bar. By 1970, less than half a dozen states allowed admission to the bar by apprenticeship without law school training. The preparation of lawyers is almost universally oriented to learning to "think like a lawyer," with neither the philosophy of early university training nor the skills of apprenticeship given much attention.

One indicator of the limits of legal education in preparation for the practice of law is the success of what are known as bar review courses. These entail short intense training to prepare law school graduates to pass state bar examinations, a requirement if one is to be licensed to practice law. Although law schools have more recently given greater attention to skills training and the relationship of law and society, the legal profession as a whole is a product of the strictly analytic training introduced by Langdell more than a century ago. The historic changes in the prerequisites to practice are arguably linked to access to the profession.

ACCESS TO THE PROFESSION

There is a difference of opinion as to the effects that changes in prerequisites to the practice of law have had on access to the profession. Alexis de Tocqueville, in his 1835 description of *Democracy in America*, observed that "if I were asked where I place the American aristocracy, I should reply without hesitation . . . that it occupies the judicial bench and bar" (vol. 1, 278). Later studies confirm the high status of the legal profession as an occupational group. Indeed, it has been portrayed as a path to higher status in a society that lauds upward mobility.

At the same time, it has been described as a profession likely to draw its members from high-status backgrounds. This is a matter of some concern, for, as noted by Reed, "the interests not only of the individual but of the community demand that participation in the making and administration of the law shall be kept accessible to Lincoln's plain people" (p. 418). As preparation for the practice of law, a college degree and three years of high-tuition professional schooling (often, if not typically, to the exclusion of income-generating employment during the school year) have been viewed by some as restricting access to the profession and denying a route of upward mobility that was used particularly by the children of immigrants in the early part of the twentieth century. At that time the only requirement was an apprenticeship with a practicing lawyer. Although comparative figures are not available, there is still a significant number of members of the bar, at least in the cities, whose fathers had substantially lower-status occupations. For many, the law is still seen as a path of upward mobility; evidence suggests that prestige and above-average income are important attractions to those seeking careers in the law. Given the geometric rise in admissions to the practice of law in the 1970s, the absolute numbers attaining higher status have no doubt increased. It should be noted that the growth in the profession beyond what would be predicted by population has, since 1974, been largely the result of the entrance of women. Through the 1960s, only 3 percent of new entrants to the bar were women; by 1983, the figure had risen to approximately 34 percent (Curran, 1985, 4).

There are contradictory views on the effects of the movement of legal training from law offices to law schools. Some argue that given the costs of law school and the prerequisite college degree, the law is less accessible than it once was. Others contend that the apprentice system demanded that personal connections to an established lawyer were necessary to obtain an apprenticeship, thereby excluding those without such connections. It should also be noted that at least in urban areas many law schools have maintained evening programs for students who need to work while attending school. However much opportunities may or may not have changed, upward mobility continues to be a strong attraction of a legal career.

LAWYER INCOME

Americans spend a great deal of money to engage the services of lawyers. According to the Bureau of the Census 1984 *U.S. Industrial Outlook*, receipts for legal services were an estimated $38.5 billion in 1983, with consumers accounting for close to half of the amount received; the remainder was from businesses. These figures are limited to private practitioners and do not include the public resources expended for lawyers who work for federal, state, or local governments or the expenditures of business corporations for legal counsel they employ.

Although anticipated high income continues to be an important attraction to legal careers, average lawyer income is not nearly as high as generally assumed. The image of extremely high income among lawyers is perpetuated by news media reporting of the cost of legal representation by a very select group of lawyers, usually in selected cases. While some lawyers bill their time at hundreds of dollars an hour and have incomes of hundreds of thousands of dollars a year, they are a distinct minority in the legal profession. The rare case that results in a judgment of several million dollars can also mean huge earnings for a lawyer whose fee is set as a percentage of the award if the case is successful. These examples, however, are not the norm.

According to a Bureau of Labor Statistics survey in 1980, the income of lawyers in private practice ranges from an average of about $20,000 at the entry level to approximately $60,000 at the management level. Other studies show a somewhat higher median for partners in law firms in some cities; several surveys indicate an overall median income of about $45,000. While these figures vary with city (New York and Washington being at the high end of the income scale) and with size of firm (with members of larger firms earning more), they do reflect the general earning levels of most lawyers in the United

States. The same can be said about the widely publicized starting salaries for new lawyers.

Although it is true that some lawyers fresh out of law school earn more than $40,000 in their starting year, such salaries are confined to a very few top graduates of elite law schools who work for the very largest law firms in selected locations (particularly New York City and Washington, D.C.). The median starting salary for new associates in law firms in cities is still less than $25,000. Those not entering firms located in major cities, including those who work for government agencies, earn substantially less.

Lawyer salaries, of course, account for only part of what is spent for lawyer services. These expenditures must cover not only direct earnings of lawyers but also benefits, overhead, and support staff. These costs are covered by billing rates of from $25 to several hundred dollars an hour, depending again upon size and prestige of firm, city in which it is located, and in some cases the reputation of individual lawyers. In some locales, minimum fees for particular services were once set by bar associations. Such fee schedules were held to be unconstitutional restraints of trade by the United States Supreme Court in *Goldfarb* v. *Virginia State Bar* (1975).

The organization of law firms is such that for the income of partners (those who have an equity interest in the firm) to continue to grow, the number of associates (nonpartners) must also grow. This is because of a combination of two factors. Partners can only charge so much for their time if they are to maintain a desired volume of business. Associates' time is billed at a rate to exceed the associates' salaries and overhead costs to the firm. The difference between what associates bring in and what they cost is profit to the firm. The more associates, the greater the total amount to be distributed among the partners. While partners also bill their time at more than they cost, thus ensuring a profit, market factors keep a ceiling on their billing rate. It should also be noted that not all partners share equally in firm proceeds. Factors such as hours billed, revenue generated, new business and clients brought to the firm, legal skills, and management role within the firm all influence the distribution of profits. While competition from other lawyers limits the hourly fees that can be charged, business corporations have recently in-

creased their in-house counsel in part to limit the cost of legal fees. Higher-priced outside counsel is then reserved for more limited use in selected areas.

THE COST OF LEGAL SERVICES

The cost of legal services is perceived as limiting access to the legal process for many Americans. Although most lawyers probably do not turn away potential clients because they are unable to pay, such questions are only rarely raised, for consumers do not seek the services they do not think they can afford. It should be noted that available evidence indicates that those who want an attorney to represent them usually find one with the assistance of family, friends, or associates who recommend particular lawyers (Curran, 1977; Mayhew and Reiss). In addition, irrespective of one's ability to pay, there is the question of whether the benefit that may be gained will be worth the cost of pursuing a case. For example, let us say that a neighbor damages your $500 electric lawnmower beyond repair. Despite admitting fault, the neighbor refuses to pay for the lawnmower. Although you may have the evidence necessary to win a case in court and can even afford to hire a lawyer to represent you, if it costs more than $500 or even somewhat less, it is not worth the trouble to pursue the amount legally due you.

The hypothetical case just described includes the expectation that each party to the dispute will pay his or her own attorney. This practice is so unique that it is known as the American rule. In British law, from which much of the American legal system is derived, the loser is generally required to pay the winner's costs, including lawyer's fees. In the United States, judicial awards collected are in fact diminished by the cost of bringing the claim. If the value of the potential award is insufficient to cover the expected lawyer's fee, no case will be brought. As in the hypothetical case, the owner of damaged property has no effective legal recourse. The defendant in a lawsuit may similarly determine that it is less costly to pay a claim than to pursue the case to a judicial decision, even if he or she might ultimately win the case.

The contingent fee substantially diminishes

the negative social impact of the apparent inability of many people to pay for the legal services needed to bring a valid legal claim. Under this arrangement, a lawyer agrees to represent a claimant in return for a percentage of the award (usually 30 percent to 40 percent). This has been an effective means of providing representation in damage cases, particularly involving personal injury to the claimant, where the amount claimed is sufficient to make the lawyer's percentage fee cover the time anticipated to pursue the case. Although the lawyer gets nothing if the case is unsuccessful, experienced lawyers know which cases are likely to be successful.

There are three limitations on the applicability of the contingent-fee arrangement. First, only legal claims likely to result in a monetary award are covered by contingent-fee arrangements. Cases that involve equitable relief are thus excluded. (Equitable relief cases involve actions intended to force defendants to fulfill acts for which they are legally responsible, such as completing a theatrical performance for which they have legally contracted. Other examples are cases seeking to stop defendants from actions that are prohibited, such as denying a divorced parent visitation rights with his or her children.) The second limitation on the contingent-fee arrangement is its applicability only to claims of sufficient size to make the lawyer's percentage worth the required time necessary to bring the case to a successful conclusion. The $500 lawnmower in our hypothetical case would, for example, be of insufficient size to attract a lawyer to the case. Finally, since the claims of the poor are often too small to be represented on a contingent-fee basis, that segment of the population may be largely excluded from gaining representation at all, even if their claims are meritorious. For cases in excess of several thousand dollars, the contingent-fee arrangement can work well.

Although consumers generally like the idea that they pay their lawyers only from proceeds recovered in a successful suit, in some areas of the law, such as medical malpractice, there has been some negative reaction to the size of lawyers' contingent fees. An example would be a case in which the lawyer gets $4 million of a $10 million award to a mentally retarded paraplegic whose condition is the result of medical negligence.

AVAILABILITY OF LEGAL SERVICES

As part of the emergence of demands for expanded social justice in the 1960s, there was a push for greater availability of legal services, particularly for those unable to afford a lawyer on the usual fee-for-service basis. The argument was, and still is, that without a lawyer to represent you, or at least the realistic expectation that one could be engaged if necessary, legal rights have little meaning. The classic "So sue me" response to a recognized violation of a legal right carries an underlying message that a lawsuit is not expected to follow. For one without access to legal counsel, it is a particularly harrowing message. Although cost is not the only factor affecting the use of legal services, it became the major focus of reform efforts.

The development of free and low-cost legal services was not, however, a new idea. Legal-aid societies for immigrants existed before the turn of the century, and some free and low-fee representation has always been done by individual lawyers or firms *pro bono publico* ("for the public good"). Although this is consistent with a lawyer's obligation under the Code of Professional Responsibility to make legal counsel available, the amount of *pro bono* work has always been limited.

The demand for greater availability of legal representation has focused particularly on civil cases. This is largely because of the involvement of government in providing legal representation to the poor in criminal cases. This, too, has been a relatively recent development. Unlike civil cases, representation in criminal cases has been based on the Sixth Amendment to the United States Constitution, which guarantees the right to counsel in a criminal trial. Although some states provided legal counsel to indigents in criminal cases before it was required, over recent decades all states have been mandated to do so by a series of United States Supreme Court decisions that made the guarantees of the Sixth Amendment applicable to the states via the due process clause of the Fourteenth Amendment. First for capital cases in which the death penalty was threatened *(Powell* v. *Alabama)* in 1932, then for all felony cases *(Gideon* v. *Wainwright)* in 1963, and finally for misdemeanor cases that result in a jail sentence *(Argersinger* v. *Hamlin)* in 1972, the United States Supreme Court has required states to provide or to pay for legal representation of the indigent. Almost all of the largest counties in the United States currently provide free counsel to indigents through a public-defender program, with lawyers serving as full-time or part-time salaried staff. Other counties use an assigned-counsel system, by which private attorneys are appointed by the courts, or a contract system, in which law firms, bar associations, or individual lawyers contract to represent the indigent for a specified dollar amount. Although an assigned-counsel or contract system may offer representation by a lawyer with little or no experience with the criminal law, professional legal counsel is provided. With counsel in criminal cases essentially guaranteed, since the mid-1960s the concern and debates over legal fees and the availability of legal services has occurred largely in the civil arena.

In 1966 the Legal Services Program was created within the Office of Economic Opportunity (OEO), as part of the War on Poverty. The congressional legislation that created the program reflected two goals: to "provide legal advice and representation . . . [and] to further the cause of justice among persons living in poverty." The latter goal encouraged a strong law-reform and social-change orientation, but the actual work funded by the program largely served poor clients with immediate problems (often divorce and landlord-tenant disputes) and little interest in social change. Many of the young lawyers attracted to the Legal Services Program were committed to seeking and achieving social change through the legal process, and their work generated sufficient political opposition to the program that the independent Legal Services Corporation was created with restrictions on the kinds of cases it could accept. Despite this change, the Legal Services Corporation continues to be the object of political debate, with its proponents arguing that it is the only means by which the poor and disadvantaged can begin to obtain the rights guaranteed them by law and its opponents continuing to object to the use of public funds to challenge public procedures and decisions (such as a cutoff of social security benefits) and to clog the courts with litigation over minor cases.

Whatever the success or failure of legal-services programs, they have all been limited to the very poor. A large portion of the population has had too high an income to qualify for government assistance but insufficient financial means to pay for legal representation on a fee-for-service basis. There followed substantial demand for greater availability of legal services for middle-income Americans.

Since the 1960s, new free-market efforts have emerged to meet the legal needs of this middle-income population. In particular, prepaid legal-services programs and legal clinics have grown substantially. Legal-services plans only began to achieve any level of significance in the United States in the 1970s. As with all insurance, the governing principle of prepaid legal-services plans is the distribution of cost among many individuals over a long period of time, thereby limiting the chance of any one person having to bear extremely high costs. Although based on the same model as medical insurance, thus far legal insurance plans have been developed largely to cover members of preexisting groups, such as labor unions. It is unclear, given the greater predictability of the need for legal services as compared to medical services and the availability of legal services on a contingency-fee basis, whether legal insurance will ever be a major mechanism for payment of legal fees in the United States.

Legal clinics may present a more widely available alternative. The emergence of legal clinics that are typically low-fee, high-volume operations has been closely tied to the lifting of prohibitions on lawyer advertising. Early proponents of legal clinics argued that low-cost services would be possible only with a high volume of cases, most particularly uncontested divorces or simple wills, for which the service could be readily standardized. The necessary volume of cases, it was argued, was possible only if the clinics could advertise. Under traditional lawyer ethical codes, advertising was explicitly prohibited. It was not until 1977, when a legal clinic successfully challenged a state ban on lawyer advertising, that clinics became a real possibility. The United States Supreme Court held that prohibitions on advertising constituted an unconstitutional restriction on free speech (*Bates* v. *State Bar of Arizona*). Since then legal clinics have proliferated, including the development of chains and franchises that can share the benefits of a single advertising campaign. As yet there is little systematic evidence detailing the productivity of these clinics. Whether they are serving a clientele that would have otherwise remained unrepresented is not known. It is also unknown whether lawyer advertising and the emergence of legal clinics have expanded the demand for legal services or whether legal work now done by clinics was previously done by other lawyers.

In addition to these mechanisms for providing legal representation, many individuals have chosen to pursue their legal claims *pro se* ("for themselves"). In many jurisdictions this has been facilitated by the creation of special procedures and even special courts designed for use by the layperson. In particular, small monetary claims and uncontested divorces are now being settled without the assistance of legal counsel. The creation of these *pro se* procedures and courts has been part of the official response to public demand for access to the courts for cases too small to interest most lawyers. At the same time, segments of the bar have been concerned that cases that once accounted for a portion of their business are now being handled without them.

LEGAL ETHICS

Codes of professional ethics are formal mechanisms that announce to the public that a profession is self-regulating and thus worthy of the autonomy granted to it by the state. These ethical standards set the profession apart, if not above, the standards of the larger society. Although words like *responsibility* and *integrity* are used to describe "professional" conduct, they are accompanied by disclaimers that terms like *legal ethics* and *professional responsibility* have very precise meanings that are applicable only within the context of the practice of law.

This alleged distinctiveness of legal ethics from general moral standards is credited by some with contributing to the traditional public hostility to lawyers. For example, it is generally considered inappropriate and unfair to impugn another person's integrity by implying lack of truthfulness when you know otherwise. Yet, in the context of defending an accused in a criminal trial, it may be deemed appropriate for a lawyer to cross-examine a truthful witness with the intent of giving the appearance that the witness is being less than totally honest or even lying. Another example is the lawyer's obligation not to

reveal anything divulged by the client. Since a good defense requires that the lawyer be as informed as possible, a relationship of trust and confidence between lawyer and client must be encouraged. Client candor is assured by guaranteeing confidentiality. Thus, all communication between client and lawyer is privileged information.

The extremes to which this obligation can lead were revealed in a highly publicized case in the 1970s in which a defendant in a case told his lawyers that he had killed two people in a separate crime and identified the location of the bodies. Although the lawyers subsequently saw and photographed the bodies, they kept their existence secret even after information was requested by the parents of one of the victims. When the lawyers' failure to reveal this information became public after a confession many months later, there was great public outrage. Although there was disagreement within the bar as to the appropriateness of the lawyers' actions, the defense that was offered argued that if client revelations are not kept in confidence, clients will not reveal all the information that is needed to best represent them.

These distinctive professional standards are closely tied to, and in fact justified by, the requirements of the adversary system. If each side is to receive the best defense, then the lawyers must consider only the interests of their clients. An advocate who considers the good of society rather than the good of the client does damage to the adversary process, which is itself presumed to contribute to the social good. Professional norms thus may dictate behavior that would otherwise be considered inappropriate.

The question frequently asked of criminal defense counsel as to how they can defend someone that they know is guilty illustrates the point. The same, of course, could be asked of the counsel representing toxic-waste companies whose disposal practices have contaminated a town's water supply. In both cases, and in many others, the lawyers' response is that their obligation as lawyers is to represent their clients to the best of their ability because the American system of justice is based on an adversarial process that in the long run will give the most just results.

Critics of this perspective on legal ethics point out that the essence of professionalism—indeed, the basis for granting any profession the right to self-regulation—is its responsibility to the social good. That responsibility is called into question by events like the Watergate scandal, in which a large number of lawyers were implicated in burglary, perjury, and the obstruction of justice on behalf of the Nixon administration.

There is in fact often an inherent tension between obligation to client and obligation to society, as noted by Karl Llewellyn:

> Duty to client reads in terms of taking advantage of each technicality the law may show, however senseless. It reads in terms of distortion of evidence and argument to the utter bounds of the permissible. Duty to court reads in terms of shaping every piece of the machinery that can be made to give, toward better functioning. It reads in terms of trying issues of fact to reach the probable truth.
>
> (1933, 181–182)

According to Llewellyn, the tension has been resolved in favor of the client. Critics argue further that even if total obligation to client were essential to an actual trial, such an obligation is much less persuasive in the context within which most lawyers practice.

The inherent conflict between obligations to client and obligations as officers of the court committed to promoting justice has remained through the continuing development of professional codes of conduct. In addition, such model codes have been unable to reflect the great diversity in law practice. As a result, the codes have continued to be more relevant to some practice contexts than to others.

The first code of professional ethics was passed by the Alabama State Bar Association in 1887. That code, like others that followed, was based on George Sharwood's *Essay on Professional Ethics* (1854), originally delivered as lectures at the then new law school of the University of Pennsylvania. The ABA promulgated its first code, the Canons of Professional Ethics, in 1908, also along the lines suggested by Sharwood. This ABA code and those it has since passed have served as models for adoption by state bar associations, courts, and disciplinary bodies. Since lawyers are licensed to practice in the states (with additional licensure required to practice in the federal system), it is the states that largely determine the rules of conduct. Over the years, most states have adopted some form of the ABA standards, with local variations.

Sharwood's essay and the early codes emphasized the high moral principles and dignity required of the profession. The traditional duties of the bar were in part derived from English practices. These included the duty to police the bar, the duty to represent the indigent, the duty not to stir up litigation, and the duty not to aid in the unauthorized practice of law (Drinker, 59–66). These duties have continued to appear with varying degrees of emphasis throughout the various reformulations of codes of conduct.

The emergence of the ABA Canons and subsequent state formulations of them came at a time when the practice of law was undergoing significant change. The growth of the American corporation was accompanied by changes in law practice to meet corporate needs. Many lawyers after the turn of the century moved away from small-town practice, in which they represented individuals, to urban practice, with its increasing representation of business corporations.

According to Drinker, the motivating force behind the 1908 ABA Canons was "the realization by thoughtful leaders of the bar of the growing commercialism all over the country. The consequent weakening of an effective professional public opinion clearly called for a more definite statement by the bar of the accepted rules of professional conduct" (p. 25). Negative reaction by the leaders of the bar to increased commercialization in the practice of law was reflected in the Canons' prohibition on lawyer advertising. The traditional view was that

> advertising, solicitation, and encroachment on the practice of others does not tend to benefit either the public or the lawyer in the same way as in the case of the sale of merchandise. While extensive advertising would doubtless increase litigation, this has always been considered as against public policy. Also, many of the most desirable clients, imbued with high respect both for their lawyer and his calling, would have no use for a lawyer who did not maintain the dignity and standards of his profession.
>
> (Drinker, 211–212)

Others have argued that "the Canons were part of an attempt to defend the better element in the bar from the inroads of a commercial spirit and the practice of those who were not gentlemen" (Macaulay, 16). This view recognizes the fact that the prohibition on advertising was particularly felt by young immigrant lawyers who were largely excluded from the developing urban firms and who at the same time did not have the established connections of the traditional small-town lawyers. Their problems were further exacerbated by their dependence on a continuing stream of individual clients to sustain their practices while the firms dealt largely with a continuing clientele. Exhortations of professional codes to await clients were thus much easier for higher-status firm lawyers to follow.

This easier applicability to one segment of the bar is not limited to the ABA Canons' prohibition on advertising. There are a number of professional ethical norms that are affected by the nature of one's practice and clientele. A study of legal ethics among practicing lawyers found that higher-status firm lawyers exhibited greater adherence to the ethical norms of the ABA Canons than did solo practitioners, who do the divorces and personal injuries that constitute much of the legal work of individual clients (Carlin). Critics have long charged that these codes of professional conduct contain both class and ethnic biases (Auerbach). It is also clear that although significant change has occurred in the distribution of lawyers in various practice contexts, ethnic and class differences have not disappeared.

The ABA's 1908 Canons of Ethical Conduct were amended over the years in response to changes in society and a series of Supreme Court decisions that reflected those changes. Developments eventually demanded a new code. During the 1960s there was increasing concern over the limited availability of legal services despite the ethical requirement to make legal services available. Indeed, some efforts to deal with this problem were opposed by the organized bar. One mechanism developed was group legal representation. Under such a plan, an individual would receive legal representation by virtue of membership in the organization. However, unlike the traditional lawyer-client relationship, an individual was represented by a lawyer chosen by the group. States and bar associations fought these plans until a series of United States Supreme Court decisions sustained their validity (*National Association for the Advancement of Colored People* v. *Button*, 1963; *Brotherhood of Railway Trainmen* v.

Virginia, 1964; *United Mine Workers District 12* v. *Illinois Bar Assn.*, 1967; *United Transportation Union* v. *State Bar*, 1971). At about the same time, the creation of the Office of Economic Opportunity's Legal Services Program called attention to the failure of the traditional duty to provide legal services to those who could not afford it.

In 1969 the new Code of Professional Responsibility was adopted by the ABA. The new code included the same traditional duties of the bar but appeared to shift its emphasis. Canon 2 provided that "a lawyer should assist the legal profession in fulfilling its duty to make legal counsel available." Although this canon constituted approximately 25 percent of the code, it continued to prohibit all advertising and to permit the establishment of minimum-fee schedules until barred by the *Bates* decision in 1977 and the *Goldfarb* decision in 1975, respectively. It has in fact been argued that the code establishes a hierarchy of interests, putting the lawyer's interest first, then the client's, and then society's (Morgan). For example, although a client's confidences are privileged, they can be disclosed when necessary to collect a fee. In addition, the protection of the public that is to flow from prohibitions on the unauthorized practice of law often appears more like protectionism.

Particular subjects of controversy have been do-it-yourself books and nonlawyer assistance in completing legal forms required in divorce, adoption, name-change, and other proceedings. The books are generally written by lawyers and even those that are not have been acknowledged as having the right to publication. Of much greater concern to the legal profession have been the nonlawyers who have established themselves in business to complete legal forms. Some are former paralegals or legal secretaries. They claim that they are doing precisely the same work they did when working for a lawyer, only now they are being paid directly and the client is charged only a fraction of what it would cost to purchase the same service through a lawyer. It is argued that requiring the use of a lawyer for these simple tasks would exclude many from using the legal process. For the legal profession these practices constitute "unauthorized practice of law," which is prohibited by every state.

Such conflicts are not unique to the contemporary scene. There has, for example, long been conflict between lawyers and real estate brokers

640

over who should be advising home buyers and sellers and who should be drafting their sale agreements. Legislatures have granted tasks that have been defined as "the practice of law" exclusively to those licensed by the state to do so. However, the practice of law is not as clearly defined as one might assume. While there is broad agreement that arguing a case for a client in a court of law constitutes the practice of law, much of the actual work of lawyers does not so obviously fall within the strict definition of that term. The work of lawyers includes advising, interviewing, and negotiating—tasks that are part of many occupational pursuits. In addition, there is the work of lobbyists, politicians, and government officials, who are often trained as lawyers and licensed to practice law. Yet it is clear that these roles are not the exclusive preserve of the legal profession, nor should they be in a democratic society. What constitutes legal services is therefore a subject of some disagreement.

The tendency to resolve conflicts between obligations to clients and obligations to the court and society in favor of the former is reinforced by the actual disciplinary practices used to enforce professional codes of conduct. The threat of actual sanction under the ABA code is quite small, with only a minute proportion of complaints against lawyers for unprofessional conduct resulting in any unfavorable action. Carlin's study of New York from 1951 to 1969 shows an average of only 4 percent of complaints going to a formal hearing, and fewer resulting in the imposition of any sanction. Carlin's figures are not unique. Another study compared official reports of four jurisdictions and found the same pattern; 91 percent to 97 percent of all complaints were dismissed without investigation, with fewer than 3 percent resulting in a sanction in any of the jurisdictions (Steele and Nimmer, 982).

Enforcement of the code is also more likely to relate to some kinds of prohibited behavior than others. Although each state has its own disciplinary agency, they are all basically reactive institutions, relying strongly on third-party complaints. Client complaints are the most common. As a result, allegations of wrongdoing are skewed toward contract disputes rather than activities that constitute more serious misconduct. Also eliminated from investigation is behavior of which the client is unaware or which is in the client's interest. Thus, for example, the bribing of a judge is

not likely to be reported to a disciplinary body. Most complaints concern fees, performance not meeting expectations, delay, lack of representation, rudeness, and conflicts of interest.

Continuing criticism of the code and of the behavioral standards of the profession led to another major rewriting of the profession's code of conduct. The new Model Rules of Professional Conduct were adopted by the ABA in 1983. Like the earlier Canons of Professional Ethics and the Code of Professional Responsibility, this is a model for the states to adopt, with or without local variations.

There are both similarities and differences between the new and old codes. Unlike the 1969 code, the 1983 code no longer contains the "ethical considerations" that were aspirational statements encouraging the highest standards of professional conduct. For example, the 1983 code omitted statements such as these from the 1969 code: "Neither [a lawyer's] personal interests, the interests of other clients, nor the desires of third persons should be permitted to dilute his loyalty to his client" (Ethical Consideration 5-1) and "The professional responsibility of a lawyer derives from his membership in a profession which has the duty of assisting members of the public to secure and protect available legal rights and benefits" (Ethical Consideration 7-1). The new code is more oriented to rules that delineate minimal standards defining behavior that can give rise to disciplinary action; these had been defined as the "disciplinary rules" under the former code.

Although the new code does not answer critics' concerns that the social good is not a sufficiently high priority of the legal profession, it does take into account some of the changes that have occurred in the nature of law practice. Thus, for example, it considers different roles of lawyers (such as counselor versus advocate) and different practice settings (such as relationships within law firms) than those previously addressed, and it recognizes the reality of lawyer advertising. In addition, the 1983 code responds to some criticisms regarding lawyer-client relations, particularly those areas that had been the basis of many client complaints. Rule 1.4(a), for example, states that "a lawyer shall keep a client reasonably informed about the status of a matter and promptly comply with reasonable requests for information." Since enforcement of the new code relies on the same disciplinary mechanisms used previously, it is likely to suffer from the same limitations. Thus, the actual impact of the new rules remains unknown.

THE PUBLIC AND THE PROFESSION

Although lawyers have enjoyed consistently high social standing, their public image has not been particularly positive. Underlying much of the criticism has been the view that the law has become curiously dissociated from justice and that lawyers are more concerned with monetary gain than with the public good. Instead of being committed to justice and the rule of law, they are, it is said, merely "hired guns."

Although contemporary criticism implies that earlier in American history lawyers were somehow more concerned with justice and the social good, there is substantial contrary evidence. For example, even before the American Revolution, colonial statutes were written in an attempt to restrict lawyers' activities. Indeed, criticism of lawyers in the early years of the Republic have a very contemporary ring; alleged offenses were malpractice, excessive fees, promotion of litigation, and the accumulation of great wealth.

Public discomfort with the bar is probably as old as the profession and is no doubt related to the power it exerts. Negative images of lawyers also appear in popular literature, including Swift's reference to lawyers in *Gulliver's Travels* as "a society of men among us, bred up from their youth in the art of proving by words multiplied for the purpose, that white is black, and black is white, according as they are paid" (Pt. IV, Chap. 5). A more contemporary example is found in the refrain from Carl Sandburg's poem "The Lawyers Know Too Much": "Tell me why a hearse horse snickers hauling a lawyer's bones."

Even so, lawyers are frequently lauded as defenders of the downtrodden and pursuers of justice willing to guarantee an individual's day in court and to protect modern-day Davids from their Goliaths. We often object to the intrusion of law and lawyers in our lives; at the same time, we look to them as a last resort to protect us. In addition, there is evidence that members of the public who have employed attorneys on their own behalf are generally pleased with the representation provided. Among individuals who have retained legal counsel, between 80 percent and 90 percent rate their lawyers good or excellent in honesty, promptness, and reasonableness of fees (Curran, 1977, 210).

Even so, modern pollsters document the low level of public confidence in the legal profession as the love-hate relationship between lawyers and laypersons continues unabated. In particular, there seems to a growing awareness of the limits of the law and lawyers in curing social ills. Yet Americans seem unwilling to give up any legal advantage and seek to protect and promote their rights under the law. In so doing, they commit themselves to the legal professionals.

CASES

Argersinger v. Hamlin, 407 U.S. 25 (1972)

Bates v. State Bar of Arizona, 433 U.S. 350 (1977)

Brotherhood of Railway Trainmen v. Virginia, 377 U.S. 1 (1964)

Gideon v. Wainwright, 372 U.S. 335 (1963)

Goldfarb v. Virginia State Bar, 421 U.S. 773 (1975)

National Association for the Advancement of Colored People v. Button, 371 U.S. 415 (1963)

Powell v. Alabama, 287 U.S. 45 (1932)

United Mine Workers District 12 v. Illinois Bar Assn., 389 U.S. 217 (1967)

United Transportation Union v. State Bar, 401 U.S. 376 (1971)

BIBLIOGRAPHY

American Bar Association, *ABA Canons of Ethics* (1908), formed the first set of ethical standards for lawyers that were intended to be applicable nationally; *ABA Code of Professional Responsibility* (1969), constituted the major midcentury overhaul of the canons; and *ABA Model Rules of Professional Conduct* (1983), is the most recent revision of ABA standards of conduct for lawyers. American Bar Association Special Committee on Evaluation of Disciplinary Enforcement, *Problems and Recommendations in Disciplinary Enforcement*, Final Draft (June 1970), approaches ethical questions from the standpoint of enforcement. Jerold S. Auerbach, *Unequal Justice: Lawyers and Social Change in Modern America* (1976), is a critical examination of the legal profession and its efforts to contain social change. "A Businessman's View of Lawyers," in *Business Lawyer*, 33 (January 1978), is the transcript of a panel discussion of corporate executives at the Program of the Section of Corporation, Banking and Business Law, American Bar Association 1977 Annual Meeting.

Jerome E. Carlin, *Lawyer's Ethics* (1966), examines how the social organization of the profession affects adherence to codes of ethics. Barbara A. Curran, *The Legal Needs of the Public* (1977), reports on a national survey of nonbusiness use of lawyers' services by adults in the United States; and *1984 Lawyers' Statistical Report* (1985), reports on national statistics on the legal profession based on 1980 data and includes demographics and nature-of-practice information.

Henry S. Drinker, *Legal Ethics* (1953), is the most extensive treatment of the historical development of standards of legal ethics, written by a longtime chairman of the ABA Standing Committee on Professional Ethics and Grievances. Monroe H. Friedman, *Lawyers' Ethics in an Adversary System* (1975), points out the conflicting values in codes of ethics for lawyers and argues the overriding importance of obligations to client in an adversary system. Cynthia Fuchs, *Women in Law* (1981), is a study of women lawyers in the 1960s and 1970s that documents their increased opportunities in the legal profession.

John P. Heinz and Edward O. Laumann, *Chicago Lawyers: The Social Structure of the Bar* (1983), provides a sociological analysis of the Chicago bar based on interviews with more than seven hundred lawyers, with particular attention on the relationship between lawyers' demographic characteristics and the nature of their legal practice. Peter H. Irons, *The New Deal Lawyers* (1982), describes and examines the central contribution of lawyers to the dramatic change in American public policy and the role of the federal government that occurred in the 1930s.

Jack Ladinsky, "The Impact of Social Backgrounds of Lawyers on Law Practice and the Law," in *Journal of Legal Education,* 16 (1963), is a study of solo and firm lawyers in the Detroit area that examines the relationship between their family origins and education and their work situations. Karl Llewellyn, "The Bar Specializes—With What Results?" in *Annals of the American Academy of Political and Social Science,* 167 (1933), is a well-known law professor's examination of the impact of specialization within the legal profession, written at a time when specialization was quite minimal compared with today; and "On What Is Wrong with So-called Legal Education," in *Columbia Law Review,* 35 (1935), is his critique of legal education, focusing on what it is that law schools do not do to prepare their students for the actual practice of law.

Stewart Macaulay, "Lawyer Advertising, Yes, but . . . ," University of Wisconsin Institute for Legal Studies, Working Paper No. 1-2, 1985, supports lawyer advertising but cautions limits. Martin Mayer, *The Lawyers* (1967), is a popular account of the legal profession, the work of lawyers, and the world in which they operate. Leon Mayhew and Albert J. Reiss, "The Social Organization of Legal Contacts," in *American Sociological Review,* 34 (1969), reports on a study of use of lawyers by residents of the Detroit area. Thomas D. Morgan, "The Evolving Concept of Professional Responsibility," in *Harvard Law Review,* 90 (1977), examines the conflicting norms within the Code of Professional Responsibility and which goals take primacy over others.

Alfred Z. Reed, *Training for the Public Profession of the Law* (1921), is an early analysis of the various modes of preparation of lawyers for practice. Douglas E. Rosenthal, *Lawyer and Client: Who's in Charge?* (1974), describes two models (traditional and participatory) of lawyer-client relationships and examines their impact on the results in personal-injury cases. H. Laurence Ross, *Settled Out of Court* (1970), an examination of automobile accident cases in which the major actors are not lawyers but insurance adjusters and layperson claimants, is an excellent presentation of the law in action and how it differs from the law on the books.

Erwin O. Smigal, *The Wall Street Lawyer* (1969), discusses recruitment, background characteristics, career patterns, and work of lawyers in large law firms in New York City, examining the internal structure of those firms. Eric Steele and Raymond T. Nimmer, "Lawyers, Clients and Professional Responsibility," in *American Bar Foundation Research Journal* (1976), reports on the enforcement of codes of professional conduct, including consideration of the nature of complaints and the frequency of sanctions. Alexis de Tocqueville, *Democracy in America,* H. Reeve, trans. (1976), is the classic examination of American society and government by a Frenchman who visited the United States in the 1830s, in which he noted the central importance of the judicial system and judges and lawyers to the system of government.

United States Department of Commerce, Bureau of Industrial Economics, *U.S. Industrial Outlook* (1984), describes the status and prospects for more than three hundred industries. Richard Wasserstrom, "Lawyers as Professionals: Some Moral Issues," in *Human Rights,* 5 (1975), considers the complexities of determining appropriate behavior when lawyers' professional rules of conduct conflict with general social rules of conduct. Frances Kahn Zemans and Victor G. Rosenblum, *The Making of a Public Profession* (1981), analyzes legal education and the professional development of lawyers, using data from more than five hundred practicing lawyers. [*See also* BAR ASSOCIATIONS; LEGAL EDUCATION; LEGAL SERVICES; *and* PUBLIC-INTEREST ADVOCACY.]

LEGAL SERVICES

Roger Billings

INDIVIDUALS and families contract for legal services by talking with lawyers who agree to accept them as clients. They often pay a lump-sum fee for defense of criminal charges or an hourly fee for handling civil matters (noncriminal), such as divorces, real estate closings, and will draftings. The lawyer usually requires a down payment, called a retainer, except in matters involving personal-injury cases. In these cases the lawyer seeks money from the person who caused the injury and enters into a contingency-fee agreement with the client. (The fee is said to be "contingent" on any award that might materialize.) In such an agreement the fee is a percentage of the money settlement or jury award, if any, and may be as high as 50 percent.

The contingency-fee arrangement makes some legal services available to rich and poor alike because no retainer is necessary. In the majority of cases, however, the cost of legal services is a barrier to the poor, who sometimes must go without representation. A study by Barbara Curran published by the American Bar Foundation (ABA) in 1977 indicated that, like the poor, members of the vast middle class seldom seek legal services when needed. The lowest 20 percent of the population in income level had no access to legal services except for lawyers provided out of charity, and the middle 70 percent were often deprived of access by the cost of services. Only the upper 10 percent of the population and corporations had easy access to legal services.

In the late nineteenth century, experiments to provide free legal counsel for the poor in New York and Chicago resulted in the first legal-aid societies to serve all people, regardless of their national origin, gender, or ability to pay. By the 1960s most major cities had legal-aid offices supported by local charities. These offices mostly handled civil, rather than criminal, cases. They began to change in the 1960s when the federal government first made public funds available for legal services.

Many cities and counties employed lawyers called public defenders to handle criminal defense of poor persons. Other defenders were appointed by the courts on a case-by-case basis and were paid standard fees out of court funds, especially after the Supreme Court ruled in *Gideon* v. *Wainwright* (1963) and *Argersinger* v. *Hamlin* (1972) that nearly all criminal defendants, regardless of means, had a right to be represented by a lawyer. The system of public defenders and court-appointed lawyers remains intact today.

The need for middle-class legal services was not perceived as early as was the need for services for the poor. Among the earliest organizations to recognize this need were automobile clubs. In the 1920s and 1930s, automobile travel between cities grew and motorists increasingly were caught in speed traps or involved in accidents. Automobile clubs sold membership contracts, which entitled holders to legal advice on the ownership, operation, and registration of their cars. Some provided for court representation. Some clubs employed lawyers directly; others published a recommended list of attorneys who would bill the club as their services were used. These early ways of providing services survive to this day, with the "staff attorney" system favored by labor unions for their members, and the "participating attorney" or "open panel" system favored by the insurance industry for policyholders. The systems are discussed in the section on prepaid legal services.

The automobile club plans were short-lived, for the ABA Committee on Professional Ethics deemed their work unethical. In Opinion No. 8 (1925) and in Canon 35 (1928) the ABA decided that it was unethical for a lawyer to accept employment with an automobile club to serve the members. Their reasoning was that these lawyers might come under control of the club instead of serving only the individual members. It was thought that lawyers must serve only their clients and not be influenced by "lay intermediaries," such as automobile clubs. The penalty for a lawyer who cooperated with a club might be loss of license to practice law.

Ultimately, the clubs were prohibited from offering legal services by local bar associations. The Chicago Bar Association sued the local motor club for engaging in the unauthorized practice of law. The bar successfully argued that the clubs, in hiring attorneys for their members, were practicing law without a license, as lay intermediaries.

State medical societies also provided legal services for physicians in malpractice suits. These faded away, too, because of attacks from bar associations. The objections of bar associations to groups hiring attorneys and, later, of state insurance departments to legal-expense insurance were powerful obstacles to the development of prepaid legal services for the middle class. Even today ethical rules reflect concern that attorneys who receive payment from one of these organizations instead of directly from the client will lose their independence. They also reflect concern that the organizations will have access to confidential client files that only the attorney is supposed to see. Counterbalancing these ethical concerns is the enlightened self-interest of many lawyers who see prepaid legal plans as a means to expand their practices.

PUBLIC DEFENDERS

Public defenders are lawyers who specialize in defending persons accused of a crime. At first such public defenders as existed were part of legal-aid societies supported by charity in big cities. These societies handled both civil and criminal matters and could accept or turn down cases as they saw fit. Perhaps the earliest was Der Deutsche Rechtsschutz Verein (the German Legal Defense Society), organized in 1876 in New York City to help German immigrants. It

was the forerunner of the New York Legal Aid Society, the Chicago Bureau of Justice (1888), and many similar organizations open to people of any national origin and gender. The societies handled few criminal cases, because they lacked money and personnel to conduct investigations and absorb the high cost of trial work. Gradually, in the 1920s, public-defender programs were established within big-city legal-aid societies, although the societies' primary thrust remained civil cases. By 1962, only 110 public-defender offices had been established.

The need for government funding was made clear in a series of Supreme Court decisions that required that criminal defendants be represented by counsel. In the landmark cases of *Gideon* and *Argersinger*, the Court held that the Sixth Amendment right to counsel is binding upon the states in any case in which conviction may result in incarceration. Later cases extended this right to those subjected to police interrogations, pretrial lineups, preliminary hearings, and parole-revocation hearings and to those who appealed from their convictions. The Court also held in *In re Gault* (1967) that juveniles had a right to counsel at the trial stage in a delinquency hearing.

Prior to these cases, only a small percentage of indigent defendants had access to volunteer counsel assigned by the court or to poorly paid defenders. Afterward, an immediate need for counsel arose in millions of cases annually. The federal government provided funds in the Criminal Justice Act of 1964 for federal judges to pay attorneys to represent individual clients. These funds were only available to persons accused of federal crimes, but the great majority of crimes were violations of state, not federal, laws. Among the states, one of the earliest to respond meaningfully was New Jersey, which enacted a statewide public-defender program in 1967, but few other states decided to pay salaries to public defenders, as New Jersey did. Instead, they relied on various schemes involving administrative offices to distribute funds for court-appointed counsel.

In cities such as New York and Saint Louis, the salaried public defenders complained that their case loads were so high as to deny effective representation. Although half of all criminal cases involved indigent defendants, the cause of creating large staffs of public defenders failed to gain significant backing at either the federal or state level. The defense of criminals seemed low in priority among taxpayers and their legislative representatives. By 1986 a debate was raging in legal literature over the failure of the legal establishment and the state and federal governments to provide funds for adequate defense of indigents. Critics complained, for example, that in 1983 in Saint Louis, twenty-two public defenders handled twelve thousand cases on a budget of $695,000 while the forty-five attorneys in the prosecutor's office had a budget of $2.4 million.

LEGAL-AID SOCIETIES

In the early 1960s there were about 250 legal-aid societies and 110 public-defender offices in the United States—very few in proportion to the population but sufficient to provide minimal coverage in major cities. They were notable for being entirely supported by charity and understaffed. A typical office had a few lawyers, a secretary, and perhaps a full-time director. Many needs of poor people went unmet, and cases potentially involving litigation were seldom handled beyond the initial advice-and-consultation stage. Divorce was discouraged because the demand exceeded the capacity of the office, and the board of directors often frowned upon divorce on moral or religious grounds. Thus, divorce clients were sent away and told to return if their situation became worse. The same inability to handle the case load was true of other common complaints, such as bankruptcy, eviction, and repossession of an automobile. Legal scholarship was just beginning to create interest in the law of consumer rights, welfare recipients' rights, and the rights of people affected by slum housing.

As the years passed and government funding brought a great increase in the number of lawyers for poor people, legal-aid offices developed expertise in these areas and could handle numerous cases efficiently. By the 1980s an office specializing in legal services for the poor had become different from the earlier legal-aid society office. It employed paralegals to handle many repetitious chores and to represent clients in hearings on denial or termination of benefits such as social security and welfare. The lawyers, supported by adequate secretarial help and research assistance from the national Legal Services Corporation (LSC), could specialize in litigation involving landlord-tenant law, consumer bankruptcy, domestic relations, and other areas of so-called poverty law.

FEDERALIZATION: THE LEGAL SERVICES CORPORATION

By the 1980s, legal services for the poor were being financed primarily by federal money. Congress authorizes about $300 million annually to the LSC, which distributes the money to local grantee offices. The LSC, authorized by an act of Congress in 1974, is independent of any government agency, but members of its board are appointed by the president with consent of the Senate.

From its beginning in 1975, the LSC has been controversial. Leaders of the bar feared that attorneys would lose their ability to exercise independent judgment on behalf of clients if they depended on the LSC for their salaries and that confidential client files might be available to unauthorized persons in the LSC or its board. President Ronald Reagan opposed the very existence of the LSC when he took office in 1981. He argued that state and local governments, charitable organizations, and volunteer lawyers should assume the burden of providing counsel for the indigent.

The changeover from private to federal funding of legal services began in 1964 with the passage of the Economic Opportunity Act as part of President Lyndon Johnson's War on Poverty. The act's administering agency, the Office of Economic Opportunity (OEO), had no congressional authorization to establish legal-services offices. In 1965, though, the OEO decided to make funds available to local projects, which were to follow certain guidelines in the delivery of legal services to the poor. These guidelines contained the seeds of controversy. In addition to requiring local programs to provide services in all areas of the law (except criminal defense), they required programs to advocate reforms in statutes, regulations, and administrative practices. This was a departure from existing legal-aid practices, which limited legal work to helping individual clients. Thereafter, OEO offices were to engage in litigation to reform laws affecting poor and not-so-poor clients as a group. The reforms also affected and alienated businesses.

At first the new OEO lawyers worked within the legal-aid offices, but gradually, as their funding and emphasis on reform increased, they began to take over the legal-aid offices. From 1965 to 1972, OEO lawyers participated in far-reaching reform cases, often working with other lawyers in the legal-rights movement. For example, they litigated the constitutionality of residency requirements for welfare, challenged antiabortion statutes, and charged a board of education with racial and economic discrimination in the allocation of funds to students. The OEO programs attracted many bright young lawyers who were motivated by altruism.

In 1974 the OEO Office of Legal Services was transferred out of OEO into the LSC. The delivery of legal services to the poor had already become institutionalized in the years 1965–1971 under OEO Legal Services Program directors E. Clinton Bamberger, Earl Johnson, Bert Griffin, and Terry Lenzner. After 1971, leaders spent much of their time preserving the system against political opposition. Among the parts of the system they preserved were backup centers, funded initially at law schools, with each designed to support litigation in a single substantive area, such as welfare or housing, or to develop expertise in handling problems of a population group such as the elderly or Indians. The centers were supplemented by the *Clearinghouse Review,* a national publication to describe poverty-law developments and national training and technical-assistance programs. A private organization, the National Legal Aid and Defender Association (NLADA), continued to be a source of information as it was before the advent of government funding.

The election of President Richard Nixon in 1968 signaled the gradual end to the War on Poverty, and the OEO began to be phased out. The sustained attack on legal services began in 1981 after the election of President Ronald Reagan. In March 1981 he proposed that the LSC be dissolved and that funding responsibility for its grantee offices be transferred to state and local governments. President Reagan's dislike of federally funded legal services probably had its origin in the late 1960s when, as governor of

California, he opposed California Rural Legal Assistance (CRLA), an OEO-funded program. CRLA was particularly successful in stopping certain welfare and Medicaid policies of Governor Reagan and in its advocacy of farm workers against growers.

As Governor Reagan was unable to put the CLRA out of existence, so President Reagan was unable to dismantle the LSC. However, he succeeded in blocking its growth and in exacting restrictions on its authority to provide legal services. By Reagan's second term, the LSC was attempting to focus local programs on services to individuals rather than on reform of the law. Riders to annual appropriations bills restrict the LSC's activities in lobbying, filing class actions against the government, and representing aliens. Although Congress reduced LSC funds by 25 percent in 1982, LSC funds are still the major source of local program funding, supplemented in some areas by charitable organizations such as the United Appeal. Finally, pro bono work sponsored by bar associations supplements the work of LSC grantee offices.

CONTRIBUTIONS OF THE PRIVATE BAR

Bar associations have long advocated a variety of programs to deliver legal services to the poor and have opposed delivering services to the poor solely through government-paid attorneys. During the LSC's struggle with the Reagan administration for funding in the 1980s, the ABA steadfastly supported the continued existence of the LSC. However, the support came at a price, for the ABA pressured the LSC into increasing the involvement of private attorneys in the delivery of legal services. As a result, the LSC began to require its local programs to spend 12.5 percent of LSC grants for private-attorney involvement. This contrasts with the early days of the OEO when the refusal to fund "judicare" programs (described below) stopped judicare from becoming the model delivery system.

Involving private attorneys requires funds for an administrator as well as for payment of the attorneys unless the attorney is a pro bono volunteer. The systems for involving private attorneys enumerated here are used by local LSC grantees, with the pro bono system being the most popular.

Pro Bono. Pro bono programs enlist private attorneys to accept from two to five cases a year without a fee. The bar association assists in signing up attorneys who will accept cases referred from the local LSC grantee. The clients usually are served in the attorney's office, but in some models the attorney works out of a neighborhood office on evenings or weekends. Occasionally, retired or practicing attorneys lend their services directly to the staff of the legal-aid office.

Judicare. In judicare systems, private attorneys join a panel of attorneys willing to provide legal services to the poor on a reduced-fee basis. The LSC grantee making use of a judicare system would allow panel attorneys to elect on a case-by-case basis to take a client and would pay them from one-third to one-half the usual rates for other members of the community. Judicare is particularly useful for routine matters that private attorneys usually handle. The disadvantages are that it requires an administrator's time to screen and assign cases, maintain records, process bills, control expenses, and perhaps obtain client-satisfaction reports and therefore does not work for more time-consuming, complex cases, which are better handled by staff attorneys of a legal-services program. The OEO originally rejected the judicare model as too expensive and unlikely to provide the aggressive, reform-minded advocates they were seeking.

Contracts with Private Attorneys. An LSC grantee may choose to handle certain types of cases by referring them to a contract attorney. For example, a grantee may choose a contract attorney to handle its landlord-tenant cases or to provide bilingual services. The contract-attorney system may be called a closed panel in that the attorney is selected by the LSC grantee to the exclusion of other attorneys. Judicare panels, by contrast, are generally open to any qualified member of the bar.

Interest on Lawyer Trust Accounts (IOLTA). Lawyers frequently hold a small amount of money for their clients for short periods of time and usually deposit it in short-term trust accounts at the bank. These do not bear interest because accounting costs for such small accounts exceed the interest. Since the 1950s the concept has developed that if all lawyers pooled these small amounts, the interest earned by the pooled account, net of service charges, could be used for charity.

Pooled accounts already existed in the Canadian provinces and five Australian states in 1978 when the Florida Supreme Court issued the first opinion approving an IOLTA program in the United States. Since then, more than two-thirds of the states have adopted some form of IOLTA. They differ greatly in whether the participation of lawyers is mandatory or voluntary and whether they are creatures of the state supreme court or legislature, but they all use the funds for pro bono legal-service projects. Examples of these projects are legal services for the poor, law-student loans and scholarships, and programs to improve the administration of justice. California and Maryland require IOLTA income to be used exclusively for legal aid, and many other states give substantial portions of it to legal aid. IOLTA income can reach several million dollars per year in large states with widespread participation of attorneys.

PROFILE OF A LEGAL-AID OFFICE

A well-run legal-aid office must use its monetary and human resources efficiently. The Legal Aid Society (LAS) of Cincinnati is such an office, and indication that this is true is apparent in a breakdown of the staff and administrators: 21 attorneys (including 2 litigation coordinators), 8 paralegals, 3 employees to screen phone requests for service (26,000 requests in 1984), 2 full-time receptionists, and 6 secretaries. Running the office are a director, an administrative secretary, administrator, assistant administrator, and word-processing manager. These LAS employees and 300 to 400 pro bono lawyers from the private bar serve three counties with a total of 148,000 people who are potentially eligible for representation. They operate out of a main office in downtown Cincinnati and one satellite office with 3 attorneys and a secretary in neighboring Clermont County. In the third, sparsely populated Brown County, private attorneys under contract with LAS provide the services.

Other indications of efficiency are careful planning of priorities and modern personnel-management systems. LAS has to allocate its resources carefully in order to cover the most important problems of clients. Every three years or so it has a retreat at which clients, staff, community organization members, social-agency employees, and client and attorney members of the LAS board of directors join discussion groups to identify community needs. The result is a statement of goals that is used as the basis for accepting cases and targeting resources. The primary goals since 1983 have been to help low-income people keep and upgrade the housing they now have and to increase the availability of decent, affordable housing generally; to help low-income people obtain and keep the income and health-care benefits now available and to increase the amounts and availability of benefits generally; and to help low-income people keep the jobs they have, to increase the job opportunities available to them, and to improve conditions in the workplace. LAS has organized teams of specialists for housing, income, and employment issues.

LAS salaries and raises are based on experience and position, and an evaluation system identifies employees' needs and weaknesses. Attorneys are expected to reach the status of senior attorney in five to six years or to be dismissed. In 1985, LAS had eight senior attorneys, but there is no limit on the number. Senior attorneys automatically become members of the legal-work committee, which oversees the legal work of the program. A management committee, with representatives from the support staff, paralegals, attorneys, and administration, advises the director on general operating policies. The director chairs both the management and legal-work committees.

Each employee is assigned a primary supervisor who evaluates him or her after the three-month probation period, again at six months, a year, and annually thereafter. During evaluation the primary supervisor posts a notice on the bulletin board asking for comments from co-workers. After collecting comments, the primary supervisor drafts an evaluation that includes recommendations for the employee's professional growth. After discussion the employee and the supervisor sign it, and a copy goes into the employee's file. The evaluation process provokes some disagreement, of course, but LAS is committed to it as the means to promote a high-quality program. Each employee has an individual work plan allocating time to types of work and to numbers of cases or intake appointments per week. The employee may draw up this plan for the supervisor's approval.

The legal-work committee oversees "impact projects." These seem similar to reform litigation programs of the OEO in the 1970s, which provoked much criticism, but they are less controversial. The committee chooses which of the litigation projects suggested by attorneys should be supported by LAS resources and then assigns attorneys to the projects. A litigation coordinator is assigned to each project. The role of the litigation coordinator varies, depending on the experience of other attorneys on the project. Projects have included a suit to get damages for former tenants of a sixty-six-unit complex who were unlawfully charged for utilities, a class action to lengthen the period during which a welfare recipient can protest a cutoff notice and still receive benefits, and assistance for a tenant group to organize itself as a job cooperative, which in fact successfully bid to provide janitorial services to a downtown building.

PREPAID LEGAL SERVICES

Prepaid legal services is a term used to describe many systems of delivering legal services, including plans for delivering legal services as an employee benefit; labor-union plans resulting from collective bargaining; legal-expense insurance sold to individuals or groups for coverage of specified legal services; and "access" plans, which include telephone advice and referrals and are often marketed by lawyers themselves as a means to increase business.

Prepaid legal plans did not develop as rapidly as the Blue Cross and Blue Shield medical plans, which have grown since World War II to become the most common type of employee benefit. There are several reasons for this. First, the need for visiting a lawyer is not always as urgent as the need for visiting a physician. Illness compels people to seek medical help, sometimes frequently, but the occasions when legal help is seen to be necessary might not occur at all: arrest, a summons to appear in court, divorce, bankruptcy, or purchase and sale of a home. Moreover, a do-it-yourself trend encourages some people not to visit an attorney when they should.

Another reason for the slow growth of prepaid legal services is the suspicion that lawyers will use the plans to escalate fees, as unions believe physicians do. To avoid this, legal plans were structured as "closed panels," with lawyers either on a salary working exclusively for plan members or under contract for specified services at a set fee. But setting up closed panels involved start-up costs and management problems, including compliance with federal government regulations for employee benefit plans under the Employee Retirement Income Security Act of 1974.

Finally, insurance companies faced opposition from state insurance commissioners and bar associations, both of which saw legal-expense insurance as being in conflict with their traditional regulatory schemes. The companies had difficulty predicting the cost of their policies because there was no data on the average fees lawyers charged for particular services. In spite of this, prepaid legal programs have begun to flourish.

The recent development of prepaid legal services may be divided into three periods: from 1963, when the Supreme Court established the right of a union to set up a legal-services plan, to 1970; the 1970s, when union plans developed closed-panel models for delivering services and insurance companies obtained legislation in many states to clarify the regulatory status of legal-expense insurance; and the 1980s, when emphasis was on growth, signaling the end of the experimental era and the availability of prepaid services to a significant percentage of the population. By the mid-1980s, prepaid or group legal services were available in some form to about 10 million people.

Employee Benefit Plans. Before unions and other employee groups could pool their resources and hire lawyers to serve their members, several obstacles had to be removed. Prior to 1963, disciplinary rules prohibited lawyers from taking payment from a group for the sole purpose of rendering service to individual group members. Early unsuccessful attempts by automobile clubs to set up legal-service plans were described above. The disciplinary rules prohibited the "corporate practice of law" and the intrusion of nonlawyers between group members and their lawyers. The Supreme Court, however, struck down the ban on group legal plans in a series of cases beginning in 1963: *National Association for the Advancement of Colored People* v. *Button* (1963); *Brotherhood of Railroad Trainmen* v. *Virginia State Bar* (1964); *United Mine Workers* v. *Illinois State Bar Association* (1967); and *United Transportation Union* v. *State Bar of Michigan* (1971). The Supreme Court in these cases upheld the right of a union (or a civil rights group) to hire an attorney to handle cases for its members, basing its decisions on the First Amendment freedoms of expression and association.

In the early 1970s other requirements for the smooth operation of union plans fell into place. The Taft-Hartley Act (Labor Management Relations Act of 1947) was amended to allow legal services to be given to union members in labor contracts in addition to medical and other benefits. State insurance laws were also held to be inapplicable to employee benefit plans. Without these changes, a state insurance commissioner could declare a union legal-services plan to be an insurance scheme and require the same investment surplus as insurance companies.

Finally, the tax laws were amended. The Internal Revenue Code exempted from taxation personal legal-service plans sponsored by employers or resulting from collective bargaining between employers and unions. Furthermore, the money employers paid into a legal-services trust fund could be excluded from income and thus escape taxation. The value of legal services used by employees and paid for by the trust would not then be regarded as taxable income received by the employee. This tax treatment paralleled that of medical benefit plans.

An experiment originally sponsored by the ABA and the Laborers' International Union (LIU) for six hundred construction workers in 1971, called the Shreveport Plan, allowed the workers to select any lawyer of their choice. The plan reimbursed the lawyer for usual, customary, and reasonable fees. However, the experiment failed, and nearly all union plans have chosen a system that restricts member choice to specified attorneys or law firms.

Early plans were financed only by members' dues. It remained for the municipal employees of New York City to establish the first large union plan that was paid for entirely by the employer. In 1978 the second large union plan, the UAW Legal Services Plan, began covering employees, their families, and retired workers of the Chrysler Corporation. The UAW eventually bargained for similar plans at General Motors, Ford, and American Motors, and the administrative office in Detroit supervised lawyers for more than 860,000 workers, their spouses, and dependents throughout the United States in 1985.

In an employee benefit plan, such as a UAW plan, the employer's commitment to pay money into a trust fund is the plan's sole source of funds. In contrast, in an insured plan, the financial resources of the insurance company stand behind the plan. If trust funds run out because of high usage of legal services, a plan might have to cease operation. To guard against this possibility, federal regulations require administrators to exercise prudence in spending trust funds. The trustees have responsibility for hiring attorneys and perhaps an administrator for the plan. Occasionally, the Department of Labor brings charges against trustees who have hired attorneys without fully checking their credentials or justifying the money they were paid.

Employee plans seldom cover all potential legal problems of members, and many cover little or no trial work. For example, business ventures of members and contingency-fee personal-injury cases are routinely excluded. Furthermore, plans do not cover disputes between union members and their employees.

Legal-Expense Insurance. When the Supreme Court said that union plans could operate with limited lists of lawyers, it left open the question whether insurance companies could do so. Ethical rules in most states still prohibit insurance companies from setting up such "closed panels." As profit-making businesses, insurance companies are considered more likely than unions to interfere with the lawyer-client relationship. Thus, they can reimburse, but not hire, attorneys to provide services to policyholders. Often the insurance company forms a panel of attorneys who agree to reduced fees, but the attorneys remain independent practitioners. Such "open panel" systems are not favored by unions, because they are expensive. Since unions are the largest source of prepaid legal services, insured plans have not flourished.

A chaotic regulatory atmosphere for legal-expense insurance has also limited the growth of insured legal-expense plans. Each state regulates insurance activity within its own borders. A state like New York has a high number of insurance company home offices that can affect legal-expense insurance greatly, yet even in the mid-1980s, New York permitted only experimental legal plans. Many other states were unclear exactly how to classify legal-expense insurance, with several allowing only casualty insurers to underwrite (sell) it and a minority of states allowing health, accident, and life insurers to underwrite it. Health, accident, and life insurers are most accustomed to selling to groups. Since the market for prepaid legal services has been mainly groups, those insurers were needed for promotion of legal-expense insurance.

During the 1970s most states refused to recognize a prepaid legal-expense plan as insurance at all. This was because they regarded many legal services as nonfortuitous; that is, the insured persons had too much power to decide when they needed legal services, especially services such as drafting a will, closing on the purchase of a house, filing for bankruptcy, and filing for divorce. Insurance, they said, is meant to cover fortuitous (unplanned) events, and the only truly fortuitous legal events were being sued or being arrested.

Bar associations were also unsuccessful when they tried to set up prepaid legal-services plans. The North Carolina bar, in particular, had to subsidize losses in its plans for several years in the 1970s. A notable exception was the Ohio Legal Services Fund, a trust set up in 1974 by the Ohio State Bar Association in cooperation with the city of Columbus for municipal employees. It is no longer affiliated with the bar association but remains a solvent open-panel plan paying usual, customary, and reasonable fees to lawyers. Its administrator during the early 1980s, David A. Baker, became a pioneer in developing computerized systems to help control costs.

Telephone Advice and Referral Plans. A few promoters in the 1970s realized that many people want to talk with a lawyer but not visit the lawyer's office. They formed organizations to market telephone advice and contracted with lawyers who would answer a toll-free telephone number. For a flat monthly fee, individuals or entire groups could purchase the right to use this toll-free number. Usually they also received the right to have a "simple will" drafted and to have a lawyer make telephone calls or write letters on their behalf. Sometimes, if further legal services were needed, the subscriber was referred to a cooperating lawyer in the community who agreed to charge reduced fees.

Because this minimal-service plan is relatively easy to set up, there are many such plans, which vary considerably. Insurance companies adopted telephone advice and referral as a device for screening insureds whose legal problems are not covered under the policy or are not legal problems at all. Some insurance companies and entrepreneurs successfully market telephone advice and referral service in mailings to credit-card holders or members of credit unions.

CONCLUSION

The feature that distinguishes private law offices and legal-service offices is that in the former attorneys receive fees for individual services but in the latter attorneys receive fixed salaries. It may be argued that in large private law firms, many associate attorneys also receive salaries, but most of these aspire to become partners and to receive a percentage of the fees collected by the firm. Both approaches are subject to criticism.

The fee-for-service model of private practice has been criticized as too expensive. In response, many private practitioners have begun to advertise fixed low fees for some relatively routine services, such as drafting simple wills, divorces, bankruptcies, probate work, and criminal misdemeanor cases. Some private practitioners have opened chains of law offices exclusively for handling these routine matters and employ lawyers on a salaried basis. In this respect, they begin to approximate prepaid legal-service-plan offices.

Since establishing a profitable law practice can take a long time, salaried positions would seem attractive to young lawyers, yet managers of legal-service offices have difficulty retaining young lawyers as employees. After a few years of doing repetitive tasks, young lawyers yearn for more challenging work. A related problem is the lack of independence each lawyer has. The lawyer works in a highly structured setting where procedures for handling client problems are set out in manuals. Creative solutions to litigation and other problems tend to be discouraged.

Management expertise is being developed whereby legal-service offices provide a challenge for attorneys, who in turn provide excellent client care. Ultimately, this expertise will be shared and contribute to a much wider availability of legal services for the poor and the middle class. The opportunity now exists for combining efficiency with quality legal care.

CASES

Argersinger v. Hamlin, 407 U.S. 25 (1972)
Brotherhood of Railroad Trainmen v. Virginia State Bar, 377 U.S. 1 (1964)
In re Gault, 387 U.S. 1 (1967)
Gideon v. Wainwright, 372 U.S. 335 (1963)
National Association for the Advancement of Colored People v. Button, 371 U.S. 415 (1963)
United Mine Workers v. Illinois State Bar Association, 389 U.S. 217 (1967)
United Transportation Union v. State Bar of Michigan, 401 U.S. 576 (1971)

BIBLIOGRAPHY

Roger D. Billings, *Prepaid Legal Services* (1981), is a treatise for lawyers, with chapters on ethics rules, lawyer advertising, unauthorized practice of law, the Employee Retirement Income Security Act, tax laws, insurance laws, and antitrust rulings. Barbara A. Curran, *The Legal Needs of the Public: The Final Report of a National Survey* (1977), is an oft-quoted national survey showing that relatively few Americans use legal services. Joel F. Handler, Ellen J. Hollingsworth, et al., *Lawyers and the Pursuit of Legal Rights* (1978), gives an in-depth evaluation of lawyer participation in various antipoverty programs. Earl Johnson, Jr., *Justice and Reform* (1975), assesses the legal-services movement from legal-aid societies to the first seven years of the OEO Legal Services Program.

Jack Katz, *Poor People's Lawyers in Transition* (1984), provides a historical discussion of what it was like to practice law for the poor in successive programs. Legal Services Corp., *Delivery Systems Study: A Research Project on the Delivery of Legal Services to the Poor* (1977), is a compendium of legal-service programs as of 1977. National Resource Center for Consumers of Legal Services, *Group Legal Service Plans* (1981), offers an introduction to prepaid legal services, followed by plan documents, statutes, and regulations. Werner Pfennigstorf and Spencer L. Kimball, *Legal Service Plans* (1981), is a collection of essays without index, containing useful legal and historical information about prepaid legal services. Harrison Tweed, *The Legal Aid Society of New York City* (1954), describes the formation and development of the first big-city legal-aid society.

[*See also* LEGAL PROFESSION AND LEGAL ETHICS *and* PUBLIC-INTEREST ADVOCACY.]

THE POLICE

Jerome E. McElroy

No component of the criminal justice network is better known to the public or the subject of more pervasive misunderstanding than the police. Much confusion and oversimplification flows from the widespread and mistaken belief that the purposes and operations of the police are clearly perceived by the average person.

In America, the police are a public institution charged with maintaining peace and order and providing a variety of services to the citizenry. They are expected to carry out their functions in a manner that is respectful of individual liberties and supportive of democratic values. Although federal, state, and local levels of government maintain police forces, the police function is most complex at the municipal level. Although the police are a part of the criminal justice network and thus influenced by the courts, prosecutors, and defense bar as well as by the correctional system, they are an independent agency of the executive branch of government, and much of their work has little directly to do with other criminal justice agencies.

It is estimated that in late 1981 there were more than 11,600 police agencies in the United States, the vast majority at the local level. These agencies employed approximately 502,000 persons, including 398,000 officers, who are sworn to uphold the Constitution and the laws of the states and municipalities they serve. As sworn personnel, they enjoy a special legal status (usually that of a peace officer) and are authorized to make arrests, carry weapons, and use force when it is necessary to enforce the law or to maintain order.

In 1979, $22.6 billion was expended by states and municipalities for criminal justice operations. Approximately half of that amount ($11.9 billion) was spent on law enforcement. While the police are universally identified as agents of the crime-control system, their actual work addresses a diversity of objectives. Herman Goldstein (1977) effectively states those objectives as follows:

1. To prevent and control conduct widely recognized as threatening to life and property (serious crime).
2. To aid individuals who are in danger of physical harm, such as the victim of a criminal attack.
3. To protect constitutional guarantees, such as the right of free speech and assembly.
4. To facilitate the movement of people and vehicles.
5. To assist those who cannot care for themselves; the intoxicated, the addicted, the mentally ill, the physically disabled, the old, and the young.
6. To resolve conflict, whether it be between individuals, groups of individuals, or individuals and their government.
7. To identify problems that have the potential for becoming more serious problems for the individual citizen, for the police or for government.
8. To create and maintain a feeling of security in the community.

(p. 35)

This formulation of the police function debunks the oversimplified belief that the police are merely law enforcement or crime-control agents. It also suggests connections between the police and public and private organizations outside the criminal justice network. Moreover, the relatively unspecific nature of some of these objectives hints at the extensive discretion exercised by the police in responding to situations brought to their attention. That discretion is affected by far more than the constitutional principles, statutes, and rules that regulate the investigation of criminal behavior and the processing of those charged with criminal offenses.

It is useful to view the police as performing a screening or diagnostic function with respect to a wide range of social problems. For each such problem, the police must decide whether to adopt a reactive or proactive posture; the circumstances under which intervention or non-intervention seems most appropriate; the objectives of immediate intervention and the long-term objectives to be pursued, if any; and the complex of public and private agencies that should be involved in effecting a final disposition.

Recognition of the enormous diversity of police responsibilities and the extensive discretion that is exercised in meeting those responsibilities is a fairly recent development among both police scholars and policymakers. From the early 1930s through the late 1960s, police administrators and scholars were more comfortable seeing the police as a neutral, ministerial law enforcement agency whose arena for discretionary action was severely circumscribed by statute and regulation. This image of mechanical law enforcement agents at first appears to insulate the police from the pressures and criticism of the political process. But the social unrest of the 1960s and the attention focused on crime and criminal justice concerns during the 1970s clearly revealed the multifaceted and discretionary nature of police work. This has greatly increased interest in how police agencies exercise and attempt to structure discretionary decision-making in their major functional areas.

The recognition of diversity and discretion also leads one to seek a common thread that distinguishes the police from other multipurpose public institutions. In *The Functions of the Police in Modern Society* (1980), Egon Bittner argues persuasively that the police are the only agents of a modern society given a general authorization to use force as a response to domestic problems.

> Many puzzling aspects of police work fall into place when one ceases to look at it as principally concerned with law enforcement and crime control, and only incidentally and often incongru-ously concerned with an infinite variety of other matters. It makes much more sense to say that the police are nothing else than a mechanism for the distribution of situationally justified force in society.
>
> (pp. 38–39)

Bittner is quick to point out that this conception is not meant to suggest that police officers are expected to use or threaten to use force in response to all the situations brought to their attention. In fact, it is expected that the actual use of force will be infrequent and proportionate to the opposing force when it is used. The point is rather that police intervention, whatever its form, is not to be opposed, and the police are generally authorized to use or threaten to use force to overcome such opposition when it is offered. Thus, asking what the police are supposed to do is identical to asking what kinds of situations require solutions that are "nonnegotiably coercible."

Two other elements of Bittner's conception need to be mentioned. He recognizes that people other than the police are sometimes authorized to use force. In defense of self, we are all permitted to use force. In addition, other special agents are authorized to use force against specific people under specific circumstances. Thus, prison personnel and hospital personnel are authorized to use force to ensure that court-ordered confinement is carried out. The police use of force to arrest a suspected criminal can be seen as an extension of this second form of authorization, but Bittner cautions against such thinking. It tends to reinforce the image of the police as merely a law enforcement agency and to tie the police use of force exclusively to that function. This not only offers an unrealistic view of what the police actually do but also stimulates the tendency to reduce all police problems to matters of criminal culpability best handled by applying the methods of criminal procedure. Such a reduction involves serious distortion of reality and procedure. For Bittner, it is essential to recognize that the authority of the police to use force is general and "essentially unrestricted" and that "their ability to arrest offenders is incidental to their authority to use force" (p. 38).

We shall now examine more closely the major police functions. For that purpose, it is useful to aggregate the more specific functions set forth by Goldstein into the following three categories: crime control, service, and order maintenance.

THE CRIME-CONTROL FUNCTION

The crime-control function of the police is the familiar one. It identifies the public expectation that the police should prevent and control the volume of crime in society and thereby ensure the public's sense of safety.

There are many different types of criminal behavior to which the police are expected to respond. Some of them are easy to define and fairly universally condemned. This is generally true of the conventional forms of street crime—homicide, rape, robbery, assault, burglary, auto theft, and larceny.

The police are also expected to deal with the problem of white-collar crime (typically, acts of fraud or embezzlement committed by professionals or business people in violation of public trust). These crimes of the economically comfortable are generally nonviolent but can result in the loss to the public of great sums of money. The detection, investigation, and prosecution of these offenses is often difficult and technically demanding. With the exception of large police agencies that can afford to develop specialization in these areas, most municipal police agencies are ill-equipped to attack this type of crime very effectively. With these considerations in mind, municipal police officials often make a minimum commitment of resources to this area, concentrating their attention on the major forms of street crime. While that judgment seems quite reasonable in light of limited resources and technical obstacles to success, it is seen by some as symbolic of uneven enforcement of the law across class lines.

There are also numerous victimless crimes that the police are expected to suppress. These include such activities as gambling, public intoxication, the use of drugs and alcoholic beverages by adults, the use and sale of pornography, and participation in various forms of prohibited sexual behavior. More often than not, there is a lack of consensus among the general public on whether these acts should be prohibited by law, what precise forms of behavior should be prohibited, what priority should be given by the police to these concerns, and what tactics should be used in enforcement. The lack of public consensus makes police decisions in this area almost inevitably controversial and can expose particular police departments and/or their chiefs to political criticism. As a result, departmental policies regarding victimless offenses vary substantially from one agency to another and tend to be politically volatile over time within any given agency.

In sum, then, the crime-control function requires the police to develop policies and procedures for dealing with many different types of criminal behavior. The capacity of police agencies to deal with white-collar crime is uneven, and their policies and procedures for dealing with victimless offenses tend to be volatile. In this context, both the expectations of the public and the inclinations of the police tend to equate the crime-control function with the suppression of conventional street crime.

Society has not always relied on the police to control the volume and types of crime. Most scholars trace the origins of the modern, urban police agency to the London Metropolitan Police Force, established by Sir Robert Peel in 1829. Prior to that time, watchmen warned of public disorders, and private citizens were responsible for protecting themselves and their property. A victim of theft was himself responsible for investigating the crime and identifying a suspect. If he succeeded in this effort, he might enlist the help of a constable in arresting the suspect and securing the property. He could then bring the person before the equivalent of a civil court and sue to recover the property. People of wealth and commercial organizations could sometimes hire private detectives to perform these functions for them, and thus the rich were thought to be privileged with respect to personal security.

The disorder and growing volume of urban crime in the English and American cities of the early nineteenth century created pressure for a more effective, honest, and reliable mechanism of control. At the same time, there was widespread fear that a formal police force would quickly become corrupt, powerful, and overly intrusive in the lives of the citizens. This last consideration produced constraints in England and America on the use of the police as a crime-preventive mechanism and especially on the use of covert methods to surveil private persons. Thus, the Metropolitan Police Force was trained to be courteous to the public, always deployed in uniform with truncheons removed from public view, and instructed to be reactive to crime complaints and service requests rather than to aggressively seek out criminal conditions and behavior.

The general British distrust of a public domestic police force was shared in the United States, so it is not surprising that the English system served as a model for American invention. The first American agency was established in New York City in 1845. Boston and Philadelphia established their own agencies quickly thereafter, and by 1855, municipal police forces had sprung up throughout the East and the Midwest. These agencies also emphasized reactive crime-control strategies, and their visibility and availability led to their increasing involvement in providing emergency services.

The nineteenth-century police forces did not wholly eliminate reliance on private protection and detective services. As anyone familiar with the history of the union movement in the United States knows, large private protection agencies were prominently involved with public order and disorder well into the twentieth century. Moreover, in their early years, public agencies were privately supported when performing investigative functions. Even today, community-based organizations engage in activities designed to prevent and control crime, often in conjunction with the police. Nevertheless, by the early part of the twentieth century, American cities had come to rely heavily on public police agencies for investigating criminal incidents and bringing those responsible before the courts.

From the 1930s through the mid-1970s, crime fighting became the character-defining function of the police both in the eyes of the public and in the vision of progressive police leaders. This development was aided by technological advances in transportation and communications. It was also furthered by the appearance in the 1930s of statistical reports that presented both the public and general government officials with an apparent means of measuring police productivity and performance. Indeed, the symbol of the modern police department came to be the well-equipped team of police officers in a patrol car moving quickly to a crime scene in response to a radio dispatch from a central communications officer.

In the late 1970s, national surveys of crime victimization rates provided what are believed to be more-accurate assessments of crime volume and an additional impetus to focus police priorities on combating conventional forms of street crime. Moreover, the 1970s witnessed a substantial commitment of federal funds to support improvements in policing and the operation of the criminal justice network generally. The Law Enforcement Assistance Administration (LEAA) was created by Congress in 1968 to assist states and municipalities in improving their capacity to control crime and administer the criminal justice process in an effective and efficient manner. The policy emphasis of LEAA, especially in the early 1970s, was on effecting real reductions in the volume of street crime in major urban areas. One of its products was the National Advisory Commission on Criminal Justice Standards and Goals, which produced documents articulating goals and standards for each component of the criminal justice system.

The police adopt two general strategic approaches to the performance of their crime-control function. The first stresses apprehension and incapacitation of criminal offenders; the second seeks to prevent crime through patrol activities.

Theoretically, to the extent that the apprehension strategy succeeds, the police contribute to the control of crime by helping to incarcerate or otherwise incapacitate criminal offenders and thereby prevent them from committing additional criminal acts. Theoretically, this strategy can bring about actual declines in the volume of crime if the number of people incapacitated exceeds the number newly embarking on criminal careers or if the people who are incapacitated would otherwise account for a disproportionate amount of criminal behavior. The first alternative stresses large numbers of arrests and convictions, whereas the second, currently known as selective incapacitation, stresses the arrest and conviction of people who are likely to be high-rate offenders ("career criminals").

A successful policy of arrests and incapacitation may help achieve crime-control goals in yet another way. It can create an impression that criminal behavior is very likely to be detected and punished, thereby making the police and the criminal justice system a credible deterrent to such behavior.

THE POLICE

The basic operations that implement the apprehension and incapacitation strategy are reasonably well known. They include providing easy access for the citizenry to report crimes to the police; ensuring a rapid police response when a report is received, especially if the crime is still in progress; attempting to apprehend the suspect as soon as possible after the crime is committed; protecting physical evidence at the crime scene; moving quickly to collect testimonial evidence from people who may have witnessed the crime or related events that might help in the subsequent investigation; conducting the investigation while the evidence is still fresh and managing the investigation to ensure persistence and continuity, especially during the first several days after the crime is committed; making sure that the investigative and arrest procedures comply with all constitutional requirements so that all incriminatory evidence is admissible in court; carefully preparing the case for presentation to the prosecutor; and cooperating with the prosecutor during the disposition process.

Since the early 1970s, most police departments have introduced new technologies and have changed procedures in an effort to implement this process more effectively. Many municipalities have introduced a simple emergency telephone number (usually 911) to contact the police. Typically, calls are received and dispatched centrally to motorized police units that are moving about designated sectors of the municipality. Computerized dispatching systems enable dispatchers to monitor the location and activity of these units and to assign the call to the unit that is positioned to respond most quickly. The same dispatching systems can be used to assess priorities among incoming calls and ensure that the most important calls are responded to first. In many departments, regular patrol officers have been trained to protect the crime scene, and teams of evidence specialists have been created to examine the scene thoroughly and protect physical evidence when it is secured. Advances have been made in analyzing evidence and improving its quality for admission in court. Techniques have been developed to improve the management of investigations by detectives and the preparation of cases for presentation to the prosecutor. Training programs have been designed for both patrol and detective personnel to improve the constitutional adequacy of the investigative and case-preparation process. Finally, a variety of special programs have been undertaken to help police officers and prosecutorial personnel to understand each other better and to cooperate more fully in the prosecution process.

Even more recently, some of the major urban police departments have established career-criminal units to maximize their contribution to the selective-incapacitation strategy. This strategy is based on the premise that people who are likely to be high-rate serious offenders over the course of a criminal career can be identified and accorded special treatment by various agents of the criminal justice network to increase the likelihood of conviction and long-term incarceration. Typically, computerized criminal-history systems are used to identify the high-rate offenders, sometimes with supplemental information from other criminal justice agencies. Most of these programs were begun on the initiative of prosecutors. However, some police agencies have attempted to tie into this strategy by creating units of investigators who, when supplied with a list of predicted high-rate offenders, either surveil these persons in the hope of catching them in the commission of a criminal act or devote special efforts to strengthening the case and increasing the probability of conviction and incarceration when candidate offenders are arrested. Some units use both tactics.

These career-criminal programs of the police are recent developments, and the returns from evaluative research are not yet in. There is evidence to indicate that improved case preparation efforts can increase the proportion of cases resulting in convictions and incarcerative sentences. Nevertheless, some observers think that long-term success is unlikely, and others have expressed concern about the tactics that might be used by police in surveilling individuals before specific complaints have been registered against them. The technical reservations usually flow from the belief that even relatively high-rate offenders spend only a small portion of their waking hours actually committing crimes and then usually with some effort to conceal them from public observation. Therefore, it is unlikely that surveillance teams will catch the person in the act. Such surveillance is invariably an expensive tactic to use.

Constitutional reservations take several

forms. In the first place, critics point out that the methods used to predict high-rate offenders are generally unreliable and tend to overpredict in a high proportion of the cases. Second, the surveillance tactics used by the police may be somewhat intrusive and thereby constitute harassment. Finally, police who are intent upon arresting a person in anticipation of future crimes may be severely tempted to engage in tactics that amount to entrapment. It is likely that all these concerns will be the subject of continuing debate as the criminal justice community acquires more experience with the career-criminal strategy.

The police also seek to control crime through a strategy of preventive patrol. The drive toward police professionalism, begun in the 1930s, stressed, among other things, the rational deployment of patrol resources to prevent the occurrence of conventional street crime. Toward that end, statistics are kept to determine where and when these types of crime are concentrated. The allocation and deployment of patrol resources is based in part on these patterns. The patrol officers are then instructed to move about their assigned sectors as much as possible to create an impression of police omnipresence and of high risks of apprehension for criminal violations. The preventive-patrol rationale is a further expansion of deterrence theory in that it seeks to increase the actual or perceived risk of apprehension.

The consensus of police officials regarding the efficacy of preventive patrol as a crime-control strategy was shaken profoundly by the research of the middle and late 1970s. Before commenting on that research, however, we shall consider what is involved in the service function of the police.

THE SERVICE FUNCTION

In the urban environment, no public agency is as available to the citizenry, or so frequently called upon to assist in as wide a variety of situations, as the police. Injured persons, medical emergencies, injured or threatening animals, missing persons, homeless children, school emergencies, heating crises, and fires are merely a few of the dozens of situations in which the police are called for assistance.

It seems likely that urban police agencies have always performed this service function; however, the volume of these calls for service has increased substantially since 1970. The widespread establishment of a simple emergency call number has contributed greatly to this trend. By the early 1980s, the New York City Police Department was receiving annually more than 6.5 million calls over the emergency 911 system; a large proportion of these was from citizens in need of some form of service.

Some observers have suggested that the increase in calls for service may also reflect greater social disorganization, especially in the neighborhoods of the urban poor. They point out that the poor are often dependent on the police for services that, in more affluent neighborhoods, are unnecessary or can be provided by other agencies. If so, improved communications have certainly made it easier for citizens to request those services from the police.

This development is not an unmixed blessing in the eyes of police officials. Although the central number was installed for emergency purposes, it quickly became the primary means by which the public seeks police assistance with every kind of request. Some police officials complain that they are now expected to respond to certain situations that should be the responsibility of other public agencies. Whatever the appropriateness of police involvement, the enormous volume of calls puts a considerable strain on the patrol resources available for response. This in turn has led to differential response strategies in many urban police departments. These strategies require the classification of incoming calls according to the type of police response required. High priority is generally accorded to calls pertaining to personal injury, crimes in progress, and a police officer in need of assistance. Normally, one or more police units are dispatched to respond as quickly as possible. Calls of lesser priority may result in setting an appointment for a later visit from the police or for the citizen's coming into the police building, or they may be handled entirely over the phone.

These differential response systems were developed in the later 1970s. In part, they reflect the practical impossibility of dispatching a patrol unit on every call received. But they also reflect two important research findings of that decade. It is now widely understood that the vast majority of calls involve non-crime-related and non-emergency service needs and that rapid police response is likely to influence outcome only in emergency situations such as crimes in progress. These research findings freed police officials from the belief that all calls must be responded to in the same way and from the use of response time as a universally relevant indicator of performance. This has provided an empirical justification for developing and testing differential response systems. Nevertheless, acceptance of such systems is likely to be tentative until the citizenry understands that not all calls require an immediate police presence in response.

The debate over what services should and should not be the responsibility of police agencies continues. It is widely agreed that any situation that involves the commission or threat of a crime, might require the use or threat of use of force to resolve, or poses a threat to life or property is indisputably a police responsibility. There is no unanimity of opinion with respect to other situations and service needs. Other public or private agencies may be better prepared to respond to such situations even though the initial call is to the police. This suggests that the police could serve as the hub of a service referral network, sorting out citizen calls and calling on more-appropriate agencies to respond either immediately or after the police bring calm to the situation. Such referrals are made informally by almost all police agencies; however, few, if any, have developed a structure for systematically performing this role.

Not only does referral expand the level of demand on police agencies, but it may also involve them in serving as an ombudsman to other public agencies. For example, urban police often receive calls for assistance from impoverished families who are freezing in their residences and in need of immediate help. When they answer the call, they may discover an apartment in which the heating and water systems are inoperative and in which the residents are inadequately clothed and fed and require various forms of medical attention. In response, the police might move the family to a temporary shelter and then refer the case to the welfare, housing, and public health departments for various services. They might even follow up on these referrals to make sure that the families' needs are attended to effectively. This role would require the police to continue their involvement with the case and expend a good deal more time and resources than is usually the case. Moreover, to the extent that they follow up referrals, they may be forced to judge the services of other agencies and prod them to better efforts. Many police administrators are reluctant to assume that level of responsibility and potential vulnerability.

THE ORDER-MAINTENANCE FUNCTION

In addition to enforcing criminal laws and providing the citizenry with needed services, the police are expected to help maintain the public order. Order-maintenance activities are the most ambiguous obligations of the police. As James Q. Wilson indicated in his important work, *Varieties of Police Behavior*,

> By "order" is meant the absence of disorder, and by disorder is meant behavior that either disturbs or threatens to disturb the public peace or that involves face-to-face conflict among two or more persons. Disorder, in short, involves a dispute over what is "right" or "seemly" conduct or over who is to blame for conduct that is agreed to be wrong or unseemly.
>
> (p. 16)

Ambiguity and discretion are the defining characteristics of the order-maintenance function. Indeed, it is not always easy to distinguish order-maintenance from law enforcement activities. In fact, the criminal law is one of the tools that the police will use in attempting to handle order-maintenance problems. Yet, in this area, the law tends to be more vague and ambiguous. As Wilson points out,

> Most criminal laws define *acts* (murder, rape, speeding, possessing narcotics), which are held to be illegal; people may disagree as to whether the act should be illegal, as they do with respect to narcotics, for example, but there is little disagreement as to what the behavior in question consists of. Laws regarding disorderly conduct and the like assert, usually by implication, that there is a *condition* ("public order") that can be diminished by various actions. The difficulty, of course, is that public order is nowhere defined and can never be defined unambiguously be-

cause what constitutes order is a matter of opin-ion and convention, not a state of nature. . . . An additional difficulty, a corollary of the first, is the impossibility of specifying, except in the ex-treme case, what degree of disorder is intoler-able and who is to be held culpable for that degree.

(pp. 21–22)

Since the early 1980s, the order-maintenance function of the police has received a great deal of attention from police scholars and police offi-cials. The reasons for this attention are many. As previously mentioned, police research in the 1970s challenged the assumptions on which the strategy of random preventive patrol was based. From October 1972 through October 1973, the Police Foundation conducted what has come to be known as the Kansas City Patrol Experiment (Kelling et al., 1974). It was designed to test the effect of random preventive patrol on crime, citi-zen fear, and community attitudes toward the police. Fifteen matched areas were selected for the experiment. In the five "control" areas, the normal level of patrol was left unchanged; in five other areas, preventive patrols were removed, so that officers entered these areas only in response to specific calls for service. Finally, in the five "proactive" areas, the level of preventive patrol was doubled or tripled. The most significant finding of the research was that "the overwhelm-ing evidence is that decreasing or increasing rou-tine preventive patrol within the range tested in this experiment had no effect on crime, citizen fear of crime, community attitudes toward the police or on the delivery of police service, re-sponse time or traffic accidents."

This research, although subject to some criti-cism and considerable debate about its implica-tions, had a profound impact on thinking about future directions for urban policing. If nothing else, it suggested that police officials need not feel bound to random patrol deployment pat-terns. That suggestion has spawned a number of specialized patrol programs targeted at particu-lar types of crimes that tend to occur in specific times and places. As of 1986, the research results on these efforts were incomplete, although there is some evidence that directed, aggressive patrol tactics may deter certain forms of street crime (Wilson and Boland). The research has also pro-duced greater experimentation with different types of patrol tactics. In short, it has led police officials to look for other ways in which to reduce crime and citizen fear.

Police reliance on general preventive patrol has been challenged for other reasons as well. Observers of the criminal justice arena have noted that the volume of conventional street crime in most urban areas continued to climb throughout the 1970s, despite the fact that the number of police officers and the volume of ar-rests also increased sharply, especially over the first half of the decade. Moreover, additional re-search has shown that the level of public fear of crime is not a direct result of the actual volume of such crime but appears to be affected even more strongly by people's perception of dis-order and incivility in their immediate environ-ments.

A careful look at the development of patrol operations since the early 1970s suggests a growing distance between the officers in the street and the residents of the neighborhoods they are expected to serve. Most scholars agree that this distance is, at least in part, an unin-tended consequence of the increasing mobiliza-tion of the patrol force. Officers in patrol cars responding to a series of unconnected calls are neither known by the people nor personally ac-cessible to them. Nor do those officers have an opportunity to develop familiarity with the pecu-liar problems, cultural characteristics, social con-cerns, and organizational resources of the neighborhoods they patrol. The ever-increasing volume of calls for service and reduced police resources in financially strapped cities serve to reduce even further the involvement of the po-lice in the daily life of the neighborhoods. In many areas, the problems of disorder have multi-plied in a context of public inattention.

Finally, some researchers have suggested that alleviating order-maintenance problems (or quality-of-life conditions, as they are also known) will not only reduce citizen fear but may also reduce the actual volume of crime in the streets. James Q. Wilson and George Kelling likened or-der-maintenance problems to broken windows that are left unattended. Such windows are a sign that no one cares and are thus an invitation to more mischief. After a few days, more windows will be broken and the building will begin to deteriorate. Unless that condition is corrected quickly, blight will descend on the whole neighborhood.

On the other side of the analogy, Wilson and Kelling also argued that problems of disorder and incivility have been generally ignored by urban police departments since the early 1970s. The festering presence of these problems has demoralized residents, reduced the use of streets and public areas, encouraged commercial entities and residents with some financial reserves to pull out of neighborhoods, and left entire communities to the predations of street criminals.

COMMUNITY POLICING

Many police scholars and administrators have focused attention on the development of community-oriented patrol strategies. The major reasons for doing so include a loss of confidence in the efficacy of random preventive patrol as a deterrent to street crime; recognition of the need to address problems of disorder to reduce citizens' fear and increase their sense of security; a belief in the relatedness of crime problems and conditions of disorder; a realization that strategies for addressing both sets of problems must be developed in the context of varied conditions and resources on the neighborhood level; and a realization that effective control of both crime and order-maintenance problems requires the active involvement of neighborhood residents and organizations.

Since the 1970s, community policing projects have been implemented in a number of communities across the nation. In some cases, the officers patrol on foot; in others, they are motorized. In some projects, the special patrol operations are carried out by single police officers, and in others, they are the responsibility of units of varying sizes. In some cases, the patrol sergeant is the principal decision-maker; other projects vest a considerable degree of discretion and decision-making responsibility in the individual patrol officer. In short, there is a fair amount of variety in the operations and structures that characterize such projects.

Community policing strategies typically emphasize the units' developing substantial knowledge about each neighborhood's problems, cultural characteristics, and organizational resources. Community policing entails continuity of unit assignment to specific neighborhoods. Stress is placed on each unit's making itself known to the people in the neighborhood and soliciting citizen involvement in analyzing and addressing local problems. Units are held responsible for dealing with both street crime and order-maintenance problems in the neighborhood and are expected to develop and apply problem-solving strategies until problems are alleviated.

The movement toward community policing has been given impetus by the demands of the order-maintenance function, but it is also emerging as a broad strategy for organizing the service and crime-control functions on the neighborhood level. Research on the actual operations and effects of community policing programs is just beginning. The Newark Foot Patrol Experiment conducted by the Police Foundation (1981) was found to have no discernible impact on reported crime levels, but it did reduce the fear of crime and enhance the sense of safety enjoyed by residents in the experimental neighborhoods. Evaluation research conducted in Flint, Michigan, revealed that a foot-patrol program had a significant suppressing effect on reported crime levels, substantially reduced calls to the central communications network, and had the desired impact on fear of crime among the citizenry (Trojanowicz). Reports on the COPE program in Baltimore County describe the unit's success in identifying, studying, and resolving neighborhood crime problems, much to the satisfaction of the people residing in those neighborhoods (Cordner and Hayeslys).

Despite the general enthusiasm for the principles of community policing and the fact that participating officers seem to find the work more satisfying than conventional patrol, there are a number of issues that require careful consideration. Much more needs to be done to describe what police officers actually do in community policing operations. The effects of specific problem-solving strategies in relation to various characteristics of the neighborhoods in which they are implemented must be studied systematically. Wilson and Kelling's hypothesis that effectively addressing order-maintenance problems will result in reduced levels of conventional street crime should be tested empirically. And there is a need to identify the types of prior experience and training that prepare officers for effective performance of community-policing roles.

ACCOUNTABILITY OF THE POLICE

Community policing as a policy raises questions that go beyond its efficacy as a means of defining problems and delivering service. The issue of accountability comes quickly to mind. In responding to an individual call for service, the police are accountable, in some measure, to the person making the request. Collectively, a police agency is accountable to the executive branch of government for a certain amount of policy direction and for effective and efficient delivery of police services. Public dissatisfaction with police efforts can affect the chief executive's entire plan for governing the municipality, as well as his or her chances for reelection. In this way, the police are accountable to the general electorate.

In a sense, police agencies are accountable to the laws and ordinances of the states and municipalities in which they operate. By defining what is illegal, the law identifies situations in which the police are expected to intervene and suggests objectives for this action. It is this understanding of accountability that the police invoke when they describe themselves as neutral ministers of the law with little discretion to exercise in performing their duties.

As indicated earlier, however, this image distorts reality. In fact, the law is not uniformly applied. The police do, and must, exercise discretion in distinguishing between those laws which will be the subject of aggressive enforcement initiatives and those which will be enforced only in response to specific citizen complaints. In addition, agency policy also informs what the police do when they intervene. For example, for many years most large police agencies attempted to calm the parties involved in an incident of family violence and to mediate some agreement designed to prevent an immediate repeat of the assault. More recently, however, in response to considerable protest from feminist organizations and the findings of a Police Foundation research project (Sherman et al., 1983), many agencies have changed policies so as to make arrest on a charge of assault the presumptive tactic in such situations.

Policies regarding when and when not to intervene and what to do when intervening are not generally the result of arbitrary decision-making by the police agency. They reflect the influence of the policies and attitudes of the executive and legislative branches of government; the perception of how particular kinds of cases are likely to be treated by the prosecution and the courts and of what the general public expects; a balancing of the resources required under alternative policy options against the resources that the agency is likely to have available in the near future; and the philosophical, moral, and social positions of the agency's administrators.

In some of its forms, community policing would formally introduce the varying needs, values, and social structures of different neighborhoods into the policymaking process. Community policing suggests that the intervention, enforcement, and tactical decisions of the police should be influenced by the needs and desires of the local community. It is argued that this kind of policymaking would reduce the distance between the police and the people, especially residents of poor, minority neighborhoods, and would enable the police to work directly with the people in improving the quality of life in the neighborhood.

Although there is not likely to be much disagreement on the general desirability of community-sensitive policing, the structures and processes created to achieve it could be controversial. Some large urban police departments are already structurally decentralized to some degree. For example, the New York City Police Department is run by a civilian police commissioner assisted by several deputy commissioners who are also civilians. Below the commissioner, headquarters consists of a number of uniformed chiefs responsible for various divisions and offices, and the people under their command. They are the ones primarily responsible for departmental policy, regulation, and oversight. Operationally, the department is divided into five separate borough commands, each headed by an assistant chief, and seventy-five separate precincts, each commanded by a captain or deputy inspector. The precincts vary tremendously in the size of the residential population and the geographical area for which they are responsible. (Precincts with populations over 100,000 are common.) They vary also by land-use patterns, character of commercial enterprises, and the racial, ethnic, and socioeconomic characteristics of the residents. Indeed, there is a great deal of this diversity within many of the precincts themselves.

Whether a department is entirely centralized or as decentralized as the New York Police Department, community policing raises questions about how the community should be defined and what structures and processes, if any, should be created in the community and in the department to facilitate exchange between the community and the police. Decisions must also be made regarding what areas of policy and procedure should be subjects for dialogue and community input; what should be done to reconcile the expectations of a community with those of the department's central command if they come into conflict; and, finally, what influence, if any, the community should have on the personnel policies and practices of the department.

These issues are addressed, either explicitly or implicitly, by all police departments. They are not peculiar to those departments which are attempting to incorporate the principles of community policing. Nor is it suggested here that these issues cannot be dealt with effectively. It does seem, however, that community policing focuses a department and a municipality more sharply on issues of this sort. Thus, a good deal more will be heard about them in the future as more departments take on the trappings of community policing.

CONTROLLING POLICE BEHAVIOR

The issue of accountability leads directly to the question of how society seeks to control the behavior of police officials. This is a particularly sensitive issue in a democratic society because, as we have seen, the police are a societal agent authorized to use, or threaten to use, force in handling situations brought to their attention. Moreover, the United States' egalitarian ethos generates special concern that the police use of power be open, justifiable, and evenhanded. Finally, the American system of criminal justice provides constitutional assurances that the civil liberties of the individual will not be abused by zealous police investigations.

Three kinds of police misbehavior are of major concern: violating the civil liberties of accused persons, corrupt behavior, and excessive use of force. The methods used in attempts to control these types of behavior differ somewhat.

During the 1960s, Supreme Court decisions in a series of criminal-procedure cases expanded the scope and content of the rights of people brought to court on criminal charges. The rights of the accused to effective legal representation, to avoid self-incrimination, and to be secure from illegal police searches of person or property were strengthened by these decisions. The principal means by which the Court attempted to control police misbehavior in these areas was articulated in *Mapp* v. *Ohio* (1961). In that case, the Court ruled that evidence obtained as a result of police behavior that violated the individual's rights would not be admissible in a state criminal proceeding brought against that person. The Court was actually extending to the states an "exclusionary" rule that had been operative in the federal system for half a century. Nevertheless, the ruling was greeted by some police officials and other commentators as an unjustifiable piece of judicial activism that would greatly limit the ability of the police to investigate serious crime and to effectively prepare cases for prosecution. Others argued that the exclusionary rule had not adversely affected federal law enforcement during its decades of operation prior to *Mapp* and that it did check police investigative abuse, while actually affecting the dispositional outcome of only a handful of cases. The rule remains quite controversial.

Perhaps because of the controversy attending these criminal-procedure decisions, there is a widespread tendency to view the courts as the control mechanism for police misbehavior. Although such decisions certainly influence police behavior, it is clear that they do not control it. To begin with, the decisions have a direct effect only if the police intend to have the suspect prosecuted in the courts. Of course, there are a great many situations in which criminal prosecution is not an intended end of police intervention and others in which it is unlikely for a variety of reasons having nothing to do with the fine points of criminal procedure. In such instances, the threat of inadmissibility would appear to have little relevance to the behavior of the police.

It is important to note, in addition, that the courts have no capacity to supervise police behavior or to reward or punish it directly. And, of course, there are ways in which police officers can make their behavior appear to be in perfect compliance with applicable laws and regulations, so that considerable litigation skills and resources would be needed to reveal actual violations. Neither are universally available to those brought before the criminal courts.

For all these reasons, court review of police practices is important to ensure the rights of the individual defendant, but it is neither reliable nor effective as a method for controlling police misbehavior in investigating, arresting, and processing criminal suspects. Genuine respect for the civil liberties of suspects requires that police agencies make the spirit of the constitutional protections a value to be served by each agency and that they then structure their systems of reward, punishment, and supervision to reflect that value.

Public concern over police behavior that violates the civil liberties of suspects is not often intense. This undoubtedly reflects the lack of public identification with, and sympathy for, those charged with criminal offenses. At times, when large numbers of middle-class citizens become involved with the criminal justice system, public expressions of concern with this type of police misbehavior increase.

Corruption, in contrast, is an object of more constant public sensitivity. *Corruption* here refers to the practice of police officials using, or refusing to use, their authority in exchange for special favors that are personally beneficial to them. Police corruption is prohibited both by law and by departmental regulations, and virtually every department of even moderate size conducts regular field audits designed to deter such behavior and to investigate and prosecute it when it is found.

Many larger police departments tend to focus their anticorruption efforts especially on those units involved with enforcement of public morals laws related to gambling, prostitution, and narcotics. These areas are often characterized by a lack of public consensus on what should be prohibited and how vigorously the offending behavior should be penalized. In addition, in major metropolitan areas, huge sums of money are involved in these criminal enterprises. Thus, the opportunities for corruption available to units operating in these areas are considerable. To limit exposure to those opportunities, many larger agencies prohibit regular patrol and investigative staffs from engaging in proactive enforcement in these areas and instead establish special units for that purpose.

Of course, corruption opportunities are not confined to the public morals arena. The work of the regular patrol force may also be distorted by corrupt influences. Moreover, many police administrators believe that if the department's intolerance of corruption is not seen by the patrol force as absolute, a permissive attitude toward low-level corrupt behavior will develop rapidly. Under such circumstances, the department may lose the moral ground needed for effectively controlling more serious forms of corruption. It is this thinking that leads some departments to forbid even the acceptance of a cup of coffee from the proprietor of the local diner and to publicly condemn such behavior when it occurs.

The movement to professionalize policing begun in the 1930s and led by O. W. Wilson in the 1950s was in part a reaction against corrupt practices and lax management in large police agencies of the time. Motorizing patrol officers, rotating working shifts, and breaking continuity in the assignment of officers to particular units and neighborhoods were policies intended not only to increase efficiency but also to reduce familiarity and special relationships between the officers and the public. The latter were thought to increase the likelihood of corrupt behavior. Today, such concepts lead some police administrators to look with caution on the movement toward community policing, which seeks to increase and strengthen interaction and familiarity between the police and the community and which may thereby increase opportunities for corruption among the regular patrol force. Others welcome the movement, arguing that the proposed openness and intensity of interaction between the police and the community will make it less likely that corrupt activities will go undiscovered.

Preventing the use of excessive force is a particularly difficult matter because it does not lend itself to absolutist definitions and monitoring systems. The threat of force is inherent in the vast majority of police contacts with the public. Thus, while a department may condemn absolutely corrupt behavior, it cannot take a similar stand with respect to the use of force. Instead, the appropriateness of the decision to use force and the nature and extent of the force employed must be judged in an almost limitless number of differing situations. Departmental control mechanisms consist of policies, guidelines, and review procedures that go into effect after force has been used or after a complaint about its unnecessary use or threat of use has been received.

It is possible to distinguish several situations in which force or its threatened use is problematic. The first and most notorious involves the use of deadly force. The concern of the public, as well as of police and general government officials, over the use of deadly force grew sharply in the wake of the protests of the 1960s. As a result of that concern, almost all departments now have policies and guidelines that are designed to restrict severely the use of deadly force. The strictest of these guidelines indicates that deadly force is permissible only when the officer is acting in defense of his or her own life or the life of someone else immediately threatened. Some departments still permit their officers to fire their weapons at a fleeing felon, but the trend seems to be to prohibit such action unless the felon poses a threat to the officer or someone else. In most major urban areas, department officials are particularly concerned about firing at fleeing felons because of the likelihood that innocent bystanders will be hit by a stray shot or ricochet.

All major police departments also have procedures for reviewing shooting incidents, whether or not they result in death. If the finding of such a review is that the use of force was unjustified, the officer can be turned over for prosecution. In fact, if there is some credible suggestion that the shooting was not justifiable, it is more likely that the prosecutor will assert original jurisdiction and direct the subsequent investigation. Most large departments reserve the right to review the case against departmental regulations, even if the criminal process results in the officer's acquittal. Actually, very few cases of police shootings ending in death result in criminal convictions.

Although instances of the use of deadly force are the most serious and the most dramatic, they are relatively infrequent and are not the kinds of cases that pose the greatest challenge to departmental control systems. Force is also used to overcome resistance to lawful orders of police officers responding to a crime call or attempting to correct an order-maintenance problem. Police guidelines typically recognize the likelihood of such situations arising in the normal course of patrol and recommend that alternative responses be tried before force is invoked and that if force is necessary, only the minimum needed to overcome resistance or stabilize the situation be used. Instances of this kind are often accompanied by an arrest, and the force is used to effect the arrest.

Police officers will also use force at times in response to provocations or insults that are not in themselves criminal acts. In such cases, an officer may be simply expressing the anger triggered by an insult or may feel that a response in defense of police authority is necessary. Neither reason justifies the use of force in law or in regulation, and if a departmental inquiry produces no other reason for the action, the officer will be reprimanded. In fact, however, it is often very difficult to distinguish these cases from those described earlier, because the officer will usually arrest the person and charge him or her with resisting arrest. The charge is designed to justify the use of force.

Police also use force unlawfully when it is applied as a form of "curbstone justice." Suspicious persons may be forcefully removed from a neighborhood; unruly teenagers or public inebriates may be beaten for moving too slowly when told to move; a neighborhood person suspected of drug dealing may be roughed up and told to move on if the police are not able to secure evidence sufficient to convict him or her. Although such behavior is clearly unlawful, it is not always clear that the officer is acting contrary to the overall objectives of the department or to the desires of the community. The words and actions of police superiors may suggest to the officer that they are primarily concerned with correcting the condition and only passively committed to enforcing the guidelines against unnecessary force. Moreover, in some neighborhoods the residents would applaud the police for physically abusing people whom they define as undesirables.

This last point suggests another source of

concern regarding the movement toward community policing. On the one hand, officers who are more visible and better known on the neighborhood level may be deterred by that heightened visibility from engaging in indiscriminate use of force. Moreover, the officer's familiarity with the people and the customs of the community may make it easier for him to prevent situations from becoming confrontational, and the people's familiarity with the officer may make them more willing to accept, rather than to resist, his intervention. On the other hand, the very familiarity with people, problems, and resources that community policing seeks to cultivate would help the officer to identify those whose prior record, current behavior, or pariah status in the neighborhood make them unlikely to complain if they are the victims of excessive force or abuse of authority. Indeed, the officer's knowledge of the community may lead him to believe that such misbehavior is precisely how the residents want him to treat the local "bad guys." That development must be resisted through periodic training sessions that continually reiterate the agency's commitment to constitutionally sound police tactics, through dialogue between the police and the community in which the constraints on police behavior and the reasonableness of those constraints are defined and explained, and through close field supervision designed to discourage unnecessary confrontation and to help the officer develop techniques for diverting and diffusing it.

Finally, police agencies have often used force to control the behavior of groups engaged in political protest. In times of political unrest such as the 1960s and early 1970s, police force becomes highly visible and controversial. In a democracy, there is great concern that the police not be used to stifle free expression and political activity. This concern is heightened when the values or political programs of the protesters are sharply different from those of the police, and the police are tempted to use their power as a political counterforce.

The experiences of the 1960s led many of the larger police departments to invest in specialized training and to develop new command and control systems for use in policing mass demonstrations. To avoid explosive confrontations, the police today often seek to negotiate with the protesting organizations long before the demonstrations take place. Both sides then have a clearer understanding of how the event will unfold, of the physical terrain in which it will take place, and of what behavior will and will not be tolerated. The police then commit large numbers of officers to assuring the orderly conduct of the protest and make certain that their behavior in the streets is closely supervised.

The antiwar and civil rights demonstrations of the 1960s heightened public sensitivity to police abuse of authority, especially the authority to use force. One of the consequences was a widespread demand for accessible and effective complaint-review systems. Some demanded complaint-review processes that were staffed and managed entirely by civilians, reasoning that police officials could not be expected to investigate and dispose of such complaints dispassionately. For their part, police organizations and agencies strongly opposed such proposals, arguing that civilians lack both the training and experience necessary to judge police behavior. The issue became a highly politicized and divisive one in many cities. In fact, very few civilian structures were established. However, many agencies did develop procedures for receiving and investigating civilian complaints about police behavior along with other policies to discourage misbehavior and to punish it when it is demonstrated. Thus, there are internal mechanisms today to check the use of force that did not exist in the mid-1960s.

THE ORGANIZATIONAL MODEL OF POLICING

The question of controlling police behavior inevitably leads to consideration of the organizational form and content of police agencies, which are often described as "paramilitary" organizations. The movement to professionalize the police was in part a reaction against corrupt, unproductive police officials who were often more responsive to private interests than to a central command. The hierarchical structure, discipline, and bureaucratic control of behavior that characterized military organization was seen as an effective corrective strategy. Moreover, by the 1950s the vast majority of men coming into police agencies had had prior military experience, and there appeared to be few alternative management models available at the time.

Whatever the historical achievements of that

model, its deficiencies have increasingly become apparent. The elaborate network of internal regulations is offset by a real dearth of standards for dealing with the problems and situations that officers encounter in the field. Therefore, there are very few standards for distinguishing between effective and ineffective police work. As a result, the management system is essentially negative, in that it depends heavily on punishments for infractions of rules rather than on rewards for handling situations effectively. The major exception to this generalization is the extraordinary weight given to arrest activity.

The number and type of arrests made by a police agency is one of the few accepted indicators of productivity. However, the preoccupation with the number of arrests made and summons given actually discourages the development of more-effective methods of dealing with problems in the community. Such methods may reduce the number of arrests made in certain situations. Moreover, when coupled with the stress on compliance with internal regulations, the emphasis on arrests may encourage officers to make arrests for the specific purpose of covering an infraction they have committed.

The weight of military-bureaucratic discipline typically falls more heavily on the patrol force than on other organizational elements in the department, primarily because the patrol officers are more visible to the public and their jobs appear more amenable to bureaucratic control. This is one of the reasons why so many young officers are anxious to get out of uniform patrol and into other work. The vulnerability of the patrol officer to being "written up" while performing tasks that do not appear to be highly valued by the department is a principal source of morale problems.

In addition, the absence of standards for handling problems in the community and the stress on compliance with internal regulations has a tendency to compromise the role of the police supervisor. It reduces his or her capacity to direct field operations and to give instructions to officers on how to deal with various kinds of community problems. The supervisor's primary tool of control may actually be the threat of punishing officers for rule infractions. This negative system of control is not likely to inspire confidence in leadership. It is instead likely to suggest that an officer's first concern should be self-protection.

It seems clear that one part of a solution to

this organizational dilemma is the articulation of acceptable objectives and effective methods to influence the de facto discretion that police officers exercise in responding to community problems. That will require much more attention to the realities of patrol practice and to the development of criteria for distinguishing between good and bad practice. Goldstein (1977) suggests that this requires, in the first instance, a recognition that the primary function of the police is the solving of problems in the community. Once that functional definition is accepted, a department can provide officers with training and support for carrying out the problem identification, analysis, and strategic planning work that is required for effective problem-solving. This premise and these methods are an integral part of the current emphasis on community policing.

It is not clear, however, that shifting the focus of police to problems external to the agency can be effected and sustained in the context of the military model of organization. The two approaches may represent fundamentally incompatible conceptions of policing.

The strains of the military model of organization are not new to American policing. They are brought into sharper relief, however, by the dominant themes shaping the directions of policy today. These include a recognition that discretionary action is an inherent and substantial part of the police officer's role and that the exercise of that discretion must be influenced by the characteristics, needs, and desires of the local community in which the officer works. In addition, policymakers are increasingly coming to believe that the role of the police is best seen as the solving of community problems and that police organizations need to develop measures of effectiveness, standards of performance, and incentives and rewards for effective performance that are commensurate with that role. Finally, those who are trying to frame policy are keenly aware of the need to control the abuses of police power, but this awareness is tempered by some skepticism regarding internal regulations that effectively preclude officers from addressing certain problems of disorder or illegality that profoundly disturb community residents.

For the future, these themes will be honed into new visions of policing as well as into the policy positions and procedural directives needed to give life to those visions. The organizational forms that will emerge are not now obvious, but it seems likely that they will represent a significant modification of the quasi-military model that typifies American policing today.

CASE

Mapp v. Ohio, 367 U.S. 643 (1961)

BIBLIOGRAPHY

Egon Bittner, *The Functions of the Police in Modern Society* (1980), is a brief but classic sociological analysis of the functional and organizational character of policing in modern America. John E. Boydstun and Michael E. Sherry, *San Diego Community Profile: Final Report* (1975), is a research report by the Police Foundation on one of the early efforts by a large police agency to implement some of the principles of community-oriented policing. Gary W. Cordner and David W. Hayeslys, "The Effects of Citizen Oriented Patrol on Police Officer Perceptions of Job Satisfaction, Police Officer Role, and the Community," presented at Society for the Study of Social Problems (1985), is a partial report of Cordner's research on the COPE program in the Baltimore County Police Department. Robert M. Fogelson, *Big City Police* (1979), is an important work on the historical development of policing in the United States, especially in the major metropolitan areas. Herman Goldstein, *Policing a Free Society* (1977), provides an extraordinarily thoughtful and thorough analysis of the functions, structure, operations, and dilemmas of policing in the United States; and "Improving Policing: A Problem-Oriented Approach," in *Crime and Delinquency*, 25 (1979), is a highly provocative article that attempts to focus police on solving problems in the community and thereby redefine organizational objectives, procedures, and reward systems.

George Kelling, Tony Pate, Duane Dieckman, and Charles Brown, *The Kansas City Preventive Patrol Experiment: A Summary Report* (1974), is a watershed report on an experiment that failed to find empirical justification for random preventive patrol practices and thereby freed police administrators to explore innovative ways to enhance the efficacy of the patrol force. Carl B. Klockars, "Order Maintenance, the Quality of Urban Life, and Police: A Different Line of Argument," in William Geller, ed., *Police Leadership in America: Crisis and Opportunity* (1985), is a tightly reasoned critique of what the author considers a too hasty and uncritical acceptance of community-oriented policing as the policy framework of the future. Mark Moore and George Kelling, "To Serve and Protect: Learning from Police History," in *Public Interest*, 70 (1983), is a well-written consideration of the history of American policing and how it has led to the current policy emphasis on community-oriented policing. National Advisory Commission on Criminal Justice Standards and Goals, *Police* (1973), is a virtually encyclopedic consideration of police operations, with hundreds of recommended standards for their improvement. Police Foundation, *The Newark Foot Patrol Experiment* (1981), reports on the effects of reintroducing foot patrol into inner city beats in Newark, New Jersey.

Albert J. Reiss, Jr., "Crime Control and the Quality of Life," in *American Behavioral Scientist*, 27 (1983), argues for the importance of focusing attention on the quality of neighborhood life and, for that purpose, treating more seriously crimes of violence against property and crimes committed by juveniles. Ruben Rumbaut and Egon Bittner, "Changing Conceptions of the Police Role: A Sociological Review," in Norval Morris and Michael Tonry, eds., *Crime and Justice: An Annual Review of Research*, vol. 1 (1979), is a provocative analysis of the major conceptions of policing that have emerged since the 1960s and a call for a sharper focus on substantive issues of police reform. Lawrence W. Sherman, Catherine H. Milton, and Thomas V. Kelly, *Team Policing: Seven Case Studies* (1973), reviews projects in several cities in the 1970s that were inspired by early formulations of community-policing concepts. Lawrence W. Sherman, Catherine H. Milton, Thomas V. Kelly, and Richard A. Berk, *Police Responses to Domestic Assault: Preliminary Findings* (1983), finds some empirical support for the efficacy of making arrests in response to domestic violence situations. Jerome Skolnick, *Justice Without Trial* (1966), is a classic articulation of the power of the police to make law by virtue of their enormous discretion in enforcing the law and of some of the concerns that this discretion generates. Douglas A. Smith, Christy A. Visher, and Laura A. Davidson, "Equity and Discretionary Justice: The Influence of Race on Police Arrest Decisions," in *Journal of Criminal Law and Criminology*, 75 (1984), is an examination of the influence of two types of alleged racial bias on police arrest decisions.

James Tien, James Simon, and Richard Larson, *An Alternative Approach in Police Patrol: The Wilmington Split Force Experiment* (1978), is a careful evaluation of a differential response system used by the Wilmington Police Department in handling citizens' calls for service. Robert Trojanowicz, *An Evaluation of the Neighborhood Foot Patrol Project in Flint, Michigan* (1983), is an early and positive evaluation of a foot-patrol program that embodied many of the principles of community-oriented policing. James Q. Wilson, *Varieties of Police Behavior* (1968), is a classic description and analysis of the different styles of policing in America (watchman, legalistic, and service) and the relationships between these styles and local political and governmental structures. James Q. Wilson and Barbara Boland, *The Effect of Police on Crime* (1979), is an empirical analysis of the effects of aggressive patrol strategies on the incidence of robbery in urban areas. James Q. Wilson and George Kelling, "Broken Windows," in *Atlantic Monthly*, March 1982, is a highly important statement of the need to focus police attention on neglected order-maintenance problems at the neighborhood level in order to increase the citizens' sense of safety and reduce the volume of conventional street crime.

[*See also* CRIMINAL JUSTICE SYSTEM; CRIMINAL LAW; CRIMINAL PROCEDURE; *and* PROSECUTORS.]

PROSECUTORS

Lynn Mather

Prosecutors in the United States, as public officials responsible for the initiation and conduct of criminal proceedings, are central actors in the American criminal justice system. They screen arrests made by police and complaints made by private citizens through their decision to proceed with formal criminal charges against defendants. Prosecutors also interact regularly with defense attorneys, grand juries, and judges in the process of setting bail, establishing probable cause, negotiating guilty pleas, arguing cases at trial, and recommending sentences for those convicted. As the linkage between enforcement and adjudication, interacting closely with private citizens and diverse criminal justice personnel, the prosecutor is often seen as the pivotal figure in the criminal justice process.

A fundamental characteristic of the prosecutor is the possession of largely unchecked discretion to shape the outcome of criminal cases, especially through decisions on charges, dismissals, and plea bargaining. This discretion has been questioned periodically and attempts have been made to limit it, but discretionary decision-making remains an essential component of the prosecutor's job. As political officials (usually elected), prosecutors also represent the views of their local constituency in setting priorities on issues of criminal and, sometimes, civil law enforcement. Moreover, prosecutors often lobby the legislature regarding statutory changes in criminal law, and they press for particular rulings in appellate litigation.

While the prosecution function in the United States is defined as a public one, this was not true in early American history, nor does it hold in many other legal cultures today. Most countries use a system that combines public and private prosecution. In such a system, the public prosecutor's responsibility for initiating criminal actions is shared with private citizens, who can also initiate their own criminal proceedings. Provision for private prosecution is especially important in situations in which the public prosecutor decides not to prosecute.

There is an important difference between a private prosecutor, who is hired by the victim to represent his or her interests by pursuing criminal action, and a public prosecutor, who is paid by the state to represent it in the pursuit of criminal proceedings that were originally initiated by the victim. Not only does the role of the victim decrease in public prosecution, but the public prosecutor confronts two serious and interrelated dilemmas in doing his or her job.

The first dilemma is found in the conflict between the prosecutor's role as chief law enforcement officer and as officer of the court. As a law enforcement official, the prosecutor acts in an adversary mode to seek conviction of those suspected of crime; like the police, the prosecutor's primary obligations are to control crime and maintain public order. In contrast, the prosecutor's quasi-judicial role is quite different. As an officer of the court, the prosecutor is sworn to uphold legal values and to see that justice is done; in this role the official must interpret the law and apply principles of due process. The tension that arises is between order and law as reflecting conflicting responsibilities of a prosecutor.

Although law and order are commonly spoken of in one phrase, the juxtaposition is misleading. Jerome Skolnick aptly commented that " 'law' and 'order' are frequently found to be in opposition, because law implies rational restraint upon the rules and procedures utilized to achieve order" (p. 7). The dilemma for a prosecutor is how to mediate between the public demand for order and the principles of legality, as articulated in judicial forums.

A second dilemma for prosecutors emerges from the conflict between the general legal rule and the needs of an individual case. Criminal laws are written in broad, abstract language, leaving to legal officials the task of matching concrete facts with general legal categories. Prosecutors, in particular, routinely choose between competing legal frameworks in their decision-making. For example, given a fistfight between acquaintances in a bar in which one party was the aggressor, should the prosecutor pursue the most serious criminal charge or consider all mitigating circumstances and file a lesser charge or none at all? To prosecute at the maximum level publicly reinforces the importance of the legal norm against physical assaults and may act as a deterrent to others in similar situations. However, full prosecution may not resolve the underlying conflict between the offender and the victim, nor may it best serve the interests of justice. The tasks of individual conflict resolution and general social control are intertwined in the criminal law. To the extent that prosecutors pursue one task, they risk compromising the other.

These tensions in the role of prosecutor should be borne in mind as we review the history of the modern prosecutor, the organizational context, decision-making and discretion, and recent trends in prosecution. Prosecutors have addressed the conflicts differently in offices throughout the country and during different historical periods.

DEVELOPMENT OF THE MODERN PROSECUTOR

In 1929, in his classic study *Politics and Criminal Prosecution,* Raymond Moley wrote that the "significance of the American prosecuting attorney has been strangely neglected by institutional commentators and historians" (p. 48). Research since that time has shed more light on the history of the prosecutor, but the origin and development of this key public official remains a matter of controversy. Records from the colonial period show various officers of government, such as deputy attorneys general and sheriffs, performing the duties of prosecutor. In 1704 the colony

of Connecticut formally created the first office of prosecutor, calling for the appointment of an "attorney for the Queen to prosecute and implead in the law all criminals and to do all other things necessary or convenient . . . to suppress vice and immorality" (Jacoby, 16). The colony of Virginia followed with the establishment of county attorneys in 1711. After the founding of the Republic, the Judiciary Act of 1789 officially designated United States attorneys as prosecutors for the federal government.

Based on records about these early prosecutors, some scholars have argued that the system of public prosecution was "firmly established" throughout the colonies by the end of the American Revolution. Other, more recent research suggests that public prosecutors existed alongside the older system of private prosecution; further, there was considerable local variation in the handling of criminal matters, with private prosecution still commonplace in some colonies but rare in others.

The specific historical origin of the public prosecutor in America is unclear. Several different theories have been advanced, but none has complete support. Some writers point to the influence of the English common-law tradition on legal development in the colonies, using this tradition to explain the derivation of the public prosecutor. What is puzzling, however, is that eighteenth-century England had no public prosecutor, and even today England operates on the principle of private prosecution. Thus, in theory at least, all English criminal proceedings were, and are, initiated by individual citizens. (In practice, police officials play a major role.) Indeed, England in the mid-1980s was considering a reorganization to shift responsibility for prosecution from the police to a crown prosecutor, thus moving to a system more like that of the United States. Hence, it is difficult to argue that the American public prosecutor is a direct product of the English system. Indirect evidence provides some support for an English ancestry from either the king's attorney general or from the justices of the peace, who performed limited prosecutorial functions as far back as the sixteenth century.

Another line of argument proposes that the American colonists turned not to England but to the civil law system of France or Holland for the office of public prosecutor. In France the *procureur publique,* a state-appointed official, investigates and prosecutes criminal offenses. While

PROSECUTORS

the American prosecutor is somewhat similar to the French *procureur,* there is no specific historical evidence to connect the two, although several reports have attempted to do so. More persuasive evidence of a civil law derivation comes from the early Dutch administration of New York and surrounding areas. According to this theory, the American prosecutor can be traced to a Dutch official, the *schout,* who was responsible for apprehending and prosecuting criminal offenders. These competing views of the origins of the prosecutor will no doubt continue to be debated and refined with further research. They will also be compared with the view that the office of public prosecutor is itself an American invention.

Regardless of the historical origin of the public prosecutor, it is important to examine the substantial changes in the office since its beginning and to understand the changing context of the criminal justice system. Following the American Revolution, private prosecution was still an integral aspect of local criminal justice systems. Victims—or their families—were responsible for securing arrest warrants, gathering witnesses, and attending pretrial hearings. Often, too, the victims hired a personal lawyer to argue the case at trial.

Judges, especially the justices of the peace, played a major role in the criminal process, frequently arranging informal settlements after interviewing the defendant. There is some question as to how common jury trials were in the early nineteenth century, but when trials were held, they were extremely rapid proceedings without defense lawyers or the extensive procedures we have today. The public prosecutor was a minor actor in the criminal process. He worked part-time, as an adjunct to the judge, presenting cases to grand and trial juries or simply expediting private prosecution. He exercised no discretion and was paid a fee for each case by the court. There was no correctional system as such. Restitution to victims was common, as was hanging, banishing, flogging, and other corporal punishment.

During the course of the nineteenth century, American criminal justice underwent a fundamental transformation, which included a much greater role for the public prosecutor. The biggest shift was in the rise of a professional police force. Urbanization and industrialization led to problems of public order that were no longer effectively handled by a private system of law enforcement. Modern police departments were formed during the 1840s and 1850s, first in big cities and then throughout the country. Police took over the responsibility for arrest and investigation of crime that earlier had been held by private victims. The victim's role was further reduced by a shift in the punishment of offenders away from restitution and toward incarceration in the newly created prison system.

Concurrently, the public prosecutor's position increased in importance. The prosecutor began making decisions about charges, possible dismissals, and the handling of dispositions. The legality of such prosecutorial discretion was initially a matter in question, with numerous lawsuits filed to challenge prosecutorial decisions. Appellate courts, however, upheld the power of the prosecutor, so that by the end of the nineteenth century the central actors in the criminal process were officers of the state (police, prosecutors) rather than individual citizens.

The professional prosecutor was further institutionalized in the nineteenth century by a change in selection. By the Civil War most states had shifted to a system of election for public prosecutors rather than appointment. The prosecutor became part of the executive branch of government, with his own source of political support, distinct from courts and the judicial branch. One means of exercising his greater power was through the prosecutor's filing of an "information" to formally charge offenders with felonies, thus displacing the once-powerful grand jury in many states. The Constitution requires grand jury indictment for accused felons in federal cases, but in the key 1884 decision of *Hurtado* v. *California* the Supreme Court ruled that the requirement did not extend to the states.

Another illustration of the increase in prosecutorial power was through the rise of plea bargaining. Case screening by full-time police and prosecutors means that evidence that once emerged at trial was now available earlier in the process. By 1880, defendants were often convicted by guilty pleas rather than by jury trial. It is not clear how much actual bargaining accompanied these guilty pleas, but surely the defendant's guilty plea in at least some of the cases was influenced by prosecutorial promises of leniency.

The prosecutor's interest in plea bargaining was aided by two factors. First, a trend in sentencing philosophy toward reformation of offenders was evident at the turn of the century. Sentencing laws were revised to introduce probation, parole, and indeterminate sentences. The emphasis was on the individualization of punishment, fitting the sentence to meet the needs of each offender. This new sentencing goal was facilitated by plea bargaining, where prosecutors could justify discretionary acts of charge reduction by reference to considerations of appropriate punishment. Second, the criminal law itself expanded tremendously at this time, as states criminalized acts that earlier had been legal or had been civil law violations. Frequent dismissals and plea bargaining by prosecutors were ways to mitigate the impact of these new laws.

That the public prosecutor had, over the course of one hundred years, achieved such a dominant and powerful position in the criminal process was a largely unnoticed fact until the 1920s. Spurred by a concern about urban crime following World War I, government officials and legal scholars initiated major surveys of criminal justice in cities such as Cleveland, Chicago, and New York. Moley's 1929 summary of these reports shows the frequency of dismissals, the high proportion of guilty pleas, and the minor role for jury trials. Writers of the 1920s expressed shock and outrage at these facts and decried the political influences and corruption that characterized many prosecutorial decisions.

Oddly, after this huge outpouring of interest in the prosecutor, little was written or done further until the late 1960s and 1970s. In those years, crime and criminal justice processes once again became political issues, leading to government commission reports and numerous scholarly studies. Each of these newer works provided valuable empirical data about prosecutors, while also offering different perspectives.

ORGANIZATIONAL CONTEXT

Prosecution at the state level is highly decentralized. Although the attorney general is the highest legal officer of each state, the attorney general rarely has control over the prosecution of crime. That official instead deals primarily with civil-law matters. State criminal law is enforced by a locally selected prosecutor. There are about twenty-seven hundred autonomous prosecutor's offices in the United States, each

serving a county or other local geographic district. The states of Alaska, Delaware, and Rhode Island are exceptions to this; the attorney general in those states also acts as local prosecutor.

The job of a local prosecutor, commonly called district attorney, state's attorney, or county attorney, varies tremendously according to the size of the community served. In rural or small-town areas, the district attorney may work only part-time as prosecutor while also maintaining a private law practice. The rural prosecutor has little or no supporting staff; decision-making tends toward the personal and informal; and there is often a substantial share of civil law work for local government in addition to the duties of criminal prosecution. According to a 1972 national survey, 37 percent of the nation's local prosecutors worked alone, with no assistant attorneys, while another 37 percent had one to three staff assistants (Jacoby).

The job of the urban prosecutor stands in stark contrast to that of the small-town prosecutor with his or her few assistants. In metropolitan areas with a tremendous volume of crime, the district attorney oversees an office with dozens or even hundreds of assistant attorneys. In 1986, Los Angeles County had the largest prosecutor's office in the country with more than seven hundred attorneys, while Cook County (Chicago) was second with about six hundred prosecuting attorneys. Attorneys in an urban prosecutor's office typically have supporting staff such as investigators, paralegals, and public relations officers to aid in their work. Procedures are institutionalized and decision-making is often specialized in these large urban offices.

The vast majority of states provides for the election of the prosecutor, typically with a term of office of four years. Where local elections are partisan, the political parties dominate in recruiting and organizing the contest for prosecutor. Even in nonpartisan elections, however, the influence of political parties is sometimes seen through the involvement of key party individuals or special-interest groups. Election as prosecutor has long been a stepping-stone to higher political office in state or national government. The public visibility of the office provides excellent exposure for those with political ambitions. Indeed, a rather large number of state judges, governors, and representatives in Congress have had prior experience as prosecutors.

Assistant, or deputy, prosecuting attorneys

are appointed by the prosecutor. In some areas selection is based on political connections, and in other areas, on legal credentials and competitive examinations. Most deputies are young and just out of law school. They seek the responsibility, professional contacts, and courtroom experience that come with prosecution. After several years, most assistant prosecutors leave the office for private law practice. Some deputies do stay on to become career prosecutors, while others leave the office to pursue political ambitions in local or state politics.

Prosecutors for the federal government are organized and selected differently. First, the Department of Justice in Washington provides some centralized control and sets broad policies for the United States attorneys who work in the ninety-four federal judicial districts. Thus, the federal prosecutor does not have complete autonomy, as does his or her local counterpart. Nevertheless, as Eisenstein's detailed study shows, United States attorneys and their assistants do possess considerable independence. Their degree of autonomy depends on the size of the judicial district, their relations with federal judges in the district, issues involved in a specific case, and the pattern of interaction between particular United States attorney offices and the Department of Justice in Washington.

Second, United States attorneys are appointed, not elected, to office. The president nominates, and the Senate confirms, prosecutors for the federal government for a term of four years. United States attorneys are nearly always of the same political party as the president, and by custom they all resign when a president of the opposing party is elected. Both the deputy attorney general's office and the senators from the state where a vacancy occurs exert great influence on the process of recruitment for United States attorneys. Those ultimately selected as federal prosecutors tend to have active political backgrounds, strong local support, some prior governmental experience, and an average age of about forty-two years (Eisenstein).

While the excitement and focus for any prosecutor revolves around the criminal process, these officials also handle civil law matters. For example, when the United States government is sued in a tort action or contract dispute, a United States attorney (or assistant) will handle the defense. United States attorneys also represent the government as plaintiff in cases of land condem-

nation, debt collection, and civil fraud. Indeed, Eisenstein estimates that civil law work accounts for about 40 percent of the activity in the United States attorney offices. While the comparable figure would be far lower for local prosecutors, they, too, handle civil cases.

In about one-quarter of the states, the prosecutor has only criminal law duties, but in the remainder the prosecutor is charged with both criminal and civil law enforcement. In these states the prosecutor may represent local governments in an array of civil matters ranging from adoption, mental health, and paternity proceedings to sewers, taxes, and zoning. However, both federal and local offices give priority to their criminal case loads over their civil law matters. Prosecution in criminal cases commands the greatest visibility and provides the greatest opportunity for influence within the courts and for political impact beyond the courts. For these reasons, prosecutorial decision-making has been examined very little in the civil process as compared to the criminal process. Discussion of decision-making in the next section will be limited to prosecution of criminal cases.

DECISION-MAKING

Decisions by prosecutors affect the processing of criminal cases in fundamental ways. Central to any empirical study of the criminal process today is the finding of widespread attrition of cases following the initial complaint or arrest. Much of this attrition can be explained by prosecutorial screening or motions for dismissal. In addition, only a small fraction of cases that do reach court are resolved by adversary trial. The remainder are handled through plea bargaining—that is, implicit or explicit negotiations between the prosecutor, defense attorney, and sometimes the judge.

Prosecutors engage in screening and negotiation for several different reasons. On the one hand, they are charged with evaluating facts and evidence according to the law to make a preliminary assessment of the likelihood of guilt or innocence. Hence, they weed out cases with weak or inadequate evidence. Yet prosecutors also must decide which crimes—both in general terms and in individual cases—warrant the most serious attention, given the inevitable limit on resources in the criminal justice system. Every violation of criminal law cannot be prosecuted (because of resource constraints), nor, many would argue, would this be the ideal policy to achieve the broader interests of justice. Consequently, prosecutors, in interaction with other criminal justice actors, make decisions that give shape and operational meaning to the formal criminal law categories. Following an overview of key decision points in the criminal process, specific factors that influence prosecutorial discretion will be analyzed.

After police make an arrest or a citizen files a complaint, the prosecutor decides whether or not to file criminal charges, and if so, which ones. The importance of this decision cannot be overstated, for it is the entry point for defendants into the criminal courts. While prosecutors and police work together in law enforcement, they also operate in very different environments with quite distinct organizational goals. Police seek primarily to maintain order. Arrests are devices that may be used toward that end. But whether or not an arrest leads to conviction is not a high priority for the patrolman maintaining order on the street. In contrast, obtaining convictions is of paramount importance to prosecutors. Knowing that the process of securing a conviction in court is bound by formal legal rules, prosecutors make charging decisions so as to avoid losing cases later on. Consequently, less than one-half of all felony arrests in many areas result in felony charges filed by the prosecutor. In the federal courts, fewer than one-quarter of all complaints result in prosecution by United States attorneys.

This pattern of prosecutorial dominance of the charging decision does not characterize all courts, however. There is great variation in how discretion is exercised, by whom, and at which stage in the process. Indeed, one of the most valuable and least appreciated lessons of empirical scholarship on criminal justice is the wide range of differences from one community to the next. All communities share an overall pattern of high attrition of cases from arrest to conviction. But the bulk of dismissals and charge reductions may occur anywhere in the charging stage, the preliminary hearing, the grand jury, or the final court hearing.

Likewise, the ones who exercise the most power over cases vary from jurisdiction to jurisdiction. For example, while the prosecutor dominates the charging process with very strict screening of arrests in Los Angeles and Detroit, there is no prosecutorial screening in some other cities; where police file cases directly with the courts, it is the local magistrates who dismiss or reduce the bulk of the felonies at the preliminary hearing. This and other variations are due to differences in local traditions, state laws, organizational resources, and relationships among police, prosecutors, judges, and others in the community.

In formulating an initial criminal charge, prosecutors have wide authority in deciding what level of charge to file or whether to file charges at all. Alschuler first wrote of the problem of overcharging, whereby prosecutors are said to inflate the initial charges in anticipation of later plea negotiations. Vertical overcharging occurs when prosecutors file charges on a single offense at a higher level than seems warranted by the facts of the case. For example, first-degree burglary may be charged in expectation of a later plea bargain to the lesser included, second-degree burglary. Horizontal overcharging refers to a set of multiple charges, or sometimes multiple counts of the same charge, filed for every possible criminal transaction that occurred. Thus, if a defendant allegedly wrote twenty bad checks, he or she could be charged with twenty counts of check forgery (or even twenty counts of forgery and twenty counts of receiving stolen property). A typical disposition in this type of case, however, would be a guilty plea to one count with dismissal of the other nineteen. Defense attorneys argue that these charging practices are unfair devices used simply to add bargaining leverage to the prosecutor's position in later dispositions. Most prosecutors, in contrast, defend charging the "highest and most" permitted by the evidence as purely part of their professional duty in law enforcement, and they deny that this would be considered "overcharging."

Prosecutors also vary greatly in their philosophy of charging. For instance, Utz (1978) found a policy of strategic overcharging in the San Diego district attorney's office but a policy of undercharging by the district attorney in Alameda County, California. Similar differences between offices can be seen in the decision whether to file criminal charges at all. Whereas prosecutors in one midwestern city file charges only "if the case will probably win at trial"

(Neubauer), prosecutors in other cities follow a much looser standard and defer more to police views of the case. Interestingly, if a prosecutor chooses not to file criminal charges, it is extremely difficult to challenge the decision. Attempts to obtain a court order to compel prosecution have rarely been successful.

Once charges are filed in court, the defendant is informed by a judge of the official accusation against him or her, and bail is set. This initial court appearance occurs soon after the arrest, usually within forty-eight hours. The amount of bail in many areas is determined by a schedule that sets bail according to the type of offense. Prosecutors frequently have input into this schedule, and they also often testify at, or else informally influence, defense motions for bail reduction and for release of defendants on their own recognizance.

In misdemeanor cases defendants may plead guilty at this initial court hearing, or they may wait for a trial date. The prosecutor engages in discussion and/or negotiation with the defense during this process about the possibility of dismissing charges, reducing charges, or recommending a lesser sentence if the defendant pleads guilty. A high proportion of misdemeanor charges are dismissed. Of those convicted throughout the country, well over 90 percent are convicted by guilty plea rather than by trial. Decision-making in lower criminal courts tends to be rapid and informal, as prosecution offices typically conserve their resources for the more serious cases.

Felony cases are those in which defendants face a possible prison term, most often of at least one year. Procedures for handling felonies are more formal and complex than for misdemeanors. Most important, additional screening of charges occurs after the initial filing of a complaint. This screening is done by a lower-court judge in a probable-cause hearing and/or by a grand jury. It is only after these hearings that the prosecutor or grand jury enters an official felony accusation in the higher court—that is, in the county or superior court in which the disposition will occur.

The probable-cause hearing (also called preliminary hearing or preliminary examination) allows a lower-court judge to review the evidence in a case to determine whether it is sufficient to proceed with felony prosecution. The legal standard used in the hearing is one of probable cause: Is there probable cause to believe that a crime occurred and that the defendant committed it? The prosecutor presents evidence and calls witnesses in an effort to establish probable cause, but rarely does the defense introduce evidence of its own. In some areas the probable-cause hearing is a formal adversary proceeding with considerable cross-examination of witnesses and a written transcript made of the hearing. Elsewhere, the probable-cause hearing is rapid, informal, and indeed, often waived by the defendant. Finally, some courts (especially federal trial courts) rarely hold probable-cause hearings, relying instead on the grand jury to screen felonies.

At the conclusion of a probable-cause hearing the magistrate holds the defendant for felony prosecution, reduces charges to the misdemeanor level, or dismisses the charges altogether. Lower-court judges in some cities use the probable-cause hearing as the major disposition point, screening out many weak cases and encouraging prosecutors to confer with defense to arrange guilty pleas to reduced charges at this stage. But in other cities, especially where there is considerable prosecutorial screening of initial arrests, relatively few felonies are weeded out at the probable-cause hearing.

If probable cause is found at the preliminary hearing, then the prosecutor either takes the case to a grand jury or files felony charges in court, depending on the jurisdiction. About one-half of the states, and the federal government, require grand jury indictment for felonies or capital offenses. The remaining states use grand juries on occasion, but most commonly rely on a bill of information to commence prosecution. An information is simply a formal accusation of felony charges issued by the prosecutor. It is the equivalent of an indictment by the grand jury.

By the time a felony case reaches the trial court for final disposition, a number of key decisions have been made: on the specific charges, on the amount of bail, and on the sufficiency of evidence to establish probable cause. The prosecutor has either made or heavily influenced these decisions, often working in close cooperation with police, lower-court judges, and the grand jury. Most important, a large proportion of cases has been screened out during the pretrial process, so that the felonies left for trial are typically quite strong. Defense attorneys in Connecticut (Heumann) and in Los Angeles (Mather) estimate that 90 percent of their felony clients in superior court are factually guilty and that for most of these, the cases present no disputable legal issues. Although some questions of guilt or innocence remain, the primary task of the criminal court lies in the determination of proper punishment for guilty offenders. As new court personnel learn this reality of their job, they adapt to the existing pattern of frequent plea bargaining.

With plea bargaining, defendants plead guilty, rather than insisting on a trial, because of an expectation of a lesser sentence or reduced charge. An explicit plea bargain involves a specific promise by the prosecutor about the sentence or charge agreement, while an implicit bargain relies on a tacit understanding of leniency in sentencing that accompanies a guilty plea. When prosecutors engage in plea bargaining, they assure themselves a criminal conviction while also influencing the sentence imposed. Cases settled by trial require more time and resources and, even more important, may represent risks to the prosecution of a possible acquittal. Prosecutors thus evaluate their cases to assess their seriousness and the likelihood of conviction. Defendants whose cases are not "worth" much can expect easy agreements to charge or sentence leniency, but prosecutors will often refuse to bargain in very serious cases.

In most jurisdictions, the prosecutor is the central actor in the plea-bargaining process. By controlling the charge, and sometimes the sentence recommendation as well, the prosecutor is the one that defense must convince about leniency in disposition. In some jurisdictions, however, judges exercise the more dominant role.

For those cases not settled by guilty plea, the prosecutor must prepare witnesses, organize the evidence, and develop an argument for trial. During the trial, the prosecutor participates in the selection of jurors, presents the case against the defendant, and cross-examines defense witnesses. Although the trial is typically viewed as a purely adversarial process, there are also opportunities at trial for cooperation between prosecutor and defense. Depending upon the case, the prosecutor may decide, for example, not to use all his or her possible challenges to potential jurors, to stipulate to certain facts alleged by defense rather than to force proof of the facts at trial, or not to cross-examine certain defense witnesses as aggressively as possible. Following conviction at trial, the prosecutor then decides whether to recommend a sentence to the judge and, if so, what kind. Here, for example, the prosecutor's decision may be influenced by sympathy for the defendant resulting from facts that emerged at trial or by desire to punish the defendant for needlessly wasting the court's (and prosecutor's) time with a frivolous or fabricated defense.

The above discussion of prosecutorial decision-making points to several notable themes: the centrality of the prosecutor in most stages of the criminal court process (with the exception of certain jurisdictions in which the prosecutor's power is substantially shared with others); the importance of organizational interactions and interpersonal relationships (such as relations with police, judges, and defense attorneys) that shape the prosecutor's working environment; and the great breadth of discretion available to prosecutors in making decisions.

PROSECUTORIAL DISCRETION

Kenneth Culp Davis, in his book *Discretionary Justice,* states that a "public officer has discretion whenever the effective limits on his power leave him free to make a choice among possible courses of action or inaction" (p. 4). Other scholars have refined or modified this definition—for example, by distinguishing between authorized and unauthorized discretion. Prosecutors may be said to exercise discretion when there are no clear rules guiding their decisions and when those decisions are not subject to review. The most obvious examples of prosecutorial discretion are the decisions to charge, to dismiss charges once made (nolle prosequi), and to reduce charges or recommend leniency in exchange for a guilty plea.

Recognizing the importance of these decisions for the entire criminal process, numerous scholars have attempted to explain empirically how prosecutors exercise their discretion; that is, what factors influence prosecutors' decisions? Given the diversity of research methodologies and in view of basic differences between prosecutors and between jurisdictions, it is not surprising that the research results are not entirely consistent. Variation lies primarily in the emphasis or importance accorded different explanatory factors. With this qualification in mind, we can summarize the general themes that have emerged from the recent literature.

Prosecutorial decisions are made on the basis of evaluation of the strength of evidence, severity of offense, defendant's background, and victim characteristics. These evaluations, in turn, are shaped by the general policies of a given prosecutor's office and by an individual prosecutor's interaction with other criminal justice actors.

Consideration of evidence is a primary factor in all prosecutorial decisions, especially initial decisions on charging and nolle prosequi. This factor exemplifies the traditional legal judgment of prosecutors to screen out cases with weak or inadequate evidence and to dismiss or to reduce charges that rest on a shaky legal foundation. In assessing the strength of a case, prosecutors ask a number of questions. Is there physical evidence such as fingerprints, stolen goods, illegal drugs, a weapon? Did the defendant confess during police examination? If so, is the confession admissible in court? Are there any search-and-seizure problems? Were there witnesses to the crime? How positive is their identification of the defendant? How credible and cooperative is the victim? Does the defendant have a credible explanation for the event that would raise reasonable doubts in the minds of jurors? In answering these questions, prosecutors decide whether the evidence is sufficient to proceed with formal charges. Analysis of the reasons given for case drop-off (screening and dismissals) suggests the significance of evidentiary or witness problems in a large number of cases (for example, in 45 percent of the declinations to prosecute studied by Frase). Prosecutorial willingness to plea-bargain is also influenced by case strength, with most research concluding that prosecutors are more inclined to bargain in weak cases (Alschuler; Jacoby; McDonald, 1985).

Decisions on charges, reductions, and plea bargains are, in nearly all studies, closely related to type of offense. Typical evidentiary differences between crimes account for some of the effects of offense type, but differences in perceived severity may account for a good deal more. The seriousness of the offense, a second factor explaining prosecutorial discretion, reflects both individual judgments and office policies on the relative importance of prosecuting various crimes. Crimes of violence are seen as more serious than property crimes, and crimes between strangers, more serious than those between relatives or acquaintances. Nearly every prosecutor's office also has a group of crimes that they consider "petty," "junk," or "garbage," in which dismissals or plea bargains are quite common. Mather (1979) found severity of offense strongly related to method of case disposition; serious felonies were more likely to be settled by adversary trial, in part because of the prosecutor's reluctance to plea bargain in these cases. Note that offense seriousness is only partially determined by statutory penalties; prosecutors also use their own values and knowledge of typical circumstances of offenses to determine what a crime is "worth."

Defendant characteristics constitute a third factor for prosecutors. In view of widespread concern about the discriminatory aspects of discretion, scholars have tried to pinpoint the effect of social characteristics of the defendant, such as prior record, race, ethnicity, gender, age, and economic status. With the exception of prior criminal record, these personal attributes have not been shown, by themselves, to be major influences on prosecutorial discretion (Eisenstein and Jacob). Testing this relationship is admittedly difficult, however, and the research findings are not entirely consistent. Most studies do suggest the importance of prior record, with prosecutors less likely to dismiss and less generous with bargains according to the severity of the defendant's record.

Finally, the identity of the victim and the relationship between the victim and the defendant influence prosecutorial discretion. The victim's role has been discussed far less than the three factors above but is increasingly the focus of greater scholarly attention. Disposition patterns have clearly shown a much higher proportion of dismissals and reductions in cases involving acquaintances or family members. Studies by Miller, Neubauer, and the Vera Institute of Justice all discuss the reluctance of prosecutors to pursue criminal cases involving prior personal relationships. Sometimes this reluctance is defended on evidentiary grounds; that is, it is sometimes said that victims in such relationships make poor witnesses or that juries will never convict in such a case. Other explanations include the availability of alternatives to prosecution (for example, telling the battered wife to "get a divorce") and the belief that the criminal sanction is simply not appropriate to resolve conflicts between those with a prior relationship.

In addition to the victim's relation to the defendant, various social attributes of the victim may also come into play to influence prosecutorial assessment of case strength and seriousness. Stanko's study of screening decisions in New York, for example, demonstrates the important role played by victim credibility, as shaped by stereotypes based on gender, race, and occupation. Thus, higher-status victims were more likely to have their complaints result in the filing of felony charges. A similar conclusion has emerged from recent research on death-penalty cases, which suggests that racial differences in the imposition of the death penalty may be explained by more vigorous prosecution and sentence severity against those who commit crimes with white victims, as against those who commit crimes with black victims.

Evaluation of these various factors may depend upon the personal views of individual prosecutors. Especially in small offices, the personal values of the elected prosecutor affect fundamentally the assessment of strength and seriousness of cases. However, in larger offices and especially in many of the huge urban prosecutors' offices, there are clear priorities or even guidelines that shape the decisions of individual deputies.

The variation in office policies affects evidentiary considerations and is illustrated by the different charging standards used by prosecutors throughout the country. McDonald (1985, 16) found that 39 percent of the offices he surveyed used a probable-cause standard, 11 percent looked for a "50–50 chance of conviction," 14 percent looked for a "high probability of conviction," and 19 percent used a standard of "beyond a reasonable doubt." Utz integrated data on decisions about charging and plea bargaining to distinguish two models of prosecution, the "adversary" and the "magisterial," which she found characterized the office policies and behavior in San Diego and Oakland, respectively.

Such broad differences in office policy also shape the assessment of offense, defendant, and victim attributes. Thus, for example, office policy may dictate vigorous prosecution of habitual offenders and/or special leniency for those with no prior criminal background. Certain criminal offenses may be targeted in response to public outcry, leading to a policy of no dismissals or plea bargains in those cases. Another common office policy is to decline prosecution for certain cases where there are alternatives to criminal processing, such as mediation or informal settlement following restitution to the victim. Frase observed a general pattern for federal prosecutors, who frequently declined to prosecute where state prosecution was available.

In establishing or modifying office policies, prosecutors respond to a host of factors, such as case-load pressure, availability of resources, type of crime problem, expectations and power of other criminal justice actors, and local geographic and political context. Relations with others, besides affecting general office priorities, may also affect prosecutorial discretion in specific cases. For instance, police pressure to file charges may override a prosecutorial judgment of insufficient evidence. Or, if the victim is prominent and well respected, the prosecutor may hesitate to dismiss or reduce charges, even if weaknesses develop in the case. The identity of the opposing defense attorney has also been found to influence prosecutors' decisions, through a personal working relationship between attorneys, knowledge of a particular defense attorney's reputation, or a perceived difference between public and private defense attorneys. Other actors who sometimes affect decisions by prosecutors include judges, court clerks, probation and parole officers, and representatives of community publics.

RECENT TRENDS IN PROSECUTION

Greater understanding and public awareness of the extent of prosecutorial discretion have led to calls for limits or checks on that discretion. Changes in prosecution since the 1970s can be explained largely as an effort to control discretion in decision-making. Not only were legal scholars unhappy with unbridled discretion, but prosecutors themselves discovered the political vulnerability that could result from discretionary decisions. Consequently, there has been a trend toward limiting discretion by internal measures within prosecutors' offices and by external action by judges and legislatures.

Prosecutors have attempted to structure and check the decisions of their deputies by several different means. Some require written records of discretionary actions with justification provided for each action. Others formalize procedures— for example, by encouraging explicit rather than implicit plea bargaining. Prosecutors have also begun to formalize policies and procedures by providing written guidelines and informal training sessions in an effort to establish some uniformity in decisions. Finally, some prosecutors have restricted the discretion available to deputies by centralizing decision-making or by increasing supervision. For example, offices might designate a few attorneys to be solely responsible for plea bargaining or else require that no deputy dismiss or reduce charges without the prior written approval of a supervisor. These efforts by prosecutors to monitor decision-making through internal management have been aided by technological and bureaucratic changes adopted by many offices throughout the 1970s. Offices shifted from paper record keeping on cases to systems like PROMIS, an automated case-tracking system that allows management to easily research discretional issues in charging or disposition.

Trial courts have provided an occasional external check on prosecutors' actions through informal or formal challenge to prosecutorial decisions. New judges, for example, may refuse to cooperate in an ongoing system of plea bargaining either by rejecting guilty pleas where bargains are involved or by rejecting recommendations of sentence leniency from the prosecutor.

Appellate court decisions represent the most well known judicial limit on prosecutors. At the initiation of defense counsel frustrated by what they consider abuses of prosecutorial discretion, numerous cases have challenged actions by prosecutors. The few resulting decisions from the United States Supreme Court have struck down certain prosecutorial strategies while legitimating others. In *Santobello* v. *New York* (1971), the Court implicitly supported prosecutorial discretion in plea bargaining, calling the process of plea bargaining "an essential component of the administration of justice," but the

Court admonished the prosecutor of the need to respect the terms of the bargain; the defendant in *Santobello* was thus entitled to relief because of the prosecutor's failure to follow through on the agreed-upon sentence recommendation.

Several other Supreme Court cases in the last decade have led to the development of a doctrine of prosecutorial vindictiveness, although the contours of that doctrine are not entirely clear. In *Blackledge* v. *Perry* (1974), the Court prohibited the prosecutor from increasing charges against a defendant who had invoked his statutory right to appeal. While the court noted there was no evidence of actual vindictiveness in *Blackledge,* they held that due process of law required the defendant to be free even of the appearance of such vindictiveness. In the next two cases, however, *Bordenkircher* v. *Hayes* (1978) and *United States* v. *Goodwin* (1982), the Court seemed to retreat from that position, allowing prosecutors to increase charges or file a habitual-offender charge against defendants who insisted on a jury trial after the failure of plea negotiations. The distinction between these three cases seems to be that the prosecutor's actions in *Blackledge* occurred in a posttrial context (where they were disallowed), while *Bordenkircher* and *Goodwin* occurred in a pretrial setting (where the Court gave prosecutors more latitude).

As a result of extensive public criticism of plea bargaining and a general cry for harsher sentencing, some states have enacted legislation to restrict or abolish plea bargaining and to increase penalties for certain offenses. Other sentencing reforms have included the passage of mandatory minimums and presumptive sentences. All of these legislative actions attempt to restrain or influence from the outside the decisions of prosecutors and others within the criminal justice process. While conclusions on the effectiveness of such measures are tentative and research is still ongoing, many studies point to the remarkable self-adjusting capacity of the court system, which allows discretion to be shifted from one stage of the criminal justice process to the next when confronted by external influences. As an example, restricting the discretion exercised by prosecutors in plea negotiation may simply result in greater discretion in the formulation of charges by prosecutors.

Another trend in prosecution has been an increased role for victims of crime. As an outsider to the criminal court, the victim has generally had negligible impact on decisions. Out of frustration and anger at their treatment by the criminal justice process, victims have lobbied successfully for greater participation and respect. In response, Congress passed the Victims of Crime Act of 1984, authorizing funds to help states establish programs for victim assistance and compensation. Whether these and other such programs will really result in a more active influence by victims on decisions by prosecutors remains to be seen.

Of particular importance in generating support for consideration of the victim's viewpoint has been lobbying and litigation by women's groups, especially in major cities. These political efforts have persuaded prosecutors to prosecute more fully defendants arrested for crimes against women, such as rape and domestic violence. These two offenses have often been downgraded in the eyes of criminal justice personnel, with a much higher than average rate of dismissal and reduction of charges. Prosecutors now are more politically sensitive in these cases, and some offices have established special task forces or charging units for rape, other sexual crimes, and crime within families.

A final trend in prosecution has been the development of informal alternatives to criminal processing. During the 1970s this idea was instituted through programs of pretrial diversion whereby defendants with social problems (who may also have committed criminal offenses) were diverted away from the criminal courts into social agencies that specialize in mental health, alcohol, or drug treatment. While the direct impact of diversion programs was minimal, they may have encouraged further thought about a range of informal alternatives to criminal punishment. Current programs, spurred by congressional legislation (the Dispute Resolution Act), include community (or neighborhood) justice centers, mediation, and arbitration. Those supporting alternative dispute resolution for criminal cases stress the cost savings for courts with the removal of minor offenses and the more appropriate and flexible processes afforded, for example, cases of interpersonal conflict.

The movement toward informal alternatives to criminal court is, oddly enough, somewhat like the movement toward increasing the severity of formal punishment: both represent efforts from the wider community to influence the policies of prosecutors and others in the criminal process, and both speak to the fundamental conflict facing prosecutors between the need to resolve disputes in the interests of justice and the need to maintain order and social control.

CASES

Blackledge v. Perry, 417 U.S. 21 (1974)
Bordenkircher v. Hayes, 434 U.S. 357 (1978)
Hurtado v. California, 110 U.S. 516 (1884)
Santobello v. New York, 404 U.S. 257 (1971)
United States v. Goodwin, 457 U.S. 368 (1982)

BIBLIOGRAPHY

Albert W. Alschuler, "The Prosecutor's Role in Plea Bargaining," in *University of Chicago Law Review*, 36 (1968), discusses plea bargaining, compares prosecutorial behavior in ten cities, and argues forcefully for the abolition of plea bargaining. Keith O. Boyum and Lynn Mather, eds., *Empirical Theories About Courts* (1983), includes recent articles discussing police-prosecutor relationships, courts as organizations, and other topics. Lief H. Carter, *The Limits of Order* (1974), presents a detailed case study of prosecutorial decision-making in California, with analysis of variation in prosecuting styles and of problems in establishing uniformity of decisions. George F. Cole, *Politics and the Administration of Justice* (1973), is an overview of the criminal justice system that draws heavily on the author's own research on prosecution in Seattle. Kenneth Culp Davis, *Discretionary Justice* (1969), emphasizes the injustices to individual parties from the exercise of discretionary power and suggests ways of confining, checking, and reducing discretion.

James Eisenstein, *Counsel for the United States* (1978), is an excellent study of the organization, politics, and behavior of the federal prosecutor. James Eisenstein and Herbert Jacob, *Felony Justice: An Organizational Analysis of Criminal Courts* (1977), analyzes and compares the disposition of felony cases in three cities, stressing the importance of the courtroom work group in decision-making. Malcolm M. Feeley, *The Process Is the Punishment* (1979), studies in detail a misdemeanor court, focusing especially on pretrial processes. Richard S. Frase, "The Decision to File Federal Criminal Charges," in *University of Chicago Law Review*, 47 (1980), presents a quantitative analysis of prosecutorial discretion in the filing of charges by federal prosecutors.

Milton Heumann, *Plea Bargaining: The Experiences of Prosecutors, Judges, and Defense Attorneys* (1978), questions the importance of case overload and shows how and why newcomers to the court learn to plea bargain. Joan E. Jacoby, *The American Prosecutor: A Search for Identity* (1980), is a comprehensive work on prosecutors, noted for its discussion of

PROSECUTORS

variation in prosecutors' offices and policies. Jack M. Kress, "Progress and Prosecution," in *Annals of the American Academy of Political and Social Science*, 423 (1976), summarizes current and historical material on prosecutors. *Law and Society Review*, 13 (1979), a special issue on plea bargaining, is an oversized collection of articles with various pieces on prosecutors.

William F. McDonald, *Plea Bargaining: Critical Issues and Common Practices* (1985), is a research report on plea bargaining, especially useful for the comparisons drawn between the author's findings and the diverse results in the current literature; and, as ed., *The Prosecutor* (1979), is an excellent collection of diverse articles on prosecutors. Lynn M. Mather, *Plea Bargaining or Trial? The Process of Criminal Case Disposition* (1979), describes and analyzes felony dispositions in Los Angeles from the attorneys' point of view, emphasizing the factors determining trial or guilty-plea disposition. Frank W. Miller, *Prosecution: The Decision to Charge a Suspect with a Crime* (1969), studies the charging decision, exploring the many reasons prosecutors have for not filing charges. Raymond Moley, *Politics and Criminal Prosecution* (1929), a classic early work on the politics of prosecution, presents fascinating material on criminal courts of the 1920s. David W. Neubauer, *Criminal Justice in Middle America* (1974), is a very readable and thoughtful overview of the criminal process, based on a study of a small midwestern city.

Jerome H. Skolnick, *Justice Without Trial* (1966), discusses police-prosecutor interactions. Elizabeth Anne Stanko, "The Impact of Victim Assessment on Prosecutor's Screening Decisions," in *Law and Society Review*, 16 (1981–1982), presents data on New York City prosecutors, demonstrating the importance of the victim to the decision to charge. Allen Steinberg, "From Private Prosecution to Plea Bargaining," in *Crime and Delinquency*, 30 (1984), presents new historical research on the early public prosecutors and the extent of private prosecution. W. Randolph Teslik, *Prosecutorial Discretion: The Decision to Charge* (1975), is a thorough, annotated bibliography on prosecutorial discretion. Pamela J. Utz, *Settling the Facts: Discretion and Negotiation in Criminal Court* (1978), compares prosecution in two California offices and analyzes the very different styles of decision-making. Vera Institute of Justice, *Felony Arrests: Their Prosecution and Disposition in New York City's Courts* (1977), describes the processing of felony cases in New York after initial arrest and explores why there is such extensive attrition.

[*See also* CRIMINAL JUSTICE SYSTEM; CRIMINAL LAW; CRIMINAL PROCEDURE; PLEA BARGAINING; POLICE; *and* TRIAL JURIES AND GRAND JURIES.]

STATE COURT SYSTEMS

Henry R. Glick

WHEN people think of the three branches of state government—the executive, the legislature, and the judiciary—they usually think of a single institution of government located in the state capital. The state legislature, for example, is usually composed of a senate and a house of representatives and typically is located in a single building. The judicial branch, however, does not involve just one institution; the state's highest court in the capital is only one of many courts in that state. The judiciary is a system of courts, located in towns, cities, and counties throughout a state and in the state capital. In a court system, various courts are connected to each other through decision-making procedures and legal policy. Therefore, understanding a state judiciary involves understanding the structure, behavior, and interrelationships of a variety of courts in a state court system.

Most crimes and civil disputes that occur in the United States become the subject of state, not federal, court cases. Compared with the states, the scope of decision-making (jurisdiction) of the federal courts is very limited, so most litigation falls to the state courts. The chances are extremely high that when Americans go to court, they go to a state court.

Each of the fifty states has its own separate system of courts with legal authority over people within the state. State courts make legal decisions in a wide variety of criminal law violations and in private (civil) disputes between people within the state. In some instances, state courts are affected by federal law and the decisions of federal courts, but in most ways they are substantially independent and separate systems of courts. Although they also are independent of each other, the fifty state court systems have much in common with each other. They all have similar levels and types of courts, with roughly comparable functions. For example, a murder trial or a serious business-contract dispute involving thousands of dollars would be heard in a state's major trial court and probably could be reviewed by the state's highest appellate court. There are variations in state law, but in general, a crime or a civil dispute in one state probably would be a crime or a dispute in another, with a comparable court available to decide it.

While the fifty state court systems share certain overall similarities, a closer look shows that there also are many important differences between them. For example, some states have relatively simple sets of courts with clear and distinct functions, while other states have many complex types of courts, which creates considerable confusion about their functions. The idea of a court system also oversimplifies the actual relationships among the courts in a state. The official role of appellate courts is to review and correct trial-court errors. However, appellate courts do not have continuous or predictable opportunities to provide legal guidance for the trial courts, since most trial-court decisions are not appealed to higher courts. Most losing litigants end their litigation with the trial courts because it is too expensive for them to continue the fight or because they believe that the chances of winning a reversal are not very good. This means, then, that most trial-court decisions are the final decisions.

There also are strong traditions of localism in American courts that prevent appellate courts from controlling local justice. Historically, the states did not create a system of multilevel courts all at once. Most early courts were local trial courts, and the few appellate courts were far away and had little authority. Today, even

682

though trial judges are parts of state court systems and receive state salaries, most of them continue to think of themselves as providers of local justice. Consequently, even when appellate judges make general rules that they expect trial courts to follow, local judges are often reluctant to fully support them if the rules conflict with local judicial policy or traditional ways of managing the work of the courts. Traditions of local control and the value of judicial independence are strong. Therefore, a diagram of an official court hierarchy that places appellate courts on top does not fully describe the reality of how state judicial systems exercise authority or create judicial policy.

THE STRUCTURE OF COURTS

There are two key elements to understanding court organization: the structure of court systems (the number and types of courts) and court jurisdiction (their legal authority to hear different kinds of disputes that people bring to court). Both the structure and jurisdiction of courts are determined by state constitutions and by statutes passed by state legislatures. These basic organizational features of courts are important because they determine the role that various courts have in state policymaking. Organization and jurisdiction affect judicial authority to deal with important state issues.

Approximately two-thirds of the states have four basic types of courts: a supreme court, intermediate courts of appeal, trial courts of general jurisdiction, and trial courts of limited jurisdiction. About one-third of the states have no intermediate appellate courts. Courts also have different names in the states. For instance, New York calls its highest court the Court of Appeals and refers to its major trial courts as supreme courts. In many states, however, intermediate appellate courts are called courts of appeals. Trial courts have many different designations. They may be called district courts, circuit courts, superior courts, or the like. Although particular courts often have different names, their functions are roughly similar. Table 1 lists the major types of courts that are found in the fifty states.

Trial Courts. Trial courts are the points of entry into the judicial process. Each side in a lawsuit or a criminal case has an opportunity to

TABLE 1
The Structure of State Courts

Highest Appellate Courts
    State supreme court

Intermediate Courts of Appeals
    Superior court, district or circuit court of appeals, etc. (found in about two-thirds of the states)

Trial Courts of General Jurisdiction
    District court, circuit court, court of common pleas, etc.

Trial Courts of Limited Jurisdiction
    Small-claims court, traffic court, family court, juvenile court, county court, justice of the peace, etc.

state its claim or complaint, to present witnesses to prove its version of the facts and circumstances, and to cite the law relevant to the conflict. Each of the opponents hopes the judge or jury will decide that his position is the correct one. Court cases involve either criminal or civil conflicts. Criminal cases occur when a person has committed an act that is forbidden by state law and is punishable, possibly by a fine payable to the government or by a jail term. Crimes are illegal acts against "the people" or the state. Civil cases include all other cases and do not involve jail terms. Civil cases often pit a government against an individual or a group, but the issues usually concern the enforcement of government policy. Civil cases not involving the government are conflicts between private parties and usually involve personal injury, property damage, debts, or some other conflict and claims for the payment of money from one side to the other. Many states have separate divisions of the same trial court to process civil and criminal cases, respectively.

Trial courts are divided into two groups: those with general jurisdiction and those with limited jurisdiction. "Limited jurisdiction" means that the particular court may hear only certain narrowly defined categories of cases. Many states have specialized trial courts that hear, for example, only traffic violations cases (traffic court), divorce and child-custody cases (family court), cases involving youthful criminal offenders (juvenile court), or cases involving small amounts of money (small-claims court). Although states are increasingly inclined to reduce the number and variety of these courts, some states have ten or more of them. Trial courts of "general jurisdiction" have broader authority to hear a large variety of cases. Any dispute involving more than a specific amount of money (for example, more than the $1,500–$2,500 limit in many state small-claims courts) may be heard by a state trial court of general jurisdiction. Most criminal cases involving serious crimes also are heard by these courts.

Appellate Courts. A person found guilty in a criminal case or a party in a civil suit who is unhappy about the outcome of a trial may appeal to another court for review of the decision of the trial court. Everyone is entitled to one appeal. Supreme courts and intermediate courts of appeals are the main appellate courts. Appellate courts do not hold new trials; they only review the written record of the lower court and hear the arguments of opposing attorneys. Appeals courts determine if the trial judge made an important error in procedure or interpretation of law that would require the appeals court to reverse the decision or to order a new trial. Exceptions sometimes occur in cases appealed from trial courts of limited jurisdiction. Appeals from these courts may require new trials in trial courts of general jurisdiction. Certain other appeals are heard by intermediate appeals courts, while others—often those involving more serious crime and more money—are reviewed by the highest court.

The formal purpose of intermediate courts of appeals is to hear certain types of cases that are considered to be less important and to take on some of the work of the highest appellate court. Some state supreme courts, for example, review criminal cases only when the death penalty is imposed. Others hear cases if the prison term handed down by the trial court is five years or more. Lesser penalties are reviewed by intermediate appellate courts. Cases involving less than certain amounts of money, perhaps $10,000, will be reviewed only by the intermediate appellate courts in certain states. Cases involving more money go to state supreme courts. In a few states, supreme courts have substantial powers to decide for themselves which cases they will decide. This is called the power of certiorari. It

is similar to, but usually not as extensive as, the power of the United States Supreme Court to accept or reject most cases. Where state supreme courts may choose the cases they will decide, the importance of intermediate appellate courts is greatly increased because these courts become the last stop for most cases in the state appellate process.

Distribution of Courts. Trial and intermediate appellate courts are distributed geographically throughout individual states, and consequently they often are viewed by local residents, judges, and lawyers as "local" courts, even though they are parts of state court systems. Trial courts have the greatest local flavor. All of the states are divided into various judicial districts, with state trial courts of limited and general jurisdiction serving local populations throughout the state. Small or sparsely populated states such as Alaska, Rhode Island, and Delaware have less than a half dozen judicial districts. Many other states have several dozen: Texas has more than 250 separate judicial districts. With few exceptions, cases are brought to courts in the area where the dispute or violation of criminal law occurs. This usually is a great convenience for local people involved in court cases, but it also means that out-of-towners who become involved in a dispute, such as a traffic accident, have to travel from their homes to a court in a distant county to participate in the case. Deciding local cases in the immediate area also means that getting justice is likely to be affected by local differences in attitudes and beliefs.

State intermediate courts of appeals usually are found in the more heavily populated and urban states, which produce many more cases than rural and sparsely populated states. However, the trend is toward the creation of more intermediate appellate courts, and we can expect more states to have them in the future. About 60 percent of the states with intermediate appellate courts have a single court with statewide jurisdiction. In the remainder, the state is divided into various geographic regions with each having its own independent branch of the intermediate appellate court. Illinois and Florida, for example, are divided into five regions, each with its own branch of the intermediate appellate court. The large state of Texas has fourteen separate intermediate appellate courts. As in the trial courts, cases are appealed to the intermediate appellate court located in the same section of the state as the trial court that first decided the case.

COURT JURISDICTION

As mentioned earlier, state courts hear most of the cases that arise in the United States. The federal courts have the power to hear only certain types of cases, and few of these affect most people. A common type of federal case is one in which people from different states sue each other for money exceeding $10,000. Because the parties to the suit are from diverse jurisdictions, such actions are called diversity cases. Few people ever become involved in these kinds of lawsuits. Other federal civil cases involve conflicts over federal law or major constitutional questions. Again, few people become litigants in such cases. There are also some (though relatively few) federal crimes, usually involving specialized and rare types of violations, such as counterfeiting, illegal immigration, and bank robbery. In contrast, the jurisdiction of the state courts is much larger and more general, and the state courts decide many everyday types of disputes.

The jurisdiction of individual courts within particular states often is very complex. Laws describing jurisdiction designate the precise types of disputes that must be heard by one court or another, but a state may permit more than one court to hear the same kind of case. The legal term for this overlapping of powers is *concurrent jurisdiction.* Where there are many different types of state courts with concurrent jurisdiction, it often is very difficult for citizens and even their lawyers to decide which court ought to hear a particular case.

We can get a clearer picture of the jurisdiction of various state courts by looking at examples of state court systems and the kinds of cases the individual courts are expected to decide. Figure 1 and Figure 2 are models of the state court systems of California and Indiana. The California system is an example of relatively simple state court systems, and Indiana represents complex and often confusing systems.

California has a state supreme court, six divisions of an intermediate appellate court distributed regionally throughout the state, a single type of trial court of general jurisdiction located in local districts (superior court), and two types

of trial courts of limited jurisdiction found in cities and towns (municipal court and justice court). The two trial courts of limited jurisdiction have exactly the same powers but different locations. The main difference between the two is that municipal courts are found in larger cities, while the justice courts are located in smaller towns and rural areas. The main role of these two courts is to conduct trials in civil cases involving less than $15,000, and the courts have separate, simplified procedures for small-claims disputes of less than $750. They also hear any criminal case designated by state law as a less serious crime (misdemeanor). A conviction for a misdemeanor usually results in a fine or very short jail sentence.

The state trial court of general jurisdiction hears civil disputes involving more than $15,000 and all criminal cases that the state has classified as serious crimes (felonies). Convictions for felonies often result in long prison terms or, in the case of murder, the death penalty. These courts also hear divorce and juvenile criminal cases. In California, and most other states, trial courts of general jurisdiction hear appeals from the trial courts of limited jurisdiction. In Figure 1, the arrow from the trial court of general jurisdiction to the courts of appeals signifies that nearly all cases decided by the major trial court may be appealed to, and must be heard by, the intermediate appellate court. An important exception is a criminal conviction carrying the death penalty. These are heard only by the state supreme court. With few other exceptions, the state supreme court has discretionary power to determine for itself which other cases it will decide. If it refuses to hear a case, the intermediate appellate court has the last word.

The Indiana court system, depicted in Figure 2, is much more complex. As in California, there is a single state supreme court and several divisions of the intermediate appellate court. However, the Indiana Supreme Court is required to hear many more cases than the California Supreme Court. In Indiana, there are two trial courts of general jurisdiction and six trial courts of limited jurisdiction. There are also special courts for particular counties as well as separate small-claims and probate courts, which deal exclusively with wills, trusts, estates, and various juvenile cases. However, a careful reading of the jurisdiction summarized in the boxes in the dia-

FIGURE 1
California Court System, 1980

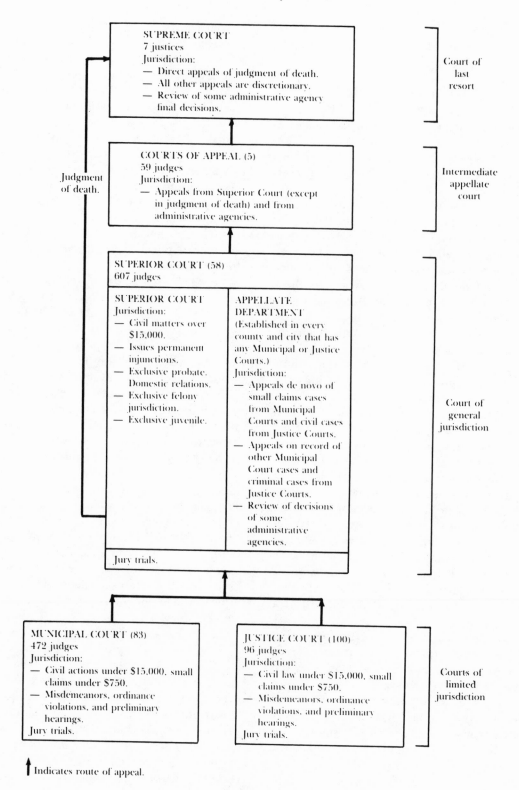

SUPREME COURT
7 justices
Jurisdiction:
— Direct appeals of judgment of death.
— All other appeals are discretionary.
— Review of some administrative agency final decisions.

Court of last resort

Judgment of death.

COURTS OF APPEAL (5)
59 judges
Jurisdiction:
— Appeals from Superior Court (except in judgment of death) and from administrative agencies.

Intermediate appellate court

SUPERIOR COURT (58)
607 judges

SUPERIOR COURT
Jurisdiction:
— Civil matters over $15,000.
— Issues permanent injunctions.
— Exclusive probate. Domestic relations.
— Exclusive felony jurisdiction.
— Exclusive juvenile.

APPELLATE DEPARTMENT
(Established in every county and city that has any Municipal or Justice Courts.)
Jurisdiction:
— Appeals de novo of small claims cases from Municipal Courts and civil cases from Justice Courts.
— Appeals on record of other Municipal Court cases and criminal cases from Justice Courts.
— Review of decisions of some administrative agencies.

Jury trials.

Court of general jurisdiction

MUNICIPAL COURT (83)
472 judges
Jurisdiction:
— Civil actions under $15,000, small claims under $750.
— Misdemeanors, ordinance violations, and preliminary hearings.
Jury trials.

JUSTICE COURT (100)
96 judges
Jurisdiction:
— Civil law under $15,000, small claims under $750.
— Misdemeanors, ordinance violations, and preliminary hearings.
Jury trials.

Courts of limited jurisdiction

↑ Indicates route of appeal.

(*Source:* United States Department of Justice. Bureau of Justice Statistics, *State Court Organization 1980,* 1982)

FIGURE 2
Indiana Court System, 1980

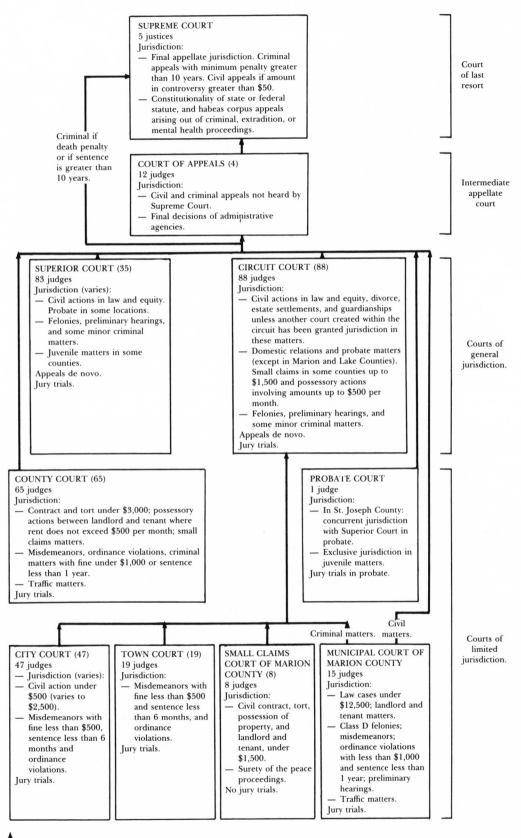

SUPREME COURT
5 justices
Jurisdiction:
— Final appellate jurisdiction. Criminal appeals with minimum penalty greater than 10 years. Civil appeals if amount in controversy greater than $50.
— Constitutionality of state or federal statute, and habeas corpus appeals arising out of criminal, extradition, or mental health proceedings.

Court of last resort

Criminal if death penalty or if sentence is greater than 10 years.

COURT OF APPEALS (4)
12 judges
Jurisdiction:
— Civil and criminal appeals not heard by Supreme Court.
— Final decisions of administrative agencies.

Intermediate appellate court

SUPERIOR COURT (35)
83 judges
Jurisdiction (varies):
— Civil actions in law and equity. Probate in some locations.
— Felonies, preliminary hearings, and some minor criminal matters.
— Juvenile matters in some counties.
Appeals de novo.
Jury trials.

CIRCUIT COURT (88)
88 judges
Jurisdiction:
— Civil actions in law and equity, divorce, estate settlements, and guardianships unless another court created within the circuit has been granted jurisdiction in these matters.
— Domestic relations and probate matters (except in Marion and Lake Counties). Small claims in some counties up to $1,500 and possessory actions involving amounts up to $500 per month.
— Felonies, preliminary hearings, and some minor criminal matters.
Appeals de novo.
Jury trials.

Courts of general jurisdiction.

COUNTY COURT (65)
65 judges
Jurisdiction:
— Contract and tort under $3,000; possessory actions between landlord and tenant where rent does not exceed $500 per month; small claims matters.
— Misdemeanors, ordinance violations, criminal matters with fine under $1,000 or sentence less than 1 year.
— Traffic matters.
Jury trials.

PROBATE COURT
1 judge
Jurisdiction:
— In St. Joseph County: concurrent jurisdiction with Superior Court in probate.
— Exclusive jurisdiction in juvenile matters.
Jury trials in probate.

Criminal matters.   Civil matters.

CITY COURT (47)
47 judges
— Jurisdiction (varies):
— Civil action under $500 (varies to $2,500).
— Misdemeanors with fine less than $500, sentence less than 6 months and ordinance violations.
Jury trials.

TOWN COURT (19)
19 judges
Jurisdiction:
— Misdemeanors with fine less than $500 and sentence less than 6 months, and ordinance violations.
Jury trials.

SMALL CLAIMS COURT OF MARION COUNTY (8)
8 judges
Jurisdiction:
— Civil contract, tort, possession of property, and landlord and tenant, under $1,500.
— Surety of the peace proceedings.
No jury trials.

MUNICIPAL COURT OF MARION COUNTY
15 judges
Jurisdiction:
— Law cases under $12,500; landlord and tenant matters.
— Class D felonies; misdemeanors; ordinance violations with less than $1,000 and sentence less than 1 year; preliminary hearings.
— Traffic matters.
Jury trials.

Courts of limited jurisdiction.

↑ Indicates route of appeal.

(*Source:* United States Department of Justice, Bureau of Justice Statistics, *State Court Organization 1980,* 1982)

gram reveals that the jurisdiction of the same type of court often varies around the state and the jurisdiction of one court often overlaps that of another court. In particular, the jurisdiction of the superior and city courts varies from place to place. Also, the powers of the superior court and the circuit court are very similar in civil cases, and the superior courts and county courts may hear some of the same types of cases. An Indiana lawyer familiar with the courts only in his home county would have to study the court system elsewhere in the state before he could comfortably take a case out of his usual territory.

The organization and jurisdiction of state courts is a major issue of judicial politics. Many legal reformers favor consolidating and streamlining state courts to obtain systems that are more like the California than the Indiana model. They believe that the presence of many different kinds of trial courts with overlapping jurisdiction is confusing and frustrating to lawyer and layman alike. It also leads, they believe, to inefficiency and disrespect for state courts. However, some lawyers and judges oppose change, because they are satisfied and familiar with the courts as they are and are reluctant to learn new law and procedures. Lawyers who specialize in trial work sometimes oppose change because their intimate knowledge of intricate local courts gives them an advantage over others in processing cases. Nevertheless, court consolidation is the current trend, and we can expect to find more consolidation in the future. About twenty states follow a system similar to California's including about a half dozen that have systems even simpler and easier to understand, and ten states have systems similar to Indiana's. The twenty remaining states have systems that lie between the two models; they usually have somewhat fewer trial courts of limited jurisdiction than Indiana but have systems that are more complex than California's.

LINKS BETWEEN STATE AND FEDERAL COURTS

Although the federal courts frequently decide certain specialized kinds of cases that rarely come up in the state courts, there are several ways that state and federal courts are tied to each other. First, there are various types of cases that

may be heard in either state or federal court. It is also possible for certain cases to move from the state courts into the federal courts. Various links between state and federal courts add to the complexity of the American legal system. For a complete picture, state and federal judicial policymaking have to be considered together and within the broader context of federal-state political relations.

There are several areas of law in which state and federal courts have concurrent jurisdiction. An important one is diversity cases. As explained earlier, these are cases in which opposing litigants live in different states and the amount of money in contention is $10,000 or more. Both federal and state courts may hear these kinds of cases. Another type of case that may be heard in either state or federal court is one that involves a substantial federal question. Federal questions concern federal statutes and/or the United States Constitution. There are many cases involving federal questions that are begun in the federal courts, although litigants may decide to start these cases in the state courts. A third area of overlap is in certain kinds of criminal cases. Certain criminal acts violate both state and federal laws, and a suspect could be prosecuted in either court. Examples of these kinds of laws are robbery and larceny, embezzlement, interstate auto theft, forgery, and narcotics violations. The odds are that federal officials will defer to local police and prosecutors if they begin prosecution for one of these crimes, but frequently, state and local officials are not as proficient in detecting and investigating certain crimes, such as organized drug trafficking, embezzlement, and interstate auto theft, so the Federal Bureau of Investigation (FBI) or other federal agency usually investigates and prosecutes these crimes in the federal courts.

Aside from the possibility that certain kinds of cases may be initiated in either state or federal court, the courts are linked through the movement of state cases into the federal court system. A major way in which this occurs is through petitions by litigants from decisions of state supreme courts directly to the United States Supreme Court. State litigants who petition the United States Supreme Court for a hearing argue that certain of their rights guaranteed by the United States Constitution have been violated and that they have not received a remedy in the state courts. Frequently, these cases involve state and local officials, such as police or other government administrators who carry out state and local law. Issues in these cases often involve the rights of criminal defendants, students' rights concerning dress codes and free speech, apportionment of state legislatures, the right to an abortion, prayer and Bible reading in the public schools, and racial and sex discrimination.

The United States Supreme Court has declared about a thousand state and local laws unconstitutional since 1800 through cases that came to the Court from state supreme courts. About one-third of these declarations have occurred since 1960. Probably the greatest impact that the United States Supreme Court has had on promoting personal freedom has occurred through its review of state cases. State and local courts and other officials are expected to support these decisions and to implement them in their own areas of policymaking. This does not always occur, nor is it usually a smooth process, but there is little doubt that the United States Supreme Court has had a lasting effect in many areas of public policy by overturning state judicial policy and by implementing its own policies at state and local levels.

Another frequent link between state and federal courts occurs when convicted criminals held in state or local jails or prisons petition federal trial courts for a review of their conviction and imprisonment, arguing that state actions have violated their constitutional rights. Their cases are based on federal habeas corpus laws. *Habeas corpus* means "you have the body," and it requires state officials to show good reason for the imprisonment. The practical purpose of these cases is to find some way of getting out of jail or getting an order for a new trial. The number of these petitions has increased over the years from approximately fourteen thousand in 1975 to more than twenty-three thousand in 1981. However, less than 5 percent are successful. These cases are last-chance attempts to overturn state court decisions, and federal judges find very few reasons to overturn most state court convictions and sentences. Despite the important role of the United States Supreme Court in setting national judicial policy through several landmark cases, most decisions of the state courts continue to stand as the final word on judicial policy.

EFFECTS OF STRUCTURE AND JURISDICTION

The existence of fifty separate state court systems, a separate federal court system, and strong traditions of localism and judicial independence have a number of important consequences for American justice. First, since state and federal courts may hear some of the same kinds of cases, there always is a strong possibility that state and federal judicial policy will differ on important and controversial issues. For example, for many years since the 1950s, the federal courts were substantially more liberal in supporting individual rights than most state courts. The United States Supreme Court in particular was severely criticized by many state and local government officials, including state judges, when it began to make controversial decisions granting greater constitutional rights to criminal defendants and requiring racial integration of public schools. Many state judges refused to apply these decisions to their own cases. However, judges in some states supported the Supreme Court and made similar liberal decisions. By 1986 some state supreme courts had become even more liberal than the Supreme Court.

Just as there are differences between state and federal judicial policy, so there are many differences between the decisions of the fifty state court systems as well as differences in judicial policy within each of the fifty states. The existence of many levels and types of courts distributed locally practically guarantees variations in judicial policy. For example, prison sentences for similar crimes often vary widely. It is common for trial judges in large cities, where crime is routine and thousands of similar cases flood the courts every year, to sentence defendants to relatively short prison terms. In contrast, in smaller towns and rural areas, where serious crime is more unusual and a more significant event, criminals are likely to face prison terms that are twice as long as those imposed in bigger cities or even longer. Variations like these can be found throughout the United States.

Appellate courts rarely control which cases are appealed, so there is generally no continuous or logical flow of cases that might stimulate appellate judges to create clear and well-developed judicial policies on many subjects. In states that have several divisions of intermediate appellate courts located in different geographic regions of the state, the chances of finding differences in judicial policy are even greater. Since these courts have taken on much of the work previously handled by state supreme courts, many cases brought to them go no further in the judicial system. The chances are good that they will develop different interpretations of law and settle similar kinds of cases in different ways. State supreme courts resolve some of these differences, but many conflicts on policy continue to exist.

Another effect of the overlap of courts is to provide litigants with certain alternatives in going to court. Decisions to use one set of courts or another usually hinge on cost and calculations about where the most favorable decisions can be found. Diversity cases give lawyers and litigants valuable options to choose the most favorable courts. The civil rights movement also discovered through using both state and federal courts over the years that federal judges generally were more supportive of civil rights. Consequently, the civil rights movement has concentrated its litigation efforts in the federal courts. If state courts had been more responsive, civil rights groups would have used them more. Overlapping jurisdiction within a state also provides litigants with some opportunities to shop for courts where judges have reputations for being more sympathetic to the legal claims brought by litigants. This sometimes occurs in large cities, where several criminal courts have citywide jurisdiction and prosecutors and defense lawyers jockey with each other to get their case decided by judges with harsh or lenient reputations.

The potential of courts to differ in judicial policy indicates that the actual operation of the legal system is closely tied to local social and political environments and is related to the characteristics of people who run the system. Courts are integral parts of the larger society in which they operate.

THE WORK OF STATE COURTS

Despite the greater visibility of state appellate courts, especially the supreme court, only a tiny fraction of all state cases get beyond the trial level. As indicated earlier, most appeals also stop with intermediate appellate courts. The flow of cases drops sharply at each higher level of court within the state court system. Therefore, even the trial courts of limited jurisdiction are important because they decide the most cases and hear the kinds of disputes and problems that are most likely to affect the most people.

A more precise picture of the work of state trial courts is presented in Table 2, which shows the number of cases filed in trial courts of limited and general jurisdiction in all fifty states and the special federal courts for the District of Columbia. The total number of cases contained in Table 2 for 1981–1982 is more than 82 million, and the trend is toward more cases. Filings in state courts have increased about 20 percent since 1977. However, not all cases decided in the state courts are included in Table 2, because some states do not keep accurate records of the cases decided by the trial courts of limited jurisdiction. There probably are several million more cases decided in the states, but no exact totals are available. Many of the cases handled by the state trial courts are for very minor offenses, particularly traffic cases. Traffic cases account for about two-thirds of the total number of cases in Table 2. Nevertheless, even with these cases removed from the total, the state courts decide more than 27 million other kinds of civil and criminal cases.

The importance of the state courts in dealing with most litigation in the United States becomes even clearer when we compare the work of the state courts with that of the federal courts. All of the federal courts, from the United States Supreme Court to the special federal trial courts of limited jurisdiction, decide fewer than 250,000 cases per year. Therefore, in terms of the probable direct impact on citizens, the state courts are much more significant than the federal courts.

There are important differences between the states in the number of cases decided and how types of cases are treated. The most heavily populated states have very large court systems and decide many more cases than the more rural, sparsely populated areas. For example, California courts hear more than 18 million cases per year, although 16 million of them are traffic cases. But even with the traffic cases removed, California courts decide more civil and criminal cases than any other state. New York has about the same number of civil and criminal cases as California, but many fewer traffic cases. Texas, which has a population roughly two-thirds that

TABLE 2
Filings in Courts of General and Limited Jurisdiction, CY 1981 or FY 1981/82

	Civil	Criminal	Juvenile	Total excluding traffic	Traffic	Total including traffic
Alabama*	216,408	140,170	46,866	403,444	227,722	631,166
Alaska	30,728	22,355	1,270	54,353	86,729	141,082
Arizona	138,621	148,395	1,076	288,092	1,153,217	1,441,309
Arkansas	99,452	147,428	13,907	260,787	479,106	739,893
California	1,639,518	923,834	102,333	2,665,685	15,599,845[a]	18,265,530[a]
Colorado*	202,775	59,578	26,153	288,506	181,873	470,379
Connecticut	212,240	109,539	14,255	336,034	303,281	639,315
Delaware	49,728	56,822	9,870	116,420	128,425	244,845
Dist. of Columbia	145,911	36,597	4,765	187,273	10,403	197,676
Florida	553,574	447,754	113,841	1,115,169	2,287,888	3,403,057
Georgia*	257,173	45,286	34,482	436,941	361,167	798,108
Hawaii	47,382	52,537	8,913	108,832	871,916[a]	980,748[a]
Idaho	52,347	32,632	7,661	92,640	209,904[a]	302,544[a]
Illinois	647,096	712,379	32,642	1,392,117	6,582,043[a]	7,974,160[a]
Indiana	388,301	144,960	26,315	559,576	354,232	913,808
Iowa	133,484	113,667	5,570	252,721	661,254	913,975
Kansas*	118,187	30,093	10,607	158,887	275,828[a]	434,715
Kentucky	187,210	217,193	36,445	440,848	274,788	715,636
Louisiana*	238,609	536,856	30,117	805,582	467,506	1,273,088
Maine*	57,938	96,449	13,404	167,791	88,372	256,163
Maryland*	590,887	171,781	29,750	792,418	646,313[a]	1,438,731[a]
Massachusetts*	465,987	657,551	118,876	1,242,414	3,243,585[a]	4,485,999[a]
Michigan*	263,863	538,014	22,131	824,008	1,313,532[a]	2,137,540[a]
Minnesota	251,062	114,986	44,672	410,720	1,448,626[a]	1,859,346[a]
Mississippi	NA	NA	NA	NA	NA	NA
Missouri	220,643	148,155	14,935	383,733	656,011	1,039,744
Montana*	6,533	1,340	576	8,449	NA	NA
Nebraska*	81,199	173,844	3,118	258,161	189,089	447,250
Nevada	81,874	52,822	2,777	137,473	225,953	363,426
New Hampshire	65,476	39,175	7,287	111,938	202,218	314,156
New Jersey*	573,166	31,719	109,881	714,766	NA	NA
New Mexico*	66,325	69,355	4,342	140,022	382,177[a]	522,199[a]
New York*	793,896	1,209,061	37,005	2,039,962	460,260	2,500,222
North Carolina	378,688	487,783	19,900	886,371	677,247	1,563,618
North Dakota	25,765	21,719	1,249	48,733	119,662[a]	168,395[a]
Ohio*	619,043	406,403	202,835	1,228,281	1,598,165[a]	2,826,446[a]
Oklahoma*[b]	208,088		8,063	NA		483,691
Oregon	155,362	149,695	NA	NA	671,893	NA
Pennsylvania	515,014	745,308	47,979	1,308,301	4,540,269[a]	5,848,570[a]
Rhode Island*	40,175	38,940	7,275	86,390	NA	NA
South Carolina	182,336	469,894	9,633	661,863	416,184	1,078,047
South Dakota	35,911	136,471	NA	NA	NA	NA
Tennessee*	94,631	37,213	NA	131,844	NA	NA
Texas	679,107	1,316,709	11,761	2,007,577	4,226,529	6,234,106
Utah*	92,894	37,366	34,848	165,108	444,421	609,529
Vermont	24,856	16,599	1,616	43,071	85,750	128,821
Virginia	770,693	399,209	133,471	1,303,373	1,014,304[a]	2,317,677[a]
Washington	218,446	170,557	24,424	413,427	1,650,194[a]	2,063,621[a]
West Virginia*	89,608	117,493	7,514	214,615	114,787[a]	329,402[a]
Wisconsin	326,920	161,645	28,336	516,901	230,680	747,581
Wyoming*	11,513	1,772	975	14,260	NA	NA

Source: United States Department of Justice, Bureau of Justice Statistics, *State Court Caseload Statistics* (1983).

*These figures represent virtually all cases filed in general-jurisdiction courts and between 70% and 80% of cases filed in limited-jurisdiction courts.

NA   These data were not available and therefore are not included in the total filing figures.

[a]Parking tickets are included in the traffic case load reported for these states.

[b]Civil cases only.

of California, has a very heavy case load, particularly in criminal cases. Texas also has one of the largest prison populations in the United States. In contrast to these larger states, small-population states such as Montana, North Dakota, and Wyoming have fewer cases and smaller judicial systems.

Differences in the case loads of the state trial courts are not accounted for only by differences in population. Local traditions and values also probably play a part. For example, perhaps in California, where the population is very mobile and there is a constant stream of newcomers, there are more impersonal and transitory relationships. Perhaps conflicts lead to court cases rather than to informal negotiated settlements. Several states, such as Texas, have many more criminal cases, which may reflect a tougher law-and-order political environment.

The work of state appellate courts is described in Table 3. The total number of cases filed for hearings in all of the state appellate courts is about 160,000 per year. About three-quarters of them are heard by intermediate appellate courts. These figures underscore the importance of intermediate appellate courts as the final appellate courts for most state cases. The overall totals in Table 3 also reinforce the point that few cases get beyond the trial-court stage. Table 3 also reveals that there are differences between the appellate courts similar to the differences between the state trial courts. California courts hear more appeals than courts in any other state, and New York and Texas also score high on the number of appeals channeled through the judicial system. The smaller, rural states have fewer appeals, and many of the small states have no intermediate appellate courts. All of the appeals heard in these states go directly to state supreme courts.

It is clear that state courts deal with most of the litigation in the United States. They also decide the cases that are most likely to involve the most citizens. This is demonstrated by the figures in Table 4, which presents a description and an approximate distribution of the kinds of civil and criminal cases that appear in most state courts. In most types of cases, there is a wide range of percentages because there are no national or even statewide totals for the types and number of issues brought to the courts.

The figures show that among the civil cases, with the exception of divorce cases, which are plentiful in some courts, those with which state trial courts deal most involve financial and commercial issues. State supreme courts also hear a significant number of cases involving the regulation of business, although a majority of state supreme court cases involve appeals concerning private economic disputes. The trial courts of limited jurisdiction (small-claims courts) also deal with a variety of commercial litigation. These courts were created to provide low cost and simplified procedures so that average citizens could go to court to recover relatively small amounts of money from other individuals or small businesses. Small-claims cases involve appliance and auto repairs, landlord-tenant disputes, and similar types of issues. While the courts do hear cases involving these issues, they are used most heavily and repeatedly by large businesses, such as banks, hospitals, and building contractors, to collect small loans and debts for goods and services. These kinds of cases range from 15 percent to 90 percent of the total case load, but in most small-claims courts in the United States the percentage of debt-collection cases probably is closer to 70 percent.

Table 4 shows that in the criminal case category the trial courts of limited jurisdiction hear relatively minor criminal cases, mostly traffic violations. Traffic cases constitute from 30 percent to 85 percent of the total case load in these courts, with the national average at about 67 percent. Precise figures are not available for other kinds of minor criminal cases. Estimates from various sources indicate that cases involving drunkenness and other liquor violations, such as possession of alcohol by minors, and disorderly conduct, which usually means rowdiness and fighting, are at the top of the list. Cases involving prostitution are common in some cities, but not in others. The percentages for drunkenness also vary from zero to 25 percent of the total, since some cities have decriminalized drunkenness, so that arrests no longer result in court cases. Instead, people intoxicated from alcohol or drugs are referred to detoxification facilities.

The state trial courts of general jurisdiction deal with most types of more serious crime. More research has been done on these courts than on others, and so we have more reliable figures for these kinds of cases. The percentages are estimates based on various sources, but they provide

TABLE 3
Appellate Court Filings, CY 1981 or FY 1981–1982

	Courts of last resort	Intermediate appellate courts	All appellate courts
Alabama[a]	1,018	496[a]	
Alaska	417	463	880
Arizona	1,143	2,436	3,579
Arkansas	446	1,194	1,640
California	4,325	14,933	19,258
Colorado	1,052	1,512	2,564
Connecticut	595	191	786
Delaware	337	—	337
Dist. of Columbia	1,663	—	1,663
Florida	1,456	13,795	15,251
Georgia	1,617	2,152	3,769
Hawaii	387	127	514
Idaho	455	—	455
Illinois	1,803	6,516	8,319
Indiana	409	1,095	1,504
Iowa	1,733[b]	(b)	1,733
Kansas	188	1,060	1,248
Kentucky	1,150	2,689	3,839
Louisiana	3,337	2,878	6,215
Maine	571	—	571
Maryland	867	1,983	2,850
Massachusetts	773		
Michigan	1,949	6,318	8,267
Minnesota	1,609	—	1,609
Mississippi		—	
Missouri	1,059	2,964	4,023
Montana	574	—	574
Nebraska	956	—	956
Nevada	732	—	732
New Hampshire	558	—	558
New Jersey	289	5,993	6,282
New Mexico	610	505	1,115
New York	708	11,638	12,346
North Carolina	989	1,994	2,983
North Dakota	309	—	309
Ohio	2,134	8,915	11,049
Oklahoma[c]	2,543	1,080[b]	2,543[b]
Oregon	812	3,403	4,215
Pennsylvania	2,254	12,830	15,084
Rhode Island	592	—	592
South Carolina	1,173	—	1,173
South Dakota	363	—	363
Tennessee	885	1,723	2,608
Texas[c]	3,395	6,151	9,546
Utah	700	—	700
Vermont	601	—	601
Virginia	2,257	—	2,257
Washington	863	2,799	3,662
West Virginia	1,549	—	1,549
Wisconsin	737	2,479	3,216
Wyoming	198	—	198

Source: United States Department of Justice, Bureau of Justice Statistics, *State Court Caseload Statistics* (1983).

Note: All available data are included in the table. Blank spaces indicate that the data were not available.

— These states did not have intermediate appellate courts in 1981.

[a]Data are incomplete: Alabama has two intermediate appellate courts, but only one, the Court of Civil Appeals, reported data in 1981.

[b]All appellate cases in Iowa and Oklahoma are filed in the courts of last resort. A portion of this case load is transferred to the intermediate appellate court for disposition.

[c]Both Oklahoma and Texas have two courts of last resort.

STATE COURT SYSTEMS

TABLE 4
Types of Cases Decided in Selected State Courts

Trial courts of limited jurisdiction[a,d]	Trial courts of general jurisdiction[b]	Supreme courts[c]
CIVIL CASES		
Payment for goods and services (15%–90%)	Divorce and family (10%–60%)	Government regulation of business (4%–64%; average = 23%)
Unsatisfactory goods and services (25%)	Debts and loans (10%–25%)	Private economic disputes (wills, estates, real estate) (6%–77%; average = 46%)
Landlord-tenant (20%–30%)	Contracts (10%–20%)	
Property damage-auto (15%–30%)	Liens (15%)	
Other property damage (3%–15%)	Personal injury and property damage (10%–25%)	Personal injury and other liability (2%–50%; average = 14%)
Debts, loans (10%)	Property foreclosures (2%–5%)	Other (average = 18%)
Wages (3%–5%)	Evictions (3%)	
Other (10%)	Government regulation (1%–3%)	
	Other (1%–3%)	
CRIMINAL CASES		
Traffic (30%–85%; average = 67%)	Burglary (15%)	Trial court error in a variety of felony cases (5%–70%; average = 31%)
Drunkenness (0%–25%)	Theft (15%)	
Other liquor laws (5%)	Armed Robbery (10%–15%)	Constitutional claims (0%–5%; average = 1.7%)
Disorderly conduct (5%–10%)	Robbery (3%–10%)	
Prostitution (1%–6%)	Assault (5%–7%)	
Other (25%)	Sale of narcotics (1%–20%)	
	Use of narcotics (2%–8%)	
	Weapons possession (4%–15%)	
	Murder (2%–4%)	
	Rape (1%–5%)	
	Gambling (1%–5%)	
	Other (7%–15%)	

[a]Adapted from Austin Sarat, "Alternatives in Dispute Processing: Litigation in a Small Claims Court," in *Law and Society Review* (Spring, 1976); John C. Ruhnka and Steven Weller, *Small Claims Courts* (1978); Robert J. Hollingsworth et al., "The Ohio Small Claims Court: An Empirical Study," in *Cincinnati Law Review*, 42 (1973); Herbert Jacob, *The Frustration of Policy* (1984); *Statistical Abstract of the United States, 1982–1983*.

[b]Adapted from Craig Wanner, "The Public Ordering of Private Relations," in *Law and Society Review* (Spring, 1974); Lawrence M. Friedman and Robert V. Percival, "A Tale of Two Courts: Litigation in Alameda and San Benito Counties," in *Law and Society Review* (Winter, 1976); *Felony Arrests*, rev. ed. (1981); James Eisenstein and Herbert Jacob, *Felony Justice* (1977).

[c]Adapted from Burton Atkins and Henry R. Glick, "Environmental and Structural Variables as Determinants of Issues in States Courts of Last Resort," in *American Journal of Political Science*, 20 (1976).

[d]The trial court of limited jurisdiction in the civil case category is the small-claims court.

a reasonably accurate overview of the work of the major trial courts. Property crimes are highest on the list, and burglary, theft, and armed and unarmed robbery are common in nearly all courts. Cases involving the sale of narcotics vary widely, depending upon the size of the drug problem and upon local law enforcement capabilities and priorities. Crimes against persons, including assault, murder, and rape, are not as plentiful as the other types. Even though these kinds of cases make the headlines most often because they are so serious and are directed against individuals, they constitute a relatively small percentage of the work of the state trial courts.

State supreme courts hear appeals from a variety of criminal cases. The range in the percentage of criminal appeals is from 5 percent to 70 percent, with a national average of about 30 percent. These cases involve a variety of issues raised during the trial or as the case was processed by police and prosecutors. However, criminal defendants do not assert many constitutional claims in their appeals, as is common in the federal courts. Most criminal appeals are based on state sentencing laws and other court procedures. They do not involve major constitutional issues. The crimes involved in cases that reach state supreme courts vary widely, according to the social characteristics of the states, the presence or absence of an intermediate appellate court below the supreme court, and the jurisdiction of the state supreme court. Generally, serious felonies involving heavy sentences are appealed most often.

POLICYMAKING IN STATE COURTS

A major function of courts is to impose legal settlements in various individual disputes and cases of crime. However, both appellate and trial courts also make policies through court decisions that have broader significance and consequences for society. "Policymaking" is governmental action designed to solve or cope with various social, economic, or political problems. Therefore, "judicial policymaking" comprises those decisions that have greater social significance than the settlement of individual cases.

Courts generally make policy in two ways. The first involves single court cases that present new, unusual, and often controversial issues. Court decisions in these cases attract news attention and reactions from other public officials and interested groups of citizens. This kind of policymaking occurs most often in appellate courts for several reasons. One important reason is that appellate courts, especially state supreme courts, have the final authority to interpret state law and constitutions and to correct errors made by state trial courts. Therefore, their decisions directly affect the policymaking of other state officials and serve as guidance for trial courts when they decide similar cases in the future. Furthermore, decisions of appellate courts are often explained in written legal opinions, so that the reasons behind the decision are set out. Written opinions also state what other officials and judges are supposed to do in current and future similar cases. Examples of these kinds of cases are state supreme court decisions that have required state governments to revise state tax laws and financing of public schools to assure greater equality among school districts, decisions on whether proposed constitutional amendments that are scheduled for a public vote meet state constitutional requirements, decisions affecting the way that police and prosecutors treat defendants in criminal cases, and rules concerning when hospitals may disconnect life-support systems to terminally ill patients. All of these individual case decisions are controversial and have major effects on society.

Courts also make policies in more subtle ways that rarely capture as much public attention or create much controversy. But the decisions still reveal how the judiciary copes with social and economic problems. This is called cumulative policymaking. It occurs when courts repeatedly make similar decisions in a long series of similar cases. Courts often develop consistent patterns of decision-making that accumulate over time and reveal court policy toward problems that repeatedly come to court. Examples of this kind of policymaking are the sentencing decisions of trial courts. Many judges in the same city tend to sentence defendants convicted of similar crimes to roughly similar jail terms, while judges in other cities often produce sentences more lenient or more harsh. Sentencing decisions reflect the policies of the courts because they demonstrate how judges have decided to cope with the crime problem. Another example concerns awarding and collecting child support in divorce cases. Some judges have recently changed from showing leniency toward fathers who have not paid court-ordered child support to imposing jail terms until fathers obtain the money needed to pay off all of their unpaid support. Both the early patterns of leniency and the change to stringent enforcement of divorce agreements are examples of court policy toward child support.

Civil Rights and Liberties. A major concern in judicial policymaking concerns civil rights and liberties. These refer to a number of constitutional rights that guarantee individual freedom and equality in the United States. Two of the most controversial policy areas in civil liberties are racial discrimination and the rights of criminal defendants and convicted criminals. However, other civil liberties involve the freedoms of speech, press, and religion; age and sex discrimination; and rights to privacy. Civil rights and liberties have become major controversial issues in the United States and in the courts in particular because of liberal interpretations of the Constitution by the United States Supreme Court beginning in the 1950s.

Civil rights and liberties are important in the state courts for two major reasons. The first is that the state courts are directly affected by decisions of the United States Supreme Court because many of its liberal policies were created by overruling conservative decisions of various state supreme courts. As part of the hierarchy of courts and law in the United States, the state courts are obligated to change their own policies to conform to the policy of the Supreme Court. Second, the state courts have opportunities to interpret provisions of state constitutions that affect individual rights. Provisions of state constitutions often are identical or similar to those of the national constitution. In recent years, a few state supreme courts have created liberal interpretations of constitutional liberties that go beyond United States Supreme Court policy. However, the large majority of the state courts have resisted past liberal Supreme Court interpretations of the Constitution, have welcomed recent conservative policies of the Supreme Court, and have interpreted their own state constitutions in ways that do not broaden interpretations of civil rights and liberties in the states.

A prominent example of the way that state courts deal with these issues involves the rights of criminal defendants. Prior to the 1960s, nearly all state supreme courts interpreted the rights of criminal defendants very narrowly. For instance, confessions and evidence seized as a result of police searches were admitted as evidence in criminal cases without much concern for how they had been obtained. Defendants had no right to attorney, and the states provided few protections against police pressure in interrogations. This began to change in 1964 when the United States Supreme Court, under the leadership of Chief Justice Earl Warren, decided *Escobedo* v. *Illinois*. This decision required that when suspects become the focus of a police investigation they must be allowed to consult with an attorney. But the decision did not specifically require police, prosecutors, or trial judges to inform defendants of this new right. State judges not sympathetic to the plight of criminal defendants refused to expand the decision to help defendants obtain lawyers. Consequently, in practice, many poor, uneducated, and uninformed defendants had no access to lawyers, despite this new ruling.

In 1966 the Supreme Court required that police explicitly inform defendants of their right to an attorney, their right to remain silent during police questioning, and their right to a court-appointed attorney if they were too poor to hire one *(Miranda* v. *Arizona)*. This decision was much clearer and more specific than *Escobedo* and gave state courts and police much less opportunity to ignore the rights of criminal defendants than the earlier decision. Most state supreme courts have followed the requirements of the Supreme Court in *Miranda.* However, even this decision did not cover all situations that arise after a suspect has been arrested and is on the way to the police station. For example, the Court's opinion did not state exactly when the police had to inform a suspect of his rights, which might give ample time for a defendant to incriminate himself through voluntary statements made upon his arrest. The decision did not automatically apply to defendants already convicted and serving jail time or to retrials of those already convicted. Generally, the large majority of the state courts did not expand the *Miranda* ruling beyond the Supreme Court's specific policy. If anything, they interpreted it narrowly so that few defendants could make full use of the Supreme Court decision. For example, in order to obtain a reversal of a conviction before a state supreme court, a defendant had to have objected to a violation of his rights during his original trial. If he had not done so, it was assumed that he had waived his rights.

In recent years, as conservative Republican justices have replaced many of the Warren Court liberals, the United States Supreme Court has become more conservative as regards the rights of criminal defendants. Like the conservative state judges, the newer justices on the Supreme Court have narrowed the interpretation of past Court decisions concerning the admissibility of evidence at a trial. Much incriminating evidence now can be admitted into court with fewer limitations on how the police obtained it. Most of the state courts have welcomed these new conservative decisions and embrace the new leadership of the Supreme Court because the decisions generally go in the direction that most state judges always have favored.

There are a few exceptions to these generally

conservative state court policies. Some supreme courts in states with heterogeneous and heavily urban populations have produced liberal policies concerning the rights of criminal defendants and other personal liberties. They frequently rely on earlier, liberal Supreme Court rulings and a legal doctrine called independent state grounds, which provides a way for state rather than federal court interpretations of the Constitution to become the basis for civil liberties decisions.

State court treatment of civil liberties policy is a good illustration of the powers of all courts to make important policy and the likelihood that judicial policy will differ throughout the United States. In most areas of law, including civil rights and liberties, there are large numbers of state and federal court cases that can serve as precedent or guidance to the state courts. There are the liberal decisions of the Warren Court era and the conservative decisions of the Burger Supreme Court. Both national and state constitutions contain general provisions concerning individual rights that can be interpreted differently by judges throughout the country. There also are various general legal doctrines or principles that judges may select as the legal basis for their decisions. Doctrine supporting the supremacy of federal law clearly provides a way for national Supreme Court policy to stand in place of state law and state court decisions. But other legal doctrines, particularly independent state grounds, provide opportunities for state law to become the basis of judicial decisions. Options in legal doctrine enhance the power and significance of the separate state court systems.

Other State Policies. Although civil liberties cases attract most news media and public attention, the state courts make policy in many other areas of law that affect more people more of the time than civil liberties policies. As indicated earlier, state courts make millions of decisions involving traffic accidents and other criminal cases, as well as a wide variety of personal disputes involving financial transactions. Few of these are affected by federal law or federal courts.

A major policymaking area in which the state courts have had a major impact on social and economic life is tort law. Torts concern rules for recovering financial awards in court for a variety of civil wrongs committed by one person or organization against another. Examples of torts involve personal injuries resulting from badly manufactured products, injuries suffered by workers on the job, and injuries sustained by patients in hospitals or by passengers in cars or on public transportation. There are about as many examples of torts as there are possibilities for injuries in a modern technological society.

Two important and similar issues in tort law concern sovereign immunity and charitable immunity. Until the 1960s, sovereign immunity prevented citizens in most states from suing a state or local government for injuries caused by negligent public employees or while using public facilities. Individuals could not sue for injuries suffered while a patient was in a public hospital or as a result of badly maintained streets and sidewalks, public utilities, or other public services. Charitable immunity prevented citizens from suing nonprofit organizations that operate schools or hospitals, such as religious organizations. By the end of the 1970s, more than three-quarters of the states had abandoned the doctrine of sovereign and charitable immunity, so that people can now recover damages for injuries. Many of these changes occurred through state supreme court decisions. Sometimes, however, the state legislatures imposed maximum dollar limits that an individual can recover from a state or local government, and some states still impose serious restrictions on suing the state government.

Another judicial policy in tort law concerns products liability. Until the 1950s, state court decisions generally prevented successful suits for injuries caused by badly manufactured products unless an individual could clearly show negligence by the manufacturer. Even then, liability was limited to the business that sold the product to the consumer. Therefore, manufacturers were successfully insulated against claims, since most products are sold through retailers. The major change in this policy occurred in 1960 when the New Jersey Supreme Court created a new policy that held manufacturers liable and made it unnecessary for consumers to prove negligence. Incurring an injury from normal use of a product was sufficient grounds for a lawsuit. Later court decisions established a policy stating that manufacturers created implied warranties in their products that guaranteed them as safe to consumers. Consequently, manufacturers became directly and strictly liable for injuries. Similar changes

697

have occurred in suits concerning defects in construction. Before the 1950s, building contractors were held blameless for any injuries caused by faulty construction after a new owner paid his final bill and accepted the property. More recent policies permit owners to sue later if injuries caused by defects in construction are not uncovered immediately.

A third area of change in the law of torts concerns the ability of members of the same family to sue each other for injuries. This policy began to change from a complete prohibition on intrafamily suits to allowance for them in the early 1900s. But it did not become a common policy in the states until after World War II. This area of policy is important because in the past it was difficult for a member of a family to recover financial losses from an insurance company when the injury occurred in an automobile accident in which a spouse or parent was at fault.

There are many other areas of state judicial policymaking in which courts can have a significant impact on society. State constitutions are very long and complex. Therefore, state supreme courts frequently receive cases in which individuals or groups challenge the constitutionality of state laws. In most cases, supreme courts approve of legislative and other governmental action, but some laws are overturned or require legislative rewriting before they become valid. Controversial cases coming to state supreme courts include no-fault insurance plans, medical malpractice laws, the legality of special local tax districts, approval of local taxes and special fees on the sale of utilities, government licensing of professions, and government regulation of business. No exact figures on the important policymaking decisions of state supreme courts exist, but there probably are a dozen or more such decisions in most of the states every year.

Local Judicial Policies. Since nearly all cases originate in trial courts, local judicial policy sometimes involves issues similar to those found in state supreme courts. Local trial courts hear cases involving zoning regulations; the conduct of elections; school board policy concerning budgets, public hearings, teacher demands, and the like; local tax laws and procedures; and other issues involving local government and politically active local interest groups. Like state appellate courts, trial courts generally approve the decisions of other local government authorities. The process of going to court and obtaining a judicial hearing frequently delays the implementation of a local government policy, but trial courts rarely stand in the way of other government action.

Although trial courts sometimes make policy in single controversial cases, they have more opportunities to affect social and economic conditions through cumulative policies. The most common types of cases involve crime, divorce, alimony and child support, creditor-debtor cases, and real estate and other financial transactions. As indicated earlier, the pattern of decisions in these cases defines the policy of local courts. Several examples will illustrate local judicial policymaking.

Local criminal justice policy is usually very different from appellate policy because relatively few defendants claim violations of their constitutional rights. It is common nearly everywhere for defendants to be protected to the extent that they are assured of having lawyers to aid in their defense and police advise them of their rights. The presence of lawyers and other constitutional safeguards, however, does not alter the fact that most defendants seem obviously guilty of having committed a crime and are willing to plead guilty in exchange for a promise of leniency in sentencing. Consequently, local criminal justice almost always results in convictions. Furthermore, the odds are high nearly everywhere in the United States that most criminal defendants are poor, disproportionately nonwhite, and accused of assault, robbery, or other theft. Relatively few white-collar crimes are detected or prosecuted.

The key differences in local criminal justice policy concern the sentences imposed by the courts. State criminal law is determined by state legislatures, which frequently allow judges broad discretion in choosing the appropriate penalty for a large variety of crimes. Therefore, it is possible for judges to impose suspended sentences, probation, or long prison terms for the same crime. State law invites and practically guarantees variation in local sentencing policy. Research on cities of similar size and with similar types of crime, often within the same state, reveals that there is enormous variation in the type and length of sentences. Judges in some cities sentence defendants in similar criminal cases to prison terms twice as often as judges in other cities. The length of prison terms in some cities also are twice as long as, or longer than, those imposed by courts in other cities.

Appellate courts sometimes develop sentencing guidelines for trial judges in their state so that sentencing policies will become more uniform, but local trial judges, jealously guarding their traditional independence and power to determine appropriate sentences, often resist efforts to standardize sentencing. Compromise guidelines frequently contain vague or general language that permits local judges to continue to do as they see fit.

Local judicial policies in economic disputes also develop predictable patterns. Generally, most economic cases are brought by individuals or businesses to collect loans and to enforce contracts and rental agreements that have been duly signed by businesses and their clients and customers. Businesses are repeat players in the judicial process. They go to court frequently in the same kinds of disputes, they seek the same kind of results, and they are experienced and able to hire legal talent to press their many routine, repetitive claims. Defendants in these cases usually are individuals who have not been to court before, are unsophisticated about the legal process, and may not have the ability or finances to hire capable lawyers to defend them. Often in these cases, they have no good defense because they signed legal agreements and have become unable, or are unwilling, to pay. Judges are normally concerned only with proof of their indebtedness, and the businesses who are repeat players normally win their cases. Local courts rarely examine the background of legal contracts to determine whether they were arrived at fairly or whether the business could have predicted that a customer would not be able to meet his or her financial obligations. If a person has entered into an agreement, the courts normally enforce collections.

Judicial policy in family law varies and is undergoing a great deal of change. Traditionally, divorces have not been very easy to obtain. It was necessary for the husband or wife seeking the divorce to prove in court that the other party had been at fault in some major way, such as committing adultery, before a court could grant a divorce. Once granted, judges would require the major wage earner, usually the husband, to pay support to his wife (alimony) and child support for his dependent children. Children typically lived with their mothers, and fathers had visitation rights. Since the 1970s, divorce has been much easier to obtain. No-fault divorce laws in many states permit divorce if the judge determines that a marriage is irretrievably broken. This very vague rule provides almost automatic grounds for granting divorces to either party seeking a divorce. Payment for alimony and child support is still common, but since larger numbers of women are in the work force, alimony is more doubtful, and levels of child support and which parent should pay is less certain.

State laws are very vague concerning alimony, child support, and child custody and visitation. Laws typically permit judges to make their own best guess about what are appropriate or fair arrangements and what is in the best interest of the children. Consequently, decisions in these cases vary enormously depending upon the values and beliefs of individual judges and informal local policies that judges may develop together concerning proper family arrangements. In most cases, mothers continue to obtain custody of their children when both parents agree, but some fathers have successfully claimed that they are the better parent. Joint custody, in which mothers and fathers share care and visitation with their children, is becoming a new judicial policy in many states.

CONCLUSION

This discussion of state court systems has described the structure and roles of state courts in the American judicial process. The structure and jurisdiction of state courts and the links between the state and federal court systems demonstrate the importance of state courts in handling most judicial business in the United States. Most crime and most interpersonal disputes that affect most people are dealt with by the state courts. State supreme courts are most visible in state judicial policymaking, and they have made important changes over the years in several major areas of law. However, state trial courts also are extremely important because they control many cumulative policies that affect most people and most aspects of life. The general independence

STATE COURT SYSTEMS

of state court systems from each other and from the federal system also indicate that state courts have many important opportunities to make policy that affects the decisions of the other branches of government and the lives of most Americans.

CASES

Escobedo v. Illinois, 378 U.S. 478 (1964)
Miranda v. Arizona, 384 U.S. 436 (1966)

BIBLIOGRAPHY

Larry C. Berkson and Susan B. Carbon, *Court Unification: History, Politics and Implementation* (1978), describes the history and implementation of major changes in state court systems and includes illustrations of individual state experiences. Malcolm M. Feeley, *Court Reform on Trial* (1983), a survey of the adoption and effects of trial-court reform, including bail reform, pretrial diversion, sentencing reform, and speedy-trial rules, concludes that most reforms fail to affect how courts process cases and defendants. Henry R. Glick, *Courts, Politics and Justice* (1983), a current and comprehensive social science text on the American judicial process that includes discussion of all levels and types of courts and judicial processes in the United States; and *Supreme Courts in State Politics* (1971), examines judicial roles in four state supreme courts, using research based on interviews with supreme court judges and examining how they view their positions and functions. Henry R. Glick and Kenneth N. Vines, *State Court Systems* (1972), is an early description of the structure and behavior of state court systems.

Herbert Jacob, *Justice in America,* 4th ed. (1984), is a short but valuable summary of major judicial institutions and processes in the United States. Fannie J. Klein, *Federal and State Court Systems: A Guide* (1977), is an overview of American judicial systems. Richard Neely, *Why Courts Don't Work* (1983), an appraisal and criticism of the performance of state trial courts, although written by a state supreme court judge, is nonlegalistic and directed to nonlawyers. Mary Cornelia Porter and G. Alan Tarr, *State Supreme Courts: Policymakers in the Federal System* (1982), includes eight essays on the importance of state supreme courts as state policymaking institutions, with much useful discussion of innovations in state judicial policymaking. G. Alan Tarr, *Judicial Impact and State Supreme Courts* (1977), discusses the responses of state supreme courts to decisions of the United States Supreme Court and how Supreme Court decisions are implemented in the states.

[*See also* FEDERAL COURT SYSTEM; SENTENCING ALTERNATIVES; STATE CONSTITUTIONAL LAW; *and* TORTS.]

THE SUPREME COURT
OF THE UNITED STATES

Walter F. Murphy

A CENTURY and a half ago, Alexis de Tocqueville wrote in *Democracy in America* that the "judicial organization of the United States is the institution which the stranger has the greatest difficulty in understanding." And by European and Latin American standards the United States Supreme Court remains a peculiar institution.

First, it operates within a system of judge-made "common law" as opposed to codes of legislatively created "civil law." In Europe, Latin America, and many developing nations colonized by the Dutch, French, Portuguese, or Spanish, the national legislature has created a systematic body of law—codes of criminal law, civil law, and procedural law with supposedly clearly written, logically arranged rules to cover all problems likely to arise. The function of judges is to apply these rules to a controversy and, if interpretation is necessary, to construe them according to principles laid down within the codes themselves. (In fact, because no "code" can be perfectly clear or cover all eventualities, the judicial function under the civil law is much more complex.)

Common-law systems—the term *system* is misleading, for common law is by nature unsystematic—are found only in Britain and its former colonies. In contrast to the civil law's ideals of a comprehensive set of rules made by legislators, common-law judges made most of the rules that they applied and interpreted, and they did so on a case-by-case basis, using experience more than abstract logic and narrowly focusing on each problem rather than constructing broadly applicable principles.

For centuries the British king and Parliament mainly concerned themselves with such overarching matters of public policy as war, peace, and taxes, and by and large left to judges the task of formulating rules to govern day-to-day activities of life. And in this context common-law judges proceeded cautiously, deciding one case at a time and citing earlier cases as authorities for decisions. They gradually built up rules by tinkering rather than by conceiving and executing a grand design.

Today legislatures in common-law countries do make rules about minute as well as broad aspects of public life; but except in areas like Quebec and Louisiana, which were originally settled by the French, these legislatures almost never try to enact comprehensive codes on the European model. What Americans call "codes" are often little more than efforts to put some order into statutes enacted over many decades. Even the "uniform codes" that have become popular among the states are seldom either uniform or all-encompassing.

The ordinary piece of legislation in common-law countries deals with a particular problem—monopoly, for example—and even then rarely claims to be complete within itself. To understand the typical statute, one has to know the earlier judge-made rules it attempts to abolish, alter, or reinforce as well as the later rules judges have made to fill in the statute's general language. An intelligent, educated citizen in a civil law system can read the appropriate code and have an accurate idea of his or her rights and duties. A similar exercise in a common-law country is a sure recipe for trouble, unless one also reads dozens of judicial opinions "explaining" the statute.

The principal point of this first distinction is that the Supreme Court, as heir to a common-law tradition, operates within a framework in which wide judicial discretion and creativity have been normal and legitimate. It is a system in which judges rely on previous decisions, on precedents, at least as much as—and usually far more than—on general legislative pronouncements.

Judicial review, a second peculiarity of the United States Supreme Court—one shared by almost all American courts, state and federal—distinguishes it from its ancestral institutions, the British courts of common law. Those tribunals fashioned and refashioned the rules of the common law as well as interpreted statutes, but they lacked authority to declare that any act of Parliament, no matter how outrageous, violated the British Constitution.

Like the "constitutional courts" of Austria, Italy, and West Germany, the United States Supreme Court plays the extraordinary role of authoritative interpreter of the national constitution, exercising the power to declare invalid acts of coordinate branches of government. But even here the Supreme Court differs from European constitutional courts. Those are specialized tribunals whose jurisdiction is largely limited to disputes involving constitutional interpretation. They cannot review and correct any other form of judgment. They do not sit at the apex of a judicial hierarchy but alongside other courts of specialized jurisdiction. Unlike those tribunals, and much more like the supreme courts of Canada and Japan and the High Court of Australia, the United States Supreme Court is also the highest court of general jurisdiction for a national legal system, with authority to interpret that government's treaties, statutes, common law, and administrative orders.

A third peculiarity stems from the federal nature of the United States and of a decision of Congress to create a separate system of national courts. Article III of the Constitution reads, "The judicial Power of the United States, shall be vested in one supreme Court, and in such inferior Courts as the Congress may from time to time ordain and establish." Congress might have provided, as the Australians, Canadians, and West Germans later did, that cases involving national law would start in state courts and have given the Supreme Court appellate jurisdiction over such issues. Instead, Congress chose to establish a federal judicial system parallel to state courts and to make the Supreme Court responsible for overseeing the administration of justice in those tribunals.

One effect of a dual set of courts is that both often apply laws relating to similar matters. A single act may violate state as well as federal statutes and result in a double prosecution—not a violation of the prohibition against double jeopardy because, the Supreme Court has ruled, federalism makes people in the United States subject to two governments.

Causing more confusion is the fact that a private citizen often has the option of starting in a state or federal court, for while Congress has provided that trials for most federal crimes will be conducted in federal courts, it has given federal courts exclusive jurisdiction over few areas of civil law. Thus, for instance, a citizen hurt by a law that she thinks violates the federal Constitution may challenge the statute in either a state or federal court. In effect, then, the Supreme Court presides not only over a national system of courts but also over fifty state systems insofar as they rule on controversies involving the United States Constitution, statutes, treaties, administrative orders, or, in very rare instances, federal common law.

Further complicating matters, if the challenged statute is that of a state and the litigant chooses to begin in a state court, he or she may allege that the statute also violates the state constitution. On that point, however, the judgment of the state's highest court is final. When the justices hear cases from state courts, they are not supposed to interpret state law, whether statutory, common, or constitutional. When state law is involved, the Court's sole task is to decide whether that law, as interpreted by state judges, is compatible with national regulations and the national Constitution. As the justices explained in *Herb* v. *Pitcairn* (1945),

> This Court from the time of its foundation has adhered to the principle that it will not review judgments of state courts that rest on adequate and independent state grounds. The reason is so obvious that it has rarely been thought to warrant statement. It is found in the partitioning of power between the state and Federal judicial systems and in the limitations of our own jurisdiction. Our only power over state judgments is to correct them to the extent that they incorrectly adjudge federal rights.

These peculiarities are surrounded by an apparent anomaly. Although officials of the United States often proclaim that the country is a democracy, with government chosen by, and responsible to, the people, members of the Supreme Court, like all other federal judges, are not popularly elected; and like most federal judges, they serve "during good Behaviour." Impeachment by the House of Representatives followed by conviction by a two-thirds vote of the Senate is the only formal way of removing a federal judge. In two hundred years of the Constitution's operation, only once has the House impeached a justice, and on that occasion the Senate refused to convict. One other justice voluntarily left the bench because of questionable private financial dealings. For all practical purposes, "good Behaviour" means as long as a justice cares to remain in office.

PERSONNEL AND PROCEDURES

The Constitution provides for the establishment of "one supreme Court" but says nothing about how many judges shall staff it. The number of justices, set by statute at six in 1789 and periodically changed during the nineteenth century, has ranged from five to ten and has remained at nine since 1869, a chief justice and eight associate justices. They are nominated by the president, and their appointment is subject to confirmation by the Senate.

Selection of Judges. Although neither the Constitution nor any statute imposes restrictions on who is eligible for selection, a president does not have a free hand. Common-law systems do not have a cadre of professional judges, as do those under the civil law; but by tradition all justices have been lawyers. There are also expectations of geographic representation. Normally, there will be at least one justice from the major regions of the country: New England, the Middle Atlantic states, the Deep South, the Midwest, and the Far West.

There are now also expectations of ethnic representation. During most of this century there has been a Catholic on the Court, and since 1916, there has usually been a Jew. The appointment of Thurgood Marshall in 1967 probably marked the beginning of a tradition of having at least one black justice; and Sandra Day O'Connor's appointment in 1981 makes it unlikely that the High Bench will ever again be an all-male sanctuary.

The power of the Court imposes additional restrictions on presidential choices. Given judi-

cial review and the invitation to discretionary interpretation that Congress opens in many statutes, only a fool or a madman would nominate a person who disagreed with the legitimacy of his policies. Richard Nixon was only being candid when he described his principal criterion for selecting judges: "First and foremost, they had to be men who shared my legal philosophy." Thus, presidents have typically chosen people from their own political party—and people whose views they think they know well. Many justices have been governors, senators, or attorneys general; and, whether or not they have held public office, the vast majority have been sufficiently active in politics to make a record that the president can assess. As Lincoln put it to George Boutwell, "We cannot ask a man what he will do [if appointed], and if we should, and he should answer us, we should despise him for it. Therefore we must take a man whose opinions are known."

Several factors have kept the Court from becoming the mirror of a president's constitutional views. First, on the average a vacancy occurs only about once every two and a half years, making it difficult for a president, even in two four-year terms, to select a majority of the justices.

Second, presidents often make mistakes about the views of the people they nominate. Woodrow Wilson, an economic liberal, nominated James C. McReynolds, who turned out to be among the most economically conservative judges in American history. Dwight Eisenhower once referred to his choice of Earl Warren as chief justice as "the biggest damn fool mistake I ever made." Moreover, the past is not an infallible indicator of the future, for what a person thinks is constitutional when a senator or cabinet official may, when he or she views the matter from the perspective of a judge, seem unconstitutional.

A third factor limiting presidential influence is that the nature of pressing political problems and their social contexts may change radically. For instance, President Franklin D. Roosevelt fought a bitter battle against the Supreme Court from 1934 until 1937, when the justices, stubbornly insisting that the Constitution required laissez-faire, invalidated many of the president's most important economic policies. As one would expect, Roosevelt nominated only justices who fervently believed that governmental regulation of the economy was constitutional. But very quickly that issue faded in importance. Replacing economic regulation was a myriad of questions about racial justice, freedom of speech and press, electoral districting, privacy, and fairness in criminal procedure—none of which Roosevelt had even remotely considered in picking judges.

The Justices. A total of 103 people sat on the Supreme Court between 1788 and 1986. Although their disagreements with each other have been frequent, public, and acerbic, most of the justices have come from remarkably similar social, economic, and professional backgrounds. All have been lawyers and most have been political activists. More than half had served as judges on other courts, but only about a quarter had spent much of their professional careers on the bench and many of those had earlier been in partisan politics. With the single exception of Sandra Day O'Connor, all have been males and, with the sole exception of Thurgood Marshall, white. Seven have been Catholics, and five, Jews. The other ninety-one have been at least nominal Protestants.

Most of the justices have come from politically active families of the upper middle or upper class; received educations at the best universities; and, when practicing law, tended to handle corporate and financial problems rather than less genteel divorce and criminal cases. When appointed they have usually been in late middle age, and curiously, they tend to outlive by a considerable margin their contemporaries, even those of the same social class.

Jurisdiction. The Court's jurisdiction—that is, its authority to hear and decide cases—is divided into two categories, original, as a trial court, and appellate, as a reviewer of the rulings of other courts. The Constitution specifies that the Supreme Court, sitting as a trial court, shall hear cases involving foreign diplomats and those to which a state is a party. Since diplomats cannot be sued and it is undiplomatic for them to sue, states tend to monopolize the Court's original jurisdiction.

In most years the Court hears several disputes between states over such matters as the location of a boundary or allocation of water from a river that flows through both. These cases could tie up the justices for many months, but the Court has devised an efficient procedure. When one of these cases is filed, the justices appoint a "special master," a retired judge or an eminent attorney,

to call witnesses, examine documents, hear arguments, and report findings and recommendations. After receiving the special master's report, the Court treats the case just as it does those that come up under its appellate jurisdiction: it allows the states to present written briefs and oral arguments contesting or supporting the master's report.

It is as an appellate tribunal that the Court does the bulk of its business. Cases come to the Court from both state and federal tribunals. But, again, the losing party in the highest state court may ask the Supreme Court to review the case only if that dispute raises questions of the interpretation of a federal statute, treaty, or the Constitution.

Below the Supreme Court in the federal judicial system are two tiers of tribunals: district courts and courts of appeals. There is at least one United States district court in each state, and its jurisdiction is limited not only by subject matter but also by territory. That is, a federal district court in New York cannot hear disputes, even about issues of federal law, that arise in New Jersey.

For supervision of district courts, the country is divided geographically into twelve circuits, each headed by a court of appeals. As a matter of right, the loser in the district court may ask the court of appeals in that circuit to review the decision. (Appeals from three-judge district courts go directly to the Supreme Court.) Usually, each court of appeals sits in panels of three judges, though, as with district courts, many more judges may be attached to the tribunal.

Although no new factual evidence may be introduced in an appeal, on occasion judges at all levels will take what is called "judicial notice" of certain kinds of notorious facts, for example, the existence of a war, a depression, or even, as in *Roe* v. *Wade* (1973), in holding that a woman has a constitutional right to an abortion at least during the first three months of pregnancy, of advances in medical technology, such as antibiotics. Furthermore, some judges—especially on the Supreme Court—have gone beyond the argument and written record to do their own homework so that they might better understand both the factual issues and the implications of certain lines of reasoning. This practice has angered some jurists, because they believe it unfair in not allowing opposing counsel to respond to what the judge has read in private. The usual response is that to depend completely on counsel would mean that issues affecting the entire country would often be determined by a single litigant's wisdom in choosing a lawyer.

The Supreme Court has appellate jurisdiction over all decisions of the courts of appeals as well as over several specialized national tribunals that hear only disputes about taxes, customs, patents, and courts martial. Much of the Court's business arises out of state supreme court decisions on federal issues.

There are three avenues to the Supreme Court. First is "certification." Here a court of appeals certifies a question to the justices for their decision; in effect, the judges of a court of appeals say that the issue is of such importance and difficulty that they should not decide it. Not unexpectedly, given judicial egos, certification is rare, and even when a court of appeals certifies a question, the Supreme Court sometimes refuses to respond, asking instead that it first have the benefit of that court's wisdom.

The second avenue is an "appeal," in a narrow, technical sense. According to federal statutes, a losing litigant can appeal to the Supreme Court and the justices must take the case when a United States court of appeals or a special three-judge district court declares a state or federal act unconstitutional or the highest court of a state invalidates a federal act or sustains the constitutionality of a state statute. In fact, because of the number of cases the justices are asked to review—more than four thousand a year—they treat appeals as being within their discretion to hear or refuse to hear.

The third and most commonly used avenue is "certiorari." The losing litigant in cases not covered by appeal may petition the justices to review a decision by a United States court of appeals or a state supreme court that has ruled on a federal issue. The next subsection describes how the Court handles these petitions; here we note only that it takes a vote of four of the justices, one less than a majority, to agree to hear the case.

The justices refuse to review more than 95 percent of all the cases brought to them, and rarely does the Court offer any useful explanation of its action. When it declines to take an appeal from a state supreme court, it typically says only, "Appeal dismissed for want of a substantial federal question." When it refuses to grant a petition for certiorari, it usually does so with a one-word opinion: "Denied." These statistics do not mean, however, that the justices treat such matters lightly.

Procedures. When a petition for review arrives at the Supreme Court, it goes to the office of the clerk of the Court. He sends a copy to each justice. From then on, practice varies, depending on the justice's preferences. Some read all or most of these petitions themselves; others divide them among their own clerks; and some have agreed to share their clerks' recommendations. Each justice may choose as many as four clerks. They work for the justice, not for the clerk of the Court, and are almost always young men or women who have recently graduated at or near the top of their classes at the most prestigious law schools. They usually serve for only one year, acting as research assistants and perhaps critics, but they have no formal authority.

Every week or so the chief justice circulates a "discuss list"—the petitions for certiorari and the appeals that he recommends the justices debate at the Court's next conference. Unless a justice objects, all other petitions received during the period covered by the list are automatically denied. If a justice wishes to discuss any petitions not included on the list, he or she merely so notes and those items are added. Refusal to review means that the lower court's decision stands; but it does not imply that the Supreme Court approved either that ruling or the principles behind it.

During the term—which begins on the first Monday in October and for all practical purposes ends sometime in July—the Court sits for two weeks, then recesses for several weeks to allow the justices to think, research, and write. During the weeks the Court is sitting, the justices hear oral arguments on Mondays, Tuesdays, and Wednesdays from 10 A.M. until noon, and from 1 P.M. until 3 P.M. Later on Wednesday afternoons and all day Friday, the justices meet in conference to debate petitions on the discuss list and cases just argued on their merits.

When the Court agrees to hear a case, each side may submit a "brief," more fully stating its arguments, and a "reply brief," responding to the other's arguments. At this stage or when the petition for review is filed, any other person or group may also present a brief to the Court as an *amicus curiae,* or "friend of the court." Those wishing to submit an *amicus* brief must either obtain the consent of the parties or special permission from the Court by showing a real interest at stake in the litigation and an intention to present arguments different from those of either side. On occasion, the Court will invite someone to appear as an *amicus,* most often the solicitor general of the United States or a state attorney general.

After the justices have granted review, the Court sets a date for oral argument. Each side is allowed thirty minutes, although in cases whose impact is likely to be especially far-reaching, the Court may permit additional time. Normally, an *amicus* is not allowed to participate in oral argument, though the Court frequently allows the solicitor general and, less often, state attorneys general to do so.

Counsel stands at a lectern facing the bench and begins, "Chief Justice, may it please the Court. . . ." These may well be the lawyer's last prepared words. The justices want a discussion, not a lecture. Most attorneys who have a case before the Court are there for the first time and erroneously assume that the justices want to hear explanations of their own previous decisions. Counsel find themselves constantly interrupted, as two or three justices simultaneously push for responses to questions that range from a decision's potential effects on public policy to more details about the case's factual background.

When five minutes remain, a white light flashes on the lectern. When time is up, a red light goes on. Counsel must stop instantly. There is a story that Chief Justice Charles Evans Hughes once cut a famous lawyer off in the middle of the word *if.* The enormousness of the Court's work load makes every second precious.

When the justices meet in conference, no one except the nine members of the Court is allowed into the room. If there is a message for one of the justices or much-needed coffee, the junior justice serves as doorkeeper and relieves the caller of his or her burden.

The chief justice opens discussion by summarizing the case and explaining his views. Then the justices speak in order of seniority. The Court keeps no formal record of these debates, but some justices take notes either to refresh their memories or to enlighten history. What Justices Frank Murphy, Harold Burton, and William O. Douglas scribbled provide the same general picture of intense, informed, and wide-ranging debate that takes place during oral argument.

Justices use the conference either to try to persuade their colleagues or, if undecided, to learn from them. Some justices make eloquent pleas; others play devil's advocate. Some sit passively, taking notes or staring out the window to relieve boredom. At times tempers flash. "We take our jobs seriously," one justice said in private, "and we do get angry. Any judge who didn't get angry when he saw the Constitution misinterpreted ought to be impeached."

The style of conferences has varied with the personality of the chief justice. Charles Evans Hughes and Harlan Stone represent extremes. Hughes disciplined himself to speak only a few minutes, and he expected similar self-control from his colleagues. He would cut off a speech with a curt "Thank you" and nod to the justice next in seniority to begin. He preferred rapid disposition of cases to give-and-take. Stone had bridled under Hughes's management; and when he became chief, he tried to turn the conference into a seminar. His colleagues sometimes turned it into a shouting match. Business that took several hours under Hughes might consume several days under Stone, but no one complained that issues were not thoroughly debated.

When the chief believes that more discussion would be fruitless, he calls for a vote. The justices vote in the same order as they speak, with the chief voting first and the junior justice last. This procedure, begun under Earl Warren, marked an important change. At least from the time of John Marshall the justices had spoken in order of seniority and then voted in reverse order, allowing the chief justice to vote last and to side with the majority.

Being in the majority is important, for one of the few prerogatives the chief has is that of assigning the task of writing the opinion of the Court if he is in the majority. If he is in the minority, the senior associate justice in the majority makes the assignment. The person who assigns the opinion may keep it himself or pass it on to the justice whom he thinks most likely to reflect the views that he wants to prevail.

Some chief justices almost never dissented. John Marshall and Charles Evans Hughes, for example, almost always found it expedient to stifle their own views when they saw they would lose, to vote with the majority, and sometimes even to assign the opinion of the Court to themselves so as to damage as little as possible the principles that they supported. Others, like Warren Earl Burger and Earl Warren, seldom suppressed their own views.

Being assigned the task of writing the Court's opinion does not guarantee that the opinion written will be that of the Court. To be so labeled and so to carry the institutional authority of the Supreme Court rather than be an expression of personal views, an opinion must have the approval of at least five justices; and all justices are free to write their own opinions, either concurring or dissenting, and to change their votes up to the minute the Court announces its decision. (If that happens, the Court does not announce its decision until the justices write new opinions.) Even later, if the losing party asks for a rehearing, justices can change their minds.

The opinion writer prepares a manuscript and circulates it to the rest of the Court. Few justices have been bashful about making suggestions for change. Sometimes these are minor; sometimes they involve recasting the entire reasoning; and sometimes suggestions from different justices are mutually incompatible. If the last is true, the opinion writer has to convert others or decide which colleague's vote to lose.

At the same time, the dissenters, acting alone or together, may circulate their opinion(s), although they may wait until the majority's opinion has approached final form. Dissents are also circulated to every member of the Court, and sometimes they persuade justices to change their votes. It is unusual, but not unheard of, for what began as a dissent to become the opinion of the Court. It is more usual for the Court's opinion writer to try to accommodate justices who plan to write separate concurring or dissenting opinions and win them over to a modified version of the Court's opinion.

In civil law systems, no matter how sharply judges disagree among themselves, decisions are reported as if they were unanimous and authors of the court's opinions are not identified. Except in the Constitutional Court of West Germany, dissents and concurrences are not allowed. The United States Supreme Court uses a somewhat similar method when it denies petitions for review; that is, it merely issues a one-word or, at most, one-sentence order. Still, justices sometimes publish dissents against denials, and oth-

ers may respond. In the past, when the justices were unanimous and either thought that the issue before them was settled or, for tactical reasons, wished to give the impression that the issue was settled, they used opinions labeled *per curiam* ("by the court"). These were terse, often only a line or two and usually no more than a paragraph, basically citing previous rulings that, the Court said, controlled the matter. Over the past few decades, however, per curiam opinions have often been much longer—that sustaining the constitutionality of most but not all of the Federal Election Campaign Act of 1971 ran to 138 pages, with an appendix that added another 90 (*Buckley* v. *Valeo*, 1976). If it takes that much space to explain the resolution of an issue, it can hardly have been settled before the Court spoke. Under such circumstances, a per curiam opinion probably indicates only that the opinion reflects, even more than is typically true, the work of a group of justices rather than a single author. Moreover, recent per curiam practice frequently involves equally long dissents and concurring opinions.

More generally, separate opinions are normal aspects of the common-law tradition; and these individual opinions sometimes propel barbed attacks on the likely effects of a decision, as well as on the majority's logic. Justice Brennan's dissent in *Paul* v. *Davis* (1976) branded the majority's opinion as "inconsistent with our prior case law," "dissembling," using "irrelevant" arguments, proceeding "by mere fiat and with no analysis," and "frightening for a free people." The decision was, he added, "a saddening denigration of our majestic Bill of Rights" and "a regrettable abdication" of the Court's role in "providing a formidable bulwark against governmental violation of constitutional safeguards securing in our free society the legitimate expectations of every person to innate human dignity and sense of worth."

In one sense, publication of a separate opinion is an appeal to history—and sometimes it turns out to be a successful appeal, for, when later justices review similar cases, they may find the minority's reasoning more convincing than the majority's and overrule the previous case. Such an overruling does not usually affect the earlier litigants, but it does mean the Court will no longer apply the principles controlling that decision.

The whole intra-Court process encourages negotiation, even bargaining of a sort. The justice who refuses to compromise seldom writes for the Court in important cases. Strong-willed, intelligent, experienced people usually have powerful views of their own and are not likely to be awed by colleagues. Sometimes the price of compromise is high. Oliver Wendell Holmes complained that "the boys generally cut one of the genitals" out of his opinions. Although he accepted such surgery with good humor, other justices have refused, allowing the case to be decided without an opinion of the Court.

A second factor encouraging compromise is the justices' knowledge that they will be working together over a long period. The average tenure on the Court is almost twenty years. The person who graciously concedes a point today can expect similar treatment tomorrow; just as the person who today refuses to compromise when in the majority can face a similar stonewall next week when he is in the minority.

Writing an opinion for the Court involves what Justice Felix Frankfurter called "an orchestral and not a solo performance." It puts a premium not only on good judgment and sound legal craftsmanship but also on skill in interpersonal negotiation—in short, on leadership rather than on command.

SCOPE OF JUDICIAL POWER

"Scarcely any question arises in the United States," de Tocqueville observed in 1835, "that is not resolved, sooner or later, into a judicial question." That observation was, and remains, only partially accurate. American judges have been sufficiently astute to avoid most issues of foreign policy, and in domestic policies, it is usually only government's action, not its inaction, that comes before judges. Still, what is left constitutes "a stately jurisdiction."

Partly because of the country's long history under the common law and its reliance on judicial lawmaking, legislators tend to speak in broad phrases, announcing general policy rather than carving specific regulations. More or less deliberately, they allow, and sometimes even invite, creative interpretation from judges and administrators.

Other factors reinforce this inclination. Frag-

mentation of power and diversity of interest groups make it difficult for Congress to enact politically significant legislation unless there are webs of compromises and sharings of benefits. What begins as a coherent attack on a problem often ends as a jumble of mutual accommodations of competing interests concealed through fuzzy language.

The constitutional document speaks in even more grandiose terms. It, too, is a bundle of compromises. Fundamentally, two different and not always compatible purposes compete for dominance within that basic law: providing for effective government and providing for limited government. As James Madison, the Constitution's principal architect, explained in the pamphlet *Vices of the Political System,* which he circulated shortly before the Constitutional Convention met, "The great desideratum of Government is such a modification of the sovereignty as will render it sufficiently neutral between the different interests and factions, to controul one part of the society from invading the rights of another, and at the same time sufficiently controuled itself from setting up an interest adverse to that of the whole Society." After the Convention, Madison described the two competing objectives as "combining the requisite stability and energy in government, with the inviolable attention due to liberty and the republican form."

Thus, the framers tried to limit power at the same time as they conferred power. Restrictions operate both by the document's "thou shalt nots" and, even more important, Madison thought, by overlapping grants of power that require public officials to share authority. Article I, for instance, confers "all legislative powers" on Congress, while Article II gives the president an independent and influential role in the legislative process. Article II makes the president the chief executive, but Article I forces him to share executive authority with Congress.

Similarly, the Constitution's divisions of authority between the nation and states are less than clear. Article VI says that congressional acts "made in pursuance of" the Constitution are, like the Constitution itself, "the supreme law of the land"; and the so-called sweeping clause of Article I, Section 8, gives Congress power "to make all laws which shall be necessary and proper" to carry out any power the Constitution delegates to any branch of the national government. On the other hand, the Tenth Amendment reads, "The powers not delegated to the United States by the Constitution, nor prohibited by it to the States, are reserved to the States respectively, or to the people." In the context of the "necessary and proper clause," that restriction means nothing at all or else it means a great deal. The words themselves do not reveal the meaning.

Because of these crosscutting grants of power, seldom can one set of public officials try to act without arousing jealousy and suspicions among others. In sum, the American Constitution separates institutions, makes them share powers, and connects the interest of the officeholder with the power of the office. The system operates precisely as Madison claimed it would: it pits "ambition against ambition" and "power against power." Whether or not judges are natural arbiters of such political disputes and whether or not the framers intended judges to act in that capacity, in fact the Supreme Court has frequently played that role, deciding where the boundaries of power run, whether between state or nation or between the branches of the federal government.

Where rights of individual citizens are more immediately involved, judges are apt to be even more active. And the relevant constitutional clauses are no more precise. The Fourth Amendment, for instance, forbids only "unreasonable" searches and seizures; the Fifth and Fourteenth forbid the taking of "life, liberty, or property, without due process of law"; and the Eighth forbids "excessive bail" as well as "cruel and unusual punishments." The Ninth Amendment is the most general of all. It forms a counterweight to the "sweeping clause": "The enumeration in the Constitution, of certain rights, shall not be construed to deny or disparage others retained by the people."

Broad public access to courts provides judges with frequent opportunities to interpret the Constitution, and the general terms of its clauses give judges a wide range of discretion in that interpretation. The charge of "government by judiciary" has echoed down the decades. Always critics allege that judges have "legislated." And always there is a considerable measure of truth in such assertions: Congress often refuses to be very precise in writing statutes and the Constitution speaks in what Ronald Dworkin refers to as

broad "concepts rather than specific conceptions." The words of the constitutional document, Frankfurter once commented, "are so unrestricted by their intrinsic meaning or by their history or by prior decisions that they leave the individual Justice free, if indeed they do not compel him, to gather meaning, not from reading the Constitution, but from reading life" (p. 30).

ACCESS TO THE SUPREME COURT

The Constitution limits the jurisdiction of national courts, including the Supreme Court, not only to the matters of federal law discussed earlier but also to "cases and controversies." These are words of art. To have a case or controversy, one must show that he or she is suffering or is in imminent danger of suffering a real injury to a legally protected right. This restriction means that federal courts are supposed neither to give advisory opinions nor adjudicate the rights and obligations of those, whether private citizens or governmental officials, who are not parties to the case being decided. (An opinion might say a great deal about the rights of others, but the actual decision will not bind them.) As the Supreme Court explained in *Massachusetts* v. *Mellon* (1923), "We have no power *per se* to review and annul acts of Congress on the ground that they are unconstitutional. That question may be considered only when the justification for some direct injury suffered or threatened, presenting a justiciable issue, is made to rest upon such an act."

There are four principal ways in which a person may bring a constitutional issue before a state or national court. First, when sued by another private citizen or by a governmental official the defendant may set up as a defense a claim that the statute, order, or treaty under which the plaintiff is proceeding violates some provision of the Constitution. Second, in a criminal prosecution, the defendant may use a similar defense, but one which may include an allegation that before the trial the police did not follow the procedures outlined in the Constitution. (It is by no means unknown for a person deliberately to violate a law that he or she believes is unconstitutional so as to provoke a criminal prosecution and then attack the provision's validity.)

Third, a litigant may directly challenge a governmental policy by asking a trial court to issue a declaratory judgment (a judgment that defines the legal rights of two parties who have a real dispute about those kinds of rights but does not order a specific action) and/or an injunction to protect a legal—here a constitutional—right. If the court is satisfied that the action complained of would violate such a right, the judge will issue the injunction. Fourth—and sometimes together with request(s) for a declaratory judgment and/or an injunction—a person may sue a public official for monetary damages because of allegedly unconstitutional action that has injured the plaintiff.

In all of these instances, a judge is supposed to interpret the Constitution and apply that interpretation in deciding the case. Nevertheless, American courts, especially the Supreme Court, shy away from constitutional issues. They do so partly because of the political checks on their power discussed below and partly because of the apparent anomaly of their position in a country that proclaims itself a democracy. As Justice Frankfurter once reminded an attorney during oral argument, "This Court reaches constitutional questions last, not first." Usually, if there is any way of disposing of a case without reaching constitutional problems, the justices will seize it.

In addition, especially if the person who instituted the suit is challenging the legitimacy of a governmental policy, the Court applies rather strict and extremely complex rules regarding what is called "standing to sue." The justices have created these rules to determine if the litigant not only meets jurisdictional criteria but also is asserting, in the context of a real controversy in which his or her personal rights are being injured or threatened with immediate injury, a question on which the Constitution authorizes courts to pass judgment.

Organized interest groups, like private citizens and public officials, may obtain access to judicial power. Under many circumstances, groups may be sued for civil damages or prosecuted under the criminal law, and they, too, may utilize the Constitution in their defense. Where the standing rules permit, associations may also sue in their own name. They may also assist someone who is already involved in litigation by paying court costs and lawyers' fees—which in the United States can bankrupt even the wealthy. Or, an organized group may ask a court to be heard as an amicus curiae. In addition, a group may actively recruit litigants who have standing to start a lawsuit, with the organization paying all expenses of litigation and directing the strategy.

SOURCES OF THE SUPREME COURT'S POWER

Max Weber, the great German sociologist, distinguished three "pure" types of authority: (1) legal, based on a set of normative rules accepted by the community as binding and the right of persons operating under those rules to issue commands; (2) traditional, "resting on an established belief in the sanctity of immemorial traditions and the legitimacy of the status of those exercising authority under them"; and (3) charismatic, resting on a peculiar personal magnetism, of being "touched with grace."

Like that of most governmental agencies that endure, the authority of the Supreme Court partakes of all three types of legitimacy. Legally, the justices base their authority on the specific words of the Constitution, most particularly Articles III and VI, and, what are to judges at any rate, the logical implications of those words. The justices' authority is also rooted in tradition in that they were, in the early days of the Republic, the heirs to a long line of common-law judges, men of some wisdom, wide discretion, and much power. In more modern times the justices have been able to reinforce that tradition by appealing to the record of great American jurists.

There is also more than a pinch of charisma behind judicial power. The notion of the judge as endowed with special talent for understanding the sacred and mysterious texts of the law, inscrutable to mere laymen in common-law systems—all enhanced by black robes and the templelike atmosphere that the architect of the Supreme Court's building (ably prodded by Chief Justice William Howard Taft, under whom planning began) succeeded in conveying—has contributed to a picture of judges as a group whom fate, if not the Deity, has set above the grit and grind of the world's ugliness.

The three specific sources of the Supreme Court's power depend on, and are related to, Weber's types of authority: its legal authority to interpret statutes and the Constitution, its prestige, and the system's need for an umpire. These are connected with each other. Without, for instance, a high level of prestige, it is improbable that the Court could fulfill its role as umpire; without authority to interpret the Constitution, it is likely the Court would lose some prestige. We should also note that these particular and more general sources of judicial power occur in the context of a blend of political theories, constitutionalism and democracy, that infuses the entire American political system. We shall look at the more specific sources and examine the underlying political theories.

Statutory and Constitutional Interpretation. As noted above, to be able to interpret statutes, especially where legislatures tend to speak in general rather than specific terms, bestows considerable power on the interpreter. Statutory interpretation had long become a routine function of British courts, and their judicial nephews in colonial America continued the practice. When it came into existence, the Supreme Court carried on such work as a matter of course. Particular interpretations might have aroused dismay or even anger, but the function itself was not controversial.

Constitutional interpretation poses entirely different problems. First of all, if Congress disapproves of the Court's interpretation of a statute, it need only enact a new one by a simple majority and secure the president's approval. Changing the Court's constitutional interpretation by amending the Constitution is more much complicated and difficult, however. Not only do opponents need a two-thirds vote in each house of Congress, they also need the approval of three-quarters of the states.

The cumbersomeness of the amending process vastly increases the importance of the question of who shall authoritatively interpret the Constitution. The text of the document is silent on this critical point. It does not mention any power of judges to invalidate an act of Congress or of the president. Neither does it, in so many words, authorize courts to strike down state statutes, although the argument that the words of Article VI plainly imply the latter power is compelling:

> This Constitution, and the Laws of the United States which shall be made in Pursuance thereof; and all treaties made, or which shall be made, under the Authority of the United States, shall be the supreme Law of the Land; and the Judges in every State shall be bound thereby, any Thing in the Constitution or Laws of any State to the Contrary notwithstanding.

In Section 25 of the Judiciary Act of 1789, the First Congress conferred on the Supreme Court jurisdiction to review and reverse state judges' interpretations of the Constitution. The justices asserted this prerogative during the 1790s, but it was not until *Fletcher* v. *Peck* (1810) that they actually held a state statute invalid.

Charges that Congress and the Court had usurped authority were both loud and frequent, with Thomas Jefferson being among the protesters. Before the Civil War, states' righters made persistent efforts to repeal Section 25, and occasionally state officials physically resisted the Court's orders. Although the Civil War should have put the issue to rest, after *Brown* v. *Board of Education* in 1954 eight southern state legislatures passed resolutions "nullifying" the Court's actions, and in 1957 the governor of Arkansas called out the national guard to prevent integration of a high school in Little Rock. President Eisenhower dismissed the guard and sent federal troops to execute the district judge's order.

Afterward, when the justices reviewed the case from Little Rock (*Cooper* v. *Aaron,* 1958), they reiterated what had long become accepted constitutional jurisprudence on the Court's relations with the states:

> The interpretation of the Fourteenth Amendment enunciated by this Court in the *Brown* case is the supreme law of the land, and Art. VI of the Constitution makes it of binding effect on the States "any Thing in the Constitution or Laws of any State to the Contrary notwithstanding." Every state legislator and executive and judicial officer is solemnly committed by oath taken pursuant to Art. VI, cl. 3 "to support this Constitution." . . . No state legislator or executive or judicial officer can war against the Constitution without violating his undertaking to support it.

The question of the Court's authority to annul acts of president and Congress has even less basis in the constitutional document than its authority to review state action. *Marbury* v. *Madison* (1803) was not the first instance in which the justices had claimed such authority, but it was the first in which they offered a lengthy justification. That power, as it has evolved over time, is immense, though it remains controversial and limited.

Prestige. Prestige can be a vital source of power. Because they do not command physical force, judges ultimately have to depend on the feeling that a party ought to obey a court's decision and that if one of the parties does not, then other public officials ought to use their power to compel obedience. Here charisma ties in with the claim to interpret the Constitution. "Among holy things," Walton Hamilton and Irene Till asserted, "likeness passes by contagion," and some of the Constitution's sacredness might have rubbed off on the justices. "Since the Constitution is America's covenant," Max Lerner has claimed, "its guardians are . . . touched with its divinity."

It is difficult, however, to gauge precisely how much (or little) prestige the Court actually enjoys. From time to time, scholars, journalists, lawyers, elected politicians, and judges themselves make statements about the Supreme Court's prestige. Unfortunately, there are few hard data to gauge the relative popularity of the Court in different periods. Some decisions irritate some groups, while those same decisions please yet others. The correlation between general public opinion and the noisy praise or condemnation of specific interest groups is doubtful. What does seem clear, is that if we were fully to believe what critics have been saying since 1789, the justices began with no prestige whatever and have fallen steadily in public esteem. With gentle irony, C. Herman Pritchett remarked that "the Supreme Court is not what it used to be, and what's more it never was."

Mass polling promises some clarification, but its use on a scientific basis goes no further back than the 1930s, and even since then, there has been scant sampling of public attitudes on judicial issues. One systematic study reveals some awareness of the Court's work. About 45 percent of national samples of voting-age adults in 1964, 1966, and 1975 could recall a recent Supreme Court action—names of cases were not asked. When a respondent could recollect a decision, it was likely that he or she disapproved of what the Court had done. Yet more than two out of three of the people who had an opinion—including 40 percent of those who had expressed only critical views of particular decisions—thought that the Court was doing its basic job very well. This difference between criticism of individual decisions and approval of the Court as an institution indicates that the justices have a reservoir of public support on which they can draw in emergencies. Other surveys of practicing attorneys and professional politicians, as well as views expressed by better-educated people in national samples, indicate that this support runs deep and is widely shared among those who might be identified as political activists and opinion leaders.

Yet three pieces of evidence from this study imply that the justices' reservoir of public support is not unlimited. First, and perhaps most significant, replies showed emotions ranging from respect, admiration, and approval, on the one hand, to disapproval, anger, and contempt, on the other. But there was no evidence of adulation that would remotely imply automatic acceptance of decisions.

Second, variations in evaluations of the Court were closely associated with respondents' overall political views, usually lumped under liberalism and conservatism. This connection indicates a complex relationship. In part, public approval of certain policies may be due to Supreme Court decisions—which is another way of saying that the Court's rulings about the constitutionality of public policies can affect the way people evaluate those policies. But, because the Court's decisions are not the only factors influencing public attitudes, this connection may also mean that certain kinds of decisions can severely drain the Court's reservoir of support and that, as general political attitudes change, so may those toward the Court if the Court's rulings do not change in the same direction as public opinion.

Third, a large portion of the public either is unaware of the Court's work or so slightly aware as to be unable to answer simple questions. As a result, we do not know how deeply, if at all, the support of this silent minority runs. Moreover, ignorance or apathy may occur among those who benefit most from judicial decisions and whose political support the Court would most need in time of crisis. In the mid-1960s, for example, one would have expected blacks to be among the most ardent defenders of the Court, and so knowledgeable blacks were. But proportionately far fewer blacks than whites had much knowledge of the Court in particular or politics in general.

The Need for an Umpire. We have already discussed a third source of judicial power: a federal system that divides power among state and national units of government, denies some power to each, and then further fragments power among units of the national government needs some kind of umpire. Governmental officials may also need the Court to help legitimize controversial decisions. In a pluralistic society any important public policy is likely to hurt the interests of many individuals and groups. Opposition will be based in part on the wisdom of a policy; but, especially when a broadly worded constitutional clause is involved, challenges to the policy's validity will occur.

To survive, every governmental structure must provide means of quieting basic constitutional doubts of this kind. In American politics the campaign speech, the ballot box, and the constitutional amendment may perform this legitimizing function, and as the discussion of the Court and public opinion indicated, so may a judicial decision. In fact, the justices are far more likely to declare a contested congressional act constitutional than unconstitutional. From 1789 to 1986 the Supreme Court invalidated federal laws in only 111 instances.

LIMITATIONS ON SUPREME COURT POWER

Technical Checks. A series of interlocking restrictions limit the Supreme Court's power. As judges, the justices must follow certain formal procedures. These are flexible, but not infinitely so. First and most important, judges lack a self-starter. Unlike administrators, judges cannot initiate action. Someone must bring a case to them and in a form that meets jurisdictional and standing requirements. The justices can, for instance, sustain the conviction of a brutal sheriff under a civil rights law, but they cannot start such a prosecution themselves.

A second restriction limits the effect of a decision. A judicial order legally obligates only the parties to that case, those who cooperate with them, and those who succeed to their office or status. A decision that the legislature of Tennessee is gerrymandered does not, of itself, legally oblige the government of any other state, even one using exactly the same representational formula. A separate suit must be brought, although the existence of the first judgment might well move the second state to act on its own.

Federal statutes and those of most states now allow a suit called a class action, a procedure that allows one litigant or a small group of litigants to sue for themselves and all others similarly situated. These kinds of options widen access to the courts, but the resulting order still binds only the specific defendants in the case. With this much said, however, the real, as contrasted with the technical, reach of any ruling by the Supreme Court is likely to be wide. As soon as a decision is announced, governmental officials, leaders of interest groups, and even private citizens are apt to use the general principles in the Court's opinion as legal weapons in fresh lawsuits or moral weapons in other arenas of policymaking.

Judges are also restricted in the kinds of orders they can issue. In general, they can far more easily forbid action than they can command action, especially where public officials are involved. The justices can hold a civil rights statute or social security law constitutional, but they cannot compel Congress to pass such a statute. To be sure, sometimes they can loosely interpret existing statutes and surprise members of Congress by discovering more policy than legislators thought they had set. In 1956, for example, Representative Howard Smith, author of the Smith Act, which punishes advocacy of violent overthrow of the United States government, expressed stunned disbelief at the Court's decision in *Pennsylvania* v. *Nelson* that this statute forbids states to adopt similar laws to protect the United States. Still, one should not be misled: Despite occasional opportunities to reap a bigger harvest than Congress has thought it has sown, limitations on the kinds of orders a court can issue are very real.

Public Opinion. If the Court draws much of its power from public esteem, popular attitudes can also check judicial power—unless the public considers the Court incapable of error, and as we have seen, there is no evidence of such adulation. Like the Lord, the public taketh away as well as giveth, and it may act considerably more capriciously than the Deity.

Internal Restrictions. The justices are also limited by their own and others' ideas of how they, as judges, ought to act. Because they come to the bench after a long period of legal training and usually a far longer period of apprenticeship in public service, the justices probably have absorbed many prevailing norms about judicial action. These norms may be vague, yet they do broadly distinguish between behavior perfectly proper for legislators and administrators but improper for judges. For instance, a legislator who, when faced with a difficult decision about how to vote on a bill, consults with experts would be looked on as imaginative and enterprising. In contrast, a judge who discusses a pending case with a person not a member of the court or his or her staff, such as a law clerk, unless attorneys for both sides are present, is skirting, and probably crossing, the edge of unethical conduct.

In addition, the justices cannot help being aware that they are appointed officials serving what amounts to life terms in a government that is in many respects democratic. The apparent oddity of this situation has caused justices to hesitate to substitute their own judgment for that of popularly elected officials.

Institutional Limitations. The simple fact that the Supreme Court is staffed by nine justices constitutes a further check. To hear a case requires a vote of four members, and to decide it requires five votes. Since nine is an uneven number, one might expect clear-cut decisions in all cases where every justice sat; but complex litigation often presents more than two options.

Furthermore, for an opinion to be labeled that of the Court, it must win the assent of a majority of the justices. It is no easy matter to persuade five or more justices to agree on a closely reasoned document based on controversial assumptions of political philosophy that may have immediate as well as long-term effects on public policy. The Court's internal procedures make it likely that a justice who is determined to write exactly as he or she wishes will write for himself or herself alone.

There are ample incentives and sanctions for bargaining within the Court. A justice's main incentive is to enshrine as those of the Supreme Court of the United States the principles he or she thinks best cover this and similar situations. The major sanction available to the opinion writer is to ignore a colleague's wishes—if he or she can still muster five votes. The sanction of those who disagree is to write separate opinions and persuade other justices to join them or to appeal to history to vindicate them.

The effectiveness of either sanction depends on the closeness of the vote and the intellectual powers of individual justices. A 5–4 division puts the opinion writer at a considerable disadvantage in dealing with other members of the majority, just as an 8–1 judgment gives the writer great latitude. So, too, a threat to circulate a separate opinion means much more from a Holmes or a Brandeis than from a less skillful judge.

That the Supreme Court rarely makes either the first or the final decision in a case imposes another set of institutional checks. As noted above, the Court's jurisdiction is almost totally appellate. It reviews a lower-court decision, reverses or affirms it, writes an opinion explaining the principles behind choices, and usually sends ("remands") the case back to the court where it began for final disposition. Thus, like the president, the justices operate through a bureaucracy, but they have even less control over their bureaucracy than does the president over his. The justices can exercise very little influence in appointing, retaining, or promoting lower federal judges and probably none whatever in state judicial selection.

The sheer volume of business, the frequency with which new issues arise, the generality of many legal rules, and the compromises within the Court that may have further blurred concepts and language mean that the justices are at most leaders of their branch of government, not its masters. The analogy of bureaucracy—judicial or administrative—to international politics, where independent and semi-independent leaders negotiate, is apt. The military model of disciplined subordinates saluting and unquestioningly carrying out orders is one that presidents and justices may sorely envy but never see.

Political Restraints. The Supreme Court can interpret statutes and executive orders; it can even declare them unconstitutional. These are great powers, but Congress and the president have weapons they can turn against the justices. Impeachment may be, as Jefferson branded it, "a scarecrow," but Congress can, and has, changed the number of justices, withdrawn some of the Court's appellate jurisdiction (although how much it can validly withdraw remains an open question), denied funds to execute decisions, enacted new statutes to "correct" judicial interpretations of old law, and proposed constitutional amendments to counter the effects of a judicial decision, as the Fourteenth, Sixteenth, and Twenty-sixth Amendments did, or even to strike at judicial power itself, as the Eleventh Amendment did.

During Jefferson's administration, Congress, although its action was flagrantly unconstitutional, abolished a whole tier of federal courts and turned the judges out without salaries. After the Civil War, when the justices seemed ready to uphold individual rights against the martial law that formed the heart of Radical Republicans' plans for the South, several Radical legislators threatened to abolish the Supreme Court itself, arguing that while the Constitution called for "one supreme Court," it did not command that there always be "one and the same Supreme Court."

For his part, the president may refuse to enforce judicial decisions. Jefferson and Lincoln were prepared to do so, and Andrew Jackson actually did refuse. They argued that the president was independent of the Supreme Court. As Jackson put it in 1832 in a message drafted by Roger Brooke Taney, who would soon succeed Marshall as chief justice,

> Each public officer who takes an oath to support the Constitution swears that he will support it as he understands it, and not as it is understood by others. . . . The opinion of the judges has no more authority over Congress than the opinion of Congress has over the judges, and on that point the President is independent of both.

Today it is unlikely that a president would openly defy the Court unless he were extraordinarily popular or Congress and public opinion perceived the Court as extraordinarily wrong in its decisions. These qualifying clauses mean that there are important limits on the Court's power. Moreover, although a situation like Little Rock in 1957 when Eisenhower used federal troops rarely occurs, it is not uncommon for the Court to need at least the president's tacit acquiescence in executing its rulings.

The president has other weapons. If he decides to do battle with the justices or merely to drag his heels, he can pardon his subordinates or anyone else convicted of criminal contempt of court for disobeying judicial orders.

Selection of new justices gives the president an additional opportunity to influence future decisions, as it does senators in confirming or rejecting a nominee. The president can also try to persuade Congress to use any of its powers against the Court, and like senators and representatives, he can draw on his own prestige to attack the justices.

Although the national-supremacy clause of Article VI of the Constitution puts state officials on a lower level than federal officers, state officials can still challenge the Court. They, too, can pass new statutes or issue fresh orders to force apparent winners back to court for additional and expensive litigation. Like federal officials, state officers may try to undermine the justices' prestige. And because the decentralized structure of both political parties makes presidents, senators, representatives, and even federal administrators to some, and often a great, extent dependent on local politicos, state officials may pressure federal officials to oppose Supreme Court decisions. Efforts to impede implementation of the Court's rulings regarding segregation and school prayers demonstrate how effectively states may retard judicial action.

THE SUPREME COURT IN A CONSTITUTIONAL DEMOCRACY

Earlier we referred to an apparent anomaly that affects judges' estimates of the way they should function in the American system of government. In a somewhat perverse sense, this anomaly, properly understood, helps explain both some of the Court's power and some of the psychological limitations on that power.

Many United States officials frequently and vociferously proclaim that their nation is a democracy, with a government chosen by, operating for, and responsible to the people. Yet the justices of the Supreme Court, like most federal judges, serve for what amounts to life tenure and are not elected. More significantly, the power they exercise in nullifying decisions of Congress, the president, and elected state officials, while not unlimited, is still immense. It would seem that the judiciary—and the Supreme Court in particular—is incongruent with the rest of the political system.

Indeed, the argument is sometimes made that judges should not have the power of judicial review at all or, even if it is legitimately theirs, they should exercise it only to keep democratic processes open. That is, they should only protect the rights to speak, publish, assemble, vote, and ensure the right to equal treatment by government for minorities who lack significant representation in policymaking bodies.

These arguments, no less than the proclamations of many public officials, fundamentally mistake the nature of the polity. It is not a democracy, not even a representative democracy. Rather, like most nations of Western Europe and like Japan since the end of World War II, the United States is a political hybrid, a "constitutional democracy." Formal political structures and the ideas on which they are based combine, on the one hand, popular rule by elected representatives and, on the other, limited government. The notion that the people should govern through those whom they elect blends—sometimes lumpily—with the notion that there are critical limitations on both what government can do and how it can carry out its authority.

Although the American political system's failings by either democratic or constitutionalist standards have been frequent and obvious, when viewed as a constitutional democracy, that system takes on more logical coherence. Popular election of senators, representatives, presidents, and their counterparts at the state level—and often at the state level of judges as well—combines with protection of the freedoms of speech, press, and assembly and a right to vote to meet, albeit far from perfectly, the institutional criteria for representative democracy.

On the other hand, federalism and equal representation of states in the Senate; staggered terms of office for presidents, senators, and congressmen; sharings of power among governmental departments; removal of some matters, such as religious belief, from all governmental control; requirements that government accord those suspected of crime certain procedural rights; and judicial review to allow nonelected officials to oversee these provisions, all reflect constitutionalist theory.

The Court, then, is limited in its power, not only by a series of institutional checks but also by gnawing reminders from democratic theory that appointed officials should be silent on many questions of public policy. On the other hand, not only the Court's institutional sources of power but also reminders from constitutionalism that human dignity and autonomy take precedence over transient popular demands make the justices important political actors.

In this intellectual and institutional context, the Court plays a series of critical roles in formulating national goals and ideals as well as more specific public policies. First, as a successor to common-law courts, it operates within a system accustomed to much judicial discretion and, in the common-law tradition, interprets and applies rules and decides specific cases falling within its jurisdiction. Although usually these cases directly involve only a few people, the principles the Court announces—such as that racial segregation has no valid place in public education or that "one person, one vote" is a constitutionally mandated requirement for electoral districting—can affect the entire nation.

Second, in interpreting the Constitution, the justices define boundaries of authority between governmental institutions and between government and individual citizens, and those rulings might also affect the entire citizenry. In a third and related fashion, in interpreting the broad concepts of the Constitution and the often equally open-ended terms of statutes, the Court must legislate. If the constitutional document does not and if Congress and the president will not formulate specific rules, that task falls to judges.

Fourth, as the head of a national judiciary, the Supreme Court must also oversee the administration of justice in that system, a duty imposed by statute as well as by logical inference from a hierarchical arrangement. Fifth, because of expectations about the composition of the Court, it also performs a representative function. It does not represent in the sense of being "chosen by" but in the looser sense of being "chosen from." Obviously, a group of nine cannot be a cross section of the population; but today, a bench composed of only white male Protestants would be as unthinkable as a bench staffed completely by men from the East was fifty years ago.

Sixth, as part of its constitutional interpretation, the Court also helps stabilize the larger political system. It offers a means of peaceful change that those who lost in the political processes may utilize to challenge the legitimacy of public policies that touch on their vital interests.

Sometimes the challengers win, and that chance makes the Court an attractive alternative to violence or to abandoning the political system. More often, the challengers lose, and the Court affirms the legitimacy of the policy and the system's normal rules for making policy. But even that decision may help cool the losers' resentment and quiet their objections.

In all of this work, the Court performs its seventh and most important function: It educates. Its decisions and opinions directly instruct the litigants, other judges, members of the legal profession, public officials, and those who follow the Court's work closely. Indirectly, insofar as news of the Court's rulings infiltrates mass media of communication and finds its way into writing and thinking about politics, the Court teaches the rest of the country. The real substance of the message relates not to technical matters of law but to visions of American society, its ideals and goals and means that are congruent with those ends. That the justices may perform this or any of their functions well or poorly may change the amount and direction of their influence; but their potential for shaping the country's present and future is an integral part of the political system.

CASES

Brown v. Board of Education of Topeka, 347 U.S. 483 (1954)
Buckley v. Valeo, 424 U.S. 1 (1976)
Cooper v. Aaron, 358 U.S. 1 (1958)
Fletcher v. Peck, 6 Cranch 87 (1810)
Herb v. Pitcairn, 342 U.S. 117 (1945)
Marbury v. Madison, 1 Cranch 137 (1803)
Massachusetts v. Mellon, 262 U.S. 447 (1923)
Paul v. Davis, 424 U.S. 693 (1976)
Pennsylvania v. Nelson, 350 U.S. 497 (1956)
Roe v. Wade, 410 U.S. 113 (1973)

BIBLIOGRAPHY

Henry J. Abraham, *The Judicial Process* (1980), offers a general introduction that helps put the Supreme Court in the context of a larger judicial system. Jesse H. Choper, *Judicial Review and the National Political Process* (1980), attempts in this interesting but controversial effort to prescribe a set of functions for the Supreme Court "proper" to the political system. Edward S. Corwin, *Liberty Against Government* (1948), written by the dean of American constitutional scholars, explores the idea of limited government and its role in American constitutional development. Archibald Cox, *The Role of the Supreme Court in American Government* (1976), presents a set of introductory lectures about the Court, originally given to a British audience.

David J. Danelski, "The Influence of the Chief Justice in the Decisional Process," in Walter F. Murphy and C. Herman Pritchett, eds., *Courts, Judges and Politics* (1985), gives a close analysis of the capacity of the chief justice to shape the Court's course. Ronald Dworkin, *Taking Rights Seriously* (1977), probes the problems of judicial decision-making in general and constitutional interpretation in particular. John Hart Ely, *Democracy and Distrust* (1980), presents an elegant but controversial effort to carve out a more limited set of functions for the Supreme Court than those prescribed by Choper. Felix Frankfurter, *Law and Politics*, edited by E. F. Pritchard, Jr., and Archibald MacLeish (1962), contains a series of insightful articles that the justice wrote while a professor at Harvard. Paul A. Freund and Stanley N. Katz, eds., *History of the Supreme Court of the United States* (1971–), was financed by a gift from Justice Oliver Wendell Holmes to the United States; as of early 1985 six of the projected nine volumes had been published: vol. 1, covering the years from 1789 to 1801, by Julius Goebel, Jr. (1971); vol. 2, 1801–1815, by George Haskins and Herbert A. Johnson (1981); vol. 5, 1835–1864, by Carl B. Swisher (1974); vols. 6–7, 1864–1868, by Charles Fairman (1971 and 1985); vol. 9, 1910–1921, by Alexander M. Bickel and Benno Schmidt, Jr. (1984).

M. Judd Harmon, ed., *Essays on the Constitution of the United States, 1978* (1978), has assembled a collection of lectures by leading scholars on the work of the Supreme Court in interpreting the Constitution. Robert G. McCloskey, *The American Supreme Court* (1960), presents an excellent, though brief, history of the Court through the early years of the Warren Court. Alpheus Thomas Mason, *Harlan Fiske Stone* (1956), a premier scholar's classic judicial biography, has become the model for such studies, and perhaps more than any other single work, it illuminates the Court not only during the critical years 1925–1946 but more generally as an institution. Walter F. Murphy, *Congress and the Court* (1962), uses a case study to analyze efforts in the 1950s to curb the Supreme Court; and *Elements of Judicial Strategy* (1964), analyzes the Court's place in the political system by utilizing the private papers of several justices. Walter F. Murphy, James E. Fleming, and William F. Harris, II, *American Constitutional Interpretation* (1986), presents an overall view of constitutional interpretation and the varying roles of the Supreme Court and other institutions in those processes. Walter F. Murphy and C. Herman Pritchett, eds., *Courts, Judges, and Politics* (1985), presents a collection of cases, articles in professional journals, and essays by the editors outlining the political functions of judges in the American political system. Walter F. Murphy and Joseph Tanenhaus, "Patterns of Public Support for the Supreme Court," in *Journal of Politics*, 43 (1981), is a systematic study of public attitudes and awareness.

David M. O'Brien, *Storm Center: The Supreme Court in American Politics* (1986), updates and goes beyond Murphy's *Elements of Judicial Strategy*. Lewis F. Powell, Jr., "What Really Goes On at the Supreme Court," in *American Bar Association Journal*, 66 (1980), describes the internal operations of the Court and implicitly denies some of the allegations in the book by Woodward and Armstrong cited below. C. Herman Pritchett, *The Roosevelt Court: A Study in Judicial Politics and Values, 1937–1947* (1948) and *Civil Liberties and the Vinson Court* (1954), two path-breaking studies, reveal the decision-making process of the Supreme Court, as well as the Court's roles in the political system. John R. Schmidhauser, *The Supreme Court* (1960), gives a collective portrait of the justices.

Bob Woodward and Scott Armstrong, *The Brethren* (1979), discloses an "inside" account of the Court's workings from 1969 to 1976, heavily based on gossip among, and leaks from, law clerks, some of which are accurate.

[*See also* COMMON LAW AND COMMON-LAW LEGAL SYSTEMS; COURTS AND CONSTITUTIONALISM; FEDERAL COURT SYSTEM; JUDICIAL REVIEW; JUDICIARY; *and* JURISDICTION.]

TRIAL COURTS AND PRACTICE

James J. Alfini

Courts are public institutions whose principal purpose is to resolve legal disputes. With very few exceptions, all disputes (cases) coming before American court systems begin in a trial court. Because no appeal is made to a higher court in the vast majority of these cases, the decision of the trial court is usually the final decision. Thus, the functions performed by trial courts are crucial to the orderly administration of justice in American society.

THE FUNCTIONS OF TRIAL COURTS

The primary function of the trial court is to conduct trials. The trial is an adversarial process governed by regularized rules of procedures and evidence. The trial court resolves cases at trial by deciding disputed factual issues and applying legal rules. For most cases, the parties have the option of having the case tried by a judge (bench trial) or a judge and jury (jury trial). At a bench trial the judge decides the facts, determines the law applicable to the case, applies the law to the facts, and reaches a decision. At a jury trial the jury decides the facts and reaches a decision by applying the law to the facts but only after being instructed on the applicable law by the judge.

Besides conducting trials, trial courts perform other, equally important, functions. In approximately 90 percent of the criminal cases filed in American trial courts, for example, there is no trial. For those cases that are not dismissed, the factual issue—whether the accused is guilty of having committed the crime with which he or she is charged—is resolved by the accused person pleading guilty. In these cases, the trial court's sentencing function is predominant and is normally performed by the trial judge. (A notable exception in some states is jury sentencing in death-penalty cases.) In fixing sentence, the trial judge considers such factors as the nature of the crime and the background of the accused and imposes an appropriate sanction such as a fine or a prison term.

Trial courts also perform remedial functions in cases involving juveniles, family matters such as child-custody hearings, and the commitment of the mentally ill. In fashioning appropriate remedies in these cases, the trial court normally relies on information obtained through such sources as diagnostic examinations or social evaluations. The trial court also performs a remedial function when it issues an injunction to prevent a threatened wrong or injury.

To perform these sentencing and remedial functions, trial courts are invested with a great deal of discretion. Because the exercise of this discretion often results in widely disparate sentences or remedies in apparently similar cases before different courts or even before different judges in the same court, trial courts have come under a good deal of criticism in recent years. To rectify this situation, trial courts have been urged to experiment with certain innovations that ostensibly would establish greater uniformity and equality of treatment of similar cases. Among the recommendations are the formulation of guidelines to be followed by judges in exercising discretion, the review of judicial dispositions by panels of other judges prior to making a disposition in a case. Such recommendations or reforms aimed at reducing trial-court discretion and achieving greater uniformity have not met with universal approval. David Neubauer, for example, worries that "there will not be as much flexibility in the system and not as much individualization of justice" (p. 486). This tension between trying to do uniform justice on the one hand and individualized justice on the other is a persistent concern in the literature on trial courts.

In addition to their trial, sentencing, and remedial functions, trial courts are sometimes required to perform what has been characterized as supervisory functions. As stated by the American Bar Association, these include "monitoring of adult probationers, juveniles under the court's wardship, persons under orders for care and treatment for mental conditions, children under custody orders, and control of the estates of decedents and incompetents over which the court has jurisdiction" (1976, 10). Normally, a trial court places great reliance on nonjudicial personnel, such as probation officers, to carry out these supervisory responsibilities.

Since the mid-1950s, some courts have employed their remedial and supervisory functions in more expansive ways to deal with extended impact cases. Extended impact cases usually involve violations of individual rights in public institutions such as prisons, mental hospitals, and schools. To help them address the conditions that are violating these rights, judges often use individuals with special expertise or insight into the problem, called "special masters." In addition to assisting the court in fashioning an appropriate remedy—such as providing for additional facilities to relieve prison overcrowding—the special master often is called upon to assist the court in its supervisory role by monitoring compliance with the judge's remedial order.

The willingness of some trial-court judges to use the remedial and supervisory functions of their courts in extended impact cases has evoked considerable controversy. Those who oppose judicial intervention in these cases claim that the courts have usurped functions of the legislative or executive branch of government in directly intruding into the operations of state-run institutions. They also argue that trial courts have neither the expertise nor the resources to correct the alleged deficiencies. Those who favor judicial intervention claim that the courts must intervene to make up for the legislative- and executive-branch shortcomings that led to the problem in the first place.

In a broader sense, the controversy over the extent of judicial intervention in extended impact cases reflects a more general debate over the proper role and functions of the courts in American society. The Council on the Role of Courts identified a "traditionalist" view and an "adaptationist" view in this debate. Traditionalists are concerned that the functions of courts are expanding so much that soon courts will no longer be recognizable as such. The traditionalist "seeks to define the appropriate limits of court function within the traditional boundaries of the adversary process." The adaptationist, on the other hand, argues that the adjudicative functions of courts are more expandable and should be continually changing to accommodate the needs of a changing society.

In furtherance of their adjudicative (trial, sentencing, remedial, and supervisory) functions, trial courts perform administrative functions. Concern over burgeoning case loads and delay in America's trial courts since midcentury has led to a heightened awareness of these administrative functions and an increased emphasis on "case-flow management." Maureen Solomon has defined case flow as "the continuum of activities through which cases move within a court." In setting forth the elements of effective case-flow management, Solomon stresses that "commitment of the judges to *court control* of caseflow is the cornerstone upon which improvements in case processing can be built" (p. 30). For many trial courts the notion that the court, rather than the attorneys, should accept the primary responsibility for such management functions as scheduling cases and monitoring their progress was a new one. In many trial courts, for example, the local prosecutor traditionally assumed responsibility for scheduling criminal cases. More radical still were the suggestions that the trial courts adopt restrictive continuance policies, which would limit the parties' ability to postpone case-related hearings and the trial itself, and case-processing time standards. Yet, such case-flow management policies have been widely adopted in American trial courts in recent years largely in response to increased public pressure to reduce case delays and backlogs.

Some commentators have become concerned over this increased emphasis on judicial management. Judith Resnik raises the specter of the "managerial judge" and argues that overemphasis on a trial court's administrative responsibilities may have an adverse effect on its adjudicative functions. She is particularly concerned that trial judges may abuse their discretionary powers in restricting the amount of time that parties will be allowed to prepare their cases and in encouraging settlement of cases prior to trial at pretrial conferences with the parties.

ORGANIZATION AND JURISDICTION

Increased emphasis on the administrative functions of trial courts has been encouraged by recent structural and organizational changes in American court systems. Grouped under the general rubric of "court unification," these changes were developed and promoted by individual reformers such as Roscoe Pound and Arthur Vanderbilt and encouraged by various national commissions (American Bar Association, 1974; President's Commission on Law Enforcement and Administration of Justice, 1967; and National Advisory Commission on Criminal Justice Standards and Goals, 1973).

These reform proposals were prompted by an increasing concern during the first half of the twentieth century that the courts were inefficient, inaccessible, and unaccountable. Many reformers argued that these conditions were occasioned by the fact that in most states there was no semblance of an organizational or administrative scheme among the various courts. Shortcomings were most apparent at the local level, where the bewildering array of autonomous trial courts with overlapping jurisdictions made it difficult for citizens and lawyers alike to know where to bring certain kinds of cases. Before the judicial reforms in Illinois in 1964, for example, there were 208 separate courts in Cook County (Chicago). Many judges ran their courts as little fiefdoms, treating those who came before them with a distinct lack of impartiality.

Proposals for the unification of court systems have been part of a larger movement during the twentieth century to make agencies of government more efficient and businesslike. Court unification calls for a centralized management scheme whereby overall administrative authority is vested in the highest appellate court with a chief or presiding judge exercising administrative control over a consolidated trial-court system in each judicial district. Arguably, such an arrangement would not only make judges accountable for their actions to others within the judicial hierarchy but would also lead to a heightened managerial consciousness within the judiciary, ultimately resulting in greater administrative efficiency.

Although many state court systems now have centralized administrative schemes, only a few have completely consolidated their trial courts into a single trial court of general jurisdiction. In this regard, the model of the state courts is the federal system, which employs a single-level trial court—the United States district court.

There are ninety-four federal trial-court districts. The size of the districts vary, depending on population and judicial business. The geographic jurisdiction of some of the federal trial-court districts is an entire state (for example, the United States District Court for the District of Maine), while others have jurisdiction over only a portion of a state (for example, the United States District Court for the Central District of California). The federal district courts hear both criminal and civil cases. Their criminal cases involve violations of federal criminal law, ranging from lesser offenses (misdemeanors) to more serious crimes (felonies). Many "white-collar crimes," such as crimes involving politicians or business executives for violations of tax or corporate securities laws, are heard in the federal trial courts.

There are several different types of civil cases that may be heard in the federal trial courts. These include cases involving diversity jurisdiction, federal questions, and suits against the federal government. "Diversity jurisdiction" cases involve those lawsuits between citizens of different states in which the amount in controversy is more than $10,000. These are cases in which there is an option between filing the case in a federal court or a state court. An example of a situation giving rise to a diversity jurisdiction case is one in which a resident of state A is driving through state B and is involved in an accident with a resident of state B. The resident of state A is given the option of suing in federal court to avoid any potential bias that a state court in state B might have in favor of a resident of its own state. "Federal question" cases are those arising under federal (rather than state) law, such as cases involving copyright or patent infringement. Finally, a common suit against the federal government would be one to establish or reinstate benefits under the social security laws.

The United States district courts exist side by

side with the state trial courts. In other words, every locale in the United States is within the jurisdiction of at least two trial courts—one federal and one state. While all state court systems have a trial court of general jurisdiction that resembles the neighboring United States district court in certain operational respects (for example, regularized rules of procedure and evidence), most state court systems also have one or more trial courts of limited jurisdiction. The state trial courts of general jurisdiction are variously named district courts, circuit courts, superior courts, and courts of common pleas. The limited-jurisdiction courts, sometimes referred to as the "lower" or "minor" trial courts, are usually named county courts, municipal courts, city courts, justice of the peace courts, magistrate courts, and police courts.

On the criminal side of their dockets, the state trial courts of general jurisdiction generally handle cases involving felonies, while the trial courts of limited jurisdiction handle misdemeanors. Many limited-jurisdiction courts also perform a screening function for the general-jurisdiction trial courts by handling preliminary hearings in felony cases. The purpose of the preliminary hearing is to ensure that there is a good reason for holding the accused. At the preliminary hearing the prosecutor must show that there is probable cause to believe that a crime has been committed and that the person accused committed the crime.

The civil case loads of the state general-jurisdiction trial courts include a wide variety of case types. Some of the more common are automobile accident lawsuits, disputes over contracts, divorces, will contests, and suits challenging the actions of state or local agencies, such as zoning commissions or transportation authorities. Some of these lawsuits can be very complex and the trials can last for several weeks. There is no limit to the amount of money that a plaintiff can sue for in these courts. The civil jurisdiction of the limited-jurisdiction trial courts, on the other hand, is generally limited to cases involving lesser claims, most commonly where the amount in controversy is less than $5,000. Civil cases that are common in these courts include disputes between landlords and tenants and between consumers and local businesses.

The vast majority of the cases filed in state courts are handled by the limited-jurisdiction courts, with the great bulk of their case loads consisting of traffic cases. Of the approximately 75 million cases disposed of in the state trial courts in 1980, for example, approximately 50 million (66 percent) were traffic matters (National Center for State Courts). Of the remaining 25 million state trial-court cases disposed of in 1980, roughly 13 million (52 percent) were civil matters, 10.5 million (42 percent) were criminal cases, and 1.5 million (6 percent) juvenile cases. These figures represented an increase over a five-year period of approximately 20 percent in civil case dispositions and 30 percent in criminal case dispositions. These increases continue a trend of burgeoning case loads that had become particularly acute in the 1960s and 1970s. The Council on the Role of Courts estimated that less than 2 percent of the cases filed in state trial courts actually go to trial. The vast majority of criminal cases are disposed of through guilty pleas or dismissals and most civil cases through settlements or default judgements (cases in which one of the parties fails to appear in court).

Although a much smaller number of cases are filed in the federal district courts than in the state trial courts, a higher percentage of the federal cases are tried. Of the approximately 239,000 cases disposed of by the federal district courts in 1983, approximately 90 percent were civil cases and only 10 percent criminal (Administrative Office of the United States Courts). Approximately 21,000 cases (9 percent of the total number of cases disposed of) were completed by trial. What is perhaps most notable about federal trial-court statistics is the staggering increase in case filings and dispositions since the late 1970s. Over the five-year period from 1978 to 1983, for example, case filings rose from approximately 166,000 to approximately 266,000, a 60 percent increase. Over this period, the increase in federal district court judgeships did not keep apace of filings. Thus, the filings per judgeship rose from 417 in 1978 to 517 in 1983, a 24 percent increase. Although median case-processing times (measures of case delay) for criminal cases increased from 3.2 months to 4.9 months over this period, median times for civil cases actually decreased from 10 months to 7 months. These statistics would appear to support the notion that there is indeed a heightened managerial consciousness in the federal trial courts; that is, the average federal district court judge is processing more cases more quickly. However, some commentators maintain that the average judge is not working much harder and is certainly not overworked, because of the legal, clerical, and technical support available to the federal judiciary.

TRIAL COURTS OF GENERAL JURISDICTION

In their handling of both civil and criminal cases, the state and federal trial courts of general jurisdiction follow specific, regularized practices at both the pretrial and trial stages. These regularized practices are known as rules of procedure and rules of evidence. Since their adoption in 1938, the Federal Rules of Civil Procedure have governed practice in the United States district courts and have served as a model for state court rules of civil procedure. The federal rules have been particularly influential in providing for simplified pleadings and broadened discovery.

The pleadings are the formal claims of the parties to a civil lawsuit. The parties, or litigants, to a civil lawsuit are referred to as the plaintiff (the person suing) and the defendant (the person being sued). In the federal trial courts and most state trial courts, a civil case is initiated or commenced by the plaintiff's filing a complaint with the court. The complaint contains the plaintiff's statements or allegations setting forth his or her claim against the defendant. The defendant is advised of the plaintiff's lawsuit against him or her when the defendant is served with a summons and a copy of the complaint. In many states, the local sheriff delivers the summons to, or "serves process on," the defendant. In other states, private process servers are commonly used.

After being served with the complaint, the defendant may attack the plaintiff's complaint for errors of either form or substance. In states using what is known as code pleading, the defendant attacks the complaint for errors of form by means of a special demurrer. The defendant may, for example, object that the complaint is too vague or ambiguous. Under the federal rules, the corresponding procedural device to the special demurrer is the more descriptive "motion to make more definite and certain." If the defendant detects an error of substance in the complaint, a general demurrer would be used to attack the complaint in a code-pleading state, but a "motion to dismiss for failure to state a claim on which relief may be granted" would be used in a trial court operating under the federal rules or their equivalent. An example of an error of substance would be the failure to allege in a contract dispute that the defendant breached (broke) the contract by his or her actions.

Motions are requests by either the plaintiff or the defendant that the trial court do something. They are used throughout the pretrial and trial stages of a lawsuit. With the motion to dismiss for failure to state a claim on which relief may be granted, for example, the defendant is asking the trial court to end the lawsuit at this early stage because the plaintiff has made substantive errors in the complaint. If the trial court rejects (overrules) this motion (general demurrer) but accepts (sustains) the motion to make more definite and certain (special demurrer), the court may allow the plaintiff to amend the complaint to correct its errors.

The defendant responds to the allegations in the plaintiff's complaint in an answer, which is the pleading used by the defendant to admit some of the facts alleged in the complaint and to deny others. The defendant may also set forth affirmative defenses in the answer. These are additional facts that would prevent the plaintiff's recovery even if all the facts in the complaint could be proven. Affirmative defenses in a case in which the plaintiff is suing to enforce a contract, for example, might be the defendant's allegation that he entered the contractual relationship under duress or was induced by the plaintiff's fraud. The plaintiff's alleged fraud might also form the basis of a counterclaim, by which the defendant seeks to recover from the plaintiff in the same lawsuit.

Just as the defendant has the right to attack the complaint, the plaintiff may attack the answer by means of a demurrer or the equivalent federal-rules motion. The plaintiff may also refute allegations in the answer through the use of a third pleading known as a reply. In many jurisdictions the reply is seldom used, because the defendant's allegations in the answer are assumed to be denied by the plaintiff.

Because the allegations in the pleadings usually are stated in general terms and do not deal with the actual evidence that will be introduced at trial, federal and state procedural rules specify a process for finding out more about an opponent's case prior to trial. This process is called discovery. The federal rules of civil procedure and subsequently adopted state procedural rules have broadened the scope of discovery on the theory that arming each side with the relevant facts through pretrial disclosures would make the trial more of a search for truth and less of a sporting event.

The most frequently used discovery device is the deposition. Both the plaintiff and the defendant may take their opponent's deposition, which consists of answers to questions under oath. The questions are posed to the plaintiff or defendant by the opposing lawyer before a court reporter. The opponent may also be required to respond to interrogatories, or written questions asking the plaintiff or defendant for certain information, including the names and addresses of their witnesses. These witnesses may subsequently be deposed as well.

Broadened discovery, a welcome reform in the 1930s, was a cause of some concern by the 1980s. Studies and scholarly commentary have identified certain problems generally referred to as discovery abuse. These problems include the unnecessary use of discovery and the improper withholding of discoverable information, resulting in increased delay and expense to the litigants. Many of the United States district courts have experimented with local rules to improve the discovery process, such as imposing time limits on the discovery process, limiting the number of interrogatories, and calling for mandatory pretrial conferences.

The federal rules of civil procedure and many state rules provide for a pretrial conference. The lawyers for each side usually attend the conference in the judge's chambers. The conference affords an opportunity to discuss possibilities for settling the case without trial and, failing that, to get the case ready for trial. At the conference, the judge attempts to refine the issues, identify and decide points of law that might be raised at trial, and deal with other matters that can be decided beforehand.

Trial may also be avoided by seeking to have the judge grant a "motion for summary judgment." This motion asks the judge to decide that there is no need for a trial because there is no genuine issue of fact. It may be made any time after the complaint is filed.

Most civil cases may be tried before either a judge or a jury. If the demand for a jury trial is not made within the time limits specified in the court's rules, it is considered to be a waiver of the right to a jury trial. The jury trial begins with a jury-selection procedure know as voir dire. This process involves the questioning of the jurors by the lawyers or the judge. In some jurisdictions the jurors are examined during voir dire exclusively or primarily by the judge, while in other jurisdictions the lawyers conduct the voir dire examination. Some argue that judge-conducted voir dire is less time-consuming and more efficient than lawyer-conducted voir dire. They point in particular to well-publicized cases, in which it may take weeks to pick a jury because many potential jurors may be subjected to lengthy questioning by the lawyers and then excused for the reason that the news coverage before the trial may have prejudiced them against one of the parties. Trial lawyers, on the other hand, argue that the lawyers must be allowed to question the jurors to ensure that their clients' right to an unbiased jury is preserved.

If it appears during the questioning of a juror that the juror cannot fairly or impartially judge the case, the juror may be challenged for cause. In addition to being able to challenge a juror for cause, each party is allowed to exercise peremptory challenges which allow a party to excuse jurors without having to state a reason. Each side is allowed a specified number of peremptory challenges (for example, some states allow twelve in a noncapital felony case). Lawyers usually excuse jurors by peremptory challenge based on their intuition that the particular juror will not favor their client. However, many lawyers have recently been using social scientists to assist them in selecting juries. Usually, the social scientists conduct surveys of the local population to determine the characteristics of potential jurors who would be most sympathetic and those who would be least sympathetic toward their client.

The use of peremptory challenges has become a source of concern in criminal cases. Most notably, prosecutors have been criticized for apparently using peremptories to eliminate minorities from juries on the theory that they would be too sympathetic to minority defendants. Although the United States Supreme Court has condemned this practice, it has made it very difficult for a minority defendant to prove racial discrimination in the use of peremptories (*Swain* v. *Alabama*, 1965). In recent years, however, some state supreme courts and lower federal courts have established less burdensome criteria for finding racial discrimination.

Once the jury is selected, the trial begins with the opening statements of the lawyers. In the opening statement, the plaintiff's lawyer explains the plaintiff's case and tells what their evidence will show. The defendant's lawyer may follow with an opening statement or wait until after the plaintiff has introduced his or her evidence. In his case, the plaintiff must introduce evidence to prove the allegations in the complaint. A principal means of introducing evidence is to offer the testimony of witnesses. The process by which the plaintiff's lawyer questions the plaintiff's witnesses is known as direct examination. When the defendant's lawyer questions the plaintiff's witnesses, it is known as cross-examination.

During the direct examination or the cross-examination of a witness, the lawyer not engaged in the questioning of the witness may offer an objection to certain testimony. An objection is a device used by either lawyer to bring an impropriety to the attention of the trial court. The objection may focus not only on the actions of the opposing lawyer but also on the actions of a litigant, a juror, a witness, or even the judge. By objecting, the lawyer is asking the court to correct or prevent an impropriety that is adverse to the interests of the lawyer's client. In deciding whether to overrule or sustain the objection, the judge may first ask the lawyer to state the grounds on which the objection is based. Permissible grounds usually include violations of evidentiary rules, such as the attempted introduction of hearsay testimony or a privileged communication. Hearsay testimony reports an out-of-court statement that the witness overheard and although such statements are considered to be unreliable as a general rule, they often are allowed if they were overheard under exceptional circumstances. A privileged communication is one occurring between individuals whose confidential relationship the law recognizes as deserving of special protection, such as that between an attorney and a client. The lawyer may offer an objection for a number of reasons—to keep certain information from the jury, to modify the manner of questioning ("counsel is badgering the witness"), or even to gain a tactical advantage.

After the plaintiff has offered his evidence, the plaintiff rests his case. In effect, the plaintiff is saying that he has proved the case against the defendant and deserves a favorable verdict. The defendant, on the other hand, may believe that the plaintiff has failed to offer sufficient evidence and may ask for a *nonsuit* or, under the federal rules, move for a dismissal or a directed verdict (in a jury trial). This motion says that even if all the facts offered by the plaintiff are correct, the law would not permit the plaintiff to recover against the defendant.

In presenting the plaintiff's case to the judge or jury, the plaintiff's lawyer is seeking to meet the plaintiff's burden of producing ("going forward with") the necessary evidence. This means that the plaintiff must meet the burden of presenting enough evidence to avoid a motion for dismissal or a directed verdict. The plaintiff's evidence must establish an issue of fact that can be sent to the jury. If the plaintiff has accomplished this, the burden shifts to the defendant, so that the defendant must now establish his case.

If the judge denies the motion for a dismissal or directed verdict, the defendant will proceed with his case by offering evidence that refutes that of the plaintiff. The defendant will also offer evidence in support of affirmative defenses set forth in the answer or in support of a counterclaim. At the end of the defendant's case, either the defendant or the plaintiff may move for a dismissal or a directed verdict.

Throughout the trial, the plaintiff and defendant will be bound by the "rules of evidence," which set forth a method by which relevant information may be presented to the trier of fact (the judge or the jury). They deal with such problems as relevancy, privilege, hearsay, competency of witnesses, opinion testimony, expert testimony, impeachment of witnesses, and objections. In most jurisdictions, these evidence rules are an amalgam of case law and state statutes. The Federal Rules of Evidence, adopted in 1975, reflect well-established evidence principles and are applicable in both civil and criminal cases in the United States district courts.

In offering closing arguments, the plaintiff's lawyer once again goes first, followed by the defendant's lawyer. Both will stress the evidence that is most favorable to their side of the case and will seek to convince the jury that they have met their burden of proof. Sometimes referred to as the "burden of persuasion," the burden of proof becomes crucial at this stage of the trial. Each side must have persuaded the jury of its version of the truth of the disputed facts by a specified standard. In most civil cases, the standard is "a preponderance of the evidence." The plaintiff, for example, must have convinced the jury that the facts alleged in the plaintiff's complaint are more probably true than not. In criminal cases, the prosecution is held to a higher standard. The defendant's guilt must be established by the prosecution "beyond a reasonable doubt."

After counsel conclude their closing arguments, the judge instructs the jury on the law applicable to the case. In some jurisdictions, the judge may also summarize the evidence for the jury. The judge's instructions to the jury have often been criticized for being so steeped in legal jargon as to be virtually incomprehensible. Some states have recently tried to improve on this situation by creating "pattern instructions," uniform instructions that may be used in all the trial courts of the state and are written in understandable language. Some states also permit jurors to take copies of the instructions with them into the jury deliberation room. Those jurisdictions that allow individual jurors to take notes during the trial also allow them to bring their notes with them to the deliberation room. Note taking by jurors, however, has not met with widespread approval. Those that oppose note taking argue that the note taker will be distracted during the trial, will record irrelevant evidence, and will have too much influence in the deliberation room.

In civil cases, juries usually return from their deliberations with a general verdict, in which they indicate whether they are finding in favor of the plaintiff or the defendant and the amount that should be recovered in damages. Sometimes, the jury is asked to return a special verdict, whereby they are given a list of questions relating to the facts at issue that they must answer.

Even after the jury returns a verdict, the trial court may entertain motions. The most common posttrial motions are the motion for judgment notwithstanding the verdict—sometimes referred to by its Latin abbreviation, judgment n.o.v.—and the motion for a new trial. The motion for judgment notwithstanding the verdict is similar to both the motion for a directed verdict and the general demurrer in that it once again raises the question of the legal sufficiency of the

evidence introduced by either side. The motion for a new trial, on the other hand, identifies procedural or evidentiary errors that took place during the trial and seeks a retrial that would avoid these allegedly prejudicial errors.

The Federal Rules of Civil Procedure and their state counterparts are inapplicable in criminal cases. Although there are important similarities between the procedures employed in the trial of criminal cases and those used in civil cases, there are also significant differences. Moreover, there is less uniformity in criminal procedure than in civil procedure across American jurisdictions. Criminal procedure has no analogue to the Federal Rules of Civil Procedure in terms of the scope of the influence of the civil rules. Indeed, more recently adopted rules of criminal procedure—such as the Federal Rules of Criminal Procedure, adopted in 1975—would appear to have been influenced at least in part by experience with the federal rules of civil procedure (for example, with respect to broadened discovery provisions).

Among the ways in which the criminal trial differs from the civil trial are the presumption of innocence, the requirement of proof beyond a reasonable doubt, the right of the accused not to take the stand, and the exclusion of evidence obtained by the state in an illegal manner. In other respects, the criminal trial is much like the civil trial, particularly with regard to the means of introducing evidence and making objections.

Until relatively recently, there were very few empirical studies of the operational realities of trial courts of general jurisdiction. However, empirical research on America's trial courts became a growth industry in the 1970s and 1980s. Most studies of trial courts have concentrated on their handling of criminal cases, because of the greater availability of federal and state research grants tied to the "war on crime."

Comparative studies of the handling of felony cases in different locales reveal significant differences in operating practices and substantive outcomes. Researchers have advanced various explanations for this diversity. Martin Levin focuses on differences in community politics and values to explain the diversity in sentencing severity in the trial courts in Pittsburgh and Minneapolis, while Eisenstein and Jacob develop the concept of the "courtroom work group" to help explain differences in adjudication and sentencing practices in the trial courts of Baltimore, Chicago, and Detroit. Work-group members include those with shared tasks and goals within the courtroom—prosecutors, defense attorneys, clerks, and bailiffs. In examining the ways in which the interactions of work-group members influence the outcomes of criminal cases, Eisenstein and Jacob introduce an organizational approach to studying trial courts.

The seemingly ageless concern over delay in the trial courts has also spawned studies that suggest new theoretical approaches. For example, Thomas Church and his associates attempt to explain differences in both civil and criminal case-processing time (delay) in large city trial courts by pointing to the "local legal culture." They argue that judges and lawyers in a particular locale become used to a certain pace of litigation and adapt themselves accordingly. Thus, local practices and expectations will have to be overcome in attempts to reduce delay. Included among recent delay-reduction innovations are simplification of procedural rules, improved case-flow management techniques, and technological innovations (for example, telephone conferencing and videotaping).

Managerial innovations have become increasingly important in handling the massive, complex cases that are becoming more prevalent in American trial courts. Because these cases often involve violations of the federal antitrust laws, they are more frequently litigated in the federal courts. Perhaps the most prominent example of complex litigation is the case brought by the United States government to restructure the American Telephone and Telegraph Company (AT&T) for alleged antitrust violations. The AT&T case lasted approximately eight years from filing to disposition and generated tens of millions of pages of documents. A key ingredient in managing this mammoth litigation was the federal judge's appointment of two special masters (lawyers acting as quasi-judicial officers) to assist in supervising certain aspects of the case, such as the discovery process, which involved more than five hundred document subpoenas and two hundred depositions. The case was settled in the eleventh month of trial.

Some believe that juries are not competent to handle such complex litigation. They argue that there should be a "complexity exception" to the right to a jury trial in civil cases. In a few recent cases, certain federal courts have denied a party's jury demand on complexity grounds and allowed the case to proceed without a jury. Although the United States Supreme Court has never upheld the denial of a jury demand, it has not foreclosed this possibility in future cases (*Ross* v. *Bernhard,* 1970).

TRIAL COURTS OF LIMITED JURISDICTION

Unlike the trial courts of general jurisdiction, the limited-jurisdiction trial courts handle large numbers of uncomplicated civil and criminal cases quickly. Delay is usually not seen to be a problem in these courts. Indeed, they are often criticized for processing cases too quickly and failing to give adequate consideration to the rights of those who come before them.

Approximately 75 percent of American courts are trial courts of limited jurisdiction. Sometimes referred to as the "inferior," "lower," or "minor" trial courts, they process the vast majority of cases, and are the average citizen's most frequent point of contact with the judicial system. However, in contrast to the trial courts of general jurisdiction, there has been relatively little attention paid to these courts by legal scholars and researchers.

In the forty-six states that have limited-jurisdiction courts, these courts are officially titled county courts, municipal courts, city courts, justice of the peace courts, police courts, magistrate courts, and district courts. A majority of states have more than one type of limited jurisdiction court. Although Idaho, Illinois, Iowa, Missouri, and South Dakota do not have limited-jurisdiction courts, these states include separate divisions or classes of judges in their general trial court to handle the kinds of cases normally handled by limited-jurisdiction courts. Within the federal court system, federal magistrates perform somewhat similar functions.

The principal business of the limited-jurisdiction trial court is the handling of misdemeanor cases. Indeed, states use the term *misdemeanor* most often to describe the criminal jurisdiction of the limited-jurisdiction court. Most states define a misdemeanor as an offense punishable either by imprisonment for less than one year or by imprisonment other than in a penitentiary.

TRIAL COURTS AND PRACTICE

In addition to misdemeanor cases, all of the limited-jurisdiction courts handle cases in one or more of the following areas: minor civil cases, felony preliminary hearings, traffic offenses, local ordinance violations, juvenile matters, and (in four states) certain felonies. Among the more common civil cases handled by the limited-jurisdiction courts are those involving disputes between landlords and tenants and between consumers and businesses.

Because most limited-jurisdiction trial courts are much less formal than general-jurisdiction courts and less likely to fit traditional notions of how a court of law should operate, they have frequently been criticized for providing "rough justice" or "assembly-line justice" (Robertson). However, some commentators have been more generous in their assessment of these courts. Susan Silbey explains that in being "more particularistic, empirical, individualized, and responsive to local communities" than the general-jurisdiction courts, the lower courts perform an important function as "official gatekeepers" for the judicial system.

What is perhaps most distinctive about the limited-jurisdiction courts is their diversity. These courts display considerable differences with regard to jurisdictional authority, case loads, available sanctions and remedies, and their case-handling practices. A good example of these differences may be seen in the various methods these courts use to handle small civil claims.

Many limited-jurisdiction courts are referred to as "small-claims courts" because they have established a simplified procedure for handling a certain range of smaller civil disputes. Although the maximum dollar amount for invoking the small-claims process varies considerably from state to state, the most common limits are between $500 and $1,000. Developed in the early part of the twentieth century, small-claims procedures were viewed as an efficient and less costly means of settling minor disputes. In particular, it was assumed that the simplified procedures would eliminate the need for a lawyer.

In their comparative study of small claims practices in fifteen limited-jurisdiction courts across the United States, Ruhnka and Weller found significant differences. Some of the courts, for example, prohibited the use of small-claims procedures by collection agencies. These courts, not surprisingly, had the highest percentage of individual plaintiffs (consumers) in their case loads, whereas in those courts that permitted collection-agency practice, business plaintiffs predominated. Ruhnka and Weller also found considerable differences in the use of attorneys in these courts by both plaintiffs and defendants. Among the fifteen courts surveyed, the percentage of plaintiffs who contacted attorneys about their claim ranged from 18 percent to 67 percent, while the percentage of defendants was from 29 percent to 61 percent. The lower percentages tended to be concentrated, predictably, in the five courts that prohibited attorneys at trial. They also found considerable differences in jurisdictional limits, the mix of cases, the size of awards as a percentage of the claims, and plaintiff and defendant satisfaction with small-claims procedures.

Although some of the trial courts of limited jurisdiction now operate within a statewide administrative system as a result of court-unification efforts, many of the limited-jurisdiction courts have retained a large degree of local autonomy, even in states in which other aspects of the court-unification movement have taken hold. This autonomy apparently has led to the development of specialized work loads among courts and judges in particular locales. Although all state limited-jurisdiction trial courts ostensibly have jurisdiction to try both civil and criminal cases, only 61 percent of the 13,221 state courts of limited jurisdiction identified by the United States Census Bureau in 1972 reported handling both civil and criminal cases, while 11 percent reported handling only civil and 28 percent only criminal (United States Department of Justice). Within those courts handling at least some criminal matters, the Census Bureau survey revealed wide variation with regard to the percentage distribution of judge time spent on nontraffic criminal cases. Although the survey indicates that state misdemeanor cases are the predominant case type (in terms of distribution of judge time), in many of these limited-jurisdiction courts, civil, traffic, or juvenile cases appear to be the predominant case type in at least an equal number of courts.

In addition to this general-jurisdictional diversity, these courts differ with regard to the mix of offenses included within their misdemeanor case loads. In particular, there is a good deal of variation with regard to the incidence of the following most frequently tried crimes: traffic offenses, public intoxication, drunk driving, disorderly conduct, narcotics offenses, petty theft, disturbing the peace, assault and battery, prostitution, and writing a bad check. The incidence of certain of these crimes may be affected by such factors as the varying success of decriminalization efforts, community mores, local politics, and community size.

Even where the incidence of certain crimes within these courts is similar, the range and severity of sanctions that may be imposed vary. Although the maximum jail sentence that may be imposed by the limited-jurisdiction courts in the majority of states is one year (with maximum fines ranging from $250 in Arkansas to $3,000 in Oregon), the maximum permissible sentence in the Minnesota courts is three months, and in the lower courts in seven states the maximum jail sentence ranges from two to seven years.

Two studies that have carefully examined sentencing practices in these courts come to very different conclusions. In his study of the handling of cases in the lower court in New Haven, Connecticut, Malcolm Feeley found that the primary sanctions were meted out in the pretrial process and that the sentences were relatively inconsequential. Feeley argues that the economic and psychological costs involved in making bail, hiring an attorney, appearing in court, and preparing the defense are the major punishment, since jail terms are unlikely and fines relatively slight in the type of cases studied. In contrast to Feeley's finding that "the process is the punishment," John Paul Ryan found that sentences in the Columbus (Ohio) Municipal Court were much more substantial and that process costs were relatively low. Ryan concludes that "the outcome is the punishment."

In the limited-jurisdiction courts, there is also considerable variation with regard to case-processing practices, the presence of prosecution and defense attorneys, the incidence of plea negotiation, the use of probation, and the legal training of judges. Many limited-jurisdiction courts support the popular notion of these courts as dispensing assembly-line justice. Cases are handled in a perfunctory, nonadversarial fashion, with the vast majority of criminal cases being disposed of by guilty plea at the first appearance. Defendants in many of these courts are seldom represented by counsel and some are prosecuted by police officers. The judges in these courts often are nonlawyers. Postverdict services such as the preparation of presentence reports and probation are either unavailable or seldom used. Practices in other limited-jurisdiction courts, on the other hand, suggest a paradigm that is closer to the popular notion of the general-jurisdiction trial court. Few cases are disposed of at initial appearance in these courts. In fact, a case may move through numerous stages with the defendant represented by counsel and prosecuted by an attorney before a lawyer judge. Presentence reports and probation are available and frequently used.

A number of legal scholars have been concerned that the assembly-line justice of many of the limited-jurisdiction courts does not give full effect to the rights of criminal defendants and have called for reforms that would inject a greater degree of procedural fairness in lower-court proceedings. These scholars have contended that there is a need for procedural reform —such as an expansion of the right to counsel— not only for theoretical but also for practical reasons. For example, Francis A. Allen explains that improvements in the administration and operation of the misdemeanor courts may be late in coming because these courts have enjoyed a "freedom from scrutiny." More specifically, those in the best position (lawyers) to analyze and critique administrative and operational shortcomings have not been present in large numbers in these courts until quite recently.

It has been argued that the few lawyers who traditionally have practiced in these courts generally lack the influence or are too corrupt to constitute a force for reform. Yet, procedural reformers have exercised a good deal of caution in calling for an expansion of the due process rights of misdemeanor defendants. They have emphasized a need to reconcile "administrative imperatives" or "problems of feasibility" with procedural changes that ostensibly would give greater effect to these rights (Allen). Recent United States Supreme Court decisions indicate a sensitivity to such "administrative imperatives" and illuminate the need to develop a better sense of how differences in adjudication practices may influence substantive rights and outcomes. In the 1970s the Supreme Court issued major decisions concerning the right to counsel in misdemeanor cases. It also decided cases relating to a defendant's right to an impartial judge, to a law-trained judge, and to a jury trial in the limited-jurisdiction courts.

In *Argersinger* v. *Hamlin* (1972), the Supreme Court held that no person can be imprisoned for any offense unless, absent a knowing and intelligent waiver, the defendant was represented by counsel. In effect, *Argersinger* extended the right to counsel, established in *Gideon* v. *Wainwright* (1963) nine years earlier, to indigent misdemeanor offenders. In the majority and three separate concurring opinions in *Argersinger,* six of the justices attempted to assess the extent of the additional administrative burdens that the decision would place on the limited-jurisdiction courts and suggested ways of easing these burdens. Chief Justice Burger, for example, pointed out that counsel need be provided to an indigent defendant only if the defendant is actually imprisoned, and suggested that the prosecutor assist the judge in predicting whether the defendant would be sent to jail if convicted. Such an approach to the provision of defense counsel to the indigent was supported by the Court's later decision in *Scott* v. *Illinois* (1979). In a 5–4 decision in *Scott,* the Court ruled that the right to counsel mandated by *Argersinger* did not extend to all cases in which there was a possibility of imprisonment but only to cases in which the defendant was actually imprisoned.

Although the impact of the defense attorney on misdemeanor court proceedings is problematic, a preliminary study suggests that the increased use of counsel in the lower trial courts has not contributed to their woes in the ways that many have assumed (Alfini and Passuth). More research is needed to examine the effect of procedural and administrative reforms on such factors as guilty-plea rates, the incidence and nature of plea negotiations, the pretrial process, and delay in the limited-jurisdiction courts.

In *Ward* v. *Monroeville* (1972), *Ludwig* v. *Massachusetts* (1976), and *North* v. *Russell* (1976), the Supreme Court ruled on the constitutionality of other limited-jurisdiction court procedures and practices. In each case, the Court considered the impact of these procedures on a defendant's substantive rights and considered the constitutional relevance of the availability of an appeal from the limited-jurisdiction trial court to a general-jurisdiction trial court.

In *Ward,* the Supreme Court ruled that the defendant was unconstitutionally deprived of his right to a trial before a disinterested and impartial judge where he was tried by the village mayor, who was responsible for village finances and whose court provided a substantial portion of village funds through fines, forfeitures, costs, and fees. The Court based its decision on principles it had laid down in a 1927 case, *Tumey* v. *Ohio.* In *Tumey,* the Court reversed the convictions when it appeared that the judge (also the village mayor) received part of the court fees and costs levied by him, in addition to his regular salary. The Court stated that "it certainly violates the Fourteenth Amendment, and deprives a defendant in a criminal case of due process of law, to subject his liberty or property to the judgment of a court the judge of which has a direct, personal, substantial, pecuniary interest in reaching a conclusion against him in his case." In *Ward,* the Supreme Court ruled that the fact that the defendant had a right to a trial de novo in the general-jurisdiction court (and that any unfairness might therefore be corrected at this level) had no constitutional significance. The Court stated that the defendant was "entitled to a neutral and detached judge in the first instance."

A trial de novo is a new trial or retrial in a higher court. The case is handled as if there had been no trial in the lower court. Historically, it was invented as a procedural device to prevent abuses in the lower courts.

Although the Supreme Court decisions in *Tumey* and *Ward* have encouraged many states to do away with fee-based compensation systems for these courts, recent studies indicate that a few states are still using a fee system. Some commentators (following the Court's reasoning in *Tumey* and *Ward*) have argued that this system of compensation results in a judge's having a financial interest in the outcome of a case, which destroys his impartiality and thus results in a denial of due process. The principal justification for retaining a fee system, particularly in rural areas, appears to be that relating the judge's compensation to his work load will give him the necessary incentive to work full-time as a judge. In states retaining some form of a fee-based compensation system, it has been argued that their systems have eliminated the constitutional objections by removing the judge's financial interest in the outcome of a case. One such system has been characterized as the "salary fund fee system," whereby the judge is paid a set salary, which is derived solely from a designated fund consisting of fines and fees imposed by the judge.

Even in courts where judges receive fixed salaries, important economic issues concerning the administration of justice in urban as well as rural misdemeanor courts remain to be addressed through systematic research. As long as judges must look to limited local funds to run their courts, the extent to which judges can remain impartial and unbiased in deciding cases and administering justice is problematic. Unlike general trial courts, limited-jurisdiction courts generate substantial revenues. Even though fines and fees may be mixed, as in many locales, with general county funds and the judge's compensation may be fixed by state statute, the judge is still required to look to local officials in most jurisdictions for the funding of court facilities and services. They may thus be encouraged to overexploit the revenue-generating potential of their courts or, conversely, discouraged from doing anything (particularly using certain sentencing alternatives) that would have an adverse effect on the amount of revenue generated by their courts. As of 1986 there had been no empirically based studies that sought to determine the effect of these and other local economic incentives and disincentives on the administration of justice in the lower courts.

Contrary to its decision in *Ward,* the Supreme Court ruled in *Ludwig* v. *Massachusetts* (1976) and *North* v. *Russell* (1976) that certain procedural shortcomings in state limited-jurisdiction courts would be tolerated as long as a de novo appeal is available in a general trial court where these shortcomings can be remedied. In *Ludwig,* the Supreme Court upheld the constitutionality of Massachusetts' two-tier trial-court system, where no trial by jury is available in the first-tier (limited-jurisdiction) court, because a de novo jury trial is available on appeal to the second-tier (general-jurisdiction) court. In *North,* the Supreme Court similarly upheld the constitutionality of Kentucky's two-tier trial-court system, where the defendant faces the possibility of incarceration by a nonlawyer judge in the first-tier court. The Court upheld the constitutionality of incarceration by a nonlawyer judge as long as the defendant has an opportunity for a trial de novo before a lawyer judge in the second-tier court.

Although the twenty-four states that utilize a two-tier trial-court system (that is, trial court systems in which the defendant has a right to a de novo appeal to the second-tier) differ with regard to the procedural rights accorded defendants in the first-tier court, the effect of the Court's decisions in *Ludwig* and *North* is to encourage the perpetuation of two-tier trial-court systems in which certain procedural rights are unavailable to the defendant in the first-tier. In other words, these decisions may encourage the continued diversity among limited-jurisdiction courts on procedural matters.

Of relevance to the *Ludwig* decision is the question of whether and how a defendant's right to a jury trial in a limited-jurisdiction court affects substantive outcomes. Available research suggests that very few defendants are actually tried before a jury in misdemeanor courts where a jury trial is available. However, in some of these courts the number of jury demands is very high. This suggests the possibility that the mere availability of a jury trial may affect negotiation and adjudication strategies in these courts and thus affect substantive outcomes.

The *North* decision raises the question of whether and how misdemeanor courts staffed by nonlawyer judges differ from those staffed by lawyer judges. The impressionistic literature suggests that nonlawyer judges (particularly in rural areas) have a greater potential for bias in deciding cases insofar as they look to others (particularly the local prosecutor) for legal assistance and may rely more on personal knowledge than the law in deciding cases.

The persistence of the nonlawyer justice courts in rural areas of the United States would argue in favor of the need for more research on these courts. Silberman's 1979 study reveals that nonlawyer judges are still authorized in an estimated 20,280 state judicial positions (approximately two-thirds of all state judicial positions) and that 13,217 of these positions were in fact filled by nonlawyers. Certainly, the *North* decision does not encourage any reduction in their number.

Although they have been subjected to a great deal of criticism, primarily for their procedural irregularities, limited-jurisdiction courts serve an important function in the judicial system.

Each year, they resolve disputes involving millions of citizens. However, at a time when many of these courts are adopting long-awaited procedural reforms and formal practices, there is a newer reform movement calling for alternate (generally less formal) dispute resolution (ADR) mechanisms for handling many of the kinds of disputes processed in these courts (Council on the Role of Courts). ADR proponents argue that the adversarial process employed in court cases discourages other than win/lose outcomes, often frustrates the search for truth, encourages delay, and is too costly. As an alternative to formal adjudication, they propose mechanisms such as arbitration and mediation. The future role of the limited-jurisdiction courts, and indeed of trial courts generally, will be largely determined by their willingness and ability to respond to these changing societal concerns and demands.

CASES

Argersinger v. Hamlin, 407 U.S. 25 (1972)
Gideon v. Wainwright, 372 U.S. 335 (1963)
Ludwig v. Massachusetts, 427 U.S. 618 (1976)
North v. Russell, 427 U.S. 328 (1976)
Ross v. Bernhard, 396 U.S. 531 (1970)
Scott v. Illinois, 440 U.S. 367 (1979)
Swain v. Alabama, 380 U.S. 202 (1965)
Tumey v. Ohio, 273 U.S. 510 (1927)
Ward v. Village of Monroeville, 409 U.S. 57 (1972)

BIBLIOGRAPHY

Administrative Office of the United States Courts, *Federal Court Management Statistics* (1983), is a statistical breakdown of the work load of the federal courts from 1978 to 1983. James J. Alfini, "Introductory Essay: The Misdemeanor Courts," in *Justice System Journal,* 6 (1981), argues that efforts in improving the lower criminal courts will be more likely to succeed if full consideration is given to their diversity; and Alfini, ed., *Misdemeanor Courts: Policy Concerns and Research Perspectives* (1981), contains articles identifying lower-court policy issues and possible research strategies for addressing these issues. James J. Alfini and Patricia M. Passuth, "Case Processing in State Misdemeanor Courts: The Effect of Defense Attorney Presence," in *Justice System Journal,* 6 (1981), reports on the results of a questionnaire survey aimed at assessing the effect of counsel on case processing in lower trial courts. Francis A. Allen, "Small Crimes and Large Problems: Some Constitutional Dimensions," in C. H. Whitebread, ed., *Mass Production Justice and the Constitutional Ideal* (1970), examines constitutional issues related to case processing in the lower criminal trial courts. American Bar Association, *Standards Relating to Court Organization* (1974), sets forth standards on court-organization topics such as unified court systems, selection and tenure of judges, rule making, and administrative authority; and *Standards Relating to Trial Courts* (1976), sets forth standards for case handling in the trial courts.

Ralph Cavanagh and Austin Sarat, "Thinking About Courts: Toward and Beyond a Jurisprudence of Judicial Competence," in *Law and Society Review,* 14 (1980), reviews arguments over the competence and capacity of courts to handle certain kinds of cases. Thomas Church, Alan Carlson, Jo-Lynn Lee, and Teresa Tan, *Justice Delayed: The Pace of Litigation in Urban Trial Courts* (1978), argues that trial-court delay can best be understood by examining the "local legal culture." Council on the Role of Courts, *The Role of Courts in American Society* (1984), gives the results of a study aimed at shaping the future role of American courts. James Eisenstein and Herbert Jacob, *Felony Justice: An Organizational Analysis of Criminal Courts* (1977), examines adjudication and sentencing practices in the felony trial courts in Baltimore, Chicago, and Detroit. Malcolm M. Feeley, *The Process Is the Punishment: Handling Cases in a Lower Criminal Court* (1979), examines criminal case processing in the lower trial court in New Haven, Connecticut, and finds, among other things, that "process costs" are high and sentences relatively inconsequential. Jerome Frank, *Courts on Trial* (1949), is a classic critique of the courts in operation, by a prominent judge and legal philosopher. Sheldon Goldman and Thomas P. Jahnige, *The Federal Courts as a Political System* (1985), contains important information on the federal courts and reviews recent research. Sheldon Goldman and Austin Sarat, *American Court Systems* (1978), is a collection of readings on various facets of American state and federal courts.

Herbert Jacob, *Justice in America* (1972), is regarded as the classic treatment of the operational realities of America's justice system; and "Trial Courts in the United States: The Travails of Exploration," in *Law and Society Review,* 17 (1983), reviews twelve years of research on trial courts. James W. Jeans, *Trial Advocacy* (1975), is a handbook on trial practice with detailed advice on the various stages of preparing for and conducting the trial. Harry W. Jones, ed., *The Courts, the Public, and the Law Explosion* (1965), is a collection of essays focusing on the courts and their problems prepared for an American assembly program of Columbia University. Yale Kamisar, Wayne R. La Fave, and Jerold H. Israel, *Basic Criminal Procedure* (1974), contains basic materials on criminal procedure. Norbert L. Kerr and Robert M. Bray, eds., *The Psychology of the Courtroom* (1982), is a collection of essays reviewing empirical and experimental research on trial-court procedures and key actors, with emphasis on the jury trial.

Martin A. Levin, *Urban Politics and the Criminal Courts* (1977), examines differences in the handling of felony cases in the trial courts in Pittsburgh and Minneapolis. David W. Louisell and Geoffrey C. Hazard, *Cases and Materials on Pleading and Procedure: State and Federal* (1979), contains cases and materials on state and federal civil procedure. National Center for State Courts, *State Court Caseload Statistics: Annual Report, 1980* (1984), reports comprehensive case load statistics for state trial and appellate courts on an annual basis. David W. Neubauer, *America's Courts and the Criminal Justice System* (1979), is an undergraduate textbook on America's criminal courts, focusing on "the dynamics of the courthouse." President's Commission on Law Enforcement and Administration of Justice, *The Challenge of Crime in a Free Society* (1967), makes two hundred specific recommendations for improving the criminal justice system.

Judith Resnik, "Managerial Judges," in *Harvard Law Review*, 96 (1982), argues that the recent emphasis on trial-court management may have adverse effects on the adjudicative responsibilities of trial courts. John Robertson, ed., *Rough Justice: Perspectives on Lower Criminal Courts* (1974), is a collection of articles on criminal case handling in the limited-jurisdiction courts. H. Ted Rubin, *The Courts: Fulcrum of the Justice System* (1976), is a primer on the American judicial system. John C. Ruhnka and Steven Weller, *Small Claims Courts: A National Examination* (1978), assesses small-claims procedures in fifteen limited-jurisdiction trial courts. John Paul Ryan, "Adjudication and Sentencing in a Misdemeanor Court: The Outcome Is the Punishment," in *Law and Society Review*, 15 (1980), examines adjudication and sentencing practices in the limited-jurisdiction trial court in Columbus, Ohio. John P. Ryan, Allan Ashman, Bruce Sales, and Sandra Shane-DuBow, *American Trial Judges: Their Work Styles and Performance* (1980), reports the results of a national survey of judges in state general-jurisdiction trial courts.

Linda J. Silberman, *Non-Attorney Justice in the United States: An Empirical Study* (1979), examines the use of nonattorney judges in American court systems. Susan S. Silbey, "Making Sense of the Lower Courts," in *Justice System Journal*, 6 (1981), argues that even though the limited-jurisdiction trial courts do not adhere strictly to a rule of law model, they have a distinct capacity for providing responsive justice for the kinds of cases they are asked to handle. Maureen Solomon, *Caseflow Management in the Trial Court* (1973), argues for increased judicial control of the flow of cases through a trial court. United States Department of Justice, *National Survey of Court Organization* (1973), contains the results of a survey of American courts conducted by the Census Bureau as a preliminary step to establishing a national program of judicial statistics. United States National Advisory Commission on Criminal Justice Standards and Goals, *Courts* (1973), sets forth standards relating to the role of the courts in the criminal justice system.

[*See also* COURTS OF LIMITED AND SPECIALIZED JURISDICTION; CRIMINAL JUSTICE SYSTEM; DISCOVERY; FEDERAL COURT SYSTEM; JUDICIAL ADMINISTRATION; JURISDICTION; SENTENCING ALTERNATIVES; *and* STATE COURT SYSTEMS.]

TRIAL JURIES AND GRAND JURIES

Jon M. Van Dyke

THE panels of common citizens assembled to serve as grand juries and trial juries are among the most democratic of American institutions. The idea itself—that ordinary citizens without experience in judicial decision-making should be brought together to decide issues of great importance—is an unusual one in the world today. The jury developed as part of a long struggle against centralized power in Britain and later in those countries that inherited the British traditions of justice. But the jury is unusual even in democracies. Most institutions of democratic governments draw their power from the people, who elect their representatives to decision-making bodies, but in the American courtroom it is the people themselves, as jurors, who make the decisions. No wonder, then, that the jury continues to be the object of controversy.

The democratic features of the jury have evolved slowly, and when juries and grand juries first began to be used in Britain and the United States, they were not selected according to the democratic principles that hold sway today. The jury has been affected by changes in society and has helped change society as well. After almost a thousand years of experience with the jury, persons raised in the Anglo-American tradition have come to view a jury trial as the right of every defendant accused of a serious crime and the jury as a body consisting of a cross section of the community, randomly selected. But the jury was originally a creation of the crown, made up of landowners. Concepts of its form and function have evolved over the centuries along with democratic government.

ENGLISH ORIGINS

The roots of the jury date back to Anglo-Saxon England, but its modern development began with William the Conqueror, who determined the countryside's wealth and population through "inquests" or "inquisitions." The king sent his barons to the villages and townships, where they summoned the important men from the neighborhood, placed them under oath, and questioned them about the community's financial affairs. The sworn men were fundamentally witnesses, supplying the information to the royal officers that eventually produced the Domesday Book, a massive census conducted around 1086. They were primarily interested in financial affairs but occasionally examined criminal matters as well.

Henry II, who ruled from 1154 to 1189 and was concerned with strengthening the crown's presence in the countryside, can probably be credited more than any other single individual with laying the foundation for the modern jury. He developed the system of inquests begun by William into the direct ancestor of the grand jury, by impaneling the "most lawful men" of every community to review the evidence against those suspected of committing crimes.

During this early period, most civil disputes over land ownership were decided by "assizes," in which a group of carefully selected men studied the case and gave a verdict. In criminal cases, however, guilt or innocence was usually determined either by trial by battle, proof by oath or compurgation (see below), or trial by ordeal, an ancient and brutal form of settling controversies that involved dunking the accused in water or forcing him to carry hot irons in his hands. These ordeals were supervised by the clergy, who would evaluate the dunking or burning to give divine sanction to the decision of guilt or innocence. The jury was used erratically according to the king's wishes until 1215, when a group of barons exacted the promise from King John, in Article 39 of the Magna Charta, that "no freeman

734

shall be taken or imprisoned or [dispossessed], or outlawed or exiled or in any way destroyed . . . except by the lawful judgment of his peers and the law of the land." The jury of 1215 was still more like the modern grand jury than a trial jury because its role was to decide whether the evidence justified further proceedings against a defendant—further proceedings in the nature of an ordeal. But in the same year as the Magna Charta, Pope Innocent III prohibited participation by priests in trials by ordeal, and the way was opened for trials by jury to take their place. A decline of religious values had in any case already brought into question the validity of the oaths taken in ordeals as well as the motives of the clergy, who were found to manipulate some of the ordeals and to profit from fees collected from them.

In the first half of the fourteenth century, the trial jury and the grand jury were finally separated. The trial jury began to be recognized as a body whose task was to evaluate the evidence and come up with a definitive verdict as to guilt or innocence, as differentiated from the grand jury, which had brought the charges. In 1352 a statute was passed stating explicitly that grand jurors could not also sit on the trial jury. After that date, when one of the king's traveling justices arrived to hear disputes, the local sheriff would choose twelve men from the immediate surrounding community to serve as jurors and would then select an additional group of twenty-four men (usually knights) from a larger area to serve as an accusing body for the entire county. After these twenty-four eliminated one member so that they could act by majority vote, they investigated incidents and soon took over the entire burden of filing indictments.

It is not known for certain why juries of twelve developed. Theorists frequently refer to the twelve prophets or the twelve disciples and to the proof by compurgation, which had frequently called on twelve men to swear that the accused's oath was trustworthy. The real reason probably was that twelve is a number large enough to ensure some reliability and impartiality and yet small enough to function with some degree of efficiency. In any case, by the middle of the fourteenth century the requirement of twelve was fixed.

As the concept of the trial jury emerged, so did the rule of unanimity. For a time, decisions reflecting an eleven-to-one split were accepted, with the dissenting juror fined for perjury on the theory that he must have been wrong if the eleven others disagreed with him. Another technique involved adding additional jurors when the original twelve were split until a group of twelve could be assembled that would agree on a verdict. But these alternatives did not satisfy the true purpose of the jury—to provide a reliable decision reflecting the view of the community in as authoritative a manner as trial by ordeal had earlier reflected the views of the divinity. Nothing short of a unanimous verdict would supply this level of reliability.

Although the Magna Charta had taken the right to use a jury out of the hands of the crown and given it to the barons, the crown retained considerable control over the jury's decisions for several more centuries. Until the early sixteenth century, jury verdicts could be overturned by a larger, specially selected, and generally more elite "jury of attaint." The original jurors were then frequently imprisoned and their lands confiscated by the crown, because they were viewed as having committed perjury in returning an "erroneous" verdict. After juries of attaint were discredited because of the harshness of their penalties, verdicts were still sometimes rejected by a judge, and jurors could still be imprisoned or fined.

In the late seventeenth century, the supremacy of the jury's verdict, and thus its independence, was finally established in a celebrated case involving William Penn and William Mead. Penn (who was then twenty-six) and Mead (another young Quaker activist) were charged in 1670 with conducting an unlawful assembly after they had held a meeting of Quakers in London that had been disrupted by others. The jury refused to return a guilty verdict, even though the judges pressured them heavily for several days to do so. Edward Bushell, leader of the dissenting jurors, was soundly scolded by the magistrate. After a series of deliberations and verdicts that were rejected by the court, the jury eventually found Penn and Mead not guilty. The magistrate then imposed a stiff fine on the jurors and ordered them imprisoned until they paid the money.

The undaunted jurors, insisting on their right to return a verdict free from judicial coercion, applied for a writ of habeas corpus. Ten weeks later, Chief Justice Vaughan, speaking for himself and ten other sitting appeals judges of the

Court of Common Pleas, freed the jurors and stated decisively that jurors cannot be punished for their decision. Vaughan's historic opinion in *Bushell's Case* emphasized that the purpose of the jury is to obtain persons from the location of the alleged crime so that they can evaluate the evidence according to their own understanding, reasoning, and conscience. Why, he asked, insist on careful selection procedures—to ensure that jurors come from the site of the incident and are unbiased—unless the verdict of the jury is to stand as the final decision on the question? The Vaughan decision articulates a principle that is now fully accepted: that if the jury is to play its intended role as an impartial fact finder to express the community's decision, it must be independent. Otherwise, it is not really the community's voice but the voice of the crown (or state), and the entire rationale for using a jury is undercut.

In 1681, eleven years after the trial jury's independence was established in *Bushell's Case,* a grand jury asserted the same power. In that year a London grand jury refused to return an indictment against the earl of Shaftesbury, who was accused of treason. After hearing the prosecution's witnesses and questioning them in private, the grand jury returned the bill presented by the prosecutor with the word *ignoramus* ("we do not know") written on the back. The royal authorities then presented the same evidence before the Oxford grand jury, which apparently did not share the politics of its counterpart in London and which indicted the earl. Despite the Oxford action, the principle that a grand jury could stand between the king and the accused was established, and the London grand jurors were not punished.

THE AMERICAN JURY

The independence of the jury from the crown was also an important aspect of the North American drive for independence from Britain in the eighteenth century. The people who settled in the original thirteen colonies considered jury trial a fundamental right, as indeed it had been in England for centuries. Most of the colonies specifically guaranteed trial by jury in their charters, although the methods of selection, size of the vicinage (the area from which jurors are se-

lected), and the extent of use differed both within colonies over time and from colony to colony.

The First Continental Congress in 1774 stressed the importance of the jury by declaring that "the respective colonies are entitled to . . . the great and inestimable privilege of being tried by their peers of the vicinage, according to the course of [common] law." The Declaration of Independence specifically included among the grievances against the king deprivation "in many cases of the benefits of trial by jury." One such deprivation was an edict by the governor of colonial New York in 1765 that jury verdicts could be appealed to the governor and his council and overruled by them if deemed incorrect. Such a claim obviously ran counter to the recognition of the jury's independence in William Penn's case one hundred years earlier. Another deprivation was the Port Bill of 1773, which gave the royal governor of Massachusetts the power to transfer trials to another colony or back to England—a move that denied the accused a jury from the community, another right that had been recognized in the Penn controversy.

The importance of jury trial was also expressed in the constitutions of the thirteen original states. Many employed phrases similar to Maryland's Declaration of Rights, which stated that "the trial of facts where they arise, is one of the greatest securities of the lives, liberties and estates of the people," among whose rights is "a speedy trial by an impartial jury, without whose unanimous consent he ought not to be found guilty." Some state constitutions borrowed language directly from the Magna Charta in their provisions on jury trial.

The great variation in practice among the thirteen colonies probably explains why the only provision relating to jury trial in the original 1787 Constitution was in Article III, Section 2, which states that "the Trial of all Crimes, except in Cases of Impeachment, shall be by Jury; and such Trial shall be held in the State where the said Crimes shall have been committed." The vagueness of this provision was one reason for opposition to the Constitution during the ratification period of 1787–1789. Many people expressed fears that jury verdicts might be reversed by appellate judges, that the vicinage requirement was too broad (calling for juries drawn within a state, rather than from smaller areas), and that no provision specifically guaranteed the right to challenge prospective jurors.

These fears were largely answered by the Bill of Rights, which was adopted as the first ten amendments to the Constitution in 1791 and refers to trial by jury in three different places: the Fifth Amendment declaration that no person can be criminally charged "unless on a presentment or indictment of a Grand Jury"; the Sixth Amendment guarantee that persons so accused shall have the right to a trial "by an impartial jury of the State and district where in the crime shall have been committed"; and the Seventh Amendment guarantee of the same right in civil cases, which says that "in Suits at common law, where the value in controversy shall exceed twenty dollars, the right of trial by jury shall be preserved, and no fact tried by a jury, shall be otherwise re-examined in any Court of the United States, than according to the rules of the common law." The Constitution thus firmly establishes an individual's right to demand the community's sanction—expressed in the jury's verdict—before he or she can be convicted of a crime and denied freedom.

The modern meaning of the constitutional protection of trial by jury was summed up by Justice Byron R. White in the 1968 case of *Duncan* v. *Louisiana*:

> The guarantees of jury trial in the Federal and State Constitutions reflect a profound judgment about the way in which law should be enforced and justice administered. *A right to jury trial is granted to criminal defendants in order to prevent oppression by the Government. . . . Providing an accused with the right to be tried by a jury of his peers gave him an inestimable safeguard against the corrupt or over-zealous prosecutor and against the compliant, biased or eccentric judge.* If the defendant preferred the common-sense judgment of a jury to the more tutored but perhaps less sympathetic reaction of a single judge, he was to have it. Beyond this, the jury trial provisions in the Federal and State Constitutions reflect a fundamental decision about the exercise of official power—a reluctance to entrust plenary powers over the life and liberty of the citizen to one judge or to a group of judges.
>
> (Emphasis added.)

The American commitment to the use of citizen panels for juries and grand juries is thus firm and based on sound policy reasons. Many disputes nonetheless remain about what roles these panels should play and how they should be structured and should operate.

THE GRAND JURY

The grand jury has been a particularly controversial body because it operates in secret and has frequently been manipulated by the prosecutor to reach a preordained result. American history contains numerous examples of independent grand juries that have confronted and exposed governmental corruption but also contains many other examples of docile, controlled grand juries that have sat idly by while elected officials enriched themselves at the expense of the public.

Prior to 1776, jurors and grand jurors were generally handpicked by the sheriff, who was appointed by the British crown, and as a result, only the largest landholders became members of these largely passive bodies. In Virginia, however, grand jurors were selected in a more random fashion, and these more independent panels frequently made unusually probing and embarrassing examinations of governmental activities. The royal governor, Francis Nicholson, became upset at this activity and issued a proclamation in 1690 instructing the local sheriffs to select grand jurors only "from the most substantial inhabitants of your counties." Nine years later, the Virginia General Assembly defined more particularly the requirements for jury service, saying that jurors in the General Court must be freeholders whose real and personal property are visibly of the reputed value of £100. These decrees substantially ended the independence of the Virginia juries and reduced the potential for embarrassment to the crown.

In the colony of Massachusetts the sheriff originally selected all grand jurors, but in the early eighteenth century the colonists were able to wrest away the sheriff's power and assign it to the town meetings held in all communities. This change became particularly important during the turbulent years before the American Revolution. When the royal governor asked the grand jury to investigate the frequent disturbances connected with anti-British activity, the colonists were able to thwart the investigation by selecting as grand jurors persons who had played leading roles in the disturbances. After the Boston Tea Party of 1773, the British House of Commons passed an elaborate statute called the Port Bill, which revised local government in Massachusetts and required that the king's sheriff choose grand and trial jurors from a list of freeholders. This move was protested vehemently, and the few token persons opposing British rule who were selected for the grand jury—men like Paul Revere and John Hancock's brother Ebenezer—refused to take their oaths as grand jurors.

Examples of abuses in the selection of grand jurors can be found throughout United States history. One instance occurred at the beginning of the twentieth century in San Francisco. A political boss named Abraham Ruef had gained control of city government through various corrupt maneuvers, and a special prosecutor was finally appointed to investigate his activities. Ruef sought to derail this investigation by controlling the 1906 grand jury, which was selected through a nominating process: each of the 12 trial judges nominated 12 persons, and then 19 grand jurors were selected by lot from the pool of 144. Several of these judges were subject to the influence of Ruef, including at least one who was directly under his control.

The grand jury secretary, Myrtile Cerf, was a confederate of Ruef. He determined the nineteen most favorable nominees before the drawing, and folded the slips bearing their names together in a packet, which he was able to feel when he placed his hand in the box at the official drawing. He was thus able to draw the names of nominees most favorable to Ruef in a process that appeared to be impartial. The editor of the *San Francisco Bulletin* later discovered this fraudulent selection process and eventually persuaded the presiding judge to discharge the panel and select a new one. Free of Ruef's influence and finally independent, the new grand jury promptly indicted Ruef; he was convicted and served a prison term with several of his confederates.

The California grand juries continued to be selected through a judicial nominating process until the 1970s, when most counties moved to a system of selecting names randomly from the voters' registration list in order to avoid the discrimination that almost inevitably results from a personal selection scheme. The specific impetus for this change in San Francisco was a 1975 rul-

ing by a federal judge who examined the statistics of the grand jurors by racial categories and sex and ruled that the "substantial underrepresentation" of nonwhite ethnic groups and women could be "the basis for a *prima facie* case of unconstitutional discrimination in selection" (*Quadra* v. *San Francisco Superior Court*).

Function of the Grand Jury. In over half the states, the grand jury has evolved from a body that reviews all criminal charges and issues formal indictments ordering accused persons to appear for trial to a body whose primary responsibility is to investigate governmental activities and major criminal schemes. This change began in the nineteenth century, and in those states that have moved in this direction, most criminal charges are reviewed by a judge in a public "preliminary hearing," in which the accused can be present and participate.

The United States Supreme Court considered this innovation in the 1884 case of *Hurtado* v. *California.* The Court tested the California change by asking whether the preliminary hearing satisfied the requirements of the due process clause of the Fourteenth Amendment of the Constitution. The Court concluded that the minimum requisites of liberty and justice were in fact preserved by a preliminary hearing in which the district attorney was obliged to establish probable guilt before a neutral magistrate. In certain respects the accused is given more protection in a preliminary hearing than by a grand jury indictment because the accused, who is barred from grand jury proceedings, can appear at the hearing with counsel and cross-examine the government's witnesses. Justice John M. Harlan, writing the single dissenting opinion, complained that an essential element of liberty was being sacrificed by this process:

> In the secrecy of the investigations by grand juries, the weak and helpless—proscribed, perhaps, because of their race, or pursued by an unreasoning public clamor—have found, and will continue to find, security against official oppression, the cruelty of mobs, the machinations of falsehood, and the malevolence of private persons who would use the machinery of the law to bring ruin upon their personal enemies.

But this concern did not convince those who preferred a more public procedure, and many states have now followed California's lead in eliminating the requirement of grand jury indictments. The grand jury may in theory be a body of citizens designed to protect people from being falsely accused; but because the grand jury meets in secret and because the potential defendant has no right to appear or refute the government's case, it provides an uncertain protection. The British, in fact, found the grand jury to be totally unnecessary and discarded the institution in 1933.

In the United States, grand juries are still active bodies, but their main role in many states is the investigation of major governmental scandals and elaborate criminal conspiracies that require extensive investigation and a greater-than-usual need to obtain private information. Colorado and Wyoming view the grand jury as such a useful investigating body that they have passed legislation authorizing statewide grand juries to be impaneled to examine wrongs that transcend county borders.

The grand jury has continued to be viewed as a useful institution, because it has a unique power to obtain evidence. A grand jury has an authority to demand answers from government officials and private citizens that go far beyond the power given to any other law enforcement body. The constitutional privileges and protections that can be asserted to avoid responding to the inquiries of the police, the Federal Bureau of Investigation, or any other law enforcement body do not shield one from a grand jury inquiry. In 1972 the Supreme Court stated that the "longstanding principle that 'the public . . . has a right to every man's evidence' . . . is particularly applicable to grand jury proceedings" (*Branzburg v. Hayes*), and in 1974 the Court applied that rule to the president of the United States (*United States v. Nixon*).

Grand Jury Abuses and Reform Efforts. The romantic image of the grand jury involves a body of citizens who gather together to investigate the crimes of the community. In fact, however, grand jurors all too often follow the prosecutor's lead completely and return indictments whenever requested to do so. Because they meet behind closed doors, are carefully guided by the prosecutor, and have almost unlimited power to demand evidence, the potential for abuse is great. During the Nixon administration, abuses of federal grand juries occurred with some regularity,

causing Supreme Court Justice William O. Douglas to write in a dissenting opinion in 1973, "It is, indeed, common knowledge that the grand jury, having been conceived as a bulwark between the citizen and the Government, is now a tool of the Executive" (*United States v. Mara*).

Efforts to reform the grand jury have faltered because most victims of grand jury abuse are isolated, with little ability to generate public attention to the problems that exist. Except during periods like the Nixon and Vietnam era, when the victims of grand jury abuse were part of a larger political movement, this institution has not been the subject of concerted political focus.

One important reform priority—as mentioned above—is to ensure that the membership of grand juries accurately reflects the composition of the population at large. When the grand jury first became a body separate and distinct from the trial jury, those selected to serve as grand jurors were wealthier and of a higher social class than their trial jury counterparts, because their jurisdiction was broader and their potential power was greater. This tradition remains intact in some areas, and, although the statutes in most states say that grand jurors are to be selected in the same manner as trial jurors, substantial differences nonetheless sometimes exist in practice and result. A "blue-ribbon" grand jury composed of elite and influential citizens may be particularly vulnerable to governmental abuse and is unlikely to protect the interests of less powerful groups in society.

Another reform proposal would allow a witness to have an attorney with him in the grand jury room. At present, a witness is permitted to leave the grand jury after a question is asked and consult with an attorney outside in the corridor, but such a procedure is awkward and seems inconsistent with the right to counsel that exists in all other phases of the American judicial process.

An accused should have greater access to the grand jury's deliberations and some right to participate in the proceeding. In some states (California, for instance), an accused will automatically receive a copy of the grand jury transcript after an indictment is filed; and, in others (New York, for instance), the trial judge is required to examine the transcript upon request by the accused. In federal courts the accused must demonstrate a special need before being shown even a partial transcript. Recent United States Supreme Court rulings require prosecutors to present "exculpatory" evidence (evidence that would tend to show the accused's innocence) to the grand jury if such evidence is in the prosecutor's possession. It is difficult to enforce such an obligation, particularly when the grand jury operates in secret.

The awkwardness of the requirement that all deliberations take place in secret—and that grand jurors say nothing about these deliberations subsequently—was illustrated by a 1984 grand jury in Brooklyn, New York, investigating the death of an individual allegedly beaten by transit police officers after scrawling graffiti in a subway station. A reviewing judge reversed the grand jury's manslaughter indictment of the officers, because one of the grand jurors pursued his own investigation of the incident and became "an unsworn witness" against the accused. The grand juror responded that his actions were proper but that his secrecy oath prevented him from defending his activities. The reviewing judge agreed that a thorough investigation of the death was essential but "abandoning the secrecy of the grand jury is not the best means to ensure that result" (*New York Times,* 21 October 1984).

One reform that has been introduced in the Hawaii state courts could provide the foundation for returning the grand jury to its original role as "the people's panel" elsewhere. In 1978 the Hawaii Constitution was amended to require the court to appoint a lawyer to serve as "independent grand jury counsel"—to advise the grand jurors directly about legal issues so that they can perform their jobs more fully without relying on the prosecutor for legal advice. The independent lawyer does not participate in the questioning of grand jury witnesses or in the grand jury's deliberations but does respond to questions posed by the grand jury and discusses difficult legal issues with them when appropriate. This device has worked quite well and has given the grand jurors more confidence about how to evaluate evidence and when and how they should question witnesses themselves. The presence of an independent lawyer in the grand jury room appears also to have encouraged the prosecutors to present their evidence with somewhat more care and thoroughness to ensure that all elements of the crime have been covered. This is a modest and relatively inexpensive reform that appears to have helped to restore the grand jury as a neutral panel of citizens standing between the government and the accused and protecting the accused from governmental oppression.

If the grand jury could be modernized, it could once again be a proud part of the American democratic tradition. When confronted with governmental overreaching, a grand jury can refuse to indict persons that the government wishes to prosecute. The grand jury also has the power to investigate the activities of governmental agencies and uncover abuses of power in a uniquely probing and thorough manner. Because the grand jurors are independent citizens who fade anonymously back into the community when their job is done, they need not fear future job reprisals or face other pressures that inevitably occur when the investigators are part of the system being investigated. Special Prosecutor Leon Jaworski, in his July 1974 brief before the Supreme Court demanding President Nixon's tapes and defending the action of the grand jury in naming Nixon a coconspirator, described the grand jury as "this body of citizens, randomly selected, beholden neither to court nor to prosecutor, trusted historically to protect the individual against unwarranted government charges, but sworn to ferret out criminality by the exalted and powerful as well as by the humble and weak." The grand jury does not always play this important role, but when it does, it reminds one anew of its importance to American democracy.

THE TRIAL JURY

The trial jury has been subjected to the same kind of exacting scrutiny as the grand jury, but the result of this scrutiny—at least in the United States—has been to reaffirm the central role of the jury in the judicial process and to underscore again the role of jurors in bringing commonsense wisdom into the legal system. The United States Supreme Court has repeatedly stressed the importance of the jury, and reforms have occurred in the state and federal systems to make it more probable that juries will be representative of their communities.

When juries were first used in England, an attempt was made to impanel persons who were the "peers" of the litigants, but this frequently meant that only men of property served as jurors. In the twelfth century, jurors were selected on the basis of their loyalty to the crown, as well as their reputed honesty and familiarity with local conditions. At the time, only freemen, and not serfs (who outnumbered freemen by about ten to one), were permitted to serve on juries. In land disputes, juries had to include four knights as well as twelve freemen, with a majority of twelve required for a verdict. Blue-ribbon juries of landowners handled appeals from other juries and disputes considered particularly complex. Until 1972, in fact, an individual had to own property to serve as a juror in England.

Many colonial courts in North America had strict property requirements for jurors as well. Even after independence, juries consisted of the more elite members of the population. Property qualifications existed for both voting and jury duty. Likewise, women were not eligible to serve as jurors, just as they were not eligible to vote. During the 1800s many states dropped their property requirements, but at least a dozen still retained them in the last quarter of that century. Some states selected their jurors from voter rolls and some from tax rolls (which automatically limited them to property owners); some jurors were selected by judges, town officials, or county supervisors, and some through a "key-man" system, wherein jury commissioners consulted prominent members of the community ("key men") for suggestions of jurors.

The federal courts impaneled elite juries through the key-man system until 1968, when Congress passed the Jury Selection and Service Act, which requires federal courts to select jurors randomly from the list of registered voters (supplemented by other lists when appropriate). Congress took this action specifically to ensure jury independence and impartiality. In the hearings preceding passage of the reform bill, Judge Irving R. Kaufman of the Court of Appeals for the Second Circuit responded to the argument that jurors should continue to be carefully selected by key men to ensure that they would have sufficient intelligence and common sense:

> Long experience with subjective requirements such as "intelligence" and "common sense" has demonstrated beyond any doubt that these vague terms provide a fertile ground for discrimination and arbitrariness, even when the jury officials act in good faith. . . . We have learned that at the present time a prospective juror may be considered unfit for jury service because he is not very articulate, or speaks with an accent, or appears nervous (something all of us experience in strange or new settings). But all these considerations are arbitrary. They have nothing to do with "intelligence," "common sense," or, what is more important, ability to understand the issues in a trial. *And they are discriminatory—usually against the poor.*
>
> The end result of subjective tests is not to secure more intelligent jurors, but more homogeneous jurors. If this is sought in the American jury, then it will become very much like the English jury—predominately middle-aged middle-class and middle-minded. . . .
>
> But, I submit, such a goal is not in harmony with our historic jury tradition. *If the law is to reflect the moral sense of the community, the whole community—and not just a special part—must help to shape it.* If the jury's verdict is to reflect the community's judgment—*the whole community's judgment*—jurors must be fairly selected from *a cross section of the whole community,* not merely a segment of it.
>
> (Emphasis added.)

As a result of the 1968 legislation, all litigants in federal courts entitled to trial by jury have the right to juries "selected at random from a fair cross section of the community." The act further states that all citizens have the opportunity to serve on juries, and strengthens this commitment by pledging that "no citizen shall be excluded from service as a . . . juror . . . on account of race, color, religion, sex, national origin, or economic status."

Most states also now use random selection systems, drawing names usually from lists of voters or holders of driver's licenses or both. It is preferable to use more than one list and to experiment to determine which lists work best to provide a cross section of the community, because no one list is likely to be adequate and different communities will require different approaches. For example, nonwhites, the poor, the less educated, and the young register to vote at substantially lower rates than the rest of the population, and so the exclusive use of the voter list is unlikely to produce a representative jury in many communities. It is also important to use recent lists in order to ensure that persons who have recently moved are not excluded from the source of names.

If a litigant challenges a jury selection process

as being discriminatory, the reviewing court will require the challenger to show both that some clearly identifiable group has been deprived of its fair share of seats on jury panels and that this deprivation occurred not by chance but through governmental design at some level. Ethnic minorities and women are examples of identifiable groups that must not be underrepresented under this test. Some courts have also heard challenges relating to the underrepresentation of young adults, daily-wage earners, the less educated, and members of specific religious groups.

The Excusing Process. Underrepresentation can also creep into the jury-selection process at the stage when excuses are granted to prospective jurors. Although jury service is a right and privilege of citizenship, many persons consider it a nuisance. Being a juror is time-consuming, inconvenient, and frequently a financial hardship. In some jurisdictions, jurors may be required to serve for several weeks or even months.

In those areas requiring long service, about 60 percent of all persons whose names are pulled from the master wheel return their questionnaires asking to be excused (or do not return them at all). How the court clerks and trial judges respond to requests for excuses and pursue those who do not answer can play a major role in determining the makeup of the panels. Some jury commissioners grant all requests automatically, because they believe that any person who does not want to serve will not be a good juror. Especially likely to be excused are women (because they are presumed to be needed for child-care duties), blue-collar workers (because their employers are less likely to continue to pay them during jury service), the young (because they are in school), and the old (because they often have health and transportation problems).

Federal jurors receive $30 a day, or $3.75 an hour, which is only slightly above the minimum wage. State courts generally pay even less, averaging slightly above $10 a day. Many employees, but not all, continue to receive their normal salaries during jury duty. White-collar professionals are much more likely to continue to receive their pay than blue-collar workers. And the larger the employer, the more likely it is that employees will be paid during their jury duty. Housewives, students, retired persons, daily-wage earners, and the self-employed are essentially asked to donate their time to the jury system.

Aside from monetary considerations, the prospect of a long period of service discourages many persons from willingly serving as jurors. Jurors in some federal courts are on call for four months and report for duty on thirty separate court days. To counter this problem, an increasing number of progressive courts have been moving to a "one day, one trial" system. Under this system, each juror is called only for one day and sent into one trial. If selected, the juror serves for the duration of the trial. (Most trials are over in a day, but some are longer.) If not selected, the person goes home and is not called again until drawn from the jury wheel at some future time. Such a system makes it much harder for a prospective juror to claim hardship and request an excuse from service, and the resulting jury panels are more likely to reflect the diversity of the community.

The states that have moved in this direction have also frequently abandoned the long list of occupational groups that are entitled to automatic excuses. These states now require an individual showing of "undue hardship, extreme inconvenience, or public necessity" before a person will be excused from service. In many states, police officers, lawyers, and even judges have served as jurors without causing any significant problems.

One example of a judicial opinion that is insensitive to the importance of impaneling juries that represent a cross section of the community is the 1984 decision of the Court of Appeals for the Seventh Circuit in *United States* v. *Gometz*. The defendant contended that 70 percent of the persons who received jury questionnaires in the federal court in southern Illinois did not respond at all and that no efforts were made by the jury clerks to send a second questionnaire or follow up in any fashion. The "qualified wheel" was thus made up entirely of the 30 percent who responded, a group that can in a sense be thought of as volunteers, who are likely to underrepresent many segments of society. The appellate court nonetheless rejected the defendant's claim that this process denied him his statutory right to a representative jury, referring to those who did not return their questionnaires as "antisocial elements" and repeating the outmoded stereotype that "a person forced against his will to serve on a jury is apt to be an angry juror and . . . an angry juror is a bad juror."

This approach harks back to the earlier days in which only the property-owning, "respectable" members of society served on juries. A jury-selection process that does not affirmatively reach out to include all members of the community will not produce the impartial juries required by the Sixth Amendment of the Constitution or the representative juries required by Congress in the 1968 Jury Selection and Service Act. Once again it should be noted that the one-day, one-trial system sharply reduces the justifications for avoiding jury duty and thereby increases the representativeness of the jury pool.

Voir Dire and Challenges. The final stage in the selection of the jury, which involves the questioning of jurors by the judge and attorneys, may also introduce unsatisfactory procedures. A prospective juror will be removed from the jury panel "for cause" if the judge determines that he or she has some deep-seated bias or partiality that would interfere with a fair evaluation of the evidence. The court's acceptance of a challenge for cause will depend upon a finding of specific bias (for example, a potential juror's relationship to the defense, prosecution, or a witness) or nonspecific bias (for example, prejudicial views on race or religion) that might play a part in the case.

Litigants can also exercise a set number of "peremptory challenges" to remove prospective jurors who appear unsympathetic to their cause, without giving any reason whatsoever. The number of these peremptory challenges varies from two to twenty-six, depending on the jurisdiction and seriousness of the crime.

Challenges can sometimes serve to restore balance when the process of selecting jurors has distorted the demographic profile of the jury panel, as is often the case. They may, however, make the jury less representative than the original jury wheel, even to the point of removing all members of a race or group from the jury. If the jury panel sent into the courtroom is indeed representative and does fairly reflect the community's diverse biases, challenging certain jurors because of their prejudices may alter the cross section of views represented.

Prior to the exercise of challenges, the attorneys, the judge, or both, question the prospective jurors about their backgrounds and their views. This questioning procedure is known as *voir dire,* an ancient term variously translated as "to speak the truth" or "to see what is said." The process of questioning varies widely from court to court. In federal courts judges tend to control the questioning, but in many states the attorneys question the jurors directly.

Court observers have engaged in heated debate over which system of questioning best serves the judicial process. Trial attorneys prefer to question the jurors directly, because they feel that their own familiarity with the case enables them to ask questions that will elicit hidden prejudices and because they want to establish personal rapport with the jurors. Judges sometimes respond that trial attorneys abuse this process by trying to persuade the jurors about the merits of the case and that questioning by attorneys takes too much court time. The proper resolution of this debate is probably to have some questioning by both the judge and the attorneys. The judge can ask the general questions, followed by more-specific questioning by the attorneys subject to judicial guidance so that the process does not become endlessly prolonged.

In the early English courts, prospective jurors could be questioned and challenged only for specific bias; this limitation survives in the United Kingdom and Canada. In the colonies that became the United States, however, litigants demanded the right to question jurors about their general prejudices or nonspecific biases as well. This issue was an important one during the revolutionary era. The right to question jurors for nonspecific bias was finally established in 1807 by Chief Justice John Marshall in the trial of Aaron Burr for treason. Marshall ruled that preconceived notions about the dispute were grounds for a challenge for cause and that the jurors should therefore be questioned to determine their feelings on the evidence. Marshall reasoned that a person who has preconceived ideas about the matter, like a person who has some relationship with a litigant, cannot be expected to be impartial. Because of the persuasiveness of this decision, virtually all state courts authorized the questioning of jurors in areas of nonspecific bias.

The voir dire must strike a balance to separate those few whose inflamed passions result in bias from those who can conscientiously concentrate on the evidence presented at trial, even though they are somewhat familiar with certain aspects of the case. In *Murphy* v. *Florida* (1975), the Supreme Court stated that "qualified jurors need not . . . be totally ignorant of the facts and issues involved" and that the governing standard was whether the prospective juror exhibited "a partiality that could not be laid aside." In that case, the Court sustained the conviction of a notorious figure in Florida known as Murph the Surf, even though some of the seated jurors had stated during voir dire that they remembered the press reports of the robbery incident and the defendant's prior criminal record.

The trial judge has broad discretion to decide which questions should be asked of prospective jurors to discover prejudices relevant to the facts at issue, and appellate courts will only rarely reverse a trial judge's decision. In 1973 the Supreme Court examined the case of Gene Ham, a young, bearded black who was active in the civil rights movement in South Carolina and who had been convicted of possessing marijuana and sentenced to eighteen months' imprisonment. Prior to the trial, the judge had asked the prospective jurors whether they were conscious of any bias for or against Ham and whether they could be fair and impartial. The judge refused, however, to ask whether the jurors were prejudiced against blacks, whether they would be influenced by the term *black,* whether they could disregard the defendant's beard, and whether they had been influenced by local publicity involving the drug problem. The Supreme Court ruled that the trial judge had erred by not posing the racial-prejudice question but that the Constitution does not require that questions about beards be asked because it is too difficult to "constitutionally distinguish possible prejudice against beards from a host of other possible similar prejudices" (*Ham* v. *South Carolina*).

In the late 1970s and early 1980s, some judges ruled that jurors should be questioned behind closed doors in order to protect the defendant's right to a fair trial and the privacy of prospective jurors. In 1984 the Supreme Court ruled that these concerns had to give way in most cases to the First Amendment rights of access of the public and press to all aspects of a criminal proceeding. This presumption of openness can be overcome "only by an overriding interest based on findings that closure is essential to preserve higher values and is narrowly tailored to serve that interest" (*Press-Enterprises Co.* v. *Riverside County Superior Court*).

Another controversy concerning peremptory challenges centers on whether a pattern of the use of challenges against a single ethnic group constitutes a constitutional violation. For almost a century after the Civil War, blacks rarely appeared on jury lists at all in the South. When, after years of litigation, they were finally included on lists of qualified jurors, the prosecution frequently used its peremptory challenges to exclude them completely from the jury box. This pattern of prosecutorial challenges was attacked in *Swain* v. *Alabama* (1965), but the Supreme Court ruling put only theoretical limits on the government's power.

In *Swain,* a black who had been convicted and sentenced to death for raping a white woman complained that although an average of six or seven blacks appeared on the trial-jury lists for criminal cases, not a single black person had served on a jury since 1950. Eight black men were among the prospective jurors called for Swain's trial, but none served; two were excused, and the prosecutor peremptorily challenged the other six. Despite these figures, the Supreme Court held that the defendant had not proved that the prosecution systematically and deliberately used its challenges to deny black persons the right to participate in the jury system and therefore affirmed Swain's death sentence.

The *Swain* decision was attacked by many commentators who viewed this heavy burden of proof—and the continued prosecutorial practice of challenging minority-race jurors—as inconsistent with the strong constitutional commitment to impartial, and thus representative, juries. State courts and some federal courts began adopting their own approaches to this problem in the late 1970s, and finally, in 1986, the Supreme Court reexamined the issue and reversed the *Swain* burden of proof. *Batson* v. *Kentucky* involved a black man who was convicted of second-degree burglary and receipt of stolen goods by an all-white jury selected after the prosecutor peremptorily challenged all four black persons on the venire. The trial judge followed the *Swain* approach in ruling that the prosecutors could "strike anybody they want to."

The Supreme Court reversed the conviction, establishing a new rule to govern this situation. If a member of "a cognizable racial group" shows that "the prosecutor has exercised peremptory challenges to remove from the venire members of the defendant's race," in circumstances that indicate that the prosecutor took this action "on account of their race," then "the burden shifts to the State to come forward with a neutral explanation" for its challenges. The prosecutor cannot justify the challenges by stating "that he challenged jurors of the defendant's race on the assumption—or his intuitive judgment—that they would be partial to the defendant because of their shared race." Instead, "the prosecutor must give a 'clear and reasonably specific' explanation of his 'legitimate reasons' for exercising the challenges."

Justice Thurgood Marshall went further in his concurring opinion and argued that the use of peremptory challenges should be abolished altogether, because their use inherently works to defeat the goal of impaneling representative panels and because the standards offered by the majority are subjective and difficult to apply. The majority declined to take this step because it felt that the use of peremptory challenges has historically "served the selection of an impartial jury" and that prosecutors and trial judges would be able to conform their behavior to the Court's new standard.

The majority's approach in *Batson* should prove effective in curbing prosecutorial abuses. States using a similar test have found that it is workable in most cases and that it establishes a new mood during the jury-selection process. The *Batson* decision is significant in reaffirming the importance of juries that are representative of a cross section of the community and in indicating that the Supreme Court will continue to monitor jury selection to ensure that all racial groups are fairly represented on jury panels.

Jury Size. As mentioned above, twelve became the fixed size of juries in England in the mid-fourteenth century. Although some of the North American colonies experimented with smaller juries in less important trials, by the eighteenth century twelve was the universally accepted number in the United States as well. In 1970, however, the Supreme Court declared that the number twelve was a "historical accident . . . wholly without significance 'except to mystics' " and not required by the Constitution (*Williams* v. *Florida*). The Court ruled that the constitutional definition of a jury should be determined by examining the function of the jury, which is to ensure that the commonsense judgment of the community stands between the state and the accused. This function, the Court explained, was served if the number of jurors was "large enough

to promote group deliberation, free from outside attempts at intimidation, and to provide a fair possibility of obtaining a representative cross-section of the community." Applying these principles to the six-person jury used in Florida in all but capital cases, the Court concluded that the smaller size did not impair the function of the jury, because there was "no discernible difference between the results reached by the two different-sized juries" and because the "reliability of the jury as a factfinder hardly seems likely to be a function of its size." The Court did not, however, make any real attempt to examine relevant social science data to test this hypothesis.

Eight years later, the Court ruled that juries with fewer than six were unconstitutional (*Ballew* v. *Georgia*). The court reviewed the extensive literature on jury size that had developed since *Williams* and concluded that a jury's size may well affect the reliability of its verdicts. Social scientists writing after *Williams* tended to criticize both the Court's result and its use of social science data. The Court summarized the literature and concluded from it that "progressively smaller juries are less likely to foster effective group deliberation," that "the data now raise doubts about the accuracy of the results achieved by smaller and smaller panels," that "the verdicts of jury deliberations in criminal cases will vary as juries become smaller, and that the variance amounts to an imbalance to the detriment of one side, the defense," and that decreases in jury size reduce the representation of minority groups of juries.

The reduced reliability of a smaller jury should be the central concern. With fewer jurors, some details in the evidence may be missed or forgotten. Studies also show that a smaller jury in civil cases rules in favor of the defendant more often than a larger jury. Apparently a larger group is needed to legitimize departures from the status quo. The decrease in minority representation on six-person juries was dramatically illustrated in Florida in the early 1980s when a series of all-white six-person juries were assembled to adjudicate charges against white police officers charged with abusing blacks. The acquittals by the all-white juries were followed by extensive rioting in the black communities and substantial dissatisfaction with the jury system.

The Court in *Ballew* also examined contentions that smaller juries saved time and money; it concluded that these savings were small or nonexistent. In sum, the Court held that criminal juries of fewer than six would violate the guarantees of an impartial jury and the equal protection of the laws found in the Sixth and Fourteenth Amendments. The Court refused, however, to take the next logical step and reexamine its 1970 decision in *Williams,* which permitted juries of fewer than twelve.

Only a few states have in fact reduced the size of their criminal juries since 1970, and most of those that have done so have reduced jury size for trials of misdemeanors only. Most state systems and the federal judicial system have remained committed to the criminal jury of twelve.

The federal courts have since the early 1970s used six-person juries for civil cases, and many important cases have been decided by only six citizens, including the multimillion-dollar defamation suit won in 1974 by Robert Maheu against Howard Hughes in Los Angeles; the $12 million damage suit won by the American Civil Liberties Union in Washington, D.C., in 1975 on behalf of 1,200 antiwar demonstrators who had been unlawfully arrested on the steps of the Capitol in 1971; and the case brought by the County of Honolulu against the city's two daily newspapers for allegedly violating the federal antitrust laws (which incidentally ended in a 3–3 hung jury).

Serious questions exist as to whether juries of only six can adequately serve the purpose of representing the community to make the sensitive judgments required in cases such as these with broad public implications. The Hawaii jury mentioned above consisted, for instance, of six women and no men, and no matter how carefully a six-person jury is selected in Hawaii, it cannot contain representatives of all the ethnic groups that make up the state's diverse population. Should a decision that could have led to the demise of one of the city's two daily newspapers have been made by a body that did not contain members of both sexes and represent the different ethnic communities in the islands? Similar questions are raised when a jury is permitted to reach a decision by a less-than-unanimous verdict.

The Unanimity Requirement. The requirement that a jury reach its decision unanimously became a firm rule in England during the fourteenth century, and the North American colonies accepted the unanimity requirement with virtu-

ally no dissent. Agreement by all of the jurors in a judgment served to legitimize the decision, giving the community a sense that the conclusion must be correct. When experimenting communities permitted a less-than-unanimous verdict and one or more jurors recorded a disagreement with the result, doubts would continue that perhaps the opposite conclusion might have been the proper one. These early experiments were therefore always short-lived.

The unanimity requirement has been criticized as wasteful and time-consuming, because it sometimes leads to a "hung jury" (a jury that cannot reach a unanimous verdict) and thus to an expensive retrial or the dismissal of charges. Louisiana, whose law is based more on the French system than on the English tradition, has permitted 9–3 verdicts in all felony cases except capital cases. In 1934, Oregon voted to permit 10–2 jury judgments in all but capital cases. The United Kingdom moved in 1967 to a system permitting a trial judge to accept a 10–2 verdict, but the British judge can do so only after the jury has deliberated together for at least two hours without reaching agreement.

Until 1972, the United States Supreme Court consistently recognized that unanimity was an essential component of the Sixth Amendment's guarantee of trial by jury in criminal cases. (*Thompson* v. *Utah,* 1898; *Patton* v. *United States,* 1930). In 1972, however, the Court upheld (over strong dissent) the Louisiana and Oregon laws as constitutional (*Johnson* v. *Louisiana; Apodaca* v. *Oregon*). The Court also implicitly ruled that less-than-unanimous verdicts would not be permitted in federal courts. When faced seven years later with the question of whether a less-than-unanimous verdict is constitutionally permissible in state courts if only six jurors are utilized, the Court said no, concluding unanimously that a 5–1 jury decision violates the safeguards that the jury is designed to provide in criminal trials (*Burch* v. *Louisiana*).

Even though the Court now permits states to use nonunanimous verdicts with juries of twelve, no other states have joined Louisiana and Oregon in allowing them in felony trials, and only a few have adopted the less-than-unanimous approach for misdemeanor trials. Strong policy arguments favor retaining the unanimity requirement. Unanimity is essential to the legitimacy of verdicts and to confidence in the legal system, because it supports the fairness of verdicts. Losing parties are much less apt to complain if their defenses have failed to convince even a single juror.

The unanimity requirement ensures careful weighing of the evidence in dispute. In a nonunanimous system, the jurors stop deliberating sooner and the majority jurors pay less attention to the jurors arguing minority viewpoints. Judge Lois G. Forer of the Philadelphia Court of Common Pleas kept records when her court system moved from a unanimous system to a five-sixths requirement for civil verdicts in the early 1980s, and she noted that the average time for deliberations dropped from four to two hours. In addition, she found that she disagreed with many of the five-sixths verdicts but found the unanimous verdicts to conform to her judgments ("Split Verdicts in Pennsylvania"). Unanimity thus reinforces the requirement that juries be selected from a representative cross section of the community, because it gives each juror, even members of small minorities, a voice.

In addition, unanimity sustains the delicate power balance between the government and the defendant. To prevent oppression by the government, which has awesome power and resources that the individual defendant cannot hope to match, the defendant is protected by certain rights and procedures. Unanimity is one of those rights. Finally, unanimity supports the constitutional requirement that no defendant be convicted except by proof beyond a reasonable doubt and the social decision that "it is far worse to convict an innocent man than to let a guilty man go free" (*In re Winship,* 1970, Justice Harlan concurring).

A number of arguments have been made for abolishing the unanimity requirement. Its abolition would arguably reduce the time and expense of trials by lowering the number of trials that result in hung juries, deal with the problem of jury tampering and juror corruption, and reduce the possibility of one stubborn juror thwarting the majority. These arguments are not convincing. Efficiency gains would be minimal, because the number of hung juries is small in general and some occur even in the less-than-unanimous systems. Although jury tampering is not unknown in the United States, not enough of this type of criminal conduct occurs to warrant preventive measures as drastic as elimination of

the unanimity principle. Less drastic alternatives, such as stricter enforcement of laws against jury tampering, are certainly available. Finally, the premise that a single stubborn juror irrationally upsets the reasoned views of other jurors was disproved by the Chicago Jury Project, which found that juries that begin with a large majority in either direction almost never hang. Only if a sizable minority—four or five jurors—disagrees with the other jurors on the first vote will a hung jury result. For one or two jurors to hold out to the end, they must have had companionship at the beginning of deliberations (Kalven and Zeisel, 462–463).

These arguments are somewhat less persuasive in the context of civil trials, where the jury must determine the verdict by a "preponderance of the evidence" instead of by the "beyond a reasonable doubt" standard used in criminal trials. Over three-fifths of the states now permit less-than-unanimous verdicts in civil cases, allowing the jury to return a judgment by a three-fourths or five-sixths margin.

No enthusiasm has developed for such experimentation in criminal cases. The legitimacy of the jury's verdict as an expression of the conscience of the community is brought into question by juries of fewer than twelve and by less-than-unanimous verdicts. The ability of juries to reflect minority viewpoints is hampered by smaller juries and will be erased in many cases in which unanimity is not required. The jury is a preserver of independence and freedom as well as a fact finder. Both functions are threatened by the Supreme Court's removal of the constitutional barriers to juries of less than twelve and less-than-unanimous verdicts. But the ultimate determination of the wisdom of abandoning these safeguards rests in the hands of the legislators and the people, and thus far they have resisted making any major changes.

Cases That Require Juries. The Sixth Amendment guarantees a trial by an "impartial jury" to all persons accused of serious crimes. The Supreme Court has interpreted this provision to apply to all criminal charges that could lead to an imprisonment of six months or more (*Duncan v. Louisiana,* 1968). Some states, such as California, guarantee a jury trial to anyone facing any criminal charges whatsoever, including traffic offenses.

As mentioned above, the Seventh Amend-

TRIAL JURIES AND GRAND JURIES

ment requires that civil cases in federal courts be decided by juries (unless the litigants agree to a decision by the judge alone) if the dispute involves $20 or more. This requirement has not been imposed on the states, and each state has established its own rules on which types of civil disputes warrant a jury trial.

In 1980 the Court of Appeals for the Third Circuit ruled that certain civil cases—involving protracted antitrust violations, for instance—are too "complex" for lay juries and should instead be decided by a judge who is better equipped to sort out evidence presented over a months-long trial *(Matsushita Electric Industrial Co.* v. *Zenith Radio Corp.).* This view has also been championed by Chief Justice Warren Burger, who said in a lecture at Loyola University, New Orleans, in November 1984 that extremely technical cases should be heard by a three-judge panel or by a jury of highly qualified people. The most competent members of a community do not serve on juries, he contended, because they do not have time for such service and because lawyers are afraid of jurors who know too much.

Most other judges have, however, rejected this view. Although it is certainly true that some modern trials do present difficult technical data, most observers have been reluctant to abandon a centuries-long commitment to the common-sense verdict of lay jurors, and suggestions that "complex" trials be given instead to "experts" for decision have not been received with enthusiasm. Chief Justice Burger's concern about the unrepresentative quality of juries should, of course, be addressed by appropriate reforms such as moving to the one-day, one-trial approach, limiting excuses, and guiding voir dire and the use of peremptory challenges as discussed above, rather than by wholesale alteration of the traditional role played by civil juries in the American judicial system.

CONCLUSION

The use of the jury and the grand jury as institutions of self-governance for eight hundred years are powerful statements of commitment to democratic institutions. Decision-making by citizens provides a level of common sense and a stamp of democratic legitimacy that cannot be attained by "experts," no matter how skilled they

may be. Discretion and sound judgment must be exercised by some group, and American society has found that these decisions are made in the most reliable fashion if made by a representative group of ordinary persons with no personal ambition or stake in the matter. Only such a random sample of community members can render judgments that are truly impartial, reflecting the community's norms and collective conscience.

CASES

Apodaca v. Oregon, 406 U.S. 404 (1972)
Ballew v. Georgia, 435 U.S. 223 (1978)
Batson v. Kentucky, 106 S. Ct. 1712 (1986)
Branzburg v. Hayes, 408 U.S. 665 (1972)
Burch v. Louisiana, 441 U.S. 130 (1979)
Bushell's Case, 6 St. Tr. 999 (1670)
Duncan v. Louisiana, 391 U.S. 145 (1968)
Ham v. South Carolina, 409 U.S. 524 (1973)
Hurtado v. California, 110 U.S. 516 (1884)
Johnson v. Louisiana, 406 U.S. 356 (1972)
Matsushita Electric Industrial Co. v. Zenith Radio Corp., 631 F.2d 1069 (3d Cir. 1980)
Murphy v. Florida, 421 U.S. 794 (1975)
Patton v. United States, 281 U.S. 276 (1930)
Penn and Mead's Case, 6 St. Tr. 951 (1670)
Press-Enterprises Co. v. Riverside County Superior Court, 464 U.S. 501 (1984)
Quadra v. San Francisco Superior Court, 403 F. Supp. 486 (1975)
Swain v. Alabama, 380 U.S. 202 (1965)
Thompson v. Utah, 170 U.S. 343 (1898)
United States v. Gometz, 730 F.2d 475 (7th Cir. 1984)
United States v. Mara, 410 U.S. 19 (1973)
United States v. Nixon, 418 U.S. 683 (1974)
Williams v. Florida, 399 U.S. 78 (1970)
In re Winship, 397 U.S. 358 (1970)

BIBLIOGRAPHY

Leroy Clark, *The Grand Jury: The Use and Abuse of Political Power* (1975), provides a history of the grand jury and then focuses on the abuses that occurred during the Nixon administration. Patrick Devlin, *Trial by Jury* (1956), is a useful historical survey of the jury combined with an analysis of certain issues about its use. Ann Fagan Ginger, *Jury Selection in Civil & Criminal Trials,* 2 vols., 2nd ed. (1985), examines the practical problems facing lawyers who are selecting juries, with many examples of strategies that have been used.

Reid Hastie, Steven D. Penrod, and Nancy Pennington, *Inside the Jury* (1983), is a fine social science analysis of how juries operate in their deliberations, which complements

Harry Kalven and Hans Zeisel, *The American Jury* (1966), a path-breaking study of the process of jury decision-making. Lloyd E. Moore, *The Jury: Tool of Kings, Palladium of Liberty* (1973), is a lively and informative survey of how juries have been used over the years. John Profatt, *A Treatise on Trial by Jury* (1877), is an earlier classic study on the subject. Rita J. Simon, *The Jury: Its Role in American Society* (1980), is a good analysis of both the social science literature on juries and policy questions about its role. "Split Verdicts in Pennsylvania," in *Center for Jury Studies Newsletter*, 3, no. 6 (1981), reports the findings of Judge Forer's study. Lysander Spooner, *An Essay on the Trial by Jury* (1852; repr. 1971), is another classic study, which focuses on the jury's power and its lawmaking role.

Jon M. Van Dyke, *Jury Selections Procedures: Our Uncertain Commitment to Representative Panels* (1977), focuses in particular on how juries are formed and the types of discrimination that still exist in the selection process; this volume also looks at questions of jury size and unanimity and jury nullification. Richard D. Younger, *The People's Panel: The Grand Jury in the United States, 1634–1941* (1963), is a useful study of the historical role of the grand jury.

[*See also* ADVERSARY SYSTEM; CRIMINAL JUSTICE SYSTEM; *and* TRIAL COURTS AND PRACTICE.]

Part IV
PROCESS
AND
BEHAVIOR

THE ADVERSARY SYSTEM

Malcolm Feeley

THE term *adversary system* refers to certain features of Anglo-American legal systems that are sometimes contrasted with European inquisitorial systems, socialist systems, and some so-called primitive law systems. The term has no fixed and precise meaning and in different contexts refers to different features of a legal system. At best it refers to a constellation of factors, not all of which are present in any one legal system and absent in others. Notwithstanding this ambiguity, it is a useful term for identifying a distinctive set of features and style of decision-making that is most fully developed in Anglo-American legal systems and particularly in the American criminal justice system.

The theory of the adversary system of adjudication is perhaps most clearly distinguished by its sharply defined roles for litigants and judge. Normally the system of judicial decision-making in an adversarial proceeding envisions two contestants—or, more precisely, their representatives—arguing their cases before a neutral and largely passive judge. The adversary process proceeds by pitting the two partisan advocates against each other and having their differences resolved by the judge, who bases his or her decision upon legal principles and the evidence presented by the adversaries. The judge has no staff or resources to make extended, independent investigation, and the norms associated with the adversary system require that the judge's decision be based upon the evidence presented by the contesting parties. What they do not present the judge cannot consider, and what they stipulate the judge cannot easily question. This same passive role extends to juries as well. Because of this the adversary system has often been likened to a battle or sporting event in which the litigants are the players and the judge and jury are the umpires.

Correlative to this, it is the task of the advocates to present their clients in the best possible light. Extending the analogy of the sporting event, the goal of the advocate is focused and limited. In the adversary system the goal of the advocate is not to determine truth but to win, to maximize the interests of his or her side within the confines of the norms governing the proceedings. This is not to imply that the theory of the adversary process has no concern with truth. Rather, the underlying assumption of the adversary process is that truth is most likely to emerge as a by-product of vigorous conflict between intensely partisan advocates, each of whose goal is to win. Thus, the duty of the advocate in the adversary system is to present his or her side's position in the very best possible light and to challenge the other side's position as vigorously as possible.

Although often criticized for elevating partisan interests above the search for truth and justice, the adversary process is also defended as the most effective means of getting at the truth and rendering justice. Defenders argue that the clash of limited and partisan interests—through the making of claims and counterclaims, challenges and counterchallenges, examinations and cross-examinations—is most likely to yield the maximum of relevant information and subject it to careful scrutiny and, in so doing, be most likely to expose falsehood and reveal truth. The sharply defined and antagonistic roles, it is felt, foster thoroughness and vigor that might be absent in a more cooperatively organized process.

In his defense of the adversary system in *Economic Analysis of Law* (1973), Richard Posner likens the adversary system to competition in the market. Just as customers, he argues, are most likely to make the best choices if they have the benefit of fiercely competitive salesmen, each of whom extols the virtues of his or her product and raises questions about the other's, so too a judge is most likely to gain the most and best information for making the fairest decision after listening to the arguments of two vigorous and fiercely partisan advocates.

The distinctive features of the theory of the adversary system are perhaps best appreciated when contrasted to other styles of adjudication. In general, the norms that govern inquisitorial systems more directly assign truth-seeking roles to each of the central actors in the process. Rather than being a by-product of the activities of fierce partisans whose conflict is umpired by a passive judge, inquisitorial systems envision a more active role for the judge and, correspondingly, a less active role for the advocates, at least in courtroom proceedings. In theory, the judge dominates the formal proceeding by actively questioning witnesses, requesting information, and in some systems—for example, the French judge d'instruction—actually supervising the pretrial investigation and marshaling the evidence. If the judge in an adversarial system can be likened to a consumer assessing the positions of competitive salesmen, the judge in an inquisitorial system might be likened to a leader of a seminar, the collective goal of which is to get at the truth and each of whose members is expected to volunteer what they know. In the criminal process, where practices in adversarial and inquisitorial systems are distinguished most sharply, this difference is underscored by the fact that in inquisitorial systems there are fewer safeguards of a defendant's interests and the judge assumes a more active role in questioning witnesses.

The adversary system of adjudication, which squarely pits parties against one another and expects passive decision-makers to resolve their disputes according to established rules, can also be contrasted to mediation, often associated with so-called primitive law systems but also gaining popularity among advocates of informality in both Europe and the United States. In mediation, a third party, the mediator, assumes the role of a broker whose task it is to try to reunite the parties or repair the damage they have done one another. The mediator may best be understood as a facilitator of compromise. As we shall see, adversary theory does allow for, if not indirectly encourage, bargaining and compromise.

However, one of the features that sharply distinguish adversarial adjudication from mediation is that the adjudicative judge is more or less passive and reactive and his or her decisions are likely to be formulated in either/or terms.

In contrast, the mediator, also a neutral third party, plays an active part in trying to reconcile the contending parties. The central task of the mediator is to act as a go-between for the two hostile parties, getting each to see the issues from the other's point of view and attempting to find areas of agreement between the two parties in order to find a formula for bringing an end to the hostilities between them. Judges in adversarial systems have an extremely limited capacity to oversee mediation or to foster bargaining, and when they do engage in this behavior, they are frequently criticized for betraying one of the central tenets of their judicial role.

Historians of the adversary process often trace its roots to early Anglo-Saxon proceedings in which legal disputes would be resolved by means of an ordeal of fire or water from which the victor would emerge unscathed or by means of a contest of strength between the disputants or their representatives. The noted jurist Jerome Frank argued that the adversary system was only a slight advance from the earlier system of resolving conflicts by means of recourse to physical prowess: once, disputes were resolved by means of physical strength; in the adversary system, words have been substituted for swords. His point was that in both instances, it is all too likely that those with the most resources in the struggle —rather than those with the most compelling cause—are likely to be judged the victors by passive and reactive judges.

However, defenders of the adversary system bridle at the allegation that it is a vestige of an early system in which actual physical combat was used to decide disputes; they point to what they see as the untenable dual roles that inquisitorial systems force upon advocates and judges. We explore these issues here as a way of identifying some of the salient features of adversary systems and to contrast them with features of other systems of adjudication.

Defenders of the adversary system claim that in an inquisitorial system an advocate's dual role as representative of client interests and coseeker of truth conflict with one another. If one is to be a zealous advocate, they maintain, he or she cannot simultaneously be an active participant in the cooperative and joint venture of discovering the whole truth. Zealous advocacy, they insist, requires that an advocate refrain from doing anything that hurts a client and requires that the advocate emphasize only those things that advance a client's interests. Perhaps the classic expression of this limited and highly focused role of the advocate in an adversary system is found in Lord Brougham's well-known observation made in the course of defending Queen Caroline:

> An advocate, in the discharge of his duty, knows but one person in all the world, and that person is his client. To save that client by all means and expedients, and at all hazards and costs to other persons, and, amongst them, to himself, is his first and only duty; and in performing this duty he must not regard the alarm, the torments, the destruction which he may bring upon others. Separating the duty of a patriot from that of an advocate, he must go on reckless of the consequences, though it should be his unhappy fate to involve his country in confusion.
>
> (quoted in Freedman, 9)

ORIGINS OF THE ANGLO-AMERICAN ADVERSARY SYSTEM

Since the adversary system cannot be defined with precision and since elements of it are found in virtually all legal systems, no concise history is possible. However, to the extent that the adversary system is associated with Anglo-American common-law systems, the history of the adversary system is in large a history of the development of the machinery of justice under the common law. In medieval and early modern England this meant the development of crown courts, which over a period of several centuries came to displace a variety of local feudal and ecclesiastical courts. But it also meant recognizing the importance and transformation of a distinctively English institution, the jury, a decision-making body comprised of laymen from the community.

In brief, the adversary system is a process dominated by the parties themselves and stands in contrast to judge-dominated proceedings. Thus, the history of the adversary process is in large the history of the transformation of the jury and later the judge from an instrument of active

official inquiry into a neutral and passive fact finder. Similarly it is found in the evolution in the role of the judge from that of agent of the crown who actively made inquiries and conducted proceedings in order to protect and promote the interests of the crown to that of neutral and disinterested fact finder. While there is no logical necessity requiring that a jury be an element in the adversary system, the jury appears to have been an important catalyst in the development of the culture of the adversary system, and it is for this reason that we briefly review its origins.

British legal historians disagree among themselves as to the origins of the first juries in England. Some suggest that the jury was an ancient indigenous institution in use even before the Saxon conquest of England in the fifth and sixth centuries. Others suggest that it was imported from the Continent in the eighth or ninth century. Whatever the case, the earliest known juries in England were around the ninth century and were quite different institutions from what we know today. Until well into the fifteenth century, jurors were selected precisely because they were knowledgeable about facts and issues in the controversy they were asked to decide. Indeed, juries were often selected well in advance of trial so that they could have time to gather additional evidence and make inquiries of the parties themselves. Under such conditions trials were essentially inquisitorial, in that the proceedings—to the extent that there even were any—allowed knowledgeable decision-makers to share information with each other. However, by the fifteenth century the character of the jury had evolved; jurors were no longer expected to rely upon privately obtained knowledge but on what they learned in court. This transformation was later reinforced by rules that prohibited pretrial contact between litigants and jurors and excluded people with prior knowledge from serving on juries.

This evolution of the jury had its parallel in later developments of the role of the judge. As the jury emerged into an independent and disinterested fact finder and decision-making body, so, too, did judges in those systems in which the jury was used. Initially, it appears that the shared fact-finding and decision-making responsibilities of the judge and jury allowed the judges, who were also representatives of the crown, to distance themselves somewhat from jury findings adverse to crown interests. This distancing appears to have fostered a desire among judges to insulate themselves still further from pressures of the crown. A series of clashes between the crown and its judges during the seventeenth century saw the crown eventually rebuffed in its efforts to remove judges who ruled against its interests. This established the independence of the judiciary and secured two important elements of the adversary system: a neutral and passive jury and a disinterested judiciary who presided over party-controlled proceedings.

The eighteenth and early nineteenth centuries saw further refinements in the adversary system, as newly developed rules of evidence spelled out in great detail the process by which parties could present evidence to judge and jury. It was perhaps during this period that a self-conscious theory of the adversary process was first articulated.

The adversary system was embraced with even greater enthusiasm and self-consciousness in the American colonies, a practice that continued after their independence. The jury, independent judiciary, and party dominance of proceedings reinforced the impulse for decentralization and served as a check on colonial authorities. The experience with summary criminal proceedings employed by royal officials during the struggle for independence served to reinforce American enthusiasm for juries and a passive, independent judiciary. Many institutions closely associated with the adversary system, especially those dealing with criminal matters, were elevated to constitutional status. It is not surprising then that today the most vigorous defenses and the most fully developed adversary institutions are to be found in American criminal law.

DISTINCTIVE FEATURES OF THE ADVERSARY SYSTEM

In American criminal law the stakes are high, the interests of the two parties are clearly divergent, and the lone defendant faces two agents of the state—the prosecutor and the judge. Indeed, even vigorous critics of the battle or sporting model admit that their greatest vulnerability to criticism is in the prosecution of the criminal law, in which the entire weight of the state is thrown against the individual defendant (Simon). To

counterbalance this obvious disadvantage, Anglo-American systems (and many nonadversarial systems as well) have erected a variety of barriers to prosecution and surrounded the criminally accused with a host of legal protections in an effort to offset the obvious advantages of state, as opposed to private, prosecution. Several of the more salient features of adversarial criminal justice systems are examined below: the standard of proof in criminal cases, the presumption of innocence, the right to confront adverse witnesses, the right to have compulsory process for obtaining witnesses, the right to silence, exclusionary rules, and the right to counsel. While none of these provisions is unique to adversary systems, taken together and in the extreme forms they often assume they do distinguish the distinctive adversarial features of the American criminal justice process.

The standard of proof in a criminal case is "beyond a reasonable doubt," a standard markedly higher than that used in civil cases ("the preponderance of the evidence") in both inquisitorial and adversarial legal systems. This high standard underscores the divergence of interests of the two parties: the state is intent on curtailing the life or liberty of the accused, and the accused in turn has an interest in avoiding or minimizing the stigma of conviction and the sting of the sanction. Given such clear-cut and opposed interests, proponents of the adversary system maintain that it is difficult, if not impossible, to imagine a proceeding in which all participants share in a search for the truth.

This divergence of interests between the parties in the criminal process is underscored by a number of other procedures as well. The presumption of innocence places total responsibility on the prosecution for proving guilt and therefore further underscores the antagonism between the state and the accused. This presumption is made meaningful by a variety of procedures, many of which in the United States have been incorporated into constitutional law. Both the Sixth Amendment's right to confront adverse witnesses and right to have compulsory process for obtaining favorable witnesses are designed to facilitate the interests of the accused in his or her battle against the state.

Perhaps the fullest and most significant expression of the inherent conflict between the accused and the state is manifest in the constitutional right of the criminally accused to remain silent, both in the courtroom and, since *Escobedo* v. *Illinois* (1964), in a variety of pretrial settings involving law enforcement officials. In the United States, the antagonistic relationship between the accused and the state has been carried to an extreme found in no other country in the world, and elements of the adversary system have been introduced early in the criminal process. Since *Miranda* v. *Arizona* (1966), not only do suspects have a right to remain silent when questioned by police, but police officers have an affirmative obligation to warn suspects of their rights to remain silent, to receive free legal assistance, and to be warned that whatever they say may subsequently be used against them. In effect, the police must alert suspects that they may soon be engaged in a battle with the state and to prepare for this battle. Failure of the police to warn suspects of these rights can lead to the exclusion at trial of whatever information the police may obtain from the suspect. Nowhere is the antagonism of interests and the adversarial nature of relationships so clearly demonstrated as in the right to be warned of the right to silence.

Exclusionary rules further underscore the battle model inherent in adversary systems. While many criminal justice systems—both inquisitorial and adversarial—exclude coerced confessions, such exclusions are generally justified on the lack of truth value of confessions obtained through coercion. That is, a coerced—whether by physical or psychological methods—confession is likely to be unreliable (Kamisar). However, in the United States this is not the only ground on which exclusionary rules rest. In *Weeks* v. *United States* (1914) and *Mapp* v. *Ohio* (1961), the Supreme Court ruled that evidence illegally obtained is excluded, regardless of its reliability. Indeed, indisputably accurate physical evidence is inadmissible at trial if it is illegally obtained by the police. Since reliability is not an issue, this exclusion must rest on other grounds, and these grounds, so the Supreme Court has ruled, are important components of the adversary process. Without an exclusionary rule, the Court majority reasoned first in *Weeks* and later in *Mapp,* the integrity of the judicial process and the ability to require meaningfully the police to follow the law would be in jeopardy. In other words, the exclusionary rule is justified as a device to assure that the contest between the state and the accused is fair and takes place according to the established rules of the game. To this end, evidence not obtained according to the rules is inadmissible even it is indisputably accurate and even if its exclusion results in a factually guilty person going free. Such a policy is highly controversial; beginning in the 1970s a series of Supreme Court decisions began to circumscribe the scope of earlier exclusionary-rule cases, and some justices are on record as favoring abandonment of the rule altogether.

LIMITATIONS OF THE ADVERSARY SYSTEM

Even the most vigorous defenders of the adversary system acknowledge some constraints upon partisan advocacy. The norms of the profession forbid advocates from fabricating evidence, encouraging their clients to lie, pursuing frivolous lawsuits, and the like. In this sense, the adversary process is more like a game in which contestants must compete within a prescribed set of rules, which limits their options, than it is like a battle, which presumably is an all-out fight to win.

Still, even the analogy to a game causes many people to question the value and ethics of the adversary system. They argue that the administration of justice is too important to be determined by a process organized like a contest and animated by the singular goal to win. This form of organization, critics continue, places too much responsibility for pursuing public interests in the hands of individual participants who are motivated by their own personal interests rather than public concerns. And perhaps more important, outcomes in adversarial contests, like those in games, are likely to be determined by the luck, skill, and resources of the contestants rather than legal merits alone. If resources are unevenly distributed between the contestants—as they often are in the criminal process, where the state opposes a sole and often poor individual, or in many civil cases when an individual must confront a large and powerful organization—outcomes will be a function of these differences rather than legal merit. As a consequence, over the years the adversary process has been modified.

Adversary theory, like the theory of the market in economics, assumes active viable participants—that is, that the adversaries are in the best position to know and pursue their own interests and that they have the capacity to do so. But just as economists recognize that there are areas in which the market does not work well, so, too, it is recognized that there can be weaknesses in the adversary system that are the equivalent of a market failure. In such instances, rather than abandoning the adversary process for something else, defenders have sought to shore up its weaknesses. We explore two such prominent efforts here: appointment of free counsel for the poor and use of pretrial discovery.

Appointment of Free Counsel. To the extent that the adversarial system is like a battle or sporting event, there is the danger that the outcome may be determined not by who has the most convincing case but by who has the most resources. If this is so, the adversary system cannot easily be defended. Hence, any gross imbalance of resources available to the competing parties is likely to be viewed with suspicion. This concern is at its height in the criminal process, and particularly in the modern criminal process, where the state has considerable resources to do battle with the criminally accused, typically a sole individual and often poor.

During the formative years of the adversary system, in sixteenth-century to early-nineteenth-century England, criminal prosecution was by and large a private affair, initiated by, and left in the hands of, the victim, usually an individual who had to mount and pay for the prosecution personally. Throughout this period both the accused and the accusor were roughly equal before the law in that both were private parties who had to pay their own legal costs. But the later eighteenth and early nineteenth centuries witnessed a shift from private to public prosecution, and with it there emerged an increasing and systematic imbalance of resources between prosecution and defense. The former had the vast resources of the state to call upon, while the latter was often without the means of obtaining even rudimentary legal advice. Rather than abandoning the adversarial process in the face of such an imbalance, Anglo-American reformers chose to try to restore (or create) some degree of balance between the parties through a variety of procedural rules and by expanding the opportunity

for right to counsel to defendants of limited means.

In the United States the expansion of the right to counsel was constitutionally guaranteed in a series of cases handed down by the Supreme Court. In its landmark decision *Powell* v. *Alabama* (1932), the Court took an important first constitutional step in trying to equalize access to legal resources by interpreting the Sixth Amendment's guarantee of fair trial and the Fourteenth Amendment's due process clause to require that counsel be appointed for poor people accused of capital offenses when "exceptional circumstances" were present. Over the years the Court expanded its list of exceptional circumstances and in 1963 held that the Constitution required appointment of free counsel in all serious criminal cases in which the accused wanted counsel but could not afford to pay for one (*Gideon* v. *Wainwright*). This ruling was later broadened to include all persons accused of offenses in which there was a possibility of a jail term being imposed (*Argersinger* v. *Hamlin,* 1972). Rather than repudiating the adversary system because of obvious disparities of resources of the participants, this line of decisions celebrates the adversary system and seeks to shore up—in the form of subsidies to one party—one of its weakest components.

This same logic has been argued with much less success in areas of civil law. With only a few exceptions, the Supreme Court has not embraced a constitutional right to counsel in civil matters, no doubt in part because the Bill of Rights does not express the same degree of concern with parties in civil suits. Still an imbalance in the civil adversary process has been recognized and has led Congress to adopt provisions providing for free counsel for the poor in a variety of areas.

Rules of Pretrial Discovery. Games often involve strategic use of the element of surprise and lore of the legal profession is filled with stories of surprise witnesses and unanticipated evidence the introduction of which caught a formidable adversary off guard and led to victory. This sporting theory of justice, as Roscoe Pound contemptuously referred to it, was modified in significant ways during the early twentieth century. With the adaption of the Federal Rules of Civil Procedure in 1938, federal courts assumed the responsibility for supervising early pretrial disclosure of evidence by both sides in a lawsuit, in order to allow each the opportunity to scrutinize the central features of its opponent's case. These pretrial discovery rules have affected the adversary system in two ways: they have reduced the likelihood that important outcomes will be the consequence of surprise or pure chance, and they have aided and facilitated the process of adjudication by clarifying issues and narrowing the scope of controversy in advance of the trial itself.

However, this reform has had important side effects that reveal the importance of resources and the protean character of the adversary system. Opposing parties can now try to "outdiscover" each other, and as a result, the party unable or unwilling to pay for the most extensive pretrial discovery may be at a disadvantage in preparing a case. Further, since discovery requires that opposing parties cooperate with one another, the party willing to invest most heavily in the process of discovery may be able to force the other to invest in the process as well and, in so doing, can significantly increase the cost of litigation and wear his or her adversary down. Some observers, such as Judith Resnick, have pointed to still another problem with pretrial discovery. Because discovery may involve close judicial supervision of the pretrial process (that is, overseeing the scope and nature of each party's inquiry to see that it remains within the bounds set by the court and setting timetables for proceedings to be completed), there is a very real potential that the neutrality and disinterestedness of the judge will be undermined. While there are ways to guard against this to the extent that judges do become actively involved in scrutinizing evidence and discussing the case with parties, the integrity of the adversary system may be damaged. Indeed, a number of scholars have argued that a new type of court proceeding has emerged, one that is neither inquisitorial nor adversarial. They label it "bureaucratic" and use the term to express their concern that judges have unwittingly abandoned their neutral and disinterested stance and now take too active a role in bringing cases to a close. Thus, justice, critics maintain, is being sacrificed to the bureaucratic concern of efficiency. Despite these concerns, there are probably very few who in the name of the integrity of the adversary system would do away entirely with some form of judicially supervised pretrial discovery and case management.

CONTINUING CRITICISMS OF THE ADVERSARY SYSTEM

The American adversary system, then, has been strengthened in order to overcome some of its obvious deficiencies or modified in order to eliminate some of its worst features. But many thoughtful observers point to still other problems and press for still more modifications to curb what they see as continuing and widespread abuses. Some critics focus upon the criminal process and argue that the barrier of protections erected around the criminally accused frustrate the ends of justice in that they exclude solid and reliable evidence. Others argue that many provisions in fact are little more than a web of technicalities that foster innumerable appeals challenging technical errors and hence frustrate finality. In both instances, critics continue, adversaries intent on winning can use such rules for strategic advantage, which has nothing to do with the quest for material truth. The implications of such criticisms are that legal—and particularly criminal—procedure needs to be drastically simplified.

Still another line of criticism argues that in the effort to be fair, so many safeguards and protections have been built into the adversary process that it has become inefficient and self-defeating. For instance, Feeley has found that in lower criminal courts, where the harshest punishment is likely to be a few days in jail, a suspended sentence, or a small fine, the very process of going through the proceeding is often more of a sanction than the final punishment itself. Others, like Fleming, have argued that we have constructed such an elaborate and expensive adversary trial system that only very few are in fact able to take advantage of it.

Still others are skeptical of the extension of adversarial hearings to grievance mechanisms in a variety of settings when traditionally they were not used, such as welfare rights hearings, social security disability hearings, and school disciplinary hearings. Here, critics say, the use of adversary procedures has fostered hostility between clients and officials and, in so doing, undercut the capacity of officials to pursue their work effectively. Some critics maintain that the heightened and expanded use of adversarial proceedings are self-defeating in that officials will find ways to subvert or avoid them.

There is certainly considerable evidence to support these views. Despite the fact that American culture celebrates the adversary trial in criminal cases, only a very small proportion of all criminal cases—perhaps no more than 4 percent or 5 percent in misdemeanor cases and no more than 10 percent or 15 percent in felony cases—are disposed of by means of a jury trial. Similarly, very few civil cases filed in court are actually disposed of by trial, perhaps no more than 5 percent to 10 percent. And in some settings administrators of social-service programs are accused of pursuing their objectives indirectly in order to avoid cumbersome and time-consuming proceedings. However, it is problematic whether the figures on trial rates are evidence of the weaknesses of the adversary system, since in fact nothing in the theory of the adversary system precludes the possibility of negotiation, and as we shall see, the adversary process, especially in criminal matters, actually facilitates it.

Another frequently voiced criticism of the adversary system is that it too easily fosters an unreasonable zealousness that leads to a desire to win at all costs. Just as some athletes and athletic programs have been criticized for putting the goal of winning above good sportsmanship, fairness, and safety, so critics of the adversary system can point to innumerable examples where attorneys, in the words of Judge Marvin Frankel, engage in a "free-for-all" well beyond the bounds of propriety. Any number of lawyers' and judges' memoirs are replete with long catalogs of tricks used by zealous advocates. Among them are how in the process of "interviewing" clients, lawyers can "prepare" them for testimony by subtly suggesting how they can lie, withhold information, and conveniently "forget" pertinent information. Attorneys can purposefully engineer delays in hopes that witnesses will die, move out of town, lose patience, or forget. And they employ a host of rhetorical tricks to intimidate and confuse witnesses and curry favor with impressionable jurors.

In recent years the issue of the limits of the extent to which counsel can use such techniques has been vigorously debated within the legal profession as it continues to attempt to reformulate its Code of Professional Responsibility. However these issues are ultimately resolved, two factors should be remembered. First, the debate within the legal profession is relatively narrow; even the most restrictive proposals still allow attorneys considerable room for zealous advocacy. This perhaps is illustrated by the fact that one of the issues seriously considered in this debate is whether the adversary system not only permits but compels a lawyer to help his or her client lie on the witness stand if it is to the client's advantage to do so. With issues such as this being debated in all seriousness, there is little likelihood that the code will impose significant restrictions on the zealousness of advocates. Second, regardless of the provisions in the code, there is no real means to enforce them, and lawyers, motivated by the desire to maximize the interests of their clients, are likely to continue to have strong incentives to employ whatever they think will help their clients and perhaps even cut corners if they think such action poses no risks to themselves and is beneficial to their clients. This attitude is what critics of the adversary system find most frustrating: once a fight or sporting theory of justice is set into motion, it is difficult to assure that the contest is played according to acceptable rules rather than fought in gladiator fashion.

One reform that has been put forward to curb the worst features of overly zealous advocacy is to invigorate the traditionally passive judiciary. That is, some reformers propose to modify the traditional party control of the lawsuit by having the judge take a more active role in managing the cases; overseeing the questioning of witnesses; and, in the criminal process, reviewing the guilty-plea process. For instance, Abraham Goldstein argues that judges have the authority, and should embrace the opportunity, to oversee more actively the exercise of the prosecutor's discretionary authority to charge and negotiate pleas of guilt. More generally, and particularly in the federal courts, judges have begun to take an active role in overseeing cases before them. While some of this has arisen as a consequence of the concern for greater efficiency, this increasing assumption of an active role by judges is also motivated by their desire to trim some of the abuses that result from the overzealousness of advocates, the imbalance of resources of parties, and public concerns not necessarily of interest to the parties themselves. It remains to be seen how many such proposals will be adopted, but it should be emphasized that few such proposals suggest any significant modification of the structure of the adversary system itself.

POLITICAL THEORY, CULTURE, AND THE ADVERSARY SYSTEM

Although the connection between political theory and ideology, on the one hand, and institutional structure and behavior, on the other, is rarely direct and immediate, social and legal institutions are shaped by theories, and in turn theories are influenced by prevailing social practices and institutions. Thus, there are strong, if not always clear, links between political theories and institutional practices. These links become discernible when we locate both the theory and practice of the adversary process in broad cultural context and compare them with the theory and practices of legal systems in other political cultures. We can demonstrate this by examining the different theoretical traditions of two distinct cultures and then contrasting them with the legal systems associated with each.

Commentators on the adversary system have frequently noted its affinity with the theory of the market and with classical liberalism. In his extended treatment of the American courts, in *Courts on Trial,* Judge Jerome Frank criticized the adversary system precisely because it took a laissez-faire approach to decision-making and, in so doing, systematically frustrated the quest for truth and justice. Conversely, Judge Richard Posner, a defender of the adversary system and of the value of a market economy, likened the adversary system to the market and extolled its virtue precisely because it operates like a market system. Thus, despite their differences, they agree that the adversary system is closely akin to the market.

Similarly, many commentators have seen a connection between the adversary system and classic liberal political theory in that both envision an essentially passive and reactive state. Classic liberalism celebrates the autonomy of the individual and justifies a political system that maximizes individual choice and minimizes governmental control. The state, in liberal theory, is an institution with a primary function to ensure that individuals have maximum opportunity to pursue their own private interests; to provide certain public goods that are not easily pursued by individual private initiative (providing for common defense, roads, and law enforcement); to establish a framework of laws (that is, establish the frameworks through which private affairs are conducted); and to provide a mechanism to see that they are enforced. The public interest or public good in liberal theory is understood as the aggregate of individual interests.

The connection of the theory of the adversary system with liberal political theory should be apparent. Both the state and the court are reactive institutions, responding to claims brought to them. Voters (politics) and litigants (the adversary system) are expected to pursue their own personal interests rather than subsume them for some larger community good or sense of justice. And as in the market, both the political process and the adversary system celebrate the clash of interests. In politics the public good is understood to be the resultant shaped by the various vectors of personal preferences or interests, and in the adversary system justice is likely to emerge as a by-product of intense partisan struggle. Both distrust the power of the state and of officials who act in behalf of others. In politics this is manifest in theories of limited government and fragmentation and decentralization of power; in the legal process this is manifest in the passive role assigned to the judge and the importance given to the litigants in presenting their cases and in the criminal law theory that views the public prosecutor as the agent for the individual victim. While the quest for justice is not wholly eliminated in either system, neither is it of central concern to the most active participants. Both systems define justice as the by-product of the pursuit of individual interests.

Perhaps the central feature that links liberal political theory with the adversary system is an intense skepticism concerning the power of the state. Liberal theory embraces limited government on the grounds that public power distorts and corrupts, and the adversary system questions the ability of disinterested parties to be sufficiently motivated to strive for complete understanding. To this end, both rely heavily upon private initiative and the intensity of self-interest. The Anglo-American adversary system provides an extensive role for lay jurors in both grand and petit juries, just as liberal political theory celebrates a wide array of opportunities for citizen participation in political life.

There are limits to this comparison. Although liberal theory expects that individual legislators, like individual voters, will represent selected interests and not the community as a whole, the judge and jury, as distinct from the parties in adversarial theory, are expected to be motivated by the pursuit of justice and not particular interests. This difference is reflected in the process of argumentation. While both voting and litigation presume ample opportunity for thorough airing of issues, it is permissible—indeed desirable—for candidates in elections to appeal to voters' self-interests. By contrast, litigants must make principled arguments, and judges must articulate principled reasons for their decisions. Still, the mobilization of facts and the clarification of principles in the adversary system are believed to best be produced by means of the vigorous pursuit of limited interests.

The affinity of classical liberalism and the adversary process becomes apparent when compared with European inquisitorial systems and the major traditions in continental political theory and institutions. European traditions of political theory are much more diffuse than the liberal British tradition of John Locke, Jeremy Bentham, and John Stuart Mill and their modern pluralist variants in the United States. Nevertheless the dominant theoretical traditions in Europe do tend to place considerably more emphasis on the importance of community and relatively less on the interests and rights of individuals. As a consequence, European traditions of political theory have been more willing to embrace the notion of an active and positive state, an institution that embodies something considerably more than, and quite distinct from, the aggregate of citizen interests. This concern with community informs traditions of European political theory, both liberal and conservative, and this concern stands in sharp contrast to the British and American traditions, which are preoccupied with the individual and individual rights. Thus, for instance, the Hegelian tradition elevates the state to central concern and gives it an autonomous status. Similarly, while the various

strains of Marxism have all predicted the withering away of the bourgeois state, they all also emphasize the centrality of the community, which is separate and distinct from the aggregation of individual interests. These various traditions of continental political philosophy are reflected in both the theory and practice of continental inquisitorial legal systems.

The structure and administration of the criminal law will serve to illustrate the impact of these traditions. The continental philosophical tradition links law quite closely with morality. A violation of law is understood as a breach of the moral order, and the community has a right—indeed, an obligation—to respond to this breach. In contrast, English philosophical tradition tends to draw a sharper distinction between law and morality, thus giving law a more limited sphere of importance. While this tradition acknowledges that the two realms often overlap, it nevertheless emphasizes that they are distinct concepts and that the state and its legal system are not to be confused with morality.

These differences are reflected in the structure of the administration of criminal justice in the two systems. In the continental tradition, where the state, law, and morality are more closely linked, there has been a longer tradition of strong centralized state authority and full prosecution. For instance, as Langbein has shown, centralized, state responsibility for criminal prosecution emerged in Germany and France in the sixteenth century, but in England responsibility for criminal prosecution long remained the responsibility of individual victims. Indeed, in England until well into the nineteenth century, complainants had to bear the cost of criminal prosecution, just as victims of torts still must. Private prosecution was justified by the theory that crime was primarily a wrong to the victim and only secondarily an affront to the integrity of the state. This view placed considerable discretion in the hands of the victim, for if he or she did not want to prosecute, the state could not easily intervene.

While private prosecution in England and the United States has long been superseded by a system of public prosecution, important residues of the earlier theory and practice of private prosecution still remain and are reflected in the adversary system. In England and Wales until 1985, there was no formal system of public prosecutors, and although prosecutions have long been paid for from public funds, important aspects of private prosecution have been retained. Prosecutors were appointed for individual cases and theoretically were representatives of the victim. While a system of public prosecution was embraced much earlier in the United States, here, too, important features of private prosecution were retained. In particular, prosecutors still have considerable discretion to set charges and prosecute, and while crime is now seen primarily as an offense against the public, in practice prosecutors often take their cues from complainants, agreeing to drop or reduce charges according to the victim's inclination.

This discretion, while not a central tenet of the theory of adversarial justice, nevertheless has an affinity to the adversary system, since both place responsibility for initiating the judicial process upon the involved private parties and view the state as a largely reactive institution. In the criminal process, not only is the judiciary largely passive, waiting for the case to be brought to it, but so is the other state agency, the prosecutor's office, which often takes its cues from complainants. All this is of course relative; prosecutors often do pursue cases irrespective of the wishes of victims, and continental prosecutors also often take their cues from complainants. Still, when British and American prosecutors are contrasted to their European counterparts, significant differences stand out. For instance, a much higher proportion of cases are dropped by prosecutors in the United States and England than on the Continent, a pattern that cannot be accounted for entirely by evidentiary problems.

Furthermore, political cultures with more pronounced political traditions of strong state authority are more likely to have stronger judges and weaker litigants, while cultures in the liberal tradition are likely to have adversary systems, which have a more restricted role for judges and a more active role for litigants. Similarly, many socialist and so-called primitive societies are likely to have a legal process that depends less heavily on the self-interest of disputants to guide the proceedings and that emphasizes communal concerns as well as the interest of the individual participants. All of these differences must be understood as matters of degree. Still, there is clearly a very real affinity between political culture and legal systems.

Finally, the theory of the adversary system encourages parties to circumvent adjudication and seek alternatives to full-fledged trials if it is in their own interests to do so. Since initiation of the suit and mobilization of the relevant facts are left to the litigants and their agents, what they do not present the court is not likely to consider. The style of decision-making in adversary systems, then, encourages this judicial passivity in civil and criminal matters. In Anglo-American systems, for example, the vast majority of criminal convictions are obtained through guilty pleas, many of which are the result of plea bargaining, or negotiation in which the accused pleads guilty in exchange for some assurance of lenient treatment, through either the reduction of charges or the promise of a shorter sentence. Roughly 90 percent to 95 percent of all criminal convictions in the United States are obtained in this manner. This mode of decision-making is in sharp contrast to the way criminal cases are handled in inquisitorial systems. On the Continent, while a great many criminal defendants plead guilty, there appears to be no appreciable amount of plea bargaining or negotiation over charges.

While a great many factors no doubt are required to explain these differences, the point to be stressed here is how easily the practice of plea bargaining can fit within the standard theory of the adversary process. Since the adversary system is animated by the interests of the parties themselves and permits them considerable discretion to pursue these interests, it easily tolerates, if not actually fosters, negotiation and bargaining. Certainly once the parties agree as to how to resolve the conflict among themselves, the judge, who is largely dependent upon the parties themselves for information, has little choice but to ratify that decision. That is, if the accused reports to the judge that he or she has accepted the charges set by the prosecution, in a very real sense there is no "contest" to umpire—hence, the adversary system's encouraging stance toward plea bargaining.

In inquisitorial systems, by contrast, a trial is not understood as a contest but is seen as an inquiry (hence, the term *inquisitorial*) in which the court is expected to gather and independently assess the evidence and make a judgment. In such a system, in a very real sense it does not matter to the court whether the defendant has pleaded guilty or not, or what, if anything, the prosecution has promised in return. The inquiry can be conducted regardless of the attitude or plea of the accused; it is not dependent upon a real contest between the parties.

In practice, at least in serious cases in adversarial systems, judges often require that the prosecution reveal its case against the accused and warn the accused of his or her right to trial. Conversely, in inquisitorial systems judges often make no sustained independent investigation if the accused does not challenge the prosecutor's case. Still, there are important differences between the two systems, the most significant one being the prevalence of plea bargaining in adversarial systems and its virtual absence in many, if not most, inquisitorial systems. These differences, it appears, are due in large part to the theories that underlie each system.

ALTERNATIVES TO THE ADVERSARY SYSTEM

Not even the most vigorous advocates of the adversary system argue that all types of disputes can or should be resolved through adversarial adjudication. As already noted, the costs associated with adversary proceedings suggest that in at least some situations a different type of proceeding might be appropriate. In this section we examine some other issues that have long posed problems in adversary proceedings. Many of these issues involve parties who have prior, and possibly continuing, relationships.

Almost everyone who has written on the topic has emphasized the winner-take-all or zero-sum aspects of adversarial decision-making and has emphasized that adversary proceedings tend to exacerbate differences between disputants. For these reasons, certain disputes between intimates and those who anticipate close and continuing relationships may best be dealt with in nonadversarial proceedings. Perhaps the classic example of such a situation is the process of awarding custody of a child following a divorce. The either/or approach typical of adversary proceedings squarely pits one parent against the other and thus may not foster the best interests of either the parents or child. For this reason, most family-law experts support mediated settlement of custody issues, in which the decision is

made through a process in which each party is expected to pursue his or her own interests in a spirit of cooperation and both disputants are encouraged to share the common goal of reducing the trauma to the child involved. Similarly, in labor disputes, mediation is often preferred to adjudication, in order to minimize the rift between labor and management and to facilitate harmonious continuing relations. More generally, the distinctive aim of mediation is to foster compromise, often for the purpose of healing or repairing the tears in the fabric of continuing social relations.

In this sense, there may be no difference in objectives between mediation and negotiation; in both, disputants are expected to pursue their own interests and a decision must be voluntarily accepted by the involved parties. However, the introduction of the third party—the mediator—gives mediation a superficial resemblance to adjudication. The comparison, however, is erroneous in that a mediator's role is to encourage parties to see that their best interests are served by compromise and to help facilitate agreement between the parties. In contrast, the judge in adjudication is charged with imposing a solution upon the parties based upon an authoritative interpretation of rules governing their dispute.

Some argue that the mediation model is intrinsically desirable and more conducive to fostering communal development than is adjudication or, more particularly, adversarial adjudication. For instance, in a wide-ranging critique of the adversary process in the criminal justice system, John Griffiths attacks the basic premises of the adversary system, labeling it the "battle model," which serves to alienate and separate still further the criminal suspect from the community. In his opinion, those most in need of being reintegrated into the community are subjected to a process that achieves precisely the opposite result, further alienating them. In contrast, he envisions replacing the adversary system with a system of dispute resolution that emphasizes the effort to deal with the "whole person," that tries to reconcile those who have grievances with one another, and that generally makes the effort to bring persons accused of offenses back into the fold of the community. Indeed something of this philosophy had long informed juvenile court proceedings.

THE ADVERSARY SYSTEM

CONCLUSION

This review has identified the salient features of adversary systems. It has also revealed that there is no clear and precise understanding of the term. At times it refers broadly to common-law systems, and at others it refers to distinctive features of American criminal procedure. Further, no clear set of characteristics unambiguously sets adversary systems apart from other types of legal systems. Still, Anglo-American legal systems are distinguishable by certain of their emphases, allowing an overall contrast with other types of legal systems. The essence of this distinctiveness can be captured in what has been called the adversary system's "by-product of truth." In adversary theory, disputants are expected to vigorously pursue their own interests before a largely passive judge who acts as umpire, and truth is expected to emerge as a by-product of this clash of interests.

The adversary system's emphasis on individual interests is reinforced in the Anglo-American culture and political philosophy, which emphasizes individual interests and is skeptical of state power. It stands in contrast to other cultures and philosophies that emphasize community and communal obligations and view government as an expression of these concerns. Thus, like so many other areas of law, the structure of the legal process reflects the larger society of which it is a part.

CASES

Argersinger v. Hamlin, 407 U.S. 25 (1972)
Escobedo v. Illinois, 378 U.S. 478 (1964)
Gideon v. Wainwright, 372 U.S. 335 (1963)
Mapp v. Ohio, 367 U.S. 643 (1961)
Miranda v. Arizona, 384 U.S. 436 (1966)
Powell v. Alabama, 287 U.S. 45 (1932)
Weeks v. United States, 232 U.S. 383 (1914)

BIBLIOGRAPHY

Richard Abel, "A Comparative Theory of Dispute Institutions in Society," in *Law and Society Review*, 8 (1973), is a theoretical analysis of the structure of various types of dispute-processing systems. Henry J. Abraham, *The Judicial Process: An Introductory Analysis of the Courts of the United States, England, and France*, 4th ed. (1980), examines the basic structure of three legal systems in a way that reveals differences between adversary and inquisitorial systems. Mauro Cappelletti and John Anthony Jolowicz, *Public Interest Parties and the Active Role of the Judge in Civil Litigation* (1975), studies the role of judges in large "public interest" cases. George F. Cole, Stanislaw J. Frankowski, and Marc G. Gertz, eds., *Major Criminal Justice Systems* (1981), is a collection of essays describing criminal justice systems in common-law, civil law, and socialist law systems. Mirjan Damaska, "Structures of Authority and Comparative Criminal Procedure," in *Yale Law Journal*, 84 (1975), compares American and European inquisitorial systems with special reference to the role of the judge in criminal procedure. Alan Dershowitz, *The Best Defense* (1982), is a lively account of cases handled by a well-known Harvard law professor and a caustic evaluation of the problems of the American judicial process.

Malcolm M. Feeley, *The Process Is the Punishment* (1979), studies the by-product costs of being a defendant in a criminal case. Macklin Fleming, *The Price of Perfect Justice* (1974), is an essay by a California judge arguing that many of the high standards of the adversary system lead to counterproductive results and miscarriages of justice.

Jerome Frank, *Courts on Trial: Myth and Reality in American Justice* (1949), is a classic critical examination of the adversary system from a reformer's perspective. Marvin Frankel, *Partisan Justice* (1980), presents a wide-ranging analysis of the strengths and limits of the adversary system by a well-known judge and scholar. Monroe H. Freedman, *Lawyers' Ethics in an Adversary System* (1975), is a thoughtful examination of legal ethics, including a spirited defense of vigorous advocacy in the adversarial system. Lon Fuller, "The Forms and Limits of Adjudication," in *Harvard Law Review*, 92 (1978), studies the role of judges in the adversary system, contrasting it with other types of decision-making systems; and "The Adversary System," in Harold J. Berman, ed., *Talks on American Law* (1961), is a brief introduction to the adversary system by a leading legal philosopher.

Abraham S. Goldstein, *The Passive Judiciary: Prosecutorial Discretion and the Guilty Plea* (1981), examines the role of prosecutors and judges in the adversary system, ending with an argument that judges should take a more active role in supervising prosecutorial discretion. Edward L. Greenspan, "The Future Role of Defence Counsel," in Anthony N. Doob and Edward L. Greenspan, eds., *Perspectives in Criminal Law* (1985), examines and vigorously defends the role of defense counsel in the adversarial system. John Griffiths, "Ideology in Criminal Procedure, or A Third 'Model' of the Criminal Process," in *Yale Law Journal*, 79 (1970), offers a wide-ranging critique of the underlying ideology of the American adversary process and a proposal for a new and different system based upon principles of mediation or what the author terms the family-law model. E. A. Hoebel, *The Law of Primitive Man* (1954), is a review of several primitive legal systems, showing their variation, by a major anthropologist of law. Yale Kamisar, *Police Interrogation and Confessions: Essays in Law and Policy* (1980), a review of the history of the law excluding confessions from trial, is by a vigorous defender of a broad approach to the exclusionary rules. Stephan Landsman, *The Adversary System: A Description and Defense* (1984), is a brief and easy to read history and overview of the adversary system, along with a strong defense of it. John Langbein, *Prosecuting Crime in the Renaissance* (1974), provides a comparative study of criminal prosecution in England, France, and Germany, pointing out their differences during formative periods in the development of the inquisitorial and adversarial systems.

John H. Merryman, *The Civil Law Tradition* (1969), is the standard treatment of civil law systems and includes a discussion of the distinctive features of the inquisitorial system. John B. Mitchell, "The Ethics of the Criminal Defense Attorney—New Answers to Old Questions," in *Stanford Law Review*, 32 (1980), examines the role of defense counsel in the adversary system. Herbert L. Packer, *The Limits of the Criminal Sanction* (1968), studies the structure and rationale of the American criminal justice system. Richard Posner, *Economic Analysis of Law* (1973), is a treatise examining substantive law and legal procedure from an economic perspective, which reveals the affinity between the market and the adversary system. Judith Resnick, "Managerial Judges," in *Harvard Law Review*, 96 (1982), is a wide-ranging critique of judges who abandon their traditional passivity and become active in managing cases before them in order to speed up processes.

Ellen Ryerson, *The Best-Laid Plans: America's Juvenile Court Experiment* (1978), studies the history, philosophy, and failure of the nonadversarial system of juvenile justice in the United States. William H. Simon, "The Ideology of Advocacy: Procedural Justice and Professional Ethics," in *Wisconsin Law Review*, 29 (1978), is a thoughtful analysis of the ethics of the adversary system. Kawashima Takeyoshi, "Dispute Resolution in Contemporary Japan," in A. T. Von Mehren, ed., *Law in Japan* (1963), relates the Japanese preference for mediation to Japanese culture.

[*See also* ALTERNATIVES TO FORMAL ADJUDICATION; AMERICAN LEGAL CULTURE; CIVIL LAW SYSTEMS; COMMON LAW AND COMMON-LAW LEGAL SYSTEMS; CRIMINAL JUSTICE SYSTEM; DISCOVERY; *and* TRIAL COURTS AND PRACTICE.]

AMERICAN LEGAL CULTURE

Joel B. Grossman

THE term *legal culture* is a social construct that describes predominant attitudes and values about law and the legal system, and that helps to define the relationship of the legal system to the structure and culture of a particular society. In the words of Lawrence Friedman (1969), the legal culture consists of

> the values and attitudes which bind the system together, and which determine the place of the legal system in the culture of the society as a whole. What kind of training and habits do the lawyers and judges have? What do people think of law? Do groups or individuals willingly go to court? For what purposes do people turn to lawyers; for what purposes do they make use of other officials and intermediaries? Is there respect for law, government, tradition? What is the relationship between class structure and the use or nonuse of legal institutions? What informal social controls exist in addition to or in place of formal ones? Who prefers which kind of controls, and why?

Although the concept of legal culture is extremely difficult to operationalize, and thus to measure, it is nonetheless useful in the understanding of how a legal system functions, what forms its normative and structural base, and how it compares to other legal systems in carrying out the basic "law" jobs of social control, conflict resolution, adaptation to social change, and norm enforcement. These functions must be carried out in any society, but there are substantial differences in how they are performed, by which institutions, with what degree of emphasis, and at what levels of success and public expectation and acceptance. In one society law may be primarily repressive, the means by which a dominant class or group maintains its power, while in another it may play an important role in enhancing and protecting individual liberties or in furthering the processes of social change. Legal culture thus sensitizes us to the need to look beyond formal rules and structures to understand why legal systems that outwardly appear to be similar may operate quite differently in practice. It also reminds us that law is not an autonomous enterprise apart from society, but—if it is to function effectively—in and of society.

The concept of legal culture is also most helpful in understanding several characteristics of modern legal systems. First, it requires us to acknowledge the perpetual gap between the official law ("law on the books") and the law as it actually operates ("law in action"). In so doing, we must examine the law's impact, the degree to which people are disposed to (and actually do) comply with legal norms, and the institutions and processes—both coercive and conciliatory—by which a society enforces its law so as to contain destructive centrifugal forces but allow enough breathing space for diversity and creative energy.

Furthermore, the concept of legal culture provides very useful insights into the close relationship between law and political authority. As Henry Ehrmann has observed, "law is always part principle and part power." Law depends on the political power of the state while providing a necessary component of legitimacy to governmental authority. In many modern states, this dualism is expressed as constitutionalism or an equivalent theory of how to assure the existence of both adequate power to govern and effective limits on the arbitrary use of that power. The "rule of law (and not of men)" is a common expression of this philosophy. But the sources of legitimacy are complex. Popular acceptance and participation are indispensable if law is to play an effective role in a democratic society. Law must at least appear to do justice and effectively carry out its other functions. It is the antithesis of a popular Brazilian expression: "For my family, everything; for my friends, justice; for my enemies, the law!"

Finally, legal culture offers special insight into the heterogeneity of virtually all legal systems. It warns us of the fallacy of legal centralism; no legal culture is homogeneous. The anthropologist Leopold Pospisil has observed, "Any human society . . . does not possess a single consistent legal system, but as many such systems as there are functioning subgroups. Conversely, every functioning subgroup of a society regulates the relations of its members by its own legal system, which is of necessity different, at least in some respects, from those of the other subgroups."

Thus, legal culture highlights not only differences between nations but also regional, local, ethnic, occupational, and class differences within a society. Likewise, it accords recognition to the interplay between the "official" law and the "law" or norms that are the primary regulators in certain groups or certain kinds of disputes. In any complex society, therefore, there will be many legal subcultures operating in both harmony and tension with the dominant culture. These subcultures are likely to be especially important in determining how people relate to, and use, the legal system. Understanding how a legal system operates thus requires some understanding of both macro- and micro-cultural elements. We need to know not only how legal cultures differ at the societal level but also what accounts for the many variations of legal attitudes and behavior within a particular society.

The United States is usually described as part of the family of nations whose laws and legal institutions evolved from the English legal system and the English common law. Americans owe so much to their common law heritage that they may easily forget just how much the United States has diverged from English law and practice in the two centuries following the Revolution. At the same time, it is easy to exaggerate the differences between the common-law culture of the United States and of Western Europe, whose civil law systems are based on Roman law. In form, the two legal families are vastly different, but shared political ideologies and common eco-

nomic, social, and technological problems have resulted in significant convergence as well.

A taxonomy of legal cultures that relies primarily upon historical development and legal structure is a helpful but not a sufficient basis for comparison. In order to achieve a more effective comparison, it would be necessary to understand norms of participation, secular and religious influences, levels of economic development, legal autonomy and how the legal system relates to the political sphere, and the degree to which the official system of a country dominates, or works with, indigenous law and culture.

BASIC VALUES

David Trubek has argued that American law rests on a foundation of three core values: equality, individuality, and community. Equality implies "equal treatment by the state," but it is not merely formal legal equality. The state, through the legal system, must assure some measure of substantive equality. This is possible because the legal system, although it is hardly free of the biases and inequities of the social and economic system of which it is a part, can nevertheless "operate independently of the social, economic, and political systems that can allocate wealth, status and power" and thus exert some influence on them. Individuality encompasses the notion of personal liberty, but it is more than mere liberty: it is the process of self-realization. The legal system promotes individuality primarily "by erecting obstacles to those who would retard it: . . . the stultifying restraints of traditional communities, the arbitrary whims of autocratic rulers, and the depredations of other self-seeking individuals." Community, Trubek says, is the sharing of an individual in a larger entity through participation in it.

Trubek's is both a critical view of the legal system and an expression of what it can attain. It is a normatively based, liberal prescription of what American law ought to be. A more orthodox and more conservative view would emphasize liberty more than equality, would prefer equality of opportunity to equality of result, and would probably not recognize "community" as a legitimate or viable goal of the law, at least not in the same sense as Trubek has used it. Moreover, there would be considerably greater emphasis on the social-control functions of the law: the maintenance of security and a stable social order and the articulation and enforcement of a viable system of duties and rights. A libertarian view would rank liberty from government restraint and intervention at the pinnacle of any hierarchy of values. A more left-radical perspective would contend that, at best, the American system can produce only "formal" equality or liberty and that emphasis on how these goals can be attained through the law merely conceals the degree to which rights are socially and economically, rather than legally, based and the improbability of attaining real liberty or equality under present constitutional arrangements.

Notwithstanding these conflicting views, law remains, at least for those who subscribe to the dominant culture, the "national ideology" (McClosky). According to Thurman Arnold, this "great reservoir of emotionally important social symbols" fulfills a widespread need for security by developing the "structure of an elaborate dream world where logic creates justice." American law is entirely secular, yet it continues to be the object of near reverence for many citizens. The "rule of law" remains an almost sacred, if necessarily ambiguous, formulation of what Americans would like the law to be but also implies a recognition of its uncertain character. Daniel Boorstin captures this ambivalence:

> One of the difficulties of talking about the relation between law and society is that in law, as in all other deep human concerns, the demands we make of our world are contradictory. We wish to believe both that our laws come from a necessity beyond our reach, and that they are our own instruments shaping our community to our chosen ends. We wish to believe that our laws are both changeless and changeable, divine and secular, permanent and temporary, transcendental and pragmatic. . . . The paradox which modern man has learned to live with is that though he can somehow make his own laws, yet they can have an authority above and beyond him.

The role of law in a society is not only complex but dynamic. Friedman (1975) reminds us, for example, that

> in traditional culture, law was a divine or time honored body of rules, which defined people's

place in the order of society. In modern times, law is an instrument; the people in power use it to push or pull toward some definite goal. The idea of law as a rational tool underlies all modern systems, whether capitalist, socialist, fascist, democratic or authoritarian.

In England, law was largely a device for the elite and business classes. The affairs of the lower class were regulated by feudal arrangements. In the United States, law rapidly became accessible to, and used by, the middle class, which had a stake in it. Law became an instrument of great power and the object of great struggles to control it. In many ways, it became the tool of those out of power to increase their status, acquire new resources, and attack those in power; thus, it became the mode and basis for important social change. In the United States one finds continued tension between the traditional assumption that law is the expression of dominant, propertied interests and the competing aspiration that law serves as an "equalizer" for the have-nots.

KEY ATTRIBUTES

It would be difficult to compare the legal cultures of Western societies solely on the basis of core values, such as liberty or equality. All such legal systems, to a greater or lesser degree, promote these or similar values. It is important, therefore, to examine those internal attributes of a legal culture that flesh out its contours and thus better account for the performance and consequences of its legal system. In American legal culture, the following attributes play an especially important role: constitutionalism, legalism, adversariness, professionalism, pluralism, litigiousness, and the unique relationship between law and politics.

Constitutionalism. As an ideology, it does not merely denote the presence or absence of a constitution (written or otherwise). Every nation has a constitution in the sense of having a set of fundamental laws that provide for the basic organization of government, a statement of that society's fundamental values, a specification of what powers government may and may not exercise, and an enumeration of basic rights that people retain, including rights against government itself. But in many countries constitutions are not highly regarded; they are manipulated or discarded to suit the political needs of the moment; their words have little intrinsic or fundamental meaning. William G. Andrews has written: "[M]any regimes in the world today have constitutions without constitutionalism. Tyrants, whether individual or collective, find that constitutions are convenient screens behind which they can dissimulate their despotism. . . . [P]rovisions that seem to be restraints can be employed to rationalize the arbitrary use of power."

The American Constitution is not entirely free of such tendencies. Initially, it sanctioned only white male suffrage and supported slavery. But fundamentally it establishes a model of compromise and accommodation that has structured American life and law. It promotes the idea that public life and public policy should be fair, open, consistent, and protective of personal, political, and religious liberty. It stands for the principle that government power should be limited and exercised in a nonarbitrary manner.

The Constitution rapidly acquired an awesome mystique that conferred a priceless legitimacy on America's political and legal institutions. In Mark Cannon's words, because of this legitimacy, "disagreement has almost always occurred within the American political system, not about that system." Even where ends were ultimately irreconcilable, as exemplified by the perennial clash between popular sovereignty and the rule of law, the Constitution provided both a means of structural accommodation and a theory to rationalize the clash of those competing ends. Each of these core values was to be prominent in the role and functions of different institutions; and intensity of preference and commitment to one or another, subject to constitutional limitations on government and constitutional protections of individual rights, was to govern the specific clashes between them.

Constitutionalism has also come to stand for an enduring and reciprocal relationship between citizens and the government. This relationship arises out of the symbolic notion of the "social contract." The citizen has both certain obligations of loyalty and support and rights that the government is bound to respect and protect. The government, for its part, is limited in both ends and means. There are certain objects that it may not pursue and aspects of individual life

and personal autonomy into which it may not intrude. To the extent that government power is invoked to promote order and other primary constitutional values, it must do so in accord with certain basic norms and procedures that, at least in theory, protect the citizen from arbitrary action and assure fair and equal treatment. This implicit promise is given life through the constitutional requirements (and the expectations created by them) that citizens be treated with due process of law and be extended the equal protections of the law.

The Constitution also made a direct structural contribution to the American legal system and legal culture. It assumed, and thereby fostered, the continuation and maintenance of state-based courts with a strong common-law tradition. But these courts were limited by the supremacy of federal law and the Constitution itself. Moreover, in establishing a national Supreme Court and providing (in the Judiciary Act of 1789) for a system of inferior federal courts, the Constitution promoted not only the fundamental concept of the rule of law but also the equally important principle that the legal system, though decentralized, was not to be unduly fragmented. If law was to be taken seriously, it had to have some agreed-upon meaning throughout the nation. All judges in the United States take an oath to defend and uphold the Constitution, but the federal courts have a special responsibility to promote the constitutional system and its primary values.

Legalism. The strong belief in the legitimacy and utility of a system of rules to resolve disputes and regulate human conduct in a manner that both maintains order and dispenses justice is called legalism. But it is also an ideology that, its critics say, tends to exalt means over ends—formal legal rationality over substantive justice. In so doing, it tends to ignore the distortions produced by the unequal distribution of resources; while promoting formal legal equality, with its emphasis on low-potency rules changes, legalism may foster and perhaps even encourage actual inequality and impede reforms designed to yield a more evenhanded justice. The dilemma between treating people equally (equality) and doing justice in an individual case (equity) can never be fully resolved. But merely changing the rules is not likely to produce equitable results; new rules tend to be absorbed into existing behavioral and institutional practices and rarely bring about any substantial reallocation of advantages and disadvantages. In this sense, rules may be merely palliatives, not cures.

Adversariness. The key structural feature of America's legal system and an important ideological component of its legal culture is adversariness. Once labeled by Jerome Frank the "fight theory of justice," the adversary system considers a court trial to be a contest between the disputants, with the judge (and the jury, if one is used) as the referee or impartial arbiter. Proponents of the adversary system assume that the best way to discover the truth is for each side to present the facts most favorable to its own position and to make the strongest argument it can.

The adversary system leaves to the court the problem of determining who is telling "the truth"—or, more realistically, which party has the stronger case. In a criminal case, the government must prove its case "beyond a reasonable doubt"; in a civil case, the plaintiff prevails by showing a "clear preponderance of the evidence." Elaborate rules bar evidence thought to be unreliable (such as hearsay testimony), although sometimes the imposition of these rules may seem to hinder the search for truth rather than promote it. Each side is permitted to cross-examine the witnesses of the other. Virtually all of the contest is carried out by lawyers, not by the disputants themselves.

In its emphasis on conflict over cooperation, in its assumption that the parties have equal access to resources and the skills of advocacy, and in its belief that the law and justice are best served by this highly regulated game, the adversary system is unique to common-law countries. In civil law countries, it is the judge's responsibility to "direct the proceedings on his own in such a way that the truth emerges" (Ehrmann). A judge may utilize the parties and hear their contentions, but it is the judge who remains primarily responsible for obtaining the truth. The search for facts cannot be impeded by what the parties see as their own best interests. The judge directs the proceedings rather than passively serving as an umpire. The role of lawyers for the parties, particularly in cross-examination and the presentation of witnesses, is given correspondingly less weight.

Critics of the adversary system note that in reality it is not so much a search for truth as a quest for victory. That the parties have equal resources is often a false assumption, and the elaborate rules designed to promote the search for truth often degenerate into a battle to exclude relevant evidence. But even more fundamental criticisms have been made. William Simon, for example, argues that the "ideology of advocacy" converts important substantive issues into charades of "procedural fetishism," which promotes a false sense of stability among both winners and losers. Losers are persuaded to accept their losses because "justice has been done," and winners are convinced of the rightness and legitimacy of their victories. For those with substantial resources, those "victories" are almost preordained. In Simon's view the "rule of law" (which is promoted by the adversary system) and the "ideal of law" are thus antithetical. The underlying purpose of the "ideal of law" is to secure justice, while the "rule of law" is designed mainly to safeguard the integrity of existing institutions.

Although American courts are formally organized along the lines of the adversary model, in fact most cases are settled consensually by an agreement between the parties before the case goes to trial. Few civil cases ever go to trial, and a very substantial number of criminal cases (including virtually all misdemeanor cases) are disposed of by a guilty plea, which is often the result of plea bargaining between the prosecutor and the defendant's lawyer. Liberal critics of plea bargaining fear that the enticement of a reduced charge or lower sentence may result in some innocent persons pleading guilty to a crime they did not commit in order to forestall a guilty verdict, which might well result in a more severe sentence. Conservative critics contend that plea bargains result in excessive leniency for criminals, who can "cop a plea" in return for saving the state the expense of a trial.

In civil settlements and criminal plea bargains, the parties to the case are still adversaries, but they also recognize a mutual interest in reducing their risk vulnerability. It might be more accurate to say that the United States has, in practice, adopted a adversary system in which the cutting edge of adversariness—the risks of a winner-take-all system—has been blunted in favor of a reduced-risk, less formal, and, on the whole, more efficient method of resolving disputes and enforcing the law. Yet the ideology of the adversary system remains predominant, and there are those who say that even a modified adversary system is unlikely to prevent the "haves" from coming out ahead, according to Galanter (1974) and Simon. Critics who claim that negotiations and settlements bypass formal legal process and thus undermine the rationality and legitimacy of the law must be reminded that the parties must, of necessity, bargain in the shadow of the law.

Professionalism. A key attribute of most Western legal systems is professionalism. In the United States, law is primarily an enterprise for trained professionals. The public plays a limited role, confined largely to electing judges in about half the states. The only role for a citizen is as a litigant, a witness, or a member of a jury. It is only by serving on a jury that citizens who are not themselves disputants participate directly in the legal decision-making process. Although the use of juries in both civil and criminal cases in the United States is declining, juries still provide a substantial basis for citizen participation.

Virtually all American judges are lawyers; this is true not only of those who preside in courts but also of those who perform other, less visible adjudicatory roles, such as private and public arbitrators and administrative law judges and hearing examiners. There is but a remnant of the lay "justices of the peace" who once constituted the primary contact point between citizens and the courts. Likewise, lawyers are the primary, if not exclusive, advocates representing individuals or groups in the various courts and tribunals of the nation. The Supreme Court has held that a citizen may defend himself or herself in a criminal case (*Faretta* v. *California*, 1975), but self-representation is widely discouraged, if not always prohibited. Only lawyers may "practice law"—that is, give legal advice and represent individuals in court.

Professionalism is less of a factor in the selection of judges. The United States has never adopted the continental model, in which prospective judges follow a career track that provides additional training separate from law graduates who aspire to private practice or prosecutorial positions. Judging in those countries is a separate vocation, and it is centrally organized along bureaucratic lines. It is a relatively closed system, with little or no political interference. Judging is truly a profession.

Judicial selection in the United States is a hybrid. In the states, judges are chosen variously by partisan election; nonpartisan election; variations of the "Missouri plan," often referred to as "merit selection"; executive appointment; or even election by the legislature. Versions of the Missouri plan have been adopted in about thirty states; judges are chosen by partisan or nonpartisan election in twenty-two states. Federal judges are chosen by the president, subject to Senate confirmation. The Missouri plan systems are the most professionalized by American standards, although they would rank far below the Continental systems on any scale of professionalism. Furthermore, they are entirely nonbureaucratic. Yet, compared with the American alternatives, the Missouri plan does emphasize the role of lawyers (through judicial nominating commissions) in selecting judges and minimizes electoral participation: the electorate can turn a bad judge out of office, but it has no say in choosing a new one. The Missouri plan tends to emphasize the technical aspects of judging. Judging is, or should be, nonpartisan and essentially nonpolitical. Judges should be chosen according to "professional" criteria: training, experience, education, age, and judicial temperament.

The alternative American model places correspondingly less emphasis on professional criteria. It embodies a more open and flexible view of the role of courts, acknowledges their essentially political role, and believes it both appropriate and inevitable for judges to be selected through the political system. Federal judicial selection is a mix of legal professionalism and political responsiveness.

Legal Pluralism. In most societies, the orthodox view is that law is primarily the province of the courts and that law and the courts are at the apex of, and dominant over, a network of dispute-resolving institutions; this centripetal image of the law is commonly known as legal centralism. A more sophisticated perspective is captured by the concept of legal pluralism, which recognizes that courts are merely "one component of a complex system of disputing and resolution" (Galanter, 1981). In this centrifugal perspective, courts and the official law are neither the exclusive sources of "norms" nor the sole arenas for the resolution of disputes. Galanter continues:

> We must put aside our habitual perspective of "legal centralism," a picture in which state agen-

cies (and their learning) occupy the center of legal life and stand in a relation of hierarchic control to other, lesser normative orderings such as the family, the corporation, the business network. Just as health is not found primarily in hospitals or knowledge in schools, so justice is not primarily to be found in official justice-dispensing institutions.

Legal pluralism does not necessarily threaten the primacy of official law, but it reminds us that the relationship between the official law and local (or occupational or ethnic) cultures is variable and problematic. Vast areas of our private and public lives are not, or not directly, regulated by official legal norms. This phenomenon is captured well by Sally Falk Moore's concept of "semiautonomous social fields," which have their own internal norms and sanctions. On the other hand, in the United States there is a strong tendency, known as legalization, for legal doctrines and procedures to be absorbed and applied by nonlegal institutions. Sometimes this is done in response to legal directives, such as the imposition of due process norms on prisons or educational institutions. But often such "legal" norms are adopted because they have become part of the popular culture and have created expectations that institutions should act in certain ways whether or not they are legally required to do so.

The idea of legal pluralism also helps us to understand and accept the variations often found in the operation of explicitly legal institutions. Legal institutions do not operate autonomously or abstractly. There is, however, substantial discretion, and that discretion is often exercised in response to regional, local, or transcendent professional norms. We know that police and prosecutors have different priorities and different styles of pursuing their respective missions. These differences are reflected in varying rates of arrest rates and plea bargains. There is ample evidence, as stated by both Martin Levin and James Gibson, that some of the variations in judicial sentencing are reflections of local popular or political cultures. "Delay in the courts" seems to some extent to be the product of "local legal cultures"—that is, the established local practices of judges, attorneys, and other court personnel (Church; Grossman et al.).

Likewise, there are substantial documented regional and local differences in the way in which citizens use the courts and respond to the decisions of courts. There is considerable variation in the propensity to use the law and to litigate to resolve disputes, and there is ample documentation that, at least with regard to specific controversial issues, there are important regional and cultural differences in willingness to comply with unpopular judicial decisions.

In the United States, tendencies toward legal pluralism are further accentuated by the federal system, which divides political—and, thus, legal—authority between the nation and the states. In reality the United States has not one but at least fifty-one legal systems, whose overlapping yields redundancy and conflict. A nationwide system of federal courts is paralleled by the court system in each state. In theory, all are subject to the supremacy of the Constitution, and state courts are inferior to federal courts in matters involving the Constitution or federal law.

But the reality is not nearly so simple. There are significant unifying trends in both doctrine and structure but also persistent local variations. For many types of cases, litigants may choose between a federal or state forum, with the expectation that disputes will be handled differently in each. There are still numerous areas in which legal doctrine differs from state to state and between state and federal courts. The Supreme Court's "nationalization" of the Bill of Rights in the 1960s was a strong centralizing force in constitutional law, but the liberal backlash of some state supreme courts against the more conservative decisions of the Burger Court swung the pendulum back somewhat toward greater local autonomy—at least in matters of constitutional doctrine. Thus, the rules that govern particular kinds of official behavior and the sanctions applied for particular kinds of official misconduct may vary widely from state to state.

Litigiousness. The propensity to use the courts to settle disputes, high in American society, is litigiousness. Many critics, employing terms such as "hyperlexis" and "legal pollution" (Manning; Ehrlich), charge that it has become excessive. Among these critics there is great fear of the growth of an excessively "adversary society" of aggressive, assertive, rights-conscious people all too ready and eager to advance their private interests through the courts. The pursuit of complete personal satisfaction, or "total redress," it is said, has replaced a more traditional view that life's misfortunes can and must be endured. Patients sue their doctors, students their teachers, convicts their jailers, and even children their parents—or so it seems. As Jethro Lieberman has written, "Anyone can sue anyone about anything."

While there can be little doubt that the United States is a litigation-prone society, there is considerable controversy over whether this litigiousness is excessive. One basis of comparison is the experience of other nations. Marc Galanter's recent study presents data suggesting that the United States is neither the most disputatious nor the most litigious of societies. Its litigation rate, measured as the per capita use of civil courts, was nearly forty-four cases per thousand—in the same range as England, Australia, Denmark, and New Zealand; somewhat higher than Germany or Sweden; and substantially greater than Japan, Italy, and Spain. The United States does have more than twice as many lawyers per capita as any other country except Israel; this suggests that if the number of lawyers may be taken as a surrogate for the total "legal activity" of a nation, Americans use the law more than anyone else, even if they do not actually litigate at an excessively higher rate. Indeed, it appears that for reasons that will be explored below, far from promoting litigation, American lawyers tend to suppress rather than stimulate litigious instincts. There is also evidence that Americans are not as prone to disputing as citizens of other nations are. Australians, for example, are much more likely to complain to officials but somewhat less likely to take those complaints to the stage of litigation.

To what extent is litigiousness a cultural phenomenon, as opposed to being merely an artifact of particular structural arrangements? Keeping in mind the analytic difficulty of separating culture from structure, how can we determine whether a nation's level of litigiousness is a reflection of a cultural propensity to dispute and litigate? Traditional, but self-serving, comparisons between the United States and Japan customarily produced a "cultural" explanation. Japan, like other Asian societies, was said to have a low litigation rate because of its cultural emphasis on social harmony and conciliation, whereas the United States, with its emphasis on redressing grievances and vindicating rights, was thought to be naturally more litigious. But more recent evidence suggests that Japan's historic preference for conciliation reflects deliberate

efforts by generations of Japanese officials to suppress litigation and keep the judge and lawyer population very low, rather than any natural or cultural reluctance to litigate. Moreover, one could hardly employ the same social harmony explanation for the low—possibly even lower—litigation rates in Spain and Italy.

Intracountry differences must also be considered. There is enough variation in litigiousness within the United States to caution against any facile cultural explanation of its litigious tendencies, at least at the national level. There are, in fact, substantial state, regional, and local—to say nothing of ethnic—differences in litigation within the United States, and there is evidence that these varying rates are linked to attitudes about the propriety of bringing certain types of disputes to court.

There is certainly no convincing evidence that the United States as a nation is excessively litigious. Yet, to understand the dynamics of the American legal and political systems, it must be recognized that as much as the people of any industrialized nation, and more than most, Americans use lawyers and the courts to resolve disputes. They are especially prone to use the courts not only for private disputes but also to promote public values and influence public policy. This is a distinctively American phenomenon.

Law and Politics. The last of the attributes is the unique relationship between law and politics. Law is inextricably linked with government and the political process, a linkage that may be especially distinctive in the United States, where courts play a key political role. What are the boundaries that define the domain of the law, what belongs to the political system, and the tasks and obligations shared between them?

Law and politics are competing but also interdependent forces that determine the allocation of values and scarce societal resources. Yet, there are distinctively "legal" and "political" processes whose legitimacy is judged by different standards. Law is often judged by its adherence to prescribed and fair procedures. In this sense, law is a customary and prescribed way of doing things; internal procedural consistency is highly valued. If things are done the right way, then on the whole the right things will be done. Results are important, but not at the expense of breaking the rules.

By contrast, politics is usually judged more by

its results. To be sure there are unwritten rules of the game in politics that must be observed. But such rules are means and not ends in themselves. Courts and judges are expected to adhere to the doctrine of stare decisis (the rule of precedent) because it links past and present, and promotes continuity and stability. Politics is not unconcerned with such values, but—at least in theory—it is less constrained by them and more open to change. Judges, even those who are elected, are not supposed to be influenced by constituent or electoral pressures in their decisions. Judicial independence admonishes them to be accountable to the law, not to political authority or public opinion. Judges should not be the agents for any particular cause except the cause of justice. Political officials, by contrast, are expected—and indeed democratic accountability requires them—to be guided largely by the wishes of their constituents. Their legitimacy depends on what they do for people rather than on how they do it.

These boundaries, however, are neither wholly clear nor fully enforceable. Law and politics are interdependent. Politics sets many of the boundaries of judicial power. Judges, whether appointed or elected, are chosen by a political process. There is a continuous movement of personnel from the political world to the legal world and, to a lesser extent, back again. A large number of American judges have been involved in politics, and an equally large number of politicians have been trained in the law. This political connection brings strength to the law but also creates considerable institutional tension.

Nowhere is this tension more graphically revealed than in the controversy over the proper role of the courts in determining key public policies, defending the rights of minorities, and serving as the focal point of challenges to established values and authority. In many societies, such an issue would not exist, for the role of courts is narrow and inflexible, and their separation from —not merely independence of—politics is taken for granted.

In a society in which courts play an extraordinarily important role, it is not surprising that the role of courts is often, indeed perpetually, controversial. In the United States, intense controversy about the role of courts in the 1970s and 1980s was fueled by two overlapping concerns already briefly described: the alleged "litigation explosion" and the consequent fear that courts have become overloaded with trivial cases; and charges that the courts have become too politicized—an "imperial judiciary" intruding improperly into the policy domains of the states and the other branches of the federal government. Courts lack the capacity to play this expanded role, critics such as Donald Horowitz charge, and they seriously risk their legitimacy by forgetting that they are courts and thus intrinsically different from other governmental institutions.

This controversy reveals a basic and probably insoluble dilemma. What are courts? And what is their proper role? Two competing models of courts have emerged to structure the debate. The traditionalist view is that courts have a specialized adjudicative structure and function that is relatively fixed both by law and tradition. The main business of courts is the adjudication of disputes within an adversary system. It is the responsibility of the parties to bring and manage a case, and the courts' responsibility to ascertain the facts and, under the law, determine the rights of the parties. Courts should not act arbitrarily; they have an obligation to produce rational and just decisions. In the words of Lon Fuller, courts must assume "a burden of rationality not borne by any other form of social ordering."

Most cases, it is assumed, will be "bipolar"— that is, between two discrete entities. So defined, litigation is an essentially private contest in a public forum, not an appropriate mode of social policymaking. The litigants represent only themselves and their own interests. "Polycentric" cases—those involving crosscutting and often continuing political and social issues not easily contained within this simple adversarial framework—are to be avoided. Courts must respect these limitations because it is only in preserving their "courtness" that they can remain legitimate. Fidelity to these norms of internal rationality is especially necessary because courts are not otherwise accountable to the political order. Moreover, when courts take over certain kinds of policy responsibilities, such as reapportionment or school desegregation, they are sapping the strength of the political order; these are decisions that should be made by the people's elected representatives.

This traditional, bipolar model of private law adjudication still defines the ordinary civil litigation that comprises most court dockets. And it was an accurate description of what American courts primarily did up through the end of the nineteenth century. But increasingly, and particularly since the 1950s and the Supreme Court's decision in *Brown* v. *Board of Education* (1954), courts have played a less constricted and more openly political role. This is often called the public-law or adaptationist model. It assumes that courts are essentially and properly hybrid institutions of law and politics, that they have considerable adaptive capacity, and that they are, and should be, judged by function and outcomes as much as by mere form. Democratic accountability, according to this view, rests on the ability of courts to do justice and contribute to the betterment of society; this is more important than preserving a fictional—or, at best, theoretical—autonomy and judicial independence. The ideology of legalism is rejected. Admittedly, complex social policy cases are difficult and perhaps not ideally suited for the judicial arena. But courts must deal with them either because they can do so better than other institutions or because if courts do not decide them, nobody will.

This overriding concern with the political role of American courts should not obscure other continuing and legitimate questions about courts and judges. For example, there is continuing discussion of how judges are to be chosen and of the consequences of any particular selection system. The debate centers on whether judges should be more professionalized in their training and preparation or whether they should continue to be chosen by the political process. Particular attention is being given to the degree of activism that judges should be allowed in supervising litigation settlements and running trials. There is perennial concern over whether American judges, traditionally "generalists," should become more specialized to meet the needs of increasingly complex cases. And there is continued discussion about informal or less formal "alternatives" to, or within, courts for processing relatively minor disputes.

After the mid-1970s there occurred a resurgence of small-claims courts and the development of various mediation and arbitration alternatives. These alternatives are often pursued for either practical or ideological reasons: they are seen as possibly reducing court dockets by siphoning off cases that do not demand full judicial treatment, or they are heralded as a more popular community-based alternative to elitist

courts. The results of these developments suggest that such alternatives are useful, but that they have brought about no radical transformations. Moreover, critics suggest that their underlying effect is to provide "second-class" justice for those without means (Abel, 1982; Auerbach, 1983).

Whatever the merits of some of these proposed reforms, their modest success affirms another important point: American courts are very stable, if immensely diverse, institutions that are quite resistant, if not impervious, to reform. They continue to perform a variety of well-defined functions. Some of these functions, such as dispute resolution, are shared with other public and private institutions. Administrative agencies play a parallel "law-ascertaining" role and make a major contribution to the growth and development of statutory law. Courts and agencies jointly play an important lawmaking role; they remain integral parts of the lawmaking process.

Recent studies have revealed some changes in the mix of cases in both state and federal courts, changes that attest to a shifting emphasis rather than a major alteration of judicial function. In general, there have been increases in public-law cases (especially in the federal courts), tort cases, and, in the state courts, cases involving domestic relations. At the same time, there have been decreases in cases involving private contracts or business relationships. There is also some evidence of increases in "routine" cases, which require judges to be little more than administrators, and proportionately less, if not fewer, truly adversarial cases.

LAWYERS AND THE LEGAL PROFESSION

Perhaps the most obvious significant fact about lawyers in the United States is their astonishing growth and number. In 1985 there were nearly 700,000 lawyers, an average of one for every 340 citizens. The number of lawyers has more than doubled since 1960; and it continues to increase far in excess of population growth. The United States is probably the most lawyered society the world has ever known.

The structure of legal practice is also changing. Traditionally, lawyers practiced alone, or in very small firms. By the 1980s only about one-third of lawyers practiced alone. The majority of lawyers in private practice are in firms, and the size of those firms is escalating rapidly. The number of "megafirms" with more than 100 lawyers in 1985 exceeded 200, and at least one firm had more than 700 lawyers. The largest growth has been among government lawyers and lawyers hired by large corporations (house counsel) —the former reflecting the increased size and scope of government, and the latter the effort of corporations, which traditionally relied on private law firms for their most important legal work, to control and reduce their legal costs. Law practice has thus become increasingly bureaucratized.

The growth and bureaucratization of the legal profession, and an increasing number of women and minority lawyers, has not yet had much effect on the social and work organization of the bar. Basically, lawyers are divided into those who serve corporations, and those who serve people and small businesses. This stratification of the bar is marked by substantial differences between the two segments in education, income, and prestige, and, of course, differences in their clients, too.

In theory, there is no formal specialization of lawyers except for patents, admiralty, and trademarks. But if there are no "board certified" lawyer specialties, as there are for other professions such as medicine, the fact is that the legal profession is specialized by subject matter, by clients and client prestige, and by styles of practice.

Lawyers and legal services are not evenly distributed across the population, and they are not equally available to all. Apart from government lawyers, lawyers hired by corporations, and lawyers who provide legal services for the indigent, in the United States law is practiced on a "fee for service" basis. Most legal work is compensated on a hourly basis, with current hourly rates ranging from $30 per hour in small firms to $250–300 per hour for the senior partners in large firms. Personal injury cases, however, are normally undertaken on a contingent fee basis: the lawyer receives nothing if the client loses, and from 25 percent to 33 percent of the recovery if the client wins. Since a client risks no money, the contingent fee system theoretically provides legal services to clients who could not afford them otherwise. But lawyers are reluctant to take low stakes

cases even on that basis, since even a full recovery may not fully compensate a lawyer for work done.

The fee-for-service system also can encourage lawyers to represent the interests of their clients to the exclusion of any ethical judgments about their clients or their clients' cases, the cause of justice, or what the public interest may require. The lawyer as "hired gun" is nonetheless a natural outgrowth of the adversary system. The client's interests are paramount; the check comes not from the lawyer's own sense of justice or right and wrong, but from the expected presence of an equally effective adversary.

Of course this classical model is something of an exaggeration. Lawyers are often involved in bargaining, and in working out compromise solutions which mediate between their client's apparent interests and those of an adversary. Yet, the model is valuable to the extent that it provides some justification for the lawyer who must defend an unpopular client or cause, and for the activities of the legal profession generally (Macaulay, 1979). It is often cited in mitigation of the organized bar's alleged lack of "social responsibility" (Auerbach, 1976). It is the "system" which produces justice, the argument goes, and it can do so only if each adversary is effectively and aggressively represented by counsel loyal to him. Thus, neither the individual lawyer nor the bar is individually "responsible" for the just resolution of a dispute or, more generally, effective justice in the society as a whole.

A number of events in the 1960s contributed to a reevaluation of the obligations of lawyers to their clients and to the public. The civil rights movement, controversy over the Vietnam War, the War on Poverty, Supreme Court decisions such as *Gideon* v. *Wainwright* (1963), which emphasized the plight of the indigent in the justice system, and the Watergate controversy, which resulted in the resignation of a president and the conviction of many of his lawyer assistants, all focused attention on the role of lawyers and the bar. If the classical, "pluralist" model was no longer a sufficient rationale for private interest lawyering, how could the bar reconcile its public responsibility and the professional self-interest of its members? What could be done to counteract the serious legal underrepresentation of minorities and the poor? Clearly, it was no longer adequate to say that this responsibility was to be discharged by the results of individual efforts. Yet the nature of legal education, the stratification of the bar, and the structure of legal practice ensured that change would be difficult.

The bar's social responsibility, such as it was, had traditionally been exercised indirectly through scattered assigned counsel and public defender programs for criminal defendants, legal aid societies in a few cities to handle some civil matters, and a symbolic but haphazardly implemented "pro bono" obligation imposed on lawyers by the canons of legal ethics.

The 1960s produced substantial improvement in the representation of indigents in the criminal justice process. Today only very minor infractions of the law are excepted from the general requirement that a criminal defendant is entitled to court-appointed counsel if he or she cannot afford a lawyer. But there is still a wide gap between the quality of legal representation offered by private counsel to those who can afford it, and that offered by court-appointed counsel or public defenders. There is no comparable constitutional right to counsel in civil cases, but OEO Legal Services programs, later absorbed into the federal Legal Services Corporation, provide a substantial increment of representation for the indigent in such matters.

Three other reform efforts began in the 1960s. First, there was a renewed effort to induce private lawyers to increase their pro bono work for underrepresented groups and public interest issues. Some large law firms developed special pro bono arrangements to lure the best law students away from other kinds of public interest work. But the effort has not borne much fruit.

A completely different approach was the development of "radical" or nontraditional law firms which were devoted to particular causes and determined to use the law as a method of political confrontation rather than to "practice it" in the conventional manner. Although some lawyers still practice this confrontational style, and it may have "worked" in a few cases, it proved—not unexpectedly—not to be viable over the long term. Such lawyering, designed to show that lawyers need not be "all case and no cause," failed to attract the funding it needed to survive. A small corps of lawyers remains concerned primarily with "public interest law."

Public interest law was once the province of liberal groups; but, in the true spirit of the adversary system, an increasing number of conservative public interest firms have sprung up to defend the interests attacked by the older liberal groups: landowners and land developers, manufacturers, energy producers, and the like. And unlike their liberal counterparts, who must compete for scarce funding resources, these conservative groups are well financed and likely to endure. It is ironic that one major impact of the liberal public interest law movement has been the development of an increasingly effective conservative counterforce—representing the very same interests that the legal profession has long nurtured so closely. But there are also friendly critics who note that, apart from funding problems, the liberal public interest law movement has suffered because it is caught in the classic trap of legal reformers: in order to be effective, it became increasingly professionalized and litigation prone. But the more professionalized and litigation prone public interest lawyers become, the more they are part of the very system which they are seeking to reform. They thus become less likely to pursue or achieve true reformist— as opposed to ameliorative—goals. In the plight of the liberal public interest lawyer one sees clearly the national dilemma of legal reform.

WHAT PEOPLE BELIEVE ABOUT THE LAW AND ABOUT USING IT

A critical element in any legal culture is what people believe about the law, and what use they make of the legal system. We have already noted the important symbolic role of law in the United States, the deep-seated attachment that Americans have to it (though not to the same degree, it should be added, to lawyers), and the high degree to which the spirit of the law, as well as much of its embodiment, has permeated the society. Americans are clearly no longer, if they ever were, quite as obsessed with the law as Alexis de Tocqueville observed in 1835 in his *Democracy in America:*

> Scarcely any political question arises in the United States that is not resolved sooner or later into a judicial question. . . . The spirit of the law, which is produced in the schools and courts of justice, gradually penetrates beyond their walls into the bosom of society where it descends to the lowest classes, so that at last the whole peo-

ple contract the habits and the tastes of the judicial magistrate.

Studies show, for example, that courts, including the Supreme Court, are not especially salient or visible to most Americans. People tend to hold the courts responsible for the "crime problem" and, to some extent, believe that courts violate the goal of equal treatment for all by treating rich people more favorably than poor people. But, on the whole, they know little about how the courts, and especially the Supreme Court, operate. Ironically, those who have had firsthand experience with the courts and who know most about them seem on the whole less approving than those for whom the courts remain remote. This may reflect only a natural disillusionment when the mythical views of courts, which Americans learn as children and which are reinforced by the media, are tested by actual contact with the legal system. Or it may indicate simply that contacts with legal institutions are inherently traumatic; they often occur at times of personal distress or misfortune, and this personal trauma yields negative views of courts that have not performed (and perhaps could not perform) as well as expected.

Yet, there seems to be an overall level of satisfaction with the courts that transcends individual experiences or disapproval of particular judicial decisions. Certainly, there is no evidence that dissatisfaction with the judiciary generally or with particular legal policies or actions has "produced deep-seated and widespread alienation from the legal system" (Sarat). One explanation for this ambivalence is that Americans believe, or are content to accept, the official myths about the courts—particularly the Supreme Court—and the legal system. Studies of attitudes toward the Supreme Court reveal that belief in these myths (of objectivity, independence, and "mechanical jurisprudence") accounts for widespread support. On the other hand, one study by David Adamany and Joel Grossman argues that the modern Supreme Court's ability to survive strong political attacks against it is not so much a product of myth or "diffuse support" for the Court as an institution as it is a product of the strategic political role of a relatively small number of liberal political activists who have blocked efforts to curb the Court's power.

The American political culture has been described by Gabriel Almond and Sidney Verba as "allegiant, participant, and civic," implying a high degree of citizen support and participation. Whether or not this applies to the legal system remains an open question. There is evidence, already described, that Americans seem particularly rights-conscious and that they do not seem at all reluctant to litigate, but there is also substantial evidence that relatively few disputes are actually brought to the legal system (Miller and Sarat, 1981). To some extent, this may reflect the costs of mobilizing the law, although these costs may not be as heavy for "middle-range disputes" as once was thought to be the case (Trubek et al.).

The highest levels of participation (other than in criminal cases, when one is more a subject of the law rather than a user of it) are found among those groups who can afford to do so and whose interests are best served by doing so. There are also important regional and subcultural differences in propensity to use the judicial system. A 1959 study by Hans Zeisel, Harry Kalven, Jr., and Bernard Buchholz of personal injury litigation, for example, revealed significant differences in "claims consciousness" in several cities. Ethnic groups such as the Chinese in San Francisco have long preferred to resolve disputes internally rather than use the official legal system, although generational change has eroded this instinct.

Litigation may or may not accord with the moral balance of a community. David Engel's study of a small Illinois county concluded that "lawsuits brought for breaches of contract [typically by members of the local establishment] were generally approved. Lawsuits brought for personal injuries [typically by newcomers and outsiders] were generally condemned and stigmatized." Contract litigation was seen as an appropriate way of enforcing an important moral precept: Pay your debts. Personal injury litigation, which was almost never brought by the indigenous population, was opposed because it was contrary to the accepted virtues of self-reliance and stoicism in the face of misfortune and because it seemed to symbolize the intrusion of unwanted newcomers and a new moral order into the tranquility and traditional life-style of that community. Future empirical studies of such local legal cultures are likely to reveal a much more complex pattern of variation.

Americans are not passive subjects of the law, yet neither are they as aggressive in using the law

779

as some have claimed. Using the law is seen as an appropriate, if complex, time-consuming, and costly, endeavor. Americans are most willing and likely to mobilize the law defensively to protect perceived infringements of their rights. Few of them see the law as the normal way of doing business or maintaining desired relationships. And even when they use the law to assert their rights, they seem willing to expect compromise as the most generally appropriate result (Miller and Sarat). What we know so far suggests the paradox that while Americans as a group are litigious people, they are also independent, self-reliant, and in many ways curiously reluctant to "mobilize the law" (Black). Thus, "it is ultimately both an empirical question and a matter of definition as to whether ours is a society of rights consciousness and conflict, or one of acquiescence and equilibrium" (Miller and Sarat, 1981).

Equivocation in the use of the law is matched by the ambivalence most Americans have toward civil liberties. Many studies have shown that Americans have a strong belief in civil liberties but that their attachment to the application of these principles wanes when they are claimed by those who are perceived as different or threatening. Maintenance of these principles is in part the result of the greater attachment to them of political elites and lawyers—those most directly involved in the formation of public policy and the operation of legal institutions. But it may also reflect the reluctance of most citizens to mobilize to deny rights to others, just as they are reluctant to mobilize the law in their own behalf unless and until threatened deprivations are especially serious. Thus, a climate of rights is maintained despite significant gaps in the willingness of some people to accord those rights to others.

CONCLUSION

Lawrence Friedman (1984) has proposed yet another basis for classifying legal cultures: two ways "in which people look at rights and duties that form the building blocks of the legal system." One is an economic or price-rationing approach to law, and the other, moral or ideological. Under the first, which may be described as a system of "interests," the law regulates by assigning weights or costs and benefits to various behaviors. Everything has its price. Behavioral and policy choices are made after assessing their relative costs. From this point of view, the legal system stands outside the world of morality; and in many respects this is how a legal system works in practice. But a second approach emphasizes moral and ideological elements. "Rights," which are in theory free and unlimited, are often the basis for the costs assigned to certain behaviors. The legal system is not neutral; it is the "enforcement arm" of a system of moral evaluation. However, no legal system is exclusively "economic" or "moral" but rather, Friedman argues, a mix of these elements. Nonetheless, the relative mix of these two approaches in a particular system may change over time, as can the meaning of the rights and duties of citizens.

It is not surprising to discover that quite often the exterior or surface of the law reflects a moral-ideological perspective, while the "living law is better described as a pricing mechanism" or a "subtle network of bargains"—principles up front, and reality to the rear (Friedman, 1984). This is certainly a fair description of the American criminal justice system, which promotes such formal concepts as due process while it relies on plea bargaining, discretionary justice, and the like. Sometimes there is a substantial equivalence: the "surface" rights describe reasonably accurately what happens in practice. But often there is a substantial disparity between what the law promises—or seems to promise—and what the legal-political process produces.

There are also instances in which the polarity is reversed. The surface of the law recognizes a plurality of legitimate interests, and legal process offers a way to determine which will prevail in a particular case or between particular parties. This is characteristic of the civil law generally and is especially seen in modern divorce-law reform: it is no longer a matter of which party was "at fault" but of acknowledging that the marriage has "failed," and the law provides a means for, and an inducement to, the parties to agree on an acceptable compromise according to their principles.

Friedman argues that while traditionally the American legal culture reflected both the moral-ideological and price-rationing features—the "double standard"—it was nonetheless firmly grounded in cultural homogeneity and a relatively widely accepted moral code of acceptable

AMERICAN LEGAL CULTURE

behavior, which made it possible to maintain a viable connection between the moral-ideological and price-rationing systems. But great changes in the composition of the populace brought corresponding changes in values and ideologies. Thus, today we recognize as legitimate a kind of "plural equality" of "multiple normative patterns"; the law and legal culture must deal with many new and conflicting claims of right and justice. Thus, as the society and its values on which the legal culture rests have become more complex, the legal culture has had to become more relativistic and more open to bargained and mediated solutions between competing principles.

CASES

Brown v. Board of Education, 347 U.S. 483 (1954)
Faretta v. California, 422 U.S. 806 (1975)
Gideon v. Wainwright, 372 U.S. 335 (1963)

BIBLIOGRAPHY

Richard L. Abel, "The Contradictions of Informal Justice," in Abel, ed., *The Politics of Informal Justice* (1982), critiques the consequences of informal justice. David Adamany and Joel B. Grossman, "Support for the Supreme Court as a National Policy Maker," *Law and Policy Quarterly*, 5 (1983), is a study of the role of liberal activists in obstructing political attacks on the Supreme Court. Gabriel Almond and Sidney Verba, *The Civic Culture* (1963), is a definitive study of the civic culture of five nations. William G. Andrews, ed., *Constitutions and Constitutionalism*, 2nd ed. (1963), collects constitutional documents.

Thurman Arnold, *The Symbols of Government* (1962), interprets symbolic politics. Jerrold Auerbach, *Unequal Justice* (1976), gives a critical history of the American legal profession; and *Justice Without Law* (1983), is a study of "alternatives" to formal legal processes. Donald Black, "The Mobilization of Law," *Journal of Legal Studies*, 2 (1973), explores why citizens use, or don't use, the law. Daniel Boorstin, "The Perils of Indwelling Law," in Robert Paul Wolff, ed., *The Rule of Law* (1971), shows the impact of natural law thinking on views about the law and legal system.

Mark W. Cannon, "Why Celebrate the Constitution?" *National Forum*, 64 (1984), discusses the basic principles of the American Constitution. Abram Chayes, "The Role of the Judge in Public Law Litigation," *Harvard Law Review*, 89 (1976); and "Foreward: Public Law Litigation and the Burger Court; The Supreme Court, 1981 Term," *Harvard Law Review*, 96 (1982), give a leading modern statement of the legitimacy of judicial activism. Thomas Church, Jr., et al., *Justice*

Delayed: The Pace of Litigation in Urban Trial Courts (1978), the best single volume on the subject of court delay.

Henry W. Ehrmann, *Comparative Legal Cultures* (1976), is the leading text on the subject. David Engel, "The Oven Bird's Song: Insiders, Outsiders, and Personal Injuries in an American Community," *Law & Society Review*, 18 (1984), gives us how and why residents of a small Illinois town use the civil courts. Malcolm M. Feeley, *Court Reform on Trial* (1983), explores the inefficacy of judicial reform. Jeffrey Fitzgerald, "A Comparative Empirical Study of Potential Disputes in Australia and the United States," Disputes Processing Research Program Working Paper, 1982–84, University of Wisconsin, compares disputing practices in Australia and the United States.

Jerome Frank, *Courts on Trial* (1949), is a classic commentary on the legal system by a prominent legal realist scholar and judge. Lawrence M. Friedman, "Legal Culture and Social Development, *Law & Society Review*, 4 (1969), is an early treatment of legal culture; *A History of American Law* (1973), a comprehensive history of American law and legal institutions; *The Legal System* (1975), synthesizes research on the legal system; "Two Faces of Law," *Wisconsin Law Review* (1984), theorizes on the interaction between the moral and economic roles of the law.

Lon L. Fuller, "The Forms and Limits of Adjudication," *Harvard Law Review*, 92 (1978), a classic statement of the traditional view of what courts are and should remain. Marc Galanter, "Why the 'Haves' Come Out Ahead: Speculations on the Limits of Legal Change," *Law & Society Review*, 9 (1974), the leading article on the use of legal institutions to achieve reform; "Justice in Many Rooms: Courts, Private Ordering, and Indigenous Law," *Journal of Legal Pluralism*, 19 (1981), states that courts are merely the tip of the iceberg: "justice" is dispensed in many ways and by both private and public institutions; "Reading the Landscape of Disputes: What We Know and Don't Know (And Think We Know) About Our Allegedly Contentious and Litigious Society," *UCLA Law Review*, 31 (1983), responds to critics of excessive litigiousness in American society.

James L. Gibson, "Judges' Role Orientations, Attitudes and Decisions: An Interactive Model," *American Political Science Review*, 72 (1972), assesses the degree to which judges' sentencing decisions are responsive to local values. Joel B. Grossman, Herbert M. Kritzer, Kristin Bumiller, and Stephen McDougal, "Measuring the Pace of Civil Litigation in Federal and State Trial Courts," *Judicature*, 65 (1981), uses data from the Civil Litigation Research Project to explore the problem of "delay" in the courts. E. Adamson Hoebel, *The Law of Primitive Man* (1954), the major work of a leading legal anthropologist.

Donald Horowitz, *The Courts and Social Policy* (1977), critiques modern judicial activism. Martin Levin, *Urban Politics and the Criminal Courts* (1977), studies the criminal courts in two contrasting urban cultures. Jethro K. Lieberman, *The Litigious Society* (1981), explores the development and reasons for the litigation phenomenon. Stewart Macaulay, "Lawyers and Consumer Protection Laws," *Law & Society Review*, 14 (1979), compares Wisconsin lawyers to the classic "hired gun" model of lawyering; "Law and the Behavioral Sciences: Is There Any There There?" *Law and Policy*, 6 (1984), critiques the concept of legal culture.

Herbert McClosky, "Consensus and Ideology in American Politics," *American Political Science Review*, 58 (1964), a study of the contrasting beliefs of citizens and political activists towards civil liberties; McClosky and Alida Brill, *Dimensions of Tolerance: What Americans Believe About Civil Liberties* (1983), updates earlier studies. Richard E. Miller and Austin Sarat, "Grievances, Claims, and Disputes: Assessing the Adversary Culture," *Law & Society Review*, 15 (1981), reports survey data from the Civil Litigation Research Project on when and how citizens seek redress for grievances. Sally Falk Moore, "Law and Social Change: The Semi-Autonomous Field as an Appropriate Subject of Study," *Law & Society Review*, 7 (1973), promulgates a theory of social ordering outside of the law.

Leopold Pospisil, "Legal Levels and Multiplicity of Legal Systems in Human Societies," *Journal of Conflict Resolution*, 11 (1967), finds that all societies have multiple systems of legal ordering. Robert L. Rabin, "Lawyers for Social Change: Perspectives on Public Interest Law," *Stanford Law Review*, 28 (1976), thoroughly analyzes the world of public interest law. Austin Sarat, "Studying American Legal Culture: An Assessment of Survey Evidence," *Law & Society Review*, 11 (1977), synthesizes many studies of how Americans view—and use—

the law. Stuart Scheingold, *The Politics of Rights* (1974), theorizes on how the law can be mobilized to maximize its utility as an agent of change.

Martin Shapiro, *Courts* (1981), a provocative exploration of the development and role of courts in Western and non-Western societies. Judith Shklar, *Legalism* (1964), applies the concept of legalism to an analysis of the Nuremberg trials. William Simon, "The Ideology of Advocacy," *Wisconsin Law Review* (1978), critiques the adversary system and argues that the ideal of law is antithetical to the rule of law.

David M. Trubek, "Complexity and Contradiction in the Legal Order: Balbus and the Challenge of Critical Social Thought About Law," *Law & Society Review*, 11 (1977), attempts to find common ground between critical legal studies and liberal legalism; Trubek, Austin Sarat, William L.F. Felstiner, Herbert M. Kritzer, and Joel B. Grossman, "The Costs of Ordinary Litigation," *UCLA Law Review*, 31 (1983), reports findings of the Civil Litigation Research Project. Hans Zeisel, Harry Kalven, Jr., and Bernard Buchholz, *Delay in the Court* (1959), explains differences in the pace of litigation by differences in the "claims consciousness" of litigants.

[*See also* THE JUDICIARY *and* PUBLIC INTEREST ADVOCACY.]

CERTIORARI

Doris Marie Provine

*C*ERTIORARI is the name of a writ, or order, that an appellate court can issue to require a lower tribunal to certify and send up the record in a case for review. Literally translated from the Latin, it means "to make more certain," a phrase that suggests the purpose of the writ: careful review of a case by a higher court to ensure that the judgment below is consistent with governing law. The writ developed early in the history of English law, but that fact should not obscure its modern significance. Certiorari is an enormously important aspect of modern appellate procedure in America, for reasons that will become clear in this article.

A court exercises its certiorari power when it accepts petitions filed by litigants disappointed with the outcome of their cases in the court below and selects a fraction of these cases for review "on the merits"—that is, reconsideration of the law applied below. This petitioning process should be distinguished from "appeal," another route to reconsideration of a case by a higher court. Litigants generally enjoy a right to at least one appeal, usually from the original decision at trial; the filing of an appeal obliges the appellate court to evaluate and respond to the legal arguments litigants put forward. Litigants enjoy no such right when they petition for certiorari.

In the Supreme Court, certiorari petitions are accepted all year long, but most decisions regarding review occur during the term (October to July) in the midst of the oral argument, voting, and opinion writing associated with the resolution of fully considered cases. The public is only vaguely aware of the agenda-setting process, though, because the Court makes its selection decisions in secret.

Yet, while certiorari decisions are much less visible than the Court's decisions on the merits, they are no less important, either for litigants or for those concerned with the causes they represent. The denial of certiorari is, practically speaking, the end of a lawsuit in most cases that come to the Supreme Court; the disappointed litigant is usually without further recourse to review and must accept the decision of the court below as final. Over 90 percent of the cases that come to the Supreme Court each year meet this fate, the Court granting full review to 150–200 cases a year out of about 4,000 applications.

Rejected litigants can only speculate about why the Court denied review. The Court issues no opinions in making these decisions, though individual justices do occasionally publish dissents from denials. Nor does the Court release the individual votes of the justices or vote totals for and against review, as it does with nearly all votes when the Court actually decides a case on the merits. The public learns who voted for review only if a published dissent from a denial makes this clear. The certiorari power, in short, gives the Supreme Court complete, unreviewable authority to select from among the cases brought to it those which it wants to decide on the merits, and it makes these selections without creating a body of precedent that might narrow its discretion in future cases.

The Supreme Court has not always had authority to set its own agenda. It had no discretion at all over its docket until Congress created the United States courts of appeals in 1891 in response to growing demands on the Supreme Court's capacity for appellate review. These new appellate courts provided a forum for hearing appeals from trial-court decisions and helped make mandatory review in the Supreme Court seem less necessary. Congress gave the Supreme

Court some power over its docket at that point, but not until the passage of the Judiciary Act of 1925 did the Court gain authority to refuse review in most types of cases. Supreme Court justices wrote this legislation, which became known as the Judge's Bill. A delegation of justices, led by Chief Justice Taft, then campaigned hard for its passage.

The 1925 act did not give the Court complete discretion over its docket. Some types of cases brought to the Court for review remained mandatory—that is, the Court was obliged to decide them. This bifurcation of review powers remains in effect today. Cases come to the Court via the mandatory route of appeal when a lower court has held a federal statute unconstitutional, when a state court has upheld a state statute against the claim that it violates the federal Constitution, and in certain other limited circumstances. Its certiorari jurisdiction is much broader, extending to any civil or criminal case from the courts of appeal and to questions from state courts involving federal constitutional or statutory law or treaties.

The mandatory cases, or appeals, now constitute about 5 percent of the cases that reach the Court. The Court has three choices in dealing with them: if it believes the appeal to be frivolous or outside its jurisdiction, it can "dismiss for want of a substantial federal question" or affirm summarily; it can overturn the result below at this stage by reversing summarily; or it can note probable jurisdiction and schedule the case for further consideration, as it does when it grants certiorari.

The justices give short shrift to most appeals, processing them much as they do certiorari cases. But the Court has not entirely eliminated the distinction between certiorari and appeal. It selects a disproportionate number of them for full, or plenary, review. In 1981, for example, appeals made up one-quarter of the cases scheduled for oral argument. These cases, together with the appeals reversed or affirmed summarily, made up approximately half of the cases the Court decided on the merits that term.

The Court's summary disposition of many appeals inevitably creates some uncertainty in the legal community, because technically speaking, these decisions have significance as precedent. But it is often unclear just what a summary decision signifies, for it occurs before oral argument or full briefing of the questions raised by the appeal. Signed opinions are rare in these cases; usually the Court simply states its result, sometimes citing the cases it deems controlling in an anonymous (per curiam) opinion.

Denials of certiorari cause no such uncertainty for the practicing bar or the lower courts. The Court issues no opinions in these cases either, but the reasons why the Court decided as it did are, legally speaking at least, not important. Denials of certiorari do not have any official significance as precedents and cannot be cited for this purpose. This does not mean that denials have no significance at all in the eyes of the attentive public. Most observers interpret repeated denials as an indication of judicial indifference to an issue.

The certiorari power is not limited to the United States Supreme Court. It exists, to varying degrees, in about half the states. In some, like California and Illinois, discretionary jurisdiction predominates. Other state supreme courts, like that of Colorado, have a case load almost evenly balanced between mandatory and discretionary cases, but in others, like those of Alabama and Georgia, mandatory cases predominate. In almost all of the states whose supreme courts have certiorari power, there is an intermediate appellate court (or courts) to handle some or all direct appeals from trial-court judgments. But appellate capacity at an intermediate level does not always spawn discretionary review at the top, as it did in the federal system. Thirty-two states have intermediate appellate courts, but only twenty-four of these states have any significant discretionary jurisdiction in their state supreme courts.

The particular arrangements by which mandatory and discretionary cases come to the state supreme court vary from state to state. A few states allow appeals directly from trial courts. In at least two others, the supreme court screens cases, deciding some appeals itself and referring others to a lower court for decision there. States attach different names to the case-selection process too. What would be a petition for certiorari in the federal setting is a petition for leave to appeal or a petition for review in some state courts.

The evidence we have suggests that the considerations involved in case selection at the state level bear a strong resemblance to those that influence certiorari decision-making in the United States Supreme Court. Judges at both levels agree on how to dispose of many review requests but differ among themselves on a significant minority, their differences following patterns that transcend specific subject matter and persist over long periods of time. Because research on certiorari at the state level is still at an early stage and because of space limitations, the remainder of this article will focus on certiorari in the United States Supreme Court.

CRITERIA FOR GRANTING THE WRIT

The certiorari power is obviously important to the litigants, whose lives are directly affected by review decisions, but it is also important to the American political community as a whole, for the Supreme Court helps set the nation's political agenda as it sets its own agenda. The cases the Court selects and then decides on the merits become the focus of attention in the mass media, scholarly journals, law schools, and the lower courts. The cases denied review are more likely to sink into relative obscurity, for it is not definite whether they represent nationally binding law.

It would be misleading to imply that the Supreme Court sets its agenda with no help from anyone. Disputants and their lawyers play important roles in the process. They determine the universe of cases from which the Court chooses, and they decide how vigorously and fully the issues raised will be pursued. The reality in all phases of the Supreme Court's work is clearly shared power.

The standards the justices use to select the tiny minority of cases they review on the merits are undefined. Some claim that they simply weed through the incoming cases and choose the most important or worthy, and others, that they grant review to correct the most egregious errors they perceive in lower-court decisions. The Court offers some guidance on its criteria for review in rules it has written and published regarding its operations. Supreme Court Rule 17 lists the following as "the character of reasons that will be considered" in granting or denying certiorari:

> *a.* When a federal court of appeals has rendered a decision in conflict with the decision of another federal court of appeals on the same matter; or has decided a federal question in a way in conflict with a state court of last resort; or has so far departed from the accepted and usual course of judicial proceedings, or so far sanctioned such a departure by a lower court, as to call for an exercise of this Court's power of supervision.
>
> *b.* When a state court of last resort has decided a federal question in a way in conflict with the decision of another state court of last resort or of a federal court of appeals.
>
> *c.* When a state court or a federal court of appeals has decided an important question of federal law which has not been, but should be, settled by this Court, or has decided a federal question in a way in conflict with applicable decisions of this Court.

Rule 17 indicates that conflict among the lower courts in interpreting federal law is an important criterion in the review decisions. Litigants shape their petitions for review to take account of this preference, alleging many more conflicts than an objective observer guided by the spirit of Rule 17 would find. A study conducted by Floyd Feeney, for example, found no genuine conflicts, direct or indirect, in 708 of the 966 cases that claimed them. Feeney showed, however, that the Court does not take up every single genuine conflict that it could. Review was denied in 66 cases presenting direct conflicts in the 1971 term and in 70 cases in the 1972 term. Sidney Ulmer has discovered that the Court has varied over time in the extent to which it makes conflicts the basis for review on the merits. The Burger Court apparently put less emphasis on resolving either conflicts between lower courts or conflicts between a lower court and the Supreme Court than the Warren Court did.

The question such statistics cannot resolve is whether the Court really should review every conflict between judicial interpretations that is brought to its attention. To allow some conflicts to stand is to permit local variation in interpretations of federal statutes and the Constitution. Such tolerance seems unfair to the individuals and organizations whose rights vary by region. Regional variation can also make legal planning difficult for litigants who operate across jurisdictions.

Yet differences between lower courts may allow some conflicts to "ripen," providing helpful guidance to the Court when it finally (perhaps

CERTIORARI

years later) does resolve the issue. The existence of conflicts, Justice John Paul Stevens has argued, can "illuminate" matters for the Court and "may play a constructive role in the lawmaking process," thus making complex cases easier to resolve. Philosophically, too, Stevens is opposed to reaching out too quickly to resolve inconsistent outcomes in the lower courts: "The doctrine of judicial restraint teaches us that patience in the judicial resolution of conflicts may sometimes produce the most desirable result."

The Court's sense of what constitutes a significant legal issue also plays a role in these decisions. The Court denies review in the face of some legitimate conflicts, apparently because it is not persuaded that the claim is important enough to merit full review. Challenges to the constitutionality of school regulations concerning student hair length, for example, seem to have fallen into this category when they first began to come before the Court: for a time, the justices failed to grant review despite a five-to-five split among the federal circuit courts.

Rule 17 does not mention errors in decisions below as an independent ground for review. The omission is no accident; simple error-correction, the justices have noted from the outset, is not the purpose of certiorari. As Chief Justice William Howard Taft described the Court's role in 1925, just after Congress had provided it with the broad certiorari power it enjoys today, "The function of the Supreme Court is conceived to be, not the remedying of a particular litigant's wrong, but the consideration of cases whose decision involves principles, the application of which are of wide public or governmental interest" (p. 2).

The certiorari power, Taft and other justices have argued over the years, allows the Court to conserve its resources for the most important cases that come to it each term. The litigant's right to appeal perceived errors at the trial level is satisfied by resort to the courts of appeals and to state appellate tribunals. It is this reasoning that lies behind the Court's frequent reminder that the denial of certiorari implies nothing as to its view of the actual merits of a petitioner's arguments.

The impact of the Court's policy of rejecting apparent error in the decision below as the sole basis for review is evident in the certiorari decisions it makes. The justices generally deny peti-

tions that simply allege a mistake or abuse of discretion in the application of existing law to the particular facts of a controversy. Such cases, whatever their significance to individual litigants, raise no broader issues that call out for the Supreme Court's attention. Capital cases are something of an exception to this rule; the Court has always been much more generous in reviewing these cases than other types of criminal cases. In noncapital cases, though, the Court looks for indications that the matter in dispute involves an interpretation of federal law that is bound to arise (or has arisen) elsewhere.

The perception that the results below were wrong does seem to have some impact on the Court's evaluation of the significance of the question, however. This can be seen in the preponderance of reversals in cases accepted for review: on the average, the Court reverses or remands for further proceedings about two-thirds of the cases it decides on the merits each term. The same pattern was evident at the individual level as well during the one period in the Court's history for which we have access to the certiorari and appeals votes of the justices. Justice Harold H. Burton, who sat on the Court between 1945 and 1958, released these votes to the Library of Congress upon his death. They are an invaluable resource for understanding how the Court sets its agenda.

Justice Burton's docket books indicate that all of the justices apparently took their views of the proper outcome of a case into account in voting for or against review. Each of the fifteen justices who sat during Burton's tenure on the Court was more likely to vote to reverse the cases he voted to review than the ones that came up for review on the merits despite his negative vote. These justices varied, however, in the extent to which they linked votes to review with the merits of the controversy. Justice Charles E. Whittaker, for example, voted to reverse 93 percent of the cases he voted to review but only 43 percent of those that came to him for a final decision despite his negative case-selection vote. Justice Burton, in contrast, voted to reverse only 56 percent of the cases he voted to review and 39 percent of the others. There is no reason not to expect similar differences in sensitivity to error below among the current members of the Supreme Court.

Even if the justices were alike in their propensity to vote for review to correct error below, they would still differ over what they perceived to be error. Even the most casual Court watcher is aware of this difference between justices. The tradition of releasing the on-the-merits votes of each justice and publishing both majority and minority opinions (and sometimes more than one of each) ensures that these differences will be obvious to everyone.

A final limiting factor in the review decision is quasi-jurisdictional. If the Court perceives a case as lying outside its competence or appropriate sphere, it will generally deny review, even where the consequences for the litigants involved are serious. The Court has been quite consistent in denying review to petitions turning on the interpretation of state statutes or case law, for example. The Court leaves these matters to the state courts. The Court also avoids correcting errors of trial courts not properly noted in the original appeal from the trial-court judgment. When, for example, a petitioner claims for the first time at the Supreme Court level that trial counsel was incompetent, the justices will not ordinarily respond. Petitioners are expected to raise their issues in a timely way in a lower appellate court to preserve them in petitioning for certiorari.

EVALUATION OF PETITIONS

Requests for certiorari arrive as petitions shortly after the entry of final judgment in the court below. The Court regulates the form in which they must be filed through its rules. Absent Court permission to file in forma pauperis, petitioners must frame their arguments within the highly structured form of a legal brief no more than thirty pages long, have forty copies of this document printed for distribution to the justices and staff, and pay a filing fee. Copies of the opinion and judgment below are attached as appendices. Respondents (those parties who won in the court below and therefore would like to avoid review) have thirty days from receipt of notice of petitioner's filing to submit a brief in opposition. Petitioners are then entitled to respond with a reply brief. The rules for cases that come to the Court as appeals are similar, the principal difference being that appellants file a jurisdictional statement, rather than a petition for certiorari.

A petitioner or appellant can avoid the formality of filing and the financial outlay it involves by asking the Court's permission to file in forma pauperis. If the Court grants the motion, the litigant need not comply with the standard format, printing, reproduction, and filing-fee requirements. The number of persons who claimed that they could not comply with standard filing requirements began to increase drastically in the late 1950s and has continued to grow since then. In forma pauperis cases now constitute approximately half of the total number filed each year. Prisoners and persons proceeding without lawyers (*pro se*) often choose this option.

The decision to proceed in forma pauperis used to have important implications for the way a case was considered by the Court. The in forma pauperis, or "unpaid," cases were recorded separately on the miscellaneous docket, while the regular, or "paid," cases went on the appellate docket. The chief justice's clerks briefed the miscellaneous docket cases and distributed their memos to the rest of the Court. Appellate docket cases, on the other hand, entered the chambers of each justice to be briefed by the designated clerk in each office. (Capital cases were the only exception to the rule of diminished consideration in in forma pauperis cases.) This two-track system ended in the mid-1960s: all requests for review now receive the same type of preconference analysis. Only the numbering system the Court uses preserves the distinction between them. Docket entries in paid cases, after a two-digit prefix denoting the year, begin at 1 each term. In forma pauperis cases begin at 5,000.

Despite the similarity in processing, unpaid cases do not have nearly as high a rate of review as paid cases do. The grant rate for unpaid cases was less than 1 percent in the 1980 through 1983 terms, and had not risen far above that rate for a decade. Grants in paid cases, on the other hand, have ranged between 10 percent and 15 percent in recent years. The differential was in the same direction, but not as large, in the 1950s and 1960s, when the case load was smaller.

The in forma pauperis litigants are less successful in getting review, in large part because they tend to raise issues the Court perceives as confined closely to the facts of particular cases; that is, they are often unimportant in the legal sense discussed earlier. But lack of financial resources inevitably takes a toll too. These litigants cannot afford to hire the legal help necessary to shape their cases to the standards the Court applies in case selection.

The rules discussed so far assume that the only way the justices have to determine the legal significance of the cases they screen is to assess the materials provided by those proposing and opposing review. This is usually the situation, but sometimes other interested individuals or groups want to make known to the Court their views concerning the worthiness of a case for certiorari. The Court regulates their participation through its rules regarding participation amicus curiae (that is, as "a friend of the court").

The requirements are very similar to those the Court applies to potential friends of the court in fully considered cases. Private individuals and organizations who want to participate must secure the permission of the named parties or get the permission of the Court itself before filing a brief in support of, or, less often, in opposition to, review. Such requests are usually granted. Government, whether state or federal, can file without asking permission.

Amicus participation at the case-screening stage has grown increasingly frequent since the mid-1960s. Before then, briefs focused on the screening decision were almost unheard of. The change is due not so much to liberalization of the Court's rules regarding an amicus as to the increasing difficulty litigants face in getting Supreme Court review. People concerned with shaping public policy through litigation have come to realize that the Court, with a fixed capacity for on-the-merits review, must be quite selective.

The Court has developed certain routines to keep the time involved in deciding review requests to a minimum. These routines have changed as the case load has increased and the justices have received more staff support. All the justices, for example, once scanned all petitions and jurisdictional statements themselves. In the 1980s, Justice William J. Brennan was the only one who still did, and even he was unable to do this over the summer months. The rest of the Court has come to rely on law clerks to summarize these materials. The clerks produce short memos outlining the facts, decision below, contentions on appeal, and recommended disposition of the case.

The law clerks are young lawyers, most of whom graduated from elite law schools and then clerked a year or two in a lower court. The chief justice currently has five law clerks, and six of the associate justices employ four each, while of the two justices remaining, one has three and the other has two. Each of the clerks works independently for a justice on opinions in fully decided cases, but the situation is not quite the same where case screening is involved. Since the mid-1970s, some of the justices have pooled law clerks for memo-writing purposes. The clerks involved produce a memo on each case, which is then shared among justices in the pool. This practice reduces the work load of the clerks; its impact on case selection has not been assessed.

The extent to which the justices rely on the recommendations of the law clerks can only be a matter of speculation. Clerks who have written on the subject generally deny that they have a significant influence on their justice's decision, but some litigators are not so sure. Philip Kurland, for example, has complained that the Court's reliance on law-clerk summaries in case-selection decisions reduces carefully drafted petitions to pap for quick judicial consumption.

Justice Burton's records indicate that he agreed with his clerks about 85 percent of the time. Agreement does not tell us who was following whose lead or whether similar judgments were arrived at independently. It seems fair to assume, though, that it is the clerks who respond to the views of their justices, rather than the reverse. The one- or two-year tenure of most clerks, the vast difference between justice and clerk in age and experience, and the inequality of their positions all point toward clerk accommodation to judicial views in case selection.

The Court convenes as a body to consider review requests and other business on most Fridays throughout the term and occasionally on a Wednesday or Thursday. These Friday conferences, which occur after a week of oral argument, are multipurpose; the Court generally devotes the morning to review requests and the afternoon to argued cases. It disposes of review requests that arrive over the summer in a series of several all-day sessions early in the Court's term.

The justices are able to dispose of large numbers of certiorari requests quickly because they have developed certain decision-making conventions, the most important of which is the "discuss list," a listing of cases that will be voted upon in the conference. The chief justice and his clerks prepare the discuss list and circulate it, though any justice is free to add cases to it. The justices can also request a delay in the disposition of any case on the conference list. All cases on the much longer conference list for that date, but not on the discuss list, are automatically denied review without discussion.

Certiorari and appeals decisions thus have two phases: an individual phase, in which each judge, usually with assistance from clerks, decides whether a case might be worthy of review and therefore should be among the minority of cases that make up the discuss list; and a group phase, in which the Court scrutinizes and rejects many of the cases that survive the first cut. In Justice Burton's day, roughly 60 percent of the cases were cut at the first phase, and another 25–30 percent in the conference. Members of the Supreme Court in 1986 estimated that about 70 percent of all cases brought before them were utterly frivolous, which suggests that this may be the proportion that failed to make the discuss list at that time.

The conferences in which certiorari petitions are considered are rather formal meetings. They begin with a shaking of hands all around, and the justices then arrange themselves around the table in order of their seniority. The chief justice starts the discussion by summarizing the case and stating his own views. After a general discussion, the voting occurs, reportedly also in order of seniority. Evidence about these conferences is scanty because they include no one except the justices themselves, and the justices tend to be very close-mouthed about conference proceedings.

It seems clear, however, that chief justices have an important opportunity for leadership at this stage. Their use of the certiorari decision-making process as an opportunity to try to push their views on the others or to seek consensus varies with the individual. Chief Justice Hughes, according to several of the justices who served with him, dominated the discussion, as much because of his preparation and formidable intellectual powers as because of the opportunity to speak first.

Other chiefs have apparently interpreted their leadership responsibilities differently. The Burton materials contain evidence on the voting patterns of three chief justices: Harlan F. Stone, Fred M. Vinson, and Earl Warren. None of these chiefs voted alone, for or against review, as often as most of their colleagues. These chiefs were also more likely than most members of the Court to contribute the crucial vote necessary for granting review in close cases. This pattern suggests that these chief justices used certiorari voting as an occasion to promote consensus on the Court, checking their own views in the process.

Four affirmative votes are required to grant petitions for certiorari and to note probable jurisdiction in appeals cases. The origins of this rule are unclear, but it appears to have been in operation even before the passage of the 1925 Judiciary Act, when certiorari cases were relatively rare. The rule could be avoided if the majority who voted against review at the certiorari stage voted, after oral argument, to dismiss the petition as improvidently granted. The justices have always felt bound, however, to honor the rule of four and give full consideration to cases that pass the screening stage, unless most or all of the Court comes to feel the petition was mistakenly granted.

The four-vote requirement obviously gives a minority of the Court the chance to force the majority to consider a case it would prefer to avoid deciding on the merits. But the evidence is strong that most certiorari decisions are not this close. In the Burton era, over half of the cases considered in conference received no votes at all for review, and a significant proportion of the rest were unanimous grants. Taking account of the cases eliminated even before the conference (through the discuss-list procedure), the rate of unanimity about review-worthiness becomes truly impressive, reaching 82 percent. The overall level of agreement at the certiorari stage may be even greater today, given the Court's much larger case load.

The justices of the Supreme Court, whose tendency to disagree with each other on the merits is well known, reach such a high level of consensus in certiorari voting because they share a basic understanding of the role the Court should play in superintending the nation's judicial system. The justices, after all, have in common their professional education and a lifetime of daily experience with the traditions and presuppositions of the profession. It is easy to lose sight of this shared intellectual tradition because so much attention is devoted to the Court's work on the merits, where close questions of law and policy often divide their votes.

Within the boundaries of fundamental agreement about the types of cases that deserve Supreme Court review, the available data suggest that the justices differ among themselves along three dimensions: in how frequently they vote for review, in the extent to which they take their disagreement with the outcome below into account in voting to review (discussed earlier), and in their interpretation of the merits of the underlying controversies. Differences along the first dimension are probably the most dramatic and certainly the least well understood of the three.

The extent to which justices might differ in their propensity to vote for review can be gauged by comparing Justices Felix Frankfurter and Harold Burton with two justices of much different persuasion, Hugo Black and William O. Douglas. Burton and Frankfurter rarely voted alone for review, each casting less than fifty votes alone in the course of ten years; they were only slightly more likely to vote with one other justice for review. During the same period, Black and Douglas each cast over two hundred lone votes for review and over three hundred apiece with one other justice.

The jurisprudential writings of these justices offer some assistance in explaining the difference in voting patterns between the two pairs. Frankfurter described his own approach in unambiguous terms in a letter to Chief Justice Warren (26 January 1956): "I am, in the main, alert against taking cases except those that obviously call for determination by this Court. By 'obviously' I mean cases about which there can hardly be a difference of opinion around the table." Black and Douglas, on the other hand, shared the view that the lower courts must be closely supervised. These justices were also less worried than many of their colleagues about the burdens a large plenary docket imposes at the argument and opinion-writing stage.

WHO WINS REVIEW AND WHY

Chances of review vary dramatically from one type of case to another. Some types, as noted earlier, have little chance of review: cases not ripe for Supreme Court decision on technical grounds, those based on competing interpretations of state law, and those of little concern to anyone beyond the parties to the action. But even among cases without such deficiencies, chances of review vary tremendously. The Court does not, for example, review many patent or bankruptcy cases, even though they raise federal questions of real significance to petitioners and others concerned with these statutes.

The Court's sense of the importance of a suit obviously operates to the benefit of some causes and petitioners and to the disadvantage of others. A comparison of the cases the Court selected for review in a given period with those eligible can help explain how the Court arrives at a sense of what is important and what that operational definition includes.

In general, the Court prefers constitutional claims to those based on the interpretation of a statute: roughly two-thirds of the cases it reviews are constitutional claims and one-third are statutory. In 1955 the proportions were just the opposite. In the constitutional realm, the court favors claims of infringed personal rights over property rights, a preference it has demonstrated since the 1930s, when it began to distinguish the level of scrutiny it would give each type of claim on the merits. Since then, the Court's understanding of what is included in the realm of personal rights has grown broader.

Changing public attitudes and legislation have been important in altering the Court's view of significance where personal rights are concerned. But the numbers of cases that come to the Court for review and the energy and imagination with which they are litigated also play important roles in altering judicial sensitivities. "Each age," Justice Douglas once noted, "brings the Court its own special worries, anxieties, and concerns. The main outlines of the life of the nation are mirrored in the cases filed with us."

Allegations of sex discrimination provide a useful example of how events, litigation, and legal development can combine to cause the Court to change its mind about "certworthiness." The Court did get occasional petitions alleging sex discrimination in the administration of the tax laws and other statutes before 1970, but it almost invariably denied them. In the Burton period, these cases did not even survive the first cut to discussion at the weekly conference. The number of filings began to grow in the early 1970s as the women's movement gained momentum and state antiabortion laws and other laws allegedly disadvantaging women came under constitutional attack. Grants of review soon began to grow at an even faster rate, in part because conflicts over the constitutional protections available to women developed among the lower courts.

The passage of far-reaching federal legislation can have a similar effect on filings and chances of review. A new law inevitably creates disputes over its meaning, some of which are likely to become lawsuits. These lawsuits are likely to spawn some petitions to the Supreme Court, and the Court may well feel the obligation to grant them to resolve significant ambiguities. The likelihood of review will diminish, though, as the broader questions are resolved.

The sophistication of the party who brings the case to the Court is also relevant to its chances for on-the-merits review. Nowhere is this more obvious than in cases brought by the United States. About 70 percent of the federal government's petitions gain review. This extraordinary grant rate is not simply an artifact of subject matter, for when the federal government's opponents are the petitioners, the grant rate does not rise much above the overall average, now less than 10 percent. Nor can the current rate at which the federal government wins review be explained in terms of the politics of the current configuration of justices, for the United States has always enjoyed enormous success in gaining review.

The federal government is successful largely because the solicitor general, who handles cases destined for the Supreme Court, is an expert and selective petitioner. The solicitor general allows only 10 percent to 15 percent of the cases the government lost below to go forward for Supreme Court review, and in those already select cases, petitions are prepared with care. The justices can thus rely on the solicitor general's sense of self-restraint in petitioning, and he or she in turn enjoys a special status with the Court. The solicitor general is, for example, the only petitioner who has an office in the Supreme Court itself.

A few law firms have become expert in filing for Supreme Court review, but most other petitioners have no expertise at all in petitioning for certiorari, for the United States has no tradition of limiting practice before its highest court to an elite bar, as Britain does with its select corps of barristers. In the United States admission to practice before the Supreme Court is required,

but this is not difficult for a lawyer with some experience in the practice of law. The negative side of this policy is that the Court is inundated with cases that have little prospect of review. The positive side is that the Court can maintain an image of openness to anyone with a legitimate grievance and thereby keep alive the often-repeated threat "I'll take this matter all the way to the Supreme Court."

The impact of the Court's policy of easy access on criminal filings is striking. Nothing prevents large numbers of prisoners from petitioning the Court, sometimes repeatedly. Unlike the solicitor general, however, these petitioners cannot afford to be selective. The result is that the Court grants only a tiny proportion of the prisoner petitions it receives each term, though the total it receives is so large that criminal cases constitute a significant fraction of the cases the Court considers on the merits each year.

The power of the Court to pass over some types of petitioners and issues entirely raises another question about who wins review and why: Does the Court sometimes use its certiorari power to dodge issues that, if resolved on the merits, might jeopardize the Court's institutional resources? Consider, for example, the problem of the enforceability of decrees. Might the Court sometimes be better advised to dodge the occasional conflict that threatens to open the Court to widespread public criticisms or open defiance? At least one constitutional scholar, Alexander Bickel, has advocated the "passive virtue" of nondecision in such circumstances.

The justices seem to have rejected the call to what one of them has described as "political self-protection" at the review-granting stage. The indirect evidence is the infrequency with which the Court is accused, even by its critics, of ducking important policy issues. Direct evidence that the Court rejects the idea of using case selection instrumentally is available in the Burton files. The files reveal that Burton's clerk recommended denials of review in several important race-discrimination cases, including *Shelley* v. *Kraemer* (1948) and *Holmes* v. *City of Atlanta* (1955), on the grounds that the public would not accept an integrationist result. In *Shelley*, which challenged judicial enforcement of racially restrictive housing covenants, Burton's clerk argued that "an abrupt and sweeping judicial invalidation of all restrictive covenants might well create about as many problems as it would solve." The clerk closed by recommending that the Court deny the petition. The Court rejected this advice, all but Justice Robert H. Jackson voting in favor of review.

PROPOSALS TO MODIFY CERTIORARI POWER

The certiorari power gives a busy Court tremendous scope to shape its own agenda each term, but at a potentially significant cost in its time and resources for considering argued cases on their merits. Time spent on review requests is obviously time not available for on-the-merits decision-making; these two aspects of the Court's work are inevitably interdependent. As the case load of the Court has increased from less than two thousand cases a year up until the mid-1960s to over twice that number in the mid-1980s, the question has been raised more and more often whether the Court can adequately discharge both functions without assistance. Erwin Griswold, for example, has warned that under current arrangements "we have been unduly rationing justice." As solicitor general from 1967 to 1973, Griswold claims to have seen at least twenty cases a year that deserved review by an appellate court with national jurisdiction but did not get it.

Others who have observed the Court closely disagree with this assessment. According to Arthur D. Hellman, "There has been a lot of attention paid to intercircuit conflicts that the Court supposedly does not resolve. In my research thus far, I have not found very many square conflicts, or even side-swipes . . . that the Court doesn't resolve. For the most part, a conflict comes up and the Court seizes the case" (Greenhouse et al., 397).

The first full-fledged report addressed to the issue of the Supreme Court's work load was commissioned by Chief Justice Burger. This report, named after its chairman, Harvard law professor Paul Freund, appeared in 1972. It recommended that the Court be relieved of case selection, which it characterized as a burdensome chore of little significance to the primary mission of the Court, which is "to give direction to the law, and to be as precise, persuasive, and invulnerable as possible in its exposition" (Federal Judicial Center, 1). The commission proposed to locate the case-selection responsibility in a new national court of appeals. The new court would certify

some cases to the Supreme Court, resolve certain conflicts between the regional courts of appeals on its own, and deny review to the rest. This drastic proposal for relieving the Court's work load met with considerable hostility, both on and off the Court, and the proposal died under the weight of adverse comment and lukewarm endorsements. Another proposal, drafted by the congressionally appointed Commission on Revision of the Federal Court Appellate System, chaired by Senator Roman Hruska, was released in 1975. It recommended a new federal court with "reference" jurisdiction. The new court would take up cases referred to it by the Supreme Court; these would be cases too important to be denied review but too unimportant to absorb the Court's limited time for on-the-merits review. Case selection would remain entirely in the Supreme Court's hands under the Hruska proposal, which may explain why it was better received than the Freund Commission report. Despite the more positive reception accorded the Hruska approach, the idea has so far failed to win congressional approval, and its prospects do not appear very bright.

Chief Justice Burger was enthusiastic about establishing a new court. He proposed a temporary court staffed with judges from around the country presently on the various courts of appeal. This court would resolve issues referred to it by the Supreme Court, most of which would involve conflicts between the courts of appeals on questions of statutory construction. Losers at this level would retain the right to petition the Court for further review.

Members of the Court did not rally behind the chief justice's proposed emergency court of appeals, though some justices do favor a new court in some form. Others propose different remedies, such as changing the rule of four to a rule of five. Nearly everyone on the Court, though, has complained of the burdens imposed by the current work load. As long as the Court remains divided about what to do about its work load, however, the chances of major structural reform are slim.

Congress is more likely to take a less controversial (and less effective) approach to the workload issue than that proposed by the chief justice or other proponents of a new court. House and Senate committees are considering bills to eliminate the Court's jurisdiction over so-called diversity cases, cases concerning the application of state law that arrive in the federal courts because an earlier era feared prejudice against out-of-state plaintiffs in state courts. This reform would have relatively little effect on the Supreme Court because the Court already disfavors diversity cases. Rule 17 emphasizes the Court's interest in federal, as opposed to state, legal questions.

Congress is also considering eliminating all types of jurisdiction that are still mandatory. All of the justices and many legal scholars have encouraged this reform, and Congress has already taken some small steps in this direction. In the mid-1970s it eliminated a few types of appeal in favor of certiorari jurisdiction. The elimination of all mandatory jurisdiction would be helpful to the Court, but it is unlikely to have a profound impact, because the justices have already developed ways to expedite their consideration of mandatory cases.

Congress could reduce the number of cases the Court gets by limiting the number of federal grounds for relief, thus eliminating some kinds of cases from the federal court system. Every grant of federal jurisdiction, however, has its defenders. These constituencies would resist any effort to eliminate federal causes of action. Major changes are unlikely to come from this direction.

The Court would benefit from a Congress more attentive to its case-management problems, but it is not necessarily harmed by Congress' unwillingness to create a new national appellate court, especially one that would lessen the Court's control over its own docket. The issues involved in evaluating and altering appellate capacity are complex, but the desirability of maintaining certiorari in the Court should be clear: the certiorari power gives the Court the opportunity to remain involved with the changing face of litigation and sensitizes it to new claims and causes. Certiorari also helps maintain the Court's image as an available forum, for it can deny review without necessarily denying the validity of a claim. The certiorari power also creates an important buffer for the Court, allowing it to time its interventions with their impact in mind. The important right-to-counsel case *Gideon* v. *Wainwright* (1963) furnishes a useful example. According to Nathan Lewin, a law clerk who served in the period, the justices chose this case from among many raising the same issue with the idea of making the result as palatable as possible:

Justice Harlan—for whom I worked—would ask, as to each case that might be resolved on the ground ultimately taken in *Gideon*, whether there were . . . unsatisfactory elements in the case that would cause greater popular resentment to the decision than it deserved. One case which seemed perfect in all other respects was rejected because it involved a charge of molesting little girls.

(p. 18)

Whatever the ultimate significance of Court-controlled case selection to the institutional power of the Supreme Court, it need not remain as secret as it has been in the past. The paucity of data about how case selection actually works has limited understanding of the work of the Supreme Court and has contributed to the tendency to view the Court solely in terms of disagreement among the justices in decisions on the merits. Voting data from the now-secret conferences where certiorari decisions are made could enable students of the Court to gain a better appreciation of how review decisions occur.

This is not to suggest that the Court should open its conferences to the public or publish its review votes as they occur. Such openness would undoubtedly inhibit the free flow of ideas in conferences and force the justices to spend much more time than they currently do in making review decisions. A better approach would be to follow Justice Burton's lead and release voting records after an interval of several years. Case selection is an important dimension of Supreme Court power, and the public deserves the opportunity to learn more about how that process proceeds.

CASES

Gideon v. Wainwright, 372 U.S. 335 (1963)
Holmes v. City of Atlanta, 350 U.S. 879 (1955)
Shelley v. Kraemer, 334 U.S. 1 (1948)

BIBLIOGRAPHY

Lawrence Baum, "Decisions to Grant and Deny Hearings in the California Supreme Court," in *Santa Clara Law Review*, 16 (1976), is the first empirical analysis of how certiorari works in a state court. Alexander Bickel, *The Least Dangerous Branch: The Supreme Court at the Bar of Politics* (1962), is a wide-ranging analysis of the Court's political role. Gerhard Casper and Richard Posner, *The Workload of the Supreme Court* (1976), analyzes the growth in the Court's case load and includes possible remedies. Commission on Revision of the Federal Court Appellate System, *Structure and Internal Procedures: Recommendations for Change* (1975), is the Hruska Commission report suggesting a new national appellate court. William O. Douglas, "The Supreme Court and Its Case Load," in *Cornell Law Quarterly*, 45 (1960), argues that there is no case-load crisis in the Supreme Court. Editors of the Harvard Law Review, "The Supreme Court," *Harvard Law Review*, is an annual survey of the Supreme Court's work and includes statistics on dispositions useful to anyone interested in numbers of grants. Sam Estreicher and John E. Sexton, "New York University Supreme Court Project," in *New York University Law Review*, 59 (1984), reanalyzes the work of the 1982 term to ascertain the Court's effectiveness in case selection.

Federal Judicial Center, *Report of the Study Group on the Caseload of the Supreme Court* (1972), is the Freund Commission report suggesting the establishment of a national court of appeals. Floyd Feeney, "Conflicts Involving Federal Law: A Review of Cases Presented to the Supreme Court," in Commission on Revisions of the Federal Court Appellate System, A-50, analyzes the extent of unresolved conflicts in certiorari petitions. Victor E. Flango, "Court Control of Access: Which Appeals Are Heard?" in *State Court Journal*, 8 (1984), briefly describes the incidence and operation of certiorari in the state courts. Linda Greenhouse et al., "Rx for an Overburdened Supreme Court," in *Judicature*, 66 (1983), discusses the Court's case load and how to reduce it and summarizes current justices' views. Erwin N. Griswold, "Rationing Justice: The Supreme Court's Caseload and What the Court Does Not Do," in *Cornell Law Review*, 60 (1975), argues for

a national court of appeals. Arthur D. Hellman, "Caseload, Conflicts, and Decisional Capacity," in *Judicature*, 67 (1983), is a well-informed analysis of the Court's case-load issues. Philip Kurland, "Jurisdiction of the United States Supreme Court: Time for a Change?" in *Cornell Law Review*, 59 (1974), discusses reform proposals. Nathan Lewin, "A Response to Goldberg and Bickel," in *New Republic*, 3 March 1973, offers a former clerk's support for the current power of Court over review.

Doris Marie Provine, *Case Selection in the United States Supreme Court* (1980), is the only book-length treatment of the subject; and "Deciding What to Decide: How the Supreme Court Sets Its Agenda," in *Judicature*, 64 (1981), briefly describes criteria the justices use in granting and denying review. Robert L. Stern and Eugene Gressman, *Supreme Court Practice*, 5th ed. (1978), is a "how-to" for lawyers, full of information on the nuts and bolts of applying for review. John Paul Stevens, "Some Thoughts on Judicial Restraint," in *Judicature*, 66 (1982), gives the justice's view that case-selection discretion should be exercised with restraint. William Howard Taft, "The Jurisdiction of the Supreme Court Under the Act of February 13, 1925," in *Yale Law Journal*, 35 (1925), discusses the certiorari power from the perspective of the chief justice who drafted the legislation. S. Sidney Ulmer, "Selecting Cases for Supreme Court Review: An Underdog Model," in *American Political Science Review*, 72 (1978), stresses the relationship between judicial attitudes toward litigants and selection behavior; and "Conflict with Supreme Court Precedent and the Granting of Plenary Review," in *Journal of Politics*, 45 (1983), analyzes the significance of different outcomes below to the review decision.

[*See also* FEDERAL COURT SYSTEM; JUDICIAL ADMINISTRATION; JUDICIAL REVIEW; JURISDICTION; STATE COURT SYSTEMS; *and* SUPREME COURT OF THE UNITED STATES.]

COMPLIANCE AND IMPACT

Bradley C. Canon

THE term *compliance* refers to whether people behave in a manner required by a judicial decision. In its most narrow meaning, compliance focuses on whether a court's specific order in a particular case is carried out—that is, did the lower-court judge to whom the case was returned issue the appropriate ruling and did the losing party change its conduct, pay damages, or do whatever else the court required it to do?

The real importance of many appellate court decisions lies not with the fate of the parties involved but with the fate of the policies announced in the decisions. *Miranda* v. *Arizona* (1966), for example, held that the police had to inform a suspect undergoing custodial interrogation that he had the right to remain silent, that anything said could be used in court, that he could have an attorney present during questioning, and that an attorney would be provided free of charge if the suspect could not afford one. The defendant in the case, Ernesto Miranda, was soon reconvicted without the use of the now inadmissible confession; his ultimate fate would have differed little if he had lost the case in the Supreme Court. As a policy statement, however, *Miranda* was directed at the behavior of all police departments throughout the United States, and in a general sense, compliance with the decision is measured by the degree to which the departments inform suspects of their rights and honor the exercise of them. In practice, the measurement of aggregate compliance is often not easily accomplished. In fact, compliance is not always easily measured even theoretically because most appellate court decisions are not as precise about behavioral expectations as *Miranda*. Nonetheless, in many instances researchers can gather sufficient information to develop some generalizations about how much compliance a decision receives. Not all judicial decisions involve compliance in the broad sense. Decisions in which a court upholds the policy or inaction complained about or otherwise takes a permissive attitude about the behavior in issue do not normally present any opportunity for noncompliance.

"Impact" is a much broader concept than "compliance." When we focus on impact we are asking: How has the judicial decision affected society? What would be different if the decision had not occurred? Compliance, of course, is a factor in determining impact. If the police did not comply with *Miranda*, the decision would obviously have little impact on society. But it does not follow that compliance produces a significant impact. If police departments complied with *Miranda* but suspects did not exercise their rights and continued to confess at the same rate they did prior to *Miranda*, the decision would have little real impact on society. Of course, if the rate of confessions declined and thus the number of unsolved crimes increased, *Miranda* would have an important impact on society.

Judicial decisions that do not involve compliance also can have an impact on society. Judicial approval of a practice may encourage others to follow it. A prime example is *Roe* v. *Wade* (1973), in which the Supreme Court upheld a woman's right to obtain an abortion during the first six months of pregnancy but certainly did not require a woman to have one. Abortions increased threefold in the decade following the decision. Impact can also occur in areas of tort law (such as product liability and medical malpractice), where compliance in the broad sense is not usually a relevant concept. Here single cases are not so dramatic as *Roe*, but changes in judicial doctrine over time can induce changes in product safety, physicians' practices, insurance rates, and the like.

There are varying dimensions to the concept

795

of impact. Some decisions may have more of a symbolic effect on society than an effect on actual behavior. *School District of Abington Township* v. *Schempp* (1963), forbidding oral prayers and Bible-reading in the public schools, emotionally aroused many segments of the population but had only a minor effect on day-to-day behavior. Judicial decisions may have an indirect impact. *Miranda, Roe,* and *Schempp* have all become political issues and may have affected the outcomes of presidential and congressional elections.

In considering compliance and impact, this essay will focus on four groups or populations of people: the interpreting, implementing, consumer, and secondary populations. The interpreting population is largely composed of lower-court judges who must decide what a higher-court decision means and apply it in subsequent cases. Through their interpretations, lower-court judges can have a major influence on the scope and meaning of higher-court decisions (at least until the higher court gives more guidance—if it ever does). The implementing population consists of those persons who perform the enforcement or service functions in society, such as police officers, prosecutors, public school personnel, welfare workers, and the like. The behavior of such persons is often regulated by judicial decisions, so compliance with such decisions and the impact of them are affected by the way the implementing population actually behaves. The consumer population is composed of people (usually in their individual capacities) who receive the benefits or suffer the disabilities that result from a judicial decision. Consumers will sometimes fail to take advantage of a beneficial court decision or even find ways to avoid its disadvantages; thus, their behavior can limit considerably the impact of a court decision. The secondary population is a residual group. It consists of all persons not in the interpreting, implementing, or consumer population. The secondary population is not directly affected by a judicial decision. However, persons in this population can influence a decision's impact through their political reactions to it.

The foregoing classification of populations is functional. Particular individuals can be members of different populations for different decisions. For instance, a teacher may have to implement the school-prayer decision, be a consumer of a decision regulating the level of public school funding, and be in the secondary population for *Miranda.* The sections below will discuss each population in turn. Much of the discussion will focus on reactions to United States Supreme Court decisions, though similar considerations apply to reactions to decisions by state and lower federal courts as well.

THE INTERPRETING POPULATION

The interpreting population consists largely of lower-court judges. (For the Supreme Court, all other courts are lower.) While there are a number of factors that induce judges to render compliant interpretations of higher-court decisions, countervailing pressures on judges not to do so often exist. And when a Supreme Court decision seems to lack clarity or when its applicability to a given situation is uncertain, lower-court judges have considerable interpretive freedom. This section will first examine those factors likely to produce lower-court compliance and then those likely to make compliance more problematic.

A major factor inducing judges to render a conscientious interpretation of Supreme Court decisions is professionalism. Judges are presumably selected for their outstanding competence in the law. If a judge were to write an opinion that patently misinterpreted a higher court's decision, it would undermine his or her reputation with other judges and with the bar. This is especially true for published opinions, wherein judges are expected to demonstrate professional craftsmanship by fashioning an honest and reasoned interpretation of a higher-court decision. Another indication of a judge's professionalism is the relative frequency with which his decisions are reversed on appeal. While all judges suffer reversal on occasion, frequent reversal is usually seen by the bench and bar as a sign that the judge cannot or will not meet professional standards. Not only will such a perception injure a judge's status, but it can also preclude career advancement. One of the most telling criticisms of G. Harrold Carswell, whom President Richard Nixon nominated to a vacant Supreme Court seat in 1970, was the extremely high reversal rate Carswell had as a federal district judge in Florida.

Another factor is a judge's sense of duty. All

judges take an oath to support the Constitution. It is now universally acknowledged that responsibility for interpretation of this document rests with the Supreme Court. And, by definition, the Court is the final interpreter of federal statutes. Thus, judges are bound by their oath of office to abide by Supreme Court decisions. This sense of duty can be a powerful reinforcement for a judge in formulating an interpretation that goes against social or political pressures—or even against his own better judgment. We enhance this sense of legal obligation and protect judges against undue pressures by significantly restricting modes of contact with them by litigants in pending cases and by according them clear physical and verbal symbols of deference.

An additional reason for lower-court adherence to Supreme Court decisions is that failure to abide by them will lead to a breakdown of the judicial system. Since judges are part of that system, its breakdown would adversely affect their own status and authority. Judges who defy or evade their superiors' decisions are inviting similar treatment from those subject to their own rulings. Moreover, overt defiance or misinterpretation affects the overall legitimacy of judicial authority. If the special competence of judges to interpret the law is not accepted by the judges themselves, lay persons can be expected to behave accordingly.

While the above factors constrain lower-court judges' freedom of interpretations, their effect is not compulsory or absolute. Unlike corporate subordinates, lower-court judges who do not follow orders very well cannot be fired by their judicial superiors. Most judges are elected or appointed for a set term and can usually be removed only through the ponderous process of impeachment. In the federal judicial system the removal of a judge by impeachment has occurred only four times, the last in 1936. Moreover, impeachment or other forms of removal are reserved for corruption or gross neglect of duty, not for refusing to follow Supreme Court decisions. Of course, the Supreme Court can reverse a lower court's interpretation if the losing party appeals. If the lower court remains stubborn, the Court can enforce its will through a writ of mandamus (a directive to the lower court carrying a contempt penalty for noncompliance). The Court occasionally threatens lower-court judges with this writ.

Quite often there is no appeal from a trial judge's interpretation. Losing parties often lack the resources to appeal. Even when they do have the resources, their appeals may not be heard. The Supreme Court and the majority of state high courts can largely pick and choose what cases they wish to review. About four thousand losing parties ask the Supreme Court to consider their cases each year; the Court does so for less than three hundred of them. In the remaining cases the lower-court rulings, many of which have interpreted Supreme Court decisions, become final. Sometimes the situation producing the legal dispute becomes moot before an appeal can be completed; thus, the lower court's interpretation becomes the effective one. For example, a planned march by the American Nazi party through the heavily Jewish town of Skokie, Illinois, in 1977, which seemed to be protected by prevailing Supreme Court decisions on freedom of speech, was effectively thwarted by lower-court interpretations.

It should be emphasized that most of the time judges make a conscientious effort to interpret Supreme Court decisions in a reasonable manner. But judges are, after all, political actors, and they can have strong views on decisions relating to controversial issues. When a lower-court judge will not accept a Supreme Court policy, he has three basic options: defiance, avoidance, or an extremely narrow interpretation.

Defiance occurs when the judge refuses to acknowledge the legitimacy of the decision. Because such behavior is highly unprofessional, it is rare. Nonetheless, when the judge feels strongly enough about an issue or when external pressures on him are great enough, defiance can occur. For example, in the decade following the Supreme Court's 1954 *Brown* v. *Board of Education* decision, which announced that racial segregation was unconstitutional, some judges in southern states ruled that the Court had no authority to make such a decision and declared *Brown* null and void.

When defiance is unseemly, judges can resort to avoidance tactics. One form of avoidance is for the lower court to dispose of a case on procedural issues, such as finding that the plaintiff lacks standing or that he is seeking the wrong remedy. In this way the court can avoid consideration of the Supreme Court decision it dislikes. Another avoidance tactic open to state courts is to settle the case on an issue of state law. These and other tactics can delay for years the necessity of having to interpret disagreeable higher-court decisions. Beyond that, a lower court may simply drag its feet. In the early 1960s, federal judges in Mississippi often waited months or even years before granting motions requiring local voting registrars to produce data or documents in suits relating to the right of blacks to vote.

When a lower court cannot or will not defy or avoid a decision, the court can try to limit severely the decision's scope by interpreting it quite narrowly. This is done by citing factual differences between the higher-court decision and the case at hand. For example, a federal judge in South Carolina once refused to desegregate city buses, by interpreting *Brown* as applying only to schools and not to other public facilities. It must be emphasized that limiting or distinguishing a higher-court decision is not always a sign of lower-court hostility. Lawyers arguing before a court cite many precedents that they think helpful to their client's case, and a judge cannot ordinarily accept all of them as controlling. It is only when a precedent's applicability seems rather obvious and the facts used to distinguish it seem rather unimportant that hostility to giving the decision a reasonable interpretation can be inferred.

Most lower-court interpretations do not involve defiance, avoidance, or a severely limited interpretation. Rather, the interpretive freedom that lower courts have exists because the meaning of many Supreme Court decisions is not completely clear or because a given decision does not address the particular situation before the lower court. To the extent that a Supreme Court opinion is ambiguous, vague, or poorly articulated, it is more likely to produce dissimilar lower-court interpretations.

Judicial decisions may lack clarity for a variety of reasons. Some decisions are ambiguous because the issue is complex or the subject matter is difficult to resolve in a judicial opinion. Decisions regarding obscenity illustrate one area in which precision is difficult. Guiding phrases used by the Supreme Court such as "patently offensive" or "without serious redeeming literary value" necessarily leave room for subjective interpretation by judges.

Sometimes Supreme Court decisions are unclear because the Court is sharply divided in its reasoning. This can result either in a single majority opinion that has to accommodate the divergent views of several justices or in several opinions none of which has majority support. The Court's initial busing decision in *Swann* v. *Charlotte-Mecklenburg Board of Education* (1971), although unanimous, was rather confusing. One lower-court judge said that it had "a lot of conflicting language. It's almost as if there were two sets of views laid side by side." Occasionally the justices themselves openly disagree on what one of their opinions means. (Cases centering on free speech at shopping centers provide a good example. In the 1976 case of *Hudgens* v. *National Labor Relations Board,* the justices devoted considerable argument to the meaning of a 1972 case, *Lloyd Corp.* v. *Tanner.*). In such circumstances, it can hardly be expected that lower-court judges will all follow a common interpretation.

Multiple opinions also tend to cloud the intentions of the Supreme Court. Around 1970 there began to appear a greater number of concurring and dissenting opinions per case. Sometimes no single opinion can command a majority of the Court. This is especially true for important decisions. For example, in *New York Times Co.* v. *United States* (1971), involving the government's attempt to prohibit publication of the so-called Pentagon Papers (a classified history of American involvement in the Vietnam War), all nine justices wrote separate opinions, none of which received the support of more than two other justices. Moreover, Supreme Court opinions that have majority support at the time they are announced can lose that support as the justices change. The history of the exclusionary rule (which prohibits the introduction of illegally seized evidence in criminal trials) illustrates this. Established as a constitutional principle in 1961 in *Mapp* v. *Ohio,* in the 1970s and 1980s the rule steadily lost favor with the Court's conservative justices, who developed exception after exception to it. In time, lower courts began developing their own exceptions to the rule.

It should be remembered that Supreme Court decisions do not stand alone. Lower-court judges must interpret each decision alongside other, related decisions that may have differing emphases or even appear mutually inconsistent. Over time, the Court may fail to provide continuing guidance about the scope and importance of goals inherent in some of its decisions. Under such circumstances, lower-court interpretations are likely to vary considerably.

When there is considerable uncertainty about how a decision is to be interpreted, lower-court judges are influenced by two types of factors (in addition to the lawyer's arguments or their own research on the issue). One set of factors involves external pressures on judges; the other involves the judges' internal attitudes and beliefs.

External influences are generally communicated indirectly and often unintentionally. Often they result from little more than the fact that judges, like other political actors, can be affected by such things as public opinion, local customs, or the attitudes of their own peer group. Because many state judges are elected, they especially must consider negative public reaction to interpreting decisions like *Mapp* or *Miranda* in such a way that a seemingly guilty defendant goes free. On occasion, this pressure can be quite overt. The Law and Order Campaign Committee, which sprang up in California in the 1970s, was successful in defeating several trial judges who were believed to be "soft on crime." Several studies have shown that state courts generally interpret Supreme Court decisions concerning defendants' rights more narrowly than do federal courts (although a few state supreme courts, such as California's and Michigan's, appear to be quite liberal in this regard). This is one of the main reasons why attorneys for unpopular clients usually choose to pursue their cases in the federal courts.

In addition to political pressures, judges receive signals from social or other nonpolitical sources. Most judges have longstanding ties with their communities; even federal judges generally serve in the states in which they were born and educated. Interaction with neighbors and associates or exposure to the local media keeps them aware of community sentiment on various issues. These pressures were felt most strongly by southern judges called upon to implement desegregation following *Brown* and have been described as follows:

> The district judge is very much a part of the life of the South. He must eventually leave his chambers and when he does he attends a Rotary lunch or stops off at the club to drink with men outraged by what they consider "judicial tyranny." A judge who makes rulings adverse to segregation is not so likely to be honored by testimonial dinners, or to read flattering editorials in the local press, or to partake of the fellowship at the club. He will no longer be invited to certain homes; former friends will avoid him when they meet on the street.
>
> (Peltason, 9)

Not surprisingly, most southern federal judges rendered decisions that only minimally desegregated schools or other community institutions. Of course, not all judges succumb to such pressures. Some southern judges, although they received much abuse, faithfully interpreted *Brown* and subsequent Supreme Court desegregation decisions. Studies indicate that in general the lower a judge is in the judicial hierarchy, the more likely it is that the influence of community pressures will be operative.

In addition to being subjected to external pressures, a lower-court judge can be influenced by his own attitudes on legal or political issues. Judges are usually intellectually active persons who have strong views on many questions of current importance. Judges who hold liberal political viewpoints may interpret Supreme Court decisions relating to such matters as workmen's compensation, labor-union rights, or product liability differently from judges with conservative values. Occasionally a judge's partisan affiliation can be significant. It is not unusual for Republican and Democratic judges to differ in their respective applications of a Supreme Court legislative-apportionment ruling, depending upon which party will benefit from which interpretation.

Lower courts may also have policy preferences based upon their own prior decisions. This is especially true when the Supreme Court makes a decision that changes the law significantly. In such an event, a lower court with an intellectual and psychological commitment to its own point of view will often minimize its differences with the High Court by interpreting a decision narrowly.

THE IMPLEMENTING POPULATION

In most cases implementation of a judicial decision is a group activity conducted by government bureaucracies, ranging from major federal departments to local school systems. In some situations, private organizations such as hospitals can be part of the implementing population. Unlike lower courts, the implementing population does not exist primarily to apply judicial decisions. Rather, the purpose of most implementing organizations is to carry out legislative or executive policies or to pursue a commercial or charitable goal. Additionally, such organizations often serve particular constituencies (for example, the Department of Education is oriented toward school administrators and teachers) and try to accommodate their needs. Because of this multiplicity of pressures, implementing organizations may give only secondary attention—or none at all—to carrying out a judicial decision. They may even resist implementing the decision if doing so interferes with their primary goals or upsets their constituencies.

It is not always easy for courts to overcome inattention or resistance on the part of implementing agencies. Judges seldom know what is happening on a day-to-day basis in places such as schools, police stations, or welfare agencies, especially if no one files a lawsuit. Even if a suit is filed, it is often not clear whether the incident complained of is an isolated one or is part of a broader pattern. While courts can usually ensure compliance in the complainant's case, many people are not able or willing to go to court to have an agency's decision reviewed. Some agencies, such as the Internal Revenue Service (IRS) or the Social Security Administration, openly acknowledge that while they will obey specific court orders in litigated cases, they will not apply the policies inherent in those orders to similar situations.

Initially, implementing agencies must interpret Supreme Court decisions. Of course, agency interpretations are not authoritative and, unlike lower-court decisions, do not have the status of law; but they are operative within the agency until overturned by a court, and sometimes they can go unchallenged for years. As with lower-court judges, agencies will have some leeway in interpreting decisions in which the language is not entirely clear or in which the general policy does not give specific guidance to the problems facing the agency. Unlike lower-court judges, however, agency personnel are more likely to ignore or grossly misinterpret a judicial

decision. Agency policymakers are often not lawyers, are not subject to the constraints of professionalism, and may have more difficulty understanding what the court is saying. Indeed, most agency employees never see the court decision they are expected to implement. Few police officers, for instance, have actually read *Mapp* or *Miranda;* research shows that they learn about such decisions through media reports, internal departmental memoranda, training sessions, or conversations with other officers. Information will often become distorted as it goes through three or four steps from Supreme Court opinion to policemen, schoolteachers, or welfare workers.

In general, agencies that are hostile to, or unenthusiastic about, implementing a Court decision are likely, through choice or selective perception in the communication process, to interpret it narrowly. For example, a study of compliance with *Schempp* in five rural communities noted that the school superintendents interpreted the decision to mean that prayers were allowed in schools so long as they were not formally required by the school board. In the decade following *Schempp,* no one challenged this narrow reading of the case, and so the behavior in all five communities followed the superintendents' interpretation rather than what the Supreme Court actually said.

When an agency is expected to implement a court decision, it must decide how it will adjust its behavior. Usually the adjustment process is at least mildly painful because most decisions needing implementation require an agency to bring to an end some practice or policy or to begin some practice or policy. The adjustment process is largely influenced by four factors: (1) the degree to which the judicial decision conflicts with agency policies or goals, (2) the need of the agency to conserve its resources to carry out its primary mission, (3) the strength of external pressures on the agency to comply or resist implementation, and (4) the likelihood and severity of sanctions against the agency for noncompliance or minimal compliance.

Most commonly, adjustment is problematic for an agency because the decision is seen to conflict with the agency's goals. Police departments, for instance, feel that decisions such as *Mapp* and *Miranda* make it more difficult for them to fulfill their primary function of solving crimes and gathering sufficient evidence to ensure convictions. One study of police behavior found that most officers believe

> the impact of the exclusionary rule . . . has not been to guarantee greater protection of the freedom of "decent citizens" from unreasonable police zeal, but rather to complicate unnecessarily the task of detecting and apprehending criminals. From the pragmatic perspective of the police, the right to conduct exploratory investigations and searches ought largely to be a matter of police-supervisory discretion. (Skolnick, 227)

The natural inclination of agencies in this situation is to adjust their behavior in such a manner that the decision intrudes only minimally on accomplishing their goals. Thus, the police may ignore the exclusionary rule or sometimes "reconstruct" the sequence of events in such a way that it appears they obtained the evidence legally. Alternatively, they may permit their compliance to become perfunctory. Before interrogating a suspect, a detective may read him his *Miranda* rights in a low monotone as if to say, "This is a little legal ritual we have to go through, but don't worry if you don't understand it because it's not very important anyway." Similarly, the IRS, whose primary function is collecting revenue for the government, is likely to make only minimal adjustments to court decisions that broadly define exemptions or "loopholes" in the tax laws.

Implementing some decisions will impose a greater strain on agency resources than will implementing others. *Miranda,* for instance, although not very popular with most police departments, imposed few costs on police time or money. Compliance with *Mapp,* by contrast, required considerable police retraining in the law of search and seizure as well as the investment of time in processing search-warrant requests. Various studies of compliance with the two decisions show that police compliance with *Miranda* is greater than with *Mapp.* Likewise, the cost of busing pupils across town or building new schools to achieve desegregation may be so great that it generates resistance on the part of school system officials who believe the funds could be better spent on direct educational needs. It should be noted, however, that some-

times the costs required to implement a judicial decision can be beneficial to an agency. Many police departments used *Mapp* and *Miranda* as a justification for requesting increased appropriations from city councils—or as an explanation for their failure to keep the crime rate down. State prison systems, while perhaps resentful of judicial interference from federal court decisions mandating better conditions for prisoners, have found a silver lining in such decisions when states scrambled to increase funding for prisons or even build new penitentiaries.

Implementing agencies do not exist in a political or social vacuum. When a Supreme Court decision is unpopular or is likely to adversely affect other segments of society, there may be considerable pressure on an agency to resist or minimize implementation. This is especially true for political agencies whose policymakers are subject to reelection. Southern school boards that showed any inclination to accommodate desegregation in the years following *Brown* were usually voted out of office. For similar reasons, school boards in many areas of the country shied away from discontinuing prayers following *Schempp.* While nonelective agencies are less subject to direct political pressure, they can be the object of orders or requests from executive officials such as the president, cabinet officers, governors, or others who are in politically sensitive positions. Moreover, agency personnel are often the object of community social pressures similar to those on lower-court judges described above. Some agencies, however, are rather insulated from political or social pressures, especially when they are staffed by professionals who are often mobile and not very attached to local values (for example, universities or military bases). They may respond more rapidly to unpopular court decisions—or less rapidly to ones that are locally popular. Many private implementing agencies can be even more protected from such pressures. Hospitals, for example, have been found to develop their abortion policy largely according to religious or commercial motivations, not community pressures.

A final factor influencing the way an agency adjusts to a judicial decision is the severity of sanctions that will result from noncompliance and the likelihood that such sanctions will be imposed. In some situations, no direct sanctions are imposed on an agency for failure to follow a court decision. For example, the police receive no direct punishment for conducting an illegal search. What usually happens is simply that the charges against the defendant are dropped. When officers are just concerned with harassing "undesirable" elements in the community, such as prostitutes or gamblers, conviction often means little to the police anyway. Even in situations in which the police want a conviction, if violating *Mapp* or *Miranda* appears to be the only way to produce the necessary evidence, the police, who have nothing to lose, will sometimes do it and take their chances. Compliance is more likely to occur when sanctions can be imposed directly on the agency or its personnel, but even here faithful implementation is not always easy to obtain. Judges cannot ordinarily fire recalcitrant or inattentive agency officials. They can, of course, enjoin administrators and impose fines or jail sentences if the injunction is violated. But courts are reluctant to impose contempt sentences except for clear violations, so agencies can often engage in halfhearted implementation without punishment. Another agency tactic is to delegate the adjustment process to a lower level in the administrative hierarchy. This reduces the visibility of noncompliance and makes it less likely that those evading the decision will receive sanctions. It is far more likely that a court would hear about and cite a school superintendent for contempt for maintaining prayers in a school system than that the court would hear about or be willing to consider jailing a teacher for saying prayers in the classroom.

Supreme Court decisions are more likely to be implemented meaningfully when the judiciary can invoke the help of another body in imposing sanctions on a reluctant agency. This is not the normal situation, but it can be done when the law authorizes it. The most common sanction is withholding money from the implementing agency. Funding is the lifeblood of most administrative agencies, and they will make many adjustments to ensure the flow of funds. Nowhere is this better illustrated than in school desegregation. In the decade between 1954 and 1964, only minuscule progress was made in integrating schools below the Mason-Dixon line. In 1964, Congress passed Title VI of the Civil Rights Act, which authorized the Department of Health, Education, and Welfare to withhold federal funds from any school system that had not adopted an acceptable desegregation plan. By the early 1970s most school systems in the South were well integrated.

Since the 1970s, some federal judges have responded to lawsuits about seemingly unconstitutional conditions in prisons or mental hospitals by issuing extremely specific orders concerning new policies in these institutions (such as square feet of living space per inmate and calories per meal). Similarly, federal judges have sometimes issued very specific desegregation plans in metropolitan areas. When such rulings are made, the judge himself becomes, for all practical purposes, an administrator. This is an effective way to secure compliance in a particular case. However, the use of such a tactic appears to be limited to decisions concerning institutions whose clientele is physically present. Moreover, many judges feel that they lack the time, expertise, or inclination to engage in such day-to-day administration.

THE CONSUMER POPULATION

Persons who are affected by judicial decisions —those who benefit from them or suffer disadvantages because of them—constitute the consumer population. The consumer population differs from the implementing population in that there is no expectation that consumers will apply a judicial decision to others. Members of the consumer population are affected in their individual capacities and not as members of government agencies. For example, police officers may be as disadvantaged by *Miranda* as suspects are advantaged by it, but the officers are affected as members of a government agency while suspects are private beneficiaries (consumers) of the decision.

On occasion, the benefits of a judicial decision accrue to the consumer population automatically. No behavior is necessary; all necessary adjustments are performed by the implementing population. Automatic consumption occurs when a Supreme Court decision requires a government agency to implement new due process or equal protection policies. This has happened frequently as Court decisions have held, for example, that indigent felony defendants must be furnished a lawyer at their trial (*Gideon* v. *Wainwright,* 1963), that public school students cannot be expelled or suspended without a hearing (*Goss* v. *Lopez,* 1975), and that widowers are entitled to the benefits of their wives' social security contributions (*Weinberger* v. *Wiesenfeld,* 1975). An advantage can also come automatically when a decision results in benefits such as lower prices, as when the Supreme Court held that state minimum-liquor-pricing laws violated federal antitrust laws (*California Retail Liquor Dealers* v. *Midcal Aluminum,* 1980). When a court decision affects the consumer population automatically, its impact is usually reasonably predictable.

More often, however, judicial decisions give persons in the consumer population an option or choice that they previously did not have. In this situation the actual impact of the decision is largely determined by consumers' decisions to exercise the new option. For many policies, potential consumers (those who fail to make the choice) will be more numerous than the actual consumers (those who do select the new option). This is particularly true when the decision addresses behavior that few persons normally engage in. Supreme Court decisions expanding the meaning of freedom of speech and press are examples. Most people do not organize street parades or take a soapbox down to the city park even though the Court's jurisprudence has enhanced their right to do so. Even when court decisions concern more personal matters, large numbers of potential consumers will not become actual consumers: many pregnant women decide to have babies even though they could choose abortion, and many adults never see X-rated movies despite their availability.

Potential consumers do not become actual consumers for a variety of reasons. Some may reject the choice because they consider the option immoral or harmful rather than beneficial. Others may not be opposed to the Court's decision but have no interest in taking personal advantage of it. Habit, inertia, or lack of information may lead people to continue their old ways. For example, in 1977 the Supreme Court overturned an ancient and rigid professional rule when it held that lawyers had a First Amendment right to advertise their services (*Bates* v. *State Bar of Arizona*), but a look at a local newspaper or telephone directory will show that only a comparative handful of lawyers actually do so. Other members of the consumer population may lack the resources to make the new choice; for example, without emotional support from her family, a woman may choose not to have an abortion.

Even a decision that offers important advantages to persons in crucial situations may have a small actual consumer population compared to its potential one. Several studies of suspects' reactions to *Miranda* warnings illustrate this. The object of *Miranda,* according to the Court, was to make the Fifth Amendment guarantee against compulsory self-incrimination more meaningful by giving a suspect sufficient information and flexibility of options to make rational decisions about his own best interest in the interrogation situation. It was also clear that the Court believed that in general the most rational course for a suspect to pursue was to remain silent, at least until he could consult with a lawyer. However, in one city studied, the proportion of incriminating statements by suspects actually increased following *Miranda* and in two others the decline was not very significant. In all cities studied, a substantial proportion of suspects questioned—from 40 percent to 50 percent—gave incriminating statements to the police despite the *Miranda* warnings. Researchers have noted several reasons for the suspects' failure to exercise their *Miranda* options. Some suspects simply did not understand the nature of their rights. Others were cynical and did not believe that they really had these rights or believed that the exercise of such rights was tantamount of an admission of guilt. Many realized what their rights were but decided that their best option was either to cooperate with the police or to try to talk their way out of the situation.

Persons in the consumer population often will take advantage of choices conferred by judicial decisions. Some suspects do remain silent or request an attorney after receipt of *Miranda* warnings. Adult bookstores or X-rated movies do attract customers (to say nothing of R-rated movies, most of which would have been banned as obscene prior to the Supreme Court's 1957 decision in *Roth* v. *United States,* which defined obscenity narrowly). As noted earlier, women's reactions to *Roe* perhaps best illustrate the actual impact a Supreme Court decision can have on the consumer population. Legal abortions climbed from around 500,000 in 1972 to over 1.5 million by 1980. As the Supreme Court never expected all women to choose abortion, these figures indicate that *Roe* had a monumental actual impact on those whom it was intended to affect. But it should be remembered that consumers' willingness to accept new choices offered by judicial decisions is governed by many factors and that the actual impact of many decisions is not as great as the potential impact.

Judicial decisions do not always confer benefits on members of the consumer population. Sometimes consumers are disadvantaged by a decision. This can occur when a court denies (or upholds a government agency when it denies) a choice or option that people had found useful (such as a type of income tax deduction) or requires people to do something they do not want to do (such as be bused to a school on the other side of town). It can also occur when a lawsuit in effect pits one group of consumers against another. Many common-law cases are of this nature. For example, in the 1960s many state supreme courts began changing one of the ancient maxims of property law, *Caveat emptor* ("Let the buyer beware"), to make builders of new homes liable to purchasers for defective or unsafe construction. Here one segment of consumers, families purchasing new homes, gained legal advantages at the expense of another segment, the home-construction industry. Likewise, antitrust cases usually pit large firms against smaller ones or against purchasers. Even when a government agency is involved in a case, it is sometimes not so much a part of the implementing population as it is a representative of a segment of the consumer population. An illustrative case is *Personnel Administrator of Massachusetts* v. *Feeney* (1979), in which the Supreme Court upheld a state law that gave preference to veterans for civil service positions. The law had been challenged as discriminatory by women's groups because so few women had been in the military service. It is also important to note that sometimes members of the consumer population who are similarly affected by a decision can feel quite differently about it. Children who were gratified by saying prayers in school would see *Schempp* as a disadvantageous Supreme Court decision, while those who did not want to say prayers would see it as advantageous.

Because people are reluctant to adjust voluntarily to a policy adverse to their interests, court decisions imposing disadvantages are often automatically imposed on the consumer population. Consumers have little opportunity to avoid certain decisions, such as those requiring local officials to assess property at full market value or permitting utility companies to raise their rates. When a disadvantageous judicial decision is not automatically imposed, persons in the consumer population can choose to accept or reject it, in accordance with their assessment of the situation. At times people will accept the legitimacy of a decision that they perceive as personally disadvantageous, because they believe that it is fair or that it serves the public interest. Many people, perhaps slowly and subconsciously, change their attitudes in the face of an unequivocal judicial mandate, as is manifested by widespread white acceptance of racial equality in the South in the years since *Brown*. But people can also accept a disadvantageous court decision without necessarily believing in its legitimacy. They accept it in the sense that they decide on a utilitarian basis that living with the policy and adjusting their behavior accordingly is better than other alternatives. Sometimes the opposite is true; members of the consumer population will decide not to accept a decision. Here they have essentially two choices: they can refuse to adjust their behavior and thus defy the court, or they can adjust their behavior so as to avoid the impact of the court decision without being defiant.

Deliberate defiance is infrequent but not unknown. It can involve violence in the form of individual resistance to a criminal conviction or a civil decision; occasionally it comes in the form of communal resistance to an unpopular court decision, such as a busing order. Generally, violence is unsuccessful in thwarting a judicial decision, although community violence may cause lower courts and implementing agencies to act gingerly in carrying it or similar decisions out. On a few occasions defiance will take the form of deliberately suffering the consequences. This is evident in the wake of *Branzburg* v. *Hayes* (1972), in which the Supreme Court held that journalists had no right under the First Amendment to refuse to answer questions about the sources of their news stories put to them in a trial court or a grand jury. Journalists saw this decision as adverse to their interests because it might well make sources who wish anonymity unwilling to reveal sensitive facts to reporters. Since *Branzburg*, a few journalists have served jail terms for contempt of court rather than reveal their news sources.

Often consumers can adjust their behavior to evade the full force of a disadvantageous decision. On occasion, evasion may be easy as for example praying silently in schools. Usually, however, there are costs to evasion. Cancer patients who wished laetrile treatment had to travel to Mexico to obtain it after the Supreme Court upheld the Food and Drug Administration's ban on the use of the substance in the United States. Some did, but many were prevented from doing so by the expense or inconvenience.

Forbidding prayers in schools and laetrile treatments are examples of prohibitive judicial decisions. Most commonly judicial decisions imposing disadvantages on members of the consumer population are prohibitive; their message is "thou shalt not." However, in making desegregation decisions, courts have found it necessary to impose "thou shalt" commands on elements of the consumer population. Busing students to schools some miles away rather than having them attend the nearest one is a prime example. Many white parents and pupils perceive, in addition to the inconvenience, a disadvantage in attending inner-city schools, which many think are intellectually and physically inferior to those in their own neighborhoods. Additionally many whites want to avoid schools in which blacks constitute a majority or a large minority. Avoiding busing is possible, although often expensive and inconvenient. Parents can enroll their children in private schools, or they can move to a suburb or another county. Even though these choices can involve tuition costs, higher mortgage payments, and longer commuting time to and from work, many white parents have felt strongly enough about busing to undergo such costs and inconvenience. There is considerable dispute among social scientists as to how much "white flight" from metropolitan public schools is motivated by opposition to busing, but there is little doubt that at least some of it is. Not unexpectedly, however, researchers have found that the single most important factor in explaining parents' white-flight decisions is not the intensity of their opposition to desegregation but their ability to afford the avoidance options.

THE SECONDARY POPULATION

The secondary population consists of everyone who is not a member of the interpreting, implementing, or consumer population. For most judicial decisions, there are numerous persons who are not affected directly. Often these people remain uninterested and perhaps unaware of the policy. Some, however, do react to judicial policies that do not directly concern them: many members of the clergy are vitally interested in the abortion decision, and many people without children in school have strong views about prayer in the public schools.

Even though the secondary population does not interpret, implement, or consume a judicial decision, it can be an important factor in determining the case's ultimate impact. Public opinion can have a considerable influence on the way in which a Supreme Court decision is treated by those populations directly involved with it. In addition, mobilized public opinion can be a factor that alters the very nature of the judicial policy. This can happen when the Supreme Court, having decided that a policy cannot succeed because of public opposition, modifies or abandons it. (Conversely, if a policy is highly popular with the public, the Court may be encouraged to expand it.) It can also happen when public opinion impels legislatures or executive agencies to pass laws or take other steps that constrain or reinforce a judicial policy.

The secondary population's interest in a decision is partly affected by the coverage the news media give that decision. If the media ignore a decision because it had little inherent drama or downplay it because of competing newsworthy events, public awareness and concern can be low. Conversely, when a decision or its implications are given considerable attention, awareness and concern will be great. The manner in which the media cover follow-up events (such as threats of violence during the implementation of a desegregation order) may further affect the nature of, and the ability to mobilize, public sentiment. While the wire services and television networks usually describe Supreme Court decisions reasonably accurately, albeit very simply, more specialized media may distort, exaggerate, or simplify their accounts of the judicial policy.

As a consequence of their concern, some persons in the secondary population will form or join organizations that seek to overturn or reinforce a judicial decision. Civil liberties, right-to-life, and environmental groups are illustrative. Few members of the American Civil Liberties Union are threatened individually with a violation of their civil liberties, many right-to-life advocates will never be personally involved in a woman's (or family's) abortion decision, and environmentalists are no more affected by air pollution than are nonenvironmentalists. Such organizations perform several functions. They may further mobilize public opinion through advertising, mass mailings, media events, or other forms of communication. They may try to get lower courts to expand or contract the interpretation of the decision by bringing litigation or supporting other litigants with amicus curiae briefs. They can direct arguments to, or bring public pressure to bear on, implementing agencies. In addition, such organizations can try to influence consumer decisions, often by informing advantaged persons (such as welfare recipients) of their rights under a court decision, giving others information about their choices (such as abortion counseling), or showing disadvantaged consumers how they might evade or resist a decision.

Perhaps the most important segment of the secondary population consists of legislators and high-level administrators who are in a position to (1) bring sufficient pressure on the court in which the decision originated to cause it to alter its stand, and/or (2) adopt their own laws or policies to modify, negate, or enhance the judicial decision's impact. This section will briefly examine congressional and presidential efforts to limit the impact of Supreme Court decisions. While there are some differences at the state level, basically similar processes of interaction exist between legislatures and governors and state high courts.

Congress can most easily modify or reverse a Supreme Court decision when the decision involves statutory interpretation. Many laws contain vague language or ambiguous implications, and the Supreme Court spends considerable time deciding what such laws mean. Nonetheless, Congress has final control over statutory meaning, and it can always change the Court's interpretation by spelling out its own intentions in clear and precise wording. When Congress has no general quarrel with the Court's interpretation of a law, it can pass legislation authorizing a particular exception to the interpretation. In the 1970s, it did this for interpretations of the Endangered Species Act and the National Environmental Policy Act, in order to save a nearly completed dam in Tennessee and to facilitate construction of the Alaska oil pipeline.

Congress does not modify or reverse most of the Court's statutory interpretations. Sometimes, in fact, Congress may deliberately adopt vague or ambiguous statutory language in order to avoid displeasing blocs of voters with conflicting viewpoints. Even when Congress is not passing the buck to the Court, the cumbersome nature of the legislative process often enables interest groups benefiting from the Court's ruling to prevent congressional action. Even when there is no great opposition in Congress to changing a low-profile statutory interpretation, efforts to do so will often get bogged down, wither, and die. Studies show that only about 4 percent of the Supreme Court's statutory interpretations in the period 1945–1975 were reversed or seriously modified by Congress. One writer concluded:

> Nearly all [successful reversals] . . . involved a return to a "common understanding" which had been disrupted by the Court's decision, and that nearly all enjoyed the unanimous support of the politically articulate groups affected by the Court's decision. The few exceptions . . . occurred either at the time of a major legislative reassessment in the area of the decision, or through the efforts of a political group powerful enough to maintain an intense, nationwide lobbying campaign.
>
> (Note, 1336)

The situation is different when the judicial policy involves constitutional instead of statutory interpretation. Congress ordinarily cannot reverse the Supreme Court on constitutional matters; it must find other ways to react. Sometimes Congress can pass legislation that minimizes the impact of undesired Court decisions. Following *Roe,* Congress passed laws to restrict federal funding for elective or therapeutic abortions. In reacting to busing decisions, Congress considered several proposals to withhold federal funds from school systems engaged in extensive busing. Still, the fiscal weapon is a limited one. Many of the Supreme Court's decisions regarded most negatively by Congress are civil liberties ones, which involve no appropriation of funds.

The most obvious way of circumventing a decision involving constitutional law is to pass a constitutional amendment changing it. It is equally obvious that changes in the Constitution are not easily accomplished. A constitutional amendment requires a two-thirds vote in each house of Congress and ratification by three-fourths (thirty-eight) of the states. Only four Supreme Court decisions in American history have been overruled by a constitutional amendment. However, the difficulty of securing an amendment has not discouraged proposals. Since the mid-1950s, Congress has considered amendments that would have overturned or seriously modified the Court's decisions in such areas as reapportionment of state legislatures, abortion, busing to achieve racial desegregation, and prayers in public schools. A couple of proposed amendments have been adopted by one house or the other, but despite repeated attempts and the unpopularity of some of the Court's decisions, no amendment in these areas has been submitted to the states.

Under Article III of the Constitution, Congress can withdraw the Court's jurisdiction to hear certain types of cases. Congress has used this drastic power only once—when it immunized certain Reconstruction policies from judicial review following the Civil War. Bills to prevent the Court from hearing cases in several areas (reapportionment, internal-security matters, busing, prayers in schools, and abortion) have been introduced in recent years, but none have passed Congress. Passage of such a bill would not negate the force of the Court's decision but would simply prevent the Court from making new decisions in that area. However, by seriously considering such a measure, Congress can "send a message" to the Court. Sometimes such messages are effective. The Court backed away from imposing rigid due process standards in some types of internal-security situations after a House-passed bill stripping the Court of jurisdiction in this area failed in the Senate by just one vote in 1958.

It should be noted that state legislatures have considerably less ability to limit the impact of a United States Supreme Court decision than they do one made by their own state's high court. During the 1950s and 1960s, southern legislatures adopted numerous laws and strategies designed to prevent desegregation of the schools, but their efforts did little more than delay the process as federal courts ultimately struck down the attempts. Similarly, many state laws designed to discourage women from having abortions (such as requiring consent by the husband or imposing a waiting period) have quickly been ruled unconstitutional. Like Congress, however, state legislatures can use the funding process to encourage or discourage implementation or consumption of a Supreme Court decision. Many legislatures have refused to fund abortions for women on welfare. Beyond that, state legisla-

tures are usually part of the process by which the United States Constitution is amended and thus can approve, or even help initiate, an amendment reversing or modifying a Supreme Court decision.

The president may have considerable interest in Supreme Court decisions that do not affect him or the executive branch directly. As a national leader and a politician, he may feel the necessity of reacting to a Court decision that generates public concern, as President Ronald Reagan did on school prayer and abortion. Through his leadership activities, he can often affect the direction and intensity of public opinion as well as help shape the course of congressional reaction. As chief executive, the president is ultimately in charge of all federal implementing agencies involved in a judicial decision. Although he may have little personal involvement with such agencies, his position is likely to influence the attitudes and behavior of agency heads. Indeed, the president may on occasion be called upon to enforce an unpopular court decision. Andrew Jackson once refused to do so with the remark that "John Marshall has made his decision, now let him enforce it." Even when a president does not defy a decision, his hostility to it may encourage others in defiance. President Dwight Eisenhower was not enthusiastic about *Brown,* and his unwillingness to condemn southern resistance in anything more than pro forma fashion probably encouraged both state and public efforts to block integration in Little Rock, Arkansas, in 1957. Eventually Eisenhower had to send in an army division to enforce the Court decision. Even more important in the long run is the president's power to appoint federal judges. By carefully choosing his appointees, especially to the Supreme Court, a president can do much to help modify or reverse judicial decisions he dislikes, as Franklin Roosevelt did in the post-1937 era and as Richard Nixon's appointees did in the 1970s in the criminal justice area.

CONCLUSION

Based largely on empirical studies about the aftermath of major Supreme Court cases, scholars have relied upon several theories to explain variations in compliance and, to a lesser extent, impact. Some of these theories have been touched upon above. For example, implementing organizations have a propensity to tailor their responses to court rulings so as to minimize disruption to their objectives and routines. This finding is consistent with a set of propositions known as organization theory. Likewise, it was noted that the content of court decisions will often become distorted as it is communicated to the interpreting, implementing, or consumer population. Communications theories generally posit that messages are often altered as they proceed from recipient to recipient. Members of the consumer population, it was noted, sometimes decide that evading a court ruling is less costly than complying. Here reliance on cost-benefit analysis, or utility theory, seems to be the best explanatory theory.

However, much remains to be learned about compliance with, and the impact of, judicial decisions. Empirical research into these phenomena began in the 1960s. Most of it focused on a small number of highly visible Supreme Court cases. Such research tells us much about patterns of compliance and impact in nationally controversial cases, but it does not illuminate or explain variation in compliance and impact more generally.

How rapidly scholars will investigate the effects of more-ordinary judicial decisions is uncertain. There is less empirical investigation being conducted in the 1980s than occurred two decades earlier. In part this is because the Supreme Court made many more controversial decisions in the era of Chief Justice Earl Warren than it did in the tenure of Warren Burger as chief justice. Undramatic rulings are less attractive to scholars than are those which pose the likelihood of major behavioral changes by members of the implementing or consumer populations. Nonetheless, scholars are continuing to carry out empirical investigations about compliance and impact, and the ability to explain these phenomena should increase with time.

CASES

Bates v. State Bar of Arizona, 433 U.S. 350 (1977)
Branzburg v. Hayes, 408 U.S. 665 (1972)
Brown v. Board of Education of Topeka, 347 U.S. 483 (1954)
California Retail Liquor Dealers v. Midcal Aluminum, 445 U.S. 97 (1980)
Gideon v. Wainwright, 372 U.S. 335 (1963)

Goss v. Lopez, 419 U.S. 565 (1975)
Hudgens v. National Labor Relations Board, 424 U.S. 507 (1976)
Lloyd Corp. v. Tanner, 407 U.S. 551 (1972)
Mapp v. Ohio, 367 U.S. 643 (1961)
Miranda v. Arizona, 384 U.S. 436 (1966)
New York Times Co. v. United States, 403 U.S. 713 (1971)
Personnel Administrator of Massachusetts v. Feeney, 442 U.S. 256 (1979)
Roe v. Wade, 410 U.S. 113 (1973)
Roth v. United States, 354 U.S. 476 (1957)
School District of Abington Township v. Schempp, 374 U.S. 203 (1963)
Swann v. Charlotte-Mecklenburg Board of Education, 402 U.S. 1 (1971)
Weinberger v. Wiesenfeld, 420 U.S. 636 (1975)

BIBLIOGRAPHY

Theodore Becker and Malcolm Feeley, eds., *The Impact of Supreme Court Decisions,* 2nd ed. (1973), contains reports from scholarly journals about research into the impact of various Supreme Court decisions. Bradley C. Canon, "Testing the Effectiveness of Civil Liberties Policies at the State and Federal Levels: The Case of the Exclusionary Rule," in *American Politics Quarterly,* 5 (1977), measures and offers explanations for different reactions in urban police departments to *Mapp v. Ohio* (1961). Everett F. Cataldo, Michael W. Giles, and Douglas S. Gatlin, *School Desegregation Policy* (1978), is a careful investigation into factors affecting parents' reactions to busing orders in seven Florida counties. Kenneth Dolbeare and Philip Hammond, *The School Prayer Decisions: From Court Policy to Local Practice* (1971), is a study of action and inaction in five rural Midwestern communities in the decade following *School District of Abington Township.* Charles A. Johnson and Bradley C. Canon, *Judicial Policies: Implementation and Impact* (1984), provides a comprehensive overview of research into the impact of judicial decisions on the four populations discussed here and of empirical support for the theories that explain variations in impacts. Samuel Krislov et al., *Compliance and the Law: A Multi-Disciplinary Approach* (1972), considers approaches to conceptualizing and testing compliance with laws or court decisions.

Neal Milner, *The Court and Local Law Enforcement* (1971), is a study of police officers' reactions to *Miranda* in four Wisconsin cities. William K. Muir, Jr., *Prayer in the Public Schools: Law and Attitude Change* (1967), focuses on how two city school systems implemented *Schempp* and how both official and private attitudes changed in the process. Note, "Congressional Reversal of Supreme Court Decisions, 1945–1957," in *Harvard Law Review,* 71 (1958), comments on both successful and unsuccessful attempts made in Congress to overturn Court interpretations of statutes by amending them. Jack Peltason, *Fifty-eight Lonely Men: Southern Federal Judges and School Desegregation* (1961), offers a very readable account of the pressures on, and the reactions of, federal district judges in the South immediately following *Brown v. Board of Education of Topeka* (1954). Harrell Rodgers and Charles Bullock, *Law and Social Change: Civil Rights Laws and*

Their Consequences (1972), details sophisticated research into the factors accelerating school desegregation in Georgia in the late 1960s. Christine H. Rossell and Willis D. Hawley, eds., *The Consequences of School Desegregation* (1983), gives several authors' reports on the impact of school desegregation in terms of such matters as white flight and black educational achievement.

John R. Schmidhauser and Larry L. Berg, *The Supreme Court and Congress: Conflict and Interaction, 1945–1968* (1972), focuses on reactions in Congress to Supreme Court decisions and the political maneuvering to pass or defeat bills to limit the Court's power. Jerome Skolnick, *Justice Without Trial* (1966), is a participant-observer's study of urban police cul-

ture and behavior, including how police react to decisions such as *Mapp* v. *Ohio*. G. Alan Tarr, *Judicial Impact and State Supreme Courts* (1977), focuses on how state high courts have interpreted and applied United States Supreme Court decisions interpreting the establishment clause. Stephen Wasby, *Small-Town Police and the Supreme Court* (1976), reports on how police and prosecutors in rural areas have reacted to *Mapp, Miranda,* and other Supreme Court decisions affecting police behavior.

[*See also* ADMINISTRATIVE AGENCIES; CONGRESS; FEDERAL COURT SYSTEM; JUDICIARY; PROSECUTORS; RACIAL DISCRIMINATION AND EQUAL OPPORTUNITY; STATE COURT SYSTEMS; *and* SUPREME COURT OF THE UNITED STATES.]

DISCOVERY

Wayne D. Brazil
Gregory S. Weber

THE word *discovery* refers to a set of procedures used by lawyers to gather information that is controlled by other parties to a lawsuit or by people who are not parties to the suit. The vast bulk of discovery is conducted well before the date on which the case is scheduled to go to trial. Thus, the principal purposes of discovery are to provide lawyers and clients with access to the relevant evidence before trial so that they can evaluate their position in the litigation; decide whether they want to attempt to negotiate a settlement and, if so, on what terms; and, if no settlement is reached, be well prepared for what will occur at trial.

It is important to understand at the outset that discovery in civil cases is quite different from discovery in criminal matters. In civil litigation (that is, in cases other than those brought by government to punish someone for violating criminal laws) discovery is very broad, meaning that most kinds of evidence that have some bearing on the suit can be discovered, and all parties (plaintiffs and defendants) are under the same kinds of obligations to disclose information that is properly requested. In current civil practice, discovery is the most important and time-consuming part of litigation.

In criminal cases, by contrast, there are more strict limits on what kinds of information one party can discover from another. The prosecution (government) generally has a much broader duty to disclose the evidence that it has developed than does the defendant, who is protected by the right not to be forced to incriminate himself or herself (a right guaranteed by the Fifth Amendment to the United States Constitution as well as by provisions in many state constitutions). Because of these substantial differences we will describe separately the two discovery systems. Because there is substantially more civil than criminal litigation in the United States and because the discovery system is broader and more elaborate in civil suits, we will devote more attention to civil discovery than to its narrower counterpart in criminal prosecutions.

Before turning to more detailed descriptions of procedures, we must emphasize one dominant fact about discovery in both civil and criminal litigation: discovery takes place in an adversary system, a system in which the parties exercise a great deal of control over the course of events and assume responsibility for much that does or does not occur. The tools of discovery are used by advocates; they are used against opponents. Discovery itself is an adversary process. In virtually all discovery systems the courts have until very recently played a largely passive role. It is the parties who use discovery tools, who ask the questions of one another, who demand that opponents disgorge information relevant to the suit before trial. A party with relevant information is generally under no obligation to disclose it unless and until another party properly asks for it. Thus, if lawyers do not use the tools of discovery well or do not respond in good faith to requests for information, significant evidence can remain hidden, and the courts generally have taken no action to be sure that all the relevant data has been brought forward. These basic facts of life about discovery have significant implications for how the system works and for the character of the problems that it has developed.

DISCOVERY IN CIVIL LAWSUITS

To understand the purposes and problems of modern civil discovery, it is helpful to know something about the system's history. That history is complex; the generalizations that follow do not do justice to its dense texture and convolutions.

Well before the American Revolution the English had developed two court systems, one called courts of law and the other called courts of equity. The law courts developed first, but they were rather narrow and inflexible. They did not recognize some kinds of rights and generally would enter only one kind of judgement: that some party did or did not owe some other party a specified sum of money. This kind of money judgement was not an adequate solution to some kinds of problems. Sometimes what a party really needed was an order from a court commanding someone to stop behaving in a certain way or to deliver a specified piece of property. Law courts generally refused to enter such orders. Occasionally someone would secure a money judgement by fraudulent representations, but law courts were not always responsive to efforts to get such judgments set aside. For these and many other reasons (some of which had to do with political power struggles), the king established a second system of courts—courts of equity—that would recognize new rights, offer more flexible kinds of relief, and correct errors made by the courts of law.

The colonists who settled America brought both kinds of court systems with them. Law courts remained relatively rigid. As court procedures evolved during the nineteenth century they provided parties with relatively few means for learning before trial what evidence other parties had developed. Thus, trial in the law courts remained to a considerable extent a game of chance; each party tried to "ambush" or surprise the other by introducing unanticipated evidence. A party who had no idea that some document or testimony would be used at trial had no opportunity to determine whether the document or testimony was reliable and thus could not help the jury or the judge determine what the truth really was. In this important respect the use of "surprise" evidence at trial undermined the adversary system: since both sides did not have a chance to explore and test its reliability, there could be no fair contest about how persuasive the evidence was. Limiting the parties' pretrial access to opponents' evidence also made it difficult to negotiate settlements rationally prior to trial. A party who knew little about the strength of the evidentiary support for his opponent's version of the facts could not rationally determine what the likelihood of winning at trial was or what the size of the judgment might be. Thus, when cases were settled before trial, it was often fear of the unknown, rather than carefully considered assessments of all the relevant information, that led to the negotiated dispositions.

During the nineteenth century, pressure from reformers led to only modest expansion of the discovery system in law courts, but equity courts developed more meaningful discovery procedures. In an equitable action, for example, a party could demand that the opponent spell out in considerable detail facts on which he or she was relying in pursuing the suit; these demands were called "bills of particulars." Equity courts also permitted parties to submit written questions to other parties and to inspect an opponent's documents. Finally, a party in an action in an equity court could "depose" another party before trial (that is, orally ask the party questions and have the party respond under oath). Such depositions could be used only to capture the testimony of someone who would not be present at the trial; they could not be used for the broader purpose of learning what someone who would be called as a witness at trial would say and how credible that person might be.

One reason American courts limited discovery in the nineteenth century is that "pleadings" performed much more substantial functions than they have come to play in twentieth-century litigation. Pleadings are the formal papers through which parties present their claims and their defenses. Nineteenth-century courts expected the parties to use pleadings to present a great deal of information about their positions in the suit. Law courts, in particular, expected the parties to go through a series of exchanges of pleadings in order to clarify and narrow the dispute between them so that by the time the case was ready for trial only a few issues would be left to be resolved.

Critics of nineteenth-century practice had harsh words for the way pleading practice had evolved, saying it had become extremely complicated and highly stylized. They argued that pleadings failed to serve their intended purpose of providing each side with essential information about the prosition being taken by the other and had become unduly expensive instruments of injustice.

It was against this backdrop that reformers, around the beginning of the twentieth century, began pushing for basic changes in the system. The upshot of the reformers' work, which climaxed with the adoption of the Federal Rules of Civil Procedure in 1938, was the merger of courts of law and courts of equity into one unified system and a dramatic shift in the functions that pleadings and discovery were expected to perform. Federal courts and most state courts no longer viewed pleadings as vehicles for exchanging detailed information about parties' positions. Under the new regime, pleadings came to serve very modest purposes. For plaintiffs, pleadings became the vehicle for giving opponents "notice" (hence the phrase "notice pleading") that a suit had been commenced and for pointing, often in very general terms, to the circumstances in the real world out of which the claims arose. Defendants used pleadings simply to announce that the matter would be contested and to reserve the right to develop a myriad of affirmative defenses. In most lawsuits the pleadings consist of no more than a simple complaint and a generalized answer, neither of which communicates a great deal about the bases for the parties' contentions. The reformers who designed this system simply abandoned the idea that pleadings could effectively serve more ambitious purposes.

Court reformers turned next to discovery. They decided that discovery should be used to perform many of the functions that pleadings had not been able to perform well. The discovery system was expanded so that lawyers could use it to learn the evidence that supported opponents' positions. The modern system was intended to equip both sides to understand fully the case before the trial. Reformers hoped that this full knowledge would result in negotiated settlements in a higher percentage of cases, would improve the fairness of those settlements, and, for cases in which no agreement could be negotiated, would make the trial more orderly and less likely to be marred by surprises. Before examining the fate of those expectations, we should describe the tools that make up most contemporary discovery systems.

THE SCOPE OF CONTEMPORARY DISCOVERY

From the 1930s until the last quarter of the century the trend in the law governing discovery had been in one direction: to expand the subject area that parties can use discovery to explore and to give probing parties great freedom to decide which discovery devices to use and how often to use them. In the early 1980s the drafters of proposed amendments to the Federal Rules of Civil Procedure took potentially significant steps that might signal the beginning of a reversal of this trend. Because it is not clear how much these changes will affect established practices, we will examine the discovery system as it has been operating in most jurisdictions before we describe the 1980s amendments and assess their implications for the future.

Under rules in effect in most states and in federal courts, the scope of discovery is very broad. Parties can use discovery not only to seek information about issues actually raised in the pleadings but also to explore material that is "relevant to the *subject matter* involved in the pending action," according to Federal Rule of Civil Procedure 26(b)(1) (emphasis added). A party may pursue information even if he or she cannot show that it would be admissible as evidence at trial. It is sufficient if it can be shown that the information sought "appears reasonably calculated to lead to the discovery of admissible evidence." This right to probe broadly into information an opponent controls is designed to reduce the likelihood that a party will fail to learn something significant because of not knowing exactly what to ask for or because the kinds of documents an opponent might generate cannot be anticipated.

In most jurisdictions there are two principal sources of limits on the scope of the matters into which a discovering party may probe. One source is the law of "privilege." The second is the power of judges to enter "protective orders."

Privilege doctrine reflects policy judgments made by legislatures or courts that have decided that in order to vitalize certain relationships, it is necessary to assure the parties to those relationships that their private communications will be kept confidential. Of the relationships protected by privilege law, the one that has the greatest effect on litigation is between attorney and client. Policymakers have decided that it is very important for clients to feel that they can talk freely to their lawyers. If lawyers could be forced to disclose everything their clients told them, clients would be forced to decide what things to tell their lawyers and what things to keep to themselves. The effect of such a system would be to force clients to act as their own lawyers; that is, clients would be compelled to make judgments about what the legal and tactical consequences would be of disclosing different kinds of information. Thus, in virtually all jurisdictions the law preserves the confidentiality of private communications between lawyer and client when the purpose of the communication is to secure legal advice. It follows that during pretrial discovery a party may refuse to disclose to an opponent these kinds of communications, even if their content is relevant to the issues in the case and would be quite helpful to the other side.

Many state and federal courts recognize privileges in additional kinds of relationships that encourage openness, such as between a doctor or psychiatrist and a patient, between a member of the clergy and a penitent, and between a husband and wife. Unlike the attorney-client privilege, most of these privileges are "qualified" rather than absolute, meaning that there are some circumstances in which a party can be forced to disclose things that were communicated in confidence to a physician, priest, or spouse. To overcome an assertion of one of these privileges, an opponent must make a persuasive showing that the information sought is not available from another source and that a serious injustice would be done if access to the information were denied.

Another doctrine that lawyers often invoke to protect information from discovery is called the "work-product" doctrine. This law is designed to encourage attorneys to do their own work, to investigate their own client's cases thoroughly, and to think independently about the legal issues. To promote these ends, the work-product doctrine generally prohibits a party from discovering documents that opposing counsel has generated while preparing a case for trial. In many jurisdictions, documents that reflect an attorney's mental impressions, legal research, or strategies about the case never can be discovered. Other kinds of documents that counsel prepare in anticipation of litigation might be dis-

coverable if an opponent could show that the information contained in them could not be acquired elsewhere and was very important. For example, federal law would include in the concept "attorney's work product" a report prepared by an expert who was hired by a lawyer to help the lawyer prepare for trial (for example, an accountant who analyzed complex financial data for the lawyer or a scientist who conducted tests on a product that was involved in the litigation). A party could force the disclosure of this kind of work product, for example, if he could show that the opponent's expert had destroyed or significantly altered important evidence when the expert conducted the analysis.

As noted above, the second important source of limits on the scope of discovery is the judiciary's power to enter "protective orders." Courts use such orders for a wide range of purposes, but most commonly to prevent sensitive information from being disclosed or to protect a party from being harassed or unduly burdened by needlessly intrusive or expensive discovery demands. In a lawsuit between two competing businesses, for example, a judge might grant the defendant's request for an order prohibiting the plaintiff from asking questions about secret manufacturing techniques if the court had concluded that the plaintiff could adequately develop her side of the case without that information, even though it would otherwise fall within the scope of discovery because technically it was "relevant to the subject matter" of the suit. Another kind of protective order permits a party to discover specified information but prohibits him from disclosing it to anyone who is not directly involved in the suit. Courts also use protective orders to prevent parties from repeatedly asking the same questions of an opponent or from needlessly protracting discovery events (especially depositions). In short, the protective order is a device that courts use to guard against unjustifiable intrusions and to impose commonsense restraints on a process that sometimes reflects too little discipline.

THE TOOLS OF DISCOVERY

In most jurisdictions rules of court or statutes provide parties with several different tools through which to conduct discovery. Of these,

813

three are the most commonly used: interrogatories, oral depositions, and requests for production of documents and other tangible evidence.

Interrogatories are written questions that one party asks another party to answer in writing. In most jurisdictions, parties may use interrogatories to seek a wide range of information, from such discrete data as the names of witnesses or the location of important documents to such general matters as the facts on which an opponent bases a claim. The latter are called "contention interrogatories" and are controversial; many lawyers resent having to answer this kind of question and insist that responses to contention interrogatories often are of little value because they are vague. When intelligently used, interrogatories can serve as an inexpensive and effective means to learn useful information from an opponent; they can be especially useful for identifying sources of information that an attorney can then use other discovery tools to explore.

Until the early 1980s, most jurisdictions imposed no limits on the number of interrogatories a party could serve on an opponent. Thus, lawyers could periodically send large sets of written questions. Word processors enable lawyers to serve long lists of questions at very little expense to themselves. The burden of answering these questions can be severe. Moreover, some lawyers are not careful to tailor questions to the specific needs of given cases; instead, they use their word processors to produce standard sets of stock questions. Inevitably, some of these questions have little or nothing to do with some of the cases in which they are used. These kinds of problems have led some courts to impose presumptive limits on the number of interrogatories a party can serve without the consent of the opponent or special permission from the court. Other courts have attempted to control these problems by restricting the kinds of information parties may seek through interrogatories; for example, some courts prohibit use of contention interrogatories until the end of the pretrial period. Because unrestricted use of interrogatories has provoked so many complaints, the trend seems to be toward imposing some limit on the use of this particular discovery tool. In the debates about imposing such limits, policymakers are pressed to keep in mind that interrogatories are the least expensive means of acquiring many kinds of information. Thus, rigid restrictions could force parties to use more-expensive means of gathering evidence and might impose unfair disabilities on clients with limited resources. On the other hand, presumptive limits on the number of interrogatories that each party can serve can protect the poor litigant from the burden of having to answer waves of only marginally useful questions.

A second commonly used discovery tool is the deposition. This device normally consists of questions posed orally by a lawyer to a party or a witness. Occasionally attorneys submit their questions in writing. In either case, the person being deposed answers under oath, and a court reporter or tape recorder captures both the questions and the answers. Unlike interrogatories, which can be served only on a party to the lawsuit, a deposition can be taken of anyone who might know something useful, such as witnesses to an important event or experts who will be called to testify at trial. Depositions usually are taken out of court, in the office of one of the lawyers or the certified court reporter. Occasionally a judge or a special officer of the court will be present to make sure that the participants follow the rules, but in the vast majority of instances the deposition takes place in a private and informal setting. Some jurisdictions permit depositions to be taken over the telephone. This procedure can be economical, especially if the person to be deposed lives a great distance from the lawyers who want to ask the questions. Many lawyers, however, prefer to take depositions in person so that they can observe the demeanor and appearance of the witness and assess his credibility. Sometimes depositions are videotaped, especially if counsel are concerned that the deponent might not appear at the trial, for example, because of health problems or because the deponent resides outside the area where the court could compel attendance at the trial.

Depositions can serve several purposes. They can be used to preserve the testimony of a person who will not appear at trial; the transcript of what the person said can then be introduced at trial as part of the evidence. Historically, the deposition was first developed for this purpose. In modern litigation practice, however, depositions are more commonly taken of people who will testify at trial. The purpose is not to preserve their testimony but to find out what they will say, to see how they stand up under cross-examination, and to uncover leads to other information that might be useful to the lawyer asking the questions. Lawyers occasionally use depositions to educate the person being deposed or the lawyer representing that person. This educational mission is accomplished by asking the deponent questions that will force him and his lawyer to confront the weaknesses of their case. Another purpose of taking a deposition can be to force a party to take a position on important disputed matters. If the party offers testimony at the trial that is inconsistent with what he or she said during the pretrial deposition, the transcript of the deposition can be read to the jury for the purpose of raising doubts about the party's honesty or accuracy of memory.

Expert witnesses can play a particularly important role in many kinds of litigation; for example, in some personal injury matters analysis offered by medical experts determines the value of the case. Nonetheless, not all jurisdictions permit parties to depose another party's expert in advance of trial. In the federal courts, for example, an expert who merely offers pretrial advice to another party but will not be called to testify at trial cannot normally be deposed. Even experts who will testify at trial may be deposed only if the party who wants to take their depositions can persuade the court that he cannot prepare adequately if he is given only a written description of the substance of what the expert will say. (Parties are entitled to these written statements.) In other jurisdictions, such as California, the rules permit parties to depose any expert who will testify at trial, without any showing of special need.

During depositions, lawyers pose the questions. Parties themselves are generally not permitted to ask questions. A person who is being deposed is required to answer only questions that are relevant to the subject matter of the suit and need not disclose communications that are protected by a privilege. If a lawyer representing the person being deposed believes that a line of questions probes an area that is irrelevant to the subject matter of the lawsuit or attempts to penetrate communications that are protected by a privilege, the lawyer will state a basis for objection and sometimes will order a client not to answer the questions. Some jurisdictions permit counsel to block testimony in this manner until

a judicial officer can decide whether the objection is well made. Another source of tension at a deposition can be the so-called speaking objection. A lawyer who engages in this practice uses objections to questions as a means to coach his witness about how to testify. The lawyer representing the deponent might say, for example, that he objects to the form of the question being posed and proceed to rephrase the question in a manner that suggests to his own client how he should answer. There is no jurisdiction that condones this practice, but it is not uncommon.

The third discovery tool that lawyers use in many cases is the request for production of documents. In most jurisdictions a party can request permission to inspect not only documents but also other kinds of physical evidence. Parties also may request permission to enter real property to examine the places where relevant events occurred. But in the vast majority of instances, requests for production focus on documents and photographs, such as medical records and X rays. The normal document-production scenario proceeds relatively informally and without the intervention of a judicial officer. A party who wants to examine documents controlled by another party simply sends a request specifying the categories of documents to be examined; then counsel for both sides work out a time and a place where the documents will be made available so that the requesting party can study them and decide whether copies are to be made. In many instances, the party responding to the request simply makes copies and sends them to the lawyer for the requesting party. A party who insists on seeing the originals has a right to do so.

Several kinds of problems can arise in connection with document production requests. Sometimes such requests are drafted carelessly or with ulterior motives in mind and result in imposing a huge burden on the responding party, either because of the volume of material requested or because the material is difficult to gather. Overbroad requests usually provoke an objection from the responding party, which in turn leads to negotiations that ultimately result in a narrower, more focused demand. But sometimes the overbroad request evokes an overwhelming response: a party responding to a broad request may simply open the warehouse where all its records are kept and invite the propounding party to start looking for material. If the warehouse is large, lawyers refer to this tactic as the "Hiroshima defense," meaning that the objective is to dump so much information on the requesting party that the cost of sifting through it will be immense and the odds of finding anything useful will be small.

Another kind of problem can arise when a party in effect "shuffles" documents before producing them. Instead of producing documents organized according to the categories in the request or as the documents are kept in the normal course of business, responding parties occasionally mix them up, hoping to make the process of examining them more onerous and less fruitful. In some jurisdictions, including the federal courts, concern about this problem has provoked rule makers to prohibit expressly such document shuffling and to compel responding parties either to produce materials as maintained in the normal course of business or to organize the documents to conform to the categories in the request.

There is one additional source of friction that may impede an exchange of documents: a dispute about whether a privilege or the work-product doctrine protects materials that otherwise fall within the scope of a request. When one party invokes a privilege as a ground for refusing to disclose requested documents, the other party usually has the right to demand that the party asserting the privilege provide sufficient information about the documents (for example, who wrote them, when they were written, and to whom they were sent) to permit an independent determination that the privilege in fact applies. Occasionally a judicial officer is forced to examine the disputed documents in the judge's office to determine whether they are protected by privilege doctrine.

The kinds of problems described in the preceding paragraphs tend to arise more often in large, complex cases than in smaller, more straightforward matters. In routine cases, the document-exchange process often goes forward with little difficulty and contributes meaningfully to the parties' ability to negotiate a rational settlement without going through a trial.

Many jurisdictions provide parties with two additional important, but less frequently used, tools for discovery. One of these is a physical or mental examination of a party who has made his or her own physical or mental condition an issue in the litigation. In many jurisdictions a plaintiff who sues to recover for injuries suffered as a result of an auto accident may be compelled to submit to a physical examination by a doctor hired by the defendant. The purpose of this requirement is to assure that the expert medical evidence about the plaintiff's condition will be fairly balanced. Similarly, if a party alleges psychological harm he or she may be compelled to undergo psychiatric examination or testing by an expert. Because physical or mental examinations are intrusive, courts sometimes impose strict conditions on how, when, and by whom they may be conducted. In many jurisdictions, including California and the federal courts, a party who has submitted to an examination by a doctor retained by an opponent has a right to a copy of a detailed written report from that physician, setting forth the findings and the results of any tests. In California a plaintiff who demands such a report incurs a reciprocal obligation to make available to the defendant any reports generated by physicians hired by the plaintiff.

The other significant discovery tool that most jurisdictions make available to litigants is the written "request for admissions." Such requests often resemble interrogatories, but this discovery tool was designed to serve an independent function and to have a more telling effect. Interrogatories are primarily used as devices for gathering information from an opponent, information about sources of evidence and bases for positions asserted. Requests for admissions, by contrast, are used primarily to narrow the scope of a dispute, to remove the need to formally prove facts about which the parties are in essential agreement. Requests for admissions are especially useful for establishing the genuineness of documents that will be used as evidence at trial. In the absence of admissions or stipulations (less formal agreements), a party who wants to introduce a document at trial must go through an expensive ritual to prove that the document is what it purports to be and has not been altered. In most situations it is a waste of the resources of both the parties and the court to go through this proof ritual. Thus, admissions of the genuineness of documents can streamline the trial.

In theory, requests for admission can be used to establish much more important facts, even such "ultimate facts" as whether a party was negligent, or whether a contract had been entered. In practice, however, it is the unusual case where requests for admission are used successfully to eliminate truly significant fact issues from the trial. Understandably, parties are reluctant to admit facts that would substantially improve their opponent's position.

HOW WELL DOES THE DISCOVERY SYSTEM WORK?

Since the 1970s this simple question has been the subject of heated debate and of a modest amount of empirical research. There does not seem to be a simple answer. In smaller cases where the parties are proceeding in good faith, the system generally works well. In larger cases the system is more cumbersome and afflicted with greater problems, even when the parties comply with the rules. But a lawyer or litigant who decides not to abide by the spirit of the rules can cause a virtual breakdown of the entire process unless a judge intervenes and plays such a vigilant monitoring role that there is little room for misbehavior.

Perhaps the principal source of problems for the discovery system is that it operates within the context of an adversary system of litigation. The principal goal of an adversary litigator is to win. He is inclined to cooperate only when he believes that cooperation will advance his client's interests and is only secondarily concerned about the health of the system, as such. These adversarial instincts often are inconsistent with the purposes of the Federal Rules of Civil Procedure, whose goals, as stated in Rule 1, are "to secure the just, speedy, and inexpensive determination of every action."

In theory, when a party launches his discovery there are two straightforward objectives: to gather information that might help support a claim or defense and to explore the quality of the evidence that supports the opponent's position. Sometimes, however, discovering parties have subtler, ulterior motives. Critics charge, for example, that some lawyers use discovery for "fishing expeditions"—that is, to snoop around in information controlled by another entity to see if there is a basis for asserting new claims. These critics contend that contemporary procedural rules permit parties to file vague, un-substantiated complaints and then use discovery to determine whether there really is a foundation for a legitimate claim or to expand what starts out as a relatively simple suit into a more intimidating, complex piece of litigation. How often parties use discovery for these kinds of purposes is not at all clear, but liberal rules of pleading make it possible for a party who begins a suit with one claim to add many others if some basis for doing so is exposed during the course of discovery.

Occasionally parties use discovery for clearly illegitimate purposes. For example, lawyers have admitted using discovery in one suit for the purpose of laying the foundation for an entirely different action against a third person (Brazil, 236). Commercial entities have been accused of filing suits against competitors in order to use discovery to try to learn trade secrets. It is not likely, however, that discovery is often used for this purpose. The potential victims of such tactics frequently are sophisticated businesses that will fight hard to get the courts to protect the secrecy of confidential material.

It probably is more common for litigants to use discovery as an economic weapon. Responding to discovery requests can be expensive and can disrupt normal business operations. Moreover, defendants in large commercial litigation usually are forced to conduct expensive discovery of their own. The cost of litigation can be so substantial (and most of it is incurred in the discovery phase) that some defendants accuse some plaintiffs of filing suits as a form of ransom—that is, of filing complaints and then threatening to launch burdensome discovery campaigns unless the defendants offer early in the case to pay a settlement, which can amount to many thousands of dollars.

It would be misleading to suggest that only plaintiffs are accused of economic abuse of the discovery system. Some plaintiffs' lawyers contend that some defendants launch massive discovery campaigns as part of a strategy of pressuring economically weaker opponents into accepting settlements that do not reflect the real value of the plaintiffs' rights. Short of such coercive strategies, lawyers sometimes use discovery to send tactical messages to an opponent; for example, early in a suit a party might decide to make a demanding discovery request for the purpose, in part, of letting an opponent know that he intends to fight hard in the suit and to make it expensive for his opponent to get the case to trial. How often motives like these affect the use of discovery is not clear, but litigants must be tempted to consider such tactics because it is so obvious that responding to, and conducting, discovery can be so expensive. Such temptations may be even greater when one party to a suit is much wealthier than the opponent.

There is another economic reason why the discovery system sometimes does not function as smoothly as its designers anticipated. Many lawyers, especially those who represent defendants, are paid by the hour. The more hours they work on a case, the more money they make. This fact gives attorneys an economic incentive to make discovery more elaborate, more thorough, and more time-consuming than the needs of the case might otherwise dictate. This economic incentive can be reinforced by a lawyer's fear of a malpractice suit. That fear provides an additional impetus to conduct discovery exhaustively and to contest discovery requests that might yield information useful to an opposing party. There is no empirical data that shows how much either of these incentives affects lawyers' behavior during discovery. At this juncture all that is known is that some lawyers perceive these factors at work in other lawyers' conduct.

Adversarial instincts also account for what many lawyers believe is the biggest single problem in the discovery system: evasive or incomplete responses to discovery requests. In one survey, lawyers reported that this kind of problem makes discovery more difficult in 60 percent of their cases. Lawyers who primarily handle large, complex matters report experiencing this problem in 80 percent of their cases; the comparable figure for small-case litigators is 40 percent (Brazil). According to the same group of lawyers the next most troublesome problem with discovery is dilatory responses. Lawyers from a wide range of practices complain that in at least half of their cases they are forced to endure "extended delays" before receiving responses to discovery requests.

It is clear that lawyers often are not forthcoming and diligent in providing information sought by opponents through the discovery process. There is no rush to disclose evidence that might be helpful to an adversary. And the knowledge that an opposing party will provide as little useful information as possible plays an important role in the vicious circle that dominates the discovery process in many larger cases: a lawyer who expects his opponent to play artful dodger will cast a wide discovery net, asking as many questions as possible in order to reduce the odds that a clever adversary will be able to avoid disclosing the key material. Thus, evasive responses spawn overbroad demands, and the process becomes more expensive, less productive, and more frustrating to all concerned.

There is one additional major source of difficulty for the system. Unlike the others, it is not directly a product of adversary instincts. Instead, it is a product of the economics of law practice, especially law practice that revolves around litigation. Litigation is unpredictable. Cases that look like they will consume substantial lawyer resources settle or are dismissed almost without notice. Moreover, no lawyer can control the pace of cases; decisions by clients, by opposing counsel, by opposing parties, by judicial officers, and by people involved in other cases that compete for the court's time all affect the pace at which cases move toward disposition. Without warning, the lawyer may face long hiatuses in several suits.

Given these facts of litigation life, lawyers feel the need to work simultaneously on many files so that they will be able to maintain a flow of income when some of their cases settle unexpectedly or are placed by someone else on the back burner. But in their effort to take on enough cases to assure a constant flow of work, many litigators accept responsibility for more cases than they can comfortably handle. They end up dashing from crisis to crisis in different cases. They have relatively little time to plan the orderly development of individual matters or to craft specific discovery requests to fit peculiar needs of individual cases. Therefore, they often resort to form interrogatories and stock responses to discovery requests. Moreover, they postpone thorough investigation of their own clients' positions, so that when they respond to discovery requests, they cannot provide all the relevant information. Eventually they have to come to more complete terms with each case, but they tend to devote their most intense energy to the cases that have the most imminent trial dates and to let the others meander along.

This picture of litigators' practices may be

somewhat exaggerated, but there is truth at its center. What it means for the system of discovery is plain enough: there is too little planning and too little order, especially in the early stages of case development. Discovery often is not done well: information exchanges are not coordinated, and depositions and document productions are handled piecemeal and often need to be repeated or cleaned up. In short, inefficiency abounds.

In smaller, relatively simple cases the toll taken by these problems consists mostly of delay in reaching a final disposition. In larger suits, however, discovery can consume vast resources and leave parties feeling unsure whether they have learned all the potentially important information. This feeling may well be justified. A research team recently asked a sizable group of litigators how often they settled cases in the belief that their opponents had not discovered arguably significant information. Lawyers who primarily handle larger suits indicated that this occurred in about half of their cases (Brazil, 811–812). If this perception is accurate, discovery is failing to achieve its principal objective in a large percentage of big cases. It is not providing the interested parties with that "mutual knowledge of all the relevant facts . . . [that] is essential to proper litigation" (*Hickman* v. *Taylor,* 1947).

EFFORTS TO CORRECT PROBLEMS OF DISCOVERY

As described in the preceding paragraphs, many of the problems that encumber the discovery process are deeply rooted in the adversary system. Because these problems are in some measure products of basic human instincts, reinforced by competitive institutions, it is unrealistic to think that they can be corrected completely. Since 1976, however, concern about the inefficiency of the discovery process and about abuse of discovery tools has become so widespread that it has inspired major efforts to improve the way the discovery machinery operates. Among these efforts, the most visible and the most ambitious has been in the federal courts. It is appropriate to conclude by describing these recent corrective measures.

The amendments to the Federal Rules of Civil Procedure that the United States Supreme Court and Congress approved in 1983 attack the discovery problem in several ways simultaneously. They discourage lawyers from unjustifiably expanding the scope of lawsuits by asserting baseless claims or defenses, and they encourage judges to play more active roles in monitoring and managing the pretrial process. They also discard the notion that parties have a right to use discovery tools as often and as extensively as they choose. In addition, the new rules attempt to create an environment in which courts will be more likely to punish those who breach discovery duties.

Taken together, these changes reflect a perception by the rule makers that in the past neither the courts nor the parties have assumed sufficient responsibility for the operation of the system as such. The people who introduced modern discovery into the federal courts in the 1930s expected the system to be largely self-executing and self-policing. They thought lawyers would make responsible, reasonable discovery demands, would forthrightly disclose properly sought material, and would be quick to detect and report violations of the rules. As the discussion in the preceding pages makes clear, these expectations have not been fulfilled, especially in large, complex, or hotly contested lawsuits.

The 1983 amendments to the Federal Rules of Civil Procedure begin by imposing responsibilities for case management, in the pretrial period, on federal judges. Rule 16, which for decades had simply authorized pretrial conferences, now actively encourages judges to hold scheduling and planning conferences early in the life of most litigation. The new version of the rule encourages judges to help the parties narrow the scope of their dispute, to establish a discovery plan that focuses on the key issues, and to keep the case-development process moving efficiently by setting deadlines for completion of important pretrial work. The theory is that if judges get more thoroughly involved in their cases from the outset they will be in a better position to deter misbehavior and to encourage litigants to come to terms promptly with their situations, thus facilitating earlier settlements.

Prior to 1983 the Federal Rules conferred on litigants a right to use the tools of discovery as frequently as they chose, subject only to the right of an opponent to seek a protective order to block abuses. The rules did not explicitly compel counsel to exercise restraint in conducting discovery. The 1983 amendments dramatically changed this situation by introducing the concept of "proportionality" and requiring lawyers to limit discovery to the real needs of the case. Rule 26(b)(1) expressly commands judges to impose limits on the frequency or extent of the use of discovery tools if they determine that the discovery sought is "unreasonably cumulative or duplicative, or is obtainable from some other source that is more convenient, less burdensome, or less expensive," or if "the discovery is unduly burdensome or expensive, taking into account the needs of the case, the amount in controversy, limitations on the parties' resources, and the importance of the issues at stake in the litigation." Rule 26(g) compels lawyers to certify that each of their requests for, or responses to, discovery is "not interposed for any improper purpose, such as to harass or to cause unnecessary delay or needless increase in the cost of litigation," and is "not unreasonable or unduly burdensome or expensive, given the needs of the case, the discovery already had in the case, the amount in controversy, and the importance of the issues at stake in the litigation."

The other major component of the rule makers' recent attack on discovery problems is designed to assure that federal judges and magistrates are more vigorous in enforcing the discovery rules. Studies conducted in the late 1970s showed that judges were reluctant to impose sanctions on lawyers who breached duties imposed by the discovery laws and that many litigators believed that this reluctance was one major reason the system did not work as well as it could (Brazil; Ellington). The rule makers responded by adding new provisions designed not only to make lawyers' duties clearer but also to increase the likelihood that breaches of those duties would result in sanctions. An added paragraph in Rule 16 empowers judges to impose financial penalties or other kinds of sanctions on counsel who fail to prepare adequately for, appear at, or participate in good faith in a conference called to plan discovery or other pretrial aspects of a case. Another paragraph in the discovery rules now compels judges to impose sanctions whenever they conclude that a lawyer has requested or responded to discovery in a manner that is inconsistent with the rules—for example,

by interposing an objection in order to cause delay or to annoy an opponent or making a discovery demand that is unreasonably burdensome or expensive.

It remains to be seen to what extent the 1983 amendments to the federal rules will have a substantial effect on the way lawyers and judges behave. There is evidence that some judges are becoming more assertive about managing the pretrial development of cases assigned to them and about imposing sanctions when counsel fail to comply with the letter and spirit of the new rules. This new assertiveness by judicial officers is causing at least some lawyers to make more responsible decisions about how they handle the discovery aspects of their litigation. These trends should significantly improve the efficiency and efficacy of the system.

DISCOVERY IN CRIMINAL PROSECUTIONS

Discovery in criminal prosecutions fulfills functions similar to discovery in civil lawsuits. Criminal discovery is designed to promote fairness and the efficient use of judicial resources. It fosters more informed decision-making during plea bargaining and helps reduce the number of issues that must be resolved in cases that end up in trial. It also reduces the incidence of surprise evidence at trial. In most jurisdictions, however, there are striking differences between the way the discovery system operates in civil and in criminal actions. These differences have two principal sources: the constitutional privilege against compulsory self-incrimination that protects defendants in criminal actions and special concerns about restraining the power of the state.

Pretrial discovery was introduced into criminal procedure more recently and more cautiously than into civil litigation. For example, Federal Rule of Criminal Procedure 16, which gives defendants limited rights to inspect documents held by the prosecution, became law in 1948—ten years after the adoption of the corresponding Federal Rule of Civil Procedure. Moreover, the discovery rights conferred by the original version of Criminal Rule 16 were quite narrow. Document discovery by defendants in criminal actions did not approach the scope and informality of document discovery in civil suits until the late 1960s and early 1970s.

During most of the history of the American system of criminal justice, defendants had no right to pretrial discovery. In the heyday of the common law in the United States (the nineteenth century), opponents of discovery by defendants successfully argued two points. First, they asserted that pretrial production of the prosecution's evidence would equip defendants to develop perjured testimony, to harass and intimidate prosecution witnesses, or to fabricate evidence in advance of trial. Second, they insisted that since the constitutional privilege against self-incrimination prevented the prosecution from discovering much of the evidence gathered by defendants, permitting defendants to discover the prosecution's evidence would give them an unfair advantage.

Today, most states and the federal courts have rejected the common-law ban on discovery. Lawmakers generally have decided that the benefits of at least some discovery in criminal cases outweigh the risks that discovery entails. They have concluded that giving defendants access to the prosecution's evidence improves the likelihood that the results of criminal cases will be fair and that a higher percentage of these cases will be settled without going to trial. Fear that broad discovery will equip defendants to prepare false evidence has not wholly disappeared, however, and vestiges of common-law restrictions on discovery rights remain in effect in most jurisdictions.

The remainder of this section describes the essential rights and procedures by which prosecution and defense may discover the evidence necessary to prepare their cases. Rules vary considerably from jurisdiction to jurisdiction. In the limited space here we can do no more than present examples of typical provisions. We focus primarily on rules developed for state court systems rather than their federal court counterparts. Unlike the situation on the civil side, where federal rule makers played a leadership role in liberalizing (broadening) discovery, on the criminal side certain states have led the movement toward expanding discovery rights.

This discussion emphasizes the scope of the parties' rights to compel pretrial disclosure. In many areas, much pretrial discovery occurs as a result of informal agreements between prosecution and defense. This is particularly true in federal courts, where the rules formally confer only limited discovery rights on defendants. Under federal law, for example, a defendant has a formal right to see pretrial statements by government witnesses only after the witnesses have testified at trial. Nevertheless, in order to prevent the delays during trial that would be necessary to permit defendants to study such statements, many federal prosecutors will disclose the statements in advance of trial. This type of informal discovery occurs most frequently where the prosecution believes that it has a very good case and wishes to encourage plea bargaining. But even when the evidence is not overwhelming, many prosecutors make disclosures in advance of trial that no statute or rule requires.

Discovery generally occurs in criminal actions only when a party makes a discovery request. There are only a few instances in which the prosecution or the defense has a duty to make disclosures without first being asked by the opposing party or ordered by a judge. In criminal matters discovery is circumscribed by the requirement of relevance and by the operation of privilege doctrines. Moreover, most jurisdictions distinguish material a party may discover merely by making a request from material that may be discovered only after demonstrating that "good cause" exists for the court to order his opponent to make the disclosure. In a few states, all discovery requests require prior court approval.

Some states impose additional restrictions on discovery in criminal matters. Some jurisdictions, for example, require a party seeking discovery to show not only that the information is "relevant" to the case but also that it is "material." The relevancy requirement merely limits discovery to items having some, even minor, connection to a case; the materiality requirement, by contrast, limits discovery to evidence that would make a difference in a juror's evaluation of the case. Some states also require the discovering party to demonstrate that the information sought will be admissible as evidence at trial.

As a further general limitation on pretrial criminal discovery, some jurisdictions, including the federal courts and Florida, refuse to permit the prosecution to discover some kinds of material unless the defendant has already asked the prosecution to disclose similar information. In these jurisdictions the prosecution has no right to compel document production from the defense unless the defense has previously requested document production from the government. And in some jurisdictions the prosecution has no formal discovery rights at all.

DISCOVERY BY THE DEFENSE

In addition to the kinds of general requirements described in the preceding section, all jurisdictions have developed special rules governing the discoverability of specific items.

Witness Statements. Most jurisdictions permit defendants to discover written or recorded statements they have made to government agents. Many jurisdictions also compel the prosecution to disclose its version of oral conversations between the defendant and government agents. In cases where the government is simultaneously prosecuting two or more people, each defendant usually has a right to obtain copies of statements made by the codefendants.

The kind of material that defense lawyers often want most to discover consists of statements that prospective witnesses for the prosecution have made prior to trial. These statements give the defense its best single opportunity to learn before trial the exact contours of the government's case. They also equip defense counsel to impeach a witness whose story changes. Jurisdictions with the broadest discovery provisions, such as the state of Washington, permit discovery of such statements. Other jurisdictions expressly preclude the discovery of government witnesses' statements. The rule in federal courts falls between these two positions: it compels prosecutors to disclose pretrial statements by their witnesses but only after their witnesses have testified at trial. This provision enables prosecutors to protect any witnesses whom they fear a defendant might harass or attempt to intimidate before trial.

States that compel the government to disclose prospective witnesses' identities and pretrial statements generally impose special requirements when a defendant tries to learn the identity of a confidential informant. For example, in California the court conducts a closed hearing at which the defendant must demonstrate a reasonable possibility that the informant will give testimony tending to exonerate the defendant. Unless the defendant can make such a showing, the court will not order the prosecutor to disclose the informer's identity. Courts also take great care to prevent intimidation of confidential informants. The greater the likelihood of harm to an informant, the more demanding courts are of defense lawyers.

Another controversial issue revolves around whether the government should be compelled to make available to a defendant a transcript of testimony he or other witnesses offered to a grand jury. In many states and in the federal courts, a defendant has a right only to a transcript of his own grand jury testimony. Some jurisdictions require the defendant to show a "special need" for the prior testimony. This rule usually blocks defendants' access to grand jury testimony. In contrast, Vermont—the state with the broadest discovery in criminal cases—compels the government to disclose the entire grand jury proceedings that culminated in the defendant's indictment.

Prior Conviction Record. In most jurisdictions the prosecution must disclose information it has about the defendant's prior convictions. Jurisdictions differ about whether a defendant may discover the prior conviction records of prosecution witnesses. The jurisdictions that require the government to disclose the identity and prior statements of prospective trial witnesses generally also require the disclosure of those witnesses' past conviction records.

Other Documents and Tangible Objects. Most jurisdictions authorize fairly broad discovery of relevant books, papers, documents, photographs, and other tangible objects. The defendant must usually demonstrate that the items are material to his case, were obtained from him, or will be used by the government at trial. In many jurisdictions defendants also are permitted to enter and inspect government property if they can show that doing so would assist their defense.

Experts' Reports. Most jurisdictions specifically authorize the discovery of test results and other reports made by government experts. Defendants most frequently utilize these provisions to obtain results of chemical, blood, physical, or mental examinations. In theory, the work-product doctrine might protect such material, but in practice prosecutors rarely assert this privilege. They know that defendants usually could make a showing of need sufficient to gain access to this kind of material.

Depositions. Jurisdictions differ widely over the availability of depositions in criminal pretrial discovery, unlike in civil cases, where depositions occur frequently. Many jurisdictions only allow depositions in criminal cases in exceptional circumstances. A defendant in a federal prosecution will be permitted to take a deposition only if he or she can show that the deponent is unlikely to testify at trial, for example, because the deponent is very ill or about to leave the country. By contrast, rules in effect in Vermont permit parties to take depositions as freely in criminal matters as in civil suits.

Potentially Exonerating Evidence. Under the landmark ruling of *Brady* v. *Maryland* (1963), a defendant's conviction may be overturned if, before trial, he or she sought discovery of exculpating evidence that the government controlled but failed to disclose. The *Brady* rule is based on a defendant's right to a fair trial. By itself, the holding in that case does not create discovery rights. Instead, it sets forth what the penalty can be if the government fails, in this way, to treat a defendant fairly. Nonetheless, a number of states have incorporated the *Brady* principle into their discovery rules. In Vermont, for example, the prosecution must disclose any evidence tending to disprove the defendant's culpability or to reduce his punishment. In the state of Washington, the prosecutor also must disclose any evidence tending to show that the government entrapped the defendant.

DISCOVERY BY THE PROSECUTION

A prosecutor's right to discover information from a defendant is circumscribed to a considerable extent by the defendant's constitutional right not to be compelled to testify against himself. This right, commonly known as the privilege against self-incrimination, extends solely to testimony—that is, to statements made under oath by the defendant. Thus, it does not prevent the prosecution from forcing a defendant to be fingerprinted and then using those fingerprints at trial. Similarly, the privilege against self-incrimination does not protect a defendant from being compelled to produce other nontestimonial evidence, such as samples of hair,

bodily fluids, or handwriting. Most jurisdictions also compel defendants to take part in lineups, to speak for voice-identification purposes, to pose for photographs, and to submit to reasonably necessary medical examinations.

The states (fewer than half) that allow the defense to discover the names and prior statements of prospective prosecution witnesses generally also require the defense to disclose to the prosecution the names and prior statements of prospective defense witnesses.

There are many differences among the states with respect to whether to permit the prosecution to force disclosure of the theories on which the defendant intends to base his or her defense. Many jurisdictions compel disclosure of certain kinds of defenses, in order to prevent unfair surprise of the prosecution. These states require a defendant to notify the prosecution of intent to assert a defense based on alibi, insanity, or incompetency.

DISCOVERY PROCEDURES

While the various time frames created by criminal discovery rules strongly resemble their civil counterparts, the discovery phase of criminal litigation usually proceeds expeditiously. Thus, while civil discovery may stretch over years, most discovery in criminal prosecutions occurs over a period of a month or less. The limits imposed on the scope of criminal discovery and the requirement that defendants receive a speedy trial prevent the kinds of delays that afflict the discovery system in civil litigation.

All jurisdictions authorize their courts to regulate discovery in order to prevent abuse and injustice. In many jurisdictions, all discovery requests require prior court approval. Other jurisdictions require court supervision of only particular aspects of discovery. Vermont, for example, does not require the defendant to seek a court order to initiate discovery; the prosecution, however, must get approval from a court for all its discovery.

Because of the limits on the scope and duration of criminal discovery, criminal prosecutions generally involve far fewer discovery disputes than civil suits. Most disputes about discovery occur after trial. It is at this stage, for example, that defense attorneys are most likely to contend

DISCOVERY

that the prosecution failed to disclose potentially exculpatory information.

As in civil cases, all jurisdictions allow their courts to issue protective orders to limit the discovery of otherwise relevant material after a showing that disclosure would unduly harass, embarrass, or intimidate the party from whom disclosure was sought. Also as in civil cases, where argument in open court of the reasons a party opposes discovery would itself require relevation of privileged or unduly embarrassing material, the court will hear the argument in private.

All jurisdictions give their courts broad power to enforce discovery rights and court orders. Penalties for discovery violations or abuses range from verbal reprimands to dismissal of the prosecution's case or reversal of a conviction. Courts generally have great discretion in deciding whether to sanction a party and, if so, how. In making such decisions courts consider the reasons offered as to why disclosure did not occur; the extent of the prejudice, if any, to the opposing party; the feasibility of rectifying the prejudice by a continuance (postponement) of trial; and the general circumstances surrounding the dispute.

Rules governing sanctions in criminal cases usually do not specifically authorize courts to compel one party to reimburse another for the expenses it incurred, including attorney's fees, as a result of a breach of a discovery duty. This kind of monetary sanction, which is becoming relatively common in civil litigation, is imposed only rarely in criminal matters. Criminal courts are much more likely to sanction serious discovery abuses by prohibiting the offending party from introducing certain evidence or calling certain witnesses.

Perhaps because the discovery system is expected to do less and to be completed in a shorter period in criminal matters, it seems to cause fewer problems and to function more efficiently than the discovery process in civil litigation. In civil suits, discovery has come to play the dominant role in the entire adjudicatory process. In criminal cases, by contrast, that role continues to be played by the trial itself.

CASES

Brady v. Maryland, 373 U.S. 83 (1963)
Hickman v. Taylor, 329 U.S. 495 (1947)

BIBLIOGRAPHY

American Bar Association, *Standards for Criminal Justice,* vol. 3 (1980), earlier editions of which served as the model for many states' efforts to revise their criminal discovery system, provides some good background authorities and analysis; and "Second Report of the Special Committee for the Study of Discovery Abuse," 92 F.R.D. 137 (1982), analyzes the problems of abuse and recommends solutions, some of which have been incorporated into the Federal Rules. Barbara Babcock, "Fair Play: Evidence Favorable to an Accused and Effective Assistance of Counsel," in *Stanford Law Review,* 34 (1982), reviews *Brady* and its progeny. Wayne Brazil, "Civil Discovery: Lawyers' Views," in *American Bar Foundation Research Journal* (1980), surveys 180 Chicago litigators' views about how the discovery system is working and what its principal problems are.

Paul Connolly, Edith Holleman, and Michael Kuhlman, *Judicial Controls and the Civil Litigation Process: Discovery* (1978), studies the volume of discovery activity and judicial efforts to contain abuses in several federal district courts. C. Ronald Ellington, *A Study of Sanctions for Discovery Abuse* (1979), is an empirical study of the frequency with which federal judges impose sanctions after alleged violations of discovery duties. Marvin Frankel, "The Search for Truth: An Umpireal View," in *University of Pennsylvania Law Review,* 123 (1975), challenges some basic premises of the adversary system.

David Louisell, "Criminal Discovery: Dilemma Real or Apparent?" in *California Law Review,* 49 (1961), discusses in depth the policies behind criminal discovery. National Conference on Discovery Reform, "Proceedings," in *Review of Litigation,* 3 (1982), reports and comments on the discovery system and proposed reforms offered by the ABA Special Committee for the Study of Discovery Abuse and about eighty federal judges, senior litigators, and scholars. Charles Renfrew, "Discovery Sanctions: A Judicial Perspective," in *California Law Review,* 67 (1979), is an important essay by a former federal trial judge about the need for vigorous judicial enforcement of discovery rules. Charles Wright, *Federal Practice and Procedure: Criminal,* vol. 2 (1982), provides one of the best single sources of material on federal criminal discovery. Charles Wright and Arthur Miller, *Federal Practice and Procedure: Civil,* vol. 8 (1970), is an annually updated treatise offering a thorough, readable, and reliable description of current procedural law in federal courts.
[*See also* COMMON LAW AND COMMON-LAW LEGAL SYSTEMS; CRIMINAL JUSTICE SYSTEM; CRIMINAL PROCEDURE; EQUITY AND EQUITABLE REMEDIES; *and* TRIAL COURTS AND PRACTICE.]

JURISDICTION

Harold J. Spaeth

Iɴ its broadest sense, *jurisdiction* refers to the authority by which a court takes cognizance of, and decides, matters brought to its attention. To establish this authority, the court must consider whether it is the proper forum for resolution of the dispute; whether the person who invokes the court's authority is a proper plaintiff; and, if so, whether the court has jurisdiction over the parties, especially the defendant.

PROPER FORUM

Determination of whether a court is the proper forum for resolution of the matter to be adjudicated depends on whether the court has subject matter, geographical, and hierarchical jurisdiction over the controversy.

Subject Jurisdiction: Federal Questions. The sources of a court's subject matter jurisdiction are constitutional provisions and statutes enacted pursuant thereto. In the case of the federal courts, Article III of the Constitution specifies the heart of this power, as "all Cases . . . arising under this Constitution, the Laws of the United States, and Treaties." Cases so arising are known as federal questions. To invoke federal question jurisdiction, a party must demonstrate to the court's satisfaction that the case substantially concerns a constitutional provision, an act of Congress (or administrative actions pursuant thereto), or a treaty of the United States.

Article III also gives the federal courts jurisdiction over disputes to which the federal government is party; disputes between states; admiralty and maritime cases; disputes involving foreign diplomatic personnel accredited to the United States; and disputes between residents of different states. For all practical purposes, when the federal government is party to litigation, the case may be considered to arise as a federal question. The other listed subjects either do not occur very frequently (for example, those involving foreign diplomatic personnel, because of diplomatic immunity to suit) or typically involve purely private disputes (such as cases in which a resident of one state sues a resident of another state, and cases involving admiralty and maritime jurisdiction). Suits between states arise infrequently also; they usually concern boundaries, water rights, or financial obligations. Accordingly, cases of national, rather than local, import surface as federal questions. That is not to say that every federal question is of earthshaking proportions but, rather, that nonfederal questions have an effect largely limited to the parties involved in the litigation.

Because the federal courts are empowered by the Constitution to hear only those cases within the judicial power of the United States, they are considered to be courts of limited jurisdiction. As such, subject matter jurisdiction is presumed not to exist. Therefore, the party who seeks access to federal court must affirmatively demonstrate that the court has subject matter jurisdiction. Insofar as federal questions are concerned, this means that the plaintiff must show that a right or immunity "arising under" federal law (Constitution, statute, or treaty) is a basic element in his cause of action and not merely a collateral issue (not involving the merits of the controversy) or introduced as a defense or in response to the defendant's counterclaim. The requirement that the plaintiff's claim show its federal basis stems from the view that if a federal court decided a case not within its jurisdiction, it would necessarily—and unconstitutionally—invade the reserved powers of the states.

Two additional results flow from the limited

jurisdiction of the federal courts. First, if the facts alleging federal jurisdiction are challenged, the burden of proof falls on the party claiming federal jurisdiction. Second, each and every federal court is obligated to notice a lack of jurisdiction and to dismiss any case on its own motion if either party fails to so move.

Subject Jurisdiction: Diversity of Citizenship. Apart from federal questions, the other major source of federal subject matter jurisdiction is diversity of citizenship—controversies between residents of different states or between a resident of a state and an alien. Needless to say, such cases contain no federal questions; rather, they consist of the ordinary, garden-variety litigation that is the staple of the state judicial systems: tort (private injury) actions. The reason for assigning federal courts diversity jurisdiction was the fear that a state court might be biased against the out-of-state litigant. Thus, to protect nonresidents from potential prejudice in the local courts, access to the federal courts is provided if certain conditions are met.

First, the amount in controversy must be more than $10,000, exclusive of interest and costs. This jurisdictional amount is set by Congress and is pegged sufficiently high so that the federal courts will not be inundated with a flood of petty lawsuits. Doubts about the adequacy of the jurisdictional amount redound to the plaintiff's benefit, however. If the sum claimed is made in good faith and if it is not a legal certainty that the plaintiff will not recover more than $10,000, the amount in controversy is met. The amount claimed, rather than the amount recovered, controls. And once the amount claimed is established, subsequent events cannot destroy jurisdiction. When the plaintiff's cause of action does not allege a dollar amount, as in a request for an injunction, the abatement of a nuisance, or specific performance of a contract, the court will determine either the value to the plaintiff of the relief sought or the cost to the defendant if the requested relief is granted.

The major complication regarding jurisdictional amount concerns the aggregation of claims. A plaintiff may aggregate even unrelated claims against a single defendant (such as two $6,000 claims), but the defendant's counterclaims against the plaintiff may not be aggregated to meet the jurisdictional amount. In multiple-party litigation, aggregation is permitted if the plaintiffs or defendants have a joint and common interest in the subject matter of the lawsuit (for example, a $12,000 painting owned by two persons) rather than an individual interest. (An example of the latter is two passengers in an auto accident each with a $6,000 injury; however, if one of the passengers suffers a $12,000 injury and the other a $6,000 one, federal jurisdiction lies only for the former.)

Second, the "citizenship" to which diversity jurisdiction pertains is a party's domicile in a state or status as an alien. If both parties are aliens or if one party is a United States citizen who is not domiciled in a state, the federal courts lack jurisdiction. (A "state," for this purpose, includes the District of Columbia and Puerto Rico.) "Domicile," however, does not mean "residence." A person may have several residences but only one domicile. The latter requires an initial physical presence within the state, plus the intent to remain there, whether temporarily or permanently. Hence, students and military personnel can establish a domicile so long as they have no immediate intention of moving elsewhere. As with the amount in controversy, diversity is established at the time a legal action commences. A person may change domicile in order to create diversity, but once established it cannot be lost because of movement during the course of litigation.

Third, in *Strawbridge* v. *Curtiss* (1806), the Supreme Court ruled that the diversity of parties must be complete. In multiparty lawsuits, therefore, no plaintiff may have the same "citizenship" as a defendant. Complete diversity is not required in class actions. The domicile of the class is that of the named plaintiff (the person who represents the class); the domiciles of the other class members are irrelevant. Neither do interpleader actions require complete diversity. Interpleader is a remedy by which a person (the "stakeholder," typically an insurance company) who admits an obligation but is unsure to whom it is owed deposits the money or property with the court and notifies the claimants that he has done so, thereby washing his hands of the matter. The claimants are required to dispute ownership among themselves. So long as at least two claimants reside in different states, diversity obtains. The amount in controversy in such actions need only be $500. Deviation from the prevailing rules is permitted because of the equitable nature of interpleader.

To overcome the difficulties that complete diversity posed to corporations, the United States Supreme Court created two remarkable legal fictions. It first asserted, in *The Louisville, Cincinnati & Charleston R.Co.* v. *Letson* (1844), that a corporation was a "citizen" of the state in which it was chartered. It subsequently reversed itself and said that inasmuch as a corporation is an artificial entity it cannot be a citizen, and that the citizenship of its stockholders must control. The Court thereupon irrebuttably presumed that each stockholder is a citizen of the state of incorporation, notwithstanding the patent falsity of the presumption. The Court's reasoning makes Delaware, the home of many major corporations, by far the most populous of the states.

A corporation has dual citizenship if its principal place of business is located in a state other than the one in which it is chartered. Regardless of the breadth of a corporation's activities, it may have only one principal place of business. This may either be corporate headquarters or wherever the bulk of the corporation's activity occurs. Each option has its judicial adherents, and the choice is made generally by that court's precedent. Unincorporated associations (partnerships, labor unions, and the like) do not enjoy the entity fiction. Instead, the domicile of each of its human members controls. As a result, national organizations (for example, the Teamsters Union) cannot avail themselves of diversity jurisdiction, because they have at least one member in every state.

Diversity jurisdiction as a means of access to the federal courts has come under serious attack since the 1960s. Its original justification—to prevent bias against out-of-state litigants—has faded as mobility has weakened parochialism. Increases in the docket of the federal courts, with resulting delay and congestion, have caused many to advocate its limitation, if not outright abolition, as the most expendable aspect of the federal courts' subject matter jurisdiction. The reformist appeal is enhanced by two considerations: diversity concerns disputes that, absent diversity, the state courts regularly resolve; and federal judges, in deciding such controversies, apply state law.

Subject Jurisdiction: Ancillary and Pendent. The federal courts exercise a third type of subject matter jurisdiction, ancillary and pendent jurisdiction, even though no statute authorizes them to do so. Ancillary jurisdiction enables claims of persons other than the original plaintiff that arise out of the same transaction to be joined together in a single proceeding (for example, the defendant's counterclaim or the interest of a third party in property that is the subject of dispute). Pendent jurisdiction permits a plaintiff to join a state claim to a federal-question claim if both stem from "a common nucleus of operative fact" (*United Mine Workers of America* v. *Gibbs*, 1966). Both ancillary and pendent jurisdiction arise in multiple-claim litigation to permit federal courts to try an entire dispute instead of just the federal portion of it, thereby promoting judicial economy and precluding piecemeal litigation. Invocation of either recognizes the presence of at least one claim sufficient to establish either federal-question or diversity jurisdiction. Both ancillary and pendent jurisdiction lie within the discretion of the presiding judge. Their exercise is appropriate if economy and fairness to the parties will result.

Hierarchical and Geographical Jurisdiction. Jurisdiction is defined not only by subject matter but also by geography and hierarchy. The last distinguishes trial courts (courts of first instance) from those that hear appeals. The latter are divided into intermediate appellate courts and courts of last resort. Geographical jurisdiction pertains to the reach of a court's jurisdiction: the state court systems organize themselves along county lines, while the federal courts do so on a state basis. The federal court structure is much simpler and displays less internal diversity than the state systems. The federal district courts, at least one of which is located in every state, are the trial courts of the federal system. They are identified by state and, if the state has more than one, by the geographical region within the state—thus, the District of North Dakota, the Southern District of New York, the Central District of California.

Appeals from the federal district courts are heard by the courts of appeals. The United States is divided into eleven numbered circuits, with an additional circuit having geographical jurisdiction over the District of Columbia. The numbered circuits have jurisdiction over the district courts in specific states. Thus, the First Circuit hears appeals from the district courts in Maine, Massachusetts, New Hampshire, Rhode Island, and Puerto Rico, and the Eleventh Circuit, created by Congress in 1980, reviews those from Alabama, Florida, and Georgia. At the top of the federal hierarchy, with jurisdiction over the whole of the United States, is the Supreme Court.

A marked difference between the federal and state court systems is that federal district courts have subject matter jurisdiction over virtually all cases the federal courts may hear. Major exceptions are monetary claims against the United States, which the Court of Claims hears, and disputes involving customs duties, which the Customs Court decides. State trial courts, by contrast, tend to have specialized subject matter jurisdiction, such as criminal cases or those concerning juveniles. In this sense, then, the federal district courts are describable as courts of general jurisdiction, while most state courts are of limited jurisdiction. Specialized subject matter tends not to exist at appellate levels. Federal exceptions are the Temporary Emergency Court of Appeals, which hears appeals pertaining to price and wage controls, and the Court of Appeals for the Federal Circuit, which includes the Court of Claims and the Court of Customs and Patent Appeals. The most unusual state exceptions are Oklahoma and Texas, each of which has two courts of last resort, one dealing with civil matters and the other with criminal cases.

Limitations on the subject matter jurisdiction of state trial courts are diverse. One court may exclusively try civil cases, while another has exclusive jurisdiction over criminal offenses; other courts may be limited to probate jurisdiction (wills, estates, and juveniles). Some states, such as New York, divide probate among more than one court. Typically, states further divide the subject matter jurisdiction of their courts on the basis of the amount in controversy and the seriousness of criminal charges. Thus, a court of common pleas may be authorized to hear only cases in which the amount in controversy is less than a specified dollar value. Or a small-claims court may have jurisdiction where the amount is less than, say, $600. On the criminal side, one court may try felonies, another misdemeanors, and a third only traffic violations. If the state contains a large city, separate trial courts may have specialized jurisdiction only within municipal boundaries. Elsewhere, the minor trial courts may have jurisdiction only over a municipality or a township, rather than throughout the county.

The foregoing divisions do not exhaust the subject matter limitations that the states impose on their trial courts. On the other hand, no state utilizes all the listed limitations.

PROPER PARTY

Even though a particular court may be the proper forum for the resolution of a dispute, that court's jurisdiction also depends on whether or not the person who invokes the court's decision-making capability is a proper party—in other words, whether the plaintiff deserves access to the court, or whether he or she has standing to sue. Resolution of this matter turns on a number of factors. Insofar as the federal courts are concerned, some criteria are mandated by the Constitution; others are viewed as prudential considerations. Questions about standing to sue rarely arise in the context of private law disputes. In such cases, whether the plaintiff is a proper party tends to be self-evident. This is not so when an interested bystander raises a public law issue, such as the constitutionality of governmental action. Hence, rules governing access primarily concern the federal, rather than the state, courts.

Case or Controversy. Paramount is the case or controversy requirement. The words of Article III of the Constitution limit federal judicial power to cases or controversies. The difference between a "case" and a "controversy" lacks practical importance. The latter is narrower in scope than the former and includes only civil suits. Like the other elements of standing to sue, the case or controversy requirement does not admit of precise definition. It requires a bona fide dispute between two or more persons whose interests conflict. As such, the federal courts have no power to decide hypothetical questions, collusive cases, or questions demanding advisory opinions. These matters are nonjusticiable.

Hypothetical questions typically result when a formerly live controversy becomes moot because of changes affecting a litigant's contentions. Thus, an out-of-court settlement moots further court proceedings. Similarly, a party's challenge to the constitutionality of a law ends with the repeal of the statute. The United States Supreme Court refused to decide the constitutionality of affirmative action programs when the issue first reached it in *DeFunis* v. *Odegaard* (1974) because the student who challenged the practice had been admitted to the educational institution in question and was assured of graduation regardless of any decision the Court might have made. Mootness does not govern criminal convictions as rigorously as other types of proceedings. The release of a convict after sentence has been served does not preclude the possibility of adverse collateral consequences. Rearrest may warrant more severe charges; reconviction may warrant a stiffer sentence. Such possibilities save the case from mootness. On the other hand, a challenge to visitation privileges would not survive the prisoner's release from custody.

The requirement that a plaintiff's dispute remain live throughout the course of litigation is perhaps most problematic in situations "capable of repetition, yet evading review." Here courts apply mootness less rigorously. Thus, short-lived controversies, such as the right of a pregnant woman to an abortion or the right of someone to vote in an election, may be addressed. Class-action suits, in which an individual sues on her own behalf as well as on behalf of all others similarly situated, also minimize the chance of mootness. Even though the status of the named plaintiff changes, the lawsuit continues. Thus, an employer's settlement with the plaintiff in an employment discrimination action, or the graduation of a child or the moving of the family to another district in a school desegregation suit, does not moot a class action.

The rule against advisory opinions (in the absence of lawsuits) to resolve legal issues dates from 1793, when Secretary of State Thomas Jefferson, at President George Washington's request, submitted to the Supreme Court twenty-nine questions of international law. Advisory opinions are considered objectionable not only because they lack liveliness but also because they have an impact on the separation of powers. If the federal courts accepted hypothetical disputes, the hypothesized questions would likely concern presidential conduct and congressional statutes, thereby increasing the potential for conflict between the judiciary and the coordinate branches of government. Nonetheless, a number of states do permit advisory opinions if requested by the governor or the attorney general.

The prohibition of hypothetical questions does not prevent courts from rendering declaratory judgments. These obviate the need for an individual to break a law in order to obtain judicial determination of his rights and duties. Although under the common law such determinations could be had only if a breach occurred, the Supreme Court reasoned that Article III of the Constitution defines and limits judicial power, not the manner in which it is exercised.

Collusive actions fail to meet the case or controversy requirement because the parties lack adversariness. Plaintiff and defendant possess a common interest—hence the labels "friendly suit" and "feigned litigation." The absence of adversariness is not always apparent. A number of landmark Supreme Court decisions appear to have been collusive cases. They commonly manifest themselves as suits by stockholders against their corporations to enjoin payment of taxes or compliance with governmental regulations. Note that the rule against collusive litigation does not necessarily require disagreement between the parties. Courts may enter default judgments and accept guilty and nolo contendere pleas. But where one party controls or finances the litigation, courts deem the case collusive.

Legal Injury. Mere dispute does not establish access to court. A conflict must concern a legal claim—a statutory or constitutional right, or some personal or property interest. That is, a proper plaintiff must demonstrate entitlement to rights prescribed by law. Ordinary commercial competition, for example, undeniably produces economic injury, but no legal injury results therefrom. One looks to legislative enactments, constitutional provisions, and the common law to identify the rights and interests that receive legal protection; and traditionally, protected interests were those on which a dollar value could be placed. Currently, aesthetic, conservational, and recreational interests may also suffice.

Thus, persons interested in a river's scenic beauty may object to the installation of overhead power lines; an organization to preserve a park may challenge highway construction through it; and conservationists may seek to enjoin the sale of timber from a national forest. If, however, "injury" results from governmental action—as when persons are subsequently found innocent of crimes for which they were convicted, or property values decline because of changes in zoning ordinances—judicial redress may not be available. Neither does the quantum of injury necessarily affect its legal character. Trifles may be legally protected. Under the common law, a single footstep on another's land, an unwanted touching, or the pointing of a gun, respectively, constitute trespass, battery, and assault—notwithstanding that the resulting damage is not discernible.

Personal Injury. A third element of standing to sue is the requirement that the legal injury complained of be suffered by the plaintiff personally. One may not bring suit solely on behalf of a third party except in the case of a legal guardian or next of kin when the injured person is legally incompetent for one reason or another. This element focuses on the party and not the issue she wishes to litigate. The question, rather, is whether the plaintiff is the proper party to litigate a particular issue, not whether the issue itself is justiciable.

Accordingly, physicians may not sue on behalf of their patients, and persons may not enjoin enforcement of a law where the statute has long existed but no prosecutions have occurred. On the other hand, organizations have been permitted to litigate their members' rights: a parochial school attacked a statute requiring compulsory public education even though the right inhered in the children and their parents; and a school board obtained an injunction prohibiting conduct that interfered with students' civil rights.

The reason for exceptions to the direct personal injury rule is that the constitutional standing requirements do not mandate its application; rather, prudential considerations are allowed to guide adjudication in the federal courts. The rule ought not apply if a substantial relationship exists between the plaintiff and the third parties, if the rights of the third parties would otherwise not be presented, or if their rights risk dilution.

The classic example of rigorous adherence to the personal injury requirement is taxpayer's suits. In the states, taxpayers have used this device to challenge governmental expenditures, bond issues, and special assessments. In the federal courts, by contrast, taxpayers, with one exception, have lacked standing to sue. The rationale is that personal injury requires that the plaintiff suffer in a peculiar and more severe fashion than the public generally, but a federal taxpayer merely suffers in an indefinite way along with millions of others. If the taxpayer can show that the challenged expenditure exceeds specific constitutional limitations on the taxing and spending power, he has standing to sue. Thus, a plaintiff successfully alleged that congressionally appropriated monies disbursed to parochial schools violated the establishment of religion clause of the First Amendment, in *Flast* v. *Cohen* (1968).

The personal injury requirement, as noted, is judicially created and not constitutionally mandated. Consequently, where a dispute is otherwise justiciable, Congress is free to authorize plaintiffs to function as "private attorneys general" who seek to vindicate the public's rights. If Congress is silent or unclear, the federal courts may infer access to private parties desiring to vindicate congressionally established rights. Thus, in *Cannon* v. *University of Chicago* (1979), the Supreme Court granted a plaintiff the right to sue an educational institution for violating a federal statute that prohibits sex discrimination in federally funded programs. The statute itself, Title I of the Education Amendments of 1972, does not expressly authorize a private remedy. Four factors, formulated in *Cort* v. *Ash* (1975), determine if a private remedy should be inferred: (1) whether Congress enacted the law to benefit a special class, one in which plaintiff holds membership; (2) whether evidence exists that Congress intended to create a private remedy; (3) whether such a remedy comports with the statute's purpose; and (4) whether a private remedy is inappropriate because the statute's subject is primarily a state responsibility. Application of this test provides courts with wide discretion.

Political Questions. Judges will not decide those questions that they deem more suitable for resolution by legislators or executive officials, calling them political questions. Courts have applied the label to a diverse range of issues; as a result, the only meaningful, though inadequate, definition is that a political question is whatever a court says it is. The label itself is a misnomer. All judicial decisions allocate society's resources, which is what politics is. Nonetheless, the label has utility. The designation of a question as political places a limit on judicial policymaking and suggests that judicial decisions qualitatively differ from those of other governmental officials. Examples of political questions include whether a constitutional amendment was ratified, the legitimacy of two competing state governments, the length of time the United States could rightfully occupy enemy territory, the deportation of an enemy alien whom the attorney general considered dangerous to the public peace and safety, the status of Indian tribes, and the termination of a treaty. One issue that originally was considered a political question but is no longer is legislative districting and apportionment. Beginning with *Baker* v. *Carr* in 1962, the Supreme Court ruled that the matter was justiciable and that private citizens have standing to sue for disparities in the population of state and local legislative districts as well as congressional districts.

Ironically, in this first decision to hold districting and apportionment a justiciable, rather than a political, question, the Supreme Court presented a set of criteria to determine whether a question is political. The list is treated as definitive, even though the criteria contain words and phrases of a markedly murky character: (1) a "textually demonstrable" commitment of the issue to the legislative or executive branch of government; (2) a "lack of judicially discoverable and manageable standards" for its resolution; (3) the need for an initial policy determination of a kind "clearly for nonjudicial discretion"; (4) a judicial resolution that would indicate "lack of the respect due" a coordinate branch of government; (5) an "unusual need" for "unquestioning adherence" to a previously made political decision; (6) the "potentiality of embarrassment" because of "multifarious pronouncements by various departments" on a single issue.

Finality of Decision. To preserve their coordinate status with the president and Congress, the federal courts refuse to decide controversies if the decision will not be final and binding on the litigants. Except for the Supreme Court's original jurisdiction, the lower federal courts and the Supreme Court receive their jurisdiction as a result of acts of Congress. Congress, however, has not seen fit to give to the courts subject matter jurisdiction over all matters that fall within the constitutionally specified judicial power of the United States. Instead, Congress has authorized various nonjudicial officials and agencies to make the final and binding decision. The classic example concerns the eligibility of a veteran for pension and disability benefits. An eighteenth-century statute vested this power in the secretary of war; today the authority lodges in the Veterans Administration.

The capability of a court to reverse the decision of a lower court does not negate this element of standing; neither does the possibility that the legislature may amend a statute already construed by a court and thereby overturn the court's decision. The same applies to a proposed constitutional amendment. The rule merely requires that, at the time of decision, the court's judgment bind the litigants and not be susceptible to review by bureaucratic or administrative officials.

Estoppel. Peripherally related to the foregoing element of standing is that pertaining to the binding effect of judicial decisions themselves. Res judicata, or claim estoppel, is the assertion that a claim has already been litigated and so cannot be made the subject of a second lawsuit. Similarly, collateral estoppel bars relitigation of an issue in a second trial. Claim and issue preclusion are based on the principle that a litigant should get only one bite of the apple—that once individuals have had their day in court, further proceedings are precluded. The principle serves several purposes: it lessens the courts' burdens; it enables litigants to rely on a court's initial decisions and thereby plan for the future; and it prevents the judicial system from being used as a tool of harassment.

To assert res judicata, a party must show that the same claim or cause of action between the same parties was resolved by a final judgment and that the final judgment was based on the merits of the controversy. Accordingly, where an initial cause of action was dismissed for want of subject matter jurisdiction, res judicata does not bar relitigation in the proper forum. The interests of judicial economy cause many jurisdictions to define causes of action broadly, thereby requiring a litigant to join all his claims against his opponent. Multiple suits are avoided inasmuch as these "transaction test" jurisdictions effectively define as res judicata claims that should have been litigated in the original proceeding even if they actually were not. Such claims remain unlitigated. The same party requirement of res judicata encompasses those who are in privity with an original litigant (for example, agency and employment relationships, as well as successors in interest). In short, res judicata binds persons whose interests are so wedded to those of an existing party that it would waste judicial time to allow a second action merely because they were not named in the initial suit.

Invocation of collateral estoppel requires showing that the identical issue was actually decided in an earlier proceeding and that deciding it was necessary to resolve the original dispute. Whether identity of issue obtains and whether it was a decided issue pose far less difficulty than a determination that the issue was necessary to the original proceeding. Because due process of law prevents use of collateral estoppel against nonparties who were given no opportunity to be heard, nonparties may be allowed to assert it. Historically, the doctrine of mutuality prevented its assertion—that collateral estoppel applied only where the parties to the second action had both been parties to the first suit. But today many jurisdictions disregard mutuality to varying degrees.

Consider an auto accident in which three passengers were injured. Passenger A establishes the driver's liability. If the jurisdiction allows collateral estoppel to be asserted offensively, passengers B and C may move for summary judgment on the issue of the driver's liability. Conversely, nonmutual defensive collateral estoppel occurs when a defendant seeks to prevent a plaintiff from relitigating an issue plaintiff previously lost against another defendant. To determine whether a previous nonparty may assert collateral estoppel against a party, courts focus on whether the party had a full and fair opportunity to litigate the issue in the first action. Increasingly, courts are tending to apply collateral estoppel only where the subsequent action was reasonably foreseeable at the time of the initial adjudication. If so, estoppel applies; if not, it does not.

Exhaustion of Administrative Remedies. In order to avoid encroaching on alternative methods of dispute resolution, courts typically require plaintiffs to exhaust any administrative remedies that the law affords. Accordingly, a plaintiff charging unfair labor practices must exhaust the remedies provided by the National Labor Relations Board, and a federal taxpayer challenging the amount of taxes owed must initially utilize the procedures provided by the Internal Revenue Service. Only thereafter will a federal court entertain the cases. Exceptions to exhaustion exist: when an agency acts ultra vires (beyond the scope of its authority); when an agency's action will produce irreparable injury; when an agency behaves in a deliberately dilatory manner; or when pursuit of an administrative remedy is obviously futile. The plaintiff bears the burden of proving an excep-

tion. Courts regularly require exhaustion when the question presented clearly falls within the agency's expertise and when the remedy sought is as likely as judicial action to provide the wanted relief.

In summary, the elements of standing—the determination of whether the litigants are proper parties—effectively limit the types of controversies courts will hear, in order that judges may avoid hypothetical, officious, and redundant questions and unnecessary conflicts with other policymakers. The rules governing standing also provide judges with a tactical flexibility that enables them to avoid issues they prefer not to resolve and to cite good legal form as their justification for doing so.

CONFLICTS OF LAW

The constitutionally prescribed division of power between the national government and the states, which made the United States a federal system, is a primary source of legal conflict. Such conflicts concern federal-state relationships and interstate relationships. Conflicts between the state and federal courts result because of overlapping, or concurrent, jurisdiction. For example, a question that is within the subject matter jurisdiction of the federal courts will frequently arise in the course of state court proceedings. Thus, a person accused of violating state law is tried without representation by counsel or is convicted as a result of illegally seized evidence; or a state law allegedly abridges First Amendment freedoms or unconstitutionally dispossesses a person of her property. Interstate conflicts occur because individuals and corporations do not limit their activities to the confines of a single state. State courts, however, traditionally reached only those persons and things within their geographical jurisdiction. How, then, could a state bring to the bar of its justice nonresidents? Is a victim denied judicial remedy in his own state courts because his injuries result from the negligence of an out-of-state business?

National Supremacy. The Constitution, in the supremacy clause of Article VI, unequivocally establishes federal law as supreme over that of the states and requires that state court judges give effect to federal law, "any thing in the Constitution or laws of any State to the contrary notwithstanding." To make this language operative, Congress, in the Judiciary Act of 1789, gave the Supreme Court jurisdiction to review state court decisions that involved a federal question. Supreme Court review was not triggered until the litigant pleading the federal question had exhausted all avenues of appeal open to him in the state court system—typically a final judgment rendered by the state supreme court. This jurisdictional grant did not settle matters. The state courts were markedly involved in deciding federal questions because Congress did not see fit to give the federal district courts first-instance jurisdiction over federal questions until after the Civil War. Only state courts could try these controversies.

To ensure the supremacy of federal law, it was especially important that the Supreme Court have jurisdiction to review state court decisions. State court judges, however, maintained that inasmuch as they were bound by the supremacy clause of the Constitution, they, as well as the Supreme Court, had the right to ultimately decide federal questions. In a landmark decision, *Martin* v. *Hunter's Lessee* (1816), which was aptly described as "the keystone of the whole arch of federal judicial power," the Supreme Court rejected the states' argument and affirmed its own power to review and authoritatively resolve federal questions.

Several results flow from *Martin* v. *Hunter's Lessee* and the facts from which it arose. First, the major link between the state and federal judiciaries is that which connects the courts at the top of each hierarchy. Second, absent this link, each state's supreme court would have been left to decide for itself the meaning of constitutional provisions, acts of Congress, and treaties of the United States. And if that were the situation, the United States would be no more united than the United Nations. Each state would long since have become a separate, sovereign entity—a nation. The meanings of due process, interstate commerce, and the First Amendment would vary from one state to another, with the likely result that any given constitutional guarantee or statutory provision would have fifty different meanings, depending on the state. Third, the link that the Judiciary Act provides is, for all practical purposes, the only glue that effectively unites the states as governmental entities. Congress provided this link, and what Congress gives, Congress may take away. Indeed, until a decade or two after the Civil War, bills to do just that were introduced on at least ten separate occasions.

Comity and the Abstention Doctrine. Mindful of the tender sensibilities of the states and their judges (which sensibilities are markedly less than those of pre–Civil War states' righters), the Supreme Court has devised a system of comity to minimize conflict between the state and federal courts. The most popular description of comity dates from a 1971 Supreme Court decision, *Younger* v. *Harris:*

> a proper respect for state functions, a recognition of the fact that the entire country is made up of a Union of separate state governments, and a continuance of the belief that the National Government will fare best if the States and their institutions are left free to perform their separate functions in their separate ways. . . . The concept does not mean blind deference to "States' Rights" any more than it means centralization of control over every important issue in our National Government and its courts. . . . What the concept does represent is a system in which there is sensitivity to the legitimate interests of both State and National Governments, and in which the National Government, anxious though it may be to vindicate and protect federal rights and federal interests, always endeavors to do so in ways that will not unduly interfere with the legitimate activities of the States.

The major instrument for effectuating comity is the abstention doctrine, formulated in a 1941 decision, *Railroad Commission of Texas* v. *Pullman Co.*, "whereby the federal courts, 'exercising a wise discretion,' restrain their authority because of 'scrupulous regard for the rightful independence of the state governments' and for the smooth working of the federal judiciary." Abstention thus requires the federal courts to avoid intruding themselves into ongoing state court proceedings or otherwise duplicating litigation previously commenced in a state's courts. Accordingly, litigants must exhaust state remedies, administrative as well as judicial, before gaining access to the federal courts. This gives the courts of each state priority in determining the constitutionality of their state's statutes and regulations and may obviate the need for federal court involvement if a state court's resolution of the federal question is compatible with federal law. On the other hand, abstention precludes prompt federal court protection of federal rights.

Occasioning federal-state judicial conflict has been the expansion of the subject matter jurisdiction of the federal courts to encompass virtually all federal questions and the increased authority of the federal district courts to enjoin state court proceedings, to issue writs of habeas corpus, and to remove cases from the state to the federal courts. Inasmuch as the abstention doctrine does not flatly require federal courts to stay their hands in all circumstances, the Supreme Court has formulated additional criteria for specific forms of federal relief.

Injunctions to stop criminal prosecutions will be granted only on a showing of "great and immediate" danger of "irreparable injury." The same difficult-to-meet standard applies to efforts to enjoin state civil proceedings. As a result, injunctions are largely limited to bad-faith prosecutions or official harassment.

Writs of habeas corpus will be granted to state prisoners by a federal district court only if they "seasonably" (that is, contemporaneously) raised their federal question at the appropriate stage of state judicial proceedings and, in addition, the state court failed to provide "an opportunity for full and fair litigation" of the federal claim. Although the quoted test is applied in the context of violations of the search-and-seizure clause of the Fourth Amendment, most habeas petitions are based thereon. Neither would it be surprising if the Court, as cases arose, extended its "full and fair litigation" standard across the full range of federal questions.

The statutory provision permitting removal of cases from the state to a federal district court that bears most directly on the system of comity concerns state denial or refusal to enforce federally protected civil rights. The Supreme Court has construed such rights extremely narrowly: the federal rights must be expressly specified, and they must grant freedom not only to engage in the protected conduct but also freedom from state arrest and prosecution. The Supreme Court has imposed an additional limitation that applies to at least one civil right—namely, removal only for violent interference with the exercise of the specified right, not merely freedom from arrest and prosecution (*Soliusou* v. *Mississippi*, 1975).

As the foregoing discussion suggests, the ab-stention doctrine applies most forcefully when state judicial proceedings have commenced and when one of the parties is the state itself. If the former condition is absent, no duplication of proceedings occurs; in such a situation, according to the Court, "principles of federalism not only do not preclude federal intervention, they compel it." If the latter condition is absent, the dispute concerns private persons and, as a result, removal of the case from state to federal court may be appropriate. In such cases, federal law permits defendants to remove if the controversy is one that could have been brought in federal court originally. This precludes removal when the defendant relies on federal law as a defense to plaintiff's nonfederal action. Federal-question jurisdiction extends only to plaintiff's claims. The major limitation on removal prohibits such in diversity-of-citizenship cases if any defendant is a resident of the state in which the action was brought. A minor limitation prohibits removal in certain classes of tort (private injury) actions where Congress wishes to give the plaintiff an unrestricted choice of forum.

Sovereign Immunity. Although Article III of the Constitution provides the Supreme Court with original jurisdiction in suits between states, the Eleventh Amendment immunizes the states from suit in federal court brought by nonresidents. The amendment, ratified in 1798 in reaction to the Supreme Court decision *Chisholm* v. *Georgia* (1793) that held that federal jurisdiction extended to such suits, lessens federal-state conflicts by denying federal-court access to those who would sue a state for damages. Even prior to the Eleventh Amendment, federal jurisdiction did not extend to suits against a state brought by its own residents. A state may waive its immunity from suit, either expressly or by implication. Waiver, however, is not required where one state sues another, but a foreign nation may not sue a state without its consent. Of course, sovereign immunity does not prevent any person—resident or not—from appealing an adverse state court decision in a suit that the state itself commenced.

Supreme Court decisions have narrowly construed the Eleventh Amendment. Immunity applies only to the states as states; it does not apply to state officials or to local governments. In general, only suits seeking to recover money from the state treasury are barred. Finally, the last section of the Fourteenth Amendment, which gives Congress the power to enforce the amendment's provisions (most especially, the rights of persons not to be deprived of due process or denied equal protection), overrides the Eleventh Amendment. Congress, therefore, may authorize the federal courts to entertain damage suits brought by persons whose civil rights a state has abridged.

Enforcement of Judgments. The full faith and credit clause of Article IV of the Constitution requires each state to give to the judgments of any other state's courts the same effect that those judgments would have in the states which rendered them. As such, full faith and credit also causes the courts of one state to give the decisions of other states' courts at least as much res judicata effect as they would have in the rendering state. Although the full faith and credit clause binds only the states, federal law requires the federal courts to enforce state court judgments. If a federal court makes the initial decision, res judicata decrees that the state court, in turn, enforce the federal decision.

The utility of the foregoing is obvious. If losing litigants could avoid liability merely by moving out of state, unity and good interstate relations would be lost. As it is, where a litigant has won a judgment that is unenforceable because the defendant has removed his property from the state whose court rendered judgment, said litigant may commence suit in a state wherein defendant does have property. Upon proof of the original judgment, the second state's court must enter an identical judgment on the basis of which the plaintiff may attach or levy on defendant's property. The second court may not reexamine the merits of the original judgment, even if that judgment misinterpreted a law of the second state.

Assume, for example, that state A construes B's laws (as applicable to the case) to permit enforcement of antenuptial contracts or imposition of strict liability in certain circumstances. In a proceeding in B's courts to enforce the wrongfully awarded damages, B's judges have no option but to grant full faith and credit to A's decision. The only exception to automatic enforcement permits B to examine A's jurisdiction over the person or property of the defendant. If such jurisdiction is lacking or has not been waived, B may refuse to enforce A's judgment.

The use of full faith and credit to establish a claim as res judicata benefits the defendant, rather than the plaintiff, in the initial lawsuit in trial court. Assume, for example, that state A renders a judgment that, by its laws, may not be relitigated. The original plaintiff then seeks to avail himself of the laws of B that permit relitigation of the claim in question. State B may not apply its law; rather, it must give A's decision the res judicata effect it would have had if plaintiff had brought a second suit in state A.

Choice of Law. In cases in which federal and state law conflict, the Constitution mandates that preference be accorded to federal law. In cases in which no controlling federal law exists—typically, diversity-of-citizenship cases—Congress has, since 1789, required the federal courts to apply the "laws of the several states." Does this phrase apply only to constitutional provisions and legislation, or does it extend to the "common law" of a state (that is, that made by judges)? Before the twentieth century, legislatures enacted few laws. Then, as now, constitutions only outlined the scope of governmental power and, in actuality, paid more attention to limitations on government rather than the exercise of power.

Consequently, if the "laws of the several states" meant only constitutions and statutes, the federal courts would need to fashion their own common law to resolve disputes based on diversity jurisdiction. The Supreme Court so held in the definitive nineteenth-century decision *Swift* v. *Tyson* (1842). Nearly a century later, in *Erie R. Co.* v. *Tompkins* (1938), the Court overruled *Swift* and held that the refusal of federal courts, sitting in diversity, to follow state common law occasioned an unconstitutional assumption of power. Nothing in the Constitution confers on either Congress or the federal courts the power to formulate and apply to the states substantive common law rules. Rather, this power is reserved to the states under the Tenth Amendment.

The practical effect of the *Erie* decision terminated the bias in favor of out-of-state litigants. Previously, rights varied according to whether relief was sought in state or federal courts. The selection of the court to resolve the dispute was made by the nonresident. He, consequently, would "forum shop" for the court most favorable to himself. *Erie*, however, required federal courts to apply the law—written, as well as judge-made—of the state in which the federal court sat, "except in matters governed by the Federal Constitution or by acts of Congress."

One matter so governed is the authority of Congress to prescribe rules of procedure for the federal courts. In 1934, Congress enacted an "Enabling Act" that delegated to the Supreme Court such power so long as the resulting rules did not "abridge, enlarge, or modify the substantive rights of any litigant." Four months prior to the *Erie* decision, the Court adopted the Federal Rules of Civil Procedure, which provided a uniform system of procedure for the federal courts. These took effect in September 1938, less than five months after *Erie.* The problem, of course, is that rules are never neutral and, as a result, invariably affect "substantive" rights.

Mindful of "the twin aims of the Erie rule, discouragement of forum-shopping and avoidance of inequitable administration of the laws," the Court, in a series of decisions, has provided guidance for the resolution of problems that the federal courts exercising diversity jurisdiction faced in the aftermath of *Erie:* (1) Federal courts are to apply the "substantive" law of the state in which they sit and federal "procedural" rules. (2) A rule is "substantive" if it is "outcome determinative"—for example, a state statute of limitations shorter than that provided by federal law, or a law barring an out-of-state corporation the right to bring a lawsuit because it had failed to comply with the state's corporation law. (3) If, however, the issue is covered by the Federal Rules of Civil Procedure, the matter is considered procedural and the federal rule applies. To date, none of the Federal Rules have been held to violate the "substantive" language of the 1934 legislation that authorized the enactment of the Federal Rules. Hence, if the Federal Rules address a matter, that matter is by definition procedural, notwithstanding the fact that it may completely frustrate the state's substantive concerns and determine the outcome of the litigation. (4) If a matter is not covered by the Federal Rules but nonetheless affects an important federal interest, the matter is to be treated as procedural, notwithstanding its outcome-determinative character. For example, the federal interest in disposing of complicated multiparty litigation in a single trial overrides a state law that prohibits suits against out-of-state corporations by nonresidents, and the "very strong federal policy" supporting jury determination subordinates a state law requiring a judge rather than a jury to determine certain factual matters pertaining to employment relationships.

Although the federal courts since *Erie* have shown sensitivity to considerations of federalism in their choice of law, no set of rules can provide clear-cut guidance. Whereas state court judges confronted by a conflict between state and federal law have no choice but to follow federal law as the supremacy clause of the Constitution requires, federal judges must attempt to weigh and balance the interests of both state and nation.

JURISDICTION OVER PARTIES

The ability of a court to render a binding, enforceable judgment in a lawsuit depends on the court's jurisdiction over the specific parties to the litigation or the property at stake. By bringing a lawsuit, the plaintiff submits himself to the court's jurisdiction. Not so the defendant. To exercise jurisdiction over a defendant's person or property, a court must meet the requirements of due process of law. Defendants are clearly entitled to notice and hearing, but those alone do not suffice. The court must also have the power to act on the defendant or his property. Whether such power exists depends on whether there have been sufficient "minimum contacts" with the forum state. Individuals having substantial contacts with the forum state subject themselves to "general" personal jurisdiction; a binding judgment may be entered against them on any claim. "Limited" personal jurisdiction, by comparison, permits binding judgments only on claims arising out of the specific minimal contacts or relationships that the defendant has with the forum state.

Minimum Contacts. If a person is domiciled or resides in the forum state, minimum contacts and general personal jurisdiction may be presumed, the rationale being that a state which affords protection to a person and his property may exact reciprocal duties. Persons may also consent to jurisdiction and thereby establish minimum contacts, either expressly or by implication. A plaintiff, for example, by initiating suit, subjects himself to a possible counterclaim brought by the original defendant. Jurisdiction attaches even though the plaintiff dismisses his action or fails to prosecute it. Persons may expressly subject themselves to the jurisdiction of a particular court even before a controversy has arisen. Thus, individuals may agree that the terms of their contract may be enforced against them only in the courts of the other party's state of domicile, and they may, in addition, even waive their rights to notice and hearing.

Obviously, application of the minimum-contacts test is much more crucial when the defendant is an unconsenting nonresident. If the defendant is within the state's boundaries, limited personal jurisdiction applies to the defendant's "contacts." Persons whose contacts involve transacting business may be sued in connection therewith; thus, motorists may be sued for the accidents they cause, and corporations, for injuries their products produce. But if the unconsenting nonresident is outside the state, jurisdiction does not attach unless, as a threshold matter, the forum state has a "long-arm statute" authorizing its courts to assert extraterritorial jurisdiction.

Long-arm statutes are of two types. One type lists in detail the kinds of intrastate activity that permits assertion of extraterritorial jurisdiction. Every state, for example, authorizes jurisdiction over nonresident motorists who cause accidents within the state. Other common acts include contracting to provide goods or services, owning land, and out-of-state acts that produce injuries within the state. The other type of long-arm statute avoids a detailed listing and grants to the state courts jurisdiction over the defendant whenever he has the necessary minimum contacts. The undefined language of the latter type allows the state to stretch its jurisdiction to the limits allowed by due process. As such, that type is readily applicable to an increasingly mobile society and its expanded business and commercial activities. On the other hand, its vagueness invites defendants to challenge the constitutionality of its reach as applied to them.

Application of the minimum-contacts test involves certain considerations: whether the defendant has minimum contacts with the forum state sufficient to ensure that maintenance of the lawsuit does not offend "traditional notions" of "fair play" and "substantial justice"; whether defendant's contacts with the forum state were voluntary; and whether defendant benefited by his contacts with the forum state. The foregoing considerations, needless to say, do not admit of precise application. They are, at best, rough guidelines.

Although the minimum-contacts test was formulated in a case involving personal jurisdiction over an out-of-state corporation, *International Shoe Co.* v. *State of Washington, Etc.* (1945), it applies to individuals as well. Inasmuch as it was established in reaction to the nineteenth-century test that virtually limited jurisdiction to personal presence within the forum state, it presumably governs defendants who were temporarily in the state when served with notice of the pending lawsuit. In addition to personal jurisdiction over individuals and corporations (that is, in personam), the minimum-contacts test also applies to jurisdiction over property (in rem).

Judgments in Personam. The policy-oriented character of the minimum-contacts test allows courts to exercise considerable discretion in determining whether in personam jurisdiction exists. Nonetheless, certain general considerations apply. If an individual or corporation regularly and voluntarily enters the state for beneficial purposes and if the cause of action also arose within the state, jurisdiction exists. Defendant's contacts exceed a minimal level; the court will be convenient as the witnesses, evidence, and applicable law are at hand. If entry is irregular, voluntary, and without particular benefit but the cause of action occurred within the state, jurisdiction likely lies, as when a traveler passing through a state in order to get to a destination in another state causes an accident in the interim state. Where defendant has more than minimum contacts with a state the specific cause of action need not be forum-related, as when a California-licensed trucker who hauls $400,000 worth of cargo into California during twenty trips per year, while en route to California, kills a California resident in Nevada. However, if defendant's activities are sporadic, then the cause of action likely needs to have occurred within the forum state.

Perhaps the outer limit of minimum contacts was reached in a case involving a life insurance policy written by a Texas company that apparently neither solicited nor did any other business in the forum state. The insurer refused to pay, claiming that the insured's death was a suicide. The insured, his beneficiary, and all witnesses resided in the forum state. The Supreme Court held that entering into this contract was sufficient to establish jurisdiction because of the state's interest "in providing effective means of redress for its citizens when insurers refuse to pay claims." Fairness to the insurer was subordinated.

Where, however, the cause of action occurred outside the forum state, fairness to the defendant receives heavier, and perhaps controlling, weight. In any event, minimum contacts between the defendant and the state must have existed. A court's convenient location or the fact that it may be the "center of gravity" of a particular controversy does not establish jurisdiction. However minimal the burden of defending in an out-of-state tribunal, "territorial limitations on the power of the respective states" preclude requiring a defendant to do so unless the requisite contacts exist.

Other considerations being equal, minimum contacts are more difficult to establish when the cause of action concerns a contract dispute rather than a tort action. In the latter situation, state interest in public safety, health, or welfare may tip the jurisdictional balance in favor of its own courts. Witnesses and evidence may not be easily moved to an out-of-state court. In contract actions, however, the defendant's contacts with the forum state may have been involuntary—for example, when a buyer must enter the state to purchase goods, or when the plaintiff is a major corporation and thus has ready access to a convenient out-of-state forum and the defendant is an individual who would be unfairly burdened traveling to the forum state.

Nonetheless, application of the minimum-contacts test remains problematic even where torts are concerned. Consider an Ohio company that made valves which it sold to another company who incorporated them into boilers. Plaintiff purchased a boiler that exploded in Illinois. Illinois' courts had jurisdiction over the valve maker on the basis that the tort was committed when the damage occurred rather than when the product was manufactured. Similarly, an Indiana company manufactured golf carts that it sold to another Indiana company. The latter sold a defective one to an Illinois country club. The manufacturer was held subject to Illinois' jurisdiction, notwithstanding the absence of any other contacts, so long as the plaintiff could show

that defendant intended to use interstate channels of commerce and that defendant could reasonably have foreseen entry of golf carts into states other than that of manufacture.

From a policy standpoint, the main concern has been the use of minimum contacts to establish jurisdiction based on a single out-of-state tort with in-state consequences, even though the consequences were foreseeable. If, for example, a retailer or other small business can be forced to defend in a distant state's courts for injuries occurring therein, availability to suit would travel with every item sold. As a result, sellers might refuse to do business with nonresidents, thereby deterring interstate commercial activity. The Supreme Court allayed such fears in *World-Wide Volkswagen Corp.* v. *Woodson* (1980). New York residents who had purchased an automobile from a New York dealer brought a product-liability action in Oklahoma against the dealer and his New York distributor for injuries suffered in an accident in Oklahoma. The Court held that the defendants' only contact with Oklahoma was "the fortuitous circumstance that a single . . . automobile, sold in New York to New York residents, happened to suffer an accident while passing through Oklahoma." Defendants closed no sales and performed no services in Oklahoma; they solicited no business there either through salespersons or media; neither did they avail themselves of the benefits of Oklahoma law, nor did they regularly sell or seek to serve, directly or indirectly, the Oklahoma market. The record therefore displayed "a total absence of those affiliating circumstances that are a necessary predicate to any exercise of state-court jurisdiction." And while foreseeability is not wholly irrelevant, the foreseeability "critical to due process analysis is not the mere likelihood that a product will find its way into the forum State. Rather, it is that the defendant's conduct and connection with the forum State are such that he should reasonably anticipate being haled into court there."

Insofar as the federal courts are concerned, their in personam jurisdiction is limited to the state in which they sit and anyplace else that that state's law permits. Congress, of course, could enact legislation governing the assertion of personal jurisdiction, but for the most part Congress has not done so. Major exceptions include suits brought under the federal antitrust and securities laws, and interpleader actions. The latter gives the district courts jurisdiction over claimants to the funds in the stakeholder's possession regardless of where they are in the United States. Causes of action involving joinder of parties other than the original plaintiff and defendant extend jurisdiction 100 miles from the federal courthouse.

Judgments In Rem and Quasi In Rem. It happens, particularly where real estate is involved, that a lawsuit does not impose personal liability on anyone but, rather, seeks to litigate the interests of persons in a specific thing (the res). On the theory that a state's "sovereignty" gives it power over all property within its borders, its courts could therefore render valid and enforceable judgments concerning ownership and title to in-state property. The same rationale applied to the status of persons domiciled within a state. Accordingly, a state's courts could issue binding decrees concerning such matters as marital status or the custody of children. The status is considered the res, and domiciliaries may commence in rem actions to alter their status, as in divorce.

Jurisdictional questions rarely arise for in rem actions. If it is established that the property is within the state or that the person seeking a change in status is domiciled therein, the state's courts may proceed. Although the minimum-contacts standard applies, it is typically met because the property or status is voluntarily acquired and protected by the state. Insofar as the federal courts are concerned, federal law allows the district courts to reach defendants nationwide "to enforce any lien upon or claim to, or to remove any incumbrance or lien or cloud upon the title to, real or personal property within the district" (28 U.S.C. 1655).

Considerably greater difficulty attends the exercise of *quasi in rem* jurisdiction. In such actions, defendant's property within the state is seized as a vehicle to adjudicate personal rights that are unrelated to the seized property; in other words, because jurisdiction over the defendant's person cannot be had, his property is attached instead, not as the subject of litigation but rather as a means of satisfying a possible judgment or establishing jurisdiction. A typical example concerns a nonresident's indebtedness to someone, here called A. A sues debtor in state X, which has no relationship with the debt and in which the

debtor has no contacts, minimum or otherwise. Debtor, however, does own property in state X. To establish jurisdiction in the courts of X, A attaches debtor's property therein. If A wins his suit to collect on the debt, the attached property constitutes payment.

Quasi in rem jurisdiction, which typically involves money damages, may be viewed as a halfway house between in rem and in personam jurisdiction: it is in rem in the sense that the court can adjudicate the case only because the defendant has in-state property and in personam in the sense that the dispute really concerns a personal dispute between the plaintiff and defendant, not title to the attached property.

The Federal Rules allow federal district courts to exercise *quasi in rem* jurisdiction compatibly with the law of the state in which the court sits. Hence, if the state's long-arm statute reaches the defendant, so also may the district court. Of course, federal courts, no less than those of the states, must meet the minimum-contacts standard to perfect jurisdiction.

Quasi in rem proceedings have unusual features. First, if the plaintiff wins, his judgment may be satisfied only out of the attached property. If, for example, defendant has a $10,000 obligation to the plaintiff but the value of the attached property is only $5,000, a new action must be brought and litigated on its merits for plaintiff to recover further—even if other unattached property exists within the forum state. Second, *quasi in rem* judgments have no res judicata effect. If plaintiff wins in one state, he may not use that judgment to escape having to litigate his claim in a second state. Similarly, if the defendant wins, she cannot use that result to bar plaintiff from initiating a new action elsewhere. Furthermore, judicial actions without res judicata effects are not enforceable by way of the full faith and credit clause except insofar as the specifically attached property is concerned. Third, if a defendant to *quasi in rem* action appears in court, he subjects himself to in personam jurisdiction and, if the plaintiff wins, the court may enter a binding judgment with res judicata effect for the full amount claimed rather than just for the value of the attached property.

To alleviate defendant's dilemma about appearing, a number of states authorize defendants to make a limited appearance. This enables defendants to contest cases on their merits but limits liability to the property attached by the court. Alternatively, some states permit defendants to make a special appearance. This allows a defendant to object to the court's jurisdiction over either his person or his property without subjecting himself to the exercise of the jurisdiction to which he objects. With regard to limited appearances, a federal court follows the law of the state in which it sits. In place of a special appearance, the Federal Rules of Civil Procedure allows a defendant to move to dismiss for lack of jurisdiction. The making of such a motion does not subject the mover to the jurisdiction he is protesting.

So long as *quasi in rem* jurisdiction was limited to real property, controversy surrounding its exercise remained limited. But with its twentieth-century extension to movable property, intangibles, and contingent obligations, quarreling intensified. Legal fictions and presumptions divorced from reality were created to identify the location of certain kinds of property: bank deposits were deemed to be located in the bank where they were made; stock where the stock certificates were held; and debts wherever the debtor happened to be. These developments, plus the alleged unfairness of *quasi in rem* jurisdiction to many defendants, have caused the Supreme Court to revamp it in recent years.

In a major decision, *Shaffer* v. *Heitner* (1977), the Court initially applied the minimum-contacts test to *quasi in rem* jurisdiction. A stockholder sued a corporation's nonresident officers and directors in Delaware, the state of incorporation. None of the activities complained of had occurred in Delaware; neither did any of the defendants have other contacts with the state. The corporation itself was headquartered in Arizona and conducted most of its activities there. The plaintiff gained jurisdiction via a statute which provided that the stock of any Delaware corporation could be attached because its stock was irrebuttably presumed to be located within the state. More than $1 million worth of stock was thereby attached. Because Delaware does not allow limited appearances, the defendants confronted a Hobson's choice: fail to defend and forfeit their stock, or defend and subject themselves to unlimited personal liability.

In its opinion, the Court focused on reality, not fiction, and ruled that all judicial action concerning "things" actually adjudicates the rights and interests of people; nowhere is that truer than in *quasi in rem* proceedings where the "thing" is merely a means to get at people. The fact that liability is limited is irrelevant. "Fairness . . . does not depend on the size of the claim." The Court concluded that "if a direct assertion of personal jurisdiction . . . violate[s] the Constitution . . . an indirect assertion . . . should be equally impermissible." Therefore, all assertions of state-court jurisdiction must meet the minimum-contacts standard. The Court also rejected various arguments supporting *quasi in rem* jurisdiction, most important, the contention that defendants ought not be able to avoid their obligations by placing their assets in states where minimum contacts preclude suit. Such attempts, the Court noted, may be countered by suing defendants in their domicile state—regardless of the presence of assets—or where minimum contacts do exist, securing a judgment, and enforcing it under the provisions of full faith and credit.

As for the application of minimum contacts in a *quasi in rem* context, the Supreme Court in *Rush* v. *Savchuk* (1980) again ignored legal fictions and emphasized a focus on fairness. *Savchuk* concerned an Indiana resident who injured another resident in an Indiana auto accident. Indiana law barred the injured party's claim. The claimant then domiciled himself in Minnesota and brought suit in a Minnesota court, claiming that *quasi in rem* jurisdiction attached because of an insurance policy issued to the defendant in Indiana by a company doing business in Minnesota, as well as the other forty-nine states. Plaintiff alleged that insurance companies are obliged to defend their policyholders (here the defendant), that such obligations are debts, and that debts may be garnisheed. The Court, however, held that the only link Minnesota's courts had to the suit was the business done by the insurer in Minnesota. The assignment of a site to the insurance company's "debt" is a legal fiction, as is the view that a corporation is present, for jurisdictional purposes, wherever it does business. Combining these two fictions makes the debt present in all fifty states, and "it is apparent that such a 'contact' can have no jurisdictional significance" under the minimum-contacts test. Furthermore, defendant's contacts may not be aggregated together. Minimum contacts "must be met as to each defendant over whom a state court exercises jurisdiction." As a result of *Savchuk,* jurisdiction over conditional obligations resulting from indebtedness shrank substantially.

On the basis of *Shaffer* and *Savchuk* one might conclude that *quasi in rem* jurisdiction has lost all utility and become merged with in personam jurisdiction. Because *quasi in rem* actions must meet minimum contacts, they will not do anything for plaintiffs that in personam jurisdiction cannot do better. This argument, however, overlooks two considerations. First, in personam jurisdiction requires a long-arm statute, in addition to minimum contacts, for the assertion of extraterritorial jurisdiction. In those states whose long-arm statutes do not go to the limits of due process, a statute authorizing attachment of instate property may permit *quasi in rem* action. Second, courts may view minimum contacts as a sliding scale whose requirements vary depending on the protections each type of proceeding—in personam, in rem, and *quasi in rem*—provides out-of-state defendants.

CASES

Baker v. Carr, 369 U.S. 186 (1962)

Burger King Corp. v. Rudzewicz, 85 LEd2d 528 (1985)

Cannon v. University of Chicago, 44 U.S. 677 (1979)

Chisholm v. Georgia, 2 Dall. 419 (1793)

Cort v. Ash, 422 U.S. 66 (1975)

DeFunis v. Odegaard, 416 U.S. 312 (1974)

Erie R. Co. v. Tompkins, 304 U.S. 64 (1938)

Flast v. Cohen, 392 U.S. 83 (1968)

Hanna v. Plumer, 380 U.S. 460 (1965)

Hanson v. Denckla, 357 U.S. 235 (1958)

International Shoe Co. v. State of Washington, Etc., 326 U.S. 310 (1945)

Louisville & Nashville R. Co. v. Mottley, 211 U.S. 149 (1908)

The Louisville, Cincinnati & Charleston R. Co. v. Letson, 2 Howard 497 (1844)

Marshall v. The Baltimore & Ohio R. Co., 16 Howard 314 (1853)

Martin v. Hunter's Lessee, 1 Wheaton 304 (1816)

Railroad Commission of Texas v. Pullman Co., 312 U.S. 496 (1941)

Rush v. Savchuk, 444 U.S. 320 (1980)

Shaffer v. Heitner, 433 U.S. 186 (1977)

Soliusou v. Mississippi, 421 U.S. 213 (1975)

Stone v. Powell, 428 U.S. 465 (1976)

Strawbridge v. Curtiss, 3 Cranch 267 (1806)

Swift v. Tyson, 16 Peters 1 (1842)

United Mine Workers of America v. Gibbs, 383 U.S. 715 (1966)

World-Wide Volkswagen Corp. v. Woodson, 444 U.S. 286 (1980)

Younger v. Harris, 401 U.S. 37 (1971)

BIBLIOGRAPHY

American Jurisprudence, 2nd ed. (1982), details the case law on federal court jurisdiction. "Federal Practice and Procedure," §§1–2609. *Corpus Juris Secundum* (1960–1961) details the case law on federal court jurisdiction, §§1–360. Kenneth Culp Davis, *Administrative Law Text* (1972), gives a detailed treatment on the subjects of proper parties and sovereign immunity. John P. Frank, *Justice Daniel Dissenting* (1964), is a biography of the United States Supreme Court's champion dissenter; Daniel's dissents substantially concerned the jurisdiction of the federal courts.

Lawrence M. Friedman, *A History of American Law* (1973), works jurisdictional issues into a scholarly yet fascinating account. John A. Garraty, ed., *Quarrels That Have Shaped the Constitution* (1962), includes the jurisdictional features of sixteen lawsuits that produced landmark Supreme Court decisions. James Willard Hurst, *The Growth of American Law* (1950), discusses the structure and jurisdiction of the state and federal courts in chapters 5 and 6. Anthony Lewis, *Gideon's Trumpet* (1964), is a journalist's account of the celebrated case of *Gideon v. Wainwright.*

Lewis Mayers, *The American Legal System* (1964), discusses aspects of jurisdiction in the first four chapters. Richard Neely, *How Courts Govern America* (1981), includes a state supreme court justice's assessment of the uses to which courts put jurisdiction; and *Why Courts Don't Work* (1982), explains the reasons for judicial inefficiency, including that relating to jurisdiction. Robert L. Stern and Eugene Gressman, *Supreme Court Practice* (1978), details, in chapters 2–4, the Supreme Court's jurisdiction. Alan Westin, *The Anatomy of a Constitutional Law Case* (1958), includes an account of the jurisdictional aspects of the famous steel seizure case of 1952. Charles A. Wright, *Law of Federal Courts* (1976), is a standard treatise on federal-court jurisdiction.

[*See also* ADMINISTRATIVE AGENCIES; ADMINISTRATIVE LAW; FEDERAL COURT SYSTEM; JUDICIAL REVIEW; STATE COURT SYSTEMS; *and* SUPREME COURT OF THE UNITED STATES.]

LAW AND MORALITY

Thomas C. Grey

THE making and application of law some-times raises theoretical or philosophical concerns, and nowhere is this more true than in connection with the question of the extent to which the law should enforce moral standards as such. This is an old practical problem in the law; in legal systems that are based, as the United States' largely is, on the political philosophy of liberalism, it is an important question of principle.

The question is not whether the law should ever enforce moral standards, for it is uncontroversial that acts of murder and rape are immoral and that they should be illegal. Rather, the question is whether law should enforce moral standards in those problematic cases involving laws against activities thought immoral but not harmful. The standard examples are laws regulating the sexual activities of consenting adults; some would put laws against gambling and drug use in the same class. Another familiar way of describing the problem is to ask whether and to what extent there should be laws creating "victimless crimes."

THE HISTORICAL CONTEXT OF THE DISPUTE

The modern debate over the enforcement of morality can be traced back to 1859, the year John Stuart Mill published his essay *On Liberty*. In that work, Mill urged acceptance of "one very simple principle" meant to "govern absolutely the dealings of society with the individual in the way of compulsion and control." As Mill stated it, the principle was "that the only purpose for which power can be rightfully exercised over any member of a civilized community, against his will, is to prevent harm to others."

From Law Reform to Philosophy. In the 1950s the debate over Mill's principle was vigorously renewed in Great Britain and the United States. The modern revival of this debate was stimulated by two related efforts at reform of the criminal law, both of which were part of a general contemporary critique of the punishment of "victimless crimes." In the United States, the drafters of the Model Penal Code proposed in 1955 to "exclude from the criminal law all sexual practices not involving force, adult corruption of minors, or public offense." In the drafters' view, "no harm to the secular interests of the community" resulted from "atypical sex practice in private between consenting adult partners." Such practices thus fell exclusively in the "area of private morals," and it was "inappropriate for the government to attempt to control behavior that has no substantial significance except as to the morality of the actor."

Two years later, in England, the Wolfenden Committee, which had been established to review the law governing prostitution and homosexuality, recommended repeal of the statute punishing homosexual acts between consenting adults. The committee argued that the functions of the criminal law were limited to the preservation of public order, the protection of the citizen against offense or injury, and the safeguarding of children and other especially vulnerable groups against exploitation. In particular, the committee stressed "the importance which society and the law ought to give to individual freedom of choice and action in matters of private morality" and concluded that "there must remain a realm of private morality and immorality which is, in brief and crude terms, not the law's business."

In 1958 the distinguished British judge Sir Patrick Devlin (later Lord Devlin) criticized the theoretical premises of the Wolfenden Report, arguing that no separate sphere of merely private morality could be marked off as in principle outside the concern of the criminal law. For him, the health of a society rested on its firm adherence to a binding moral code, so that the entire system of prevailing moral beliefs must be in principle subject to legal enforcement, though prudence might suggest limits on morals legislation.

The Model Penal Code drafters, the Wolfenden Committee, and Lord Devlin did not mention Mill's *On Liberty*. Nevertheless, the position of the reformers was recognizably in the spirit of Mill, and Lord Devlin's counterattack was recognizably critical of that spirit. At this point, the British legal philosopher H. L. A. Hart entered the dispute. In his book *Law, Liberty and Morality* (1963), Hart placed the controversy around the Wolfenden Report in the wider context of the century-old debate over Mill's principle, noting the similarity between the views of Lord Devlin and those expressed by Mill's nineteenth-century critic Sir James Fitzjames Stephen in his *Liberty, Equality, Fraternity* (1873).

At the same time, along with his review of the controversy, Hart offered a modern revision of Mill's principle. Lord Devlin responded, expanding his original position while criticizing Hart's views, in *The Enforcement of Morals* (1965). The Hart-Devlin debate attracted the attention of a number of the best-known Anglo-American writers on legal philosophy, and succeeding years saw a flurry of theoretical work on the modern implications of Mill's principle.

Transformation in Philosophy. The Hart-Devlin debate came at an important juncture for Anglo-American social philosophy. Over the preceding two decades, English and American philosophers had primarily pursued the technique of ordinary-language analysis, an approach that focused philosophers' professional attention on close examination of the use and meaning of the terms of everyday speech. The central thesis of the ordinary-language school was that traditional problems of philosophy could often be shown to result from the extension of ordinary terms outside their context in normal usage. A corollary was a consensus that philosophers had no special competence to speak on the merits of controversial moral and political questions. By the early 1960s, this consensus was ready to break down, and the Hart-Devlin dispute marked the renewal of debate by professional philoso-

phers over live ethical and political issues. The hectic politics of the late 1960s accelerated the trend thus begun. Anglo-American academic philosophers have since addressed a wide range of social and political issues—income distribution, capitalism and socialism, race and sex discrimination, conservation and the environment, and the morality of war, among others.

The issues of the Hart-Devlin controversy reflect in microcosm a central concern of contemporary social philosophy—the question of the continued viability of liberalism, a world view identified with the spirit of Mill's principle. Thus, recent liberal theorists like John Rawls and Ronald Dworkin have defended versions of Mill's theory, while libertarians like Robert Nozick have advocated an unregulated marketplace by expanding Mill's principle to encompass "capitalist acts between consenting adults" (p. 163). Libertarians have also argued that the classic common-law refusal to establish duties of rescue embodies a general principle of liberty prohibiting redistributive egalitarian measures. On the other hand, opponents of liberalism, both conservative and radical, have seen in Mill's principle what they find to be the vices of liberal theory generally: an abstract and unhistorical character, an excessive individualism, and a blindness to economic power as distinguished from formal political authority.

From Philosophy to Constitutional Law. The modern dispute over Mill's principle began in the law with the Model Penal Code drafters and the Wolfenden Committee. The debate entered academic philosophy through the mediation of a judge and a law professor, Lord Devlin and H. L. A. Hart. The philosophers' controversy has now had its own reciprocal influence on the practice and theory of law in the United States.

The Hart-Devlin debate was triggered by proposals for legislative reform of the law governing sexual behavior. The continuation of this reform movement has achieved striking success in the years since, particularly with respect to the law concerning homosexual conduct. But it would be difficult to say that the revival of Mill's principle itself has played a large role in these legislative developments. The growth of a women's and later a gay political movement, a (temporary) decline in power of the conservative churches, the changing technology of contraception, and other sociopolitical factors of this kind have no doubt been the dominant forces behind recent changes in the legislation governing sexual behavior.

But along with these legislative changes, American constitutional law has moved toward incorporating something like Mill's principle. Constitutional case law, because it is developed through opinions in which judges purport to justify their decisions, has always provided a bridge between practical politics and more abstract theory. At the constitutional level, the contemporary rebirth of normative moral and political theory inaugurated by the Hart-Devlin debate has become intertwined with the development of new legal doctrines about the power of government to regulate morals.

The new doctrines were born with the United States Supreme Court's decision in *Griswold* v. *Connecticut* in 1965. In *Griswold*, the Supreme Court declared unconstitutional a Connecticut statute that prohibited to married couples, as to others, the use of contraceptives. The Court held that implicit in a number of constitutional provisions was a "right of privacy," which was violated by this sort of governmental intrusion into marital life. The dissenting justices did not defend the justice or wisdom of the law but argued that the courts had no business inventing individual rights not to be found by reasonable exegesis of the text of the Constitution. They noted the parallels between the "right of privacy" invoked by the majority and the "liberty of contract" that a conservative Supreme Court had used to strike down economic regulatory legislation earlier in the twentieth century.

The *Griswold* dissenters were reflecting what had become an important strand in American constitutional thought during the 1940s and 1950s. This was the view, formed out of the clash between liberal legislatures and conservative courts during the Progressive Era and the New Deal, that the Supreme Court was expected to defer to legislative judgment except where laws infringed specific limitations expressed in the text of the Constitution or clearly inferable from its history. Accepted as such specific limitations were the protections of freedom of speech and religion in the First Amendment, the specifications of fair criminal procedure in the Bill of Rights, and the prohibition of official racial discrimination implicit in the equal protection clause of the Fourteenth Amendment. What was rejected by this view was the doctrine of "substantive due process"—that is, the use by the

Court of the due process clauses of the Fifth and Fourteenth Amendments as a vehicle to protect judicially selected "basic liberties" against legislative infringement, as the earlier Court had done with liberty of contract.

In the face of this New Deal–Progressive orthodoxy, the majority of the Court in *Griswold* revived a version of substantive due process with the new constitutional right of privacy, and in the years since, the Court has continued to expand the scope of that right. Thus, the right to use contraceptives without state interference was extended from married to unmarried couples and from adults to minors. The Court has also extended the rights of privacy in order to strike down restrictions on the right to marry, limits on the custodial rights of fathers of illegitimate children, and zoning restrictions on the right of extended families to live together in a single dwelling. Many lower courts have found that the new right of privacy protected individual autonomy in such matters as dress and hairstyle. The most dramatic extension of the new constitutional privacy came in 1973, when the Court in *Roe* v. *Wade* struck down the restrictive abortion laws existing in a majority of American states, holding that these laws unduly infringed the right of women to determine their own procreative destiny.

From the first, the Court's development of a right to privacy has suggested to philosophical-minded commentators the possible elevation to constitutional status of Mill's principle of liberty. Critics of the new privacy developments have adapted a remark that Justice Oliver Wendell Holmes made while opposing the earlier doctrine of liberty of contract: "The Constitution does not enact Mr. Herbert Spencer's *Social Statics*" (*Lochner* v. *New York*, 1905). Nor, argue contemporary critics, does it enact John Stuart Mill's *On Liberty*. On the other hand, commentators friendly to the development of the privacy doctrine have argued that Mill's theory of liberty provides a sound theoretical basis for the doctrine, rebutting the charge that the new developments represent no more than the arbitrary invalidation of laws a majority of the justices find distasteful. Any number of academic legal commentaries in the years since *Griswold* have suggested that the Court is moving (or should move) to enshrine in the Constitution Mill's principle or one of its contemporary versions.

Since the 1960s, the trend in academic philosophy toward taking sides on controverted moral and policy issues has begun to affect constitutional-law commentary generally. Philosophers have analyzed and debated the issues in Supreme Court decisions—for example, abortion and affirmative action—while constitutional commentators have increasingly drawn on moral and political theorists as sources of legal doctrine and argument. John Rawls's reworking of social-contract theory in *A Theory of Justice* has been especially popular with legal commentators. Emerging as the most influential legal philosopher in the United States in the later 1970s, Ronald Dworkin has argued that many difficult and controversial legal issues—particularly issues of constitutional law—are simply issues of normative moral and political philosophy. This trend has lent support to the idea that Mill's principle might be part of American constitutional law.

The Supreme Court itself has been less ready than have academic commentators to read philosophical theories in general—or Mill's principle in particular—into constitutional doctrine. In 1976, in its first confrontation with the precise question that began the Hart-Devlin debate, the Court upheld the constitutionality of laws punishing private homosexual acts between consenting adults against a challenge based on the *Griswold* privacy doctrine (*Doe* v. *Commonwealth's Attorney*). Earlier the Court had held, though over vigorous dissent, that the Constitution did not prevent states from prohibiting the exhibition of pornographic movies to adults, in a decision with strongly Devlinesque overtones (*Paris Adult Theatre I* v. *Slaton,* 1973). But neither the civil liberties lawyers nor the academic commentators have been willing to take these decisions as the Court's last word on the constitutional version of the Hart-Devlin debate. Lawyers and critics have continued to argue that once the Court began to protect the rights of consenting adults in *Griswold,* it could not consistently stop short of reading into the Constitution some version of Mill's principle.

The New Issues. The Hart-Devlin debate had its origins in, and was conducted largely in terms of, questions of the enforcement of traditional sexual morality by law. But Mill's principle has obvious application beyond sexual freedom for consenting adults. The principle purports to erect a clear barrier against all legal moralism, all coercive enforcement of communal ideals of de-

cency or the sacred. Individual freedom can be legitimately constrained, according to Mill, only to protect the rights of individuals to life, liberty, and property.

While legally enforced sexual repression had retreated substantially by the 1980s, other regulatory impulses had arisen that seemed to conflict with Mill's principle. Many of these impulses spring from advances in medicine and biology. Consider the movement to prohibit research on recombinant DNA, research that is aimed toward the artificial creation of new life forms. Some of the opposition to this kind of research is based upon traditional harm-based concern for public health and safety. However, others oppose DNA research on the ground that life-creating technologies violate some sense of the sacred, the idea that human beings should not play God. Similar objections are raised against research and development on extrauterine conception and gestation of human beings.

As in the days of the grave robbers, the development of medicine has generated public opposition to new uses of human cadavers. It is becoming technically feasible to maintain most of the functions of a human body by artificial means after the person in question has "died" (in the sense that the brain has irreversibly ceased functioning). Maintenance of bodies in their functioning state as objects of experiment, medical teaching devices, sources of organs for transplantation, and the like would at the present time provoke widespread public outrage and ultimately legal prohibition. It is doubtful that the consent of the persons in question or that of their families to this treatment of their bodies after death would be thought sufficient.

In this case and others like it that arise in the biomedical area, the grounds for prohibiting the practices are hard to square with Mill's principle. It is difficult to locate harm to the concrete interests of individual human beings in research on physiologically functioning dead bodies. What seems to be operating is a generalized sense of revulsion at the practice, akin to the nonrational "indignation, intolerance and disgust" that Lord Devlin believed justified the legal prohibition of homosexual acts.

But there has been no general rush by proponents of Mill's principle to defend the right of researchers to make free use of human cadavers. Instead, at least outside the research community itself, there has been a general acceptance of the propriety of regulation protective of public sensibilities. The general failure to place this new set of issues in the context of Mill's principle may mean only that there is a lag in casting new issues in traditional forms of dispute. Or it may suggest a decline in the Millian discourse itself.

THE CONTEMPORARY DISPUTE

With its recent history in mind, it is now time to look at Mill's principle with an interpretive and critical eye. What is the principle and what can be said for and against it?

Policy and Principle. The debate between Mill's supporters and his critics has not been over the propriety of particular laws. For example, the two sides do not divide fundamentally over the issue of whether there ought to be laws against private adult homosexual acts. Most of Mill's supporters oppose such laws, but it is by no means necessary that his opponents should generally favor them. What characterizes the Millian side of the debate is adherence to some general and reasonably definite principle of liberty of action. The exact formulation of the principle remains a matter of debate within the Millian camp.

The Devlinite camp then can be defined negatively as all those who deny that there is any such defensible general principle. The position is stated by Sir James Stephen ("I have no simple principle to assert on this matter"; p. 137) and by Sir Patrick Devlin ("I think . . . that it is not possible to set theoretical limits to the power of the State to legislate against immorality"; p. 12). For the Devlinites, the question of whether to have a particular piece of morals legislation is an open-ended matter of policy, to be decided by weighing all factors that might seem relevant in the circumstances. Such a weighing-up might lead to the conclusion that a particular law—for instance, prohibition of adult consensual homosexuality—does more harm than good, in which case Devlinites will oppose the law. But they have no theory, no general principle, that condemns the law in advance of their detailed examination of its effects and circumstances.

This formulation makes the line between the two camps seem clearer than it really is. A principle is not a mechanical rule. At the same time, for

Devlinites each case is not unique; general policies are invoked in large classes of cases. For example, Stephen and Devlin both assert standards, more or less definite, to guide the decision whether to punish immorality. Stephen proposes that we consider "whether the object for which the compulsion is employed is good? whether the compulsion employed is likely to be effective? and whether it will be effective at a reasonable expense?" He notes some general dangers of prohibiting immorality: vice seldom does enough harm to be worth the suffering inflicted by criminal punishment, and its detection is typically expensive and threatening to privacy. Stephen urges that these considerations ought always to be taken into account, and he believes they will often tip the balance against invoking the criminal law against immorality as such. Devlin states three cautionary notes himself. Before immoralities are punished, the lawmaker should be satisfied that the vice in question lies "beyond the limits of tolerance. It is not nearly enough to say that a majority dislike a practice; there must be a real feeling of reprobation" (p. 17). Second, "in any new matter of morals the law should be slow to act." Finally, "as far as possible privacy should be respected" (p. 18), though this is not a "definite limitation" but rather "a matter to be taken into account" (p. 19).

How do these Devlinite policies differ from Millian principles? Devlin's own words can serve as a working formulation of the difference between the two camps. Millians assert "definite limitations" upon morals legislation; Devlinites only note "matters to be taken into account" in deciding for or against it. Modern Millians characteristically concede that principles are not absolute but only establish strong presumptions against their infringement, making the issue between the camps become less a sharp division and more a question of degree. Is it enough of a division to justify the metaphor of two camps? Let us resist trying to answer in the abstract. First, we should work our way through some of the actual debate. But we are now alerted to examine proposed Millian principles for something more than their substantive appeal. We will focus as well on how determinate they are. If initially clear-sounding Millian formulations collapse into "matters to be taken into account," then the Devlinites have won the debate, for they have defeated the claim that a definite general principle restricts the power of the state to enforce morals.

The controversy over whether liberty of action is a definite principle or a mere policy factor has a legal analog. Mill's principle purports to be at the very least a limitation on legitimate law-making authority. It is put forward, then, essentially as a constitutional limitation. The very question is raised of whether some version of Mill's principle is now being incorporated into American constitutional law. In the American scheme of government, constitutional limitations are enforced by courts as legal restrictions on legislative power. Such limitations must thus be sufficiently definite to operate as legal rules in the decision of ordinary lawsuits. Not every verbal formula proclaiming a human right or a political ideal has seemed sufficiently definite to be judicially enforceable. For example, the courts have declined to enforce the constitutional requirements that federal spending must be "for the general welfare" and that each state must be guaranteed "a republican form of government." On the other hand, constitutional limitations apparently no more precisely worded than these have been found judicially enforceable (or "justiciable," as legal jargon has it). For example, courts interpret and apply the requirements that searches not be "unreasonable," that punishments not be "cruel and unusual," and that governments provide "due process of law" and "equal protection of the laws." History lends some content to these abstractions, but no one would pretend that the courts have clung close to the records of the past in their interpretations. Indeed, one may fairly doubt whether there is anything but arbitrariness in the line drawn between justiciable and nonjusticiable general principles; one may suspect that the notion of "undue vagueness" is itself unduly vague. In any event, the debate over whether a proposed standard is definite enough to be applied in concrete cases is familiar to constitutional lawyers.

As these considerations should suggest, the discourse of the Millian-Devlinite debate takes on a characteristic form. First, Millians propose some version of the principle of liberty as a kind of constitutional limitation on the ordinary law-making power. Devlinites respond that the principle proposed is too broad, that it disables the polity from passing laws that all would agree should be within legislative discretion. They

offer examples. Millians agree that some of the suggested results are unacceptable but argue that the principle of liberty as proposed has been too broadly interpreted; it can be qualified or amended to meet the difficulty. Now the Devlinites may respond that the amendment or reinterpretation has softened the proposed principle to the point where it is no longer definite enough to be a real principle; it has been reduced to a vague admonition against excessive moralistic zeal in lawmaking, a sentiment Devlinites can endorse but a sentiment that is only a "matter to be taken into account" and no longer an enforceable "definite limitation." Millians respond that the Devlinites are creating an artificially rigid conception of what is to be a principle . . . and the dialogue goes on.

Decency and Offense. Does making someone uncomfortable count as harming him? As all participants in the debate have recognized, if the answer is an unequivocal yes, then no version of Mill's principle can survive, for it will always be the case that some people are upset and made uncomfortable that deviant activity is going on subject to no legal prohibition. If no one is bothered by an activity, there will be no pressure to prohibit it, and no issue of liberty can arise.

Millians thus seem driven to the position that "harm" must mean more than psychic discomfort. What then does it mean? One suggestion has been to confine the concept of harm to deprivation of property and physical injury. (The concept of "deprivation of property" is itself problematic, as discussed later in this essay.) But surely this is unacceptably narrow. It is, for example, a crime (assault) to put someone in immediate fear of injury by threat of force. Are actions that cause only the psychic distress of fear to be protected by Mill's principle? Or consider laws that prohibit making obscene or threatening phone calls; surely these laws are not barred by Mill's principle. But if they are legitimate, what is the line between the psychic distress that they are meant to prevent and the distress generated in moralists by their knowledge that deviant sex is occurring with legal impunity?

More generally, there is the problem of conduct that is prohibited because it offends public sensibilities. The point can perhaps best be made with respect to prohibitions of public indecency, as applied, say, to public sexual intercourse. Can behavior that is embarrassing or distasteful to the majority when viewed in public be prohibited on that ground alone? Few Millians have come forward to argue that there can be no prohibition of public conduct on grounds of offense. Mill himself accepted the legitimacy of this sort of prohibition, as does Hart in his modern restatement of Mill's principle. Millians have typically drawn the line between public and private conduct. Public indecency can be suppressed; private deviance cannot.

The problem is to justify prohibition of some conduct on the basis of offended sensibilities without admitting offense or mental distress as a general ground for coercion, a concession that would wholly defeat Mill's principle. Hart has given the best-known justification for disallowing "offense at the thought" as a ground for restriction:

> The fundamental objection surely is that a right to be protected from the distress which is inseparable from the bare knowledge that others are acting in ways you think wrong, cannot be acknowledged by anyone who recognizes individual liberty as a value. . . . To punish people for causing this form of distress would be tantamount to punishing them simply because others object to what they do; and the only liberty that could coexist with this extension of the utilitarian principle is liberty to do those things to which no one seriously objects.
>
> (pp. 46–47)

On its most natural interpretation, this argument breaks down. Allowing people's distress at the thought of an activity they dislike to count as a ground for prohibition does not mean that every activity anyone seriously dislikes will be suppressed. Those who enjoy the activity will have their say on the other side, as will those who sympathize with them, those who love abstract liberty, and those who just dislike bluenoses. These forces, taken together, will frequently prevail in the political arena—as they have in Great Britain and many American states in effecting the repeal of antihomosexual laws.

Perhaps Hart did not mean to say that all liberty would disappear if pure distaste were admitted as a kind of harm. Perhaps he meant that no firm right to liberty, no principle protecting general individual freedom could survive under these circumstances. He would surely be right to claim that, but if offered as an argument against

the Devlinites, it begs the question. For it is precisely the Devlinite position that there is no general right to liberty as a matter of principle, that the question of whether widely disapproved private activities shall be made criminal must be determined politically on an issue-by-issue basis.

Finally, Hart may mean that even generally accepted liberties, such as freedom of speech and religion, could not exist if pure distaste were a legitimate ground for suppression. A Devlinite response might be that it is only with respect to peculiarly important forms of human conduct that we create the special protection associated with the idea of a constitutional right. Speech and religious practice are immune from suppression on the ground of general offense only because substantive psychological, political, and moral arguments identify them as general realms of activity that deserve such extra immunity. No such special immunity can be claimed for the supposed all-embracing liberty of individuals to do as they please.

It may be that other spheres of human conduct can be brought within the category of special protection—for example, private adult sexual activity. But to accumulate discrete particular rights is to abandon the Millian position that "nonharmful" behavior is in general protected, independent of any consideration of the value of that behavior.

Some Millians, recognizing the difficulties created for their principle by the prohibition of offense, have argued that even the suppression of public conduct on the grounds of decency must be rejected; if it is not, a prohibition against, for example, interracial couples' appearing together in public could be justified on the basis of the horror aroused in the breasts of racists at the very sight. But it is the racist aspect of the prohibition, rather than its foundation in offended sensibilities, that makes it especially objectionable. It is hard indeed to defend the notion that no public display, however disgusting to average sensibilities, can be prohibited on grounds of decency.

Property. Why should spouses and relatives of the newly dead have anything to say about what is done with the remains? Suppose one dies without making any provision for one's burial or expressing any wishes about it. Why should not the hospital where the death occurred simply keep the cadaver and use it for dissection in the medical school anatomy classes, whatever the feelings and wishes of the family of the deceased?

There are two ways to answer this question. The straightforward way is to observe that the sensibilities of the relatives are protected by law, which gives them a limited veto over uses to which the body is put. This respect for their feelings is not absolute; for example, if the deceased died in suspicious circumstances, public authorities can require an autopsy, even against the wishes of the family.

Another and more convoluted way of characterizing the matter introduces the familiar yet ultimately mysterious concept of property. It seems natural to determine what can be done with a body after death by asking who owns the body. Traditional law governing human remains is sometimes summarized in the statement that the next of kin own the body of the deceased, though this is usually qualified by saying that the relatives do not have "full ownership" but only a "quasi-property" right. What this murky language adds up to is that the "ownership" of a dead body does not include any right to sell the body, to give it away, to feed it to the hogs, or to keep it embalmed in the front parlor and charge admission to see it. The relatives' "ownership" means only that they have a legal duty to see that the body receives a prompt, decent burial and that if anyone interferes with the body in a way that causes family members emotional distress, they can recover compensatory money damages. This is very far from what we usually mean in ascribing property ownership to someone.

In interpreting Mill's principle, it is common to assert two paradigms of harm—injury to the person and invasion of property. The law of cadavers suggests some of the difficulties that lurk below the surface of the notion of property invasion. The first account given above of this area of law made no reference to property, but it raised a serious difficulty with Mill's principle. The hospital was forbidden by law to do something (dissect the body) on the sole basis that someone else (the relatives) would be shocked at the thought that the act was taking place. If the relatives are to have this control, must we not make the Devlinite concession that coercion based on distress "at the thought" is sometimes valid? If coercion is valid here, what in principle distinguishes coercion based on shock at the thought of deviant sex, drug use, and the like?

On the other hand, the second formulation seems to avoid the assault on Mill's principle by recasting the right to protect sensibilities as a property right. And of course, it is uncontroversial that an invasion of a property right counts as a harm. But the very ease with which the reformulation is carried out should invite suspicion. Cannot every sensibility be recast as a property right, hence destroying Mill's principle? Why not legislatively create a property right in each person that will be infringed by anyone who engages in homosexual acts or who uses marijuana?

Before exploring possible Millian responses to this line of argument, let us consider a story that raises a related problem. Squatter moves in on an unused corner of Rancher's land with his tent and settles down. Rancher discovers he is there and tells him to leave. Squatter says he is not hurting Rancher in any way; he is not injuring the land or frustrating any practical purpose Rancher may have. He will move if and when Rancher wants to use the land in any way inconsistent with his remaining there. Rancher admits that he suffers no tangible injury or even inconvenience from Squatter's presence—he simply wants no one camping there, and it is his land. When Squatter will not go, Rancher sends for the sheriff to arrest him for criminal trespass. Does Mill's principle protect Squatter, who insists he is not harming Rancher (or anyone else) in any way?

Of course not—so would say everyone accustomed to the property notions of Western culture. Squatter is harming Rancher. He is trespassing on his land, thereby infringing his property rights. This is harm in the most classic and straightforward sense. But we must ask why Rancher is unaffected by Mill's principle while the postulated statutory "property right" that no one shall have sex outside marriage would be dismissed by everyone as a play on words, a sham.

In order to answer this question and resolve the dilemma posed by the law of cadavers, Millians must be able to formulate an intelligible concept of property rights. They must be able to say that not every entitlement a legislature enacts thereby becomes a property right, that indeed we have a definite and restrictive concept of what makes a legislated entitlement really a right of property.

Twentieth-century legal theory lends little

849

help to Millians in their efforts to formulate such a conception. Two centuries ago, Blackstone defined property as "that sole and despotic dominion which one man claims and exercises over the external things of the world, in total exclusion of the right of any other individual in the universe." That definition may have made sense when it was written, and no doubt it closely corresponds to some inchoate popular sense of what property is today. But it is wholly inadequate to capture present legal-economic arrangements.

First, it does not cover joint ownership. Ownership can be divided up in an almost infinite number of ways: different people can have property in parts of something, rights to use it, rights to profits from it, rights to time slices of it, and so on. Thus, property is constituted of rights, not of things. Second, and more significantly, property rights need not have any connection with "things" (material objects) at all. Indeed, present-day property is mostly made up of intangibles, such as checking accounts, certificates of deposit, bonds, corporate shares, accounts receivable, pension rights, insurance policies, licenses, franchises, trademarks, copyrights, and business goodwill. It is still common to think of this kind of property in physical metaphors. An insurance policyholder "owns a piece of the rock"—but actually he has a complex set of legal claims against an abstract corporation whose wealth itself is largely in the form of bonds, stocks, and the like. A bank depositor imagines herself to be "putting some money in the bank," as though she were placing some valued objects in a safe place. In fact, she is engaging in a complex transaction that gives her abstract contractual claims against an equally abstract financial institution. Shareholders in a corporation may think of themselves as part owners of the company's factory buildings outside of town. But really the corporation could sell off the buildings and still be the "same" corporation. And the corporation's most valuable assets might not be its buildings but its name, its patents, and its trade secrets. Some businesses are valuable property, though they own nothing and produce nothing, because they have lost money in prior years and can provide tax benefits to another corporation that acquires them. The short of all this is that property rights can no longer be thought of as necessarily or even typically "rights

in things." What, then, does property mean today?

The people who deal with the structures of the economy as professionals—lawyers, economists, financiers—have a multiplicity of technical definitions of property that have little correspondence to the classical Blackstonian definition. The following are examples of current technical usages. The Constitution prohibits infringing rights of "life, liberty, or property without due process of law." The Supreme Court decided in *Goldberg* v. *Kelly* (1970) that this constitutional provision required that before individuals can lose their welfare benefits, they must have the opportunity for a hearing on the question of eligibility. It was held that the statutory right to receive welfare when the stated conditions of eligibility were met was "property" within the meaning of the Constitution. Since then, the Supreme Court has apparently concluded that all entitlements created by statutes are property—including, for instance, a young person's statutory right of attendance at public high school.

To take another of the disparate current conceptions of property, some lawyers have defined property rights as rights that are good against the world, as distinguished from rights (such as those established by contract) that are good only against certain people. If your neighbor sells you an easement to pass over his land, your right is good even against someone to whom he later sells the land. But if he merely makes a contract with you to let you use his land for a period in return for certain payments, that right cannot be enforced against someone who buys the land from him during the contract term. The first right is a property right; the second is not. This definition of property as all rights against the world is much broader than the popular concept of property; it includes, for example, your right not to be murdered or assaulted as a property right.

In summary, legal theory can no longer offer any generally accepted concept of property. Yet all versions of Mill's principle presuppose such a concept. Along with physical injury to the person, invasion of property rights is one of the two central categories of harms. Why is Squatter's trespass against Rancher a harm? If we are saying nothing independent of existing legal arrangements when we say "because it violates his property rights," then we are driven to seek another answer. Mill's principle is meant to be a critical standard by which existing legal arrangements may be evaluated.

Paternalism, Exploitation, and Economic Freedom. Do minimum-wage laws violate Mill's principle? Most contemporary defenders of the principle would say no and, indeed, would abandon the principle if it were thought to require economic laissez-faire. On the other hand, left-wing critics sometimes argue that the personal freedoms liberals support are just window dressing for the fundamental core of liberalism, which is the "freedom of contract" of the capitalist marketplace. And classic liberals, or libertarians, echo this left-wing position, urging that those who argue for sexual freedom on liberal grounds cannot consistently abandon freedom to make voluntary economic transactions. In the words of the libertarian philosopher Robert Nozick, economic regulations such as minimum-wage laws "prohibit capitalist acts between consenting adults."

Mill himself, though he supported laissez-faire as a matter of policy, believed that market transactions fell outside the protection of his principle of liberty. He said, "Trade is a social act. Whoever undertakes to sell any description of goods to the public does what affects the interest of other persons, and of society in general; and thus his conduct, in principle, comes within the jurisdiction of society."

What justifies Mill's saying that trade is a "social act," so that regulation of trade falls outside the principle of liberty? It might be argued that laws like the minimum wage restrict only the employer and do not interfere with the liberty of the worker but confer the benefit of higher pay on him. But this cannot be correct in all cases. The effect of a minimum wage must sometimes be to prevent a job being offered to a worker who is willing to work at less than the law requires, where the potential employer would rather do without the potential employee than pay the minimum. Here that state steps between two willing transactors, and the question of justification must arise: What harm is prevented?

An indirect answer is suggested by the fact that some workers will assuredly benefit from the minimum wage. While some who otherwise would have had jobs will go unemployed, other employees who would otherwise have received less will be raised to the minimum unless highly unusual market conditions prevail. Exactly who will benefit and who will lose, and by how much, will generally be a technical and controverted economic question. This suggests a ground for Mill's conclusion that market regulations are "public" and hence outside the scope of the liberty principle. Such regulations are invariably redistributive, and this is typically part of their purpose. Some people benefit while others lose from such laws, just as with public taxing and spending programs. The fact that the redistributive effect of the minimum wage may be, on widely shared economic assumptions, anti-egalitarian (creating unemployment among the poorest class) may be a policy argument against it, but it does not render the conduct regulated "self-regarding" in Mill's sense. Similar arguments would affect many other market regulations, including maximum-hour laws, and maximum- and minimum-price regulation. Such laws can quite realistically be seen as taxes on those who lose and subsidies to those who gain by their redistributive effect.

On the other hand, many economic regulations seem to have no such purpose, and if they redistribute income or wealth, they do so only incidentally. Regulations of product or workplace safety are within this category. Thus, requiring that new cars be sold with airbags or that the workplace be free of harmful asbestos or radiation seems primarily aimed at protecting people against harming themselves. Mill, at least, saw such laws this way and included them within the prohibition of the principle of liberty. All that could be allowed in such cases was the requirement that persons choosing an unsafe product or job be fully warned of the dangers before making the choice.

Most of Mill's modern supporters have deserted him on this point. For example, Hart has proposed a major amendment to Mill's principle, striking out of it any condemnation of paternalistic regulation. Mill's principle, as modified by Hart, would allow coercive intervention to prevent harm to others or to the actors themselves. Hart justified this modification—a very substantial one, given the extent to which the argument of *On Liberty* was directed against paternalism—on the ground that the century since Mill wrote has seen "a general decline in the belief that individuals know their own interests best" (p. 32). Hart says that Mill saw the normal human being as "a middle-aged man whose desires are relatively fixed" (p. 33). We have had a century to learn that people are driven by unconscious desires and that their judgment about their own actions is deeply distorted by cognitive blind spots. We may still distrust paternalism, but few of us are any longer willing to accept a principle prohibiting it.

Such arguments expand on points Mill himself made. He excluded from the scope of the principle of liberty children and those not in full possession of their faculties. He allowed that the state could prohibit persons from selling themselves into slavery, recoiling from the paradox that a principle of liberty might protect a right to extinguish all liberty. He conceded that persons could be forcibly restrained from taking a risky step where it appeared that they might not know the risks involved. In the twentieth century we are more ready to see ourselves as in many respects children or idiots where our own welfare is concerned; as potential slaves to various addictions; and as incorrigibly unable to assimilate and properly weigh information about certain risks to our lives and safety.

Consider the question of automobile seatbelts. It can be shown that if people always fastened their seatbelts when they rode in cars, death and serious injuries occurring in accidents would be greatly reduced. This fact has been widely publicized, and almost all cars are now equipped with seatbelts. Nevertheless, actual use of seatbelts remains very low. There is only a moment of inconvenience involved in fastening a seatbelt, and a slight sense of constriction, which for most people soon passes, involved in wearing one. The objective possibility of collision is a fact for anyone who rides in an automobile. What can explain the general pattern of nonuse?

The proponent of the Millian view that people know their own interests best must urge that seatbelt nonuse results from a rational weighing up of expected benefits from use (the preventable injury, discounted by its improbability) and expected costs (the actual inconvenience of buckling up). Into this equation must also be factored each individual's attitudes toward risk of this sort: does he enjoy a gamble with life and health for its own sake, or is he averse to taking this kind of chance?

It is difficult to assign numbers with any assurance of accuracy to all these factors, but most people would agree that only rarely would anyone's fixed and considered views on the relative value of health and life, inconvenience, and risk lead to a decision not to wear a seatbelt. To explain the phenomenon of nonuse, we must take account of irrational factors. In the age of Freud, it is not difficult to postulate what these might be. First, Freud said that we cannot truly imagine our own death. The same might be said, by extension, of very serious injury. Perhaps we are systematically unable to take effective account of the likelihood of drastic misfortune to ourselves in the subjective weighing process that underlies our daily decisions; in Freudian terms, we repress the possibility of our own death or injury. Second, many of us associate taking explicit health and safety measures with parental control, and freedom from such measures with adulthood and autonomy; thus, driving without a seatbelt or riding a motorcycle without a helmet reenacts the psychic drama of the struggle to emancipate ourselves from our parents.

Of course, to assert these psychological claims is not to prove their truth. Perhaps equally familiar as denial of death and childish acting-out are compulsive hand washing, safety obsession, and hypochondriasis. The point of introducing considerations of neurotic and unconsciously motivated behavior is not to settle the question of paternalism but to argue that it must be treated as an issue of policy, to be resolved case by case in light of detailed facts and flexible guidelines rather than prohibited once and for all as an issue of principle. We have strong grounds to doubt Mill's presumption that people are generally best able to decide in their own interests; very often others can, by virtue of their detachment, have clearer sight about rational behavior for an individual than he does.

If this sort of argument is accepted, so that Mill's principle is no longer read to prohibit paternalism, laws like the requirement of passive restraints (such as airbags) in cars, the requirement that motorcyclists wear helmets, and the prohibition of known dangerous addicting drugs all fall outside the scope of the principle. This is the conclusion that Hart, among others, has reached, and it is probably the dominant position among contemporary Millians.

Once this concession is made, the question arises whether Mill's principle in its surviving aspect can stand by itself. In its original formulation the principle prohibits two kinds of coercive interference—the moralistic and the paternalistic. In its weaker version, it prohibits only legal moralism, leaving paternalism in the realm of policy.

Lord Devlin has argued that the same grounds Hart cites as justifying paternalistic protection of health and safety likewise justify what he calls "moral paternalism." Does Hart mean to distinguish between "physical" and "moral" paternalism? Devlin asks. No such distinction can be sustained in principle. The same psychological discoveries that have led us to see that adults are not always the best judges of their own interests in matters of health and safety support similar conclusions in the sphere of morals. "If paternalism be the principle, no father of a family would content himself with looking after his children's welfare and leaving their morals to themselves. . . . If, on the other hand, we are grown up enough to look after our own morals, why not after our own bodies?" (pp. 136–137). And yet, as Devlin says, if "moral paternalism" is accepted, this leaves nothing to be protected by Mill's principle. It makes little difference in practice whether we say we are prohibiting immoral acts for the sake of morality itself or to protect persons against their own moral weaknesses.

Against this argument of Devlin's, the response must be to draw an empirically based distinction between the state's authority to presume what individuals' best interests are in matters of health and safety, on the one hand, and on matters of morals (Devlin has in mind chiefly sexual morals), on the other. A person who suffers serious physical injury that a fastened seatbelt would have prevented will regret not using the belt. He will unequivocally wish the injury had not happened; he has no doubt that he was harmed. Contrast the sexual sinner (you may choose your sin). In some cases he will regard himself as a compulsive person and wish he could stop; but in many others he will not. No longer is there a consensus as to what counts as "moral self-harm" in sexual matters. Any effective consensus would have to include the typical "perpetrator-victims" of the supposed self-harmful act. In the sexual case, even if 90 percent of the population thinks that some sexual practice amounts to moral self-harm but most of the 10 percent who engage in the practice do not see

it that way, then the analogy to physical paternalism does not hold. In the case of health, but not in the case of sexual deviance, we can say that the persons subject to paternalist restraint are injuring themselves on their own view of their interests.

Some paternalistic laws are also antiexploitative. Laws against sweatshop working conditions are aimed at exploitation, whereas laws requiring every new car sold to be equipped with an airbag are not. What is meant by "exploitation" is that one side of a transaction is taking advantage of some weakness in the other party. Housing codes, the unenforceability of contracts made by children with adults, and prohibition of psychiatrists' seducing their patients are other examples of prohibiting exploitation.

Mill himself was prepared to consider making an exception to his antipaternalistic stance in cases where people made exploiting human weakness their livelihood:

> Fornication, for example, must be tolerated, and so must gambling; but should a person be free to be a pimp, or to keep a gambling-house? . . . On the side of toleration it may be said, that the fact of following anything as an occupation, and living or profiting by the practice of it, cannot make that criminal which would otherwise be admissible. . . . In opposition to this it may be contended, that although the public, or the State, are not warranted in authoritatively deciding, for purposes of repression or punishment, that such or such conduct affecting only the interests of the individual is good or bad . . . they cannot be acting wrongly in endeavoring to exclude the influence of solicitations which are not disinterested, of investigators who cannot possibly be impartial—who have a direct personal interest on one side, and that side the one which the State believes to be wrong, and who confessedly promote it for personal objects only.

The point is that where A has a financial incentive to close a transaction with B that is likely to be against B's interests but toward which B is impelled by some recognized powerful motive known to have special power to override one's better judgment, there is an especially strong case for paternalistic intervention. In cases of economic exploitation, B's weakness is poverty, and his judgment is distorted by a powerful need for money in the short run. In the case of transactions between adults and children, we recognize the undeveloped impulse control of the young. Where the temptation offered is sex or gambling, there are again familiar distorting drives and compulsions at work.

Causation, Action, and Omission. Does Mill's principle allow every coercive intervention that is reasonably calculated to prevent harm from occurring? Or does it allow only coercion aimed at preventing the doing or causing of harm? In ordinary life, we draw a distinction between someone's causing harm and merely allowing it to happen.

The distinction between causing and allowing harm presupposes that someone does suffer harm. We may imagine that someone dies or is badly injured. The distinction does not involve the degree of loss to the victim but the casual contribution to it on the part of the person whom we are considering subjecting to coercion. Thus, this is not the distinction between causing harm and merely withholding a benefit. The harm-nonbenefit distinction presupposes some benchmark of normal or appropriate welfare and designates a person's falling below that benchmark as harm, while misfortune that leaves the person above the benchmark is considered merely the absence of a benefit. The two distinctions are often confused with each other, especially under the terminology of "positive" versus "negative" duties.

A third distinction, variously phrased as the action-inaction, act-omission, or misfeasance-nonmisfeasance distinction, may or may not be separate from the first—the distinction between causing harm and merely allowing it to happen. Some would say that the notion of "cause" is so intimately linked to the notion of "action" that it would not make sense to say that someone caused an injury to someone else by inaction. But most would agree that where there is an independent duty to act, the inactive failure to discharge that duty causes harm in any case where discharge would have prevented that harm. Thus, where a jailer is obligated to feed a prisoner and fails to do so and as a result the prisoner starves, most people would say that the jailer's inaction caused the prisoner's death. Few would seriously argue that any principle of liberty would protect the jailer from being held legally responsible.

What many do believe is that liberty is violated where people are coerced to prevent harm they have not caused. Suppose that A needs a kidney transplant to survive and asks B, a stranger, to donate one. B refuses; no other donor comes forward; and A dies. Can B properly be said to have caused A's death? Nowhere does the law now hold B causally responsible for A's death in this situation; the question is, Would a principle of liberty be violated if B were made responsible?

It is not clear whether Mill himself would have thought coercion in these circumstances to violate the principle of liberty. What is clear is that Mill thought coercion could be properly used to compel action where inaction would, in his words, "cause evil." He thought such duties to act for the aid of others should be the exception rather than the rule, but this was for him a matter of policy, which turned on the "special expediencies of the case." His language leaves open the possibility that there might be cases in which we would say that one person's inaction did not cause injury to another but merely allowed that injury to occur and that in such cases holding the inactive person responsible would violate his liberty. Perhaps he would have seen the hypothetical reluctant kidney donor as raising such a case.

On the other hand, it is possible that Mill would not have thought there was any important distinction between "causing harm by inaction" and "merely allowing it to occur." One conception of causation would regard B, in the hypothetical kidney case, as unequivocally the cause of A's death through his refusal to donate a kidney, since a course of action was open to B that would have averted A's death—that is, donation of the kidney. This is what lawyers call the "but-for" conception of causation. Under it, event X is the cause of event Y if "but for" the occurrence of X, Y would not have occurred. Logicians would call it the "necessary condition" test; X causes Y if X is a necessary condition of Y. Under such a conception, we might not want to force B to donate his kidney to A, but we would have to say that B killed A—excusably or justifiably killed him, perhaps, but killed him nonetheless—in refusing to donate it.

Such a conception of causation is profoundly counterintuitive. To confirm this, consider another example. Each of the readers of this passage could, by dint of personal effort and expense, no doubt save some one of the many children who will die of malnutrition or disease throughout the world in the next year. To do it, you might have to give up your present station in life, at least temporarily; raise all the money you can; and travel to Bangladesh or Somalia. Or it might turn out that you could be assured of the result if you just gave half of your income to a reliable charitable organization. It would take some considerable time and effort to find out how one could be reasonably sure to save a single child, but you could do it.

It is a fair prediction that few readers of this passage will follow this course. Shall it be said of each of you, and also of me, that we have each of us caused the death of the child (presently unknown to us) whom we each would have saved had we undertaken this enterprise? Note that the argument is further subject to reiteration. Even the person who does undertake the saving mission for one child could presumably, with greater effort and expense, save two. Indeed, the only limit placed on the saving capacity of each of us is our need for survival: in this version of causation, we cause the deaths of children as long as we leave ourselves any margin of money, time, or energy above what is needed to avert our own death.

Does this story make out a successful reduction ad absurdum argument against the conception of "causing harm" under which B has caused harm to A as long as there is some action to B that would save A from harm? The notion that each of us causes all the death and misery in the world that we could conceivably prevent almost entirely eliminates the usefulness of the concept of causation in the ascription of human responsibility. It may be that we will want to accept this consequence and admit that each of us has caused the death (that is, killed) those children; we will certainly depart from ordinary usage if we say so, but perhaps this is a reform of ordinary language we will want to undertake. Dropping causation as a limiting concept forces us to confront in more explicitly normative terms the scope of our responsibilities. We would no longer be able to say of each dead child, "Well, *I* didn't kill him." We will have to conclude that we value our comfort, our plans, our range of individual options more than we value the lives of children personally unknown to us, and we will then have to justify these priorities to ourselves.

I suspect that no such reform of ordinary language and ordinary moral thought can possibly be carried through with any consistency. The consequences of sincerely attempting it would not be more altruism or wider moral vision but helpless anxiety and endless hypocrisy on the part of most of those making the experiment. If this is so, some limiting notion of what it is to cause harm by inaction must be recognized. When that is done, it will be plausible to say that Mill's principle prohibits coercion to prevent harm that is not caused or threatened by the person against whom the coercion is directed.

Some have argued that no such intelligible line can be drawn between those events that are actually caused and those that are merely occasioned by inaction. The argument is that the common notion of human causation is intimately linked to the common notion of action; only when persons act can it be intelligibly said that they have caused consequences. Persons holding this view may argue that Mill's principle ought to be extended to protect against any coercive requirement that persons take positive action to avert avoidable harm. On this view, associated with modern libertarianism, the state violates liberty if it imposes civil or criminal sanctions on a doctor who refuses emergency treatment to a badly injured patient, even when no other doctor is available and however trivial the reasons for the doctor's refusal to give treatment. As the passage quoted above indicates, Mill held no such view; but he did not address himself to the difficult question of what the limitations were to be on the extent to which inaction could be said to cause harm. The Anglo-American common law has long incorporated a general principle that inaction (or as the legal jargon has it, nonfeasance) will not give rise to criminal or civil liability. That doctrine has long been subject to intense criticism because it legally permits instances of dreadful callousness and selfishness. But at the same time, it has been defended by libertarians as a necessary if troubling consequence of the principled protection of individual liberty and autonomy.

Collective Institutions. Under Mill's principle, what is the justification for punishing espionage, perjury, contempt of court, or tax evasion? Very often these crimes do no direct harm to any individual. Take the case of someone who perjures himself, so that a criminal escapes punishment. Who is hurt by this? The natural answer, easily accepted by most defenders of Mill's principle, is that this action tends to undermine the deterrent effect of the criminal law, which in turn is needed to protect individuals against concrete injury to person or property.

But this natural answer opens up what is in many ways the most sweeping of objections to Mill's principle. Perjury against the state or any of the other crimes cataloged above typically causes harm to individuals only indirectly, through the undermining effect such actions have on important collective institutions. Furthermore, the concrete injury to these institutions of any particular violation is typically undetectable; one can locate the harm justifying coercion only when one considers that many people may perjure themselves or not pay taxes if these matters are left to private decision.

Opponents of Mill's principle urge that many of the main examples of "moral legislation" or "victimless crime" are justified as laws protecting collective institutions. For example, it is said that the laws prohibiting sex outside marriage are designed to protect the family. If one believes that stable monogamous marriage is a socially valuable institution and that the institution is in part defined by the designation of sexual relations outside marriage—fornication, adultery, and homosexuality—as illegitimate, then the argument for these laws has exactly the same form as the argument for the laws against perjury or tax evasion. The claim is not that isolated nonmarital sex acts harm particular individuals or that these acts are punishable because they violate some abstract moral code; rather, the claim is that some legal restraint is needed in addition to social or customary sexual mores to protect the social structure of monogamous marriage against being undermined by general disregard of its limitations.

It is not necessary here to resolve the factual issues that this argument raises. It can be debated how important sexual fidelity is to marital stability and how important marital stability is to child-rearing and the other social goals promoted by the family. The usefulness or necessity of legal sanctions in enforcing sexual mores can also be debated. The various sorts of sexual aberration can be further separated: perhaps adultery is more threatening to the stable family than fornication, and so on. The point is not the result of entering into these factual and value disputes;

the point is that as soon as the venture onto the terrain of balancing values and guessing at debatable social facts begins, the Millian position is in jeopardy. Where the legitimacy of particular laws against sexual activity turn on the assessment of such contingent, debatable, and fluctuating matter, it becomes increasingly difficult to treat the question as one of principle; the question looks more like one of policy, one in which sexual liberty, privacy, family stability, and so on are all "matters to be taken into account" in striking the legislative balance.

Devlinites need not conclude as an empirical matter that criminal punishment is a useful deterrent to adultery or that widespread adultery is threatening to the family as a stabilizing social structure. Some of them will come out one way and some the other on this question. They will all agree, however, that the question is one that will be answered differently from time to time and from place to place; none of them will believe it is a question that can be answered independent of the facts and outside of history and concrete politics by an abstract principle such as Mill's.

Contemporary Millians have seen the threat to their position in the argument that conduct should be prohibited because, if generalized, it will undermine valued collective institutions. Their response has been to attempt to place the argument under a double handicap. They have dubbed the argument from collective institutions "the disintegration thesis"—the thesis, that is, that society will disintegrate if the law does not protect its central institutions by legally enforcing the mores that constitute them. Millians have not generally denied that it would be right to prohibit a social practice that had so disastrous an effect, but they have urged that the burden of proof must rest on the proponents of coercion to demonstrate a serious threat of social disintegration before interference with liberty on this ground could be justified. Such a burden is in practice impossible to meet.

Why should the proponents of legal regulation have the burden of proof, and why must they prove a threat of disintegration? To answer the second question, it seems absurd to say that society can protect one of its valued institutions against injury only if there is a threat of the total disintegration of society itself. Take the example of perjury. Suppose we removed all criminal penalties against committing perjury in favor of a defendant in a criminal trial, on the ground that such perjury is a victimless crime. No one could believe that the system would be very seriously damaged, much less that society would disintegrate. Many witnesses would continue to testify truthfully because they thought it wrong to lie generally, because they felt especially bound by an oath to tell the truth, because they wanted the defendant punished, or because they feared humiliation and disgrace if their false testimony were exposed. Many other witnesses would lie, probably more than do now. But many witnesses lie under oath today anyway; they are very rarely prosecuted and less often convicted.

We cannot be sure that any serious negative consequences would result from the decriminalization of perjury against the state; perhaps the only thing we can be sure of is that society would not disintegrate as a result. Yet no one would think of arguing that making perjury against the state a crime violates some basic principle of liberty because it neither harms individuals nor threatens social disintegration. It is enough that there is some betrayal of a valued collective institution.

Similar stories can be told with respect to other crimes against the state, such as bribery and tax evasion. In many countries there is a virtual decriminalization of practice of certain forms of these two activities. Those societies do not disintegrate as a result. Indeed, some of them have flourished as great civilizations with essentially no legal suppression of some varieties of bribery or tax evasion for hundreds and even thousands of years. That this is so provides no argument for striking these victimless crimes off our statute books in the name of some principle of individual liberty. In short, we do not need a threat of disintegration to find ourselves justified in protecting collective institutions. Minor injury will suffice.

Now let us return to the first question: assuming that collective institutions may be legally protected against injury if they are merely useful to society's functioning, though not necessary to its survival, why should the proponents of such legal protection bear the burden of proof that any concrete injury will result? Suppose this burden were placed upon defenders of the law against perjury or bribery. Could they show, with any sort of convincing scientific evidence, that

decriminalizing these activities would lead to any serious social detriment at all? You may believe that a society is better where the law tells witnesses they must not lie under oath and tells officials they must not use their office for private gain. Many people likewise believe that societies are better, cleaner, more vigorous where strict sexual morality is practiced and enforced by law. In neither case could the proponents of these views prove their case conclusively; in either case, they could give examples from history and comparative politics that would cut in their favor, examples that could be countered by competing examples from their opponents. Do you prefer Sparta or Athens; republican or Augustan Rome; contemporary China or contemporary Italy?

Mill recognized that his principle of liberty could be realized only in an advanced and complex society, one characterized by stable collective institutions. He never doubted that society could legitimately protect its basic institutional fabric by law, in addition to punishing acts that harmed individuals directly. The difficulty with his position is in drawing any principled distinction between those customary institutional norms and practices that are, and those that are not, part of the fundamental fabric. We think of the courts and government fiscal apparatus as unquestionably fundamental, legitimately to be protected by the law, even against victimless crimes. Should the traditional family be seen in this light? The evidence of history and anthropology suggests that all known societies have placed some restrictions, flowing from their kinship and family structure, on sexual activity. The content of the restrictions has varied with the different family structures that have existed—just as the content of the law of theft has varied with the different property structures in effect in different cultures.

What about the social structures defined by burial customs? Again, all known societies have had established procedures and rituals for disposing of the bodies of the dead. In most cases, breaches of these procedures have been treated as serious offenses against the social order. Do our traditions with respect to the handling of human remains deserve similar legal protection, apart from any particular harm to an individual that might be caused by breaches of these traditions? To modify an example used earlier, suppose a group asked that bodies unclaimed at the

LAW AND MORALITY

morgue be turned over to them so that they might remove and shrink the heads, which would then be used as objects of amusement. On what basis would the law say no to this? Doubtless reasons of health or hygiene would be given, but surely all can recognize that such grounds would be specious. Human burial is treated differently from the disposal of the bodies of animals for reasons other than health. Are not those reasons rooted in a sense that collectively defined and transmitted restrictions on burial customs are part of what makes up the institutional framework of our society? No harm would be done by shrinking human heads for souvenirs in a society in which that was customary, but in ours that is not what is done with human remains. The "harm" or "injury" from the practice is the inconsistency with our collective self-definition. Here, no more than in the case of our approach to taxes or witnesses' oaths, can we do more than guess that a different collective self-definition might not be, in some Olympian sense, just as good.

CONCLUSION

People are individuals, separate from one another; people are social beings, connected to each other. The main project of the political philosophy of liberalism is the attempt to work out a boundary between the domains of these two propositions. In practice, this has meant the attempt to define and protect individual rights, conceived as spheres of personal autonomy into which the state, the organized representative of society, must not reach.

Among the classic documents in the history of Anglo-American law and politics are the few basic attempts to express the boundary that separates individuals from their governments. One of these was John Locke's statement that people retain their natural rights to "life, liberty and property," a formulation that has been enshrined in the due process clauses of the United States Constitution. Another is the Declaration of Independence, in which Thomas Jefferson spoke of the individual's "inalienable rights" to "life, liberty and the pursuit of happiness."

Mill's principle that the state can act coercively only in order to prevent "harm to others," though now a century and a quarter old, remains perhaps the most current classic statement of the liberal principle. One of its virtues is that it is not sanctified by official acceptance. It has remained controversial and has produced lively debate in our own time. This is altogether appropriate, for liberalism itself is controversial, today as much as ever.

CASES

Doe v. Commonwealth's Attorney, 403 F. Supp. 1199 (E.D. Va. 1975), affirmed, 425 U.S. 901 (1976)
Goldberg v. Kelly, 397 U.S. 254 (1970)
Griswold v. Connecticut, 381 U.S. 479 (1965)
Lochner v. New York, 198 U.S. 45 (1905)
Paris Adult Theater I v. Slaton, 413 U.S. 49 (1973)
Roe v. Wade, 410 U.S. 113 (1973)

BIBLIOGRAPHY

American Law Institute, *Model Penal Code, Tentative Draft No. 4* (1955). Patrick Devlin, *The Enforcement of Morals* (1965). Ronald Dworkin, *A Matter of Principle* (1985); and *Taking Rights Seriously* (1977). Joel Feinberg, *The Moral Limits of the Criminal Law* (1984–), is the most thorough modern discussion and reworking of Mill's principle of liberty. The first two of its projected four volumes are *Harm to Others* (1984) and *Offense to Others* (1985); the last two are projected as *Harm to Self* and *Harmless Wrongdoing*. Great Britain, *Report of the Committee on Homosexual Offences and Prostitution* (Command 247) (1957) (The Wolfenden Report).

Herbert L. A. Hart, *Law, Liberty and Morality* (1963). Robert Nozick, *Anarchy, State, and Utopia* (1974). John Rawls, *A Theory of Justice* (1971). James Fitzjames Stephen, *Liberty, Equality, Fraternity* (1873).
[*See also* CRIMINAL LAW; AMERICAN JURISPRUDENCE; PRIVACY; PROPERTY LAW; *and* SEXUALITY AND THE LAW.]

LAW AND SOCIAL SCIENCE

Wallace D. Loh

THE scope of "law and social science"—a specialized area within the field of law, on the one hand, and the disciplines of anthropology, political science, psychology, and sociology, on the other hand—is quite broad. Nonetheless, two distinct approaches or subareas can be distinguished.

The first is "law and society." This subarea consists of scholarly studies of law and legal institutions from the perspective of the social sciences. Beginning in the latter part of the nineteenth century, sociologist-lawyers such as Emile Durkheim and Max Weber and anthropologists such as Sir Henry Maine published classic essays on the origins and legitimacy of law, founded upon analyses of society, economy, and culture. Contemporary social scientists have developed, especially since the 1960s, a growing body of empirically based knowledge on the social organization of the legal profession, the operation of formal and informal means of dispute resolution, the effectiveness of legal sanctions, and the public impact of legal rules, to mention only some of the main topics of inquiry. All these studies have the common purpose of developing and testing social theories of law and its administration.

The second subarea is "social science in law." The driving force here is the deployment of social science findings, methods, and theories in the service of law. Although there is no sharp division between basic and applied social research, there is a difference in emphasis. In basic research, the goal of developing scientific generalizations about the role of law in society leads researchers to frame theoretically interesting issues for investigation. In applied research, the concern with practical applications prompts researchers to pursue questions shaped by the needs of lawyering and legal policymaking. Thus, in the judicial process, social science has been used to determine the facts of the issue under adjudication, to sustain or criticize the law applicable to those facts, and to justify in a written opinion the reasons for the conclusion reached.

With respect to fact-finding, psychologists since the start of the twentieth century have proposed methods to assess the reliability of courtroom witnesses. At present, they play an active forensic role by offering expert testimony on the reliability of eyewitnesses and conducting studies to improve fact-finding procedures at trial.

Also since the turn of the century, lawyers and judges have relied on social science to arrive at or to justify legal decisions. The use of extralegal information in appellate briefs was pioneered by attorney (later Supreme Court Justice) Louis Brandeis in *Muller* v. *Oregon* (1908) for the purpose of showing the reasonableness of a statute limiting women's working hours in industry. The brief presented evidence on the social and economic effects of sweatshop hours for women. Today a "Brandeis brief" refers to any brief that contains empirical research information in addition to traditional legal arguments. Starting in the 1950s, there has been a steady increase in the use of social science to challenge, as well as to support, existing legal policies. This development coincided with improvements in social research and with expansion of judicial protection of the rights of racial minorities and of criminal defendants. Cases that raise due process and equal protection claims provide the main context in which social science and law come together. Social science serves not only to illuminate the factual background of legal issues, as in *Muller,* but also to evaluate the anticipated impact and the social costs of existing or proposed legal policies. For example, the debate over the exclusionary rule—the rule that excludes from trial any evidence illegally seized by the police—is framed in utilitarian terms (*United States* v. *Leon*, 1984): Does the exclusion deter future police misconduct? How many arrested criminals are set free because the state's evidence is suppressed?

This essay focuses on the role of social science (the realm of social facts) in constitutional adjudication (the realm of social values). However, a generalized account of this role is difficult to formulate. For every judge who embraces social science as a basis of decision, there is another judge—or the same judge in another case on a different subject—who decries such reliance. There is no consensus on the extent to which research evidence influences constitutional decision-making, since courts have not announced the general conditions under which such evidence is deemed essential.

In consequence, issues concerning when, how, and why the courts do or do not use research data in reaching or justifying their decisions cannot be addressed in the abstract. They have to be considered in the context of a particular topic. The role of social science in the judicial process depends on many circumstances, such as the availability and quality of the research, the legal precedents, the importance of the policy issues at stake, and the social-political temper of the times. Instead of reciting different instances where social science and judicial decisions have commingled, this essay examines in some depth the applications of social research in one legal area: school desegregation. From desegregation's early rural, southern beginnings to its present urban, northern manifestation, empirical evidence (drawn from a variety of social science disciplines) has been used extensively in the litigation. Social science is perhaps nowhere woven so tightly into the fabric of judicial decisions as in school desegregation. This topic provides a springboard for addressing broader issues on social science in law.

SOCIAL SCIENCE IN SOUTHERN SCHOOL DESEGREGATION

In 1954, in the landmark case of *Brown* v. *Board of Education*, the Supreme Court declared that "separate educational facilities are inherently unequal" and ruled that the separate-but-equal doctrine of *Plessy* v. *Ferguson* (1896)—which for half a century had legitimated Jim Crow legislation—had no place in the public schools. The Court also found that segregation of schoolchildren "solely because of their race generates a feeling of inferiority" and tends to retard their educational and mental development, citing in footnote 11—possibly the most renowned footnote in all of the opinions of the Court—the writings of social scientists as the "modern authority" for these findings. *Brown* gave modern social science its first big splash in constitutional waters.

In the trial-court proceedings, several noted social scientists testified on behalf of the plaintiffs, who were challenging segregated schools. They described studies purporting to show the harmful effects of segregation on children's personality and learning. For example, psychologist Kenneth Clark, the plaintiffs' leading expert, presented white and brown dolls to sixteen black children aged six to nine years in Clarendon County, South Carolina, where one of the trials was held. He found that most of the children identified with, and preferred, the white doll, even though they recognized that the brown doll was more like themselves. From this result, Clark inferred that the children had feelings of self-rejection and inferiority. His study is subject to pointed methodological criticisms, which the defendant school board failed to raise at trial: the absence of a comparison group of nonsegregated black children; the small sample size, which limits generalizability; the questionable inferences from the data (for example, why is preference for a doll of a color different from oneself necessarily indicative of psychopathology?); and the legal nonrelevance of the results (that is, there was no showing that school segregation, rather than segregation in society at large, was responsible for these psychological effects).

Consequently, no mention was made of the dolls or other similar clinical demonstrations in the appeal to the Supreme Court. Instead, Clark prepared an appendix to the appellants' (plaintiffs') brief, which was signed by thirty-two distinguished social scientists, entitled "A Social Science Statement: The Effects of Segregation and the Consequences of Desegregation." It summarized the available knowledge on the subject, and it included the results of a national poll of social scientists showing their nearly unanimous belief that segregation has negative social and psychological effects. The basic predicate of this "Statement" was the hypothesis that greater interracial contact, beginning at the elementary school level, would decrease black psychological damage, lessen white prejudice, and ultimately improve society. This was the source of the "modern authority" cited in footnote 11. The Brandeis brief, used initially to sustain the constitutionality of progressive social-welfare legislation, was resurrected a generation later by civil rights advocates to strike down discriminatory legislation in schools—and it worked.

Reactions to the "sociological decision," as some columnists and legal scholars characterized the *Brown* decision, were not altogether favorable. Critics who were otherwise in favor of desegregation were unsparing in their attack on footnote 11. They derided the "Social Science Statement" as literary psychology, as consisting of information that was more social than scientific. They feared that the people might come to think that the Court's decision rested on the empirical data tendered in the brief, so that a change in research results in the future would force a change in the constitutional findings regarding segregation. They argued that the constitutional rights of blacks—or of other Americans—should not be made to rest on the flimsy foundations of the studies presented. Today, some social scientists recognize that the original signers of the "Statement" may have been blinded by their ideology and that their recommendations at the time were based not on well-established data but mostly on well-meaning rhetoric.

The secrecy that surrounds all judicial decisions precludes our knowing the precise role that social science played in the *Brown* decision. There is extensive scholarly debate on the issue. Many scholars saw footnote 11 as superfluous, as no more than a consolation gesture to Clark and company for their fidelity to the cause. These skeptics undoubtedly had the better part of the argument in disclaiming any direct impact of social science on the decision itself. If, as the Court said, segregation is inherently unequal, its wrongfulness is self-evident. The holding represents a moral judgment not grounded in factual proof. This is not to say, however, that the data may not have exerted an indirect effect on the final outcome. What was said to have been but

common knowledge about the psychological consequences of segregation was the product, at least in part, of the substantial corpus of research information that had accumulated over the years and had worked its way into popular consciousness and then into the living law.

The imprimatur of "modern authority" served other functions as well. It added legitimacy to the overruling of the separate-but-equal doctrine in education, which was originally rationalized in terms of the psychological knowledge of its time—namely, the nineteenth-century social Darwinist ideas about the biological bases of racial attitudes and their imperviousness to change by legislation or judicial intervention. The united front of the social scientists reinforced the image of broadly based agreement on the evil of segregation that the Court sought to convey in its own unanimous opinion.

One year later, during arguments on the implementation of *Brown,* both sides relied heavily on social science. Clark urged immediate desegregation with iron-fisted enforcement by federal officials, on the theory that change in public attitude follows change in conduct, rather than vice versa. The southern states, which until then had felt no need to marshal social science support, now presented their own Brandeis briefs to argue the opposite theory. They proposed a gradual approach to desegregation under the aegis of local authorities. Faced with a politically sensitive matter, the absence of legal precedent, and conflicting social science recommendations on the timing and mechanics of desegregation, the Court trod a fine line between resoluteness and accommodation. The second *Brown* decision, *Brown II,* reached a compromise solution without any mention of empirical findings: desegregation by local school boards, under the supervision of federal district courts, conducted with "all deliberate speed"—a formula that combined opposite ideas for epigrammatic effect.

During the next decade, the lower federal courts began to strike down segregation in nearly every other area of public life (such as parks, beaches, and transportation), and the Supreme Court affirmed these orders on the authority of *Brown I.* The application of that case to these other areas was problematic because the opinion had focused narrowly on public education. The Court, however, was untroubled by the logic of invoking the detrimental psychological effects of segregated schools for the purpose of ending, say, segregated beaches. *Brown I* became the catalyst for the civil rights movement of the late 1950s and the 1960s.

Ironically, when this movement was over, the one institution that remained essentially segregated was the local schoolhouse. Ironically, too, social science was now used to perpetuate dual schools or delay desegregation. A major test of footnote 11 occurred some ten years later in *Stell* v. *Savannah-Chatham County Board of Education* (1963). Psychologists and sociologists for the defendant school board testified that "differences in physical, psychical and behavioral traits" made it "impossible for Negro and white children of the same chronological age to be effectively educated in the same classrooms," because otherwise all would suffer "grave psychological harm." In a reversal of pre-1954 roles, the plaintiffs called no experts. Instead, they simply argued that social science evidence was irrelevant because *Brown I* had proclaimed that "segregation itself injures Negro children." The Court of Appeals for the Fifth Circuit nimbly sidestepped the school board's attempt at factual impeachment of *Brown I.* It ruled that the holding in that case rested on an authoritative judgment and that judgment stood even if its factual underpinnings were proved to be erroneous. Many other courts have since recast *Brown I* in normative terms, so that the mandate of desegregation has become independent of the empirical research.

SOCIAL SCIENCE IN NORTHERN SCHOOL DESEGREGATION

For almost twenty years after *Brown*, the courts generally ignored racial imbalance in barrio and ghetto schools. Desegregation was deemed a southern problem. So long as the imbalance was not the product of official action and did not have a history of state-sanctioned separation, it was not subject to constitutional attack. Two demographic trends, however, made the racial disproportion increasingly acute: the northward migration of southern blacks and the exodus of the white middle class to the suburbs. In 1973 the Supreme Court finally put the North on notice that it too had to comply with *Brown.* It ruled that intentional (de jure) segregative acts by the Denver school board in a mostly black neighborhood created a presumption that other

segregated schooling within the system was not accidental *(Keyes* v. *School District No. 1).* The Court ordered citywide desegregation when school officials were unable to overcome the presumption that the wrong done in one part of the system had infected the whole.

Detroit is more representative of the northern urban metropolis than Denver because, unlike Denver, racial minorities constitute a more substantial segment of the city's population. Detroit has a bull's-eye population pattern—that is, a predominantly black inner core surrounded by rings of white suburbs. A steady out-migration of whites has left a school population that is largely black and is forecast to be virtually completely black by 1990. Thus, in Detroit and other major cities, the problem is not only racially separate schools but also racially separate communities within a single metropolitan area. Against this background, a federal district court judge found that the Detroit school board had purposefully segregated the city's schools. He then ordered the most sweeping metropolitan busing program in the history of the Republic, involving tens of thousands of students in more than fifty suburban school districts and in Detroit itself. The Supreme Court quickly struck down the metropolitan remedy but affirmed the finding of intentional discrimination in Detroit, thereby limiting desegregation to within the city's boundaries, then already 64 percent black and growing *(Milliken* v. *Bradley,* 1974, or *Milliken I).* Subsequently, the Court approved a decree requiring substantial state expenditures to improve the educational quality of Detroit's mostly black schools *(Milliken* v. *Bradley,* 1977, or *Milliken II).* The Detroit case was the first major setback for integration since *Brown,* and it signaled the start of a modern version of *Plessy:* mostly separate but equal, at least when the alternative is large-scale interdistrict busing.

The appellate opinions in the Detroit case and in some other northern cases make scant or no reference to social science. However, examination of the trial transcripts often reveal that voluminous expert testimony had been presented at both the trial and remedy proceedings. The testimony and briefs typically cover one or more of the following areas: the causes and extent of residential and school segregation; the educational effects of desegregation; the social psychological effects of desegregation; and the purportedly wrongful conduct of school officials in maintaining racially separate schools. The empirical literature, especially in the first three areas, is vast. Only some of the findings and their legal relevance will be highlighted here.

Residential Segregation and School Segregation. For nearly six weeks during the Detroit trial, plaintiffs' expert witnesses expounded on the dynamics of urban demography and the causes of ghettoization. Their theory was that discrimination by public officials (prior to the promulgation of fair housing legislation) and private parties (such as lenders and real estate agents), and not voluntary preferences of blacks or their lower income, was the prime cause of residential segregation. The seemingly neutral policy of assignment to neighborhood schools, coupled with the fact of residential segregation, resulted in racially imbalanced schools, so that de facto ("naturally" occurring) segregation is really de jure (intentional) segregation once removed. Hence, there is a reciprocal, causal relationship between the racial composition of schools and of neighborhoods. Essentially the same theory was presented in a Brandeis brief entitled "School Segregation and Residential Segregation: A Social Science Statement," signed by thirty-seven social scientists and introduced in the Columbus, Ohio, school desegregation case (*Columbus Board of Education* v. *Penick,* 1979). In both cases, although the experts claimed broad scholarly agreement, they acknowledged that the evidence was incomplete and that the causal connections were only dimly perceived. Social science, they admitted, lacks the tools to disentangle the effects of governmental action from the welter of demographic, economic, and attitudinal factors that influence residential choice.

Most courts have avoided facing squarely the issue of racial containment in housing. *Milliken I* dodged it on the technicality that the issue was not formally before the Court. One possible reason for the judicial evasion is a reluctance to avoid blurring the already razor-thin distinction between de jure and de facto, which would occur if the state's role in causing or perpetuating segregated housing is recognized. Thus, a concurring opinion in *Milliken I* characterized the dynamics of housing segregation as not only "unknown" (despite the voluminous trial testimony) but also as "unknowable." To say that a demographic process is beyond cognition may

be a cryptic way of suggesting that nobody can be blamed for it. Similarly, a dissenting opinion in *Columbus* declared that racially imbalanced schools result "primarily from familiar segregated housing patterns which—in turn—are caused by social, economic, and demographic forces for which no school board is responsible."

There is also no need for the courts to deal directly with the housing evidence, because it is not legally relevant. The basic issue is whether school officials engaged in intentional discrimination on account of race. Given this narrow and technically correct formulation of the legal question, the data on residential segregation is not necessary. School officials tend to limit their defense to the absence of intentional wrongdoing, while the plaintiffs typically broaden the focus of inquiry to include evidence on societal patterns of racism.

Underlying the debate on demography and school segregation is the preoccupation with "white flight"—the transfer of white students out of schools that are being (or are about to be) involuntarily desegregated and into private or suburban public (and mostly white) schools. There is no consensus among social scientists, however, on the extent of the white exodus attributable directly to busing or on the percentage tipping point above which resegregation would quickly accelerate. Thus, in the Boston school desegregation case, abundant empirical evidence was introduced by both parties and summarized in the opinion of the Court of Appeals for the First Circuit (*Morgan* v. *Kerrigan,* 1976). One side concluded that large-scale and rapid desegregation by court-ordered busing defeated the goal of increasing interracial contact, because white flight would simply produce resegregation. The other side criticized the methodology of the studies from which the conclusion was drawn. It argued that white flight was a short-term phenomenon and that the general decline in the proportion of whites in urban areas was the result of long-term demographic trends independent of school desegregation. Faced with the rounds of evidence and counterevidence, the court said with more than a hint of exasperation,

> Throughout this series of submissions this court has been burdened with reports written for sociologists by sociologists utilizing sophisticated

LAW AND SOCIAL SCIENCE

statistical and mathematical techniques. We lack the expertise to evaluate these studies on their merits. We do come to one conclusion, however. The relationship between white flight and court ordered desegregation is a matter of heated debate among experts in sociology, and a firm professional consensus has not yet emerged.

The court then proceeded to "reject all these materials as irrelevant to the issues before us." It opined that "what the layman calls 'resegregation' is not constitutionally recognized segregation."

The range of disagreement among experts has narrowed at present, and there is virtually no dispute on one key point: At least some noticeable decline in white enrollment goes hand in hand with court-ordered desegregation. A few years after mandatory busing was begun in the Boston public schools, the number of white students had dropped by about one-half.

Some courts have begun to allow consideration of white flight in desegregation plans, so long as it is not used as a subterfuge to avoid desegregation. For example, in Queens, New York, members of minorities constituted less than one-fifth of school students in the 1950s; by 1980 they constituted over two-thirds. The increase resulted from residential demographics, not de jure violations. To stem the trend to an all-minority population, school officials limited the enrollment of minority students so that it would not exceed 50 percent in any desegregated school. The Court of Appeals for the Second Circuit upheld this school policy. The factual dispute, involving sophisticated statistical analyses and conflicting interpretations of the data, centered on whether there was empirical justification for the 50 percent cutoff point as opposed to 60 percent or some other higher figure (*Parent Association* v. *Ambach*, 1984).

Educational Effects of School Desegregation. In the first two decades after *Brown*, a key justification for school desegregation was its favorable impact on the educational performance of minority students. The attainment of equal educational opportunity was measured in terms of raising the scores on standardized achievement tests of disadvantaged pupils. The so-called Coleman Report was enormously influential in shaping the public debate (Coleman et al.). It was a cross-

sectional survey of over half a million students across the nation, one of the largest studies in the history of social science, and it examined the relationship between academic achievement and (naturally occurring, not court-mandated) school desegregation. The principal finding was that family background and school peers affected a student's achievement the most; school expenditures and the physical resources of the school affected achievement the least. The clear implication of this result, which was testified to in many school desegregation trials, was that interracial contact in the schools would enhance minority achievement. Of course, the drawback of this or any other nonexperimental research is that the relationship may be a spurious one because of the effects of uncontrolled variables. For example, black children who voluntarily attend schools with a white majority are usually not there by chance. If they outperform their counterparts in segregated schools, it may not be because their middle-class schoolmates are more stimulating but because they themselves possess characteristics that influence achievement.

By the early 1970s, coincident with the emerging white consensus against involuntary busing, some social scientists began to cast doubt on the claimed academic and psychosocial advantages of biracial schooling. Studies on the effects of mandatory (not naturally occurring) desegregation reached the conclusion that desegregation did not enhance achievement as measured by standardized tests. Reanalyses of the data of the Coleman Report showed that naturally integrated (nonbused) black pupils were still significantly behind white pupils in the same schools. The policy implication was that court-ordered busing for promoting student achievement was not effective and should not be adopted. Antibusing social scientists charged that their probusing colleagues who were testifying otherwise were misleading trial judges into believing that racially mixed classrooms were educationally justifiable.

Busing proponents promptly counterattacked by questioning the methodology and the findings of these studies. They complained that the achievement gains of black students in desegregated schools should be compared not with gains of white students in the same schools but with those of black students in segregated schools. This quarrel over the criterion of deseg-

864

regation success illustrates how the fact of measurement can subtly redefine the basic policy issue. It solidified the role of achievement scores as a critical test of whether mandatory desegregation is effective. Faced with dissension among the experts, the Supreme Court since *Brown* has not expressly relied on social science evidence on academic harms or benefits in determining whether there is a constitutional violation or in fashioning remedial decrees when such a violation is found.

On balance, the best that can be said at this time is that sometimes desegregation improves black academic achievement and sometimes it does not. Whether or not it improves achievement depends on a host of circumstances related to when and how the desegregation process is carried out. For example, does it start in the early elementary school years or in the later high school years? Does the desegregation imply changes in the quality of interracial interaction, such as the creation of a social climate conducive to learning and the availability of support services, or does it entail nothing more than racial mixing of students?

Psychosocial Effects of Desegregation. The *Brown* premise that segregated schools generate a negative self-image among black children had wide currency until the late 1960s. Then social scientists began reexamining this proposition and discovered little or mixed empirical support for it. There are now few who believe that segregation impairs black self-esteem, but there is no clear evidence that desegregation, in itself, raises self-esteem. Another claim made at the time of *Brown* was that desegregation would reduce racial prejudice. One-race schools were said to nurture intolerance in children, so that in the long run it has a fallout effect on the level of prejudice in society as a whole. Integrated schools were thought to be incubators of racial harmony. Again, the evidence on school desegregation and interracial attitudes is inconclusive. For every study that shows a certain result, another study can be found that reaches a conflicting conclusion. The poor quality of many studies contributes to the uncertainty. In addition, there are countless factors inside and outside the school setting that could influence self-esteem and racial attitudes. Prejudice in American society has a long history. It seems unrealistic to expect that school desegregation would usher in the mil-

lenium. Schools mirror the conditions of the society of which they are a part.

Unconstitutional Conduct of School Authorities. A basic teaching of post-*Brown* cases is that the courts may not create a remedy for segregated schools without first establishing intentional discrimination by school officials. This intent to segregate, or de jure violation, need not involve malice or prejudice; the intent to bring about the forbidden result is sufficient. The intent is inferred from objective circumstances, such as building new schools, busing black but not white pupils, manipulating boundary lines to perpetuate racial separation, and using optional attendance zones in changing neighborhoods to enable whites to avoid going to mostly black schools.

Social research is not available or actually needed to establish some of these circumstances. Recent decisions make clear that plaintiffs' burden of proving de jure violations can rest on the slenderest of evidence. In the *Columbus* case, for instance, the schools were highly segregated. Before 1954, schools in historically black neighborhoods contained mostly black students and teachers. There was no proof that these school locations were initially chosen with race in mind. After 1954, the racial composition of these schools remained unchanged. At the time of the trial in the latter half of the 1970s, the faculty had already been desegregated and over one-half of the black students in the school district were attending integrated schools. The students in the schools in question were mostly black, but the result would have been the same regardless of how attendance boundaries were originally drawn because of the mostly black neighborhoods. Nonetheless, the school board was found to have caused and perpetuated the mostly black schools. The presence of racial imbalance and the delay by school officials to rectify it in post-*Brown* years gave rise to the inference of discriminatory intent. Once the showing of improper purpose was made, the school board was saddled with the exceedingly heavy burden of proving that its actions (and the actions of its predecessors decades ago) did not cause the contemporary racial disproportions. The Court ruled that the school board had an affirmative duty to integrate as a result of the inference that pre-1954 board actions were related, no matter how tenuously, to post-1954 conditions.

The elusiveness of the definition of intentional discrimination belies the ease with which it can be proved. In other words, the distinction between de jure and de facto is now exceedingly thin and fragile. A trial judge, troubled by the moral questions posed by de facto segregation, can readily find a de jure violation. The judge in *Bradley* admitted that "if racial segregation . . . is an evil, then it should make no difference whether we classify it de jure or de facto." Since no-fault liability is impossible under present law, the litany of school board violations could be a reluctant concession to the requirements of legal precedent. The accordionlike quality of the concept of discriminatory purpose gives judges considerable discretionary power. Different judges faced with similar facts might well arrive at different conclusions regarding the purity of a school board's motives.

The presumption of temporal causation in *Columbus* (pre-1954 violations caused post-1954 conditions) and the presumption of spatial causation in *Keyes* (violations in one part of the school district infect the entire district) are difficult to prove or justify empirically. The presumed linkages between de jure violations and segregated schools are not, and probably could not be, empirically substantiated. Legal "causation" in this context is a concept that rests more on moral grounds than on quantitative measurement. The nearly conclusive presumption of causation and the allocation to school authorities of the burden to rebut it serve to create, in effect, a presumption of guilt on the part of the school authorities.

If proof of de jure violations is relatively easy and if proof of housing segregation and of the social-educational benefits of desegregation are not legally necessary, one would think that plaintiffs would dispense with the costly and time-consuming attempts at presenting such social science evidence at trial. After all, such evidence often goes unmentioned in appellate opinions. However, plaintiffs continue to introduce extra legal information on the societal sources and social consequences of school segregation, perhaps because of felt pressure to offer some plausible justification for mandatory desegregation beyond reliance on case precedents. The social science may well exert an indirect influence on the trial outcome. After studying trial transcripts, one sociologist concluded that in

Detroit, as in some other cases, the extensive and often emotionally moving testimony on racial discrimination in housing and its effects on school segregation helped to arouse the trial judge's sense of wrong. The testimony prompted the judge—who was on record prior to the trial as being opposed to involuntary busing—to find de jure violations by the school board, thereby triggering massive busing. (Ironically, the "guilty" school board consisted of members committed to integration and the trial-court opinion devoted more space to praising their prointegration efforts than to condemning their purported violations.) In essence, "social science was an important aspect of [the judge's] indoctrination" (Wolf, 119). After the trial, the judge indicated that the evidence on residential segregation was the key to understanding the case and, presumably, to his remarkable change of heart as to the need for interdistrict busing.

Thus, the practical relevance of legally irrelevant empirical evidence is that it may help sensitize judges to the broader picture of racial discrimination in society. To persuade a judge to decree social change, the artful advocate needs to convince both the mind and the emotions of the judge. Intellect and feelings together inform a person's sense of justice. Legal arguments are addressed to the mind, and legal doctrines provide the analytical means for reaching the desired result. But to impel the judge to undertake such action in the first place may require an appeal to the judge's emotions. Social science evidence can serve as a catalyst for awakening feelings of right and wrong.

SOCIAL SCIENCE, SOCIAL VALUES, AND SCHOOL DESEGREGATION

There are two basic value-laden questions that underlie school desegregation. First, does the United States want to have an integrated society, relying on integrated public schools as a stepping-stone toward that ultimate goal? Second, if yes, is compulsory busing the desired means for achieving integrated schools?

Traditional liberal ideology answers both questions affirmatively. The societal ideal is "one [racially integrated] nation, indivisible, with liberty and justice for all." As *Brown I* declared, public education "is the very foundation of good citizenship," the "principal instrument in awakening the child to cultural values." Because of widespread residential segregation, busing becomes virtually synonymous with integrated schooling. This ideology has long been associated with social science, in part because of the nature of the discipline. Social science seeks to understand and predict social and behavioral phenomena; hence, the profession tends to attract into its ranks those who are more interested in shaping the future than in preserving the past. Theory and research usually focus on social change, not on the status quo.

Social scientists have offered expert testimony and helped draft Brandeis briefs far more often on behalf of those challenging existing practices than on behalf of those defending them. In desegregation lawsuits involving both small and large school districts, plaintiffs in the majority of cases have used expert witnesses to prove a violation, whereas defendants only rarely have relied on experts to refute the charge of discrimination. In addition to the ideological tilt of the experts, the participation of institutional litigants suggests another explanation for the use or nonuse of social science. Plaintiff attorneys are usually associated with the National Association for the Advancement of Colored People, the American Civil Liberties Union, or the Department of Justice, organizations that specialize in civil rights litigation and have a ready network of seasoned expert witnesses to call upon. Defense counsel typically consist of a local law firm that represents the school district on labor relations or other routine business, but not on school desegregation matters. A similar imbalance is found in other areas of law. For example, in litigation involving the death penalty, there is more expert testimony against the sanction and the method of its imposition than there is in favor of the system of capital punishment. In criminal trials involving identifications made by eyewitnesses to the crime, psychologists often testify on behalf of criminal defendants regarding the probable unreliability of such identifications. Rarely do psychologists appear for the prosecution to inform the jury about the circumstances when eyewitnesses are generally reliable (Loh).

The alliance between proponents of judicial activism (who hark back to such hallowed epigrams as "The Constitution is what the judges say it is") and liberal social scientists (who pro-

vide the empirical justification for legal change) came to the fore in the 1950s and 1960s when the Supreme Court, under Chief Justice Earl Warren, spearheaded far-reaching reforms to ensure equal treatment for racial minorities, voting rights for the disenfranchised, and fair procedures for criminal suspects. However, in the 1970s and 1980s the Supreme Court under Chief Justice Warren Burger shifted toward a more passive role in social policymaking. In this approach, constitutional principles are seen as antecedent to judicial decision-making; judgments are the product, not the cause, of law. The proponents of judicial restraint are critical of decisions that rely on social science. They urge that decisions rest on principled or nonempirical grounds. The function of the courts is to preserve the social peace and the existing order by interpreting standards of the past rather than by following uncertain empirical predictions. These lines ascribed to Sir Thomas More exemplify the philosophy of judicial nonintervention: "The law, Roper, the law. I know what's legal, not what's right. And I'll stick to what's legal . . . I'm *not* God."

The disavowal of the integration-*über-alles* philosophy finds favor not only with many whites who oppose court-ordered busing but also with some segments of the black community. For example, in the Dallas school desegregation case, a group of blacks opposed any escalation in the use of racial balance remedies to cure the effects of segregation and sought, instead, alternative solutions to improve educational quality and to eliminate the disparity in academic performance (*Tasby* v. *Wright,* 1981). In the Nashville litigation, the usual roles were reversed when a white majority of the school board, acting on the advice of a white expert, recommended to the court more busing to achieve more racial balance, while the black plaintiffs urged less busing and more neighborhood schools, even if the result should be schools with a black majority (*Kelley* v. *Metropolitan County Board of Education,* 1980).

Confronted with the rising neoconservatism of the 1980s, proponents of integration have become increasingly estranged from social scientists, their erstwhile allies. One of the sharpest critics has been Kenneth Clark, plaintiffs' chief social science expert in *Brown.* At the time of that decision, he declared that proof of the wrongfulness of segregation had to come from social psychologists. A quarter of a century later, he reversed himself. He warned that "the business of social justice is too important to be left in the hands of . . . social scientists who are primarily responsive to majority fashions, prejudices, and power"; instead, he urged that citizens "put their faith and trust in our federal courts" (1977, 9). The irony, of course, is that his fear that a change in social science conclusions might force a change in constitutional policy was precisely the alarm that critics of footnote 11 sounded in the mid-1950s.

INTERPRETATIONS OF THE *BROWN* DECISION

The promise of *Brown* has undergone different interpretations as social-political conditions have changed. One interpretation of *Brown* is that it proscribes color-conscious policies and actions that result in racial exclusion or imbalance. Official segregation is inherently wrong because it rests upon assumptions of racial superiority and inferiority that are repugnant to American aspirations of equality. The remedy for its violation is color-blind decision-making: equal educational opportunity (*Brown I*) or equality of access. This is an "input perspective" on the system of segregation. It seeks to eradicate the cause of the wrong.

A second interpretation of *Brown* is that it safeguards minority children against the social, psychological, and educational harms said to result from racial segregation. The constitutional right is defined in terms of the consequential injury. The remedy for its breach is color-conscious decision-making: racial integration. This relief promises more than just open access and an end to racial barriers. It mandates deliberate racial mixture in order to bestow upon the underclass the purported advantages of exposure to the classes above it. This is an "output perspective" on segregation. It looks to the results of segregation, irrespective of its cause.

Through the years, liberals have clung steadfastly to the original understanding of *Brown* that racial integration and equal educational opportunity are inextricably related—the former guarantees the latter. When schools were in fact separate and unequal, black children had to go to the same schools attended by white children in

order to receive the same educational package. Today, with equalization of educational funding to schools within a district and substantial white opposition to involuntary busing, neoconservatives do not equate the right to equal educational opportunity with the right to an integrated education. Instead, they reinterpret *Brown* as promising only the color-blind remedy of nondiscriminatory access: to them, desegregation does not necessarily mean integration. Massive racial balancing, they fear, would determine the social-political consensus of America's multiethnic society.

The Supreme Court has steered a middle-of-the-road course between color-conscious and color-blind remedial strategies. *Milliken II* affirmed the trial court's decree that the state of Michigan and the Detroit school board each expend $5.8 million for compensatory education and counseling programs in city schools, in addition to any intradistrict busing and in lieu of any interdistrict busing. It signaled the end of the integration line of *Brown* and the start of the neo-*Plessy* doctrine of mostly separate but equal, at least where demographic conditions such as those of Detroit prevail.

The outcome in Detroit suggests a third way of interpreting the promise of *Brown:* a "process perspective." The preceding two perspectives tend to slight the "education" component in *Brown* v. *Board of Education.* They focus on the inputs of discriminatory actions that produce racial imbalances or on the outputs of new racial balances and social-educational improvements. The process perspective attends more to the quality of the schooling than to racial considerations. There is a small but growing "effective education movement" in the black community that rejects racial integration as necessary to black educational achievement. Adherents of this movement subscribe to the belief that predominantly black schools can be changed to foster academic excellence. They also recognize that integration of low-income blacks into upper-income, mostly white schools involves racial assimilation and that the process of socializing nonwhite students to behave like white students can wreak psychological and educational havoc on the black children. Some school administrators, acknowledging that their schools have always been segregated and that they will probably continue to be segregated because of residential demographics, are now shifting their efforts to address education rather than desegregation.

The apparent difficulty with this process perspective is that it offers a new remedy without a corresponding redefinition of the underlying right that triggers it. One can sue a school system because it is segregated, but one cannot sue it because it is educationally ineffective. The *Milliken* Court, however, nimbly circumvented this difficulty by finding de jure violations and using this fiction as the constitutional peg upon which to hang the effective education remedy.

These perspectives on *Brown*'s meaning bear implications for empirical inquiry in school desegregation. So long as the remedial objective' was integration, social science also adopted an output perspective on research. In the mid-1950s, psychologists conducted small-scale experimental studies on the social and personality effects of segregation. In the mid-1960s, liberal sociologists gathered extensive cross-sectional data and applied sophisticated statistical analyses to examine the social and educational effects of "natural" desegregation. In the mid-1970s, similar large-scale surveys were done by neoconservative sociologists on the effects of induced desegregation via mandatory busing. In all these instances, the basic research issue was the effect of school segregation or desegregation on social and educational outcomes. The issue presumed a global impact of racial and/or social-class composition on the outcome measures. There is a certain allure to the idea that heterogeneity in the schools based on race and/or social class can bring about the educational and social millenium.

After the mid-1970s, coincident with the emergence of the effective-education movement, social scientists began to pay more attention to conditions inside the schools. They noted that factors such as the nature of intergroup contact and the social climate in the classroom can be as important as simple racial balancing, if not more so. Social psychologists differentiated between merely desegregated and genuinely integrated schools. The former refers to the mere mix of races and implies nothing about the quality of racial interaction that is a precondition to effective learning. The latter involves the presence of those conditions deemed necessary for favorable intergroup relations: equal status, common goals, noncompetitive atmosphere, and institutional resources. Researchers began to examine the circumstances under which schools can maximize the desired outcomes.

The third perspective directs social scientists to think about the remedy in terms of an ongoing process rather than a final product. It focuses attention not only on what goes into, and what comes out of, the school system but also on the myriad events that transpire in between. School desegregation, in short, cannot be thought of as a kind of experimental treatment in education, because desegregation programs are not all alike. The quality of education may be entirely different in schools with the same racial balance, because the conditions of learning and interracial contact are different. It is unrealistic to expect desegregation to have any across-the-board impact on educational performance or any other outcome. The emphasis now is on the conditions of effective biracial learning. The renewed attention to school variables that intervene between input and output—variables that the Coleman Report rejected—mirrors the judicial trend toward restoring the educational component of *Brown.* The role of social science in school desegregation in the coming years will be more for the purpose of helping frame the remedy (for example, designing genuinely integrated schools) than for establishing the wrong.

SOCIAL SCIENCE IN JUDICIAL DECISION-MAKING

The role of social research in the courts is part of the broader subject of how information about social reality contributes to shaping the way society should be ordered. It deals with both the objectively true and the morally right. There is no single, elegant, and consensual link between the realms of fact and value. One way to map this role is in terms of what courts do: determine the facts of a case, create or modify the law applicable to those facts, and rationalize or justify the conclusion reached in the case.

Judicial Adjudication. When the applicable legal rule in a case is uncontested and only the facts are at issue, social science evidence aids in determining the applicability of the rule—that is, in judicial fact-finding. For example, if studies show unequal resources in black and white schools within a jurisdiction, the rule requiring separate-but-equal educational facilities might lead to a decree of equalization of funding. Or, to take another illustration, if scientific surveys show that the population eligible for jury service in a particular community is highly prejudiced against one of the litigants, the law guaranteeing a fair trial might lead to a decision to move the trial to a different venue. It is a kind of programmed or prefabricated decision-making—a jurisprudence of antecedents. Once the specific facts are ascertained, the judge reasons from the governing rule to the inescapable conclusion. The use of social research here is not problematic—it does not lead to any change in legal doctrine or policy.

Judicial Legislation. A more unsettled role of social research is in the creation or modification of law—that is, in judicial legislation. When both the applicable law and the facts are at issue, as they were in *Brown,* a court must resolve conflicting claims of fact and decide between opposing interests. It is a kind of unprogrammed decision-making, used in new types of cases. The presentation of empirical data on the disputed facts can influence judge-made law either directly or indirectly.

A direct or instrumental role of social research is in ascertaining the impact of decisions. One ground for choosing between different legal premises is an evaluation of their anticipated social and behavioral effects. Decision implies choice, and choice implies prediction. Impact research can help shape decisions because of the reciprocal relationship between issues of fact and law. It is a central feature of the nature and growth of law that the "issues of fact arise out of the law but, at the point of application of law, the issues of law also arise out of the facts" (Hart and McNaughton, 61). Existing legal rules give facts their legal significance, but facts, in turn, can also beget new legal rules.

The "chicken-and-egg relationship" between issues of fact and law suggests a method for collaboration between lawyers and social scientists in reform-oriented litigation. In the course of identifying the legal issues, a lawyer can indicate to the social scientist the kinds of empirical data that might be needed. Legal rules define the types of facts relevant for adjudication. An antisegregation rule might state, for example, that there is wrongful discrimination if there is substantial racial imbalance in a school system as a result of deliberate actions by school officials. It is only when segregation is deemed wrong (a normative judgment embodied in the rule) that one needs to inquire about the facts of racial imbalance and official conduct—"The issues of fact arise out of the law." Although the initial factual questions of investigation are posed by the lawyer, the social scientist does not remain in a handmaiden's role. He may call attention to other facts that the lawyer had not considered and that could alter the character of the legal issues. He might do research that shows that segregated schooling produces harmful effects on minority children irrespective of whether the segregation came about by deliberate action or fortuitous circumstances. The lawyer could use these findings (if well established) to challenge the existing rule by arguing that these effects are sufficient to find unlawful discrimination, without any further showing of improper official motive. Here is an instance of using social research to help create new law. This is possible because "at the point of application of law, the issues of law also arise out of the facts." Hence, neither the lawyer nor the social scientist can be in complete command. Each contributes to the other in developing the analysis.

Another direct role of social research is in formulating and implementing remedies for proven constitutional violations. Although empirical data may not be the key factor in establishing a wrong, it may help shape the design of remedial decrees. Some courts, for example, now take into account the potential for white flight in determining the extent of desegregation, and expert assistance has been used in preparing compensatory education programs as alternatives or supplements to integration.

Social science may also have an indirect effect on shaping the outcome. What was claimed by legal critics of *Brown*'s footnote 11 to have been common information about the psychosocial effects of segregation was the result, at least in part, of the empirical research that had developed over the years and seeped into popular learning. Social research is a cumulative enterprise. Its findings can have a long-term and indirect influence on social judgments. An example of this oblique influence is found in the area of capital punishment.

In the mid-1960s, following the path taken a decade earlier by civil rights lawyers who used social scientists to mount an equal-protection challenge to racial discrimination in schools, criminal defense lawyers also retained social scientists to assist in an equal-protection challenge to racial discrimination in capital sentencing of rape defendants. Teams of lawyers and sociologists conducted statistical studies in southern states that showed that black defendants convicted of rape were much more likely to receive the death penalty than their white counterparts, even though the two categories of defendants were otherwise equivalent with respect to prior criminal record, degree of force used, and other relevant characteristics. The courts rejected the statistical proof of unequal treatment in capital sentencing, even though they had relied upon less systematic and less sophisticated empirical evidence of inequality in striking down segregated schools. To accept the data would have been tantamount to branding hundreds of rape juries in the South as prejudiced; in effect, the courts would have acknowledged that rape convicts were sentenced to death because of their race rather than their crime. The Court of Appeals for the Eighth Circuit opined, "We are not certain that, for Maxwell [the black defendant], statistics will ever be his redemption" (*Maxwell* v. *Bishop,* 1968).

However, in the late 1970s, the solicitor general of the United States made a remarkable concession in a legal brief in support of capital punishment. He agreed that the earlier studies were valid, and he did not question their conclusion that during the period covered by the studies, there had been racial discrimination in capital sentencing. However, he hastened to add that the current research did not show that racial discrimination was continuing. Thus, the federal government belatedly admitted to what state officials have always denied, though it also argued that racial discrimination in imposing the death penalty was an event of the past and not of the present. These studies may not have saved Maxwell, but they may have spared subsequent black rape convicts. The effect of social science in the cycle of law reform may not be discernible until many years after its application. First, there is the presentation of empirical evidence of the racial disparities in sentencing; second, there is vigorous denial by state officials of any racial bias and the upholding of this denial by the courts; and third, there are changes in sentencing dur-

ing the ensuing years that result in the diminution or elimination of the racial disparities, changes that represent a tacit admission of the very bias that was denied initially.

Whether intended or not, the use of social science can also frame or redefine the policy issue. In school finance litigation, for example, the opposing sides disagree on the impact of greater expenditures on educational quality, but implicitly they (and the court) agree that educational quality is measured by performance on standardized achievement tests. Social research channeled thinking about the issue as a technical matter of improving test scores of low-income minority children rather than as a moral dilemma posed by economic inequality. Expert testimony can be a factor in persuading the judge that improved achievement scores make school desegregation worth the effort.

Judicial Rationalization. The judicial function involves two distinct processes: judging and rationalizing. Judging consists of reaching decisions by applying existing law or by creating new law. Rationalizing consists of explicating the reasons for these decisions. A similar distinction is made in the philosophy of science between discovery and justification. Discovery involves the conception or invention of a scientific theory; justification consists of elaborating a rationale to support the new theory. The genesis of scientific insights or of new legal rules may not be susceptible to logical reconstruction, but the post hoc explication of the discovery requires the operation of logic and reasoning.

Judicial creation of law usually implicates choices or accommodations between competing social values—for example, integrated schools versus neighborhood schools and equal rights versus property rights. These value choices are, at bottom, political choices. Vexing policy issues are often converted into the form and language of a lawsuit. Questions of legitimacy arise when appointed judges in a democratic society decide what are essentially issues of political choice. A justification for judicial policymaking in situations not governed by determinate precedents is the requirement of a written opinion. The judiciary is the only branch of government that must give reasons for its decisions. An opinion explains how the decision was arrived at, places it in relation to past decisions in analogous cases, and looks into the future in terms of its effect in

LAW AND SOCIAL SCIENCE

furthering societal purposes. By obligating judges to lay bare for public scrutiny the whys and wherefores of their decision-making, an institutional check is built into the judicial process. It forecloses or minimizes the risk of ad hoc judgments that merely express transient or personal feelings of what is right.

Judicial rationalization can be in normative (that is, principled, reasoned) terms or in instrumental (that is, empirical, utilitarian) terms. Normative analysis involves the conscious pursuit of explicitly defined social values and an elaboration of the means of attaining them. It consists of developing arguments that are analytically reasoned and ethically persuasive in terms of shared moral principles of the community. The test of a decision lies in the quality of the normative arguments used to justify it. Instrumental analysis involves a consideration of the possible consequences of alternative courses of action, the cost-benefits of the chosen decision, and the means of effective implementation. Such utilitarian calculations invite the use of social science evidence. Judicial rationalization can also be framed in both normative and instrumental terms. In *Brown I* the assertion that segregation is "inherently unequal" was a normative justification, and footnote 11 exemplified an instrumentalist rationale for desegregation. Thus, to the extent that rulings are predicated—at least in part—upon empirical premises, social science has a role in the legitimation of judicial lawmaking.

Since judges can frame the legal issues before them in normative or instrumentalist terms (or both), they can predetermine the relevance of empirical data in the rationalization process. Proponents of principled judicial decisions, and they include both liberal and neoconservative scholars, object to the use of social science justifications. They recognize that social science has had an impact on adjudicative and legislative functions of the courts. Every decision contains, explicitly or implicitly, factual premises that control it. Social science has a role in aiding judicial fact-finding. However, because the articulated rationales in the opinions provide a basis for public evaluation of the legitimacy of the decisions, they insist that these justifications be conditioned on principle rather than data. The "major crisis for the judiciary," in the view of this normative jurisprudence, "may not arise with the incompetent use of empirical evidence, but rather simply because the judiciary bases its decisions on social science evidence" (O'Brien, 19).

Liberal critics of judicial reliance on social science fear that constitutional rights may become more uncertain and precarious when they are placed on the proverbial slippery slope of social science. This was the perspective that informed the critique of the early dolls studies at the time of *Brown* and is still urged today with respect to other basic freedoms. Thus, if the Fourteenth Amendment right to nondiscriminatory schooling depended on whether integrated schools raised minority students' achievement scores and self-esteem, if the Fourth Amendment right to exclude illegally seized evidence depended on whether the exclusion deterred police misconduct, or if the Sixth Amendment right to a trial by jury (of twelve members rather than some smaller number) depended on whether the size reduction impaired the functioning of the jury, then these constitutional rights may be undercut by studies that challenge the respective factual predicates.

Neoconservative scholars in law and in the social sciences have deplored social policymaking by the courts, which they characterize as government by judiciary. In their view, courts ought to exercise self-restraint and not engage in the kind of lawmaking that should flow from the elected representatives of the people. To abide by this passive role, judges are expected to engage in sharply reasoned and principled decision-making (code words for judicial self-restraint) and eschew reliance on social science materials. It is not surprising that critics of judicial activism are also critics of judicial use of social science, since social scientists as a group have usually been associated with liberal reforms, governmental intervention, and social engineering. As one critic put it, "The propriety of courts functioning like social reform agencies and the greater prospects for judges deferring to social science when justifying their decisions strikes political conservatives as unconscionable and antithetical to representative government" (O'Brien, 14).

Judges have been known to cite studies the way they cite cases, treating scientific conclusions as highly malleable holdings that can be assimilated into a normative scheme. Courts often do use empirical findings the way a drunk uses a lamppost—for support rather than illumi-

872

nation. The findings in such instances serve to ornament decisions reached on other grounds. If the final business of law is normative preference rather than scientific truth, then courts should explicate the normative bases of their conclusions rather than justify them in instrumentalist terms.

However, instrumentalist justifications need not necessarily be ad hoc, any more than normative justifications are by definition principled. Decisions can be conditioned, at least in part, on well-established facts, and done so in a consistent and coherent fashion. Indeed, if social research influenced judicial thinking—for example, by helping to diagnose the nature of the social problem, to anticipate the possible consequences of alternative choices, or to inform on the prospects of public compliance—it would be unjustifiable to pretend that such considerations never entered into the decision-making. The "ought" cannot be derived from the "is," but accurate knowledge of social reality can discipline or condition thinking so as to make possible the normative leap. The explication of these factual predicates is not incompatible with normative analysis, unless an unbridgeable gap is posited between facts and values.

There is both a chasm and a bridge between the realms of fact and value. Without the chasm, there would be no place for purposive analysis; normative issues would surrender to empirical inquiry. Without the bridge, social research would have nothing to contribute to the moral choices that preoccupy the law. The role of empirical inquiry in judicial decision-making is not an either-or matter. Both instrumentalist and value judgments are implicated because the empirical and the normative are interwoven.

Thus, the sanction of scientific authority in *Brown* helped to justify the avoidance of the *Plessy* doctrine, which was itself rationalized in terms of the psychological knowledge of its time. The consensus among the social scientists, documented in footnote 11, served the political purpose of reinforcing the image of broadly based agreement on the wrongfulness of segregation. A lesson of *Brown* is that judges are more likely to use social research for rationalization when the evidence is agreed upon by the experts, it clearly supports or refutes the legal matter at issue, and it implies a solution that is within the court's control. Absent these attributes, as in the northern school desegregation cases, judges avoid any overt justification based upon social research and rely instead on flexible legal fictions such as de jure violations.

CONCLUSION

A theme that emerges from the long history of school desegregation from *Brown* to the present is that things are no longer as simple as they appeared back in 1954. With respect to both legal policy and the associated empirical research, there is now more dissension than consensus, more complexity than simplicity, more indeterminacy than certainty. The original promise of *Brown* has been redefined and somewhat diminished over the years. Racial justice in schooling has taken on different meanings at different times, in different localities, and in the course of different implementation policies.

So long as social science is expected to provide guidance in policy decisions—that is, to serve a deterministic role in the judicial process—there is bound to be disillusionment and the desire to cast (as some judges had done) a pox on both liberal and revisionist houses of social science. On the other hand, if social science is seen as playing mainly an oblique role in policy matters, educating the courts and society at large about the factual dimensions of the issue at stake, its uses and limits in judicial decision-making begin to be appreciated. It can expose the varied facets of social problems and stimulate further reflection on the adequacy of society's preconceptions. It might prompt a different view of the issue and expand the range of alternative solutions. In short, it can inform and make more responsible the exercise of judicial judgment, even though it should not and cannot displace the act of judging itself.

CASES

Bradley v. Milliken, 338 F. Supp. 582 (1971)
Brown v. Board of Education of Topeka, 347 U.S. 483 (1954) [Brown I]; 349 U.S. 294 (1955) [Brown II]
Columbus Board of Education v. Penick, 443 U.S. 449 (1979)
Kelley v. Metropolitan County Board of Education, 492 F. Supp. 167 (1980)
Keyes v. School District No. 1, 413 U.S. 189 (1973)

Maxwell v. Bishop, 398 F.2d 138 (8th Cir. 1968)
Milliken v. Bradley, 418 U.S. 717 (1974) [Milliken I]; 433 U.S. 267 (1977) [Milliken II]
Morgan v. Kerrigan, 530 F.2d 410 (1976)
Muller v. Oregon, 208 U.S. 412 (1908)
Parent Association v. Ambach, 738 F.2d 574 (2d Cir. 1984)
Plessy v. Ferguson, 163 U.S. 537 (1896)
Stell v. Savannah-Chatham County Board of Education, 220 F. Supp. 667 (1963); 333 F.2d 55 (5th Cir. 1964)
Tasby v. Wright, 520 F. Supp. 683 (1981)
United States v. Leon, 104 S. Ct. 3405 (1984)

BIBLIOGRAPHY

Noreen L. Channels, *Social Science Methods in the Legal Process* (1985), a primer on how to conduct and evaluate social research in legal settings, is organized according to the steps in the research process, from the formulation of questions to the analysis of results. Kenneth Clark, "Social Science, Constitutional Rights, and the Courts," in R. Rist and R. Anson, eds., *Education, Social Science, and the Judicial Process* (1977), presents the traditional, liberal social science critique of the neoconservative arguments against desegregation by compulsory busing; the volume also contains other essays on the role of social science in school desegregation litigation. James Coleman et al., *Equality of Educational Opportunity* (1966), the first massive, nationwide survey of the social and educational effects of voluntary school desegregation, provided the scientific justification for integration. Lawrence Friedman, *The Legal System: A Social Science Perspective* (1975), examines legal institutions and procedures in behavioral terms, such as legal acts, legal impact, and legal effectiveness. Lawrence Friedman and Stewart Macauley, *Law and the Behavioral Sciences* (1977), contains excerpts of dozens of articles and editorial commentary that explore the interrelationships between law and society.

Henry Hart and John McNaughton, "Evidence and Inference in the Law," in Daniel Lerner, ed., *Evidence and Inference* (1959), is a graceful analysis of the nature of legal reasoning and a comparison of it with statistical and scientific modes of reasoning. Irwin A. Horowitz and Thomas E. Willging, *The Psychology of Law: Integrations and Applications* (1983), an undergraduate textbook that provides an overview of psycholegal research, emphasizes the psychology of the jury, the functions of psychologists in court, the applications of psychology to legal negotiations and interviewing, and the institutional roles of psychologists and lawyers. David L. Kirp, *Just Schools: The Idea of Racial Equality in American Education* (1982), develops an analysis of how constitutional principles, consensus politics, and social science are intertwined in the implementation of school desegregation in five Bay Area communities. Richard Kluger, *Simple Justice* (1976), a compelling narrative of the *Brown* case told as a morality tale, details the involvement of social scientists at the trial on pages 315–366, 415–422, 480–507, 555–557.

Richard Lempert and Joseph Sanders, *An Invitation to Law and Social Science* (1986), an undergraduate textbook that introduces students to "law and society" research, attempts to synthesize existing theory and research in the field in ways that should be useful to specialists. Wallace D. Loh, *Social Research in the Judicial Process: Cases, Readings, and Text* (1984), a systematic introduction to the uses and limits of social science in areas of legal policy (such as school desegregation, capital punishment, and police procedures) and of courtroom processes (such as jury selection and reliability of witnesses), provides a comprehensive bibliography on social science in school desegregation and examines the history and the current state of social science in legal education and legal scholarship. John Monahan and Laurens Walker, *Social Science in Law: Cases and Materials* (1985), covers some of the same topics as Loh but highlights the uses of clinical psychology in areas of law that relate to mental health. David O'Brien, "The Seduction of the Judiciary: Social Science and the Courts," in *Judicature*, 64 (1980), argues against judicial reliance on social science evidence in justifying constitutional decisions, on the grounds that such instrumentalist rationales tend in the long run to undermine principled decision-making.

Paul Rosen, *The Supreme Court and Social Science* (1972), a history of the Supreme Court's use of social science in the areas of equal protection, due process, and the First Amendment, provides an extensive treatment of the social science in *Brown*. J. Harvie Wilkinson III, *From Brown to Bakke: The Supreme Court and School Desegregation* (1984), chronicles post-*Brown* developments leading to the decision on affirmative action. Eleanor Wolf, *Trial and Error: The Detroit School Segregation Case* (1981), critically reviews—from a neoconservative perspective—the extensive social science testimony presented in *Milliken* in support of interdistrict desegregation. Hans Zeisel, "Race Bias in the Administration of the Death Penalty: The Florida Experience," in *Harvard Law Review*, 95 (1981), discusses the statistical evidence showing that the death penalty is disproportionately imposed on black convicts.

[*See also* LEGAL REASONING *and* RACIAL DISCRIMINATION AND EQUAL OPPORTUNITY.]

LEGAL REASONING

Lief H. Carter

WHEN rules of law provide no single dispositive solution to a legal dispute, judges choose a solution. The term *legal reasoning* refers to the theory and practice by which judges justify their choices. To understand legal reasoning one must appreciate that judges do choose what the law means. Legal reasoning is the process by which judges persuade us that these discretionary choices are impartial.

IMPARTIALITY AND LEGAL REASONING

All complex human systems contain institutions and routines for resolving conflicts between people. In most organized sports, umpires and referees resolve the conflicts and disagreements that inevitably arise in the play of the game. In commercial life, employment contracts, often negotiated through a union representing employees, establish grievance procedures for settling disputes about conditions of employment. In government and public affairs, legal institutions have the responsibility for preventing and resolving conflicts.

All institutions that solve conflicts rely in varying degrees on rules. In simple systems and relationships, a few clear rules (such as the order of winning hands in a poker game) prevent or resolve conflicts almost automatically. However, in complex, institutionalized conflict control, the rules cannot anticipate and govern unambiguously in advance the many different conflict situations that occur. Thus, people—judges—must be prepared to exercise "judgment" in order to resolve conflicts. These people—umpires, arbitrators, judges, and so forth—must act impartially if they wish to keep conflict within acceptable bounds. Impartiality ensures that losers in disputes trust the fairness of the decision, at least in the minimal sense that they do not rebel against the regime the judge represents. Martin Shapiro concludes that when the decider appears simply to take on the winner's side against the loser, the dispute-settling mechanism becomes "politicized." Individual cases become "causes" in escalating political conflicts that can destroy the structure of institutions and polities. The failure of trust in conflict-resolving mechanisms has with some frequency contributed to the collapse of political regimes not only in developing nations but also in the United States during the Civil War era.

Impartial decisions must appear to be consistent with rules, procedures, and values that the institution and therefore the conflicting parties within it have previously accepted as applicable to the dispute. In Herman Melville's great story *Billy Budd,* the innocent hero, Billy, so trusts the rightness of the rules and the impartiality of his ship's captain that he calmly accepts his own hanging for striking and killing a ship's officer, Claggart. The ship's company, which reveres Billy, does the same. That Claggart was an evil bully, that he provoked Billy's blow, that the unforeseeable way he fell after receiving the blow contributed to his death, that the sentence of hanging could have been mitigated—none of these facts destroys Billy's faith in the captain's impartiality. Hence, impartiality depends upon the capacity of the judge and the formal trappings of the judgmental process to persuade the audience that the decisions are made not on the basis of the judge's own will but in terms of broader rules, customs, and values that the community shares. Short of the brutal use of force and coercion, only this maintenance of trust can keep social conflicts within manageable bounds.

The legal systems of the American nation, the

fifty states, and thousands of local governmental units are all highly developed. That is, these systems all purport to govern with reference to a complex network of rules applied by people with political authority to do so—hence, the popular slogan "We live under the rule of law, not under the rule of men." Legislatures, executive and administrative agencies, and courts all make, and purport to follow, the literally millions of rules that fill law libraries. The impartiality of judges who decide cases depends on their honoring these rules in application.

The vast majority of potential human conflicts do not, however, become publicly visible lawsuits. Clear and authoritative legal rules permit citizens and their lawyers to anticipate and resolve most problems privately and usually in their early stages. Lawsuits cost money, and when a rule speaks unambiguously to a case, the involved parties have little incentive to pay a judge to tell them what they already know. Thus, the very success of governance through rules—rules concerning estates, insurance, business and financial dealings, liability for negligently hurting others, and so on—screens cases from the courts and prevents students of the judicial process from seeing the power of "the rule of law" firsthand.

In the main, two kinds of disputes do get to court. The first is a factual dispute between parties. A plaintiff injured in an automobile accident insists that the defendant hit him after running a red light. The defendant insists the light was green or perhaps that he ran a red light while rushing a choking child to the hospital. Such factual disputes often raise no conflict about the interpretation of legal rules, and no judicial justification is required. The rules of trial procedure and evidence are very detailed and specific so as to minimize the chances for judicial error. The other kind of dispute involves the meaning of the legal rules themselves. Granting, for the sake of argument, that a certain set of facts is true, the plaintiffs and defendants make contradictory legal arguments, each arguing that a rule or legal principle related to the presumed facts dictates that his or her side should win.

And so a fascinating paradox in legal reasoning emerges: if political stability depends in part on judicial impartiality, but if impartiality depends on decisions consistent with rules, how can judges decide impartially if the rules in fact give no answer or give conflicting and inconsistent answers? If rules conflict or are worded ambiguously, then the judge must choose among them. Precisely because the tension is so great between the ideal of impartiality, on the one hand, and the reality of legal indeterminacy, on the other, judges (particularly appellate judges) provide published reasons, or "opinions," for their choices. *Legal reasoning,* therefore, refers to the justifications of choices that judges express in these opinions. Ultimately, judicial impartiality and the efficacy of the judicial system itself depend on the persuasiveness of legal reasoning.

Legal reasoning, in theory and practice, does not deal directly with the actual psychological process by which judges choose legal solutions. The neurobiology of human decision-making is still in many ways mysterious to experts in psychology, and how judges decide remains at bottom just as mysterious. In an oft-quoted passage from 1929, Judge Joseph Hutcheson wrote, "The judge really decides by feeling and not by judgment, by hunching and not by ratiocination, such ratiocination appearing only in the opinion" (Golding, 15). Hutcheson used the metaphor of an "intuitive flash" of electric current that makes the connection between a legal question and a judicial decision.

Behavioral studies of the American legal system have established through empirical research that judicial backgrounds, values, role models, and political aspirations do influence judges' legal choices, but this descriptive research hardly specifies how individuals actually make particular choices. The term *legal reasoning* thus will here be used for the observable characteristics of the reasons judges give for their choices. Legal reasoning thus provides an ideal model of how judges ought to decide, but it does not describe how judges actually decide.

Jerome Frank went so far as nearly to divorce the psychological process of choice from its justification, as if a judge who chose a solution by flipping a coin would commit no sin as long as he or she could provide an adequate justification for the choice after the fact. More recently, however, Richard Wasserstrom has pointed out that the forms of justifications influence the way people search for their decisions. Because experimental reproducibility is the test of justification in science, scientists search for truth by doing experiments; they do not flip coins. Discussions of legal reasoning can directly describe and analyze only published judicial justifications. These discussions may in turn affect the way judges reach their hunches through processes we do not yet understand.

Legal reasoning operates at both analytical and theoretical levels. It analyzes the logical patterns that judges seem frequently to use when they publish reasons for their decisions. It also differentiates between more and less desirable techniques of reasoning that judges ought theoretically to follow. The theoretical and necessarily ethical level at which legal reasoning operates is part of the field of political philosophy. It is considerably more controversial than the empirical workings of this kind of reasoning.

AMBIGUITY IN LAW

Legal reasoning occurs whenever rules of law, in their practical operation, fail to provide judges and lawyers with obvious and automatic solutions to factual disputes. Ronald Dworkin has argued that courts must act as if there were one correct solution to each legal dispute and that in a world of cost-free, completely available information, such solutions presumably exist. In practice, however, many forces work against the judge who tries to deduce from principles, rules, and facts the correct solution in each case. Appellate courts, as opposed to trial courts, hear and review questions of law—they do not retry the facts of cases—and litigants on both sides invest their money in the costs of an appeal because they believe they have a chance to win. In appellate courts the principles and rules of law are arguably ambiguous at the outset. It is certainly true that to reach legal closure in a case, a judge must appeal to something, but the something often turns out to be a principle of the judge's own making. Sometimes the judge does no more than give hints in his or her opinion as to the nature of that principle.

In the American system legal rules originate in all branches of national, state, and local governments. Legislatures make statutes; city councils and county commissions make ordinances; and executive agencies and independent regulatory agencies make rules to further the policies they are created to execute. Moreover, the American practice of following precedent, the most prominent characteristic of modern common-law systems, gives judicial decisions themselves the force of law in future cases that seem factually to resemble earlier cases.

Each of these kinds of law have characteristics that engender legal uncertainty. Statutes and similar rules tend by their nature to create ambiguous applications. A statute is a political command that attempts to provide a solution to a class of problems, not a unique conflict. In defining this class, questions inevitably arise about the location of its boundaries. Thus, in one famous case, *McBoyle* v. *United States* (1931), Congress had made it criminally punishable to transport knowingly a stolen motor vehicle across state lines. The statute, the National Motor Vehicle Theft Act, defined *motor vehicle* to "include an automobile, automobile truck, automobile wagon, motor cycle, or any other self-propelled vehicle not designed for running on rails." The defendant had knowingly transported a stolen airplane across state lines. He argued in the Supreme Court that because all the vehicles specifically mentioned in the statute ran on the ground, it was not fair to punish him for transporting an airplane, something the statute might not cover. Justice Oliver Wendell Holmes agreed with him: "Although it is not likely that a criminal will carefully consider the text of the law before he murders or steals, it is reasonable that a fair warning should be given to the world in language that the common world will understand, of what the law intends to do if a certain line is passed." Had McBoyle knowingly transported a stolen automobile, the rule would have covered him unambiguously, but he argued successfully that it did not cover airplanes.

Another possibility is a hypothetical case of a Federal Bureau of Investigation (FBI) agent who recovers a stolen automobile and drives it back to its owner across a state line. He has fallen within the letter of the law, but he does not represent the class of problems the statute tries to resolve. Must the law apply to him anyway?

Statutes may also speak in language that raises doubts about the application of the words in any context. Words are inherently crude and inexact communicative tools. Statutes may speak so uncertainly that judges cannot distinguish the statutory core from its periphery. Thus the 1970 Occupational Safety and Health Act defines an "occupational safety and health standard" as a standard that is "reasonably necessary or appropriate to provide safe or healthful employment." It directs the setting of standards for toxic materials and substances that "most adequately assures, to the extent feasible, on the basis of the best available evidence, that no employee will suffer material impairment of health or functional capacity." But what do phrases such as "reasonably necessary," "extent feasible," and "material impairment of health or functional capacity" mean? The Supreme Court justices could not agree on the statute's meaning in cases involving benzene, in *Industrial Union Department, AFL-CIO* v. *American Petroleum Institute* (1980) and *American Textile Manufacturers Institute* v. *Donovan* (1981).

Constitutional rules, particularly in the Constitution of the United States, address fundamental questions about the nature of the polity at a more general and abstract level than do statutes. Therefore, constitutional rules are even more open-ended and uncertain in their application than are statutory rules. It is inevitable that the Supreme Court, not the Constitution, shapes constitutional meaning in practice. Thus, Charles Evans Hughes remarked, "We are under a Constitution—but the Constitution is what the Judges say it is."

The primary reason judges face the inevitability of choice concerns the nature of judicial precedent. For every choice an appellate judge makes, there exist prior judicial decisions (precedents) that arguably govern the result. This happens both in case-law situations (tort and contract law, for example) and when judges choose between competing applications of constitutional, statutory, and administrative rules.

To reason from a precedent is to reason by example. The judge must decide whether the case or issue put before him or her factually resembles a prior case that a party has argued resolves the current dispute. Unfortunately, the legal system provides no clear formula telling judges how to decide whether a prior case is factually similar enough to the current case to serve as precedent (Levi). A judge faced with a decision in the case of a hypothetical defendant charged under the National Motor Vehicle Theft Act with the transportation of a motor boat across state lines might find the airplane precedent determinative. If so, the judge would hold the accused not punishable under the terms of

the statute by the authority of *McBoyle.* But nothing in the law obligates this judge to treat *McBoyle* that way. He or she is free to articulate a factual difference. If the stolen boat was either driven across a lake or river or transported on a truck across state lines, the judge could freely argue that *McBoyle* did not cover this defendant because the act of transport did not take place in the air.

Reasoning from precedents is the primary source of legal indeterminacy. This form of reasoning by example makes judicial choices inevitable. It is therefore particularly necessary for judges to justify their choices persuasively in order to maintain judicial impartiality.

THE LOGICAL STRUCTURE OF JUDICIAL JUSTIFICATIONS

Judges do not make choices by "doing" statutory, common-law, or constitutional reasoning. These phrases merely describe the outer contours of legal reasoning; they denote categories of reasoning problems, not the logical structure of the justifications themselves.

Martin Golding provides a useful dissection of the varying forms of the logic of judicial justification. He reviews the common logical forms that most arguments take. These include both determinate and indeterminate forms. The standard deductive syllogism ("If all A are B and all B are C, then all A are C") is a determinate argument. An argument by inferential observation ("All observed cases of A are B; therefore, the next observed case of A will be B") is not determinate.

Four important observations stand out in Golding's analysis. First, it is possible to find judicial opinions that appear to take the form of any and all conceivable logical forms, including fallacious ones. Second, most judicial opinions are indeterminate. They do not meet the criteria of what logicians call a "sound deductive argument," which is one in which all the premises are true; the premises are arranged in valid form (not, for example, "If all Americans are humans and all French are humans, then all Americans are French"); and no other premises need be asserted to establish the truth of the conclusion. Reasoning by example is inferential and indeterminate ("The new case is more like precedent 1 than precedent 2; therefore, precedent 1 governs"). In cases where judges do not resort to precedent, it is difficult, if not impossible, for them to prove either the truth or the exhaustiveness of an opinion's stated premises.

Third, judicial opinions frequently fail to state and support a premise on which the logical structure of the argument depends. (A logical statement that leaves unstated or implicit a premise on which the conclusion depends is an "enthymeme.") Although it is often possible to analyze an opinion in such a way that the analyst supplies a plausible implicit premise, judges by no means necessarily make plain the logic of their opinions.

Finally, the most common single form of judicial argument does not meet standards of determinate logic. Judges tend to engage in an assertive and implicitly ethical form of logic known as "practical reasoning."

Judges rarely receive formal training in logic, and the legal community (including the bar and law-school associations) has not seriously demanded of judges that their decisions meet the criteria of determinate logic. The flawed syllogisms and reductiones ad absurdum should not surprise anyone, nor do they necessarily constitute failures in impartiality. The elements of practical reasoning suggest how legal reasoning may be impartial at the same time that it employs a technically illogical structure.

Consider first the well-known 1954 desegregation case, *Brown* v. *Board of Education.* Its legal question was, Does the equal protection clause of the Fourteenth Amendment ban racial segregation of public school children? The Court's answer runs, in effect, as follows: Racial equality is a desirable social goal and a protected individual right as well. Racially segregated schools impede progress toward racial equality. Therefore, the law ought to bar public racial segregation in schools. Note that this argument does not prove deterministically that the equal protection clause, either by its words or by prior precedents applying it, prohibits racial segregation. Instead, the Court argued that the law ought to do so.

This is the essence of practical reasoning. It is, as Golding points out, value-laden and action-oriented. Practical reasoning asserts that the law ought to say something in order to achieve in action a desired state. Often the court contents itself with asserting the desirability of the asserted state, not proving it by either deductive or inferential means. Thus, the legal reasoning that the mix of ambiguity in law and the political demand for impartiality makes mandatory becomes on close inspection an operation in which judges articulate their beliefs about the way society works and how it ought to work.

The observable structure of judicial justifications thus takes many forms. These justifications tend, however, to have important normative assertions at their cores. The remainder of this essay therefore describes the normative issues, often controversial ones, that commonly arise in judicial justifications.

THE DOCTRINE OF STARE DECISIS

Lay people—and, for that matter, more than a few lawyers and judges—have more misunderstandings about the nature and role of precedents than about any other aspect of legal reasoning. As many people understand it, when primary rules do not on their own terms resolve a specific conflict, the judge should find a previous application of the rule in a case whose facts most resemble the facts of the current case and then decide the current case in the same way. This is the conventional but incomplete doctrine of stare decisis.

The perception of factual similarity or difference between the conflict in court and any prior case depends, as we have seen, on the judge's perception of which facts in the cases are pertinent. In making comparisons, the judge may already have decided, at least roughly, how the case should come out. It may serve the cause of impartiality for a judge to assert that his or her decision is consistent with at least one prior decision, but this does not mean that the new decision proceeds from the past case or that the past case is, when compared to other cases that the opinion may ignore, a more persuasive or dispositive precedent. Hence, the doctrine of stare decisis cannot merely involve "following" precedent.

Stare decisis is indeed a useful legal reasoning tool, but its role is very different from the conventional perception of it. Specifically, *after* a judge concludes from reasoning by example that the holding of a previous case does determine the result, the judge should then ask whether this holding must be followed. He will of course want to follow the precedent if doing so would achieve the "right" result. Indeed, he may well choose one factual similarity as opposed to others precisely because that choice produces the outcome he desires.

Nevertheless, cases arise where a well-developed line of precedents states a rule that is so clear and well known that judges cannot ignore it, *and* the judge feels that the original rule, as a matter of practical reasoning, produces the "wrong" result—that is, it serves no useful public purpose or protects no valid individual rights. To illustrate, the Supreme Court held in 1922 and again in 1953 that the business of professional baseball did not need to comply with the antitrust laws, laws prohibiting unfair and monopolistic competition in commerce. Everyone in the baseball business knew these precedents, and in 1972 the Court reiterated the position for a third time *(Flood v. Kuhn)*. Yet, many doubts existed about the wisdom of the precedents. In the interim, the Court had held that all other professional sports did need to comply with the antitrust laws, and the commercial character of baseball had expanded tremendously.

Thus, the doctrine of stare decisis really provides reasons for judges to follow precedents that state "bad law," precedents whose practical reasoning the judge, unburdened by the weight of precedents, would question or reject. There are two kinds of circumstances under which judges should do so. First, whenever a lower-court judge establishes that an authoritative precedent from a higher court in the same jurisdiction disposes unambiguously of the case in court, he is in nearly all circumstances normatively obligated to follow it. This strong norm of "vertical stare decisis" follows from the hierarchic nature of judicial systems. But the same judge is not similarly obligated to follow a precedent from a court in another jurisdiction or from a court on the same level in the same jurisdiction.

Second, when (as in the baseball cases) a state or federal supreme court is tempted to overturn an outmoded precedent of its own making, one or more of the following five social norms, each itself a statement of practical reasoning, may justify "horizontal stare decisis." The first is the preservation of the stability of social institutions. The second is the protection of specific reliance on law; individuals actually do make plans (business arrangements, tax investment decisions, wills, deeds to property, and so forth) on the

basis of announced law. The third is the promotion of efficient judicial administration; the judicial work load would become overwhelming if judges had to decide each and every legal issue anew. Fourth is the protection of equality, and fifth is the promotion of the image of justice. Impartiality depends on giving the appearance of treating people equally and justly by deciding on general, not individual, grounds. Following precedent helps maintain the appearance of impartiality.

It is often said, as the Supreme Court did in the baseball cases, that when these norms apply, legal changes should come from the legislature because the legislature can act without upsetting plans made in honest reliance on past law. However, there is a growing consensus that in many cases the five reasons just given for following outmoded precedents apply only weakly, or not at all. In such cases, courts should embrace opportunities for change. Viewed in the light of these five principles, the baseball cases should probably have come out the other way (Carter, 1984).

STATUTORY INTERPRETATION IN THE FIRST INSTANCE

A statute or local ordinance is an attempt by an elected lawmaking body to remedy some perceived evil. Such rules solve problems by a variety of means. Some rules command people to behave in a particular way in certain circumstances; for instance, most Americans who earn over a certain number of taxable dollars in a year must file a federal tax return. Other rules prohibit certain behaviors; as an example, certain statutes prohibit the willful taking of another's life in the absence of a legally recognized defense. Some statutes command the expenditure of public funds for certain programs in the hope that these programs will better the human condition.

Although statutory commands vary widely, important political norms underlie their application. In a democracy it is presumed that elected lawmaking bodies are the primary source of law. Absent conflicts with constitutional commands, statutory rules ought to determine how courts should apply them to concrete situations.

Where a statute speaks clearly to a situation, conflicts about statutory meaning do not arise.

When a statute fails in its own terms to resolve a problem, because of the generality of its language, because it conflicts with other statutory commands, or because of any of the causes of legal uncertainty noted above, then judges must choose what the statute means. If precedents exist, the judge may conclude that they are wise in themselves or that the doctrine of stare decisis requires that precedents be followed, despite doubts about their wisdom. If, however, the judge finds no dispositive precedents or concludes that the existing precedents need not be followed, then the statute itself must be examined. This process is called statutory interpretation in the first instance. To interpret a statute in a manner that is consistent with the democratic norm, the judge must ask and answer these questions: What is the social evil the statute (or statutes) bearing on this case seeks to remedy? What remedy has the statute commanded? Is the case before me an instance of the problem the statute seeks to remedy?

Judges in recent English and American practice have developed an astonishing array of theories about statutory interpretation. Many of them seek to evade the issues just posed. Judges are uncomfortable with these questions because they believe that judges have no lawmaking authority in a democracy. Judges often believe that once a legislature has spoken, they ought to have no choice in the matter. The solution to the legal problem must somehow exist in the statute itself and in the legislative action that brought the statute into being. The judge must discover that solution, not choose it; to choose would substitute the decisions of less democratically responsive judges for those made by more democratically responsive elected officials.

One technique for evading the obligations of legal reasoning in the application of ambiguous statutes is to apply statutory language literally whenever possible. A literalist judge would thus hold the hypothetical FBI officer liable under the National Motor Vehicle Theft Act for returning the stolen car to its owner by driving it across a state line. Such a judge might agree that the result is absurd and that to so apply the act does not serve any discernible public purpose. This judge would also argue, however, that a statute is a statute and that once courts assume the power to say what statutory words do not say, undemocratic courts can say anything they like. The practical reasoning implicit in this argument

would hold that legislatures ought to make clear laws and that courts should reach absurd decisions so as to teach legislatures to make clear laws.

Fortunately, American judges have tended not to follow the literal approach as often as English judges have. Unfortunately, American judges have more frequently employed a second approach, called the plain-meaning rule, which is not much better. This rule holds that when the words of a statute do not produce an absurd result in application and when one reading of the words seems more direct and less tortured than others, then statutory commands must be followed according to that reading.

The plain-meaning rule is an unworkable concept in both theory and practice. In theory it cannot work because words have no plain meaning except in context. A basketball player who says to a teammate during time-out, "I can get free underneath. When I do, feed me the ball," is not asking his teammate to place a spherical rubber snack in his mouth during play. The judge who invokes the plain-meaning rule without looking at the problem-solving context of the statute makes no better than a stab in the dark. Judicial invocations of the plain-meaning rule have proved neither coherent nor consistent.

A third method for pretending that ambiguous statutory language is certain allows a judge to invoke one or more "canons" of statutory interpretation. The judge can say that the legislature intended its language to be read with the canons in mind. These rules for interpreting rules, like the plain-meaning rule, seem sensible from a safe distance. For example, the canon of ejusdem generis holds that where a statute contains both general and specific language (for instance, "vehicle" and "automobile" in *McBoyle*), the general language covers only those things which possess the characteristics that all the specifically mentioned things have in common.

The list of canons is, however, a lengthy one. Karl Llewellyn listed fifty-six of them in twenty-eight pairs and showed how, in a given case, for each pair the two canons yielded opposite results. Like the plain-meaning rule, canons disguise judicial choices but do not eliminate the fact that judges make them.

The fourth and most common method by which judges pretend that uncertain statutes are certain is to attempt to discover how the legislature intended the courts to apply the statute in practice. Judges explore statements made in legislative debate, the reports of committees that drafted the legislation, statements in the record of the sponsors of the bill, and so forth.

The concept of legislative intent suffers from severe logical and practical defects. First, the question before the court always concerns a unique case. In all likelihood, the legislature never intended anything regarding the unique case because the facts of the unique case never crossed any legislator's mind. The late-nineteenth-century authors of the Sherman Antitrust Act almost surely did not anticipate the growth of the sport of baseball into a major commercial enterprise in the twentieth century. To hold that baseball is not covered because Congress did not intend to cover it belies the very generality of statutory problem-solving commands.

Second, only a duly constituted majority of a legislative body possesses the legal power to enact a law, and only the bill duly passed and enacted has the force of law. One sponsor or one committee constitutes a legislative minority that lacks any lawmaking power of its own. To hold that such a sponsor's or committee's intent governs is to admit lawmaking by minority. Put another way, if intent counts, it is the intent of the legislative majority. But the only measure or poll of this majority's intent is its vote to convert the words of a bill into law. This merely returns a judge back to the starting point: the words in the context of the unique case are ambiguous.

Third and finally, legislatures are political and practical places. Ambiguity in statutes often reflects political compromises necessary to get a bill passed. In effect, the legislative process creates bounded ambiguities and then transfers the responsibility of clarifying what the words really mean to the courts.

The core of the difficulty in much modern statutory interpretation arises from the assumption that legislatures, not courts, "make" statutes. Judges are tempted to grasp any concept that reaffirms at least the appearance that judges honor this democratic norm. This practice, however, cannot logically coexist with a central feature of the American legal system: that each appellate case represents a potential precedent for future similar cases. If, in the literal reading of statutory words, the mechanistic application of a canon, or the superficial assertion of legislative

intent, an appellate court produces a result that does not promote the social goals of the statute, then such a court, probably without appreciating the fact, creates case law for the future that undercuts the "will of the people" expressed in the statute. Ironically, the techniques for giving legislative acts the appearance of clarity and primacy in reality have precisely the opposite effect. They undermine legislative primacy in favor of judicial face-saving. Because common-law political systems traditionally accept judicial lawmaking, the effect is even more ironic. A legislature unhappy with a judicial application of its statute remains politically free to rewrite or amend the legislation.

When statutory language does not resolve a problem, judges must interpret not the statute but the context in which the statute arose. Interpretation is a practice that Clifford Geertz calls "thick description." To interpret a statute in the first instance, judges must explore the social history surrounding the passage of an act. In 1890 the monopolization of businesses was perceived to cause higher prices and lower wages than would competitive business conditions. When the National Motor Vehicle Theft Act was passed, it had become clear that the jurisdictional boundaries of states prevented state law enforcement officials from acting swiftly against crimes carried on through movement from state to state. Federal officials, who could cross state boundaries without losing their legal authority to enforce, could therefore assist in the apprehension of those taking easily moved items across state lines.

Statutory words, canons, the statements of sponsors, committee reports, and the like may assist in the thick-textured effort to diagnose the targeted social evil, but these are rarely conclusive. Justice Holmes, in the airplane theft case, did not really inquire into the purpose of the statute. He did not ask the following questions: Are stolen airplanes easily moved from state to state, like stolen cars? If so, on what basis would the purpose of the act not cover airplanes? If airplanes fall within the act's purposes, on what basis should we excuse McBoyle? Does McBoyle have a moral claim that what he did was otherwise lawful? Similarly, if the two major baseball leagues conspire to prevent the development of competition from a third league in the twentieth century, on what basis does this conspiracy differ from the monopolization of sugar or steel in the nineteenth century? These are precisely the questions judges frequently evade despite the fact that the common-law political system presumes that the courts will resolve them.

Two further points about judicial articulation of statutory purposes deserve mention. First, not even exhaustive interpretive efforts, efforts far greater than those which judges have time in their daily schedules to undertake, reveal one, and only one, correct decision in a given case. Judges may honestly disagree about the nature of statutory purposes. Thus, Justice Holmes might have argued in *McBoyle* that the statutory exclusion of trains must have some purposive significance. Presumably the significance lies in the easy traceability of stolen trains by following their tracks. He might then have cited a general norm favoring localism in law enforcement and pointed out that one can easily trace airplanes to airports. If so, he would have reached the same result (excusing McBoyle), but he would have done so by reasoning about statutory purpose.

Second, the misunderstandings about the legislative process just described have led some scholars, including Edward Levi, to advocate a more rigid adherence to stare decisis in statutory interpretation. Levi argues that if courts have freedom to reinterpret legislation, legislatures will be relieved of the pressure to update and improve their statutes. Legislatures and courts must cooperate in the lawmaking effort, and a clear-cut division of labor makes that cooperation possible.

Indeed, there are instances in which legislators heave a sigh of relief that courts have taken a delicate political problem off their hands. But the assumption that most interpretive problems raise highly charged public issues that deserve legislative rather than judicial responses is inaccurate. Most statutory interpretations lie either at the margins of a policy problem, where busy legislatures concerned with general policymaking will not really care which way courts go, or the issue will be so intertwined with the never-ending pulling and tugging of lobbyists, bureaucratic agencies and legislators, and their committees that it will receive occasional reexamination, regardless of judicial decisions in specific cases.

Of course, there are exceptions, but the better rule, when a judge is satisfied that the five reasons for horizontal stare decisis listed above do not apply, is to ignore precedent and treat the problem as a new one; Guido Calabresi has elaborated this position.

NORMATIVE PROBLEMS IN COMMON-LAW REASONING

In 1881, in a book entitled *The Common Law*, Oliver Wendell Holmes wrote:

> The life of the law has not been logic: it has been experience. The felt necessities of the time, the prevalent moral and politcal theories, intuitions of public policy, avowed or unconscious, even the prejudices which judges share with their fellow-men, have had a good deal more to do than the syllogism in determining the rules by which men should be governed.
>
> (p. 1)

Holmes was reporting his understanding of centuries of common-law history. Throughout its development from the Battle of Hastings on, common-law principles and the methods by which judges reach them mirror the thought patterns of their times. Earlier common-law thinkers, whose work culminated in the treatises of Blackstone, attempted to codify principles of common law into "correct" legal principles. Pervasive religious beliefs made the absence of "correct principles" unthinkable. But that era has given way, as Holmes predicted, to a more rational and pragmatic, hence open-ended and indeterminate, approach to law.

In the twentieth century, common law has become, according to Karl Llewellyn, not a reservoir of "right rules for human conduct" but a process that permits a healthy compromise between legal predictability and legal change. Ambiguities in law seem not merely inevitable but desirable. Ambiguities encourage those with opposing interests to go to court with arguments about what the law ought to say. Ambiguity, in other words, provides the necessary incentive for people to bring new ideas and factual information to court. Contestants invest in the presentation of a believable case because they have a chance to win. The normative principles that guide judicial thinking may thus change with the times.

One dramatic illustration of a change in legal

doctrine that appears to mirror broader social and political changes is the shift toward protecting personal liberty and physical safety in contests pitting the claims of business interests against those of individuals. The common-law tendency to "let the buyer beware" had in the nineteenth century produced a variety of holdings that protected the interests of businesspeople in the youthful days of corporate capitalism. A person injured by a product purchased from a retailer but made negligently by the manufacturer had, with the exception of things the courts found "inherently dangerous," no cause of action against the manufacturer because his contract was with the retailer. But the retailer was rarely a negligent party, so the retailer was liable only to the extent he guaranteed the product.

Courts today, however, are much more likely to protect the consumer in such instances. Owners of shopping centers have been held liable for damages to the nighttime victims of muggers and purse snatchers, on the theory that the shopping center parking lots were not so well illuminated as to prevent the crime. It is possible to associate these changes in law with changes in democratic ideology, with the growing realization that losses of health and property can be spread across society through insurance coverage, and with increasing technological and economic complexity, which necessitates increased reliance on the care exercised by those with whom the public has no direct contact.

These modern common-law dynamics—incremental legal changes in relation to changing social conditions and ideologies—apply in theory to all judicial decisions, statutory and constitutional as well as judge-made common law. Because judges accept both the inevitability and propriety of judicial lawmaking in a common-law framework, judicial justifications in common-law cases often articulate with candor and clarity the ethical assertions and factual assumptions, the practical reasoning, on which the legal conclusions rest. In a particularly compelling recent example, *Soldano* v. *O'Daniels* (1983), an intermediate appellate court in California held, contrary to more than a century of common-law rulings, that one citizen with no relationship to a second citizen may in certain circumstances be liable in tort for failing to aid the second. In *Soldano* the court held a bar owner potentially liable to the heirs of a man who died from injuries suffered in

a fight across the street when the owner's bartender refused to allow a Good Samaritan to use the bar's telephone to call the police.

The principal debate in modern common-law reasoning involves the extent to which, in a legislative age, courts should cease extending common-law principles of tort, contract, and the like, in deference to the legislature's presumably superior lawmaking position. Judges hotly debate the issue. In *Tarasoff* v. *Regents of the University of California* (1976), California Supreme Court Justice William Clark, later prominent in the administration of President Ronald Reagan, argued in dissent that a psychiatrist has no legal duty to warn the potential victims of his patients: "The Legislature obviously is more capable than is this court to investigate, debate and weigh potential patient harm through disclosure against the risk of public harm by nondisclosure. We should defer to its judgment."

This primary question in contemporary common-law reasoning becomes, on close inspection, a variation on the themes discussed above in the section on statutory interpretation. Is a legislature in fact a superior fact-finding body? Levi wrote, "Despite much gospel to the contrary, a legislature is not a fact-finding body. There is no mechanism, as there is with a court, to require the legislature to sift facts and to make a decision about specific situations" (p. 22). The key to Levi's statement is the word *require*. Legislative committees often make thorough and complete analyses of the arguments for and against pending legislation, but they are not required to do so. The slower but more orderly and public exchange of information and debate of ideas, and particularly the custom of justification in judicial but not legislative policymaking, make courts relatively effective fact-finding bodies. (Indeed, in the *Tarasoff* case Justice Clark rather effectively refuted his claim of legislative superiority by digesting in considerable depth the professional literature analyzing the dynamics and consequences of confidentiality in the doctor-patient relationship.)

Thus, the real issue is neither one of political or constitutional deference by courts to legislatures nor one of comparative institutional capacity. Whether courts ought with some confidence to venture to initiate legal innovations, common-law or otherwise, really depends on the nature of the issues before the court. If the issues and the language that expresses them fall within areas of traditional judicial training, competence, and experience, there seems little reason for courts to abandon the common-law tradition (Horowitz; Carter, 1977).

REASONING ABOUT THE CONSTITUTION

The United States Supreme Court's constitutional rulings have throughout American history helped to shape political and social events. Of all judicial decisions, the Court's receive the widest press coverage. In the belief that judges at this most powerful and most public level must, in order to preserve political trust, be particularly impartial, both the press and scholars pay a disproportionate amount of attention to the quality of constitutional reasoning.

Despite, or perhaps because of, the Supreme Court's prominence, constitutional reasoning is highly controversial. The legal reasoning perspective adds some important insights to this debate. Chief among them is the observation that the very nature of the Constitution inevitably induces judges to justify constitutional decisions in ways that tend to differ, in theory and in practice, from legal reasoning in other areas of law.

The Constitution consists of a set of legal commands. Indeed, it claims to create "the supreme law of the land," and the legal system has come to accept it as the law that governs the government. Many of these commands—"Congress shall make no law respecting an establishment of religion, or prohibiting the free exercise thereof," for example—are general, ambiguous, and capable of colliding with each other in specific application. Indeed, the two phrases within the amendment just quoted do collide if, for instance, a public schoolteacher who wishes to exercise his religious commitment to evangelism asks all his students to pray in the classroom with him. Because the Constitution articulates the fundamental values of the nation—values that potentially apply to an unimaginably broad range of specific conflicts—constitutional generality, ambiguity, and the potential for collision among rules should not be surprising.

Since the Constitution has a statutory form— its clauses are rules made by a "constitutional" legislature—judges often attempt to interpret it by using statutory interpretation techniques. Often enough, judges pretend that they need not choose what the Constitution means at all. They claim to read the words literally or to discover the intent of the framers, for example. They pretend, as Max Lerner once put it, that constitutional decisions are delivered by "constitutional storks." When judges reason this way, they hide from their audience the reality that they have chosen, not discovered, the result. Given the paramount importance of constitutional impartiality, the temptation to so hide is understandably great. But if judges in fact choose, then, as in statutory interpretation, their method of justifying their choices should reflect that reality.

Because practical reasoning involves, implicitly or explicitly, an estimation of the consequences of certain choices, the judge content with a legalistically determined "discovery" may not pay adequate attention to the consequences of his or her choice. This, we have seen, is true for all kinds of legal reasoning; however, constitutional reasoning here takes a twist. Although in statutory interpretation the judge ought to seek out the purpose of statutory language—the class of social problem that the statute has historically seemed to address—and then determine if the issue in court belongs to that class, judges should not, and usually do not, do so when they reason about the Constitution. Whereas the statute in its historical context defines the problem for the judge, in constitutional law the judge may change the definition of the problem altogether.

Three forces produce this twist. First, some judges and scholars believe that constitutional clauses ought to change meaning with the times. Chief Justice John Marshall's opinion in *McCulloch* v. *Maryland* (1819) said as much. Thus, assuming even conclusive proof that the First Amendment's religion clauses did not react to the mischief of prayer by officials in government in the eighteenth century, it would not follow that a modern court must, as a matter of law, deny that the amendment prohibits prayer in public schools today. Second, the political realities of constitution-making obscure beyond reconstruction either what a majority of founders may have intended a given clause to mean or, more deeply, the scope of the purpose of that clause. Third, the machinery for amending the Constitution operates so infrequently and unpredictably that courts cannot "defer" judgment on constitutional questions to other governmental institutions. When citizens present an appealing constitutional claim, such as a claim that their tax monies should not be spent to support schools operated by a religious denomination, as in *Flast* v. *Cohen* (1968), the courts cannot defer to the legislature. The constitutionality of its statute is the very issue in question.

Scholars have recently escalated the debate over whether the phrase "constitutional interpretation" has any meaning—that is, whether the Court does, or should, interpret the Constitution at all. The technical definition of the interpretive act—"thick description"—suggests that courts rarely interpret in any legal area. In the looser legal sense of interpretation the weight of scholarly opinion seems, in the mid-1980s at least, to tip toward the proposition that courts should justify constitutional conclusions in terms of normative propositions about the character of contemporary American social and political life. However, in 1985 Attorney General Edwin Meese and other conservative politicians argued the opposite view that courts should decide according to the historical context in which a specific clause was drafted and adopted.

No doubt this debate will continue indefinitely. As an empirical matter, however, there is little doubt that the Supreme Court throughout constitutional history has justified its landmark constitutional decisions primarily in relation to contemporary values and experience, and not to history. For example, from about 1880 to the middle of the Great Depression the Court believed that societal well-being depended upon minimizing the power of government to affect private decisions about the use of property and labor in commerce. The Court therefore struck down or severely limited the scope of statutes that sought to correct perceived commercial abuses. The Warren and Burger Courts' emphasis on individual rights and liberties follows from a different and partially incompatible set of premises, according to John H. Ely. Organized commercial interests are well represented in the pluralistic, money- and vote-driven processes of political policymaking and implementation; and individuals and insulated minorities deserve access to the courts because they lack the resources to be heard elsewhere.

Neither approach is demonstrably correct or incorrect in any absolute sense. The point, rather, is that Holmes's "felt necessities of the time, the prevalent moral and political theories, [and] intuitions of public policy" stand out prominently in constitutional reasoning.

CONCLUSIONS

This essay began by emphasizing the importance of judicial impartiality and, hence, of legal reasoning within a larger political framework. Subsequent descriptions, however, seemed at every turn paradoxically to underscore the political realities of legal reasoning, realities that raise doubts that judges can decide impartially after all. Judges do not regularly honor the criteria for determinate logic. Judicial justifications tend to take the form of practical reasoning, but even here judicial opinions often fail to state their premises clearly. Analysts must supply the missing premises, and they may themselves disagree. Judicial obscuring of logic, if deliberate, seems motivated to hide from the audience the political and, hence, partial character of many judicial decisions. Indeed, the internal compromises necessary to get different appellate court judges on the same bench to agree with each other enough to sign a common opinion resolving a case can obscure key premises in the opinion (Murphy).

Furthermore, judicial justifications exhibit little patterned consistency in the theories that judges employ. Judges follow prior precedents blindly in the face of powerful evidence that the five reasons given for horizontal stare decisis pose no obstacle to a decision to overrule. Judges also speak of legislative intent or the "plain meaning" of statutory words as if these phrases denoted some reality. Few formal norms consistently guide the justification process. Judges disagree about when, whether, and how actively courts should intervene on behalf of a constitution in legislative matters. They do not even agree about the role either a constitution or a legislature ought to play in lawmaking. It would seem that theories and norms of legal reasoning amount to no more than a hegemonic device to maintain the political power of the legal profession.

Such an assessment is misguided. Legal reasoning does indeed possess all the characteristics just described. Holmes's description is apt, yet the system seems to persist, and despite occasional criticisms, complaints about the quality of appellate court justifications are not very widely shared.

Perhaps we overestimate the political importance of legal reasoning. If only lawyers, judges (and their clerks), and a few professors (and their students) pay serious attention to opinions, then the substance of the result—which interests win and which lose—will shape the public's assessment of appellate court impartiality more than the fine points of the opinion. No matter how well reasoned it is, large segments of the public will oppose a ban on voluntary public school prayer. No matter how poorly reasoned it is, large numbers of the public will approve the reintroduction of the death penalty. Perhaps trust in the judiciary rests on only a minimal kind of impartiality. As long as the courts do not, over many cases and jurisdictions, appear to take sides consistently with one political party or one political ideology, as long as a "Nixon Court" votes to bring down President Nixon, as long as free-speech doctrines protect Ku Klux Klansmen and Communists alike, legal reasoning will pass public muster.

The public unquestionably knows little or nothing of the reasons courts give in opinions. Yet, if judges believe it is their job to justify within an isolated framework of legal language but in reality their decisions significantly affect policy, then their chosen forms of legal reasoning will prevent them from attempting effective practical reasoning about the consequences of their choices. Furthermore, a merely minimal impartiality will suffer the long-term consequences of professional and scholarly criticism. If the legal and academic professions increasingly condemn the judicial process wholesale, that condemnation will spill over—as criticism of the Supreme Court spilled over during the Great Depression—into overtly politicized reactions.

Perhaps political satisfaction with legal reasoning arises from the fact that judges are nobody's fools. If most appellate judges know quite well that they are part of the political process, if they consider as carefully as their resources permit the practical consequences of their choices, then we should not object if they couch justifications in an artificial language of political impartiality so as to preserve public trust.

This approach might suffice in a one-court world, a world of only horizontal stare decisis; but in a common-law system, lower courts and private parties do base plans on what they believe the law permits and requires. The political culture seems widely to endorse the proposition of equality, that differential treatment of individuals should have a rational basis. Planning, particularly by trial judges and practicing attorneys, seeks to predict the consequences of specific actions through reasoning by example. Judicial opinions must therefore contain reasons that permit planning and preserve some sense of equal treatment. Reasons proffered only cosmetically, without real relation to the substance of the decision, increase political and social unpredictability. Ultimately, too, they risk increasing unnecessarily the number of costly lawsuits.

In the 1980s a solution to these paradoxes of legal reasoning began to emerge, in part through the much publicized work of a group of liberal law professors loosely designated "the critical legal studies movement." The solution offered by many critical and noncritical scholars in the 1980s makes the following assertions about the legal process and legal reasoning. First, Holmes not only described correctly the character of legal reasoning but also prescribed, without intending to do so, how legal reasoning ought to operate. Impartiality means acting so as to satisfy audience expectations of the decision-making process. Since by definition legal rules have failed to resolve conflicts in their own terms, it is entirely proper, indeed inevitable, for judges to justify results by resorting to deeper cultural beliefs and values that provide a coherent resolution of the case (Gusfield).

Second, one central criterion of a "good" practically reasoned judicial justification is that it expresses as accurately and candidly as possible both assumptions about empirical reality and assertions about what society ought to resemble (Nonet and Selznick). Third, "good" justification must also claim to reach normative or moral closure on the issue at hand. Unlike scientific research, legal reasoning must resort to such devices as theatrical staging (robes, judicial benches, and the like) and the poetic use of language to persuade its audience, if only temporarily, that it has achieved closure (Ball; White).

Finally, each instance of judicial practical reasoning should seek to contribute to an ongoing ethical narrative about the nature of the American polity. It is not possible, desirable, or necessary for any one justification to end the narrative. Rather, the social value of good judicial justifications lies in keeping the narrative alive. Justifications should, by harmonizing rules, empirical data, and cultural values within the facts of a given case, reassure the polity that it possesses a coherent and enduring character (Carter, 1984 and 1985; Cover).

If this view is correct, it is (except for those who believe in natural law) no rebuttal to argue that an opinion's substantive accuracy and normative attractiveness amount to no more than the "felt necessities" of the late twentieth century. If they amount to no more, they nevertheless provide a framework for understanding and accepting many important legal justifications since World War II. To take perhaps the most significant example, *Brown,* the issue is not whether the framers of the Fourteenth Amendment intended to proscribe separate-but-equal racial discrimination; rather, the question is whether the Court accurately appreciated the human costs of segregation and whether, through such affective phrases as "we cannot turn back the clock to 1868" and "separate educational facilities are inherently unequal," it helped prolong the public conversation about the meaning of equality in American life.

CASES

American Textile Manufacturers Institute v. Donovan, 452 U.S. 490 (1981)
Brown v. Board of Education, 347 U.S. 483 (1954)
Flast v. Cohen, 392 U.S. 83 (1968)
Flood v. Kuhn, 407 U.S. 258 (1972)
Industrial Union Department, AFL-CIO v. American Petroleum Institute, 448 U.S. 607 (1980)
McBoyle v. United States, 283 U.S. 25 (1931)
McCulloch v. Maryland, 4 L. Ed. 579 (1819)
Soldano v. O'Daniels, 190 Cal. Rptr. 310 (1983)
Tarasoff v. Regents of the University of California, 551 P.2d 334 (1976)

BIBLIOGRAPHY

Milner S. Ball, *The Promise of American Law* (1981), is a provocative argument for recovering law's poetic and spiritual dimensions by an author trained in law and theology. Raoul Berger, *Government by Judiciary* (1977), offers the conservative argument for constitutional interpretation in terms of the original historical meaning of constitutional clauses. Guido Calabresi, *A Common Law for the Age of Statutes* (1982), argues for greater judicial willingness to change and update interpretations of statutes. Benjamin N. Cardozo, *The Nature of the Judicial Process* (1921), is the classic statement of the inevitably creative and discretionary character of judicial decision-making.

Lief H. Carter, "When Courts Should Make Policy: An Institutional Approach," in John Gardiner, ed., *Public Law and Public Policy* (1977), calls for varying degrees of judicial activism depending on characteristics of the policy environment of the case at hand; *Reason in Law,* 2nd ed. (1984), provides further elaboration of all points in this essay; and *Contemporary Constitutional Lawmaking* (1985) reviews competing theories of constitutional interpretation and proposes evaluating the work of the Supreme Court in explicitly aesthetic terms. Robert Cover, "Foreword: *Nomos* and Narrative," in *Harvard Law Review,* 97 (1983), chastises the Supreme Court for failure to acknowledge the power and significance of myths and nonrational beliefs in private communities.

Alfred Rupert Cross, *Statutory Interpretation* (1976), and F. Reed Dickerson, *The Interpretation and Application of Statutes* (1975), are comprehensive critical analyses of standard issues in statutory interpretation. Ronald Dworkin, *Taking Rights Seriously* (1977), makes a widely discussed and controversial philosophical justification for active judicial protection of fundamental human rights. John Hart Ely, *Democracy and Distrust* (1981), attempts to explain the circumstances in which judicial activism is consistent with democratic political theory. Jerome Frank, *Law and the Modern Mind* (1930; repr. 1963), uses early psychological theory to criticize many conventions and procedures in courts and in the legal profession.

Clifford Geertz, *The Interpretation of Cultures* (1973), explores the nature of interpretation in the social sciences. Martin Golding, *Legal Reasoning* (1983), gives precise descriptions of the various forms judicial logic (and illogic) can take. Joseph R. Gusfield, *The Culture of Public Problems* (1981), reveals how unexamined moral assumptions determine the funding and credibility of scientific research. Oliver Wendell Holmes, Jr., *The Common Law* (1881), cleared the way for positivists, realists, and pragmatists in jurisprudence. Donald Horowitz, *The Courts and Social Policy* (1977), is an important early study of institutional weaknesses of courts as policymakers. Edward Levi, *An Introduction to Legal Reasoning* (1949), raised many fundamental questions in modern legal reasoning theory for the first time.

Karl Llewellyn, *The Common Law Tradition* (1960), is an excellent integration of legal realism and traditionalism by one of the great law teachers of the twentieth century. Walter Murphy, *Elements of Judicial Strategy* (1964), describes the negotiating and compromising necessary to generate agreement among United States Supreme Court judges. Philippe Nonet and Philip Selznick, *Law and Society in Transition* (1978), states a sociological case that law should move away from abstract legal formalities and concern itself more directly with the substantive rationality of policy. Michael J. Perry, *The Constitution, the Courts, and Human Rights* (1982), argues that the Constitution can be interpreted to permit the Supreme Court to decide in terms of modern values and social conditions.

Martin Shapiro, *Courts: A Comparative and Political Analysis* (1981), provides an excellent comparative analysis of courts in different cultures. Richard A. Wasserstrom, *The Judicial Decision* (1961), carefully analyzes the procedures of justification courts should follow within a utilitarian philosophical framework. James Boyd White, *When Words Lose Their Meaning* (1984) and *Heracles' Bow* (1985), assert that we can understand judicial opinions best by treating them as literary and poetic expressions.

[*See also* ALTERNATIVES TO FORMAL ADJUDICATION; BEHAVIORAL STUDIES OF THE AMERICAN LEGAL SYSTEM; COMMON LAW AND COMMON-LAW LEGAL SYSTEMS; CONSTITUTIONAL INTERPRETATION; *and* JUDICIAL REVIEW.]

PLEA BARGAINING

Milton Heumann

P LEA bargaining is the process of negotiation by which the defendant in a criminal case agrees to give up his or her right to go to trial in return for a reduction in charge or a real or anticipated reduction in sentence. Although it is a major mode of disposition of most criminal cases in most courts in the United States, plea bargaining continues to be the subject of much scholarly, policy, and legal debate. Opponents call for its outright abolition; proponents include those who view it as a necessary case-management expedient in the nation's always overwhelmed courts as well as those who go further in endorsing it in the belief that it is a preferable way to resolve many of the disputes that work their way into the criminal justice system.

This essay does not take a specific position in the debate about the propriety of plea bargaining but, instead, adopts a descriptive analytical approach to help inform judgments on the costs and benefits of plea bargaining. Moreover, by describing the process of plea bargaining in some detail, we will be able to consider its implications for sentencing reform, an issue of much current concern.

THE ACTORS

In the typical image conjured up by the term *plea bargaining,* a prosecutor and a defense attorney haggle over a case's disposition in a corridor, a courtroom, or occasionally an office. These attorneys work something out and sell it to both the client and the judge, and the deal is thus completed. As a rough approximation of the pattern of plea bargaining, this is accurate; however, there are a substantial number of exceptions to this model as well as refinements that need to be made if we are to accurately appreciate the way plea bargaining works in the court.

First, it is useful to identify who is doing the bargaining. On one side, at least in instances in which explicit bargaining takes place, there is a representative of the prosecutor's office, usually an assistant prosecutor. The amount of discretion allowed the assistant prosecutor depends on the size of the office, its policies, and probably traditions within the jurisdiction as well. In some prosecutors' offices the assistant is given complete discretion to negotiate a case. The assistant prosecutor is considered a professional who will make responsible decisions by weighing all the competing values at stake. These offices afford the professional staff maximum latitude. In contrast, some offices prohibit assistant prosecutors from indiscriminate plea bargaining. This increasingly fashionable posture, in turn, takes several forms. In the strictest version, neither the assistant prosecutor nor the chief prosecutor engages in plea bargaining; the office adopts a "no plea bargaining" policy. However, even within this model, prosecutors and attorneys discuss a case—indeed, even "negotiate," "reappraise," or "reevaluate" it. It is only the actual bargaining that they are not doing, or so they claim. Other jurisdictions adopt more moderate restrictions on plea bargaining, such as forbidding the assistant to bargain but allowing his superior to do so, allowing limited forms of plea bargaining that are severely circumscribed by prosecutorial policies and directives and reserving plea bargaining for a designated unit of the prosecutor's office and/or the chief prosecutor. The point here is that even in the straightforward "prosecutor plea bargains" model, the nature and extent of the prosecutor's participation is not a simple matter.

PLEA BARGAINING

Similar complexity is evident when we consider the defense attorney side of the model. Too often the popular literature stereotypes the plea-bargaining defense attorney as either a harried public defender without the time or motivation to devote to a case or as an unscrupulous private attorney whose practice depends on turning over a large number of cases quickly. Though these stereotypes may sometimes comport with reality, on balance they are unfairly critical of public defenders in particular and many private practitioners as well. It is true that many public-defender organizations and other offices set up to represent indigent defendants (the bulk of the defendants processed in the courts) are overworked and may have to dispense with some of the "handholding" commonly associated with a lawyer-client relationship. It is also true that the defendants themselves, perhaps because they have little choice in selecting assigned counsel, tend to view public defenders as less than full-fledged attorneys. (In an oft-quoted response to an interviewer, one defendant replied, when asked if he had an attorney when he went to trial, "No, I had a public defender.") But the data do not generally support the proposition that when comparable cases are examined in terms of outcomes, public defenders on average provide inferior representation. Similarly, it is wrong, though easy, to stereotype unfavorably the private attorney who plea bargains. Suffice it to say that elite defense attorneys, not just struggling criminal practitioners, end up negotiating the dispositions for most of their clients' cases.

Not all defense attorneys plea bargain in the same way. Styles of plea bargaining vary quite substantially. On the one hand, some attorneys file extensive formal criminal motions prior to the plea sessions or raise substantial legal issues during plea negotiations. On the other hand, there are attorneys who argue their motions orally and do not devote a great deal of time to case preparation and research.

Other matters affect the defense side of plea bargaining. As is the case in some prosecutors' offices, assistant public defenders may be assigned to cases on either a "zone" or a "person-to-person" basis. In the latter, a defendant receives counsel when he first appears in court, and the assigned attorney is normally his for the duration of the proceedings. In the zone defense, a defendant receives different attorneys at different stages of the proceedings. Although typically one public defender will handle the plea bargaining, it is possible for a different member of the office to attempt to reach a disposition. Again, the important point is that even in a very simple model of prosecutor–defense attorney plea bargaining, very different patterns of plea bargaining are possible depending on the particular prosecutor–defense attorney mix.

If we move beyond the simple model, the two major additional actors who need to be introduced are the judge and the defendant. The assumption in the simple model (often one that is not unwarranted) is that if the prosecutor and the defense attorney reach an agreement, the judge will in almost all instances ratify it. Departures from this model and this assumption arise in terms of the extent of judicial participation in generating the particular plea or pleas in general. Some judges feel it inappropriate to get involved in plea bargaining, whether it is charges, sentences, or both that are being discussed. These judges feel that this is a task appropriately left to the adversaries and inappropriately participated in by judges, though these judges will acquiesce in plea bargains offered by the prosecutors and defense. Other judges take a more active posture in generating pleas. Some allow prosecutors and defense attorneys to speak to them in chambers about the difficulties they are encountering in reaching agreement; others call counsel in to encourage the plea-bargaining process. Finally, some judges plea bargain (even in felony cases) on the bench in court (though off the record) at the time cases are called.

Most plea agreements are now put on the record and the defendant no longer needs to falsely state that he or she is pleading with no expectation of charge or sentence reduction. A judge now informs the defendant that if, upon reading the probation report (prepared before formal sentencing in felony cases), he cannot abide by the terms of the agreement, the judge will allow the defendant to withdraw his plea of guilty. This commendable openness in the rules of plea bargaining certainly marks a significant step forward; however, beyond these changes, judges continue to differ rather drastically in the extent to which they inquire about the details of the plea-bargaining process and, more important, about the details of the offense. Does the plea fit the facts the defendant is willing to admit to? Must the plea fit the facts? Must the defendant admit to the facts of other offenses with which he was charged? These are questions that remain open about the plea-bargaining process generally and about judicial inquiry specifically. There has been little systematic research on differences between judges with regard to the extent to which they make inquiries and the amount of time they devote to accepting pleas (whether or not various inquiries are undertaken). Some judges do pride themselves on being able to take pleas in under two minutes, assuring observers (quite correctly) that their inquiries of the defendant meet all state and federal constitutional requirements. Other judges engage in a far more deliberative process, some communicating sincerely that they want defendants to understand what rights they are waiving; still others seem determined to make the record immune to subsequent challenge. A systematic survey of these practices, particularly in light of the attention given to the matter of the factual inquiries that ought to be included as part of the plea canvass, remains one of the most pressing research needs in the plea-bargaining field.

The final and, curiously, often overlooked participant in the plea-bargaining process is the defendant. Critics of plea bargaining address what they believe to be the coercive forces that encourage defendants to plead, notably the fear of a substantially higher penalty if defendants do not plead and go to trial. While acknowledging that the final choice of a disposition is the defendant's, proponents of plea bargaining focus on the professional judgments of the defense attorney and the prosecutor about the strengths and weaknesses of the case. What is often lost in these discussions is the issue of the pressure defendants put on attorneys to "work out a deal." It is certainly true that the way defense attorneys frame the choices when presenting plea bargains to defendants can substantially affect a defendant's calculus. But defendants are often learned in the ways of the criminal court (particularly those defendants who have committed felonies) and are not naive buffoons who can be easily misled by an attorney, especially since defendants often mistrust assigned attorneys to begin with. They have a sense of what is "a good deal." This is not to say that their choices are unaffected by a fear that they will be penalized with a higher

sentence simply for going to trial. It is to say, however, that the independent input of a defendant is a factor—occasionally a major factor—that affects the plea-bargaining system. Defendants often want to plead; the sections that follow will examine some of the reasons why this is so.

REASONS FOR PLEA BARGAINING

Traditionally, plea bargaining has been explained as the practice of crowded urban courts, courts in which case loads were too large to be processed by trials. Plea bargaining was viewed as an unattractive, quasi-legitimate expedient necessary for processing the volume of cases but not really an appropriate means of case disposition in an adversary system. This conception of the nature of the criminal justice system and of the development and role of plea bargaining within it is not totally inaccurate. It is indeed the way plea bargaining has been perceived, and to an extent it remains a popular perception. However, the social science research of the past two decades, along with a number of notable developments on the appellate level, have done much to debunk the mythical components of the model and to suggest alternate explanations for the centrality of plea bargaining in the criminal courts.

The first problem with the hypothesis that case pressure explains plea bargaining is that the data do not support it. Both crowded and uncrowded, urban and rural courts dispose of most of their cases by pleas. And it appears that reliance on nontrial disposition is not a new, "crowded urban court" phenomenon at all but one that has characterized most American courts at least since the Civil War. A number of alternative explanations have been developed for why plea bargaining appears to dominate the disposition practices of most criminal courts. A cornerstone of these explanations is the argument that adopting an adversary posture in court is not likely to be fruitful. It is simply the fact—and an encouraging fact if one reflects on what would exist were it otherwise—that most of the defendants brought to court are factually guilty of the charge or of some related charge. Of course, in a system in which procedural protections loom large, factual guilt does not always equate with legal guilt. The burden is on the state to establish the defendant's guilt, and if the state is unable to do so because of procedural defects (illegal searches and seizures, involuntary confessions, and the like), the consideration that the defendant is factually guilty is in a sense irrelevant. The argument against adopting an adversary posture suggests that of the many cases in which defendants are factually guilty, few contain realistically contestable legal issues. Although one can never be sure about claims of contestability either in a particular case or across a range of cases, research does support the proposition that there are many cases without meaningful factual or legal issues to be contested. Such cases are said to be "born dead." The collective task of the prosecutor, defense attorney, judge, and defendant is to negotiate a disposition; the guilty plea itself is almost a foregone conclusion. Under this conception of the disposition process, the frequency of pleas is a function not of case volume but of the contestability of cases. Advocates of this view hold that it is futile to go through the motions on cases in which the outcome is clear; and there is widespread agreement that everyone's time is best spent on cases that raise real factual or legal questions.

In addition to this general understanding of plea bargaining, there are several actor-specific explanations for plea bargaining that have been advanced by various court scholars. Some of these are related to the theme of reducing uncertainty for the parties in the plea-bargaining process. Specifically, prosecutors, defense attorneys, and defendants are well aware that their expectations about trial outcomes can go awry; plea bargaining affords these actors the opportunity to reduce the uncertainty of trial. The prosecutor does not run the risk of an acquittal; the defense attorney and the defendant do not run the risk of conviction on the highest charge (when they are able to charge bargain) or an uncertain sentence (when they are able to sentence bargain). Similarly, the judge, by acquiescing in the negotiated disposition, can appear to manage his docket efficiently, a concern of judges in crowded and uncrowded courts alike. Also, although the argument is probably overstated in some of the popular literature, there is more than a kernel of truth to the notion that judges do not like to be reversed on appeal. A plea bargain in most circumstances immunizes a judge against appeal, thus increasing the judge's

confidence in the finality of the decision. Some judges stress this finality in outcome, along with the swiftness potentially afforded by the plea-bargaining process in contrast to the trial process, as important additional arguments in favor of the criminal justice system's reliance on pleas. Some judges believe that certainty and celerity of punishment are related to the efficacy of criminal sanctions with respect to individual deterrence and that plea bargaining allows the system to achieve its goals more successfully than would a greater reliance on trials.

A host of other role-specific explanations for plea bargaining are found in the literature. Prosecutors are said to be able to maximize "batting averages" for pleading (the ratio of convictions to total cases) and perhaps even to maximize total person-years that convicted defendants must serve in prison. (Even if a "discount" is given for pleading, as discussed below, the expected value of cases after trial would include those cases in which the defendant was acquitted.) Similarly, prosecutors are portrayed as being concerned about individualizing dispositions. Whether the concern stems from their sense that legislative penalties are too high (particularly in mandatory-sentencing cases) or just from a more general tendency to feel that they are "close to the case" and as capable as (maybe more capable than) the judge in tailoring dispositions need not concern us here. What is of importance is that prosecutors often work with defense attorneys to tailor general laws to particular defendants—in effect, to seek "substantive justice" while at the same time disposing of the business.

It is of course in the defense attorney's interest to work with the prosecutor who wants to individualize dispositions by mitigating the potential punishment. It is also in the defense attorney's interest to not become an annoyance to the prosecutor. An adversarial relationship can exist within a framework of mutual accommodation, up to a point. For example, both prosecutors and defense attorneys will occasionally need a postponement in a case. The prosecutor's witness may not have shown up, or the private defense attorney's fee might not be forthcoming. (Judges can call postponements to await the arrival of "Mr. Green" or "pursuant to Rule Number 1 of this court" to give private attorneys time to collect their fees.) On any given day, one side could make it difficult for the other in terms of a particular motion. However, because it is likely that these same attorneys will be adversaries in many cases, it is in the interests of each to cooperate as long as neither is sacrificing professional obligations (to the state or to the client).

These are, then, some of the more persuasive or at least justifiable reasons for participation in the plea-bargaining system. No discussion of the reasons for plea bargaining would be complete, however, if it did not at least note some of the other, far less defensible reasons that some argue animate the plea-bargaining system. In the views of those who advance these explanations, judges are seen as lazy and eager to get cases out of the way as quickly as possible and with a minimum of effort; prosecutors are portrayed alternatively as overwhelmed, lazy, or too accommodating. The overwhelmed prosecutor is eager to plead simply to manage a large case load or the lazy prosecutor wants to dispose of cases because he or she has something better to do; the accommodating prosecutor is eager to obtain the support of defense attorneys who may be helpful when the prosecutor attempts to become a judge. The prosecutor, in these arrangements, adjusts professional responsibilities to realize none too laudatory goals. Finally, the defense attorney, if a public defender, is depicted as not very competent, very overwhelmed, or both. Plea bargaining allows the public defender to process a heavy case load, notwithstanding minimal skills and limited time. If the attorney is in private practice, by plea bargaining he can carry a heavy case load through the courts, generating far more in fees than would be possible even with the higher charges that could be levied for trials. Although there may be a kernel of truth to these explanations for some judges, prosecutors, and defense attorneys in some courts, they do not usefully or accurately explain why plea bargaining characterizes the courts, nor do they do justice to the majority of attorneys practicing in the courts.

CENTRAL CONCERNS OF PLEA BARGAINING

In this section, four themes from the plea-bargaining literature are discussed. Two of these —the issue of discounts for pleas and the question of the inevitability of plea bargaining—are currently being actively debated by social scientists who study plea bargaining as well as by attorneys concerned about the propriety of discounts in the first instance, and about the feasibility of abolishing plea bargaining in the second. The other two issues—the actual sentences associated with plea dispositions and the relationship between plea bargaining and the recent flurry of sentencing innovations in the states— are less frequently discussed and are presented here precisely because of their centrality and the fact that they have often been overlooked.

Plea Discounts. The issues raised in connection with discounts for pleading guilty are both normative and empirical. Should defendants be rewarded for waiving their right to go to trial and opting to plead guilty? In other words, should defendants who go to trial receive higher sentences (be penalized) for going to trial? Answers to these normative questions vary. A principled case is made by some that the exercise of a constitutional right should never be associated with a penalty, here a higher sentence for exercising the right to trial. At the other extreme, some argue that it is perfectly appropriate to reward defendants who plead guilty with a discount from the sentence that the defendant would be expected to receive after trial. The justifications for this reward, however, vary among its proponents. Some argue that pleading guilty is the first step to rehabilitation and that the defendant who so pleads should receive a shorter sentence than the defendant who is found guilty after a trial. Also, the case of the defendant who goes to trial may simply look worse after its details are revealed in open court. Further, if defendants take the stand in their own defense, they may, upon conviction, be viewed as having perjured themselves during the trial. Others defend the discount for a plea because of the time and money it saves the state or because of what is termed a "provability discount": with pleading, problems of proof for the state are removed. A middle position argues that only for the defendant who opts to pursue a "frivolous trial"—one in which provability for the state is easy—should the penalty for trial loom large. By this argument, it is not that the defendant is using the state's time and resources; rather, he or she is wasting them. Plea bargaining helps send a message for these kinds of cases.

The perception that the defendant who pleads fares better than the defendant who goes to trial is widely shared in most courts. Marshaling empirical evidence to support this perception is a different matter. The case characteristics or prior record of defendants who plead as compared to those who go to trial may be different in systematic ways. (For example, some argue that only the weakest state cases go to trial, whereas others argue that the state only takes it strong cases to trial and pleads the rest.) Because assignment to trial or plea is not random and because it is possible to argue that systematic differences do exist, one must be cautious in comparing groups of defendants. Of the comparisons that have been made, most support the notion of some plea-trial differential, although at least one prominent study has questioned these findings (Heumann). What does seem unarguable is that most court actors do believe that there is a difference, that defendants who plead generally do better than defendants who do not plead. The extent to which this belief is fueled by the reality of systematic differences, by some isolated cases of dramatic disparities between plea offers and trial sentences, by differences in some categories of offenses but not in others, or by some other dynamic remains an important question for future research.

The Inevitability of Plea Bargaining. Most plea-bargaining research since the 1960s falls squarely on the side of the argument that maintains that plea bargaining of some sort is likely to remain a cental means of case disposition in the criminal courts for the foreseeable future. This argument does not rest on the notion that overburdened courts must plea bargain to survive. This is accurate for some courts but inaccurate for others; low-volume, well-staffed courts seem to plea bargain at a fairly high rate. Some plea bargaining may be a product of habit and tradition. But more important are notions that have already been touched upon—namely, the widely shared perception that many defendants are both factually and legally guilty, that they have few plausible issues to contest, and that they expect to benefit from a plea. Included in this understanding are pleas entered with an expectation of a reward even if no explicit negotiations take place. This kind of implicit plea bargaining seems to be different in degree but not in kind from the explicit variant.

Support for the proposition that plea bargaining, either implicit or explicit, will persist into the foreseeable future comes from several different bodies of research. First, a number of studies have evaluated the success of various efforts to abolish plea bargaining. These studies teach several lessons. When prosecutors have strictly adhered to proscriptions on charge bargaining, judges typically have gotten more involved in the plea-bargaining process and increasingly have negotiated sentences with the defense attorney. In those few jurisdictions that have imposed further restrictions on this kind of judicial plea bargaining (for example, the Alaska Supreme Court prohibited judicial sentence bargaining, which increased dramatically after the Alaska attorney general prohibited prosecutors from charge bargaining), the guilty-plea rates remained high despite the prohibitions on explicitly negotiated dispositions. Although trial rates have increased slightly in some of these jurisdictions, for the most part defendants continue to plead. Their pleas are animated by implicit plea bargaining, by the general expectation that they will fare better by pleading than by contesting their cases. Moreover, with knowledge of a jurisdiction's preprohibition norms, defendants can make reasonably good guesses about what sentences they will receive with a plea before particular judges. They or their attorneys are aware of the "going rates," or sentencing norms, of a jurisdiction and of a judge; and even without the preferred option of explicit negotiation to ensure that the case is correctly handled, defendants apparently still plead under the reasonable expectation that they will receive a particular going rate or, at a minimum, that what they will receive will be a benefit compared to the possible sentence after trial.

A second part of the argument about the centrality and inevitability of plea bargaining derives from the results of a number of studies outside the United States. Plea bargaining or functional equivalents thereof seem to be quite common in England, Scotland, Israel, and perhaps (there have been heated debates about this) on the Continent as well.

Additional findings of import for the theme of plea bargaining's centrality and inevitability are those from studies that have examined jurisdictions purported not to rely extensively on plea bargaining. The results of a number of these studies suggest that often, but not always, what looks like a greater reliance on adversary procedures, most notably bench (nonjury) trials, is illusory. The high rate of bench trials is not conclusive evidence of a more adversarial system, for it has been found that in many of these jurisdictions many of the bench trials are nothing more than "slow pleas of guilty." They seem to serve as a means for defendants to plead before a judge in a truncated procedure that may not, and often does not, take longer than a guilty-plea hearing. It is important to qualify these findings in two ways. First, even in jurisdictions in which the bench trial commonly serves as a functional equivalent of a guilty plea, not all bench trials are necessarily slow pleas. There are circumstances in which contesting a case before a judge alone, without a jury, is preferable to the parties. Also, there may be jurisdictions—there is some evidence suggesting that Philadelphia is one such example—where real bench trials are used at a fairly high rate and consequently the percentage of plea bargains is substantially lower than in most jurisdictions (Alschuler, 1981).

Some observers of such bench-trial practices use the existence of these trials to raise questions about the centrality and inevitability of plea bargaining. Lest anyone make too much of these bench trials, several things about them ought to be noted. At least in Philadelphia, one factor responsible for the high bench-trial rate is the seeming pattern in the assignment of judges: "harder" sentencing judges to jury trials, "softer" judges to bench trials. The coerciveness of this practice of directing defendants away from jury trials is obvious and troublesome. Furthermore, the bench trials that are held, even if they are not slow pleas, are often brief, truncated proceedings. It may be that adjudicating a disposition in this manner is different, perhaps importantly so, from the plea process. Indeed, some may well prefer this more adversarial practice, but in light of the coercive context in which such bench trials are generated (at least in some jurisdictions), it is a preference with which not many informed observers would readily join.

Nonetheless, these "real" bench trials are legitimately introduced as a limit on the inevitability hypothesis. Cases are plea bargained in some communities but at a rate significantly below that in most others. And it is interesting to speculate why these communities opt for ab-

breviated trials rather than following the usual plea-bargaining pattern. Notwithstanding plea bargaining's centrality in most American courts and in many other countries as well, its perseverance in the face of efforts to abolish it, and its close kinship to many "functional equivalents," it is possible to point to settings that do function without a heavy reliance on plea bargaining. It remains far from certain, however, whether these exceptions are exportable practices or whether it would be desirable to export them.

The Outcomes of Plea Bargaining. To the chagrin of many of its proponents, plea bargaining suggests by its very name that defendants receive a bargain. Indeed, it is this specter of "bargain-basement justice" that makes plea bargaining, when raised in a political campaign, a potent issue to use against its practitioners and advocates. The problem with this view is that the link of plea bargaining to "bargain" justice may often be incorrect in practice, and it is certainly wrong in principle. To appreciate the relation of plea bargaining to its outcome, the sentence, one must begin by asking about the origins of the sentences imposed. Legislative indeterminate-sentencing schemes typically define penalties in terms of wide ranges of years of imprisonment for particular offense classes. Thus, judges and prosecutors have traditionally been left with the responsibility to choose a sentence from within these broad ranges. Many factors guide this sentencing decision, and we would need to range far afield to cover them all here. But it is clear that different court actors emphasize different goals (rehabilitation, deterrence, and so on) and that personal proclivities and hunches about defendants and about the efficacy of different sanctions are also at work. What is important to emphasize is that no single sentence is necessarily the right one for a defendant.

Whatever sentence is meted out by a typical plea-bargaining or trial system is neither required nor right. The sentence could be higher or lower, and the differential in plea and trial sentences in most cases could be large, small, or even nonexistent. Clearly, some defendants' sentences are lower than they would be if they had gone to trial. But is this a bargain objectively, and must it be set at a particular price? The answer is no. Because no price is right, the plea-bargain price may be harsh or lenient, fair or unfair, and it might be raised or lowered without having a substantial effect on plea rates in a specific jurisdiction.

Recent attempts to raise criminal sentences have not been accompanied by a decrease in pleas. New and more severe prices have been set in jurisdictions, and defendants still plead. But as long as uncertainty can be removed, as long as the court continues to process many clear-cut cases, and perhaps as long as actors continue to believe there is a plea-trial differential, plea bargaining will continue to characterize many courts' dispositional processes, however harsh the sentences in the particular jurisdiction.

Sentencing and Plea Bargaining. The years since the mid-1970s have been a period of great change for the sentencing codes of the states. Indeterminate-sentencing schemes, which afford judges wide latitude in sentencing, have been replaced, piecemeal or as a whole, by various less discretionary systems. No state has adopted a complete mandatory-sentencing plan, but some have passed mandatory sentences for a fairly wide range of crimes (for instance, firearms use) or criminals (such as repeat offenders). Other, somewhat less severe sentencing changes that impose constraints on judicial discretion include those based on empirical or prescriptive sentencing guidelines as well as those that include determinate or presumptive sentences that call for a specific sentence rather than a range of years.

What is important here is the focus reformers accord judicial discretion. To decrease discretion in sentencing, they decrease judicial discretion; to decrease the perceived leniency in sentences, they sometimes remove judicial discretion altogether. To the extent that judges sentence—a not surprising perception that legislatures have of the judicial role—these reforms, for better or worse, ought to achieve their objectives. The problem is, of course, that in many systems judges do not sentence or at least do not have the control over the sentencing process assumed by the reformers. It is the prosecutor who, through the initial charging decision and subsequent charge and sentence bargaining, controls in large measure the sentences that defendants receive. If prosecutors and judges disagree with the aims of a new sentencing code, they can use the plea-bargaining process to undermine the reform's intent.

Plea bargaining is the Achilles' heel of sentencing reform. Narrowing judicial discretion

simply and directly enhances prosecutorial power as it shifts more discretion to the prosecutor's office. Although some prosecutors claim to have eschewed this power to charge- and sentence-bargain (particularly vis-à-vis cases directly affected by new reforms in the jurisdiction) and some have promulgated voluntary guidelines for assistants within their offices, for the most part prosecutors have remained silent about their enhanced prerogatives under the new sentencing codes. Whether this silence reflects an acceptance of the new order or indicates that prosecutors and judges are quietly circumventing these new sentencing schemes is a question that we can set aside. It is sufficient to note that plea bargaining remains the Achilles' heel of efforts to reform sentencing by focusing only on reducing judicial discretion. Although prosecutors and judges may indeed feel obligated to observe both the letter and the spirit of the new sentencing schemes—and many do—plea bargaining lurks as a potent and tempting means to adjust a new code's strictures to former practices and norms.

A LOOK AHEAD

What directions for future research and reforms of plea bargaining practices are suggested by these observations? There is, first, a need for more research on how case pressure affects plea bargaining. Earlier this essay argued that plea bargaining did not result from case pressure, that it was not caused by overworked and understaffed courts. This is different from saying that case pressure does not affect plea bargaining. It seems clear that case pressure beyond some point may well affect the way some or all cases are processed in a court. This relationship may be straightforward: in a system that begins with no case pressure, as the number of cases increases, plea bargaining increases to cope with the new imbalance of cases and resources. Or the relationship might be far more complicated: a penalty for trial might be introduced, or the former penalty for trial might be increased in an effort to ensure that defendants are aware of the gap between plea and trial results. Interestingly, since the plea price can be kept the same, there is no reason for prosecutors to reduce the sentence associated with a plea by "giving away the store" when case pressure increases. Alternatively, screening of cases for trial may increase through outright dismissals, more diversion programs, or other such mechanisms. The general point is that more research is needed into how different case loads affect plea-bargaining practices.

A second matter in need of more research is the issue of differences between plea-bargaining systems. Plea bargaining can mean very different things in different jurisdictions. In some, it can be quite adversarial, a process in which defense attorneys vigorously contest, perhaps informally in the prosecutor's office or more formally in the context of pretrial motions, the state's claims; in others it can be a far more cooperative system in which working out a solution or "doing substantive justice" is given primacy and the adversary process is simply not used as often and perhaps not valued as highly. In certain jurisdictions, as some have suggested, plea bargaining may be likened to a bazaar in which prices fluctuate with demand; in others (probably most), a supermarket metaphor might be more appropriate. Prices for the different products are on the shelves, and these prices, or "going rates," more than the haggling of the bazaar, are what lead to the settling of cases with particular sentences.

Finally, with respect to understanding these differences in jurisdictions, we need to devote more attention to the elusive but important notions of courtroom culture, courthouse culture, and local legal culture. Court participants seem to share a set of values, norms, perceptions, and beliefs about the way a community's courts should operate. Whether these beliefs are simply the product of tradition or reflect a more complex interplay of courtroom, courthouse, and community values and expectations shaped by the criminal code, case types, crime rates, case load, and so on is a question that merits further study.

The agenda for work on plea bargaining ought not be limited to social science research. More attention needs to be given to the abuses of plea bargaining and to legal and policy reforms of plea-bargaining practices. Since the mid-1960s the United States Supreme Court has brought plea bargaining out of the closet, recognizing it as a common method of case disposition, legitimizing it as an appropriate practice, and, in the eyes of some, applauding it as a pref-

erable means of dispute resolution. It is not yet evident what limits if any the Court will impose, nor is there a consensus as to what these limits ought to be.

More research must also be done on the question of "truth in plea bargaining." The days of the guilty-plea charade, when defendants were forced to deny in open court the promises just made to them behind closed doors, are largely over; plea agreements are put now on the record. However, there remains some ambiguity about the extent to which a factual basis for the guilty plea must be established before a judge can accept the plea. Should a plea be accepted only for the real offense, or should artificial pleas to decreased charges be acceptable even when they conflict with the facts of the offense, such as allowing pleas to unarmed robbery despite assertions in the record that a gun was used? To what extent should a defendant be afforded an opportunity to contest specific facts at the sentencing stage even though the defendant chose to plead guilty to the charge? With the narrowing of judicial discretion through guideline-sentencing schemes and determinate sentencing, plans that are sometimes coupled with the abolition of parole, defendants can be less assured that judges will tailor sentences to particular facts in the file and that parole boards will use case facts to individualize sentences. Thus, the opportunity for a defendant to set the factual record straight while still having the opportunity to plead seems all the more important.

The policy components of the plea-bargaining agenda ought to include efforts to develop prosecutorial guidelines or some other method of rationalizing and regularizing prosecutorial discretion. Other policy matters worthy of new or increased attention include according victims and/or defendants a larger role in the plea-bargaining process; working on ways to make explicit the sentencing norms of a jurisdiction so that novice attorneys do not lose out on the "standard discount" generally given to experienced attorneys and so that defendants are not misled by their attorneys or by the prosecutor into believing that they are obtaining an unusually good deal (which the attorneys or prosecutor can use to justify an unusually high fee); and continuing the trends toward increased discussion of plea bargaining and more training in negotiation skills in law schools.

Much has been accomplished by the research since the 1960s into plea bargaining and the criminal justice system. We have learned about plea-bargaining dynamics, and we have become increasingly sophisticated and realistic with respect to our ability to frame the questions in need of further research and thought. The challenge that confronts us in the decades to come is to work on informed responses to these research questions and related policy issues.

CASES

Blackedge v. Allison, 431 U.S. 63 (1977)
Bordenkircher v. Hayes, 434 U.S. 357 (1978)
North Carolina v. Alford, 400 U.S. 25 (1970)
Santobello v. New York, 404 U.S. 257 (1971)

BIBLIOGRAPHY

Albert Alschuler, "Implementing the Criminal Defendant's Right to Trial," in *The University of Chicago Law Review,* 50 (1983), vigorously opposes plea bargaining; and "The Changing Plea Bargaining Debate," in *California Law Review,* 69 (1981), discusses the bench trial alternatives to plea bargaining. John Baldwin and Michael McConville, *Negotiated Justice* (1977), discusses plea bargaining in Great Britain. David Brereton and Jonathan Casper, "Does It Pay to Plead Guilty? Differential Sentencing and the Functioning of Criminal Courts," in *Law and Society Review,* 16 (1981–1982), is the best summary of existing research on the issue of a penalty for going to trial. Jonathan Casper, *American Criminal Justice* (1972), presents the very mixed views that defendants have about plea bargaining.

Thomas Church, Jr., "Plea Bargaining, Concessions and the Courts: Analysis of a Quasi-Experiment," in *Law and Society Review,* 10 (1976), evaluates attempts to abolish selectively plea bargaining in the United States. James Eisenstein and Herbert Jacob, *Felony Justice* (1977), and Martin A. Levin, *Urban Politics and the Criminal Courts* (1977), are two valuable comparative studies of felony courts containing important insights into plea bargaining. Malvina Halberstam, "Toward Neutral Principles in the Administration of Criminal Justice: A Critique of Supreme Court Decisions Sanctioning the Plea Bargaining Process," in *The Journal of Criminal Law and Criminology,* 73 (1982), critically summarizes the case law on plea bargaining.

Milton Heumann, *Plea Bargaining* (1978), develops the argument that prosecutors and defense attorneys believe that defendants who plead guilty fare better than those who go to trial. *Law and Society Review,* 13 (1979), published as part of a National Conference on Plea Bargaining held in June 1978, is an excellent collection of articles reporting on studies of plea bargaining in different jurisdictions and on the attempts to reform or abolish plea bargaining. William F. McDonald and James Cramer, eds., *Plea Bargaining* (1980), also treats these issues. Lynn Mather, *Plea Bargaining or Trial?* (1979), Arthur Rosett and Donald R. Cressey, *Justice By Consent* (1976), and Pamela Utz, *Settling the Facts* (1978), are book-length empirical studies of plea bargaining in felony courts. William M. Rhodes, *Plea Bargaining: Who Gains? Who Loses?* (1978), articulates the view that the state gives away little and gains much in the plea-bargaining process.

[*See also* SENTENCING ALTERNATIVES.]

PUBLIC-INTEREST ADVOCACY

David F. Chavkin

I N the late 1960s and early 1970s, public-interest law achieved a high level of public attention, as the popular media and scholarly law
journals examined public-interest law in great
detail. Television shows romanticized "store-
front lawyers." Editorials furiously debated such
public-interest law victories as the effort to save
the snaildarter. An unlimited future was predicted for this new field.

While public-interest law did go through a remarkable expansion during this period, it is a
field with a long history in the United States.
Despite that history, the parameters of this area
of law remain ill defined today. Such basic questions as the definition of the public interest and
the kinds of advocacy that it encompasses can
elicit nearly as many answers as there are public-
interest lawyers.

IDENTIFYING THE PUBLIC INTEREST

Underlying the American legal system is the
notion that truth can be established through an
adversarial judicial process utilizing skilled advocates to represent the interests of private parties.
Divorce cases, commercial litigation, and contract issues all place lawyers in the role of ad-
vocating on behalf of private interests against
other private interests. Through the legal process, disputes can be settled in an orderly manner without undue disruption. Ultimately, it is
hoped, justice will prevail. If one accepts this
underlying premise, any legal advocacy can be
viewed as furthering the public interest. This
broad view places great importance on the role
that the legal system plays in a pluralistic society.
Under this view, then, the public interest is furthered whenever recourse is had to that system

to the exclusion of other dispute resolution devices such as guns.

Short of such a broad view of the public interest that would encompass nearly all lawyering,
the legal community has historically recognized
that lawyers sometimes play a different role from
that of private advocate. For example, in 1975
the American Assembly on Law and a Changing
Society II, cosponsored by the American Bar Association (ABA), noted in its report, "While
there may be ambiguity of definition and scope,
a serious void in our legal institutions is being
filled by the activities of lawyers who engage in
representation of groups and interests that
would otherwise be unrepresented or underrepresented."

Long before the introduction of the term *public-interest law* in the mid-1960s, lawyers representing such unrepresented or underrepresented groups and interests were referred to as
acting *pro bono publico.* In performing such a role,
the attorney was thereby acting "for the public
good" or "for the welfare of the whole." Unfortunately the historical term *pro bono publico* is no
more helpful than the term *public-interest law* in
deciding what advocacy advances the public
good or the welfare of the whole. Such a definition necessarily depends on the development of
a consensus as to public goals, but such a consensus is difficult to achieve.

In 1970, the *Yale Law Journal* published an
expansive article on the then state of public-
interest legal activity. The following story, re-
counted in that article, illustrates the problems
inherent in developing such a public consensus:

> Lloyd Cutler, a Washington lawyer of considera-
> ble professional stature, led a firm team which
> obtained a consent decree on behalf of automo-

900

bile companies, settling before trial a government antitrust action which charged the companies with conspiracy to impede the development of pollution control systems. Through [Ralph] Nader's promptings, a number of law students picketed Cutler's firm to draw attention to the settlement, which they felt to be a Justice Department sellout of the public interest. The students felt that the settlement prevented a proper public airing of crucial issues, and noted that the settlement also prevented the possibility of private treble damage actions based on the original judgment, which would have been possible had the government gone to trial and prevailed. In the midst of a press conference, in which a clearly upset Mr. Cutler accused the picketing students of violating legal ethics, he asked an especially difficult question: "Why do you think you have a monopoly on deciding what is in the public interest?"

In an interview, Mr. Cutler said that the negotiations were not "secret," as the students had alleged; that public objections were heard and amendments made; and that the final settlement was unanimously affirmed on appeal. According to Cutler, the government received the relief it had sought, and it was by no means clear to those involved that the government would have prevailed had the case actually been tried. Cutler's press-conference question, then, appears to mean the following: if we agree that the pluralistic political system is a fair one, the public interest can only be defined as the outcome of the political *process* in which various private and group interests compete. Thus any lawyer representing *any* substantive interest in the process can with equal justification claim to be working towards the "public interest." Assuming that the process operated properly, the pollution case settlement, which was the outcome of the process, must have been "in the public interest."

(Borosage et al.)

The extent to which the public interest will be furthered by any specific legal advocacy may exist only in the eye of the beholder. However, some underlying areas of agreement with regard to a definition of public interest law have been developed.

ABA Criteria. In 1974, reflecting the post-Watergate self-analysis of the legal profession, the ABA began to take a more aggressive role in encouraging lawyers to provide "public interest legal services." The ABA's Special Committee on Public Interest Practice proposed to define public-interest practice to include legal services for the poor, representation without fee or at a substantially reduced fee in "cases seeking the vindication of an individual's fundamental civil rights" and "rights belonging to the public at large," and representation of charitable organizations. This definition of public-interest practice proved to be relatively noncontroversial. The Special Committee also proposed that each lawyer be required to spend a specific amount of time in such public-interest work. As might be expected, the legal community was extremely resistant to such a mandated public-interest obligation, despite the fact that lawyers would have been free to choose the subjects and activities they would undertake.

A study done at that time pointed up part of the reason for professional resistance. The study, cosponsored by the National Science Foundation and the Office of Economic Opportunity (OEO), surveyed a random sample of lawyers across the country. Since information was obtained from interviews with attorneys, the expected bias in such a study would be to inflate the actual commitment to public-interest work. Nevertheless, the study found that over 60 percent of all lawyers spent less than 5 percent of their billable time doing public-interest work; 30 percent spent no time at all. Even when nonbillable hours were considered, 70 percent of the lawyers surveyed reported spending one hour or less per week in public-interest work.

In 1975 the House of Delegates of the ABA, the policymaking body of the organization, approved a resolution that expanded the definition of "public legal service" to mean:

legal services provided without fee or at a substantially reduced fee, which falls into one or more of the following areas:
1. Poverty Law: Legal services in civil and criminal matters of importance to a client who does not have the financial resources to compensate counsel.
2. Civil Rights Law: Legal representation involving a right of an individual which society has a special interest in protecting.
3. Public Rights Law: Legal representation involving an important right belonging to a significant segment of the public.
4. Charitable Organization Representation: Legal service to charitable, religious, civic, gov-

ernmental and educational institutions in matters in furtherance of their organizational purpose, where the payment of customary legal fees would significantly deplete the organization's economic resources or would be otherwise inappropriate.

5. Administration of Justice: Activity, whether under bar association auspices, or otherwise, which is designed to increase the availability of legal services, or otherwise improve the administration of justice.

The inclusion of poverty law and civil rights law reflected the traditional focus of public-interest law on "representation of the unrepresented and underrepresented." Codes of professional responsibility for attorneys have traditionally required lawyers to make legal representation available to all persons. These two areas of public-interest law are therefore consistent with the concept of public interest embodied in such codes.

Ethical standards also emphasize the distinction between providing legal representation to those who might otherwise go unrepresented (the public-interest goal) and attorney responsibility for the actions of an individual client. While controversy may arise in an individual case involving, for example, a particularly notorious defendant, most people recognize that representation is needed to ensure the accountability of the legal system. Thus, whether provided by a public defender to an indigent criminal defendant, by a legal-services attorney to an indigent civil litigant, or by a private attorney in either setting through a reduced fee or free representation, important public goals are advanced.

Similarly, legal services for charitable organizations further important public goals. American society has decided to further the efforts of charitable organizations through such devices as the establishment of a tax deduction from income for charitable contributions. Attorneys who provide inexpensive or free legal representation reduce the amount of money that the charitable organization must spend on legal services and thereby free additional monies for furtherance of the organization's charitable goals.

A similar situation exists with regard to legal services that further administration of justice. Again, specific provisions of most codes of professional responsibility are involved here as well.

Whether directed toward improving access to, or the quality of, legal representation or toward increasing public trust in the judicial system, legal services in this area again further societal goals.

The key expansion in the 1974 proposal and the 1975 resolution was therefore the inclusion of public-rights law. This area of public-interest activity was described as "legal representation involving an important right belonging to a significant segment of the public. . . . Where society needs to have the rights vindicated but as a practical matter the would-be plaintiff or defendant will take action to vindicate or defend those rights only if he receives aid, and does not have to bear the costs himself."

IRS Standards. It was advocacy in the public-rights area of public-interest law that drew the greatest attention in the late 1960s and early 1970s. Since most of the new organizations engaged in this activity were nonprofit corporations seeking the benefits of tax-exempt status, the growth in this area also did not go unnoticed by the Internal Revenue Service (IRS). In addition, since most of the litigation engaged in by these new public-interest law firms involved challenges to governmental action, some government officials welcomed tighter regulation by the IRS to control these new entities.

In October 1970 the IRS suspended the issuance of tax-exempt determinations to public-interest law firms. This was to be part of a broader effort to limit the ability of existing and future public-interest law firms to qualify for a tax exemption. Although this effort was ultimately unsuccessful, the IRS moratorium on new tax-exempt determinations did destroy or discourage several organizations.

The final guidelines issued by the IRS generally parallel and implement the ABA definition of public interest law. These guidelines require that a public-interest law firm represent broad public interests, rather than private interests. The guidelines generally prohibit such an organization from accepting fees for services and require that the offices be distinct from that of any private law firm. Perhaps most significantly, the guidelines require that the policies and procedures of the organization be set by a board or committee representative of the public interest.

One of the telling distinctions emphasized by the IRS between public-interest law firms and

902

other legal entities is the nature of the client's interest in the outcome of the litigation. As enunciated by the IRS, a public-interest law firm may not accept cases "in which private persons have a sufficient economic interest in the outcome to justify retention of private counsel." The interest being advanced must therefore be significant and broadly shared but must not be significant enough, in economic terms, to justify individual retention of counsel.

This formulation of the definition distinguishes such services from traditional legal activities. Whereas private litigation involves the resolution of disputes between private parties over private interests, public-interest law must involve, on at least one side of the dispute, public interests advanced by private parties.

The debate seems to have come full circle. The 1985 ABA Model Rules of Professional Conduct contain the following requirement in Rule 6.1:

> A lawyer should render public interest legal service. A lawyer may discharge this responsibility by providing professional services at no fee or a reduced fee to persons of limited means or to public service or charitable groups or organizations, by service in activities for improving the law, the legal system or the legal profession, and by financial support for organizations that provide legal services to persons of limited means.

The comment to this model rule emphasizes that its intent is to implement the 1975 resolution of the ABA House of Delegates. However, the comment also evidences the resistance to a mandated *pro bono publico* obligation that was noted after the 1974 report. The comment emphasizes that this rule, unlike the other rules of professional conduct, is not intended to be enforced through disciplinary process.

Despite more than ten years of deliberations and despite the IRS and ABA definitions, considerable uncertainty still reigns as to whether specific activities are "in the public interest." For example, the middle and late 1970s saw a growth in conservative public-interest law firms. These firms were similar in structure to the early public-interest law firms and were often funded by conservative foundations. One of these is the Pacific Legal Foundation. In 1976 the Pacific Legal

Foundation filed a lawsuit against the United States Department of Health, Education, and Welfare to prevent further funding for welfare payments to families with unborn children (*Plumas County* v. *Califano*, 1979). Such payments had been authorized by the federal government for more than thirty years as an optional program for states participating in the Aid to Families with Dependent Children (AFDC) program. Funding had been established by the federal agency, with congressional support, to improve nutrition during pregnancies and to permit indigent mothers to purchase clothing and equipment that would be needed when the baby was born. When the lawsuit was filed, public-interest law firms intervened on behalf of poor families who would be affected by a termination of the program.

In applying the ABA definition to this litigation, the public interest that would be furthered by a termination of funding as sought by the plaintiffs had to be identified. In fact, the only interests that could be enunciated by the plaintiffs were their moral opposition to such payments and their desire to limit federal expenditures. By contrast, the public-interest defendants could demonstrate the statistical improvement in the health of mothers and their offspring that occurred because of the federal financial support. It was therefore not unexpected when the lawsuit was dismissed on the grounds that the plaintiffs did not have a sufficient interest to even challenge the legality of the program. Liberal public-interest law firms are no less immune from such questions. For example, few people could see the public interest at issue in Ralph Nader's proposal that the salary of a United States senator be withheld during the period that he prepared for a shuttle flight.

Public accountability therefore remains an elusive goal for most public-interest law firms. This problem is heightened when significant public interests are present on both sides of a dispute. For example, rural electrification may be advanced at the expense of environmental interests. Occupational safety and health interests may be opposed by those concerned with international competitiveness and the free-enterprise system. Two significant and competing interests are involved here. However, even in such cases, we can return to the goal that is the basis for public-interest law: the desire to articulate the competing interests in a case before a court. Public-interest law firms help to ensure the realization of that goal.

THE TYPES OF PUBLIC-INTEREST PRACTICES

The types of public-interest law firms are nearly as varied as their activities. Occasionally one type of public-interest practice will complement another. In other situations, the goals of the law firms may be very different.

Private Law Firms. The oldest type of public-interest practice involves the attorney in private practice who devotes a portion of his or her time to cases or other legal activities that do not yield compensation from clients. This assistance may take the form of participation on the board of directors of a nonprofit charitable organization or acceptance of referrals for voluntary representation of indigent clients. These roles have been strongly urged by organized bar associations as an essential way of fulfilling public responsibilities acknowledged in the various codes of professional responsibility.

Some private law firms have taken a very structured approach to fulfilling responsibilities to the public. For example, in Washington, D.C., the law firm of Covington and Burling, one of the largest and most prestigious firms in the country, has placed younger associates in legal-services organizations serving the poor. During this externship the firm continues to pay the salary of the associate and provides other support services. Meanwhile, the associate gains valuable client contact and litigation experience that would otherwise take years to acquire. Hogan and Hartson, another major Washington firm, has taken a slightly different approach. Rather than place its staff outside to engage in a public-interest practice, Hogan and Hartson pays one of its partners to engage solely in a public-interest practice and rotates its staff through this aspect of the firm's work. Both of the firms, as well as many others, also provide additional forms of public-interest legal assistance. Counseling small public-interest law firms and charitable organizations as well as working in a cocounsel capacity with public-interest attorneys in litigation are examples of such forms of service.

Despite these efforts, the organized bar continues to grapple with the question of how to increase the extent of such *pro bono* work. In a society that has made lawyers indispensable for so many activities, the degree of responsibility that attorneys have to make their services more accessible to the poor and to the lower-middle class is an especially acute problem. Although these questions continue to be asked, satisfactory answers have yet to be found.

Some private attorneys have tried a different approach to public-interest law. These attorneys have established small law firms that focus on, or engage exclusively in, public-interest law. At a time when many lawyers are being criticized for representing any client for a fee, a practice sometimes described as being a "hired gun," some law firms will only represent clients in matters that are consistent with the political and philosophical views of the law firm staff. Thus, such a firm might decline to represent a corporation alleged to have violated environmental laws or a business sued for unfair labor practices.

Representation that passes such a litmus test might be financed in part by client fees, although generally such fees would be far less than the going rate in that area of law. Supplemental funding might depend on foundation support or on the ultimate availability of attorney's fees. To further compensate, attorneys in such firms generally accept salaries that are below those commanded by attorneys in comparable private practice positions.

Most such private public-interest law firms have found maintaining such a practice very difficult. The realities of funding often force such firms to supplement their revenues through the handling of other, politically neutral matters. Firms that have been able to secure one or more large attorney's fees awards have been able to use such awards to establish their own endowment and thereby protect themselves from the vagaries of funding by the public-interest sector.

Government Lawyers. Government lawyers, whether at the federal, state, county, or municipal level, constitute the majority of public-interest lawyers. Although some might disagree with the inclusion of government lawyers in this category, the role of government lawyers, at least in theory, is to further the public interest by enforcing laws and by representing the interests of their governmental clients. To the extent that these laws and governmental actions are consistent with the public interest, the public interest will thereby be advanced by their effective advocacy.

A far less traditional type of governmental public-interest lawyer works for the relatively new breed of governmentally funded public-interest law firms. One of the leading examples of this type of practice is the New Jersey Department of the Public Advocate. This state-funded public-interest law firm was created in 1974 "to represent . . . the public interest in any proceeding." Moreover, to the extent that competing or inconsistent public interests may be involved in a particular matter, state law authorizes the public advocate to utilize different divisions within the department to represent competing interests. The primary goal of such an office is, in many ways, not to achieve particular outcomes but to ensure that whatever outcome is achieved occurs only after full consideration of the public interests affected. Since its creation in 1974, the Department of the Public Advocate has utilized different divisions to further the public interest by appearing in rate-setting cases involving businesses and utilities, by providing legal services and medical consultation to indigent mental-hospital patients, by mediating and resolving disputes without litigation, and by providing legal services to disabled children and adults.

Although the New Jersey legislation represents the broadest mandate in the United States for such public ombudsman activities, many states have created more limited public-interest agencies. Probably the most common of these are the public counsel offices, charged with representing the public interest in utility rate cases.

Legal Services for the Poor. With the exception of government attorneys, the largest and most comprehensive public-interest law firm is funded by the national Legal Services Corporation. The corporation was established in 1974 by the United States Congress as an independent government agency. Through this agency, funding is provided in the form of grants and contracts to agencies and individuals who deliver legal services to the poor.

The legal-services program originally started in 1965 as a part of the "War on Poverty." As community-action programs grappled with the political powerlessness of the poor, they sought ways to empower that population. One of the approaches that was utilized with increasing frequency was the funding of neighborhood law firms or legal-services offices. Rather than simply provide individual legal representation, the expressed mission of these programs was to change the condition of the poor through legal advocacy.

Although there is wide room for disagreement about the extent to which this goal has been achieved, there is no disagreement that significant victories have been won by the hundreds of legal-services programs across the country.

For example, in the early days of legal services, welfare benefits represented a form of charity that was provided without procedural safeguards for the recipients. Through coordinated litigation efforts, legal-services attorneys and other public-interest attorneys were able to establish rights to notice and a hearing before welfare benefits could be terminated. In establishing these important procedural guarantees, important checks were provided against arbitrary and improper governmental actions.

In addition to the local legal-services programs, national support centers were established to improve the level of knowledge and expertise available to local legal-services attorneys and paralegals. These national centers, established in such areas as health law, welfare law, consumer law, and housing law, not only provide training and technical assistance for local programs but also provide needed information for government-appointed and elected officials on the needs of the poor and on the impact of proposed actions on the poor.

These national support centers have also fulfilled an important role by identifying potential areas for legal advocacy. For example, the National Health Law Program (NHeLP), the national legal-services support center on health problems of the poor, identified a federal statute that required hospitals and other nonprofit health care facilities to provide free or reduced-cost care to indigent patients. NHeLP publicized this statute through articles and mailings to legal-services programs across the country. It also developed strategies to force health care facilities to meet their obligations under federal law and assisted local attorneys in implementing these strategies through litigation and administrative and legislative advocacy. Ultimately, this approach forced health care facilities to make millions of dollars of free care available to the poor that would otherwise have been denied.

The Civil Rights Defense Funds. A major forerunner of the public-interest law movement is the NAACP Legal Defense and Education Fund. The structure and approach utilized by the NAACP Legal Defense and Education Fund formed the model for such other organizations as the Mexican-American Legal Defense and Education Fund (MALDEF), the Native American Rights Foundation (NARF), the Disability Rights Education and Defense Fund (DREDF), and similar civil rights public-interest law firms. The NAACP Legal Defense and Education Fund, Inc., which came to be referred to as the Inc. Fund, was originally set up to take advantage of the tax-exempt status available to nonprofit organizations that did not have lobbying as their principal purpose. The Inc. Fund was originally headed by Thurgood Marshall, who later became a Supreme Court justice.

One of the pioneering approaches of the Inc. Fund was to develop and implement a long-term strategy to battle segregation. Most lawyers litigate cases as they are brought to them. By contrast, the Inc. Fund attorneys decided which cases to bring and when. One of these decisions was to challenge segregation in public education (thought to be an especially sensitive area) only after successful challenges to discrimination in such fields as public transportation and higher education had been made. This carefully choreographed strategy was advanced another step in 1948 by the unanimous decision of the Supreme Court in *Shelley* v. *Kraemer,* barring judicial enforcement of restrictive covenants, private agreements that barred transfers of property to certain races or religions. This victory emphasized another significant contribution by Inc. Fund attorneys to the field of public-interest law.

In the *Shelley* litigation, the Inc. Fund attorneys made extensive use of economic and sociological data demonstrating the destructive effects of segregation. The purpose of the data was to frame the issues not merely in legal terms but also in light of the political, philosophical, and religious underpinnings. That strategy would become a frequent element of public-interest litigation from that time forward and played a significant role in the victory in *Brown* v. *Board of Education.*

Finally, in 1954, the five cases that were consolidated under the name of *Brown* v. *Board of Education* reached the Supreme Court and were argued and then reargued. Fifteen years after the Inc. Fund was created, the Supreme Court ruled that "separate but equal" educational programs were inherently unequal and violative of the equal-protection clause of the Fourteenth Amendment to the United States Constitution. That victory in *Brown* not only altered the social fabric of American society but also represented a success story that numerous public-interest law firms would attempt to repeat through litigation strategies built on the Inc. Fund model.

In part because of their successes, the NAACP and the Inc. Fund became targets for attack by those opposed to their goals. In this area as well, a significant legacy was left to the public-interest legal community. All codes of professional conduct for attorneys bar improper solicitation of clients. This practice is often referred to as "ambulance chasing." In public-interest litigation, clients are often unaware of their rights or of the availability of legal redress. There are a number of factors that can account for this unawareness, including the poverty of the client and the intricacy of the law. The NAACP and the Inc. Fund attorneys made a deliberate effort to seek out clients and to inform communities of the possibility of legal recourse. Since legal advocacy is only as good as the clients whose interests are being advocated, opponents sought to control the civil rights lawyers at this source. Complaints of unethical activities against the civil rights attorneys were filed in a number of jurisdictions and prosecutions of these complaints were initiated in many states. In *NAACP* v. *Button* (1963), the Supreme Court ruled that such client education was authorized by the First Amendment's protection of free speech. The Supreme Court explained that

in the context of NAACP objectives, litigation is not a technique of resolving private differences; it is a means for achieving the lawful objectives of equality of treatment by all government, federal, state and local, for the members of the Negro community in this country. It is thus a form of political expression. . . . And under the conditions of modern government, litigation may well be the sole practicable avenue open to a minority to petition for redress of grievances.

As a result of this decision, public-interest law firms can now take an aggressive role in informing their client constituencies of legal wrongs and the availability of legal recourse. The NAACP and the Inc. Fund served as the lightning rod for this aggressive action.

Today the civil rights defense funds represent the interests of numerous groups that cannot fully protect their rights through the political process. Although the massive scope of the success in *Brown* dwarfs nearly every other victory since 1954, the civil rights defense funds are still a vital element of the public-interest law community.

Freestanding Public-Interest Law Firms. The most recent entry into the public-interest arena is the freestanding public-interest law firm. Some of these offices specialize in specific areas, such as environmental law. Other law firms handle a wide variety of legal problems. These newer public-interest law firms tend to be relatively small, generally with less than ten attorneys on staff. They also tend to be less hierarchical in structure than their private law firm counterparts. On the negative side, attorneys in these firms tend to be paid less than half the salary they could command in private practice. Despite that fact, they must work as hard as the private bar under far less glamorous and often more trying circumstances.

The key reason for the growth of this network of public-interest law offices is the ability for such lawyers to create a situation in which their legal practice is an extension of their political and philosophical beliefs. Lawyers in such firms can, and frequently do, decline representation in cases that are inconsistent with this value system. Law under such circumstances is viewed as a way not merely to achieve client goals but to realize shared client-attorney goals through client representation. This element, which is present to a greater or lesser extent in all public-interest advocacy, is not without its pitfalls. For example, lawyers have an ethical responsibility to allow their clients to make decisions regarding the handling of their cases. If a settlement offer is made to a client that will address that client's individual needs but will not achieve broader goals, a conflict of interests must be solved.

This problem is not unique to public-interest lawyers. Attorneys in class actions must protect the interests of their individual named clients as well as the class members that those individuals purport to represent. Unfortunately, the interests of the individual and the class may not necessarily be identical. For that reason, court supervision exists in such class actions to ensure that actual conflicts will not prejudice either group. No similar impartial supervisor is available in public-interest law, however. Moreover, public-interest clients may be especially at risk in such potential conflicts because they are often poorly educated and may be excessively deferential to advocates on their behalf. While public-interest lawyers have not found a simple solution to this problem, nearly all public-interest law firms have taken steps to ensure that individual client interests are not sacrificed to broader concerns.

The potential for conflict in public-interest law received national media attention in the case of *Westmoreland* v. *Columbia Broadcasting System* (1984). General William Westmoreland was represented by the Capital Legal Foundation, a conservative public-interest law firm that was funded for this case through conservative foundation support. By most informed views, Westmoreland could not achieve a victory against CBS because of the constitutional impediments to recovery for defamation of a public figure.

The Capital Legal Foundation has long supported efforts to challenge coverage of the news by so-called liberal media. The desire to further this political view may have overtaken the Foundation's obligation to advise the general of the likely legal consequences of litigation and the effect on his reputation. This illustrates that public-interest lawyers across the political spectrum will continue to grapple with the potential for conflict.

FUNDING PUBLIC-INTEREST LAW

As with any other legal practitioners, public-interest lawyers must pay salaries, rent, and other expenses. Just as the types of public-interest law firms vary from practice to practice, so do the funding approaches utilized by these firms. Many firms use a combination of revenue sources. Although the funding approaches described in this section have led to an enormous increase in the number and type of public-interest law firms, funding remains a critical concern for most organizations. As United States Supreme Court Justice Thurgood Marshall noted in 1975:

> Public interest law practice has had one major problem: funding. Almost by definition, public interest lawyers represent persons or groups who cannot compete in the ordinary market for legal services. Often the cost of public interest lawyering exceeds the *economic* benefit to the *individual* client. In these circumstances, the funding of public interest law is a problem without an easy solution.

Attorney's Fees for Private Attorneys General. During the initial surge in public-interest law, one of the brightest funding possibilities was the "private attorney general" theory of attorney's fees. Attorney's fees are not generally available for prevailing parties in litigation in the United States. The private attorney general theory suggests that courts could award attorney's fees to prevailing parties in litigation brought to advance significant public interests. Attorney's fees remain an important source of income for many public-interest law firms, but the national potential of the private attorney general doctrine was dealt a crippling blow by the United States Supreme Court in 1975 in the case of *Alyeska Pipeline Service Co.* v. *Wilderness Society.*

The *Alyeska* case involved a challenge by organizations concerned with the environment to bar construction of the trans-Alaska pipeline. These organizations successfully argued that the granting of right-of-way and special land-use permits by the secretary of the interior would violate the provisions of the National Environmental Policy Act of 1969 and the Mineral Leasing Act of 1920. The environmental plaintiffs prevailed in their lawsuit. (Congress subsequently amended the legislation on which the challenge had been based.) They then sought an award of attorney's fees against the defendants.

In overturning a lower court award of fees, the Supreme Court first noted that the general "American rule" barred attorney's fees in most litigation. The Court also emphasized that the exception to the American rule permitting an award of fees against a party who acts in bad faith was inapplicable here since the defendants had proceeded in good faith. The plaintiffs had argued, and the Court of Appeals for the District of Columbia had agreed, that they were entitled to an award because they had successfully proceeded as "private attorneys general." In justifying its award, the court of appeals explained that the environmental plaintiffs had acted to vindicate important statutory rights of all citizens, had ensured that the governmental system functioned properly, and were therefore entitled to an award of fees. It explained that a denial of fees in such costly cases would deter private parties desiring to see proper administration and enforcement of the nation's laws.

Although the Supreme Court acknowledged that the other exceptions to the general American rule had been created by the courts, the Court refused to expand these exceptions. To do so, the Court stated, would be to "jettison the traditional rule against nonstatutory allowances to the prevailing party and . . . award attorneys' fees whenever the courts deem the public policy furthered by a particular statute important enough to warrant the award." The Court then concluded that this policy matter should be reserved to the Congress for further action.

Attorney's Fees Under Federal Law. The congressional response to the Supreme Court's invitation in the *Alyeska* decision was not long in coming. One year after that decision, the Congress enacted the Civil Rights Attorney's Fees Award Act. This provision has become a major source of funding for public-interest lawyers. Although not as broad as the private attorney general theory, the act does permit an award of fees to a successful plaintiff in a civil rights action. The relevant portion of the act provides that "in any action or proceeding to enforce a provision of [the civil rights statutes] . . . the court, in its discretion, may allow the prevailing party, other than the United States, a reasonable attorney's fee as part of the costs." This provision has been interpreted by the courts generally to require an award of fees to the prevailing party, absent exceptional circumstances.

Many public-interest law cases involve challenges by plaintiffs to protect significant constitutional or statutory rights guaranteed by the civil rights statutes. For example, a public-interest law firm that successfully attacks discrimination on the basis of sex in educational programs would ordinarily be entitled to a fee award. These cases might be described as the bread and butter of public-interest practice. For many pub-

908

lic-interest law firms, the Civil Rights Attorney's Fees Award Act has provided an important tool in financing public-interest law. This is especially true in light of the decision of the United States Supreme Court in *Blum* v. *Stenson* (1984). Public-interest lawyers traditionally work for salaries far below their counterparts in private practice. In *Blum* the state of New York argued that this fact should be used by the courts to reduce attorney's fees awards to public-interest law firms. The Supreme Court rejected this argument and held instead that it was the value of the work that should be rewarded. Such a reward must therefore be based on the comparable worth of the legal work performed by the attorneys for the prevailing parties, the Court concluded.

Although the government of the United States had traditionally been exempt from attorney's fees awards under federal law, it also did not escape unscathed in the wake of the *Alyeska* decision. In 1980, Congress enacted the Equal Access to Justice Act, which directed courts to award fees against the United States unless the court found that the position of the United States was substantially justified or that special circumstances made an award unjust. The parameters of the Equal Access to Justice Act were in 1986 still being defined in judicial decisions. However, the potential that it presents for public-interest lawyers seeking to force the federal government to obey its own laws is significant.

Attorney's Fees Under State Law. Not all states followed the lead of the United States Supreme Court in the *Alyeska* decision. One of these states was the state of California. At the same time that the *Alyeska* case was pending before the United States Supreme Court, the California Supreme Court was considering the validity of the private attorney general theory under California law in the case of *Serrano* v. *Priest* (1977). The *Serrano* case involved a successful challenge to the method of funding public education in California. The plaintiffs had successfully argued that the funding system discriminated against poorer school districts in violation of the equal-protection clause of the California Constitution. The plaintiffs were represented by Public Advocates, one of the original Ford Foundation–funded public-interest law firms, and the Western Center on Law and Poverty, a Legal Services Corporation–funded regional support center.

In analyzing the private attorney general the-

ory, the proponents described the rationale behind it as a way "to encourage suits effectuating a strong congressional or national policy by awarding substantial attorney's fees, regardless of defendant's conduct, to those who successfully bring such suits and thereby bring about benefits to a broad class of citizens." Initially, the California Supreme Court decided to refrain from ruling on the validity of this rationale until the United States Supreme Court ruled in *Alyeska.* After the *Alyeska* decision was announced, the burden on the public-interest plaintiffs in *Serrano* was substantially increased. The most powerful court in the country, the United States Supreme Court, had decided to defer to the legislative branch to establish such a rationale for fee awards. Many observers predicted a similar result in California.

The plaintiffs in *Serrano* did not give up, however. In a brief that was strongly supported by numerous diverse elements of the bar appearing as friends of the court, the plaintiffs again stressed the importance of the private attorney general theory and the underlying importance of the public-interest law movement:

> Because the issues involved in such litigation are often extremely complex and their presentation time-consuming and costly, the availability of representation of such public interests by private attorneys acting *pro bono publico* is limited. Only through the appearance of "public interest" law firms funded by public and foundation monies . . . has it been possible to secure representation on any large scale. The firms in question, however, are not funded to the extent necessary for the representation of all such deserving interests, and as a result many worthy causes of this nature are without adequate representation under present circumstances. One solution . . . is the award of substantial attorneys fees to those public-interest litigants and their attorneys.

The California Supreme Court accepted this argument and concluded that the public-interest law firms involved in *Serrano* had advanced a significant public interest by protecting the rights of all Californians to have public education funded consistent with the California Constitution. The fee award was then upheld as a proper exercise of judicial power when such significant constitutional rights were protected.

After the *Alyeska* decision, the United States Congress had acted to undo the holding in that decision by expanding opportunities for fee awards. After the *Serrano* decision, the California legislature had a similar opportunity to either accept or reject that ruling. The California legislature not only accepted the *Serrano* holding but greatly expanded its scope by authorizing fee awards in any case enforcing important regulatory, statutory, or constitutional guarantees affecting the public interest.

The approach adopted in California, and to a lesser extent in the federal system, has also been used in other jurisdictions. The result is an important source of renewable funding for public-interest litigation.

Government Funding. Numerous federal and state statutes have provided financial support for public-interest law activities. One significant type of support is the treatment of public-interest law firms as nonprofit charitable organizations. Through this recognition the federal and state governments subsidize public-interest law firms through the tax-deductible nature of such contributions. The federal government also provides several forms of direct support.

The most significant contribution is in the area of legal services for the poor. Since the middle 1960s, the federal government has funded organizations to provide legal services to the poor, first under the Economic Opportunity Act of 1964 and then under the Legal Services Corporation Act of 1974. This financial support now involves hundreds of millions of dollars.

The federal government also subsidizes other forms of public-interest law practice. For example, the Developmental Disabilities Assistance and Bill of Rights Act provides federal financial support for organizations to protect the rights of developmentally disabled persons. Every state now has such a protection and advocacy agency.

These agencies take several different forms. In Maryland, the protection and advocacy agency is a nonprofit corporation, the Maryland Disability Law Center. This program receives a federal grant and state and private assistance to protect disabled children and adults. For example, the Maryland agency received a complaint that a forty-three-year-old deaf woman had been confined to a Maryland state mental hospital for twenty-two years without treatment. No treatment had been provided because the facility had no ability to communicate with her. In fact, the treatment plans developed for her recommended that she learn to listen better. Along with the National Center for Law and the Deaf, a public-interest law firm funded in part by the National Association of the Deaf, a lawsuit was filed against the state of Maryland (*Doe* v. *Wilzack*, 1986). That lawsuit resulted in the creation of a specialized inpatient unit for deaf patients, expanded services for hearing-impaired persons throughout the entire mental health system, the creation of community-based mental health and housing programs for hearing-impaired persons, and compensation for the woman whose confinement had set things in motion.

At the state level, funding has been provided for public-interest lawyers to protect similarly vulnerable clients. Some states have funded public-interest law firms to protect nursing-home residents, residents in state mental hospitals, or residential centers for the mentally retarded. The goal of these ombudsman programs is to make the legal process available to those who would otherwise be unable to protect themselves.

Foundation Funding. In the spring of 1974 a meeting was convened by the Ford Foundation to consider critical issues in public-interest law. This meeting of public-interest lawyers, foundation executives, and private attorneys led to the creation of the Council for Public Interest Law. The council was cosponsored by the ABA and by three major foundations active in funding public-interest law firms—the Ford Foundation, the Edna McConnell Clark Foundation, and the Rockefeller Brothers Fund. This council served as a clearinghouse for information on developments in public-interest law and as a focus for common action. One of the primary goals was the development of secure funding sources for public-interest law practices.

The initial list of public-interest law firms funded by the Ford Foundation reads like a who's who of major litigation in the 1970s. The Center for Law in the Public Interest, the Citizens Communications Center, the Education Law Center, the Environmental Defense Fund, the Institute for Public Interest Representation, the International Project, the League of Women Voters Education Fund, the Legal Action Center of New York, Public Advocates, the Sierra Club Legal Defense Fund, the Women's Law Fund, the Women's Rights Project, and the Research Center for the Defense of Public Interests all

910

grew out of the first wave of increased Ford Foundation funding. Other public-interest law firms, such as the Center for Law and Social Policy, were added in the next few years.

Since the late 1970s, foundation funding for public-interest law has not significantly increased. This has inhibited further growth in this segment of the legal community. Two factors have contributed to this effect. First, economic conditions in the late 1970s and early 1980s had a significant effect on the available funds of many foundations. Second, as with other foundation activities, foundation funding for public-interest law was seen as seed money to test out new ideas and new approaches. Generally, foundation support does not exceed three years.

The hope of these foundation-funded programs was that other funding sources would take the place of foundation funding once the success of public-interest law activity had been demonstrated. Unfortunately, that goal has not been fully realized. As a result, many foundation-supported programs have been forced to greatly scale back operations in the 1980s.

Membership Support. Another common source of funding for public-interest law is membership support. Since public-interest law firms generally qualify as nonprofit charitable organizations under the Internal Revenue Code, contributions to such organizations are tax-exempt. This aspect has been featured in fund-raising efforts by many public-interest law firms. This feature also points up the reason why public-interest law firms fought so hard against the more restrictive guidelines proposed by the IRS in 1970.

Some public-interest law firms, such as the Southern Poverty Law Center, have made concerted efforts to build up national membership bases to finance their activities. Unlike many membership organizations, the membership in such a public-interest law firm is rather removed from the setting of program priorities. However, even with such a broad-based membership, accountability for program activities may be felt through reduced contributions in response to specific program activities. For example, contributions to the American Civil Liberties Union (ACLU) suffered significantly after it sued the city of Skokie, Illinois, to force the city to grant permits to allow the American Nazi party to march.

Membership support may also take a slightly different form. Some preexisting membership organizations utilize legal advocacy as an additional tool for achieving some of their goals. A public-interest law firm may then closely align with its parent organization or may simply represent one type of activity of that parent organization. The initial development of the Inc. Fund is an example of the former type of approach. The National Association for the Advancement of Colored People (NAACP) is a membership organization that saw legal advocacy as a tool for combating discrimination. Later, the Inc. Fund was spun off as a separate organization for tax reasons. Eventually, the Inc. Fund formed its own membership base to help support its activities. By contrast, the Sierra Club Defense Fund has remained closely aligned with its parent organization, the Sierra Club. The ACLU is an example of the latter model. It receives most of its funding through membership support. Members concerned with protection of the Bill of Rights support the organization to litigate, to lobby, and to engage in other activities to advance organization goals. In this model, litigation is simply one facet of the organization.

Membership is an important form of financial support for many public-interest law firms. However, efforts to establish such a membership base have not been uniformly successful. In addition, fund-raising efforts can be extremely costly.

Law School Funding. Another funding model used by some public-interest law firms utilizes law school support. A public-interest law firm may be established as part of a school's clinical law program or may be viewed as a vehicle for channeling social responsibilities of faculty and students. Sometimes the public-interest law firm combines both of these goals.

The Institute for Public Interest Representation (INSPIRE) is an example of this type of funding model. Originally established with Ford Foundation support, INSPIRE is affiliated with Georgetown University Law School. Staff attorneys in the law firm also serve on the school's faculty. Students receive credit for working in the law firm and also gain valuable experience.

The Center for Law and Social Policy developed an even more ambitious approach. The center established a structured legal education program in 1970 in cooperation with five law schools—Yale University, the University of Pennsylvania, the University of California at Los Angeles, Stanford University, and the University of Michigan. Students spend clinical semesters at the center. Through these externships the students gain valuable practical experience and the law firm expands its resources for public-interest legal work.

Private Bar Support. In addition to the contributions to public-interest law made by private attorneys who provide legal representation at a reduced fee or for free, many bar associations have provided direct financial support for public-interest law activities. Probably the oldest form of such support is the bar-supported legal aid society. These programs, which long predate federally funded legal services for the poor, traditionally provided legal representation for indigents in such areas as family law. In some areas, these programs still exist. In others, they have been merged with the Legal Services Corporation–funded program in that area.

In 1971 the Beverly Hills Bar Association decided to utilize a somewhat different approach by establishing the Beverly Hills Bar Association Foundation. This public-interest law firm is supported by the bar association in several ways. Initial onetime start-up money was provided directly by the bar association. Ongoing financial support for the foundation was provided through solicitation of contributions from private firms. In addition, private bar staff resources are made available to supplement and assist the bar foundation staff.

Interest on Lawyer Trust Accounts. The newest, and perhaps the most encouraging, form of financial support for public-interest law comes from interest on lawyer trust accounts (IOLTA). Lawyers are required to maintain trust accounts to ensure that client funds are not commingled with funds belonging to the law practice. These client funds are deposited to pay for such costs as filing fees, expert-witness fees, and other litigation costs. Client funds generally are kept in these trust accounts for short periods of time before they are disbursed. Since the amount of monies belonging to any one client are generally small and since the amount of time that these monies remain in the account is generally short, it has traditionally been very difficult to identify interest attributable to any single client. For that reason, client trust funds were traditionally maintained in non-interest-bearing escrow accounts.

Under the leadership of the Florida bar, lawyers in that state received authorization to deposit these client funds in interest-bearing accounts. Interest generated by these accounts is then transferred to a quasi-public entity. That entity distributes the IOLTA monies to support such public-interest law activities as legal services for the poor.

Following Florida's lead, many other states have now implemented IOLTA programs. Since clients did not receive interest from these accounts previously, the IOLTA model has proven to be a relatively painless way of providing financial support for public-interest law. Millions of dollars are now being generated by IOLTA programs, and the funding will only increase in the years ahead. Moreover, since most IOLTA distributions are in the form of continuing grants, IOLTA-supported programs do not face the periodic vagaries of funding from other sources.

TOOLS OF THE PUBLIC-INTEREST LAWYER

Private attorneys use a variety of tools on behalf of their clients. Client counseling, negotiating, and administrative advocacy all are utilized to advance client goals. Litigation is viewed as only one weapon in a varied and effective arsenal available to advance private interests. Although public-interest attorneys were aware of these other approaches, it took some time to lessen an excessive public-interest law focus on litigation on behalf of clients. In fact, this lesson was not brought home to many public-interest law firms until they saw hard-earned legal victories in the courts being overturned by simple changes in federal or state legislation or in administrative agency regulations.

One of the public-interest law firms that led the way in utilizing a multifaceted approach was the Children's Defense Fund (CDF). This Washington-based organization was begun as a spin-off from the NAACP Legal Defense Fund. Originally known as the Washington Research Project, it was created because of the belief of its director that an ongoing Washington presence was necessary to address public-interest goals effectively. In the case of CDF, those goals include increasing access to quality health care for pregnant women and for children, protecting children in foster care from abuse and neglect, and improving public educational programs for low-income children.

One of the best examples of a multidisciplinary approach to public-interest advocacy is CDF's work to improve health care for poor children through the Medicaid program. This program provides federal financial assistance to states willing to follow federal guidelines in reimbursing health care providers for health services provided to eligible children and adults. In 1967 a new federal requirement was added to the Medicaid statute. That requirement mandated states to provide early and periodic screening, diagnosis, and treatment (EPSDT) for children under the age of twenty-one.

This new program was not greeted with enthusiasm at the Department of Health, Education, and Welfare (HEW), the federal agency charged with implementing its requirements. Since implementing regulations would be needed before states could reasonably be expected to comply with EPSDT requirements, CDF staff began urging the department to initiate rule making. When HEW continued to drag its feet, CDF, in conjunction with the National Health Law Program, filed litigation against the secretary of Health, Education, and Welfare to force him to publish regulations for the EPSDT program. That litigation in 1971, *National Welfare Rights Organization* v. *Weinberger,* was ultimately successful in forcing the publication of federal regulations.

At this point, initial efforts at administrative advocacy (agency lobbying) had proven unsuccessful. Litigation had achieved the desired goals. The focus now shifted back to administrative advocacy to try to obtain the best possible set of EPSDT regulations. Frequent contacts with agency staff and regular public meetings finally resulted in the issuance of acceptable, if not ideal, regulations in 1971. CDF utilized administrative advocacy and legislative advocacy at the state level to secure state implementation of these new regulations. Neighborhood legal-services offices and other organizations across the nation were enlisted in this effort.

Again, a multifaceted approach was utilized. Some states that were generally receptive to the EPSDT program were persuaded to implement the program through lobbying of the agencies administering the Medicaid programs in those states. Other states proved far more recalcitrant. In these states, litigation often proved necessary. In most cases, these lawsuits were filed in conjunction with local legal-services programs.

While this national implementation effort was under way, CDF also recognized that the importance of the program needed to be emphasized in Congress and in the federal bureaucracy. A national research project culminated in the publication in 1977 by CDF staff of *EPSDT: Does It Spell Health Care for Poor Children?* The media attention generated by the publication of this report helped increase public awareness of the program and provided an effective tool for improvement in the program. Again, two approaches were utilized for improving the program. Initial efforts were begun to improve the federal legislation governing the program. Several congressmen and senators were persuaded to introduce legislation to establish a new program—the Child Health Assurance Program, or CHAP. At the same time, efforts continued to improve the program through regulatory reform.

Legislative efforts over nearly ten years culminated in 1984 with the passage of the CHAP legislation. This program expanded the prior EPSDT program to include additional hundreds of thousands of children and pregnant women. The effort to improve access to health care will continue as administrative advocacy will be necessary to ensure the best possible regulations under the CHAP program, as litigation will likely be necessary to ensure that states and the federal government fully comply with the statutory requirements, and as research will be necessary to monitor implementation and to identify areas needing improvement.

The lesson of this and similar efforts is that it is generally not possible to achieve desired results in a single test case. Public-interest lawyers cannot assume that a problem is solved simply because a case is won. Frequently, a victory is only the start of a long battle for change.

CONCLUSION

When public-interest law burst on the scene in the late 1960s, an almost limitless future was predicted for it. After the setback in the *Alyeska* case, many of these same observers predicted that public-interest law would disappear from the American legal scene. Both of these predictions were wrong. As public-interest law came through its adolescence in the mid-1970s, it developed a more realistic assessment of its potential impact on the American legal system. That impact is already reflected in an increased accountability of government institutions to the public. At the same time, in its newfound maturity, public-interest law continues to grapple with fundamental questions regarding the nature of this area of the law. Probably foremost among these is the question of how to ensure public accountability for the work engaged in by these independent entities so that the public good and the welfare of the whole are truly advanced.

CASES

Alyeska Pipeline Service Co. v. Wilderness Society, 421 U.S. 240 (1975)
Blum v. Stenson, 465 U.S. 886 (1984)
Brown v. Board of Education, 347 U.S. 483 (1954)
Doe v. Wilzack, Civil Action No. H83-2409 (D. Md. 1986)
NAACP v. Button, 371 U.S. 415 (1963)
National Welfare Rights Organization v. Weinberger, Civil Action No. 2091-71 (D.D.C. 1971)
Plumas County v. Califano, 594 F.2d 756 (9th Cir. 1979)
Serrano v. Priest, 20 Cal. 3d 25, 569 P.2d 1303, 141 Cal. Rptr. 315 (1977)
Shelley v. Kraemer, 334 U.S. 1 (1948)
Westmoreland v. Columbia Broadcasting System, 601 F. Supp. 66 (S.D.N.Y. 1984)

BIBLIOGRAPHY

American Bar Association, "Implementing the Lawyer's Public Interest Practice Obligation," in *American Bar Association Journal*, 63 (1977), discusses the ethical issues underlying public-interest obligations of attorneys. H. Craig Becker, "In Defense of an Embattled Mode of Advocacy: An Analysis and Justification of Public Interest Practice," in *Yale Law Journal*, 90 (1981), strongly defends public-interest lawyers, especially legal-service attorneys, from the attacks undertaken by conservatives during the early 1980s. Edward Berlin, Anthony Roisman, and Gladys Kessler, "Public Interest Law," in *George Washington Law Review*, 38 (1970), describes the work within a small private law firm practicing public-interest law in Washington, D.C.

Martin Bierbaum, "On the Frontiers of Public Interest Law: The New Jersey State Department of the Public Advocate—The Public Interest Advocacy Division," in *Seton Hall Law Review*, 13 (1983), describes the law establishing the New Jersey Public Advocate and the initial accomplishments

of that office. Robert Borosage et al., "The New Public Interest Lawyers," in *Yale Law Journal*, 79 (1970), interviews many of the founders of public-interest law firms in the late 1960s and through these interviews analyzes many of the issues that public-interest lawyers continue to face. Steven Brill, "Doing Well by Doing Good," in *Esquire*, 1 August 1978, describes the public-interest work performed at one of Washington's major private law firms. Edgar S. Cahn and Jean C. Cahn, "The War on Poverty: A Civilian Perspective," in *Yale Law Journal*, 73 (1964), provides the philosophical underpinnings for the development of neighborhood legal services offices; and "Power to the People or the Profession? The Public Interest in Public Interest Law," in *Yale Law Journal*, 79 (1970), discusses some of the philosophical dilemmas facing public-interest lawyers.

Charles Halpern, "Public Interest Law: Its Past and Future," in *Judicature*, 58 (1974), describes the early accomplishments of public-interest law firms and discusses major issues for public-interest lawyers. Charles Halpern and John Cunningham, "Reflections on the New Public Interest Law: Theory and Practice at the Center for Law and Social Policy," in *Georgetown Law Journal*, 59 (1971), describes work at the Center for Law and Social Policy, one of the early Ford Foundation–funded public-interest law firms. Joel Handler et al., "The Public Interest Activities of Private Practice Lawyers," in *American Bar Association Journal*, 61 (1975), discusses the need to fund public-interest law firms through foundation and bar support.

Sanford M. Jaffe, "Public Interest Law: Five Years Later," in *American Bar Association Journal*, 62 (1976), details some of the accomplishments of public-interest law firms and some of the questions raised by public-interest practices. Gerald Lubenow, "The Action Lawyers," in *Saturday Review*, 26 August 1972, reviews some of the accomplishments by the new breed of public-interest lawyers. Thurgood Marshall, "Financing Public Interest Law Practice: The Role of the Organized Bar," in *American Bar Association Journal*, 61 (1975), argues that the organized bar must expand its support for public interest law. Michael Meltsner and Philip Schrag, *Public Interest Advocacy: Materials for Clinical Legal Education* (1974), a textbook for law students interested in public-interest advocacy, discusses many of the issues faced by public-interest lawyers.

Mitchell Rogovin, "Public Interest Law: The Next Horizon," in *American Bar Association Journal*, 63 (1977), discusses the need to increase organized bar support for public-interest practices. A. O. Sulzberger, Jr., "The Naderites of the Other Side," in *New York Times*, 30 September 1979, describes the work of the conservative public-interest law firms. Washington Research Project, *EPSDT: Does It Spell Health Care for Poor Children?* (1977), is the influential EPSDT report. Stephen Wexler, "Practicing Law for Poor People," in *Yale Law Journal*, 79 (1970), describes the work of a public-interest lawyer serving as counsel to the National Welfare Rights Organization.

[*See also* ADVERSARY SYSTEM; LAW AND SOCIAL SCIENCE; LEGAL PROFESSION AND LEGAL ETHICS; *and* RACIAL DISCRIMINATION AND EQUAL OPPORTUNITY.]

SENTENCING ALTERNATIVES

Elyce Zenoff

THE sentence is the penalty society exacts from an offender who has been found guilty of a crime after a public trial conducted in conformity with various rights guaranteed defendants by the Constitution. What sentence is given a particular offender depends on a variety of factors, including the objectives of the criminal justice system, constitutional and statutory limitations, the seriousness of the offense, and characteristics of the offender.

Condemnation, retribution, incapacitation, deterrence, and rehabilitation are generally asserted to be objectives of the criminal justice system. However, these objectives usually have not been specified in legislation or court decisions because there is no public consensus on which objective is paramount. In contrast to today's objectives, restitution to the victims was the primary goal in ancient civilization. Later, retribution became the principal objective. But in the eighteenth century, deterrence was advanced as the most appropriate goal and remained so until the twentieth century, when rehabilitation increasingly became recognized as the major, if not the only, appropriate goal of the criminal justice system. Since the mid-1970s, however, because of a large increase in reported crime, especially violent crime, and the belief that efforts to rehabilitate offenders had been unsuccessful, increasing emphasis has been placed on the objectives of retribution, incapacitation, and deterrence. Concurrently, there is also increased interest in the victim's needs, and so, for the first time in several hundred years, restitution is increasingly mentioned as a sentencing objective.

ACTORS IN THE SENTENCING PROCESS

Most people think of the judge as the person responsible for sentencing. However, there are a host of other actors—the legislature, victim, prosecutor, jury, probation officer, and clinicians—who either make a contribution to the initial sentencing decision or have the power to subsequently modify that decision. Legislatures initiate the sentencing process by deciding what activities are to be considered criminal. By denominating those activities that are criminal, legislatures determine whether any criminal sanction can be imposed for engaging in, or refraining from, that behavior. Provisions in the state or federal constitution may limit the legislature's power to enact criminal laws. For example, a legislature cannot make it a crime to criticize the government, because the law would violate the First Amendment guarantee of freedom of speech. A second limit on the freedom of the legislature to criminalize or to increase or reduce penalties from various activities is public opinion. The decriminalization of sexual relations between consenting adults and the relaxation of marijuana laws have been responses to such public pressures, as has the adoption of more severe penalties for drunk driving.

Legislatures also play a major role in sentencing by setting the limit for the sanctions that may be applied to various crimes. It is the legislature that decides whether an offense is punishable by incarceration or a fine or whether capital punishment may be imposed for murder. Similarly, the legislature decides whether the sanction of probation can be used for a particular offense or for recidivists. The legislature also decides, at least in the first instance, whether sentences for multiple offenses are to be served concurrently or consecutively.

How much sentencing authority judges should exercise is also a legislative decision. The legislature may delegate a great deal of authority to the judge. For example, the judge may be allowed to impose a sentence of from one to twenty years for robbery. On the other hand, the legislature may arrogate most of the sentencing power to itself, allowing the judge to decide only whether the offender is to serve four, five, or six years in prison. Still another alternative used by some legislatures is to divide sentencing responsibility between the judge and an administrative agency. Under this type of system, the judge sets the maximum sentence within legislative guidelines, but the sentence may be shortened by a parole agency.

Although it was commonplace during the nineteenth century for juries to impose sentences, juries now sentence in noncapital cases in only a handful of states. The American Bar Association (ABA) and many other national legal groups have strongly protested the practice of jury sentencing, because jurors have no chance to acquire sentencing expertise. In capital cases, however, this practice is preferred, but not required, by the United States Supreme Court.

By choosing whether or not to report a crime, the victim is instrumental in determining whether an offender will receive any sanction for the crime. The crime of rape, for example, may be undetected or unpunished because many victims do not notify the police or are unwilling to testify. In the past, victims had no role after guilt was determined. Now, however, a number of jurisdictions permit victims to testify at the sentencing hearing.

The prosecutor may influence the sentence before and after the trial. If an offender is charged with several offenses, the prosecutor may decide to seek convictions on one, two, or all of them. Also, the prosecutor selects the exact crime with which the suspect is to be charged. Choosing between a prosecution for murder and manslaughter may make a significant difference in the penalty imposed upon conviction. Recommending a sentence to the judge after conviction of the offender is a third way in which the prosecutor can influence the sentence.

But perhaps the most influential role that prosecutors play in the sentencing process is in plea bargaining. The overwhelming majority of defendants plead guilty, often as the result of a plea bargain. The defendant frequently is willing to admit responsibility for an offense for which a lighter sentence is imposed, instead of taking the risk of being convicted of a more serious crime. The prosecutor may accept the plea to the lesser charge in preference to a time-consuming trial and the always present chance of an acquittal. This process is called charge bargaining. Charge bargaining also occurs when the defendant pleads guilty to one charge in return for an agreement to dismiss other charges. A third type of plea bargaining involves the situation in which an offender admits guilt to the offense charged in exchange for the prosecutor's recommendation of a light sentence.

The probation officer usually compiles information about the offender's criminal record, background, and personal characteristics for the judge's consideration in designing the sentence. In some jurisdictions the report also contains the probation officer's opinion about the appropriate sentence.

If an offender is placed on probation, a probation officer monitors his activities. If the probationer violates any of the conditions of probation, the officer decides whether the violation should be reported to the judge. Accordingly, the probation officer may stimulate a change in the offender's sentence because the report may result in the revocation of the probation and the imposition of a jail or prison sentence by the judge.

Increasingly, judges request a psychiatric or psychological evaluation of an offender in order to obtain information about the type of rehabilitative program an offender needs and about his "dangerousness." Consequently, the opinion expressed by the clinician may influence the choice of sanction, probation, imprisonment, the death penalty, or the length of the sentence the offender receives.

The president of the United States, governors, and parole boards usually are not thought of as having a role in sentencing, because they do not make initial sentencing decisions. However, they are able to modify the decision. For example, the president has the power to pardon federal offenders. He also has the power to remit fines, penalties, and forfeitures and the power to commute sentences. A commutation moderates a sentence, while a pardon completely absolves the offender of guilt and restores him to the legal position of a defendant who has been acquitted. Governors have similar clemency powers over persons convicted of violating state laws. Although clemency powers were once exercised frequently, they have been replaced to a large extent by the practice of parole.

In most states, the parole board may shorten the time served in prison by releasing prisoners to the community under supervision. The amount of time a person must serve before becoming eligible for parole varies from state to state. In some states and the federal system, the parole board's authority to decide when an offender should be released has been eliminated.

The final and most recent actor in the post-sentencing process is the offender. In many states the offender may have his prison term reduced substantially by complying with "good time" policies. In some states the offender can earn the reduction simply by maintaining good behavior, but in others he must participate in educational or training programs to accrue good time.

SENTENCING PROCEDURES

Criminal trials, where guilt or innocence is determined, are governed by a variety of rules required by the Constitution, legislation, or court rules of criminal procedure. Most of these rules, however, do not apply at the sentencing stage. For example, in most jurisdictions the defendant has the right to exclude illegally obtained evidence and to cross-examine witnesses at trial but not at sentencing. Sentencing procedures can be best examined by dividing them into three stages: the presentence investigation, the sentencing hearing, and postsentence review.

The belief that the sentence should be designed to "fit the offender," as well as "fit the crime," is the reason for the presentence investigation. Typically, immediately after a verdict or plea of guilty, the judge asks a probation officer to investigate the offender's criminal and social history and to present a report of the results. The goal of this report is to assist the judge in

evaluating the risk of allowing the defendant to remain in the community or in determining the length of the period of incarceration. The typical report contains the defendant's criminal history, with all official records of prior convictions; details of the offense, including the police version (from police records), the defendant's version, and statements of the victim, witnesses, and codefendants; biographical information, including family, school, employment, military, and marital data obtained from records and statements of the offender's friends, acquaintances, and relatives; treatment plan resources, especially if probation is the recommended or likely sentence; and recommendation of the probation officer.

In the past the defendant was not entitled to know the contents of a presentence report. However, an increasing number of jurisdictions now require its partial or complete disclosure. In the federal system, for example, disclosure is required, but information obtained by a promise of confidentiality, information diagnostic in nature, and information that if disclosed could be harmful to the offender or others may be withheld, but the defendant must be given a summary of any withheld information upon which the judge expects to rely in determining the sentence.

After the presentence report has been submitted to the judge, the sentencing hearing takes place. In the past, it was a brief, informal proceeding. The offender merely was asked if he had anything to say before the sentence was announced, and the offender's lawyer, if he had one, made an appeal for leniency. Then the judge would announce the sentence.

The sentencing phase of the trial is now more structured and formalized. Representation by counsel at the sentencing hearing has been recognized as a constitutional right (*Mempa* v. *Ray,* 1967), and counsel now take a more active role at this stage than they did in the past. It is now common for the offender's attorney to present witnesses and to offer a treatment plan. The prosecutor also has a more extended role at sentencing and may present witnesses and make a sentencing recommendation to the judge. Victims, too, now often participate in the sentencing hearing.

Offenders have more rights at sentencing when the death penalty is a possible sanction. For example, in capital cases the Supreme Court has held that the presentence report must be disclosed to the offender or the offender's counsel prior to the sentencing hearing, the offender must be allowed to introduce any mitigating evidence, and appellate review of death sentences is required (*Gardner* v. *Florida*, 1977; *Bell* v. *Ohio*, 1978; and *Gregg* v. *Georgia*, 1976).

In addition to requiring the probation officer's presentence report, some states authorize a psychiatric examination of the offender as part of the presentence procedure. At least in death penalty cases, where the defendant's dangerousness is at issue, the Supreme Court has determined that due process entitles the defendant to a presentence psychiatric examination on this issue, the assistance of a psychiatrist in preparing for the sentencing hearing, and the psychiatrist's testimony at the hearing (*Ake* v. *Oklahoma*, 1985).

The third stage of sentencing, the post-sentence review, was unavailable in most jurisdictions before 1970. Extensive criticism of sentencing disparity during that decade produced a significant change in the law. More than half of the states now authorize appellate review of sentences in at least some circumstances, and in the remaining jurisdictions, the failure to develop such measures seems to be the result of inertia, not opposition.

In 1986, sentence review was so new that most states were still trying to devise appropriate procedures for it. Despite the lack of detailed procedures, there was general acceptance of the view that the same courts that decide other appeals should handle sentence appeals and that substantially similar procedures should be used.

There has been considerable controversy over the issue of whether the government as well as the defendant should be allowed to appeal a sentence. However, the ABA, whose views have been influential with legislatures and courts in criminal justice matters, has taken the position that the prosecution should not be able to appeal a sentence on the grounds that it is too lenient. Nor would the ABA permit the reviewing court to increase a sentence, only to reduce or affirm it.

TYPES OF SENTENCES

A judge may choose from a variety of sanctions, including death, incarceration, probation, restitution to the victim, and fines, when designing a sentence. The judge's choice of a penalty is limited by the applicable statute, and both the judge and the legislature are restricted in their choice of sanction by the state and the federal Constitution. For example, the Constitution specifically prohibits the passage of bills of attainder and ex post facto laws. A bill of attainder is a legislative act that inflicts punishment without a judicial trial, while an ex post facto law is one that imposes punishment for an act that was not a crime at the time it was committed. A law that imposed more severe punishment than that permitted at the time of the crime would also be an ex post facto law.

Cruel and unusual punishments also are prohibited by the Constitution. There are three ways in which this prohibition affects sanctions. First, it limits the method of punishment that may be imposed. Branding an offender, cutting off his hand, or depriving him of citizenship would be considered cruel and unusual punishment.

The second way in which the Eighth Amendment affects sanctions is that it limits the amount of punishment that may be used. For example, six years in prison for cutting flowers in a public park would be out of all proportion to the offense committed.

The third restriction is a prohibition against any penalty in some circumstances. This was illustrated by the Supreme Court when it said that even one day in prison would not be allowed as punishment for having a cold (*Robinson* v. *California*, 1962).

Capital Punishment. The most severe sanction, the death penalty, cannot be imposed for most offenses. Thirty-seven states and the federal government allow imposition of a death sentence for certain types of murder, currently the only offense that the Supreme Court has recognized as warranting the death sentence, which therefore cannot be said to violate the cruel and unusual punishment clause (*Gregg*). Two sentencing objectives, retribution and deterrence, justify this sanction.

Most states allow the death penalty for persons who have been convicted of murder as minors; between 1975 and 1985, at least eighteen youngsters received this sentence, and at least one of those sentences was carried out. By 1985 the Court had not decided the constitutionality of this penalty for minors.

Although a few states authorize capital punishment for other crimes, such as kidnapping, the constitutionality of such statutes is doubtful because in 1977 the Supreme Court forbade the use of the death penalty for rape on the grounds that the victim did not die (*Coker* v. *Georgia,* 1977). Under this reasoning, treason and espionage, when they result in death, may be the only offenses other than murder for which the death penalty will be approved.

Incarceration. Incarceration is the most frequently imposed sanction for serious criminal offenses. There are four rationales for its employment: deterrence of other potential offenders, protection of society by the incapacitation of offenders, rehabilitation of the offender, and retribution for the crime.

Authorized periods of incarceration or confinement vary from a few months to life imprisonment. Historically, confinement was always in a correctional facility and was a full-time penalty. Since the 1960s, there have been variations both in the place and the extent of confinement. It is now not uncommon to hear of "confinement in the community" and "partial confinement."

Although it is generally agreed that the length of incarceration should correspond to the seriousness of the crime, it is well known that the penalty structure of many states does not meet this goal. Some states have revised their laws to rectify this situation, and others will undoubtedly follow their lead. One method is to divide all the offenses into five or six groups, each group containing crimes of similar seriousness, and to assign sanctions accordingly. Table 1 illustrates this approach.

It is also well documented that the length of confinement imposed by sentences in the United States is longer than in the rest of the Western world. However, this disparity may be reduced because of extensive use in America of parole and "good time" to shorten the incarceration period.

Life imprisonment, which frequently means a period of twenty or thirty years instead of the actual life of a particular offender, is normally reserved for violent offenses, such as murder, rape, and kidnapping. However, in many states life imprisonment may also be imposed on offenders who have been sentenced on three or more occasions, even if their crimes were neither violent nor involved a substantial amount of property. The propriety of imposing this severe penalty for the repetition of other than very serious crimes is beginning to be questioned both on policy and constitutional grounds. The sanction of life imprisonment for three thefts of less than $100, for example, may be found to be disproportionate and thus offend the Constitution's prohibition against cruel and unusual punishment.

The states employ a variety of systems to determine the length of the prison term to be imposed. The legislature, the courts, and the parole authorities have differing degrees of control over whether the offender must be imprisoned, and, if so, the length of the sentence, depending on which type of system is in operation in that state.

In some instances a judge may be required to sentence an offender to prison. Forty-three states mandate a prison term for certain violent crimes, such as murder and rape. Other common mandatory prison laws include the use of a gun while committing a crime (in 1985, thirty-seven states and the District of Columbia) and narcotics offenses (twenty-nine states and the District of Columbia). In addition, these mandatory-imprisonment laws frequently specify a minimum term of imprisonment.

Some states use an indeterminate sentencing system. In those states, the judge sets a minimum and a maximum term to be served (for example, five to ten years). Within the range set by the judge, the parole agency decides the actual time of release and therefore determines the actual time to be served. Instead of the judge speculating at the time of sentencing when the offender will be sufficiently rehabilitated to deserve release, the correctional authorities make this determination, presumably on the basis of prison behavior.

If a state has a determinate sentencing system,

TABLE 1
Offense Levels and Penalties

Class of Offense	Maximum Term
A level	Life
B level	20 years
C level	10 years
D level	5 years
E level	1 year
F level	6 months

the judge sets a fixed term, which must be served in full. Under this system, parole officials do not have the authority to release the prisoner before the expiration of the sentence. One form of determinate sentencing is called presumptive sentencing. In presumptive sentencing, a convicted offender always will receive a particular sentence assigned to the offense committed, unless the judge finds that specified aggravating or mitigating factors exist that should lengthen or shorten the sentence by a specific amount. Any deviation from this pattern must be justified by the sentencing judge in a written opinion, which is subject to review by an appeals court. In 1985 nine states used determinate sentencing.

Some states employ a sentencing guideline system, under which the judge is to consider both the severity of the offense committed and the offender's criminal history in designing the sentence. These guidelines are used to form tables, which provide recommended sentences to the judge. Approximately ten states have such guidelines.

An offender sentenced to a term of imprisonment is usually able to serve a portion of that term outside the prison, by means of either parole or good-time reduction. All but the nine determinate-sentencing states allow the parole authorities to release an offender prior to the expiration of his sentence. During the remainder of the sentence, paroled offenders remain subject to the parole system and under the supervision of a parole officer. Parole may be revoked and the offender returned to prison if any of the conditions of the parole release are violated.

Of the states that allow parole, about one-fourth allow it at any time during the sentence, within the discretion of the parole board. Other states require that a specified portion of the sentence be served before the prisoner can be considered for parole. Still others require a minimum term to be served before the prisoner is eligible for parole. Fifteen jurisdictions use parole guidelines, similar to sentencing guidelines, to assist the parole authorities in making the parole decision.

Time actually spent in prison may also be reduced by involving other policies, collectively referred to as good-time programs. Even states that do not allow for early release on parole reduce the period of incarceration through good time. The maximum amount of good time that can be awarded varies widely from state to state, with extremes ranging from five to forty-five days for each month served.

Partial Incarceration. Partial incarceration is a relatively new sanction, lying between total incarceration of the offender and leaving him free to live in the community. It has several forms. In one, the offender is never totally incarcerated but is placed in a jail or prison only in the evening and/or on weekends. The purpose of this sanction is to allow the offender to support himself and his family or to enable him to earn money to make restitution for his offense. A variation of this sanction would permit the offender to be placed in a halfway house in the community, which is supervised by correctional personnel. Although not free to live where he chooses, the offender has more freedom than if he were in jail or prison.

Some states allow partial incarceration only after the offender has spent some time in total incarceration. Still another variation is sentencing the offender to prison but allowing him, usually after having served some of his sentence, to leave the correctional facility for a part of each day to work, receive employment training, or to attend school.

Probation. Probation is a sanction that does not involve confinement but imposes conditions and allows the judge to retain authority over the offender, to modify the conditions of the sentence, or to resentence the offender if its conditions are violated. It is essentially a twentieth-century development.

Two separate rationales are offered for the use of probation sanctions. For one group of offenders, probation is imposed primarily for symbolic reasons, while for the second group, probation putatively serves rehabilitative goals. For the first group, a judge uses probation because no further criminal conduct is anticipated, yet considerations of restitution and deterrence require some sanction. The judge will use probation for the second group when it is thought that the offender needs some supervision and treatment, which in the opinion of the judge can be provided in the community.

During the term of probation, which seldom exceeds five years, the offender must abide by all of the conditions set down by the sentencing judge. These conditions are usually related to the crime for which the offender was convicted. For example, those convicted of drug abuse may be required to participate in a clinic or hospital treatment program. If the conditions are violated or another crime is committed, the judge may revoke probation and impose another sentence.

The probationer remains under the supervision of a probation official to whom the offender usually must make regular visits. Ideally, the probation officer is to aid in the rehabilitation of the offender. The official is also responsible for notifying the court of any probation violations which warrant the court's attention. Probation is often combined with other types of sentences, such as a fine or restitution.

Restitution. Restitution is another sentencing alternative available to a judge. Restitution can be defined as court-ordered compensation to the offender's victim for damage caused by the offender's criminal conduct. Most often, restitution entails actual financial compensation to the victim. It may involve returning stolen property or donating services to the victim, to a value equivalent to the loss sustained. Restitution is commonly limited by statute to the amount of actual loss suffered by the victim and does not compensate for pain and suffering or provide a vehicle for punitive damages. Actual loss may include destroyed or stolen property, services fraudulently obtained, medical expenses incurred as a result of an injury caused by the offender's crime, and wages lost because of time absent from work as a result of victimization. Although some suggest that restitution be combined with incarceration, with funds being taken from the inmate's earnings from work in prison industry, restitution is usually coupled with a sentence of probation.

Community Service. Sentencing an offender to perform services benefiting the community, rather than an individual victim, is relatively new. In many instances this sanction is more appropriate than either a fine or restitution, the other nonincarcerative sanctions that require the offender to make amends for his criminal act.

Community service may be a more effective penalty than a fine for the middle-class offender, for whom the sum involved may have little significance. It may also be a better alternative for indigent offenders or those who have only moderate means, because the unintended conse-

quence of fines on offenders with low incomes may be to penalize their families.

Ordering an offender to perform community service also may be a better disposition at least in some circumstances than restitution. For some offenses, such as selling liquor to a minor or drunken driving, there is no appropriate action the offender can take that will benefit the victim, while for other offenses, such as white-collar crime, often no individual victim can be identified. Even when the victim is known and a specific amount of money that would repay the loss can be established, the objectives of deterrence and rehabilitation may be better served by having the offender perform some noncompensated service for a segment of the public.

Service projects vary widely and may involve work to improve public parks and highways or services to charitable and civic organizations. The following are examples of community service sentences: A self-employed cleaner convicted of petty larceny charges agreed to provide $250 worth of services to a home for the elderly. A judge assigned graffiti scrawlers to clean-up chores. A president of a college, convicted of manslaughter for killing a pedestrian while driving under the influence of alcohol, was sentenced to lecture for a stipulated period of time on the consequences of drinking and driving.

Fines. Fines are the most commonly employed of all criminal sanctions, making up as much as 75 percent of all sentences. Like other sanctions, fines may be the sole sentence given an offender or may be combined with other penalties such as imprisonment or probation. Most frequently a fine is the only sanction imposed. Fines differ from restitution in that they are paid to the government rather than to the victim of crime and therefore serve as a source of revenue for the state.

Usually the court may exercise some discretion in setting the fine. Statutes usually set only the upper limits on the amount of the fine that may be imposed for a particular offense. The only constitutional limit on the judge's discretion to impose a fine of a lesser amount is that the fine may not be so grossly excessive that it amounts to a deprivation of property without due process of law.

Theoretically a fine is due as soon as it is imposed by the court. However, the court usually sets a reasonable time, which varies depending on the circumstances of the case, within which the fine is to be paid. In recent years, some states have started to permit payment of fines in installments, which helps avoid defaults and financial hardship in the case of poorer offenders.

If the offender does not make a reasonable effort to pay the fine within the required time, he may be jailed until payment. Imprisonment in this situation is not part of the sentence for the offense but is only a means of enforcing the sentence of the fine. The offender may secure his release at any time by paying the fine. Some states set a maximum time limit on imprisonment resulting from failure to pay a fine.

TRENDS IN SENTENCING

The task of devising a sentencing system that will achieve the goals of deterrence, retribution, incapacitation, and rehabilitation and will also function with fairness to offenders, victims, and the community is an old one. However, public recognition that this is an exceedingly difficult goal to achieve is relatively recent. Throughout most of the first two-thirds of the twentieth century the underlying premises of the sentencing system were that offenders should be given a sanction that would reform them and that they should be under state control until reformation was achieved. The indeterminate sentence was developed to facilitate this aim. It was based on the beliefs that most criminals could be rehabilitated, judges could determine which criminals could be reformed and by what sanction, and correctional officials could determine when offenders were "cured."

In the late 1960s all of these beliefs came under attack. The view that we do not know how to rehabilitate offenders has become dominant. Many people who have come to this conclusion argue that rehabilitation should be abandoned as a sentencing objective and that more emphasis should be placed on retribution, deterrence, and incapacitation.

In addition, there is considerable controversy about the ability of judges, correctional officials, or clinicians to identify offenders who will or will not commit crimes again. Consequently, the indeterminate sentence is considered to be unfair, no matter what its length, because similar offenders may be incarcerated for different periods of time.

The following practices have been suggested for implementing more evenhanded sentencing practices: offenders committing similar offenses and who are equally blameworthy should receive the same punishment; offenders should know the duration of their punishment when they are sentenced; sentences based on prediction of future criminality and expectations of cure should be abolished; parole should be abolished; and treatment programs should be available to offenders but not required.

Not everyone subscribes to these views. There are those who argue that the resources necessary to achieve the rehabilitative objective have not been available. Instead of abandonment of the rehabilitative ideal, they seek a new commitment to this goal and an increase in the amount and kind of rehabilitative services for offenders, especially for those offenders who can remain in the community without threatening public safety. Proponents of this view often are convinced that the sanction of imprisonment is used too often and for too extensive a period. Members of both groups seem to agree that offenders should be given increased procedural protections at the sentencing stage and that sentencing review should be made available to reduce sentencing disparity.

CASES

Ake v. Oklahoma, 105 S. Ct. 1087 (1985)
Bearden v. Georgia, 461 U.S. 660 (1983)
Bell v. Ohio, 438 U.S. 637 (1978)
Coker v. Georgia, 433 U.S. 584 (1977)
Gardner v. Florida, 430 U.S. 349 (1977)
Gregg v. Georgia, 428 U.S. 153 (1976)
Mempa v. Ray, 389 U.S. 128 (1967)
Robinson v. California, 370 U.S. 660 (1962)
Solem v. Helm, 463 U.S. 277 (1983)

BIBLIOGRAPHY

Francis A. Allen, *The Decline of the Rehabilitative Ideal* (1981), discusses the decline and the future of the role of rehabilitation in sentencing. American Bar Association, *Standards for Criminal Justice* (1980 and 1982 Supplement), provides model sentencing procedures, extensive commentary, and references. Marvin E. Frankel, *Criminal Sentences: Law Without Order* (1972), is the seminal book on sentencing reform. Nicholas N. Kittrie and Elyce H. Zenoff, *Sanctions, Sentencing and Corrections* (1981), contains articles, cases, statutes, statistics, and commentary on sentencing objectives, procedures, types of sanctions, and proposed reforms.

Norval Norris, *The Future of Imprisonment* (1974), analyzes the problems and expectations of imprisonment as a sanction. Charles Renfrew, "The Paper Label Sentences: An Evaluation," in *Yale Law Journal*, 86 (1977), describes the reasons for and reactions to Judge Renfrew sentencing five corporate executives convicted of price-fixing to make twelve oral presentations about their offense to civic and business groups. Twentieth Century Fund, Task Force on Criminal Sentencing, *Fair and Certain Punishment* (1976), describes the merits of presumptive sentencing. United States Department of Justice, Bureau of Justice Statistics, *Sourcebook, Criminal Justice Statistics* (1983), contains comprehensive statistics on criminal justice, including the number of offenders imprisoned, executed, and paroled. Franklin E. Zimring, "Making the Punishment Fit the Crime: A Consumer's Guide to Sentencing Reform," in *Hastings Center Report*, 6 (1976), criticizes presumptive sentencing and other determinate sentencing proposals.

[*See also* CRIMINAL JUSTICE SYSTEM; CRIMINAL LAW; JUVENILE LAW; PLEA BARGAINING; *and* PROSECUTORS.]